# LOVRO ARTUKOVIĆ

## STAGINGS

Reproductions in the book are marked with numbers and letters according to the catalogue of works with descriptions, printed on pages 242 — 250.

Reprodukcije u knjizi označene su brojkama i slovima prema katalogu djela s opisima, koji se nalazi na stranicama 242 — 250.

contents

# FOREWORD

VANJA ŽANKO, Nomad Team

You are holding in your hands the first monographic publication about Lovro Artuković, conceived to celebrate the artist's singular talent as well as provide an extensive history of his work. It is a story which begins in the 1980s, when Zagreb was still a city in the former Yugoslavia, and ends in present day Berlin.

Lovro Artuković is considered a leading Croatian and Central European painter and graphic artist whose artistic expression investigates figuration and intimacy, weaving together an iconography of urban civilisation. He was born in 1959 in Zagreb, where his education led him through both the Classical High School and then the graphic department at the Academy of Fine Arts. After his school years, he worked in the city as a freelance artist until 2003, teaching graphic techniques at the School of Applied Arts, which ultimately led to an assistant professor role at the Academy of Fine Arts, where he taught drawing. Beyond his oeuvre receiving a number of prestigious awards, his artworks have been both presented in and collected by iconic collections, such as  the National Museum of Modern Art Zagreb, Albertina Museum Vienna, Deutsche Bank Kunsthalle Berlin, Museum of Fine Arts Split, Museum of Modern Art Dubrovnik, Museum of Modern and Contemporary Art Rijeka, Museum of Contemporary Art Zagreb, and Museum of Arts and Crafts Zagreb. They are also included in esteemed private collections in Zagreb, Vienna, Zurich, Berlin and New York. His work has been the focus of two films: the experimental work *The Theft* (Lukas Nola, 2004) and the documentary *L.A. Unfinished* (Igor Mirković, 2008). In 2012, he created the scenography for the play *The Yellow Line* by Juli Zeh and Charlotte Roos, directed by Ivica Buljan (Zagreb Youth Theatre).

Arriving in Berlin in 2001, Artuković has since been living and working in the city as a freelance artist.

The transformative moment in the relationship between Lovro Artuković and myself was catalyzed by his retrospective *Lovro Artuković: The Best Paintings* at the Galerija Klovićevi dvori Zagreb (2008). The exhibition was organized by patron Tomislav Kličko, whose previous collection I had been curating, and thus on this occasion I was coordinating the show. A significant part of Lovro Artuković's practice between 1984 and 2008 was luckily documented by the photographer Fedor Vučemilović for the Galerija Klovićevi dvori Zagreb, who has generously shared rich visual materials that feature in this publication.

The next milestone in our relationship was the inauguration of Tomislav Kličko's Lauba House Zagreb in 2011, where we had historically organized solo and group exhibitions, most notably *Das Magazin* (2012) and *The Face of the Painting* (2013). Ever since, Lovro Artuković has been generously sharing his specific philosophy of painting and vast knowledge of history of painting with me - an invaluable tool which not only helped me relearn how to look at art, but more broadly at the world itself. Looking back, we remain beyond lucky to have had the talented photographer Damir Žižić photograph the contemporary art world during this time. As a result, Lovro Artuković's works have been meticulously documented through time, across an array of different media and formats - from the drawings made in the 1980s up to the most recent installations like *Underworld Party* (2023).

Nomad itself was born in 2014, with the social and cultural intent of building a platform that contributes to the promotion of our contemporary cultural discourse. It is our goal to shape the market of regional artists from and around Croatia, and in the process build long-lasting cohesive networks around it. With a special dedication to cross-disciplinary collaborations, our practices include fundraising, commission management, producing exhibitions and publications, building collections as well as artist promotion.

In Autumn 2021, Lovro Artuković invited our Nomad team: Ana Petričić Gojanović, Andrea Šarić, Daria Darmaniyan, Dora Zane, Jelena Tamindžija Donnart and myself, to celebrate his 20th anniversary in Berlin. This was the moment we began building this book together. It was as such not only a beautiful and celebratory coming-together moment, attended by many *Friends of Nomad*, but a moment of synchronicity which fused our community. It marked a crucial first step towards the great futures possible to us, and to the empathetic potential of the art world.

Our team has managed this process of the book making with great resourcefulness and care, bringing them together exceedingly with talented collaborators: text authors Boris von Brauchitsch, Leonida Kovač and Lovro Artuković; graphic editor Damir Gamulin; translators Andy Jelčić and Marina Schumann; and proofreader Ivana Sor. I am grateful to Anna Ebner-Quadri and Silvia Jaklitsch at the Verlag für Moderne Kunst in Vienna for publishing this book. We owe deepest thanks for the creativity, dedication and collaborative spirit that everyone has brought to this ambitious project, as we have collectively acknowledged the urgency of producing this monograph.

Special appreciation goes to *Friends of Nomad*, the institutions and individuals to whom we are deeply indebted: Zagreb Tourist Board, Grand Park Hotel Rovinj, Museum of Fine Arts Split, National Museum of Modern Art Zagreb, Adris Foundation, Ministry of Culture and Media of the Republic of Croatia, Croatian Cultural Center Sušak - Gallery Kortil, Gallery Trotoar Zagreb, and Cerin Antonić Collection, as well as Ivana Andabak and Siniša Šare, Martina Bienenfeld, Stanka and Vedran Braun, Davor Bruketa and Tina Fras, Nives Cavić and Vice Mandarić, Aleksandra Cvetković, Gordana and Igor Čičak, Andrea and Hrvoje Fajdetić, Mario Furčić, Damir Gojanović, Ana Kričković, Saša Lui, Sanja Ljubičić and Luka Tomasković, Iva and Michael Markota, Tihana Milas and Peter Lösch, Goran Pikunić, Adriana Prlić Belay and Zhan Belay, Mihael Šutalo, Tatiana Wiesner-Pavlova and Manfred Wiesner, Neda Young, Ivana and Borna Zane. The realisation of the publication would not have been possible without their generosity and partnership.

Lovro Artuković has been with us during all the key moments of our Nomad journey and we are exceptionally grateful to him for dedicating so much time to this exciting project.

We at Nomad Platform believe that ambitious cultural projects can come to life only through a long-term synergy, fueled by curated partnerships and the linking between the profit and non-for-profit sectors. The success of this book is restoring our faith in the cultural field as a space for dialogue and encounter, as well as a space of economic and environmental sustainability.

Vienna, 2023

ARTIST'S ACKNOWLEDGEMENTS

LOVRO ARTUKOVIĆ

I would like to start with thanking Nomad Platform for their trust and unyielding support in creating my first monograph. Thank you to Vanja Žanko and her entire team for planning and overseeing the execution of the fundraising, production, and editing of this publication.

My gratitude goes to the authors Boris von Brauchitsch and Leonida Kovač for their texts and Damir Gamulin for his thoughtful design.

I also thank photographers Gunter Lepkowski and Damir Žižić, who documented my work over the years. This monograph would also not have been possible without Fedor Vučemilović and the kindness of Galerija Klovićevi dvori, who provided photographs of some of my major works initially exhibited in my 2008 solo exhibition The Best Paintings. My special thank you to Boris Cvjetanović for photos from my exhibition Alphabet of Narcissism (1988).

The development of the database for my oeuvre was in the capable hands of Natascha Schoenaich. Thank you for your friendship.

My special appreciation goes to Dražen Karaman, who has always been available for constructive discussions about my texts. His help with editing and translating of my writing, as well as the years of meticulously working on my website, are indeed invaluable.

This publication features many works that have found their home in public institutions and collections. It goes without saying that I am grateful to all the institutions and individuals who have made those works available for publishing and who have trusted me over the years, especially Stanka and Vedran Braun, and Tomislav Kličko.

My dear friends have some of my deepest gratitude. Suad Arifagić and Sulejman Kurtagić, you have endlessly supported and helped with my work, from framing my paintings, setting up exhibitions, and even building my entire studio. Jeannine Simon, you have selflessly offered your creative input for some of my paintings, for which I am greatly indebted.

And, finally, all my love goes to my partner Constanze Krüger and my sister Sanja Artuković. Thank you.

Berlin, 2023

Boris von Brauchitsch

# SISYPHUS WITH A CIGARETTE



Some reflections on Lovro Artuković's paintings

When Correggio captured Ganymede floating away or when Rubens portrayed Caesar, these painters presumably modeled people from their environment who embodied the mythological or historical figures in the studio. Why, says Lovro Artuković, should he have done otherwise when he composed the great history painting depicting a significant moment in the history of his former homeland. Without much ado, he re-enacted the signing of the Dayton Agreement, supposed to end the war and political fractures in Bosnia-Herzegovina in 1995, in a Berlin pub with friends, transforming the political ritual into a religious one. The pompously staged but ultimately dramaturgically boring Parisian reality - where three suspicious figures sign a treaty under the critical gaze of their Western colleagues - is in Berlin transformed into a kind of multi-ethnic Last Supper with clear borrowings from Leonardo da Vinci and Veronese (for whom a Last Supper without a dog seemed unthinkable).

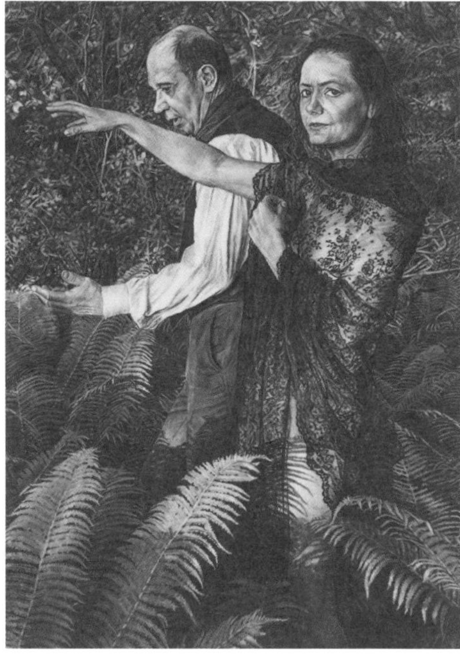

The impetus for the painting, however, was more a German than a Croatian state of mind: artists from the region of former Yugoslavia were expected "in the West" - particularly in Berlin - to take a political stance in their art. Consequently, a Croatian artist had to be a political artist. Lovro Artuković's monumental painting is therefore to be understood first of all as a commentary on this expectation, which it ironically undermines.

*Signing of the Declaration on the Annexation of West Herzegovina and Popovo Polje to the Republic of Croatia (Who ordered beer?)* is the correct title of the work, with the crucial part of the title in brackets. Art is obviously supposed to ask questions.

The obscure and inextricable political situation is reduced to a simple investigation to which all those present can easily give answers and which suddenly seems central, even elementary, with regard to the madness that the disintegrating Yugoslavia experienced in the years after 1991.

The question about the beer orderer may seem politically incorrect and absurd in the context of the gruesome war scenarios, but it reveals the actual absurdity - the one of historical reality. By gathering 22 friends of the most diverse origins at a table under a board where national borders become a secondary matter in view of a menu that has something tempting in store for very diverse tastes, Lovro Artuković's painting also seems to be a very direct statement for peaceful or at least respectful coexistence, like the one offered to the Croatian painter by his new home Berlin. If one has an ashtray in front of him instead of a paper maze and a cigarette in his hand instead of a penholder, the culture of discussion becomes more pleasant, even if the need for discussion may seem urgent and the confusion may be ever so profound here and there.

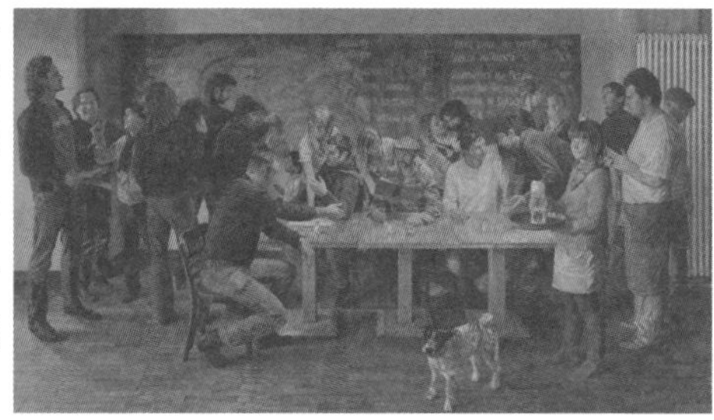

When Lovro Artuković for once gets carried away copy-
ing Old Masters, it's not to demonstrate his brush skills
to himself or someone else, but because he has a living
work of art in mind, a party, for instance, in which the
guests, bathed in black light, move between underworld
scenarios from art history. They dance not on the volcano
but under it, between Ixion and Sisyphus, Persephone
and Proserpina. But these copies remain marginal notes
in the work of the painter. They are rather reinterpreta-
tions of myths and fairy tales that occupy him over the
years, archaic stories of happiness and eternal love, of
betrayal, loss and aberration that exist in all cultures.
The artist finally becomes Orpheus himself, who intends to lead his Eurydice out of Hades, whereby he and his companion transform themselves
into Hansel and Gretel, who wander through a forest that apparently has
no spatial or temporal end, for the lost children have long since become a
grandparent-aged couple, who make their way through the thicket without
encountering a witch's house supposed to save them.

The black light that Artuković planned as studio lighting for his underworld performance is repeatedly found in his paintings as well, as if the
spooky illumination had been absorbed by the canvas. Such is the case
in *"Women's Bath"*, which depicts seven female figures, all wrapped in a
single long swath of fabric, draped around a tin tub of neon tubes where
goldfish cavort. Again, a note in brackets is added to the title, again it is a
question, and again it seems to be the decisive clue: *(Diana and Actaeon?)*.
The viewer may answer this question himself by recalling the myth of the
youthful hunter Actaeon, who surprised the goddess of the hunt while
bathing, was transformed by her into a deer as punishment, and torn to
pieces by his own dogs, who no longer recognized him.
Since there is no man in the picture, male viewers may
assume that they have slipped into the role of Actaeon
viewing the painting and now, after Diana has discovered them, they become the victims of their own picture
viewing, so to say in seven stages of reaction to their
looks. The ghostly light has long since transformed the
improvised idyll, including the graceful goddess, into a
ghost train ambience, so that it is only a matter of time
before the divine revenge befalls the viewer.

Light is constituent anyway. For observation and painting in general, for
Lovro Artuković's paintings in particular. For example, when he paints the
same scene three times with different lighting - a woman in a nightgown
doubled into a pair of twins - once in front of a bright, roughly plastered wall,
once with the light turned off, and once with a star map of the constellation
Gemini projected onto her. The two heroes Castor and Pollux, catapulted
to principal stars in the firmament, appear as two bright, colored spots,

respectively, on the faces of the twin female figure. The studio with its floorboards, the universe, the ancient mythology of the horse tamers, and the staging of the young woman in the nightgown from the second-hand store in the light of a projector merge, or rather overlap, to form a multi-layered narrative.

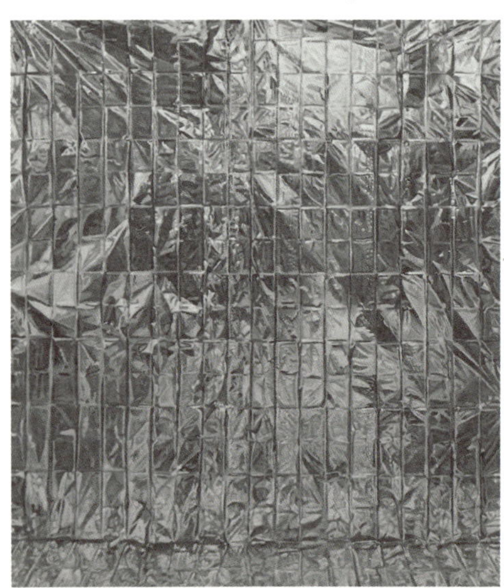

And then the haunting is gone, what remains is the bare wall. This wall over plank floor is known from many Artuković's paintings, it is located in a backyard 52°29'11" north latitude and 13°25'30" west longitude. If the frequency of its appearance were a decisive criterion, it would play the main role in the oeuvre of the painter. And indeed, this background repeatedly comes to the fore, the flat canvas transforms into that plaster wall parallel to the painting that can be completely self-sufficient, accentuated at best by an electrical outlet or bathed in the bluish light of the night. Then someone has placed a sofa in front of it, captured as coarse and crumpled, with all the signs of dissolution, as if that which was happening on this studio stage were completely indifferent and therefore worthy of a picture.

Lovro Artuković does not paint fire or water or starry sky, but projections of fire or water on his studio wall or the projection of a map of a starry sky on rough plaster. The elements, the cosmos, the world are guests in his studio. It is possible, but not necessary for art to leave this space. Thus, the studio space always remains part of his paintings.

Occasionally, Lovro Artuković appears as a gregarious hermit. Armed with a resistant charm in the face of the distortions of an outside world that masquerades as reality, he develops the dimensions and stratifications of his own perception in front of and on that wall, which repeatedly becomes a canvas, only to leave the studio as such and announce an intimate universe outside.

The hermit in his hermitage corresponds to the process of artistic work, which the painter describes as slowing down. While outside things are moving faster and faster, he allows himself more and more time. He himself attributes this to a growing obsession with detail, and he may be right. It suits him that it is precisely there, where seemingly the non-objectivity enters the scene, that the richness of detail is at its peak. In the mirror foils, which he has repeatedly chosen as his motif since 2018, the images are fragmented, distorted, blurred and dissolved. Not through abstraction, but through reflection.

More details guarantee a longer creation time, more time for reflection as well, for immersion in the images. The physical reflection corresponds to a spiritual reflection. Through the folds of the mirror foil, the before is refracted as in a kaleidoscope. The before are again the old masters, motifs from the religious holdings of art history,

his own works, torn figures and spaces. Behind it, that much as we know by now, is the wall, the bare wall of the studio. And in between, the foil: gossamer, fragile, a gold ground as if from a medieval panel painting. This time in the form of the finest matter, in which injured people in a traffic accident or boat refugees are wrapped after being rescued.

The gauzy layer between prosaic, hard, whitewashed wall and reflective imagination thus becomes a rescue foil. For the artist, for the viewer, perhaps for a fundamental perception of the world.

7

Leonida Kovač

# THE EVENT OF THE IMAGE

There is a black-and-white photograph, obviously staged with meticulous attention, from which three pairs of eyes stare unblinkingly into the gaze that observes them. These eyes, gazing back at the gaze that transforms them into an image, belong to two living individuals and a painting hanging on the wall behind them. The painting depicts a frontal close-up of a young man's face. It is titled *Giacomo* and painted in 2019. The vertical axis of symmetry in the photographic image in question is clearly defined by the distance between his wide-open eyes, as in some Renaissance *sacra conversazione*. This distance between the eyes of the face painted in oil on canvas corresponds to the distance between the heads of the two physical bodies of persons seated in front of the wall on which the painting is displayed. The painted image literally gazes over their shoulders into viewer's gaze, which transforms all of them together into

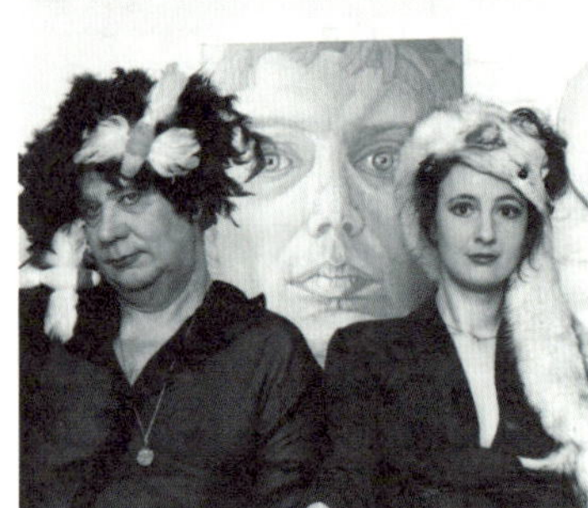


A

an image. The photograph I am referring to is a re-enactment of a photographic portrait taken by Denise Colomb in 1952 in Paris, featuring two Surrealist painters. In this re-enactment of the photographic image, Leonora Carrington and Leonor Fini, who posed for the photographer donning peculiar animal head-dresses, are here impersonated by Lovro Artuković and Natascha Schönaich, and the gaze from the picture hanging behind them belongs to the face that appears in Artuković's painting *Who is Looking at Whom Here*, shown in 2004 as part of his exhibition *Repository*. In contrast to that exhibition, which took place in public space with a large audience, the photograph taken in the artist's studio was reproduced on a flyer advertising the exhibition *Some Things Just Stick in Your Mind*, held in the same studio in 2019. During this exhibition, Artuković presented to his friends and colleagues his recently completed painting *Let Me Show You My Dream (after Leonora Carrington)* – a re-enactment of Carrington's *Self-Portrait* from 1937/38, now housed in the Metropolitan Museum in New York. The title of that "chamber" exhibition, which is also a quote (of the title of a song written by Mick Jagger and Keith Richards in 1965), indicates numerous questions raised by Artuković's artworks over the past four decades.

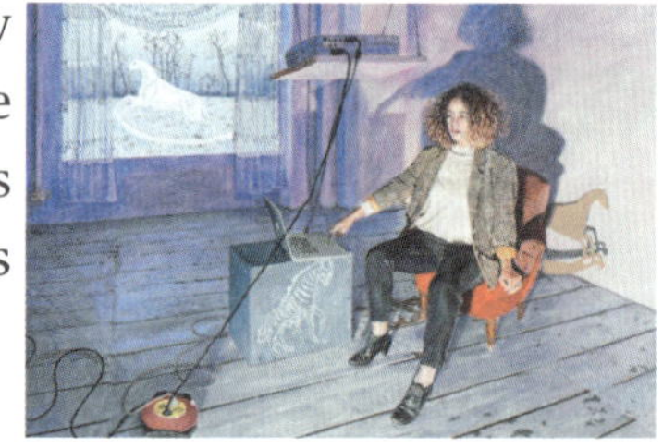

Lovro Artuković categorically claims that he is dealing with images, not the painting, although the history of painting resides in every particle of his paintings, or at least that's how I see it. His paintings confront me with the same question that Georges Didi-Huberman asked in 1990 at the beginning of his groundbreaking book *Devant l'image*, which aimed to "interrogate the *tone of certainty* that prevails so often in the beautiful discipline of the history of art."[1]

8

He asks: "[...] what obscure or triumphant reasons, what morbid anxieties or maniacal exaltations can have brought the history of art to adopt such a tone, such a rhetoric of certainty? How did such a *closure* of the visible onto the legible and of all this onto intelligible knowledge – and which such seeming self-evidence – to constitute itself? [...] In short, the said 'specific knowledge


1   Georges Didi-Huberman, *Confronting Images: Questioning the Ends of a Certain History of Art*, trans. John Goodman (University Park, PA: Pennsylvania State University Press, 2005), p. 2.

of art' ended up imposing its own *specific form of discourse* on its object, at the risk of inventing artificial boundaries for its object - an object dispossessed of its own specific deployment or unfolding. So the seeming self-evidence and the tone of certainty that this knowledge imposes are understandable: all it looks for in art are answers that are *already given* by its discursive problematic."[2]

2   Ibid., pp. 3-4.

In 2004, Lovro Artuković commented on the paintings in the *Repository* exhibition with words that were in stark contrast to that "specific knowledge of art" that was the subject of Didi-Huberman's critique: "Painting resides in the Repository, which dwells within our collective, total soul. All the ways of applying paint, all the tricks of the trade, everything 'new' or 'old', exists eternally in that Repository, timeless and enduring, as long as there is that collective, total soul, i.e. humanity. The first painter already encompassed within himself all the painters who would come after, just as an individual born at this very moment contains within himself all those who came before. A painter takes from the Repository what he needs, or what he can reach with his ability, and brings it to the light of the unique moment in which he lives. What emerges from the Repository and how it is used, how it materializes in the Painting, depends on this distinctive fragment of time and on the painter himself."

How did the *Self-Portrait* of Leonora Carrington, for instance, materialize in Lovro Artuković's studio in 2019, transforming into the painting *Let Me Show You My Dream*? Since the early 2000s, that studio had often been denoted as the place of action, yet the place of action is not the same as the place of the event of the image. That painted spot does not function in the dramaturgy of the painting as the *mise en scène* of the event. The image of the studio is there to show the staging of the scene, and the staging of the scene is not the same as the staging of the image, because the image cannot be staged: it occurs and is excessive in that occurrence: not on the formal, but rather on the molecular level. In the painting *Let Me Show You My Dream*, whose title implies a dialectics between the intimate and the extimate, the *Self-Portrait* of Leonora Carrington occurs in the studio of Lovro Artuković. Unlike the artist sitting in an armchair dressed in rider pants and pointing with her index finger to the gap between herself and a hyena approaching her while looking at something outside the picture, the woman in Artuković's painting is pressing a key on the laptop placed on a pedestal with a hyena drawn on its front. The laptop is connected by cables to a projector, which instead of the window with curtains in the painting of Leonora Carrington, through which one sees a galloping white horse, projects an image of a window with curtains through which one sees a white wooden swing horse. In the original painting, such a horse is floating in front of the wall behind the artist's back, casting its dark shadow on the wall. In Artuković's painting, this shadow has been replaced by the large shadow of the seated woman, and the wooden horse

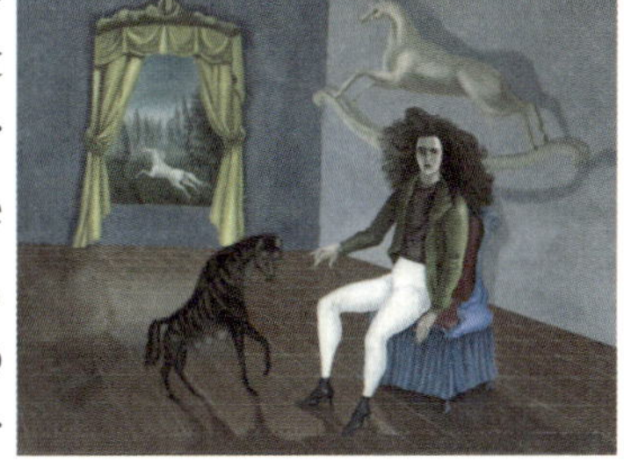

B

by a flat, cardboard one peeking behind her armchair. In the painting *Let Me Show You My Dream*, the dis-enacting appropriation of the self-portrait of a fugitive does not connote the notion of Surrealism in terms in which it is described by the "beautiful discipline of the history of art." I prefer to understand this re-enactment in terms of the question posed in one of Sebald's novels: "And might it not be, continued Austerlitz, that we also have appointments to keep in the past, in what has gone before and is for the most part extinguished, and must go there in search of places and people who have some connection with us on the far side of time, so to speak?"[3] In this atopic location "on the far side of time," I recognize the event of the image, which manifests itself as a *mise en abîme* in Lovro Artuković's painting. The abysmal.

3   W.G. Sebald, *Austerlitz*, trans. Anthea Bell (New York: Modern Library, 2011), pp. 441-442 (e-book).

A year later, in 2020, Lovro Artuković set up the installation *Underworld Party* at Berlin's Kewenig Galerie. In a room lit by ultraviolet light, he arranged a small round table covered with a white tablecloth, upon which there were two unopened bottles of wine, several glasses, an ashtray, and a vase with a flower. Adjacent to the table were an armchair and an upturned wooden chair. The arrangement was positioned in front of a wall where Artuković affixed, in two rows, six charcoal drawings on paper, made during 2019 and 2020. These drawings depicting scenes from Greek mythology occurring in the underworld were made after paintings created between the 16th and 19th centuries. Specifically, these were Titian's *Sisyphus*, Frederic Leighton's *Return of Persephone*, Ribera's *Ixion*, Corot's *Orpheus Leading Eurydice from the Underworld*, Rembrandt's *Rape of Persephone,* and *Psyche Bringing Back the Box of Beauty to Venus*, based on Antoine Maurin's lithograph derived from a painting by Claude-Marie Dubufe.

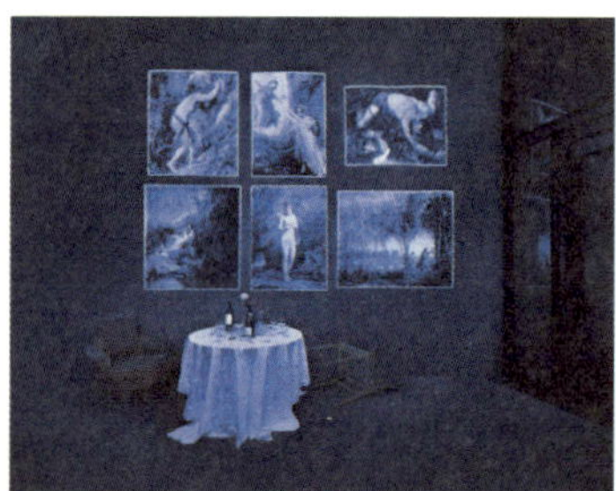

9

In a statement regarding the staging of the underworld party, the painter said:

> "I had the idea to organize a party in my studio titled 'Underworld'. I envisioned the space illuminated by ultraviolet light, the so-called 'black light'. The walls would display charcoal drawings on paper, their whiteness emanating an unnatural bluish glow under the UV light. These drawings were to be replicas of the Old Masters' paintings depicting scenes from the underworld of Greek mythology. I imagined how the party guests, all dressed in black and white according to the mandatory dress code, wandered around the studio through a fog of cigarette smoke, resembling shimmering spectres. In itself it would be a trivial club or disco scene, but I liked to think it could bear something mystical nonetheless.

However, as I began working on the first drawing, I realized that, although I imagined to have accumulated lots of
experience in my work, I was still childishly naive. The
production of copies true to the original turned out to be
so time consuming that the date for the party was postponed
into an indefinite future. Also my wish to give a party
in the first place slowly decreased. But I continued the
work although I felt I was doing something utterly absurd.
Why in God's name would I want to waste my time with some
copies? To be nicknamed 'Rembrandt' by someone? And would
the concept be right if the party was cancelled? Moreover,
I knew that a 'true professional artist' would delegate
such painstaking tasks to others while focusing on more
intelligent endeavours.

But while I was working on the copies, a certain joy started to grow inside me about the lack of purpose and sense
of this whole venture. Apart from that, I did not want to
waive the pleasure: firstly of working with charcoal and
secondly of the gradual 'entering' into the original which
I took as my master copy. Eventually this experience became
a descent into the underworld itself – if not as a wild
party, then still as a kind of conversation with those who
do not roam our world anymore."

When reading this artist statement, several questions
emerge. Firstly, can the performative process he describes
be reduced to mere replication, or does it entail something
else? Additionally, was the endeavour of meticulously translating paintings by artists from past centuries into charcoal
drawings on paper truly devoid of purpose? In 2022, Lovro
Artuković created a charcoal drawing on paper titled *Persephone*, depicting a scene from his own studio. In the foreground, a young girl dressed in a faux fur coat appears, tightly
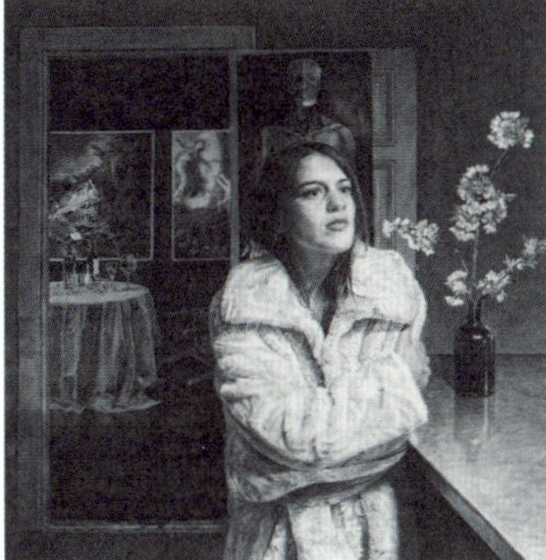
clutching it as if trying to ward off the cold. Her gaze is directed into the
distance, fixated on someone or something that remains unseen within
the painting. On the kitchen counter, against which she leans slightly,
there is a glass bottle with a branch from a blossoming fruit tree. Behind
the girl's back, an anatomical model of the male body made of paper, often
present in Artuković's other paintings, is attached on the open door of the
artist's studio. Through this door, one can glimpse the staged setting of
the *Underworld Party*, with clearly recognizable drawings of Rembrandt's
*Rape of Persephone* and Leighton's *Return of Persephone*. The question that
arises here is what is signified by the term "Persephone" in Artuković's
painting. The young girl in the foreground? Sexual violence normalized

by the narrative of Greek myth and by the discourse of its countless pictorial representations? Return of the repressed? All that together? Or something totally different?

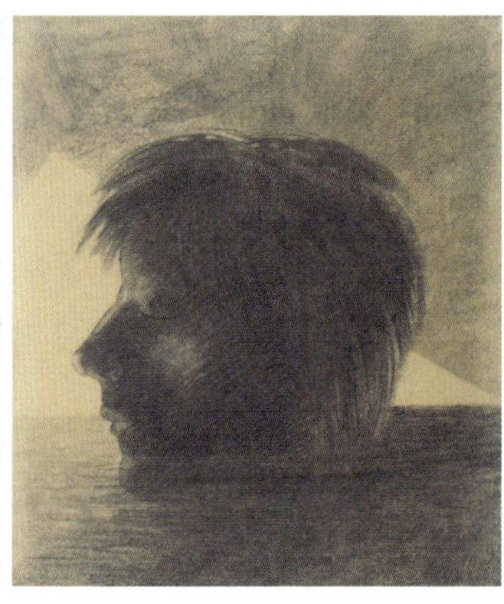

In 2020, Lovro Artuković re-enacted the symbolist painter Odilon Redon's drawing *Head of Orpheus on the Water, or The Mystic* (1880) using charcoal on paper. His two drawings, non-identical depictions of the same motif, were titled *In the Water.* The format of each drawing was approximately twice the size of Redon's original, and the head, almost photographically realistic in contrast to Redon's sketchy portrayal, was reflected on the water's surface, revealing its de-formed counterpart. Notably, the head depicted was that of a woman, not a man, and her perfectly relaxed face floating from a profile view in one drawing to an almost frontal in the other, as if she were turning. Through that subtle, barely perceptible turning, visualized through two painterly frames, I recognize the articulation of Orpheus' transgression against the prohibition to turn, which resulted in irreversible loss. The gender inversion present in this visual translation of the Greek myth raises a question, paraphrasing the title of Artuković's previously mentioned painting from 2004: Who is leading whom from the underground (or perhaps underwater) world? Furthermore, why is she turning? She, not he, is also turning in a drawing from 2021 titled *Orpheus and Eurydice (or Hansel and Gretel - Doesn't Matter),* in which Orpheus and Eurydice (or Hansel and Gretel), moving with opera-like gestures through a dense fern, are impersonated by Lovro Artuković and Jeannine Simon. While he appears to be saying something, or perhaps singing, her outstretched right hand grasps something invisible as she gazes directly at the viewers of the picture. Or, perhaps, at the participants of the underworld party?

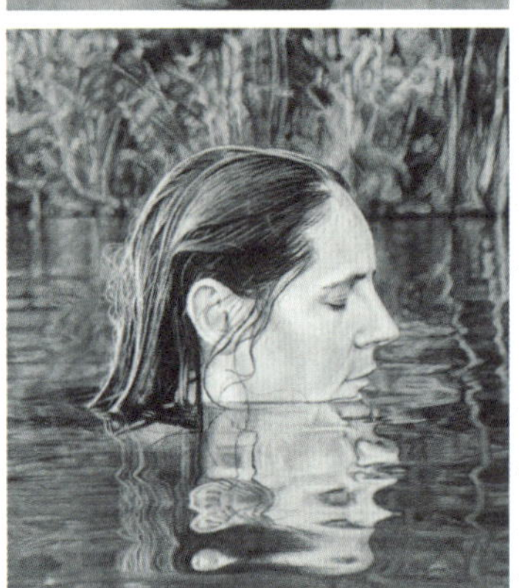

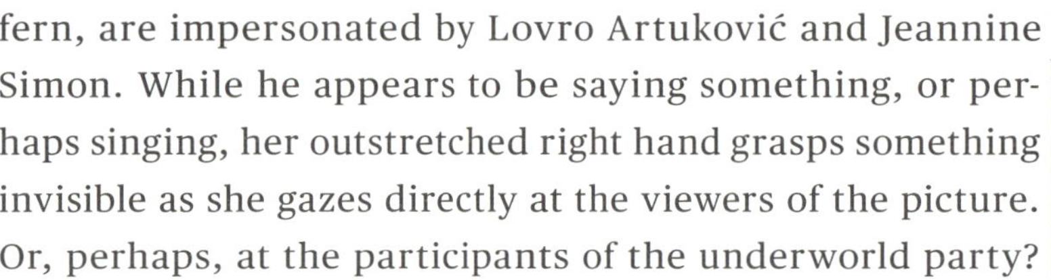

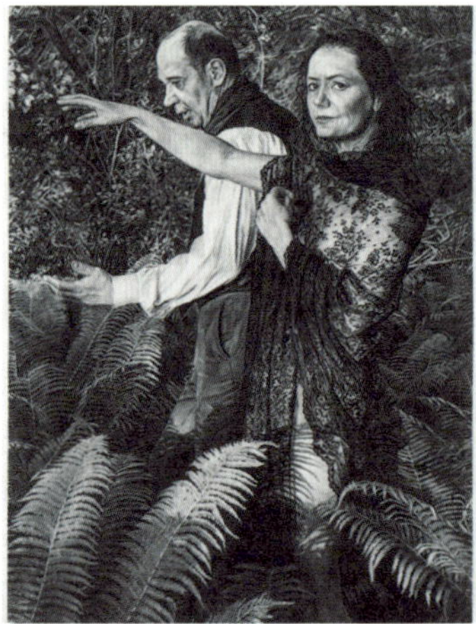

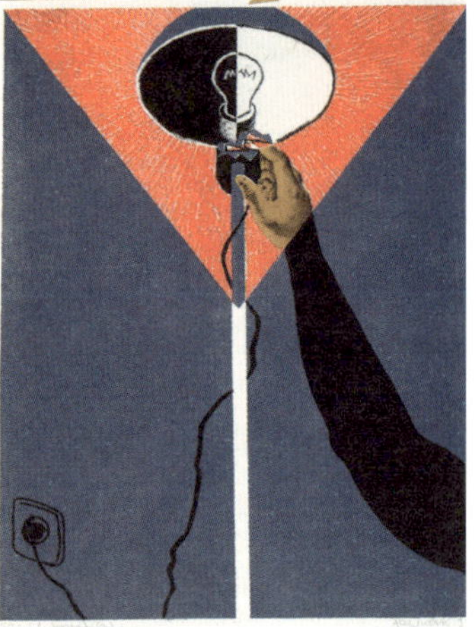

Artuković's *Underworld Party* immediately brings to mind a cinematic gathering, the opulent and debauched party organized by Cardinal Scipione Borghese, a patron and art collector, in the Vatican underworld, staged in Derek Jarman's film *Caravaggio* (1986). Among other things, Cardinal Borghese commissioned the sculptural composition *The Rape of Proserpina* (1621) from the young Bernini. Jarman meticulously reconstructed Caravaggio's light and insisted on veristic details typical of the painter when depicting human figures. At the time it was shot, the film achieved a

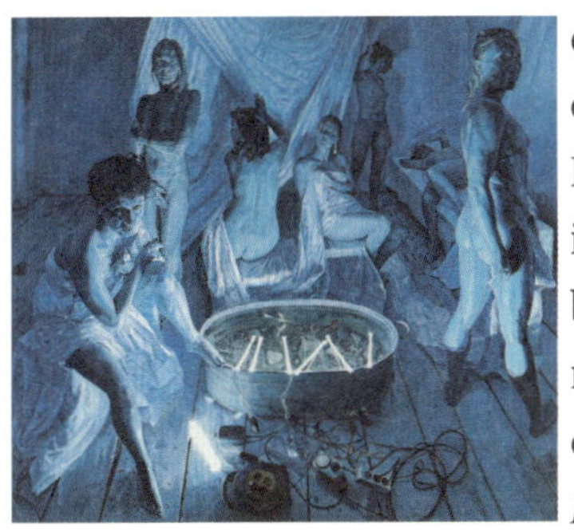

defamiliarizing effect through the blending of historical and contemporary time, articulated in the set design and costumes. In some of the scenes, Caravaggio's life situations were staged in 20th-century environments, visibly illuminated by electric bulbs. Notably, the electric light bulb emerges as a recurring motif, even a protagonist, in Lovro Artuković's artworks. It can be traced back to his early series, such as the *Alphabet of Narcissism* and *Constructed Everyday Life* from the early 1990s, and continued through the paintings presented at the *Repository* exhibition in the early 2000s. Variations of the motif appear as neon tubes in the *Women's Bath* series (2014-2017), as well as in the presence of street lights, traffic lights, car headlights, and bar lights that invariably feature in his *Night Lights* series (2019-2020).

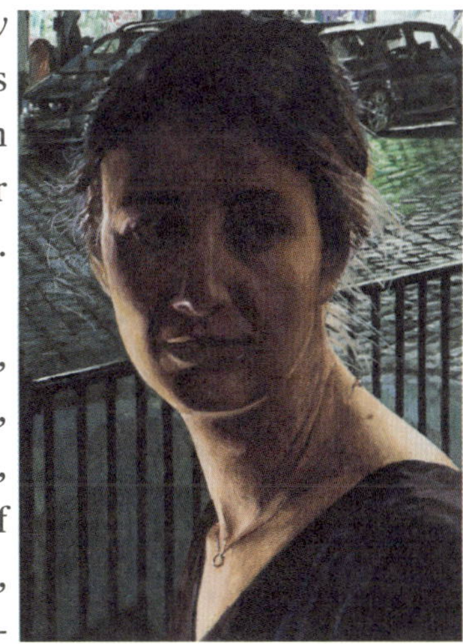

Around the time when Derek Jarman was filming his *Caravaggio*, Lovro Artuković began exhibiting works in Zagreb galleries that, despite a kind of comic-pop-art articulation of the painterly field, clearly referred to themes from the history of painting. One of these paintings was the *Party* (1985), measuring 180 x 260 cm, made with egg tempera and charcoal on paper. The represent-

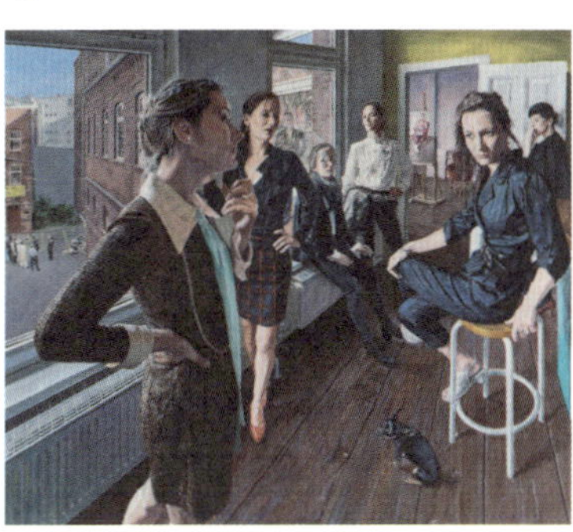

ed  space of a private apartment where, in the mid-1980s, a large group of girls and boys are having fun at a party, is structurally analogous to the depicted space of Artuković's Berlin studio, a recurring motif in his paintings from the 2010s to the present. Here I would single out the aforementioned drawing *Persephone* (2022) and the oil paintings *Dispute about the Meaning of Figurative Representation* (2015), *Dispute in the Studio* (2015-2020), *Anne (Royal)* (2015), and *Girl with Apple* (2017). In both cases, a closed space is represented, featuring a room with a door in the back wall that offers a glimpse of a seemingly secondary event occurring in another room. Additionally, there is a window on the left, allowing the outside atmosphere to permeate the picture. However, unlike the depiction of the Berlin studio, the room in the *Party* is painted in a schematic manner, resembling a box with its front removed. Its walls are adorned with an ornamental pattern reminiscent of a stylized Florentine lily. And no, it is not a depiction of wallpaper. The same ornamental pattern can be observed in Artuković's gouache *Primavera* (1985), which is an evident re-semanticization of Botticelli's painting. When viewed from a distance of forty years, in an era marked by the hegemony of information technology, it takes on the appearance of UV mapping for texturing in the process of computerized 3D modelling. In this piece, Artuković presents a virtual space, a cube with ornamented walls inhabited by silhouettes of characters

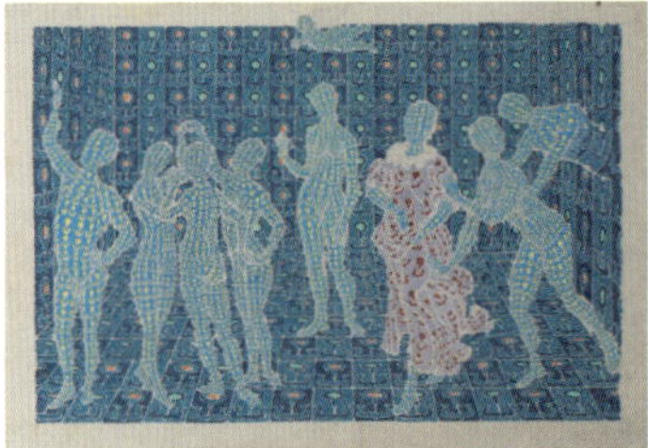

from Botticelli's painting whose bodies are filled with the same ornamental pattern found on the walls within which they are imprisoned. As such, they resemble spectres, effectively visualizing the meaning behind the title of the 2019 chamber exhibition - *Some Things Just Stick in Your Mind*.

The indication that Artuković's 2020 underworld party took place in the realm of the unconscious is evident in another early variation of Botticelli's theme, a painting titled *Apprehension* (1986). Artuković re-enacted a fragment of a fresco by the Renaissance master, currently housed in the Louvre, titled *A Young Man Being Introduced to the Seven Liberal Arts*. In Botticelli's fresco, a female figure leads the young man by the hand towards a group of seven women allegorically representing the Seven Liberal Arts. In *Apprehension*, Artuković clearly establishes his replica of Botticelli's composition as a phantasm. The man ascending the stairs and the woman guiding him are depicted clothed, while the seven women seated in poses mirroring Botticelli's Liberal Arts are naked, resembling the eroticized bodies often seen in paintings of women's baths rather than the allegorical figures of Grammar, Rhetoric, Logic, Arithmetic, Geometry, Astronomy, and Music. In Artuković's painterly performance, the hybridization of these two iconographic themes is accompanied by the dissolution of boundaries between representations of physical and and phantasmal space. His bathers, or if we like, the Liberal Arts, are positioned on a stage - in a box whose walls are also painted with an ornament that repeats on the principle of the infinite pattern. Isn't myth itself a kind of infinite pattern?

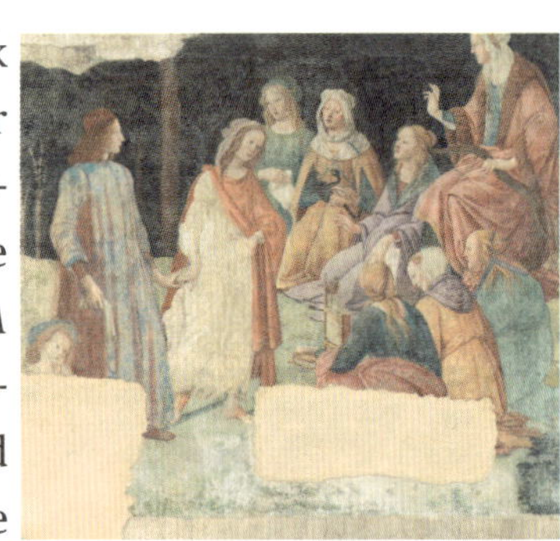

D

E

Botticelli's fresco painted in the late 15th century, which Lovro Artuković re-semanticized with his painting *Apprehension*, was originally made for a wall in Villa Lemmi, owned by Giovanni Tornabuoni, Lorenzo Medici's uncle. There was another fresco next to it, titled *Three Graces Presenting Gifts to a Young Woman*. Both artworks were commissioned for the wedding of Tornabuoni's son, Lorenzo, and Giovanna Albizzi. A quote from the latter fresco appeared in Artuković's 2001 oil on canvas and glass shards titled *God, I Love Botticelli*. The dialectics of colour and non-colour, functioning as a fundamental compositional postulate in that painting, articulates a specific kind of temporality: non-chronological time, the simultaneity of different times in the same place of the event of the image. This active, non-chronological time blurs the boundary between factual vision and phantasm. Similar to Botticelli's fresco, the action unfolds in front of a wall. However, in Artuković's painting, this wall is distinctly depicted as surrounding a house adorned with blossoming fruit trees in its garden. There is a closed door in the wall, and a young man stands before it with his eyes closed,

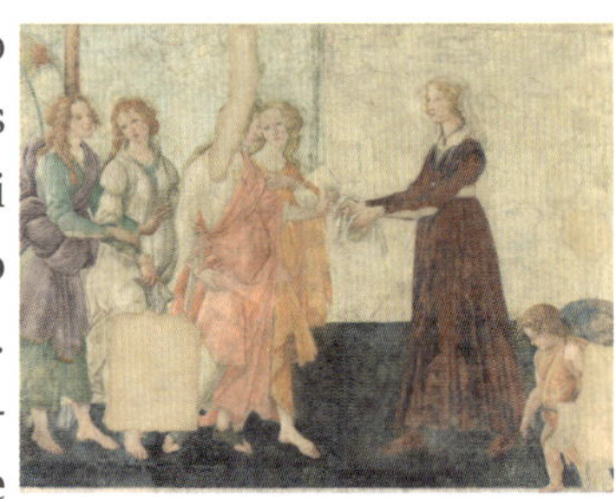

18

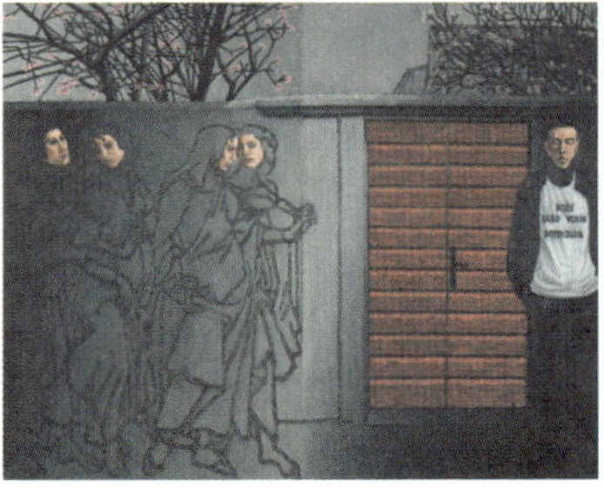

wearing a white T-shirt with the words "God, I love Botticelli" written on it. His frontal position in the composition corresponds to the spot where Botticelli's fresco depicts a profile view of a young woman to whom the Graces present gifts. The four female figures, outlined with relief contours of thick grey paint matching the colour of the painted wall, gracefully approaching from the left side of the painting, are a literal quotation of the movement of the figures in Botticelli's fresco. They are in the process of arriving. The delineation of their translucent bodies signifies their status as apparitions. The grey monochromy of the painting is interrupted only by the faces of all five human figures, painted in the hue of human skin, the brick-red door within the surrounding wall, and the pink and white blossoms of the fruit trees. It is worth noting that the eyes of Artuković's Graces are not painted, but rather resemble slits in masks, so that instead of their gazes, the spectator faces the greyness of the wall that is visible through them.

Botticelli's Graces, whose transparent bodies are outlined like apparitions, made appearances in several other paintings from the series *Pictures Seen by Someone Else*, which Artuković produced during the 2000s. One notable canvas within this series is *Painting for Teeth (Shhhh)*, where the Graces move in front of a house with a blue wooden front door marked with the number 62. There is also a painting from 2006 titled *64*, which is, in fact, a self-portrait of the painter with his daughter. The number 64 is depicted as a house number on a brick building, against which the transparent Graces of Botticelli's appear. However, the number itself signifies the concept of the future. The painting was created when Lovro Artuković was forty-seven years old, yet he portrayed himself frontally as a sixty-four-year-old man, with grey hair and closed eyes, wearing a red unbuttoned jacket with a white T-shirt underneath reading "God, I love Botticelli." Standing beside him and gazing out of the picture is a young girl, also dressed in a red jacket, with a few autumn leaves in her hair, shown at the age at which the painter's daughter actually was at the time.

Paintings from the series *Pictures Seen by Someone Else* - a title that implies the question "who is that other?" - once again delve into the realm of the unconscious, specifically Lacan's (inaccessible) Real. These artworks often feature frontal figures of a woman, a man, and a girl with their eyes closed, and their meticulously painted, coloured faces stand out against their transparent, contoured bodies, seamlessly merging with the surrounding grey backdrop. Among them, there is a self-portrait of the artist titled *The Deer Hunter's Dream* (2001), which establishes a connection not only with the *Forest Scenes* and *Artists in Nature* series, painted in the second half of the 1990s, but also with a sequence of staged and carefully directed scenes that Lovro Artuković painted between 2015 and 2021, uniting them under the title *Excursion*.

19

The *Forest Scenes* also include the paintings *Beech* (1996) and *Scarred Beech* (1997), which the artist reflected upon many years later in his text *Thanks to the Beech*:

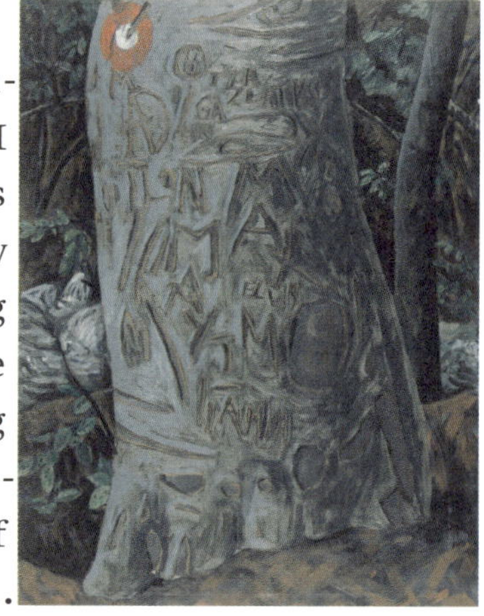

"[…] At one time, I had a rather intense connection with trees. I didn't hug trees, but I did draw them, and those three or four years of frequenting forests undoubtedly benefited my physical wellbeing. The fresh air and walking kept me in a good shape, while drawing in the peacefulness of the forest, carefully observing the chosen subject and its almost imperceptible yet constant changes, became a form of contemplation that nurtured my mental health.

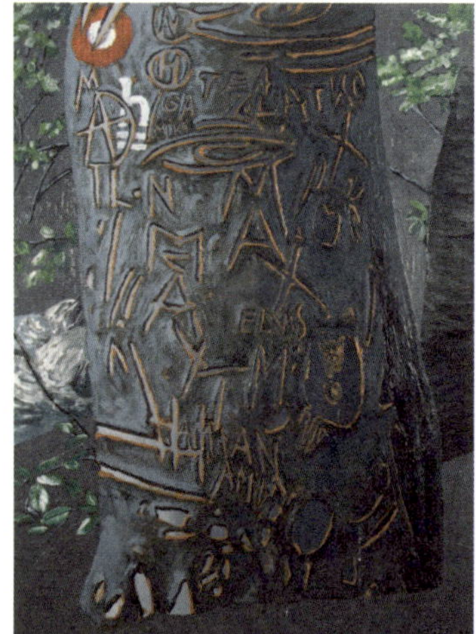

I drew different trees during that time – young and old, oaks, chestnut trees, and hornbeams; but I am writing all this because of a beech tree. It stood next to the hiking trail, and judging by the girth of its trunk, it was quite old. Its bark was full of wide gaping scars: engraved names and initials, simple lines and signs. Fresh scratches stood out in intense orange against the grey bark. It had what they call 'tree eyes' in places where branches had fallen off or been cut, and bulging horizontal scars that resembled tattoos. It also displayed hikers' markings and other signs – likely made by the foresters. I painted it several times, and through that repetition, the way I painted gradually evolved. Thanks to this new experience, I started to think differently about the surface of the painting and the act of painting itself. For that, I am immensely grateful to that beech. If I ever hike that path again and it still stands there, I will give it a heartfelt embrace."

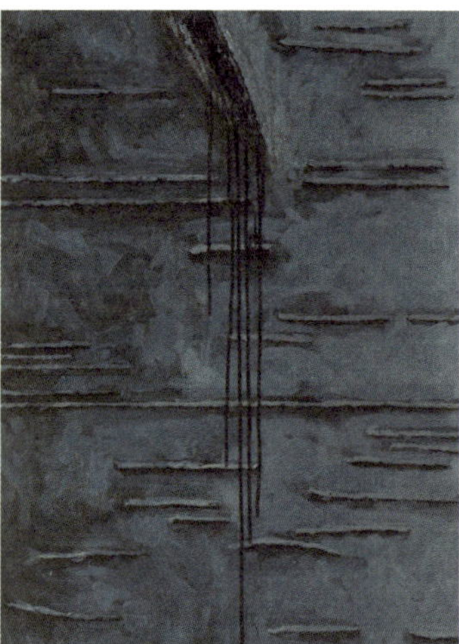

At the time when Artuković painted the *Beech* and *Scarred Beech*, he also embarked on a series of nearly monochromatic grey paintings. These pieces, characterized by close-up views that emphasize the drama inherent in the painting matter itself, diverge from everything he had painted before and after that. I am specifically referring to the *Scar* series, which includes two self-portraits - depictions of Artuković's own seated figure, seen through a kind of foreground in the painting that resembles a veil composed of scars copied from the beech tree.

They are titled *Self-Portrait* (1996) and *Self-Portrait (as a Beech)* (1997). The scar, of course, alludes to the concept of trauma, and the agency of trauma (which, by definition, is mute; like a beech tree?) is inseparable from what Sigmund Freud refers to as *Nachträglichkeit* - deferred action. While Freud did not provide an explicit definition or a comprehensive theory of the concept, it stands as an extremely important element within his conceptual apparatus. In a letter to Fliess dated December 6, 1896, he wrote:

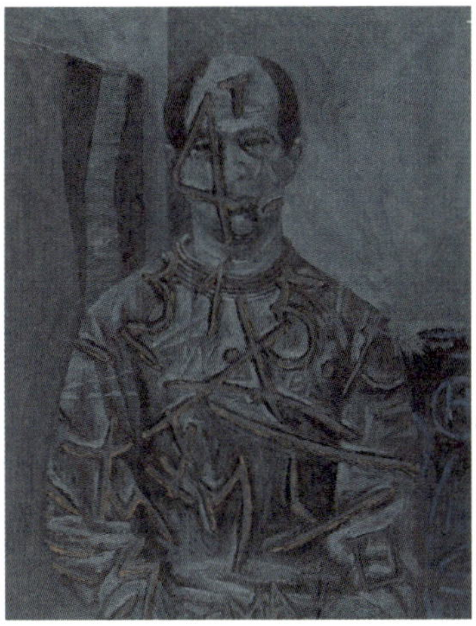

"[…] I am working on the assumption that our psychical mechanism has come into being by a process of stratification: the material present in the form of memory-traces being subjected from time to time to a *re-arrangement* in accordance with fresh circumstance – to a *re-transcription*."[4] Summarizing the main features of this Freudian term, Laplanche and Pontalis conclude: "It is not lived experience in general that undergoes a deferred revision but, specifically, whatever it has been impossible in the first instance to incorporate fully into a meaningful context. The traumatic event is the epitome of such unassimilated experience. […] Deferred revision if occasioned by events and situations, or by an organic maturation, which allow the subject to gain access to a new level of meaning and to rework his earlier experiences."[5]

4  Freud's letter to Fliess, quoted from Jean Laplanche and Jean-Bertrand Pontalis, *The Language of Psychoanalysis*, trans. Donald Nicholson-Smith (London: Karnac Books, 1988), p. 112.

5  Ibidem.

Artuković's assertion that "a painter takes from the Repository what he needs, or what he can reach with his ability, and brings it to the light of the unique moment in which he lives" is analogous to this psychoanalytic elaboration of one of Freud's pivotal concepts. However, it is crucial to delve into the very notion of an image. In the Croatian language, there exists no terminological distinction in the designation of various meanings associated with the term, as English does with the words *picture*, *painting*, and *image*. W.J.T. Mitchell has elucidated the distinctions between these terms through the notorious ambiguity of the word *image*, which can denote "both a physical object (a painting or sculpture) and a mental, imaginary entity, a psychological *imago*, the visual content of dreams, memories, and perception. It plays a role in both the visual and verbal arts, [and] can even pass over the boundary between vision and hearing in the notion of an 'acoustic image'."[6] In psychoanalytic theories, the *imago* is often defined as an "unconscious representation," but rather than an image, it is an acquired imaginary set, a stereotype through which the subject views the other person.[7] In Artuković's paintings, the dissolution of such imaginary sets occurs in the process of staging. Therefore, it is not surprising that his exhibition held in

6  W.J.T. Mitchell, *What do Pictures Want? The Lives and Loves of Images* (Chicago and London: The University of Chicago Press, 2005), p. 2.

7  Laplanche and Pontalis, *The Language of Psychoanalysis*, p. 211.

2014 at Zagreb's Lauba, where he showed paintings created since 2006, bore the title *Stagings*. In these paintings, Artuković had elevated the art of painting the incarnadine to its zenith.

Painting the incarnadine does not entail the representation of skin, as it does not involve mimesis. The purple pigment employed by Artuković is known as *caput mortuum*, a colour utilized by the Old Masters. Alchemical practice also acknowledges *caput mortuum*, sometimes referred to as *nigredo*, which denotes a useless waste substance formed in the process of sublimation. It is synonymous with dissolution and decay, leading the alchemists to associate this residue with the symbol of a stylized human skull. The Impressionists banished *caput mortuum* from painting, which in the coming period definitely witnessed its secularization.

The term *incarnadine* is a commonplace in the discourse of the discipline of art history. The Croatian language borrowed it from German, where it denotes the materic assemblies that create the illusion of the colour of human skin. The German language also employs the term *Fleischfarbe* - which literally means "the colour of flesh." The English denotes the same concept with the noun *incarnadine*, used for a light crimson or rose-red hue. It entered the English language in the 16th century from French and Italian, where the word *incarnatino* originated from the Latin term *incarni*. It is, of course, associated with the concept of incarnation and thus leads to the conclusion that Lovro Artuković, when painting the incarnadine, does not represent the surface of the body. Even if modernist rhetoric attempts to convince us that a painting is nothing more than a flat surface covered with paint.

At the *Stagings* exhibition, Artuković also presented several incomplete works. In this context, incompleteness does not imply that a particular painting lacks something; rather, it could be said that in all aspects of the performance, Artuković deliberately avoids what is referred to as *closure* in film terminology – an ultimate ending. He never ceases to paint the same image on the same canvas, even at times when the painting, having found an "owner", departs from his studio. The temporality of these unfinished paintings reveals that sameness is never truly identical, and that what appears on the surface of the canvas is not the essence of the painting. The painting is not and cannot be concluded, for it is not a representation (of something), but a (trans)figuration that, pretending to be a realistic representation, goes beyond realism where it establishes a relation with the Real. Here, of course, I am referring to Lacan's Real. And that is exactly why what exists on Artuković's canvases is closer to a permanent performance occurring beneath the threshold of perception, than to the category of a picture. It is a live performance in which mimesis becomes a stage prop. This event, blurring the border between the animate and the inanimate, generates uneasiness within the painting or, more accurately, the uneasiness of being in front of a painting that transports the spectators from the realm of externality to its own stage.

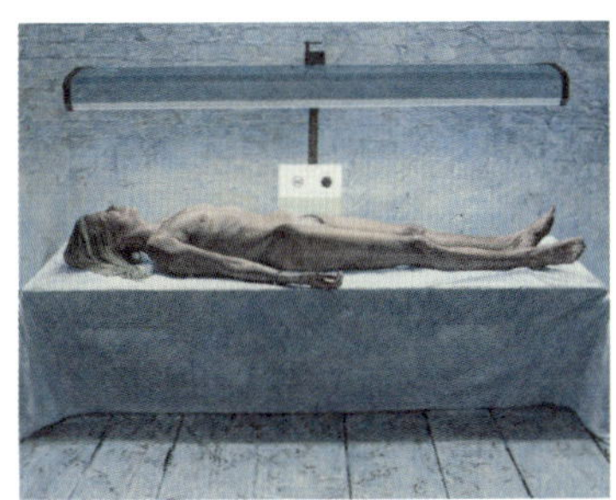

In the painting *Solarium* (2013-2014) from the *Women's Bath* series, a nude female body stretches across the entire width of the painting frame. Like Holbein's dead Christ in his shallow, narrow grave. Julia Kristeva has written one of her reflections on depression and melancholy, published in the book *Black Sun*, by approaching Holbein's *Dead Christ* through the lens of Prince Myshkin, a character from a novel by Fyodor Mikhailovich Dostoevsky, who concludes that "some people may *lose their faith* by looking at that picture."[8] In the face of that dead Jesus of Nazareth, Kristeva identifies "the expression of a hopeless grief," and in his blue-green complexion, she perceives a man who is "truly dead," forsaken by the Father and "without the promise of Resurrection."[9] She highlights Holbein's radical departure from the Italian Renaissance and Mannerist iconography of the Passion. Italian iconography - she writes - "embellishes, or at least ennobles, Christ's face during the Passion but especially surrounds it with figures that are immersed in grief as well as in the certainty of the Resurrection, as if to suggest the attitude we should ourselves adopt facing the Passion. Holbein, on the contrary, leaves the corpse strangely alone." It is in this *act of composition*, rather than in drawing and colour, that the painting is endowed with its "major melancholy burden." Concluding that the artist depicted Christ in the worst kind of abandonment - forsaken by the Father and separated from all of us - Kristeva wonders whether Holbein invites us to "change the Christly tomb into a living tomb, to participate in the painted death and thus include it in our own life, in order to live with it and make it live? For if a living body, in opposition to a rigid corpse, is a dancing body, doesn't our life, through identification with death, become a 'danse macabre'?"[10]

8  Julia Kristeva, "Holbein's Dead Christ," in *Black Sun: Depression and Melancholia*, trans. Leon S. Roudiez (New York: Columbia University Press, 1989), p.107.

9  Ibid., p. 110.

10 Ibid., p. 112-114.

In Artuković's painting, a nude female body is depicted lying on a table covered with a white sheet, which takes on a bluish hue under the illumination from above. Unlike Holbein's depiction of the Nazarene, the woman's eyes and mouth are closed, and her outstretched right arm rests along her body with slightly bent fingers, her palm facing the elongated horizontal lighting fixture positioned above the table. The proportions of this elevated object correspond to those of the body beneath it. However, in contrast to Holbein's spatial confinement where the tableau only reveals the contents of the burial niche, Artuković portrays the surrounding space in which the motionless naked body lies under what appears to be the metallic lid of a coffin. The frame of the *Solarium* painting resembles a film frame captured in two planes. The mise-en-scène is highlighted: it becomes evident that the table stands on a wooden floor, with a white-painted brick wall behind it. The whiteness of the wall, painted in shades of blue and purple, results from the reflection of the "artificial sun" - the ultraviolet light of a solarium lamp. If the title of the painting did not suggest otherwise, I might interpret the scene on the threshold of which I am standing, in front of a large-sized canvas, as an autopsy room setting - an essential backdrop in TV series since the late 20th century- intended for interrogating "mute witnesses." If in today's visual culture the impact of mass-media moving images is analogous to the influence exerted by painting compositions with sacred subject matter around the middle of the second millennium, then these images prompt us to identify with lifeless matter that was once a human being. In a coexistence with omnipresent screens and projectors, in an era where the line between biological and technological bodies is blurred, erasing the distinction between the real and the virtual, the very act of living, driven by the imperative to pursue pleasure, becomes a "danse macabre" that Julia Kristeva, writing about Holbein's painting, apostrophizes while discussing the genesis and effects of melancholy. Perhaps that is why the motionless body stretching across the entire width of Artuković's painting - captured in the stage of "embellishment", in the induction of the body's chemical reaction to artificial sunlight, a transformation that will first manifest on the skin - irresistibly evokes both Holbein's entombed Christ and the heroes of Ridley Scott's film *Prometheus*: Kane on the medical bed of the spaceship Nostromo and the archaeologist Elizabeth Shaw who, despite everything, still holds onto her faith in God and performs a surgical procedure on herself within a hermetically sealed medical apparatus (in its proportions analogous to the narrow tomb in Holbein's painting), aborting the monster.

Jean-Luc Nancy posits that every image is fundamentally "monstrative" or "monstrant", and as such functioning as a monstrance (or pattern), referred to as an *ostensoir* in French. He further concludes that the image is of the order of the monster, because the *monstrum* is a prodigious sign that warns (*moneo, monstrum*) of a divine threat: "What is monstrously shown (*monstré*) is not the aspect of the thing; it is, by way of the aspect or emerging from it (or drawing it up from the depths, opening it out and throwing it forward), its unity and force. Force itself is nothing other than the unity woven from a sensory diversity. The aspect is in this diversity, it is the relation that extends between the parts of a figure; but the force lies in the unity that joins them together in order to bring them to light. That is what all painting shows us, tirelessly and in constantly renewed modes: the working of or the search for this force. A painter does not paint forms unless, above all, he paints the force that takes hold of forms and carries them away in a pres-ence. Under this force, forms too deform and transform themselves. The image is always a dynamic or energetic metamorphosis. It begins before forms, and goes beyond them. All painting, even the most naturalistic, is this kind of metamorphic force."[11]

11  Jean -Luc Nancy, "Image and Violence," in *The Ground of the Image*, trans. Jeff Fort (New York: Fordham University Press, 2005), pp. 21-22.

During the period between 2006 and 2012, Lovro Artuković created a series of twelve paintings titled *The Face of the Picture*. These are frames measuring 145x105 cm, executed in oil on canvas, where a woman's face appears painted in extreme close-ups. These works are not portraits of specific persons, as the relationship between the painter and the model in the process of creating a painting here becomes the relationship between a director and an actress (Karin

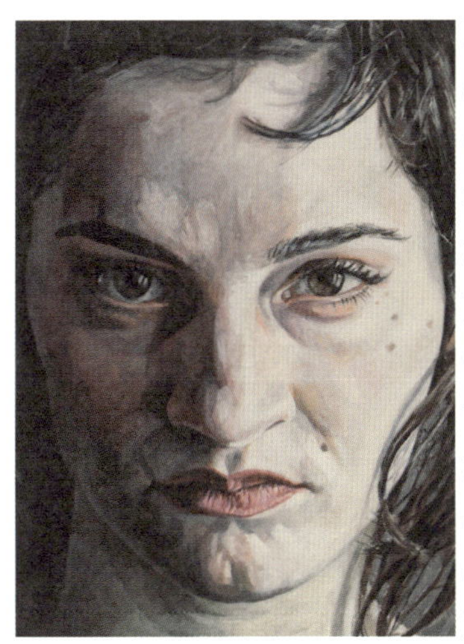

Enzler), the latter's task being to convey a specific emotional state through facial expressions. To embody a dramaturgical demand. The painterly procedure then transforms that state into the energy of matter, which explicates the presence of force by expressing it on the surface of the face as a constantly pulsating colour that cannot be contained within the boundaries of the outline. This vibrant colour acts as a de-forming and trans-formative force. One may say that each individual frame in Artuković's *Face of the Picture*, where one and the same face ceases to be identical to itself, articulates a particular aspect of that metamorphic force described by Nancy, because what happens with the pictorial matter should indeed be considered in terms of de-forming transformations. The matter, driven by this nameless force, is literally de-forming here. The face is stepping out from of its own contours, and its matericity pierces through them. The skin, stripped of its epidermis in the transformation, becomes synonymous with the metamorphic carnal force portrayed, which has truly been in-carnated and become incarnadine. Its eruption on the surface of the face of the picture is manifested as *caput mortuum* - the pulsation of living tissue within an inanimate picture.

25

Nancy argues that there is an unimaginable imagining in the ground of every image: dying as a movement of self-presenting: "At the far end of all imagination, there is access without access to what is never-yet-imaged of the one, and to an interminable in-figuration of every finite figure. The image always promises more than the image, and it always keeps its promise by opening its imagination onto its own unimaginable. [...] In the ground of the image there is the imagination, and in the ground of the imagination there is the other, the look of the other, that is, the look onto the other and the other as look - which also opens, consequently, as an other of the look, a fore-seeing non-look."[12]

12 Nancy, "Masked Imagination," in *The Ground of the Image*, p. 97.

Nancy's "other", which I understand as tangentially related to Lacan's Other, i.e. the Real, leads me to the *Twins* that appear in Artuković's canvases from 2006 to 2014. There is a black and a white variant of the *Twins*; there is a Twin depicted in front of an image of the Gemini constellation, while a soccer ball with the number 90 flies in from an undisclosed location; there is a girl in the Twin's nightgown who, by striking a match, illuminates a segment of the projected galaxy; and finally, there is a nightgown (as if floating) - a white nightgown (against a white background) - that the body has abandoned. To become what?

The melancholy of the *Twins* primarily stems from Artuković's act of composition, which dispels the illusion of a fairy tale by revealing it as a painted image - two distinct canvases joined together at their vertical edges, the line being visible within the fabric of the painting and articulating the notion of

31

a cut. That cut is not the same as a cinematic cut and should be considered in the context of Freud's or Lacan's concept of *Spaltung,* as Artuković paints the scene split in its own coherence. It is the coherence of projection, for *projection* is a concept found in the referential field of each of his paintings. Whether explicitly painted or not, projection becomes a protagonist of the painting - a medium, neither new nor old, but a non-chronological agency that induces the dramaturgy of permanent performance in the Real.

The *Twins* (2009) pose (seemingly pretending not to) in front of a white wall, clad in white nightgowns, standing barefoot on a wooden floor. The wall and the wooden floor are a kind of trademark in all of Artuković's 21st-century paintings. Painted, they denote that the observed scene has been staged in his studio, and what becomes visible as a realistic image will always remain a projection capable of inducing further projections. What is projected into what I see? And what does the painting project back onto me? The *Twins* (2009) show exactly this reverse gaze; leaning towards each other - distinct yet paradoxically identical - they look at us beyond us, inviting our gaze to extend past their presence. Towards the white wall before which they stand, and which resembled a sheet of clean yet crumpled 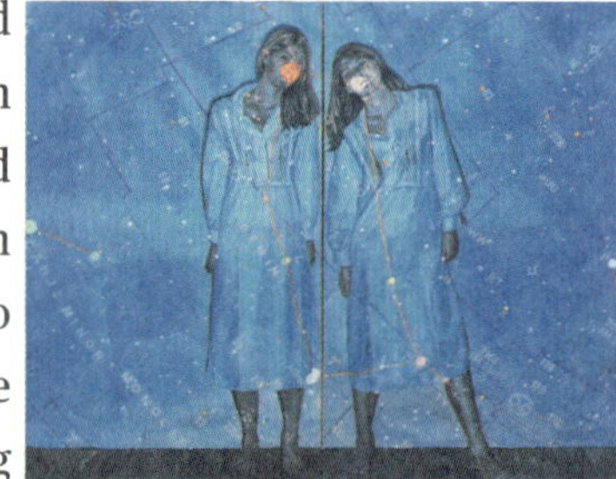 paper. Their white nightgowns exhibit folds painted in an even whiter colour, indicating that the garments were ironed and neatly folded before being worn for the scene visible in the painting. The texture of the fabric is almost identical to the texture of the wall on which the painted, barely visible shadows of the Twins' bodies are projected. In a painting made two years earlier and titled *Gemini* (2007), the Twins, dressed in identical nightgowns, adopt the same leaning pose in front of a wall onto which an image of an indigo-blue starry sky is projected, with the names of constellations inscribed in white letters. In this instance, the bodies of the two girls, together with the wall behind them, become the projection screen. The Gemini constellation, highlighted in orange, is thus divided by an irreconcilable residue, a gap resulting from the connection of the two canvases that do not form a diptych, but a figuration of the total space of the painting.

The notion of total space emerged in the discourse on modern painting around the mid-20th century, and in the splitting of the "total space" of the painting in the works of Lovro Artuković, I perceive his response to the demand that Clement Greenberg sets before painting. By insisting on the "norm of the medium," specifically flatness as a unique property of painting, on the purity of the medium, Greenberg's rationalization implicitly imposes normativity on desire as well: "Space, as an unbroken continuum that connects instead of separating things, is something far more intelligible to sight than to touch (whence another reason for the exclusive emphasis on the visual). But space as that which joins instead of separating also means space as a total object, and it is this total space that the abstract painting, with its more or less impermeable surface, 'portrays'."[13] Green-berg further explains the rationale behind banishing narrative from painting: "Pictorial space has lost its 'inside' and become all 'outside'. The spectator can no longer escape into it from the space in which he himself stands. If it deceives his eye at all, it is by optical rather than pictorial means: by relations of color and shape largely divorced from descriptive connotations, and often by manipulations in which top and bottom, as well as foreground and back-ground, become interchangeable. Not only does the abstract picture seem to offer a narrower, more physical and less imaginative kind of experience than the illusionist picture, but it appears to do without the nouns and transitive verbs, as it were, of the language of painting."[14] However, Mark Rothko, arguably the most radical of all abstract painters, challenged this institutional normativity of experience with the following statement: "If you are moved only by the color relationships in my paintings, then you miss the point. I'm interested in expressing basic human emotions - tragedy, ecstasy, doom."

13 Clement Greenberg, "On the Role of Nature in Modernist Painting," in: idem, *Art and Culture* (London: Thames & Hudson, 1973), p. 173. The essay was first published in 1949.

14 Greenberg, "Abstract, Representational and So Forth," in *Art and Culture*, pp. 136-137. The essay was first published in 1954.

27

Tragedy, ecstasy, and doom are nouns that achieve their ef-fect in conjunction with transitive verbs. This effect renders the surface of the painting permeable (as exemplified by the movement of Rothko's elemental particles of paint), and that permeability leads to the palpability of the force acting from the ground of the image.

26

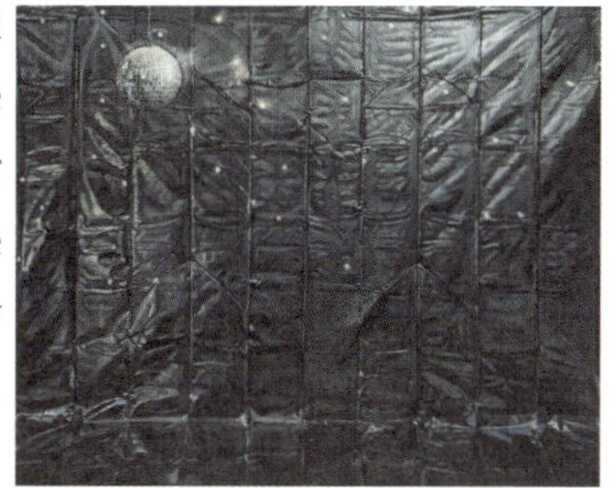

The words "surface" and "ground" are also nouns and as such become the represented motifs, moreover, the dram-aturgical backbone and the mise-en-scène of the event in Lovro Artuković's paintings. This is most evident in those paintings where the subject is explicated through the rela-tionship between two words strategically placed in the title: *as if*. This "*as if*" denotes the illusion as the substance of what is given to be seen in realistic painting. *As if* spells its own staging. As if they were *False Twins in the Night* (2013), *As if It Were a Starry Night* (2007), although it is actually impermeable black plastic foil (akin to the one standing for the sea in Fellini's *Casanova*) and a rotating silver disco ball. And all this is painted in such a way that the space seems to touch us, although the *act of composition* clearly shows us that we stand outside the picture. On its threshold.

Unlike Greenberg, who appears unwavering in his belief in painting's ability to portray total space, which should also be a total object, Nancy implicitly rejects the possibility of a portrait, because "a painter does not paint forms unless, above all, he paints the force that takes hold of forms and carries them away in a pres-ence." And flatness and presence are mutually exclusive.

28

33

In his book *Corpus*, which is actually a reflection on the incorporating sentence - *Hoc est enim corpus meum* - Nancy argues that the "anxiety, the desire to see, touch, and eat the body of God, to *be* that body and *be nothing but that*, forms the principle of Western (un)reason. That's why the body, bodily, *never happens, least of all when it's named and convoked.* For us, the body is always sacrificed: eucharist."[15] Arguing that the body is weight and that the laws of gravity include *bodies* in space, he wonders whether we invented the sky for the sole purpose of making bodies fall from it. At the same time, he posits that the "Body" is our naked agony and might serve as another name for the Stranger. Reflecting on how the programme of modernity once consisted in not writing about the *body*, the body itself, Nancy underscores touch and interprets the act of writing as touching.[16] He ultimately concludes that painting is the art of the body in that it solely knows skin, being skin through and through: "Another name for local color is *carnation*. Carnation is the great challenge posed by those millions of bodies in paintings; not *incarnation*, where Spirit infuses the body, but carnation plain and simple, referring to the vibration, color, frequency, and nuance of the place, of an event of existence."[17] Bodies do not take place in discourse or in matter, Nancy argues. They do not inhabit "mind" or "body", but take place at the limit - external border, the fracture and intersection of anything foreign in a continuum of meaning, a continuum of matter.[18]

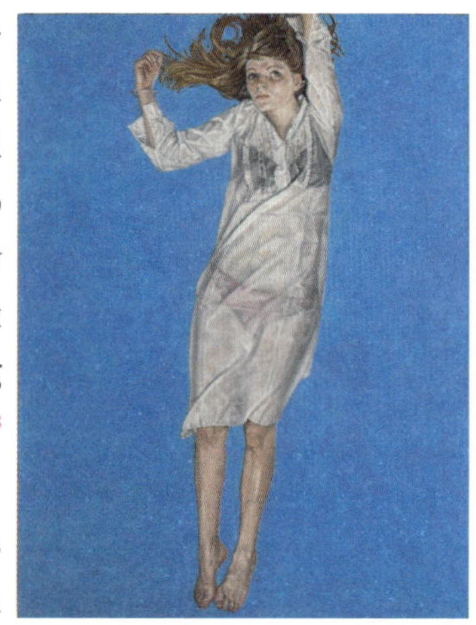

Similar to Nancy's writing, Artuković's painting is touching. In his canvases, the sky is nothing but a projection; bodies do not fall from it. *As if Floating* - and apparently it is no coincidence that the background against which they float is consistently monochromatic - sometimes blue, another time white, and at times red: like the colours in the title of Krzysztof Kieślowski's melancholic trilogy.

There is no trace of illusionism in Lovro Artuković's paintings; they intentionally expose their "special effects." In the painting *Winged*, his painterly performance creates the impression of audible sound emanating from the painted aluminium foil, which functions as an opaque but reflective background. Against this backdrop, the figure of a girl in a white dress appears to be flying. The wings, even whiter than the perfectly white dress, strapped to her back, are painted with such veristic precision that one can almost feel the soft touch of their feathers on one's skin. Artuković does not paint a flight, whether real or fake, but a sensory sensation, a transformative force - that "unity woven from a sensory diversity" that the gaze, that

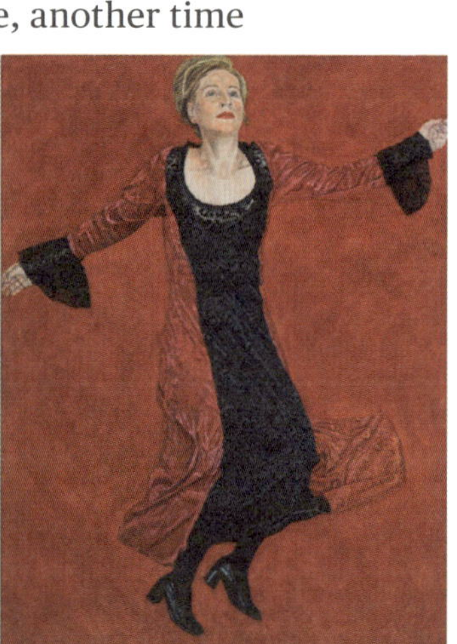

15  Jean-Luc Nancy, *Corpus*, trans. Richard A. Rand (New York: Fordham University Press, 2008), p.5.

16  Ibid., pp. 8-11.

17  Ibid., pp. 15-17.

18  Ibid., p. 17.

29

30

31

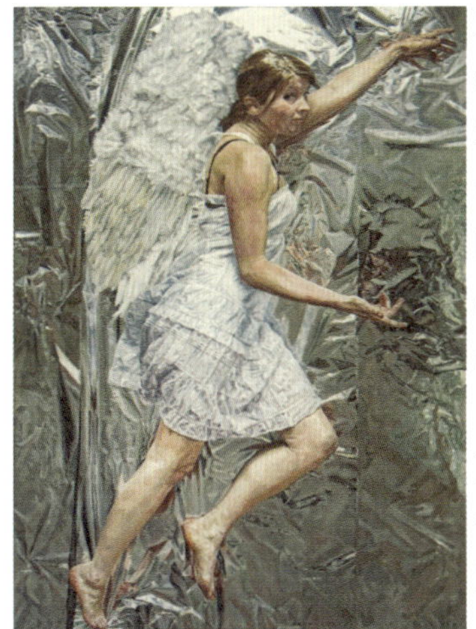

is, the retina of the eye, cannot verify. This reaffirms once again Nancy's thesis that the image is the obviousness of the invisible.[19] Consequently, it is completely irrelevant whether the painted wings connote the wings of an angel or Icarus, because the focus lies on the fall, the body in the abyss of its own carnality, an abyss that Artuković's paintings, re-semanticizing various aspects of familiar myths, bring to presence.

Re-semanticization was literally performed with the painting *Pietà Inverted* (2011), which has its "double" – the painting titled *Models Posing for a Pietà* (2011). Both paintings undoubtedly allude to the most famous depiction of the Virgin with the body of the dead Christ in her arms, that of Michelangelo. However, Artuković's act of composition, wherein he situates the protagonists of the Passion in front of the same white brick wall that is actually the main character in many of his paintings, clearly shows that it is a theatrical staging in which the Passion denotes physical passion rather than Christ's torment. The scene is structured in two picture planes. The background is dominated by "stage lighting," a representation of a vertically positioned, luminous neon tube affixed to the wall, connected by a power cable to a meticulously painted socket in the same wall. In the foreground, an eroticized scene unfolds, featuring a woman dressed in a voluminous black robe holding the weighty body of a completely nude man on her lap, his genitals uncovered by the loincloth that traditionally functions as a signifier of the Crucifixion in Christian iconography. Unlike Michelangelo's Madonna, she does not avert the gaze downwards at her "burden", but looks directly at the spectators from the painting. The weight of the reclining body is here directly related to touch: the painter emphasizes the taut muscles of the woman's left arm as she supports the heavy leg of the man reclining in her lap. In the second painting, *Pietà Inverted*, the mise-en-scène remains unchanged, but the positions of the man and woman are swapped. The man, still nude and seated, firmly rests his feet on the wooden floor, while the woman, swathed in the same black drapery, throws her head back and raises her left leg, bent at the knee, as she reclines in the man's arms. As the drapery falls from her right shoulder, which the man is embracing, it is revealed that she is wearing a bathing suit. This positioning of the reclining female figure in the *Pietà* composition, rather than the dead Christ, evokes Bernini's *Ecstasy of Saint Teresa*. The eroticization of the scene is enhanced by the painted red flower petals scattered across the woman's draped body, with one petal stuck to the man's lips.

19  Jean-Luc Nancy, "The Image the Distinct," in *The Ground of the Image*, p. 12.

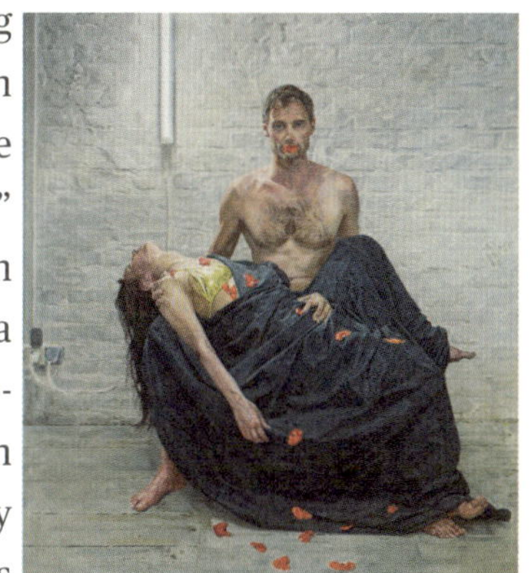

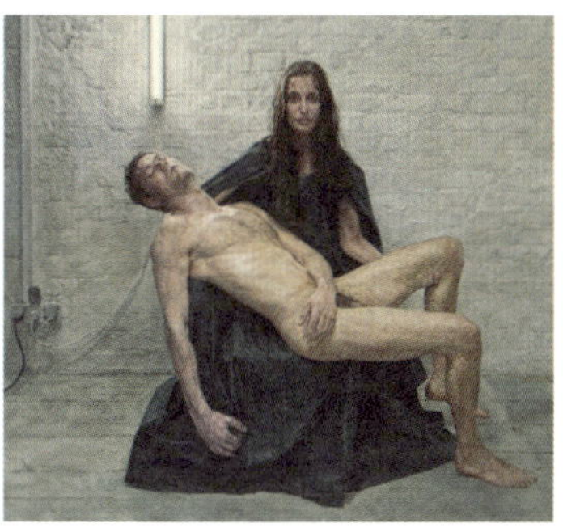





34

Reading the *Dead Christ in the Tomb* in the context of melancholy characterized by identification with an abandoned object,[20] Kristeva brings in another painting by Holbein, an almost monochromatic diptych with depictions of *Christ as the Man of Sorrows* and the *Virgin as the Mater Dolorosa*.[21] Analysing the paintings, she notes that "the body of the man of sorrows, strangely athletic, brawny, and tense, is shown seated under a colonnade; the right hand, curled up before the sexual organ, seems spasmic; the head alone, wearing a crown of thorns, together with the aching face with gaping mouth, expresses a morbid suffering beyond vague eroticism." Reflecting on these aspects, Kristeva poses the following questions: "From what passion did such a pain arise? Would the man-God be distressed, that is, haunted by death, *because* he is sexual, prey to sexual passion?"[22] I am inclined to recognize the same question in Artuković's variations on the theme of *Pietà*, in which the faces of the protagonists enacting the classic scene of Christian iconography, referenced extensively in works of modern and contemporary art - from Eisenstein to Picasso and Sam Taylor Wood - do not reveal the slightest hint of distress.

An explicit depiction of "tormentum" does appear, however, in Artuković's *Hanging Self-Portrait* (2009-2013), a picture embedded within a painting measuring 270 x 360 cm titled *Apollo and Marsyas (Triumph of the New Media over Painting)*, made between 2009 and 2011. In the *Hanging Self-Portrait*, painted in life-size proportions (250 x 110 cm), the body occurs on the borderline between theatrical staging and media image, specifically referencing footage of sadistic atrocities committed for the amusement of torturers in detention camps, opened at the beginning of a never-declared world war following the infamous September 11 events, which ushered in an era of necropolitics and total (media) control. In this canvas, the artist literally portrays himself as hanging meat, let's say, in a refrigerator, suspended by ropes attached to a mountaineering harness tightly fastened around his nude body. The harness connotes extreme sports, an aspiration to climb and reach unchartered territories, but also alludes to sadomasochistic equipment. The painting's backdrop consists of a crumpled, off-white linen curtain hanging parallel to the artist's body, concealing a wall behind it. A canvas from which the body has slipped away? Or perhaps the Shroud of Turin, with the incarnation of a completely different image? There is *caput mortuum* on the flushed head, the chest and palms extended towards the spectator, whose body is allowed to approach the edge of the painting.

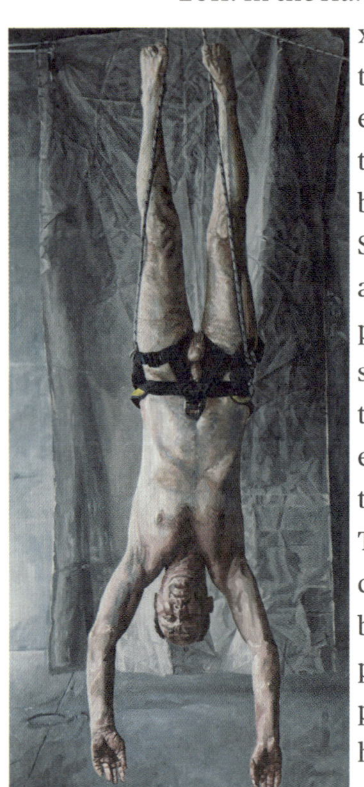

21  The diptych, dated ca. 1520, is housed at the Kunstmuseum Basel.

22  Julia Kristeva, "Holbein's Dead Christ," p. 112.

35

20  Sigmund Freud associates melancholy with loss, its distinguishing mental features being "a profoundly painful dejection, cessation of interest in the outside world, loss of the capacity to love, inhibition of all activity, and a lowering of the self-regarding feelings to a degree that finds utterance in self-reproaches and self-revilings, and culminates in a delusional expectation of punishment." Unlike in mourning, where "it is the world that has become poor and empty, in melancholia it is the ego itself." But the free libido is not displaced on to another object; it is withdrawn into the ego. In this process, there is an identification of the ego with the abandoned object, and thus an object-loss is transformed into an ego-loss, and the conflict between the ego and the loved person into a cleavage between the critical activity of the ego and the ego as altered by identification." Sigmund Freud, *Mourning and Melancholia*, trans. James Strachey, SE, vol. XIV (London: Hogarth Press and The Institute of Psychoanalysis), pp. 244 and 249.

In the *Triumph of the New Media over Painting*, which the artist himself has referred to as a "bulky painting," thus calling into mind the numerous examples of the so-called historical painting - enormous canvases that fill the halls of museums in European metropolises - the *Hanging Self-Portrait* assumes the role of the satyr Marsyas. In Greek mythology, Marsyas was flayed by the god Apollo after being deceitfully defeated in a musical contest, as he naively picked up the double flute crafted from deer bone that the goddess Athena had thrown away upon catching sight of her reflection in the water and realizing that her distorted cheeks, livid from blowing into it (*caput mortuum*?), marred her beauty. Marsyas' skilful playing had won him admiration as he journeyed through Phrygia accompanied by Cybele - the Great Mother of the Gods - so Apollo, fuelled by envy, challenged him to a competition, proposing that they play their instruments in reverse, with the victor granted to do as he pleased with the loser. Since the flute could not be played in reverse like Apollo's lyre, the Muses sided with Apollo, and Marsyas' flayed skin was affixed to a pine tree.

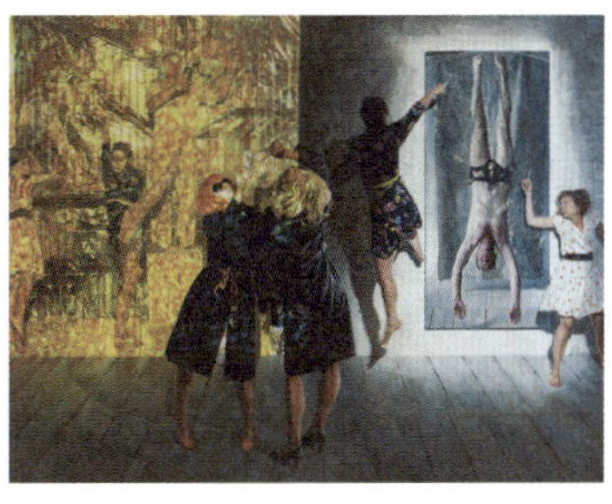



This mythological narrative reminds me of the concepts articulated by Clement Greenberg, the most influential American critic of the mid-20th century, who constructed a modernist myth around the possibility of attaining purity within a specific artistic medium and advocated for the prohibition of narrative in painting. He thus wrote: "Cubism undertook a completely two-dimensional transcription of three-dimensional phenomena, in defiance of everything the Impressionists had learned about light and verisimilitude through light; but by being *sculpturally* exhaustive, by showing in shaded relief the back and sides as well as front of an object, Cubism ended up with an even more radical denial of all experience not literally accessible to the eye. The world was stripped of its surface, of its skin, and the skin was spread flat on the flatness of the picture plane. Pictorial art reduced itself entirely to what was visually verifiable, and Western painting had finally to give up its five hundred years' effort to rival sculpture in the evocation of the tactile. And along with the tactile, imagery and imaging had to be renounced too, insofar as anything taken from the world of nonpictorial space brought with it connotations and associations that the retina could not of itself verify."[23]

23 Greenberg, "On the Role of Nature in Modernist Painting," in *Art and Culture*, p. 172.

Drawing a relation between Greenberg's notion of "cleansing", i.e. the metaphor of stretching the flayed skin in place of the unique picture plane, and Artuković's narrative, specifically his *Hanging Self-Portrait* featuring an explicit depiction of an inverted penis and the suspended fabric that could be that stripped skin of the world that suddenly became a painterly canvas through a mystical discursive transfiguration, I cannot help but recall the context in which Lovro Artuković began his career. Today it is evident that the rhetoric of high modernism had a distinct aim: the depoliticization of art. In the second half of the 20th century, this depoliticized, "abstract" art became mainstream in Croatia, a Yugoslav republic at the time. Lovro Artuković, who emerged on the Croatian art scene in the early 1980s, was never interested in modernist formalism; his works always contained a "story" that led to other stories. I am reminded of his ironic, even critical painting titled *Kitschmonger in the Shade* (1999) from the *Artists in Nature* series, which undoubtedly connotes Greenberg's dichotomy of avant-garde and kitsch,[24] where the so-called "figurative art" was implicitly associated with kitsch. Today, we still witness similar superficial binary oppositions and the resulting biases. One such division is the categorization into the so-called "traditional" and "new media". The painting *Apollo and Marsyas* directly addresses this issue, which is why the defeated Marsyas, in the multimedia performance staged on the canvas, is actually a painting - a self-portrait of the (self-)hanged painter. However, the act of composition in both pictures defies any definite conclusion regarding whether it represents punishment or erotic pleasure.

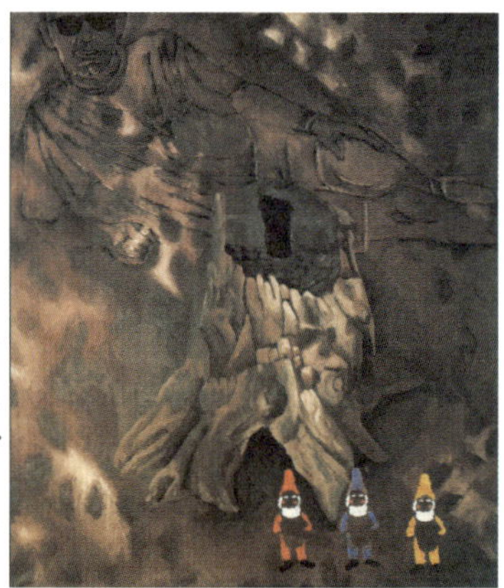

24 Greenberg's essay "Avantgarde and Kitsch" was first published in 1939.

The scene in the painting *Apollo and Marsyas (Triumph of the New Media over Painting)* is divided into three parallel planes, none of which can be clearly identified as front, middle, or back. The entire painting functions as an interplane where several stage performances unfold simultaneously. Those stage performances are painterly performances at the same time. Lovro Artuković paints here the levels of a performance where the boundaries between real and virtual, truth and falsehood, become blurred, and this irrelevance of truth highlights the notion of the performative. Regarding the performative, from which the term performance is inseparable, it is important to note that Shoshana Felman distinguishes three semantic connotations of the English word *performance*: linguistic, theatrical, and erotic,[25] all of which are present in Artuković's "fake historical painting."[26] The painting *Apollo and Marsyas (Triumph of the New Media over Painting)* also explicitly shows its own staging on the very same stage where all of Artuković's "events of the body" occur - his studio, characterized by a white brick wall and wooden floor. What the painting gives to be seen is a re-enactment of a theatrical performance, and in this painterly re-enactment, the binary opposition between the painted, painterly image and the digital, electronic image projected onto the painted screen within the painting itself has been annulled. The motif of the wall connects the performance that took place in a different space and time with the painterly canvas that re-semanticizes that performance. The models posing for *Apollo and Marsyas* are dancers from the group *Nightmare before Valentine*, performing the piece *Früchte im Koma* in a theatre, with a choreography based on jumps that involve body impacts against the wall. On the right side of Artuković's canvas, one sees the *Hanging Self-Portrait*, which in this new painterly dramaturgy assumes the role of the satyr Marsyas

25 Shoshana Felman, *The Scandal of the Speaking Body: Don Juan with J.L. Austin, or Seduction in Two Languages* (Stanford, CA: Stanford University Press, 2003 [1st ed. 1980]), p. 15.

26 Artuković referred to his *Apollo and Marsyas* as a fake "historical painting" in an interview conducted by Patricija Kiš, *Jutarnji list* (February 21, 2011), http://www.jutarnji.hr/ lovro-artukovic--ovo-sam-ja- sa-64--htio-sam-znati-kako- cu-izgledati-kad-ostarim-- plasi-me-prolaznost-vremena-- i-smrt/926802/ (last accessed on July 20, 2014).

as two dancers rush towards him with knives in their hands, replicating the same jumps performed in *Früchte im Koma*. Are they impersonating the Muses who declared Apollo the winner and thereby allowed him to skin Marsyas? On the other, left side of Artuković's canvas, Apollo, standing on the "victor's pedestal," is opening a bottle of champagne. However, the space in which Apollo celebrates is a virtual space of projection. His "triumph" is projected onto a folded, reflective golden foil that serves as a screen. On this screen, a telescopic shot of explosions on the surface of the Sun is projected, causing the figure of the winner, as well as the figures of the two dancers performing before "Apollo", to dissolve into vagueness. The champagne that the winner opens in the space of the screen is actually consumed in the space of the artist's studio, where the performance of the "painting abuse" takes place. Two women wearing elegant black leather coats, their eyes concealed by sunglasses, are shown in a chore-ographed movement of raising their champagne glasses. They are positioned almost into the geometric centre of the picture, into the interspace between triumph and punishment. Nancy argued at one point that art "is not a simula-crum or an apotropaic form that would protect us from unjustifiable violence. [...] It is the exact knowledge of this: that there is nothing to reveal, not even an abyss, and that the groundless is not the chasm of a conflagration, but imminence infinitely suspended over itself."[27]

27 Nancy, "Image and Violence," in *The Ground of the Image*, p. 26.

In Artuković's costumed and choreographed "performances" of the image, a peculiar relationship between the body and garment emerges. Or, rather, between the metamorphic force and its ever-changing attire. In his artworks, the notion of the garment of the painting (which always keeps its promise) is connoted by the protective packaging material used to safeguard artworks from mechanical damage, such as plastic wrapping with air bubbles. The girl with the blue wig in his *Ari in a Trashy Costume* (2012) dons such an outfit, enveloped in the same ma-terial as depicted in the composition *Ari Dances with Plastic Cups* (2012-2013). The body as a painting? Tunica as a pigment? Picture as a costume? Or, the body itself as a costume – foreign to itself? As if were a melancholic *Alien*, or a *Shy Cowboy* (2005-2010), which is the title of one of Artuković's self-portraits. In this particular self-portrait, he represents himself frontally, with a gaze cast downward. With his upper body exposed, shield-ing his bare chest with crossed arms, he stands before a paint-ing turned towards the wall, concealing its content from view. Positioned above the concealed picture are two painted photo-graphs with clearly recognizable scenes from Western movies.

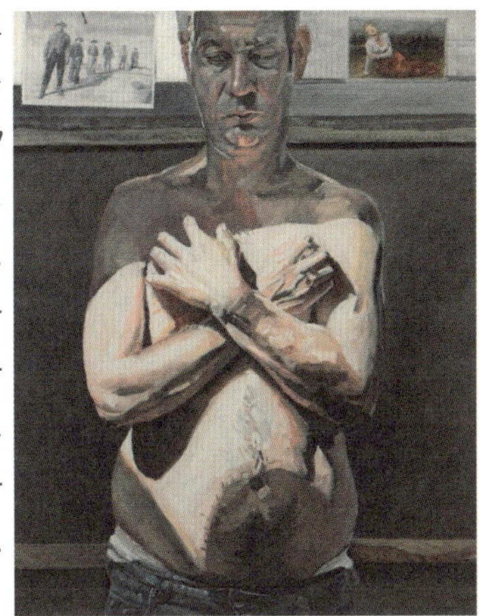



39

In 2022, Artuković painted two completely different self-portraits. The first, titled *Self-Portrait – Thinking of Marino Tartaglia*, is a re-enactment of one of the most significant paintings in the history of Croatian modern art, an expressionist self-portrait of very small dimensions painted by Marino Tartaglia in 1917 and first exhibited in 1918 at the *Mostra d'arte indipedente* in Rome's gallery L'Epoca alongside artworks by Giorgio de Chirico, Carlo Carrà, and Enrico Prampolini. Artuković's second self-portrait, which literally visualizes the futuristic concept of bewildering speed, is chromatically akin to the first one and is titled *Self-Portrait - At the Moment When I Am Trying to Recall Something*. The depiction of an exploding head visual-

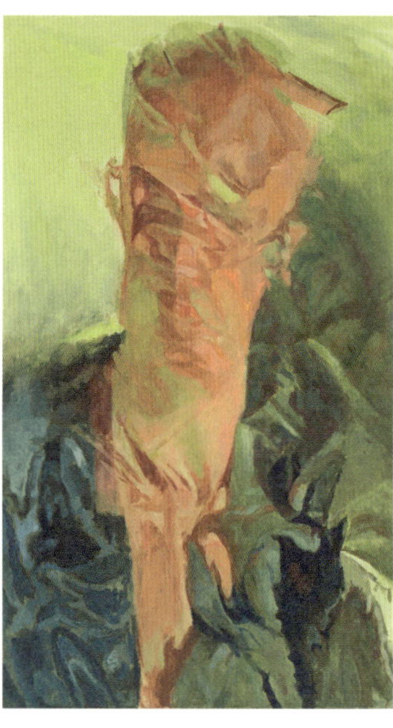

ly represents the exertion of memory. In their execution, both self-portraits are related to the paintings from the *Reflections* series, produced a few years earlier and displayed, together with the series *Studio Visit*, *Night Lights*, and *Excursion*, in Artuković's 2020 exhibition *Deceleration* at the National Museum of Modern Art in Zagreb.

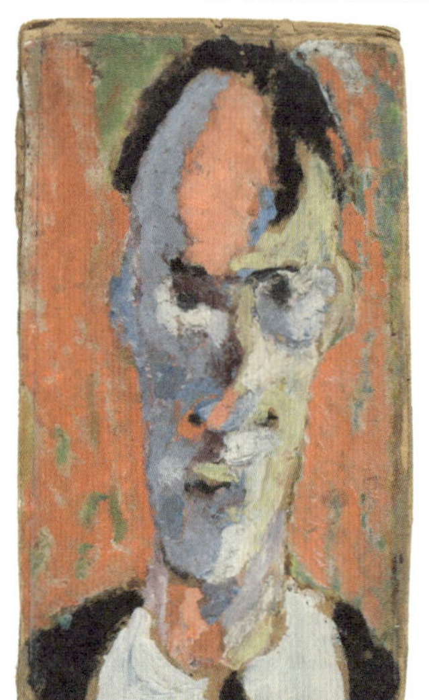

F

Speaking about these works, Artuković said that what he intended to achieve with his paintings was becoming increasingly time consuming. "The paintings are swarming with details and my way of painting, which involves countless brushstrokes with varnish on the same spot to achieve the desired presence and density of the painted image, takes hours and hours that somehow pass unnoticed. Often, while sitting fixed for days on a single detail of a painting, I think I should speed up the painting process, be more productive, and work more adequately in a time where everything is happening at a frenetic pace and where, I'm afraid, no one will have the patience or concentration anyway to indulge in the old-fashioned viewing pleasure when looking at my paintings."

40

6

My own, perhaps old-fashioned, viewing pleasure when looking at his paintings, which feature reflections on polyester metallic foil such as is obligatory in every car's first-aid kit, leads me to the question of difference, of the enigma of the unnamed that Lovro Artuković has been "trying to reach" when painting. The polyester foil commonly known as the *Rettungsdecke*, first-aid blanket, or survival blanket, usually 210 x 160 cm in size, was invented in 1964 as part of NASA's space programme and is a multi-purpose product. This waterproof and windproof blanket is golden on one side and silvery on the other, and it keeps your

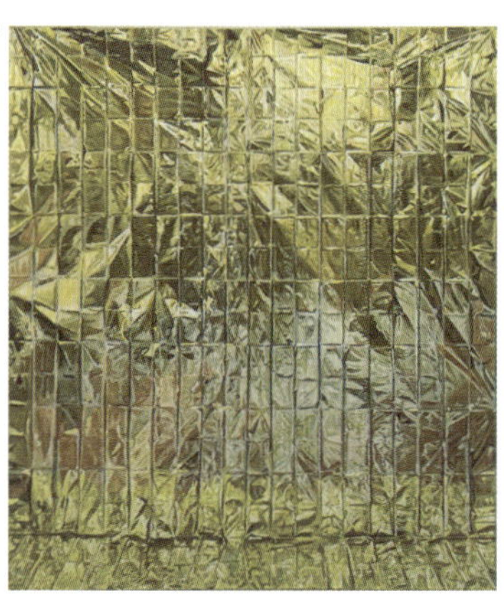

body temperature stable while its shiny surface makes it easier for lifeguards to find injured persons. In Artuković's art, its portrait first appeared in 2009, in a painting from *The Place* series titled *Gold (First-Aid Blanket)*. The place is, of course, the artist's studio while the gold is the polyester foil, attached to the wall and descending to the floor. Its surface is broken down into a regular grid of rectangular facets created by the folding, i.e. packaging of the blankets. In this painting, the motif of glistening fake gold occupies a full frame sized 145 x 125 cm. That same year, the first-aid blanket appeared again in Artuković's painting *New Year's Eve Gown* as a golden background, with the green dress from the *As if* series floating in front of it. The painted motifs in this series, as well as its very title, connote delusion or optical illusion by representing scenes in a state of staging. Delusion in its multiple appearances would become one of the main themes in the paintings that Lovro Artuković has been working on since 2018. In them, the painted reflections on the surface of the golden first-aid blanket disfigure various scenes from the artist's studio. This disfiguration is manifested as an infinite multiplication of different images within one and the same image. *Mise en abîme*?

When speaking of difference, I am reminded of the installation *Tragedia civile* that Jannis Kounellis set up at the Lucio Amelio Gallery in Naples in May 1975. The gallery wall, with its entrance to the left, was entirely lined with square golden leaflets. Next to the wall, the artist had placed an antique wooden hanger of the so-called Viennese type, with a black man's coat and hat on it. On the right-side wall, he had attached a petroleum lamp to discreetly counter the dominant neon illumination of the gallery. The golden wall radiated a specific light and at the same time incorporated the dark shadows of the hanger and the garments. There are numerous interpretations of Kounellis' installation in which, among other things, references to the use of golden leaflets have been found in ancient mythologies, the tradition of medieval painting, and the artist's admiration for the work of Andrei Rublyov. Furthermore, the title and placement of the objects in this enigmatic work have been linked to theatricality, with the historical transversal extending from the Greek tragedy to Brecht's epic theatre. In these interpretations, the *Tragedia civile* has also been contextualized by referring to the use of gold in the conceptual art practices of the 20th century, with a particular emphasis on the golden leaflets that Beuys used to coat his face as he contemplated on how to explain pictures to a dead hare.[28]

28 Giorgio di Domenico, "'Una partecipazione che va trovata': Jannis Kounellis, Tragedia civile, 1975," *Studi di Memofonte* 21 (2018), Fondazione Memofonte, pp. 216-242, https://www.academia.edu/38567354/_Una_partecipazione_che_va_trovata_Jannis_Kounellis_Tragedia_civile_1975 (last accessed on February 18, 2020).

Unlike Kounellis, who covered the wall with real gold, Lovro Artuković attaches cheap polyester foil of golden colour to the wall of his studio, which becomes a kind of screen against which the disfiguring reflections take place, becoming the object of painterly representation. However, real golden leaflets did appear in his work twenty years earlier, in paintings from the *Artists in Nature* series. These include *The Bunny and the Creek* (1999) and *The Bunny and the Frozen Creek* (2000), in which the artist painted Joseph Beuys with a dead hare in his arms after the photographs taken on November 26, 1965, during that famous performance at the

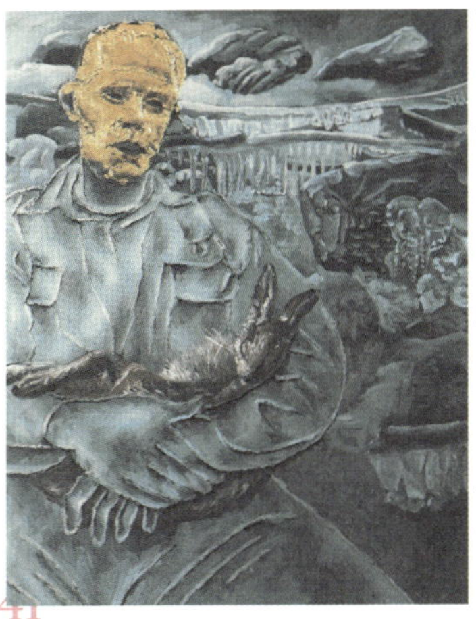

Schmela Gallery in Düsseldorf, situating him in a landscape reminiscent of the setting of the saddest Croatian song for children, evoked by the titles of Artuković's paintings. In these oils on canvas, Beuys' face is shaped by golden leaflets. *The Bunny and the Frozen Creek* disappeared without a trace in 2002, when the vehicle transporting Artuković's paintings from the Lisbon exhibition to Zagreb was stolen.

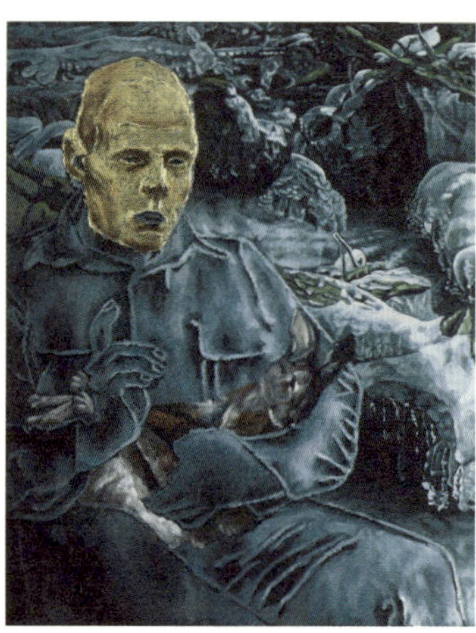

Today, looking at the paintings featuring the grid of reflective surfaces of a survival blanket, I wonder if that which Lovro Artuković is trying to achieve by painting is analogous to Beuys' silent endeavour of explaining pictures to a dead hare? More precisely perhaps, is it possible to explain pictures at all? History of painting is full of dead hares, and Lovro Artuković repeatedly tells me that he is dealing with images, not the painting.



The disfiguring reflection that occurs in Artuković's paintings crystallizes the question of translatability; of the relationship between what is visible and what is seen articulated by the dynamics of macro and micro planes of the painting.

The very act of painting yields an irreducible difference between seeing the picture (*confronting the image*) and the event of the image; the rift in which resides that what makes Artuković's work theatrical. For, however successful the illusion may be, the mimesis occurs only in order to expose the image to the unstoppable whirlwind of trans(re)lations. It is not by chance that the golden, reflective surface of the first-aid blankets is painted in different sizes and on different material supports, in particular oil on wood and oil on canvas. In this fact I might detect a reference to the history of painting, the trajectory of images from the medieval times to modernity. For example, the painting entitled *Fairy Tale Creature - Cubist* (2018) is made in oil on wood and measures 33.5 x 22.5 cm, whereby its surface is divided into nine rectangular squares, resulting in fragmentation and, consequently, the dis-figuring of the depicted figure. Its dis-figuring makes it impossible to determine with certainty whether it is a reflection of someone standing in front of the painting or someone who, from a depth of space within the painting (separated from the outer space by a kind of transparent partition), approaches the one who is viewing the image. The *Captured Spectre* (2019) - a charcoal drawing on paper made in a slightly larger format that same year - apparently solves this dilemma, since in the dark configuration on the left side of the paper it is possible to recognize (or imagine) something like a palm of a hand on which the depicted spectre rests against the gridded membrane separating it from the observer, who is perhaps identical to the spectre itself. The act of the disfigured face of that spectre, coming extremely close to that



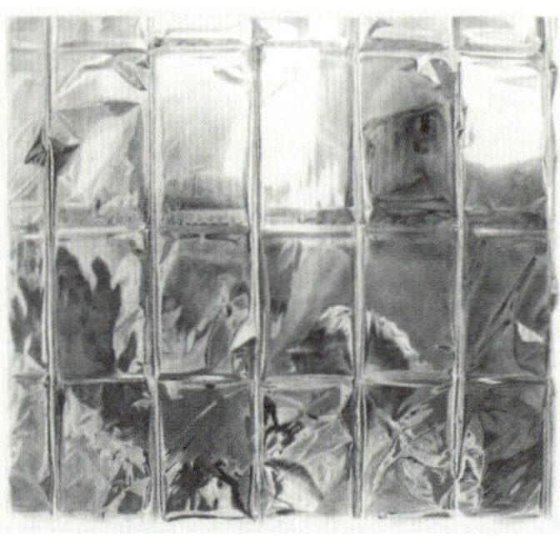

of the supposed observer, reminds me irresistibly of the blurred boundary between the intimate and the extimate in Courbet's youthful self-portrait *Le Désespéré*, painted between 1843 and 1845. The historiography of art says that the artist did not separate from this painting until his death, just like da Vinci from his Mona Lisa. With the title of his most celebrated painting, which in its format appropriated the prerogatives of the then most revered genre - historical painting, Courbet complicated the definition of realism to the extreme. The full title is *L'Atelier du peintre. Allégorie Réelle determinant une phase de sept années de ma vie artistique (et morale)*, or in free translation: *The Painter's Atelier: A Real Allegory that Sums up Seven Years of my Artistic (and Moral) Life*. Real allegory would be an oxymoron by definition. But what if one tried to ask what reality the definitions create? And furthermore, what is the relationship between the reality thus created and what Courbet called moral life?

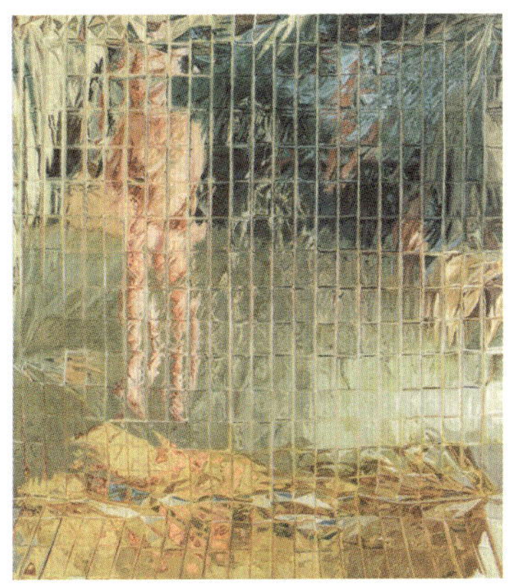

Unlike Courbet, Lovro Artuković titled his oil on canvas sized 220 x 190 cm *Studio Reflection in Golden Sheet* (2018). What is reflected are some naked bodies. Or the reflected forms only seem to be that. The regular grid of the depicted lines made by packaging, or rather folding of the foil, divides the painting into 432 rectangular fields, each of them with a different image. Some of them resemble what the history of art has categorized as monochrome painting, or abstract expressionism, or Cézannean landscape, while others are reminiscent of the sceneries of German expressionist film. In the painting titled *Io and Jupiter,* the first-aid blanket reflects figures whose bodily gestures remind me of Picasso's *Les Demoiselles d'Avignon*, and in some facets of the *Black Silhouette* I see scenes that seem like city vedutas. One of the images in the *Reflections* series is titled *The Annunciation*. This title, as well as the quite evident painting procedure of image dissolution, evokes to me Richter's series *Verkündigung nach Tizian* (1973), in which the performative gesture of paradoxical erasure of the painting surface successively, from canvas to canvas, has disfigured one of the central themes of the Christian myth, bringing it down to its very essence articulated by the translation of red colour, with which Titian figured the Archangel's swirling attire into a hazy field of particles. In this haptic yet elusive haze, a dissolution of contours occurs that blends all colours and hues in a way reminiscent of Rothko's monochrome fields. By the way, in the geometric centre of Artuković's *Annunciation*, something unknown has taken place, chromatically bicomponent, painted in bright and dull tones of red. The recliner in the atelier? Behind that something, a green depth opens. In the collapse of the compact image, with an effect analogous to Richter's and Rothko's osmosis, the particle quality articulated in the works of Lovro Artuković raises the question of the image and its multilevel interferences with the living body. It is the question about the enigma of the image, not its definitions, because it does not refer to what

46

47

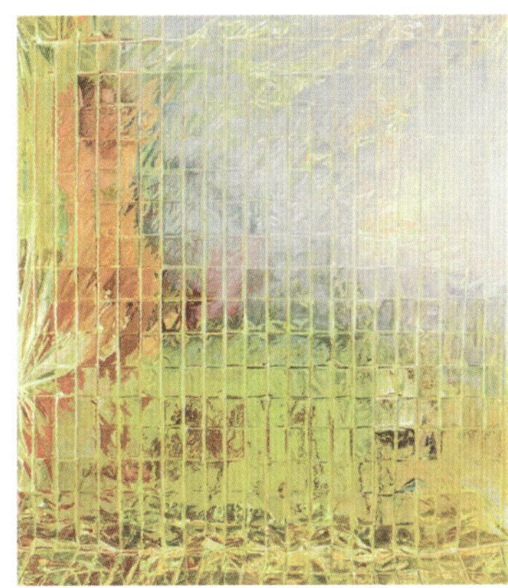

I see and how I see it, but to the substances that reside in the sediments of the ground of my vision. The ground of vision is *mise en abîme*, and it plays a key role in the event of the image in Lovro Artuković's painting.

*Mise en abîme*, as the principle of an infinite multiplication of micro-narratives within a canvas saturated by painting, also appears in the seemingly formally completely different, "compact" paintings, where the condensation

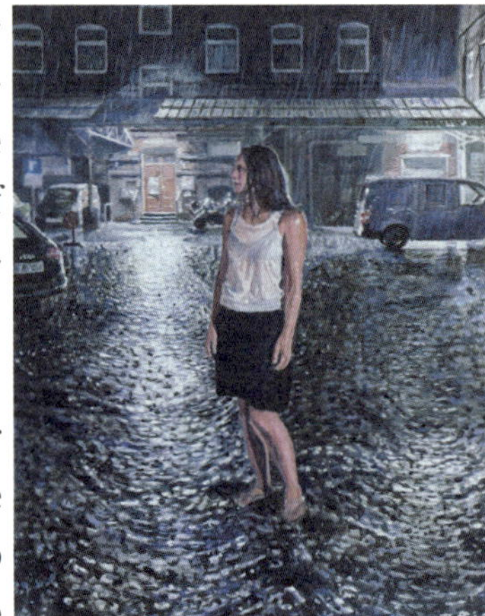

of mimetic and diegetic register of scenes occurs. Thus, in the *Full Moon in My Kitchen* (2019), a dark shadow of the artist's body is mirrored in the invisible glass of the studio window. Unlike in the opaque *Black Silhouette*, this shadow allows us to see through it the windows of the surrounding buildings glowing in the darkness. The same windows, visible from the kitchen of the artist's studio, appear in the paintings *In the Yard* (2019) and *Lene in a Deluge* (2019). Perhaps it is these three paintings taken together, paintings in which the vantage point is successively lowered to focus the notion of a variable position of vision, that raise the question of the place of the event of the image, the topography that resides beyond iconography.

The position "on the far side of time," which I identified earlier in this text as the space of the excessive event of the image manifested as *mise en abîme* in Artuković's painting, is also encrypted in his *Dispute in the Studio* (2019-2020). Barely visible in its reflection in the window pane, a tiny transparent figure is watching the scene from the other side of the reflection with its arms crossed. The author? Unlike Courbet's "real allegory," in Artuković's painting the notion of art is not subject to symbolization. Art is not signified here by the figure of a naked woman - a numb signifier that points to everything but itself, a passive body before

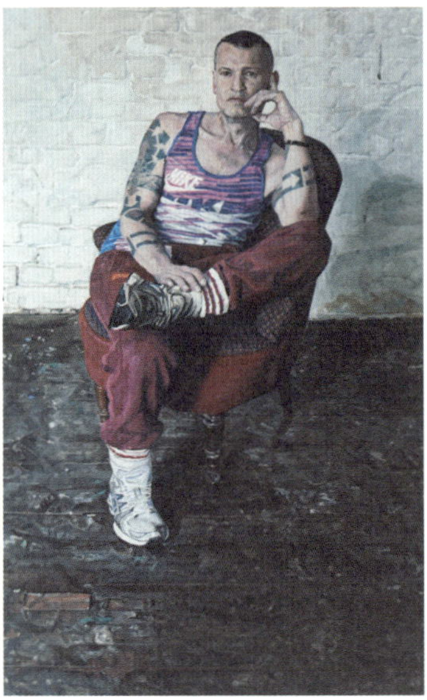

the powerful gaze of the artist. Are the six female characters represented in the picture of the artist's studio perhaps in search of an author? Pirandello's theatre piece is also a sort of *mise en abîme*, a play within a play. The presumed author - whose position in the space of the represented scene, but located outside the painting, may be revealed by his (or her) reflection in the window pane painted in the background - seems to be discovered only by a small dog gazing at him (or her) from the foreground. This canine gaze brings to my mind the dramaturgy of the Dutch Baroque genre scenes, in which animals play an important role and not without reason. Artuković's six human figures - women silently "debating" in the kitchen of his studio - are portraits of one and the same actress, Jeannine Simon, who, for the purpose of performing in the painting, changes her clothes, position in

48

49

50

space, gestures, and facial expressions. This sameness of the model, which is nevertheless not the identity of the portrayed figure, introduces into the painting a dimension of simultaneous, non-chronological time manifested as deceleration. This deceleration, which in Artuković's painting seems like cinematic découpage, multiplies the seemingly accessory scenes. In one of these scenes, one sees the studio workspace with an unfinished portrait of a man (known from the painting *Runar*, 2015) through the open kitchen door, while in another, a window painted behind the back of a woman in the foreground opens a view to a street where a group of people is discussing something vigorously. In the fight scene, their tiny but minutely crafted figures remind me of the narrative structure of Renaissance paintings, in which the unnamed story in the background draws attention more strongly than the title theme of the painting. What is going on in the street?

There is something painful, reminiscent of Fassbinder's films, in the timbre of Artuković's paintings of Berlin streets and bars. In the tenderness with which his figures are texturized and the quietness with which they inhabit the scenes, in the sombre lights of devastating intensity that draw their bodies out of invisibility. I say texturized, not textualized (because I understand texture as divergent to text), referring thereby to Proust's distinction according to which writing is completely opposite to describing. By analogy, Artuković's painting is not a depiction; that is why I am not speaking about the scenes of Berlin's streets and Berlin's bars, but about the images of streets and bars. Speaking about Proust's fatal fascination with Vermeer, figured by the "little phrase" of *petit pan de mur jaune*, Didi-Huberman writes the following: "Proust was very far from looking for some pseudo-'photographic time-still' in the visible; he sought there on the contrary a trembling duration, what Blanchot called ecstasies - the 'ecstasies of time'. Correlatively, Proust did not seek in the visible the arguments of *description*; he rather sought there a fulguration of *relations*."[29] Lovro Artuković is likewise far from searching for such pseudo-photographic time-still, although each of his paintings is preceded by an extensive photo session - a performance for the camera, so to say. And what follows is: how should one trigger the event of the image out of a petrified moment, a mortifying shot?

Anne Carson has counted that in the novelesque series *In Search of Lost Time* Albertine's name occurs 2363 times, and that she is present or mentioned in 807 pages of the novel.[30] Should I try to count the number of times and paintings by Lovro Artuković where the figures of Ari, Jeannine, Charly, or Natascha appear? Although they do not ride bicycles in these scenes, under the street lighting by night in his *Apparition in Neukölln* (2019), behind the back of a woman dressed in something like a wedding dress, which is in

29 Didi-Huberman,
*Confronting Images*, p. 245.

30 Anne Carson,
*The Albertine Workout*
(New York: New Directions,
[2014]).

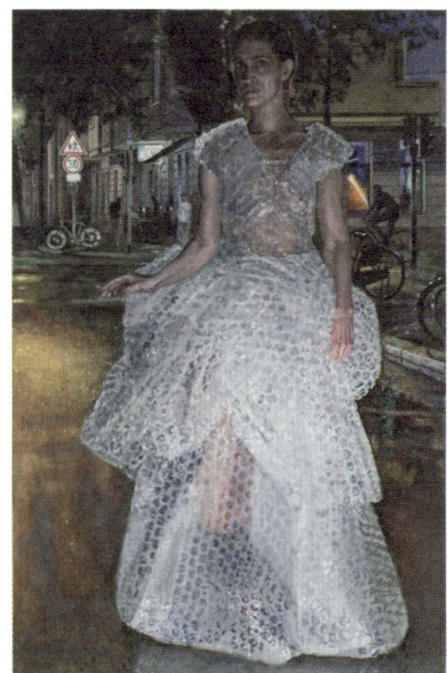

fact a plastic foil with air bubbles such as used for wrapping artworks and other fragile items, I see a cyclist and several parked bicycles. Instead of the artist's studio, as in the paintings *Ari in a Trash Costume* (2012) and *Ari Dancing with Plastic Cups* (2013/14), Ari is now sitting, dressed in the same kind of foil, in the middle of the road in Berlin's district of Neukölln, her back turned to the terrace of a bar that is here an embedded quote from Van Gogh's *Terrasse de café sur la place du Forum*, painted in 1888 in Arles. The same quote, but with a completely different intonation, appeared decades earlier in *My Friend Vincent*, which Lovro Artuković painted in 1986. In this painting, the apparition of Van Gogh's terrace occurs in Zagreb, in Medulićeva Street.





Where do the *Late Night Tales* (2019) take place? At the *Tier* bar in Berlin, in whose interior many photographic frames were taken in order to be painterly transfigured generating the erupting particles in the event of the image? Where does the dim red light come from under which Natascha, her back turned to the observers, gazes through the smoke of a cigarette at a huge, strange photograph attached on the other side of the counter like wallpaper? Charly and Anian look at her in amazement, she may be saying something. In another sequence of Artuković's "film", her face is illuminated by a mixture of bar and streetlight, fully occupying the painting *Night Lights* (2019). The green glare on a granite cube of the street paving, visible through the bar window, links the painting to the *Flower Dress* (2019), in which Charly, illuminated by the light of a scented candle, taps the ashes of her cigarette into an ashtray with a focus and slowness of Vermeer's *Milkmaid*. In another painting (*At the Bar*, 2020), the painter's gaze glides slightly backward and offers a scene seen from a slightly greater distance, so that the painting shows Charly, dressed in a black dress with yellow floral pattern, is still in the same pose, with the same facial expression, but now Natascha and Anian are sitting at the table next to which she is standing, their eyes fixed on something not visible in the picture. In the third frame, the two of them are watching her attentively, and the artist has titled this painting *The Storyteller* (2020).

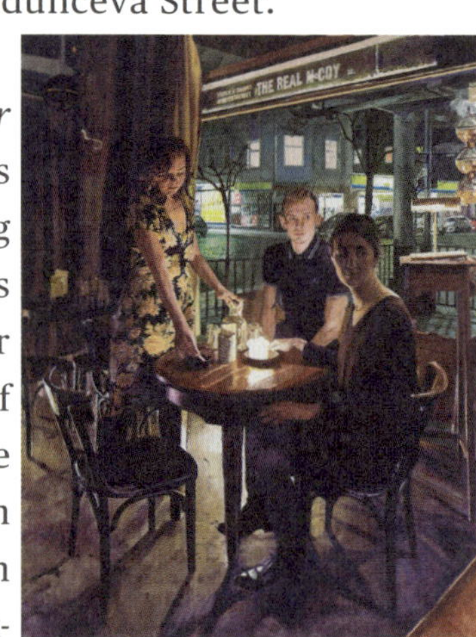

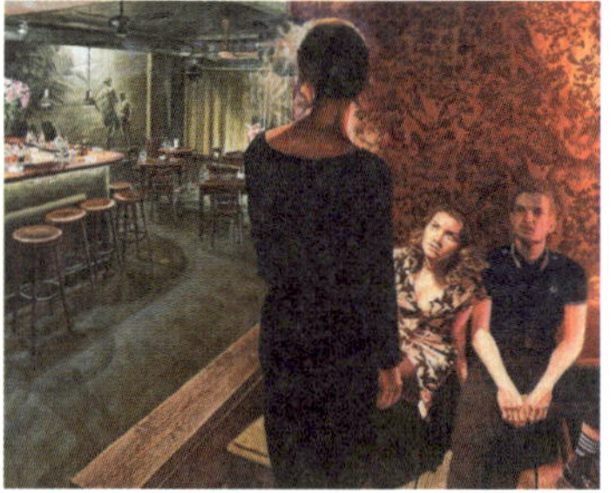



In 1936, Walter Benjamin, a Berliner himself, wrote an essay called *The Storyteller* in his Paris exile, saying that the art of storytelling had become rare and is even about to die out as we have lost an ability that once seemed inalienable - the ability to share experiences. The price of experience has fallen and continues to plummet - he writes - and the image of not only the external, but also the moral world has undergone changes overnight that we would have never thought possible.[31] Is the abyss mentioned by Benjamin in relation to the price of experience also the subject of Artuković's *Late Night Tales*, painted in the second decade of the 21st century? How to paint a conversation? Or what has been spoken, but will never reach audibility? The *Tragedia civile*?

31 Walter Benjamin, "The Storyteller," in *Illuminations*, ed. Hannah Arendt, trans. Harry Zohn (New York: Schocken Books, 1968), p. 83.

In the foreground of one of the bar scenes, there is a self-portrait of Lovro Artković. He has painted himself in profile, sitting at a bar, dressed in a windbreaker and immersed in his thoughts, glancing at the empty glass he is holding in his right hand. His face is frontally illuminated by the red lights of the bar and laterally by the blue reflection from his windbreaker. Natascha, Anian, and Charly are also on the stage. None of them is looking at anyone else and nobody is talking; Natascha is smoking, Anian is washing the glasses, and Charly is absent-mindedly pressing the edge of the sink with her hands. The title of the painting is *Bad Thoughts* (2019). Here, too, there is a quotation embedded in the ground of the image, but this time it is not a specific visual, but a verbal motif that he is citing - the title of a series of performative photographic images produced by Gilbert & George in 1975, in which the colour that immerses the performers' figures - the

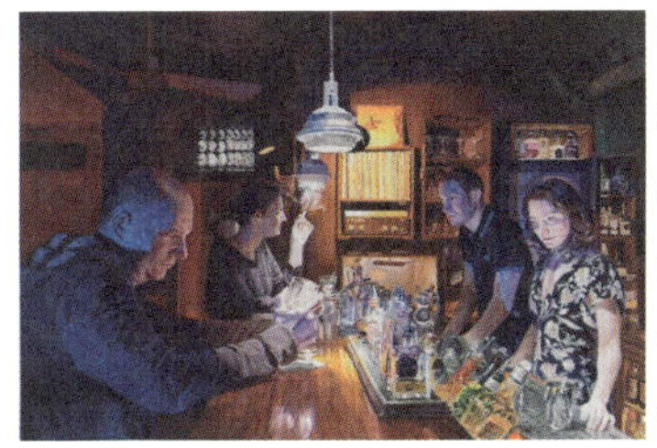

two of them, with glasses in their hands, and their home studio - is blood red. The series was preceded by a sequence of works titled *Drinking Pieces*. It is worth mentioning here that at the very beginning of their career, Gilbert & George, who have since declared themselves a living sculpture, "portrayed" themselves in a typical English landscape. Made in large format, these charcoal and chalk drawings on paper are titled *The Nature of Our Looking* (1970), while the oils on canvas, painted a year later, are simply called *The Paintings (with Us in the Nature)*. These titles are, of course, ironic because the subject of their interest has been and remains the culturally produced naturalization of the discourses of power. These paintings, like the works of Lovro Artuković today, articulated questions about the place of the event of the image: the visible reflections and the flashes that pass below the threshold of perception.

55

56

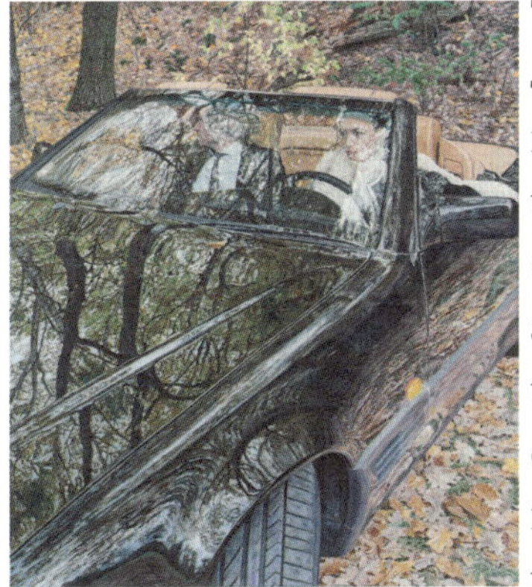

The *Excursion* series was made simultaneously with the *Studio Visit*, *Night Lights*, and *Reflections*. To paraphrase, I might say that these also raise the question about the "nature of our looking." What do I see in the *Autumn Excursion* (2019) and why? A luxury cabriolet whose polished metal and windshield mirror the forest - its half-bare canopy and the golden leaves on the ground? Through these reflections one can barely see the figures of a woman and a man sitting in the car, dresses more appropriately for an evening outing than a trip to nature. She is at the wheel, staring in front of her, while his face is turned to the left, toward the forest. A movie scene? What genre does it belong to? The "story" continues with the next image,

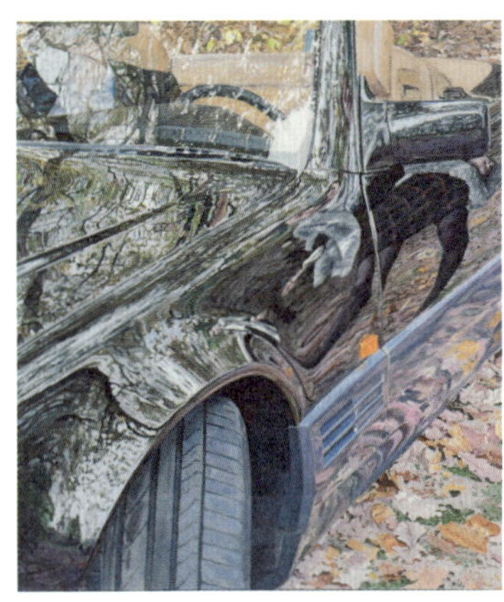

which "zooms in" on the car wheel, the fender, the door, and the empty driver's seat. The painting is entitled *Hydra (in an Autumn Landscape)*. The painter did not, like Goya, insert the inscription *El sueño de la razón produce monstruos*, but painted a microscopic scene in the exterior rearview mirror, calling it (internally) *A Brandenburg Landscape with a Figure (Reflection)*. With the *Hydra (in an Autumn Landscape)* Artuković has syncopated the phenomenon of anamorphosis. Anamorphosis, of course, occurs in reflection.

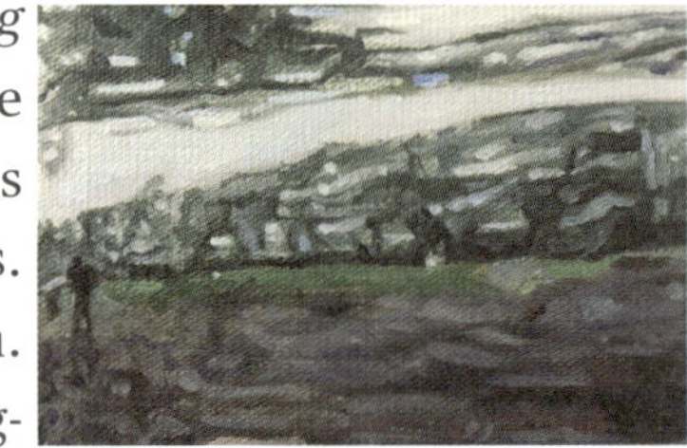

That is why it is completely irrelevant whether I will recognize the mythical being of lethal odour in the gleaming fender, among the reflections of autumn leaves, or an absent driver dressed in a plaid skirt, or something completely different, because it is in Artuković's *Spring, In Grunewald*, and *On a Summer Day in the Heidelberg Forest*, in the "trembling duration" or the "ecstasy of time," that the event of the image resides - a presence that, in the density of the painted, takes the painter "hours and hours that somehow pass unnoticed."

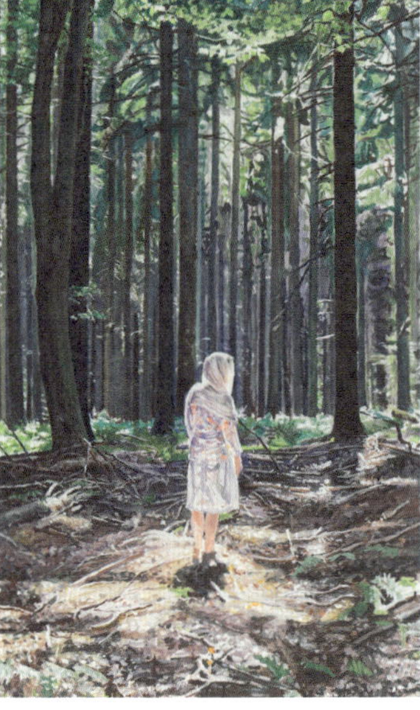



57

58

Notes

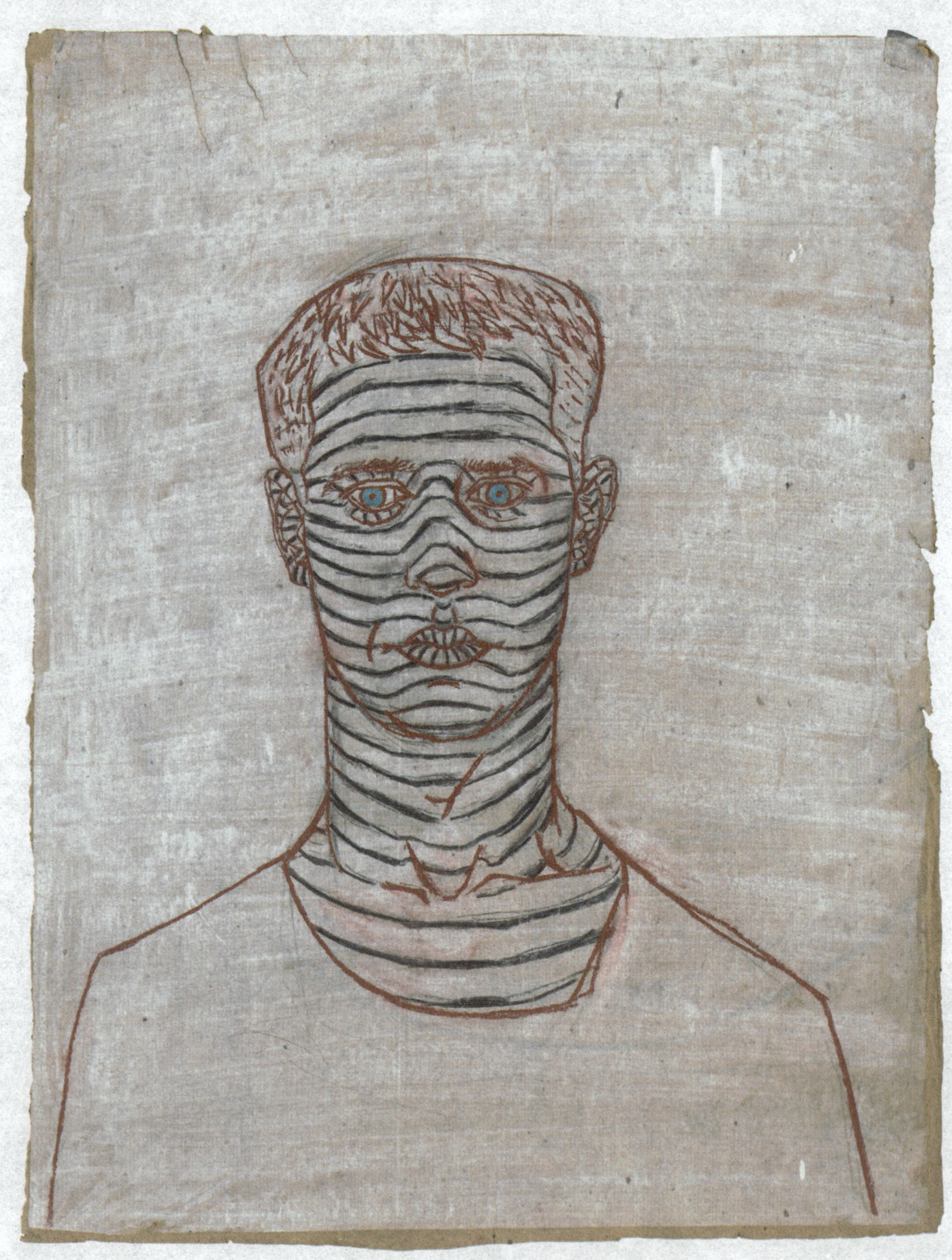

59

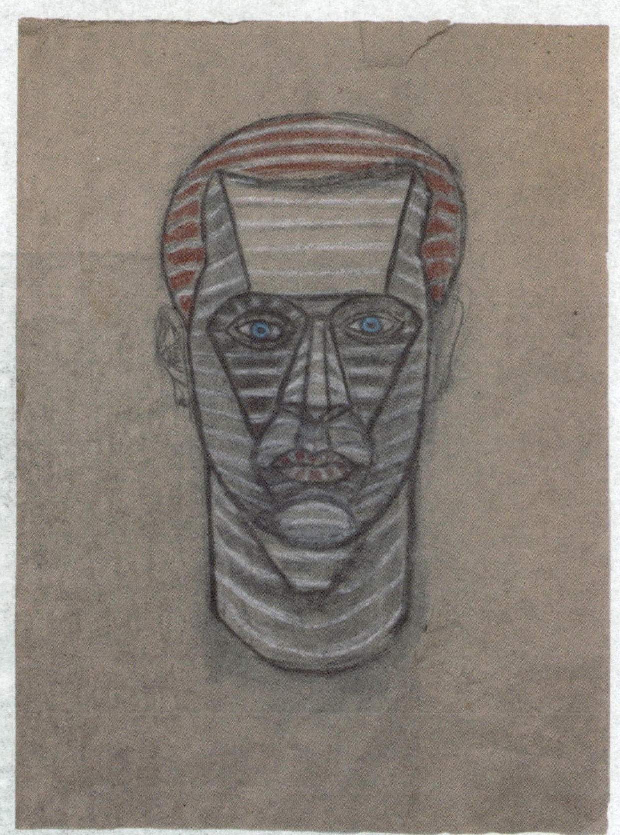

61

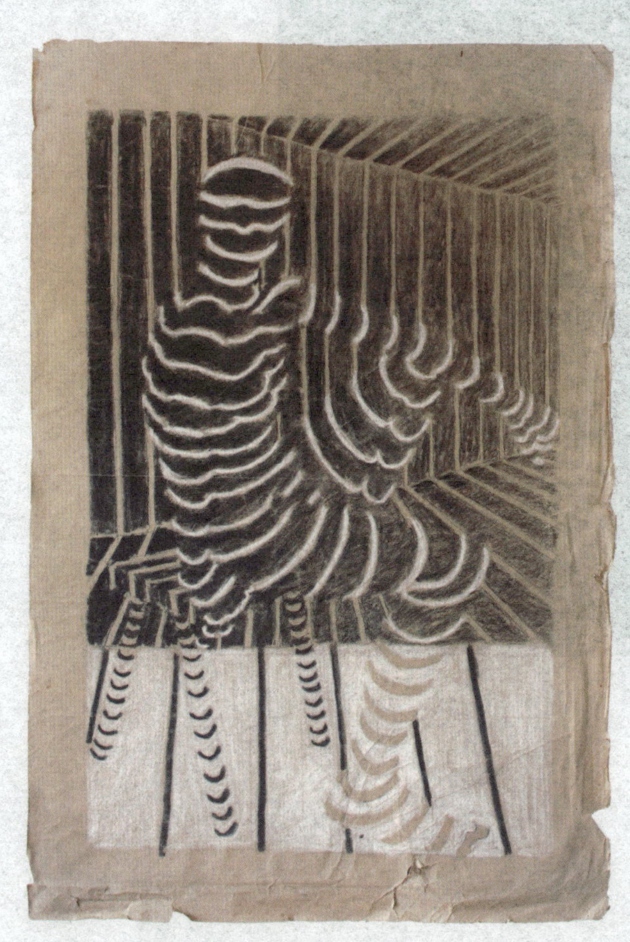

62

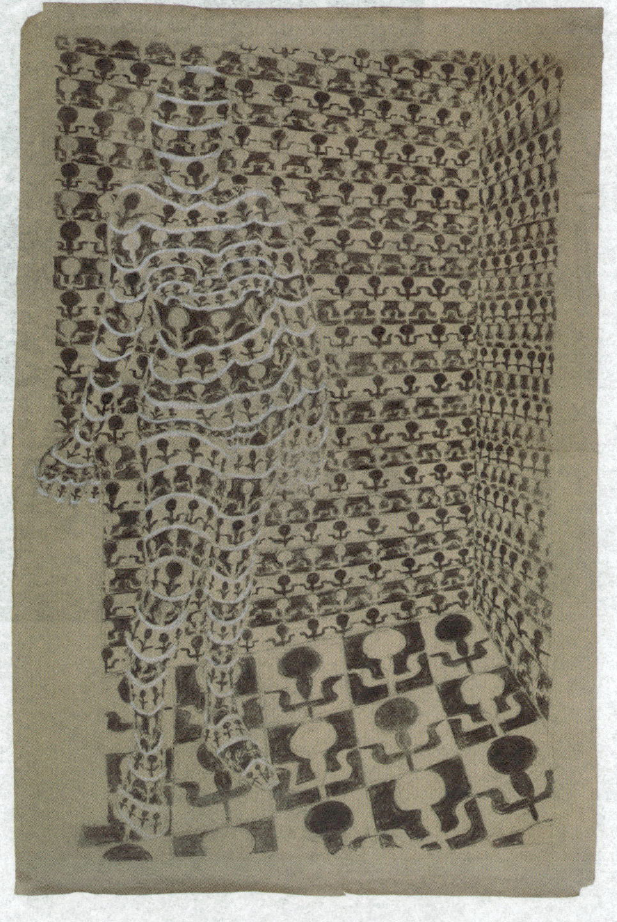

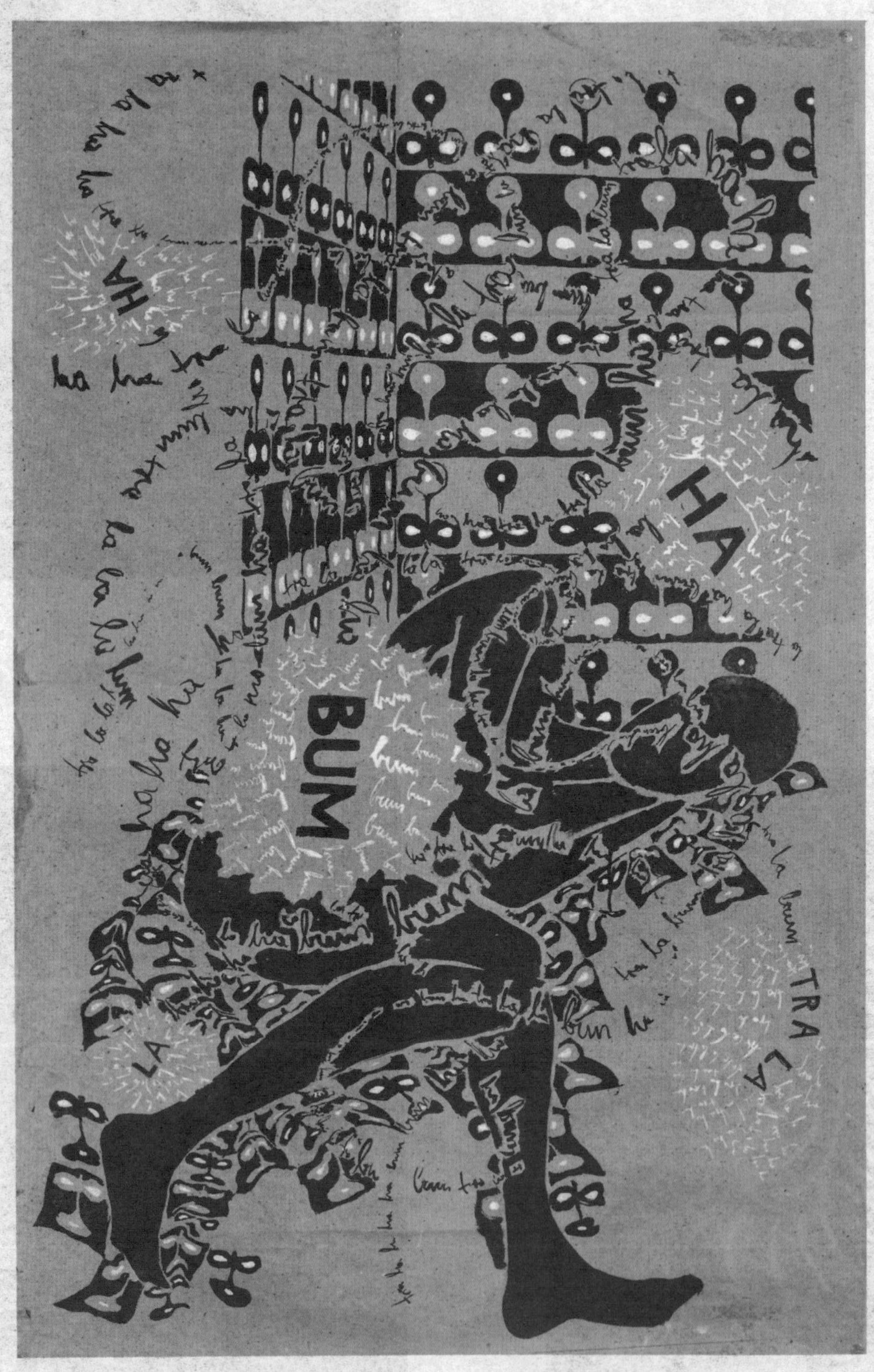
HA
HA
BUM
TRA
LA
LA
BUM

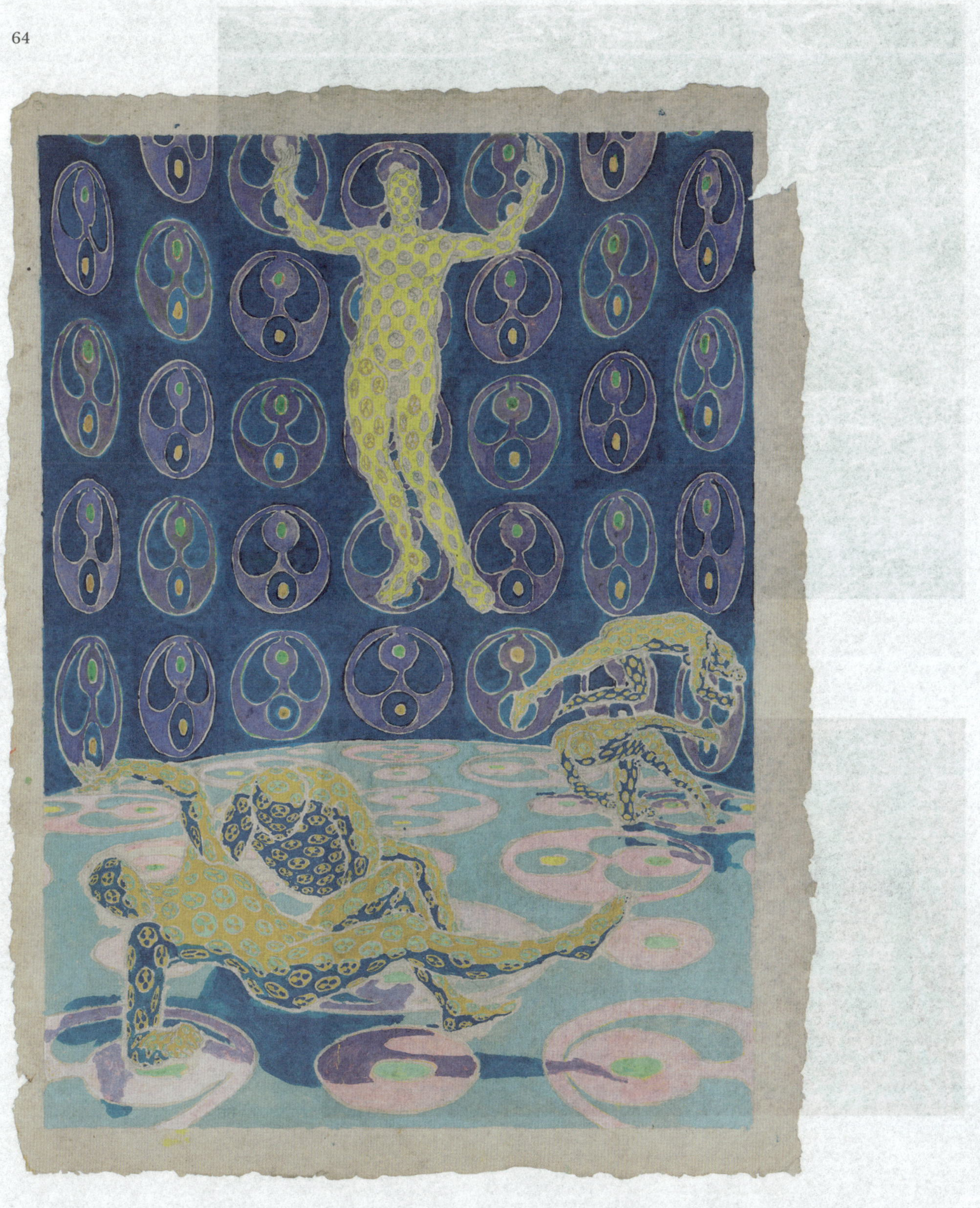

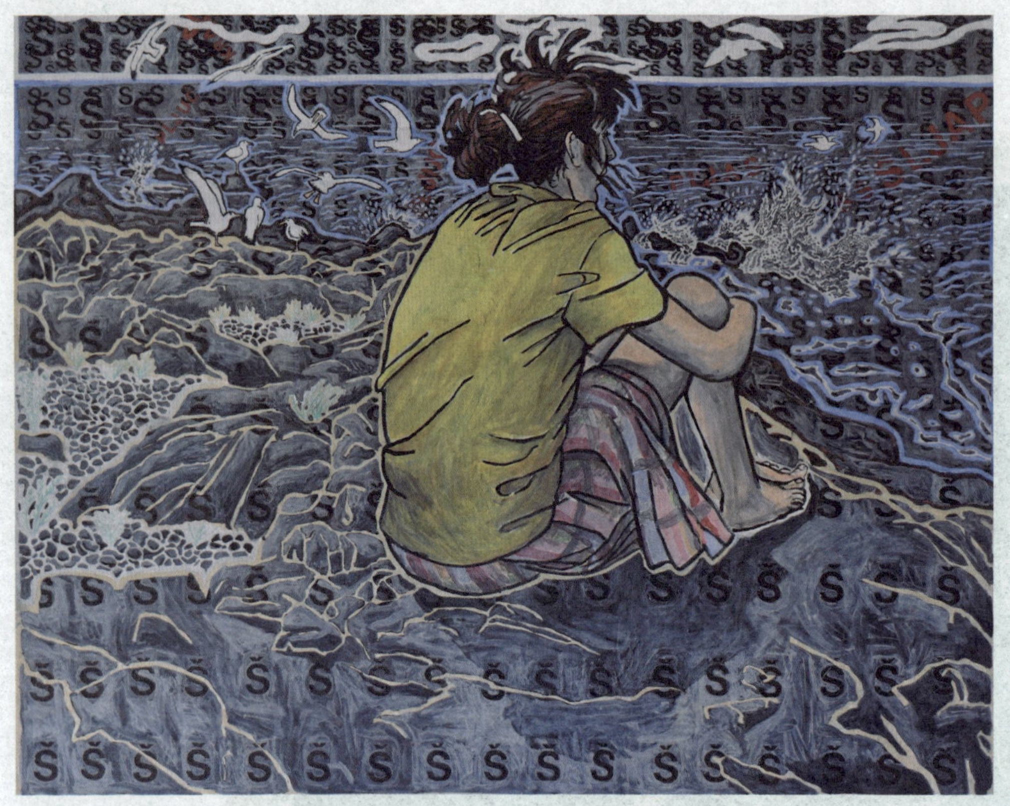

65

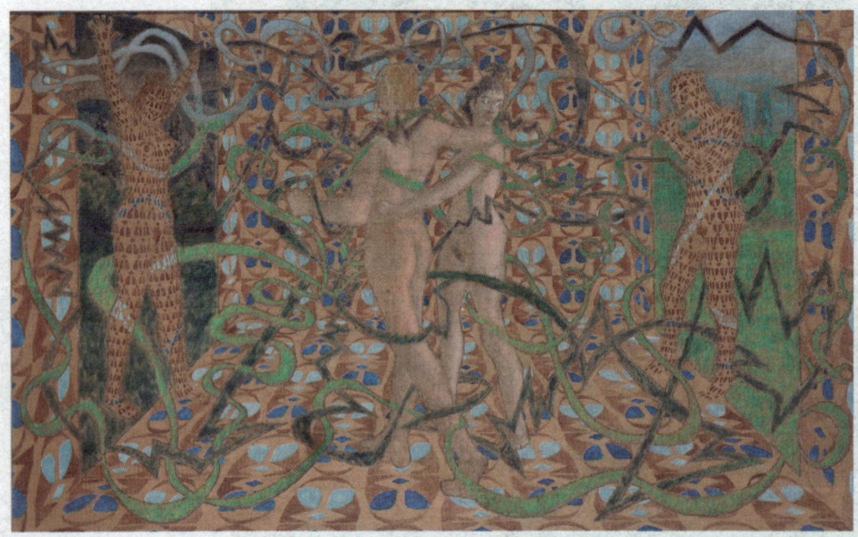

66

Paintings

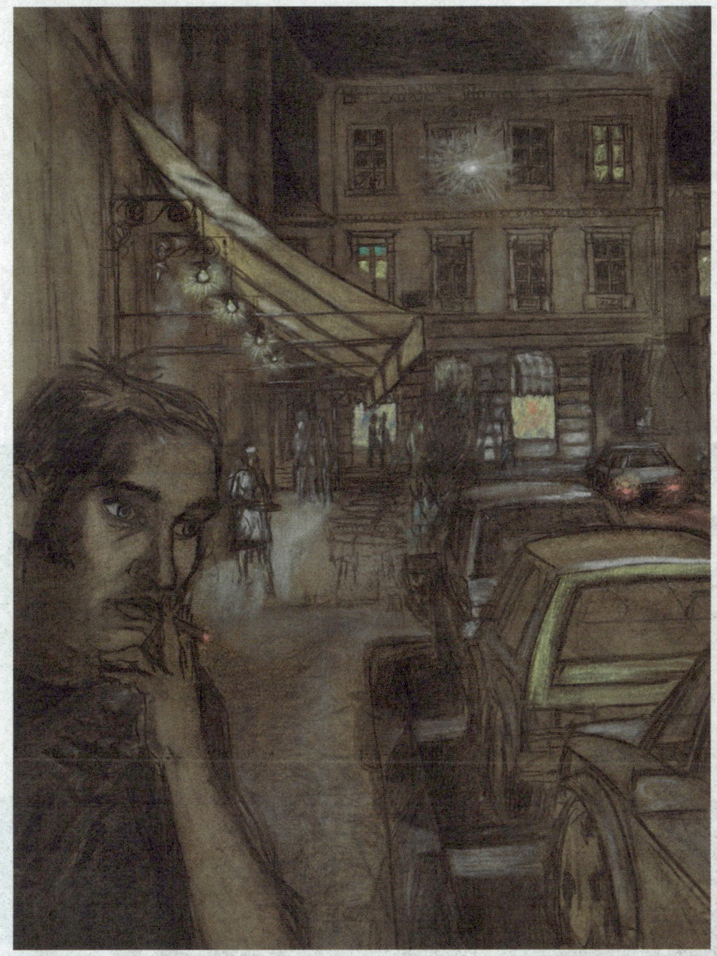

67

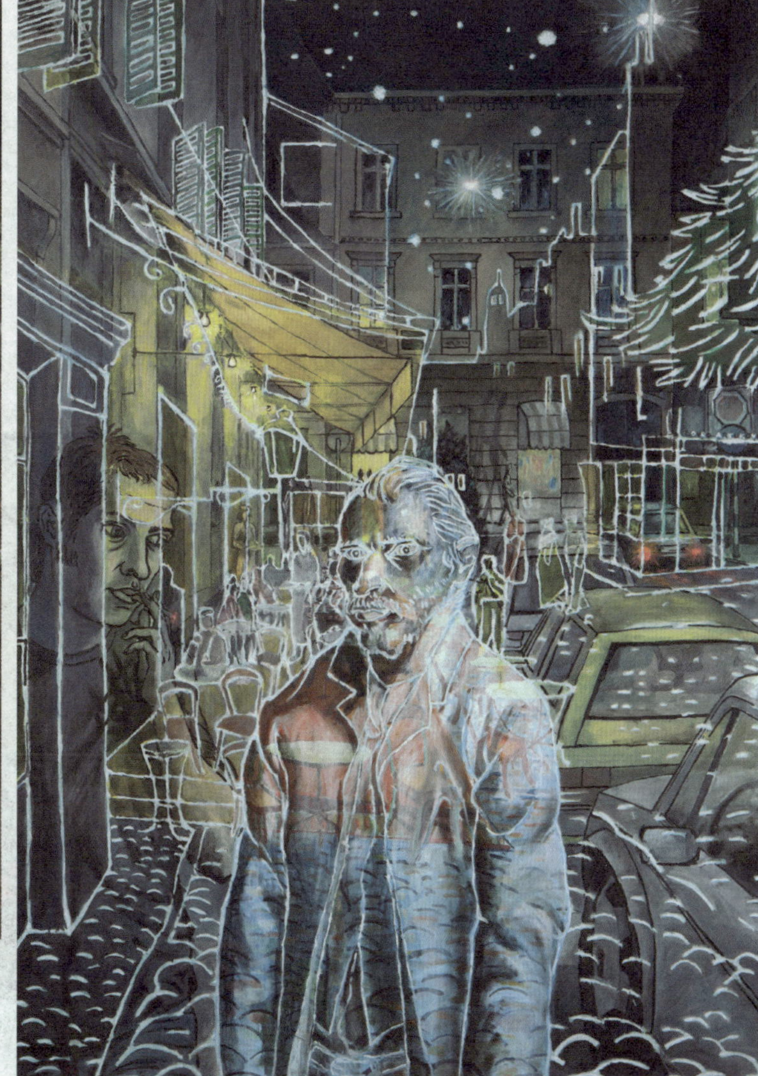

68

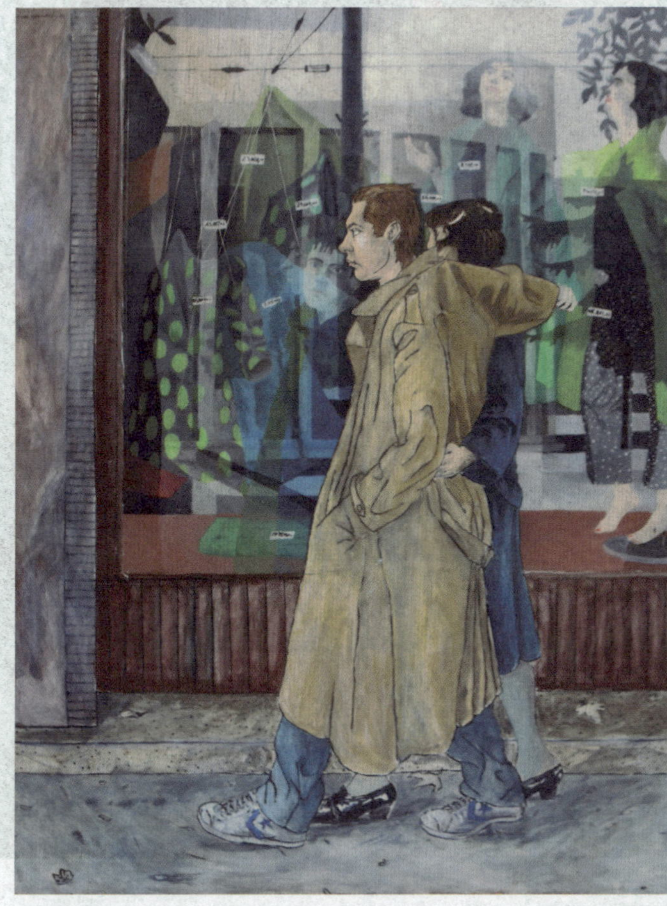

69

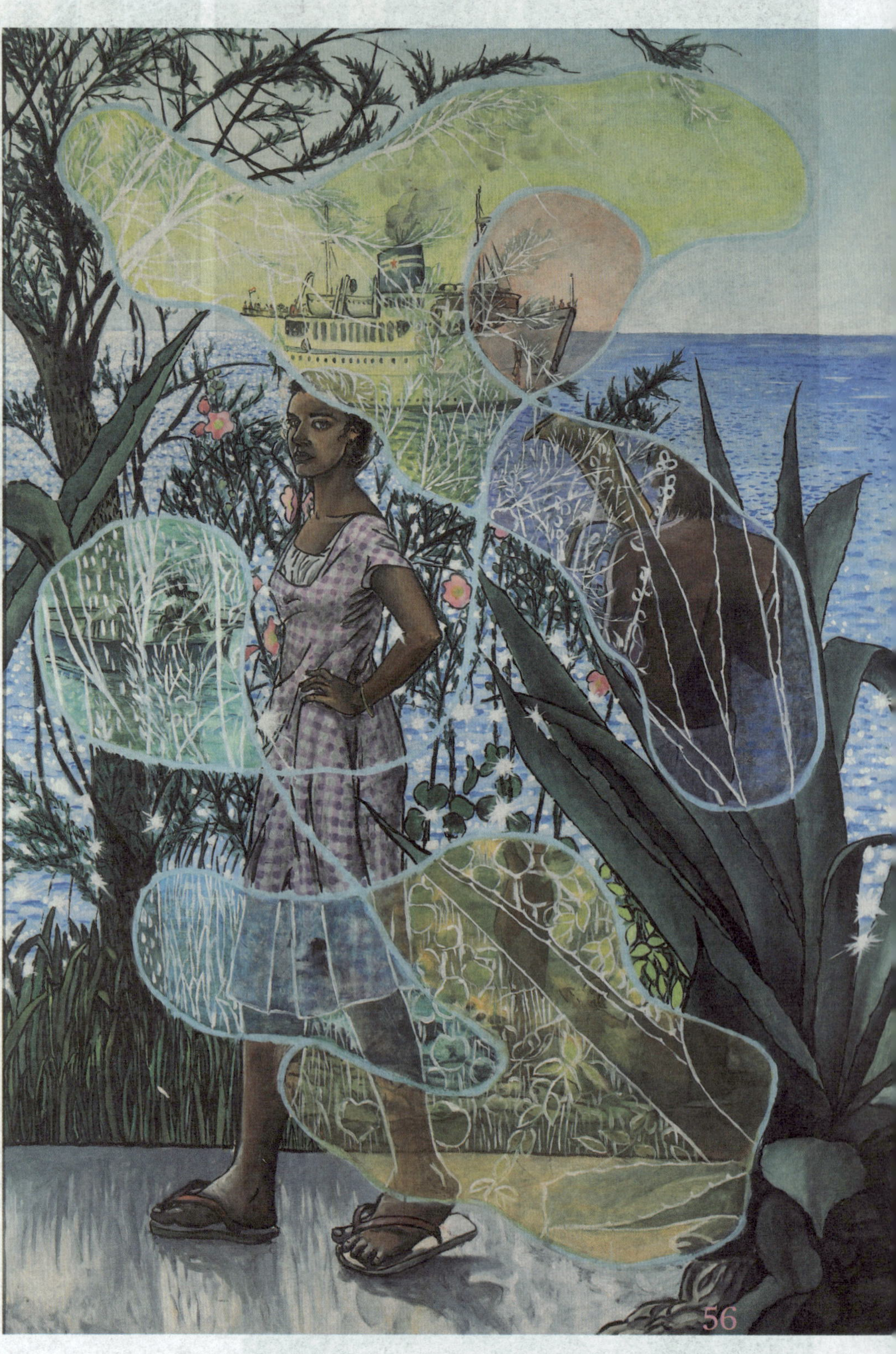

56

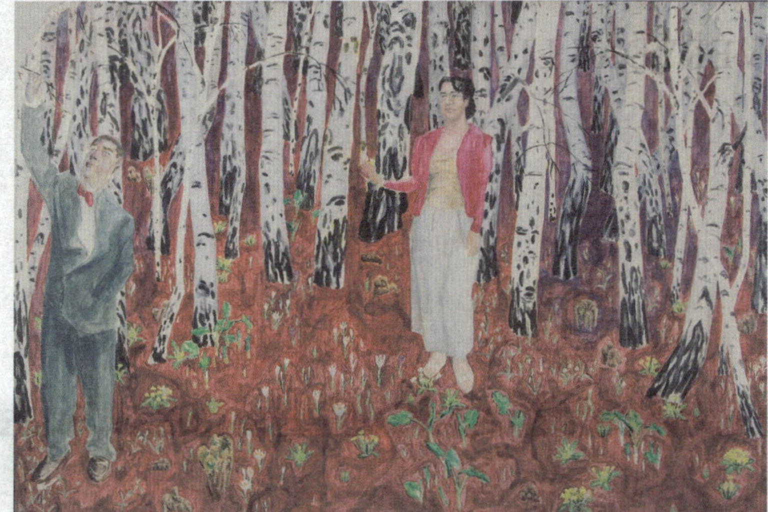

71

72

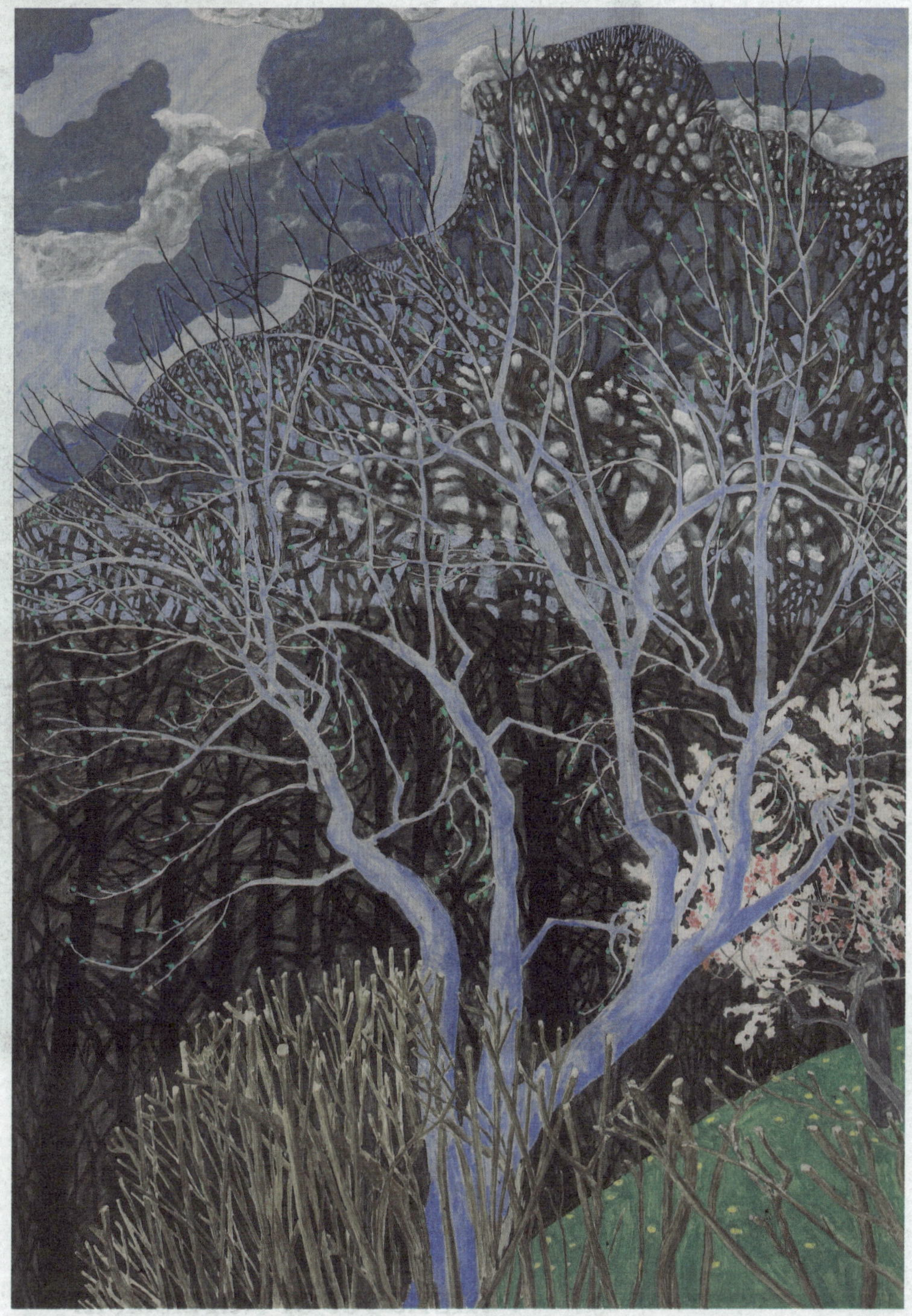

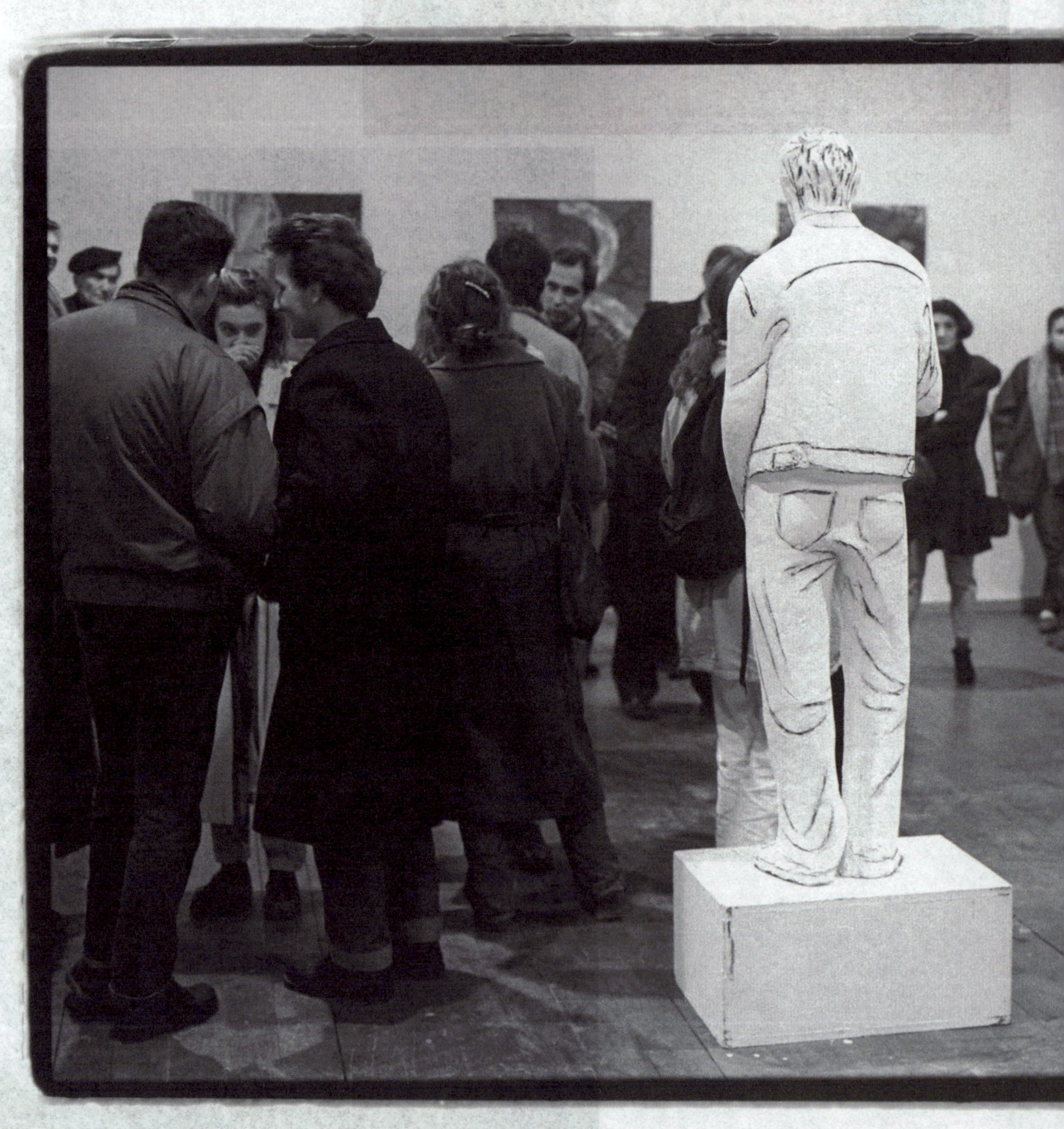

Alphabet of Narcissism

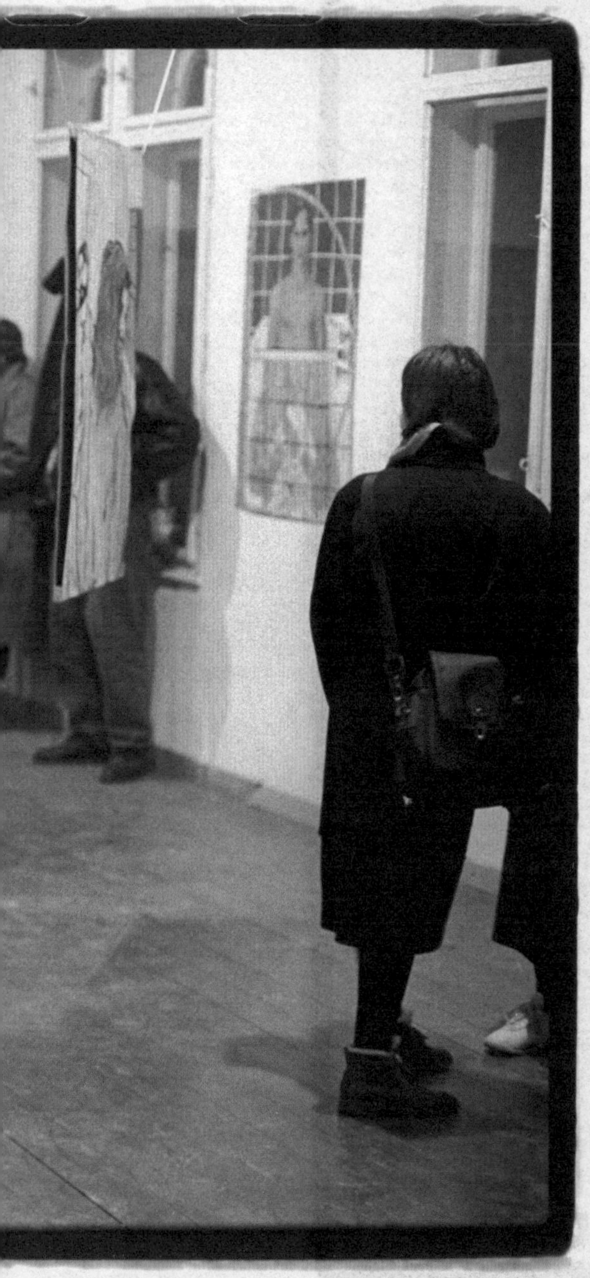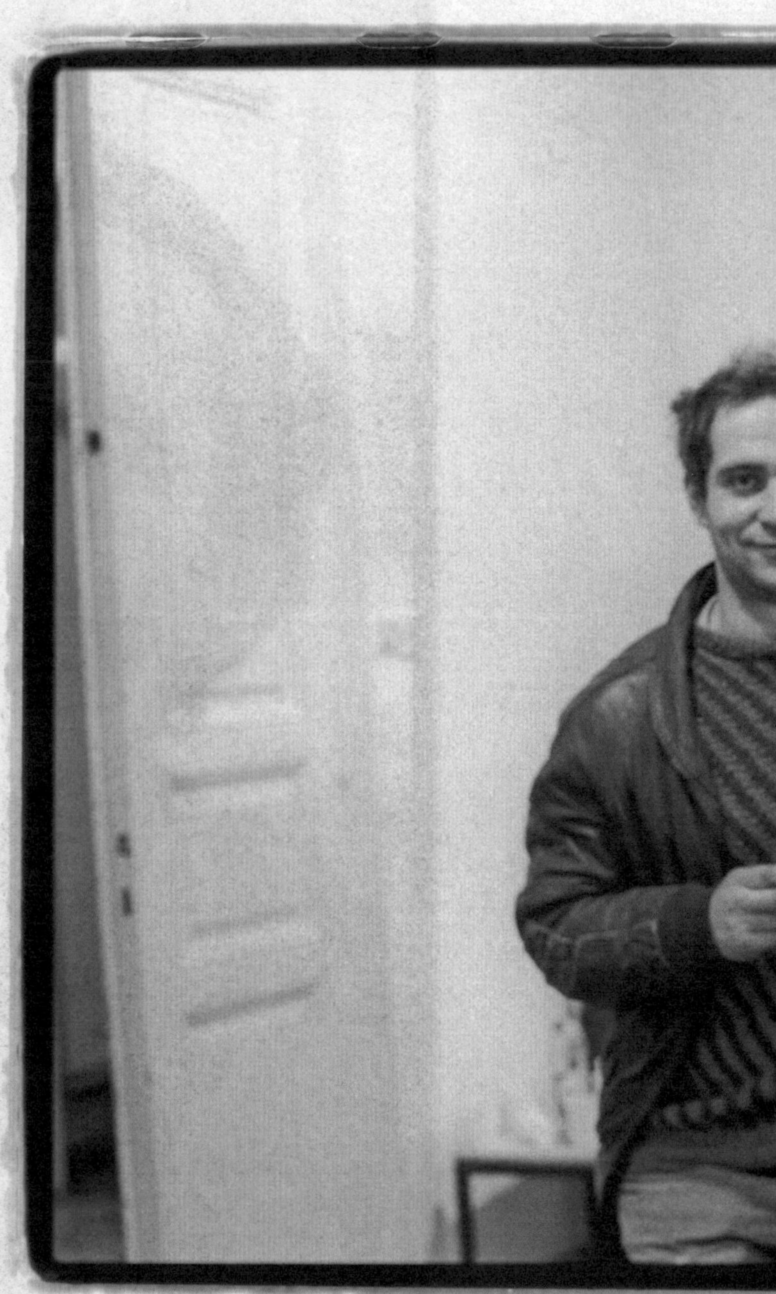

Boris Cvjetanović, Lovro Artuković Exhibition at Gallery PM, 1988

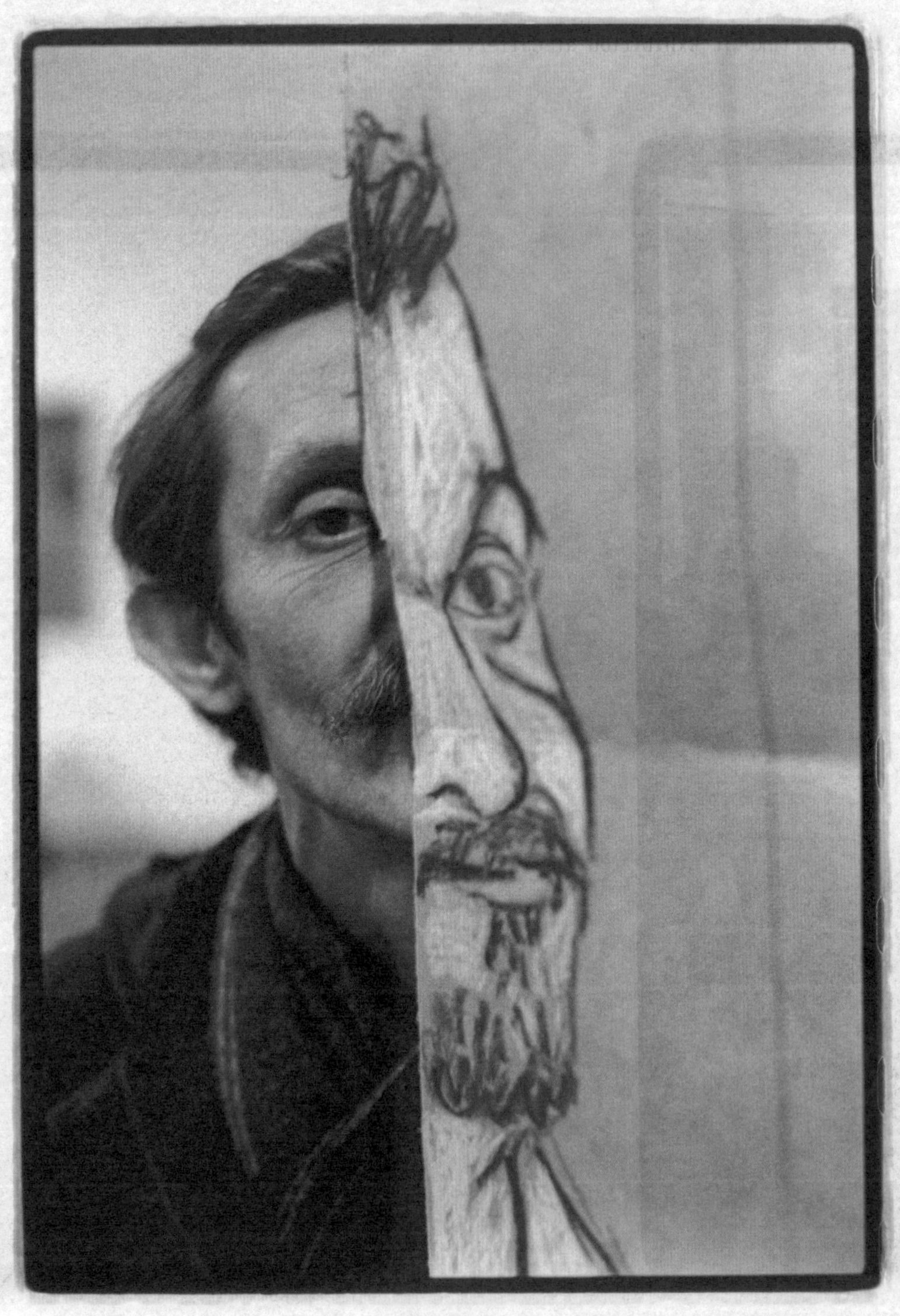

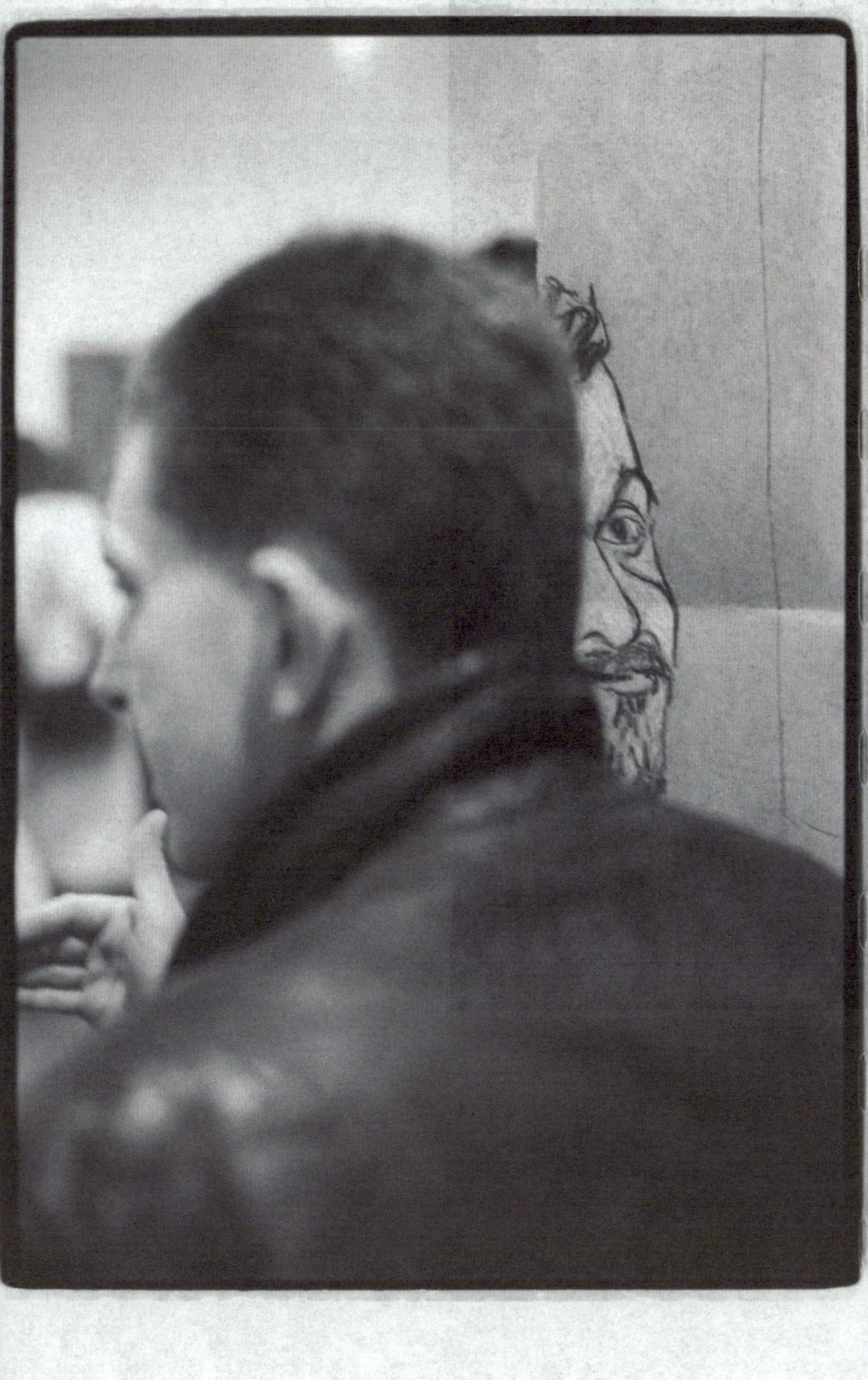

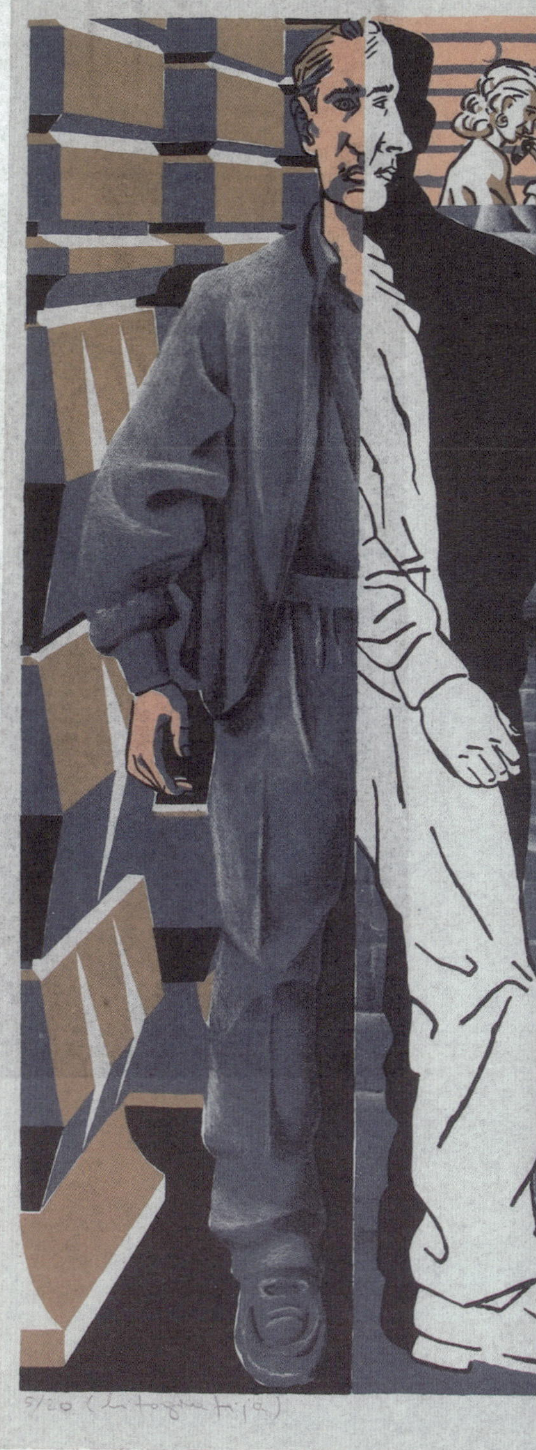

9/20 (litografía)

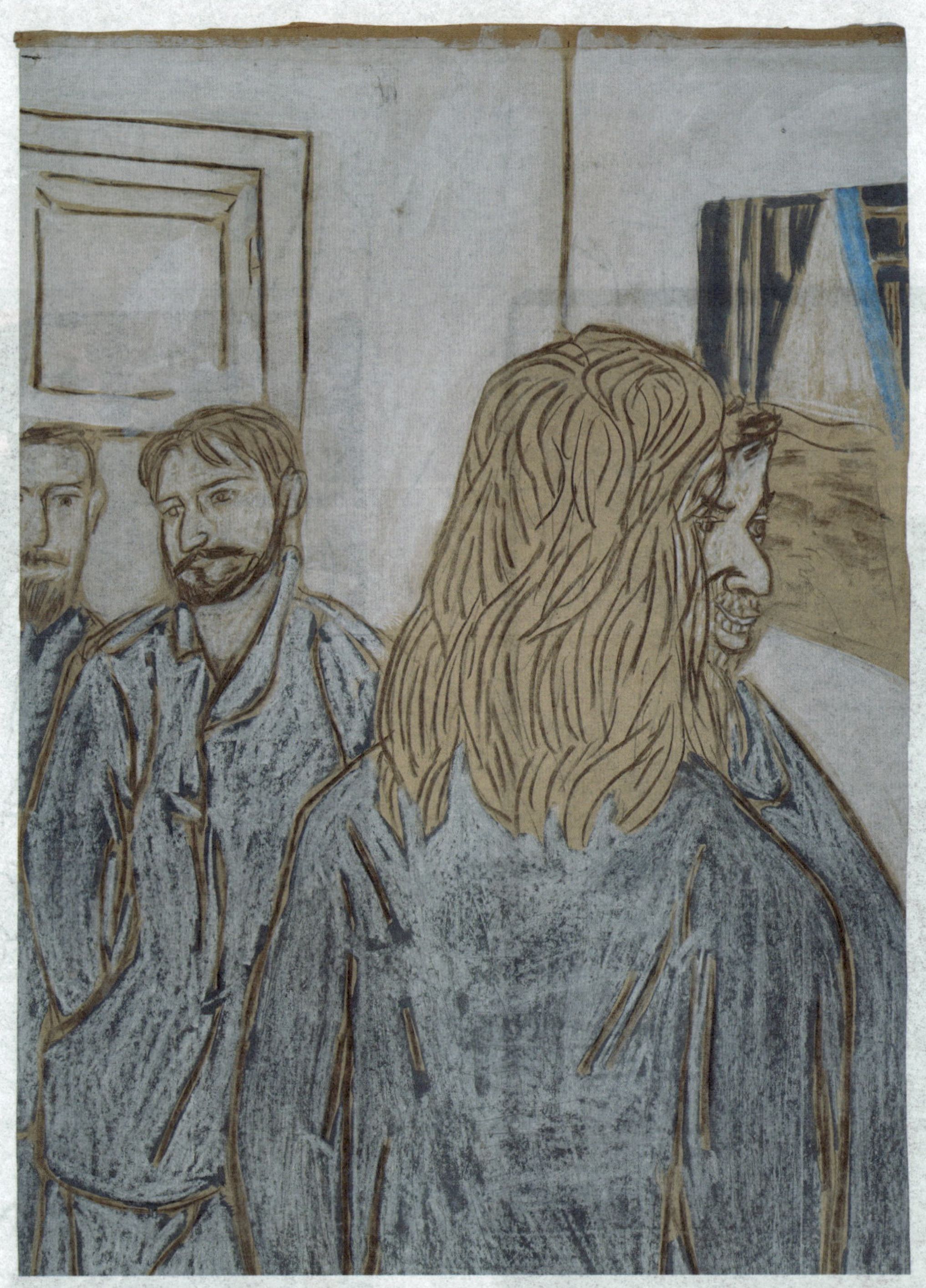

74

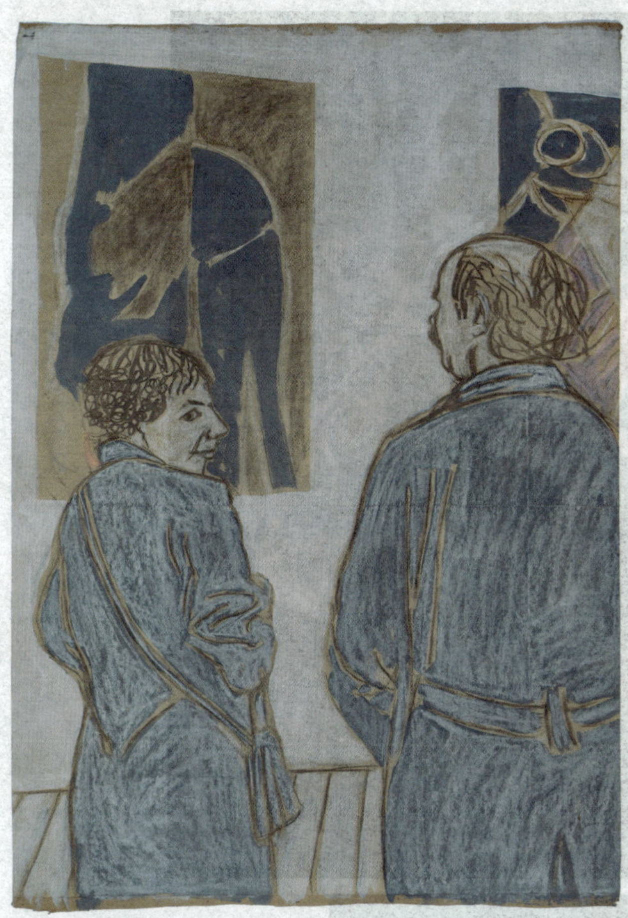



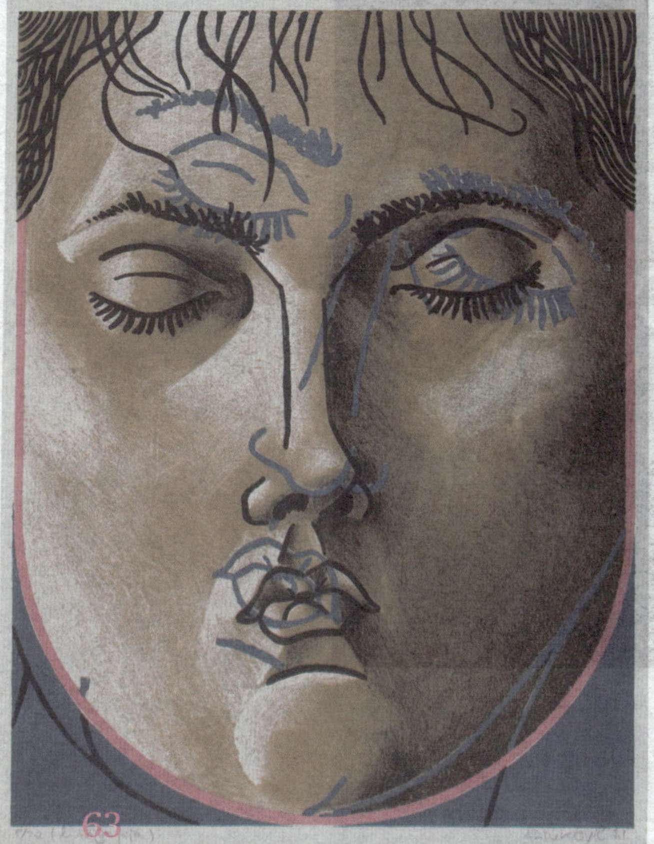



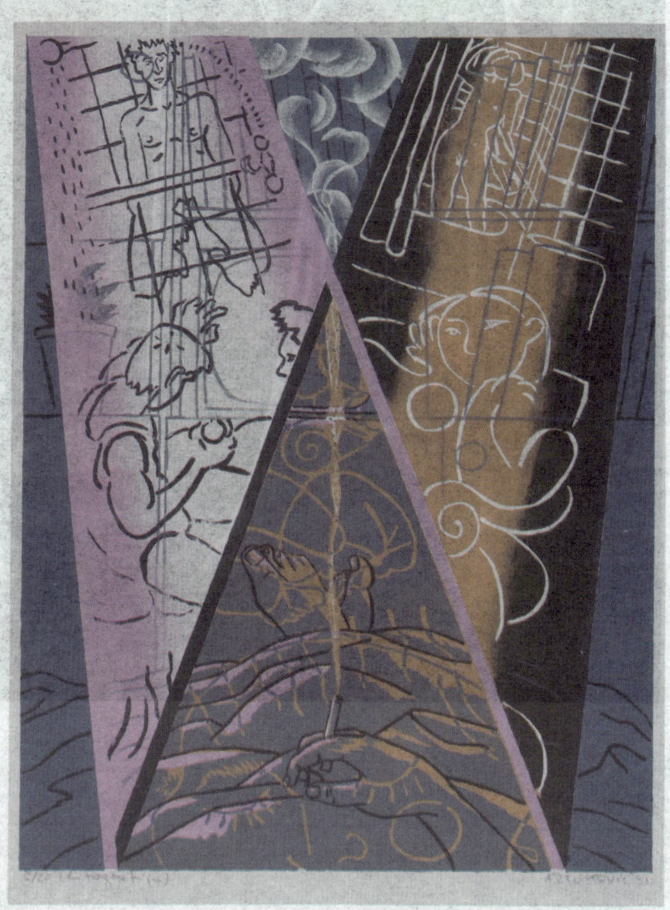

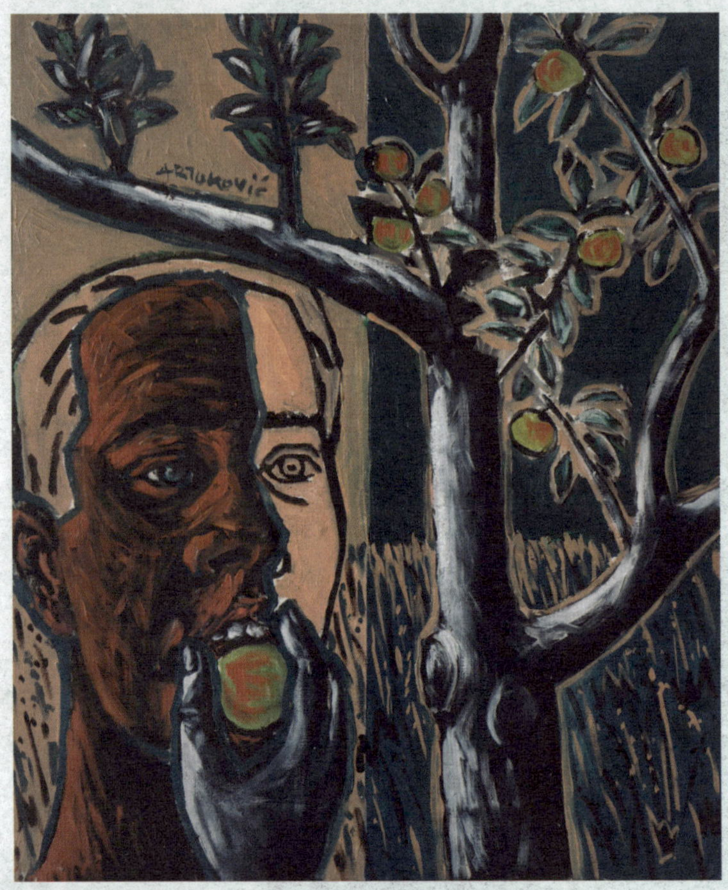

78

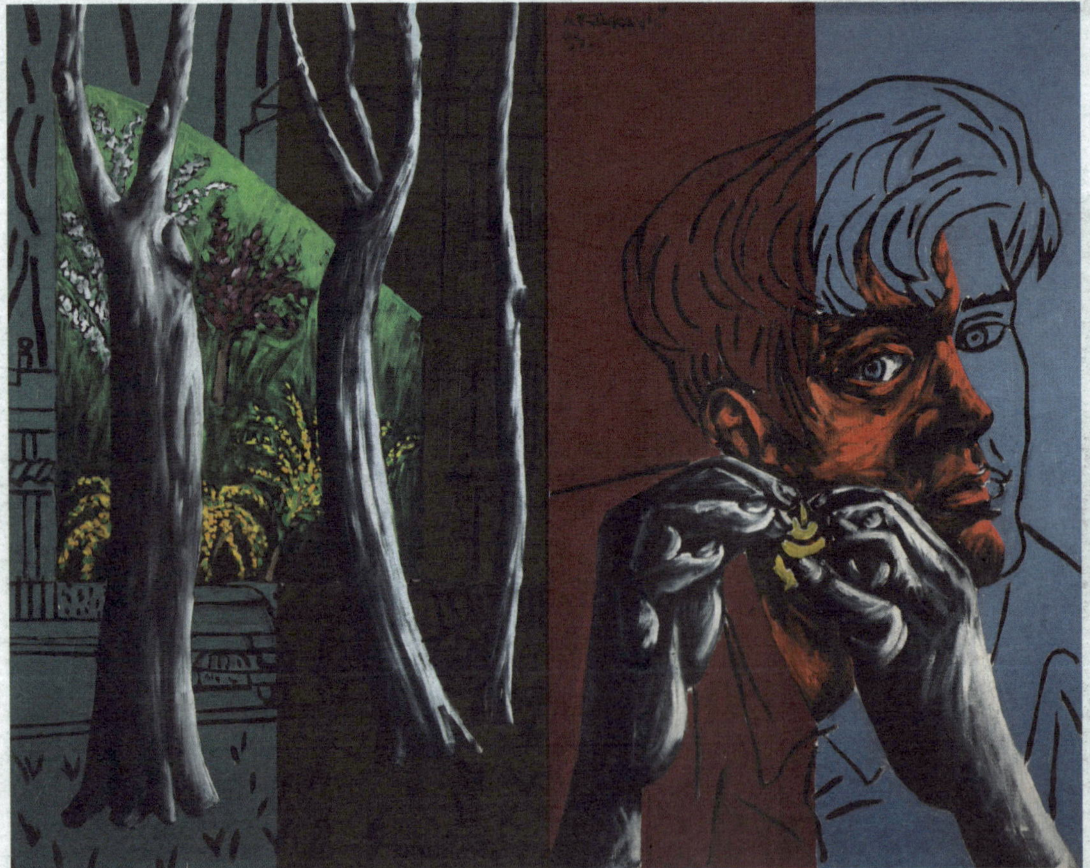

79

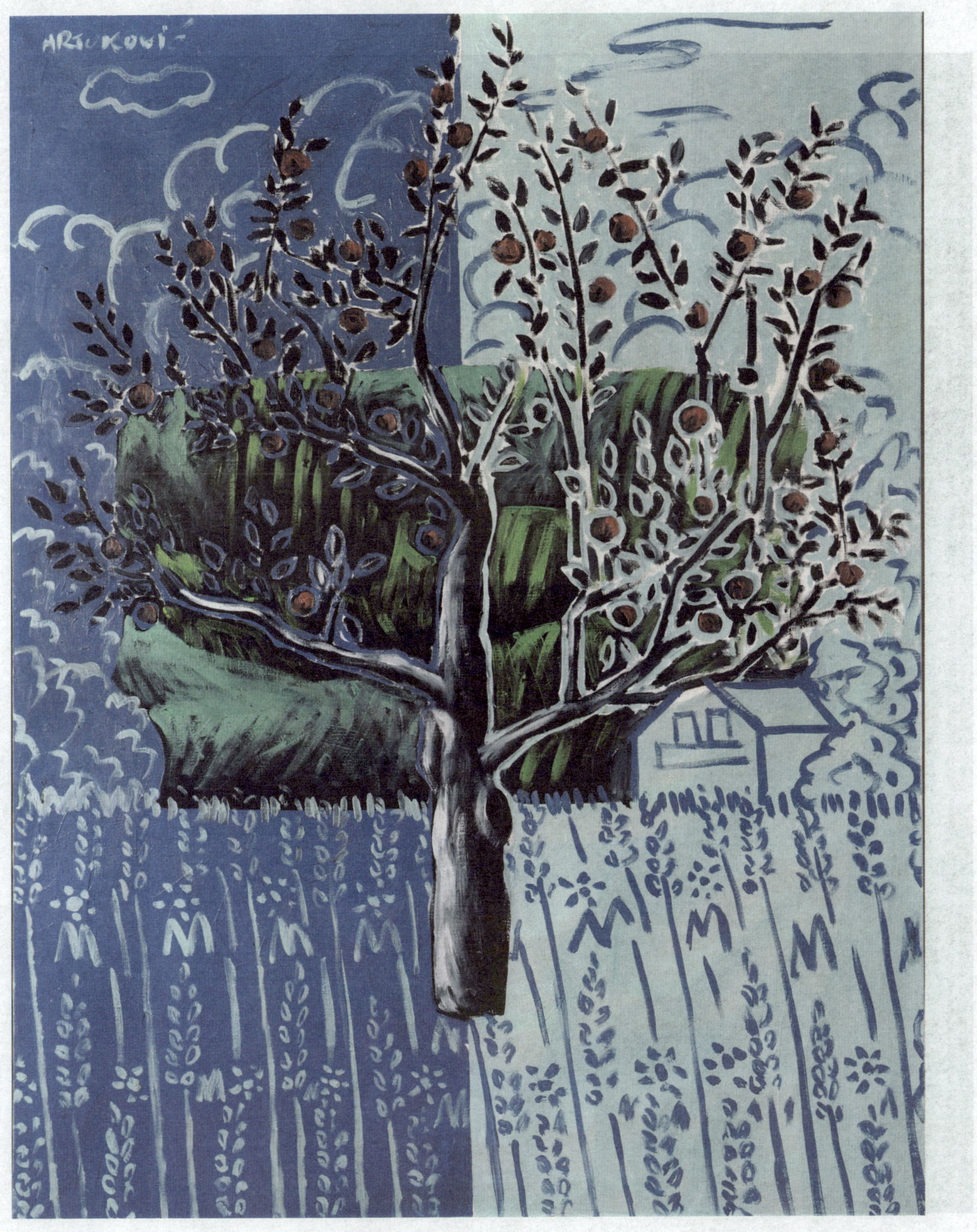
ARTUKOVI

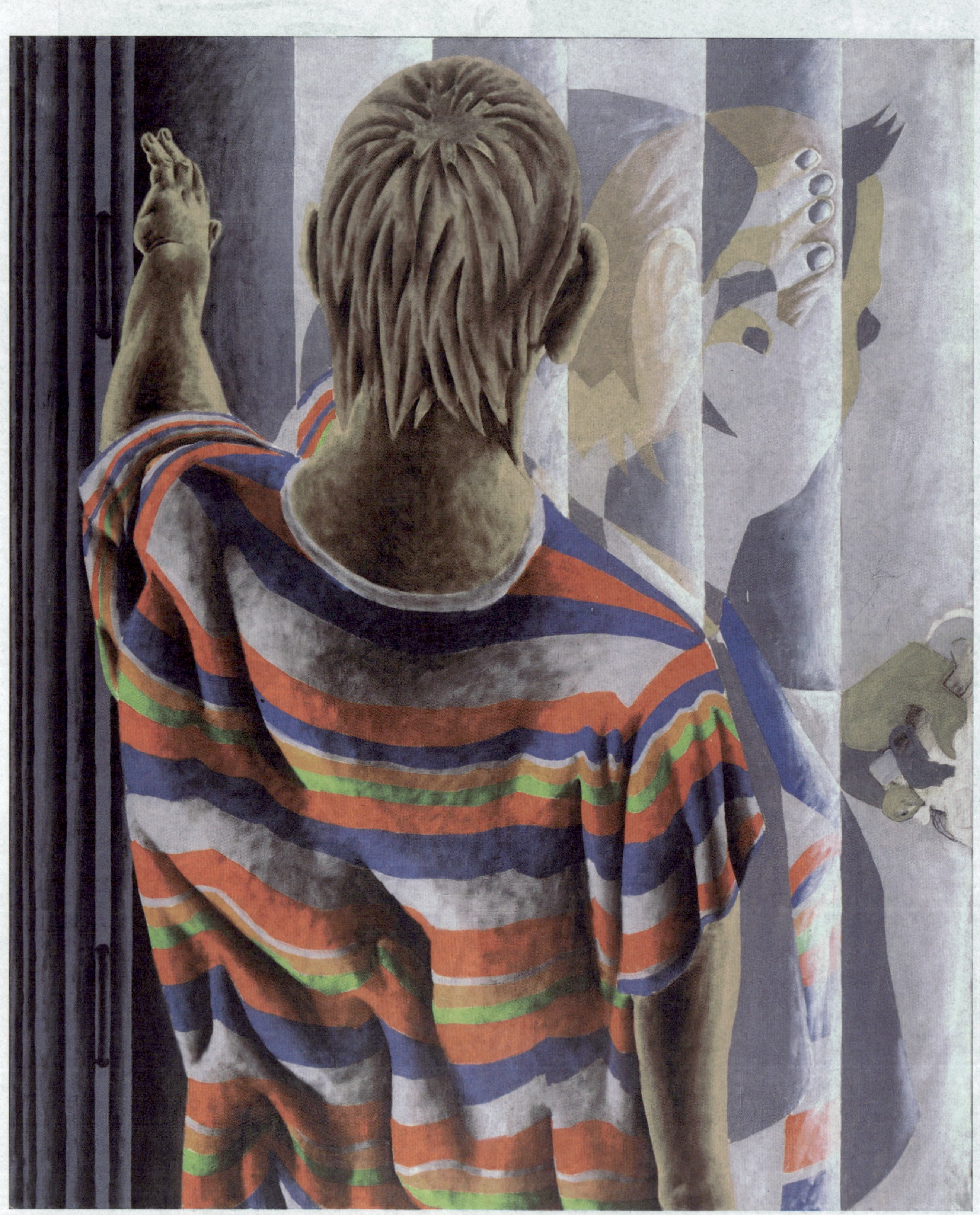

83

82

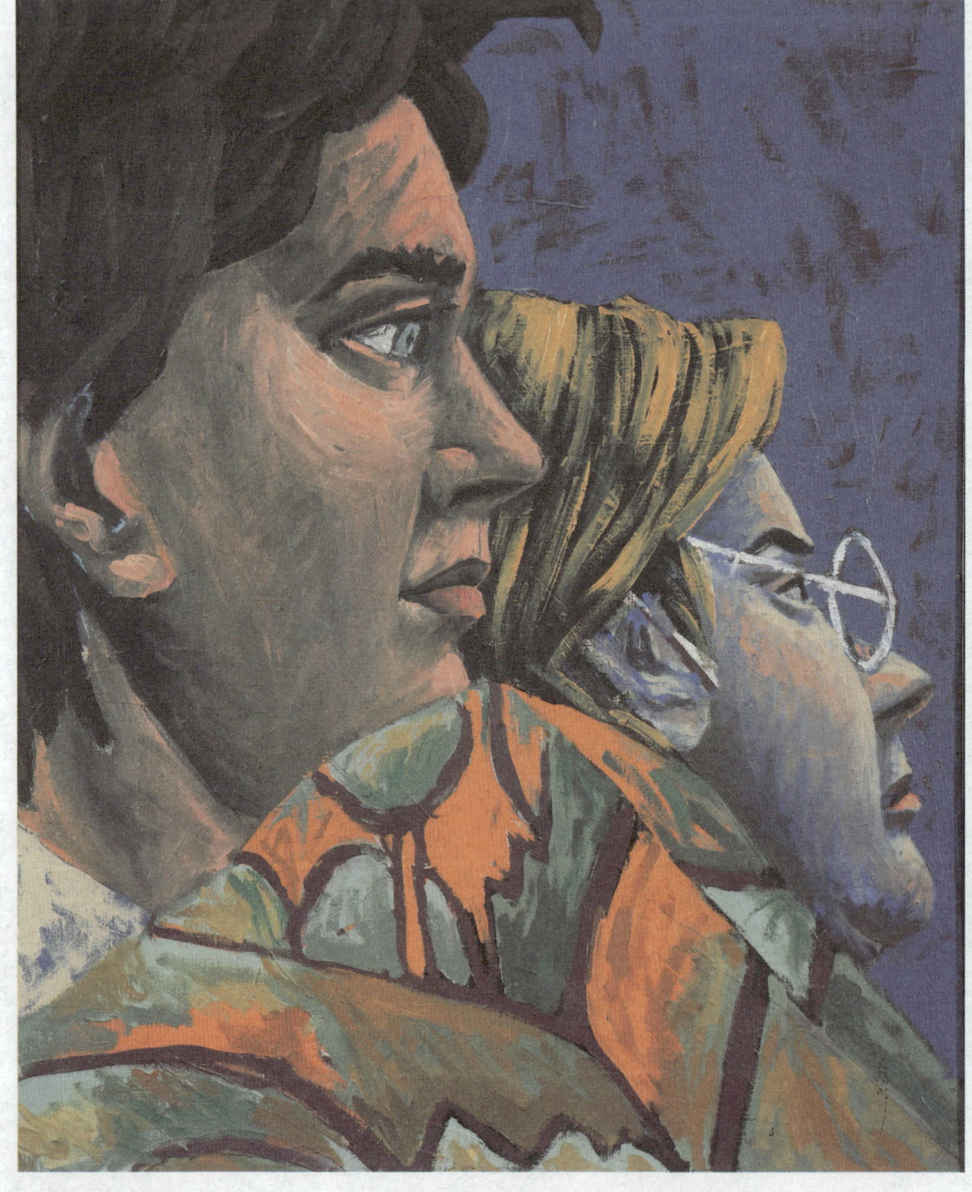

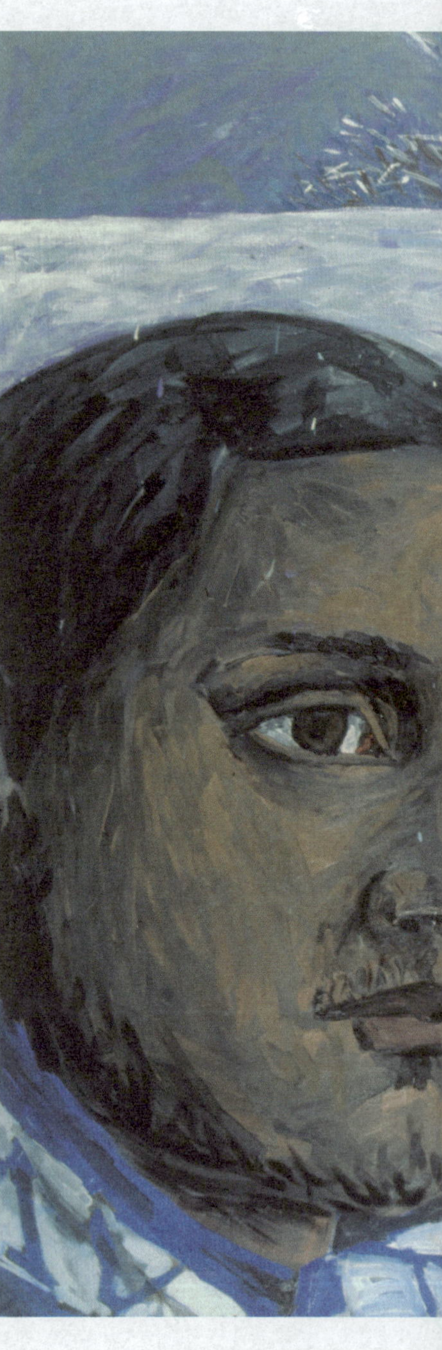

SCENES

Portraits

68

When I submitted those paintings for a jury selection at one of the exhibitions designed to show the current trends at the local art scene, I was glad that my works were accepted and displayed, although they differed from everything that surrounded them. I don't know if that was the reason, but when someone addressed me, I could feel mockery in his question: "Soo, you are painting portraits now?" At that time, painting portraits was considered uncool.

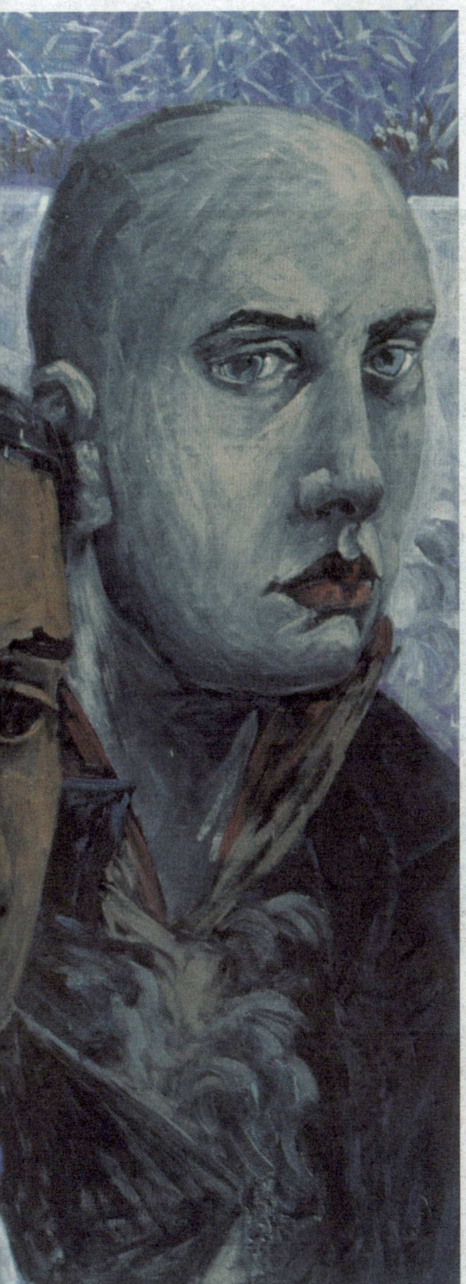

Personally, I did not see portraits in those paintings. They came about very naturally, as a continuation of my previous work, following the development of my painting procedures and my experience of the atmosphere of that particular moment. What made them different from others was their ability to force the viewer to concentrate only on the figures and the manner in which they had been painted. As a friend of mine said, "there is no bluffing with portraits", they are what you see.

I have to admit that in my youth I also a bit mockingly called my school friends from better Zagreb houses, in which family members stared from the walls, "the ones with paintings at home". This was probably more an expression of frustration coming from a child whose parents came from the province than an ideological standpoint or even if it was, its origin was in the former fact. I don't know if already then - when someone "introduced" me to a figure in Austro-Hungarian uniform, his late great-grandfather, in which I saw only a clumsily done painting - I started asking myself if with the time a portrait liberated itself from the painted person, becoming just a picture? A good or a bad one. Or are they tied together forever, so that we, passing through exhibition halls of a museum, do not only look at the portraits as paintings, but also feel purely human curiosity, attraction or repulsion towards the depicted persons?

Of course, we should also not forget that we are trained to see their author in the portraits. But it seems to me that I have started to complicate things, I am not much of a thinker. Looking at things from their purely practical side, thanks to the paintings at the exhibition I started to occasionally receive orders from people who wanted to be portraited and in that way I earned a few bucks, which I found cool.

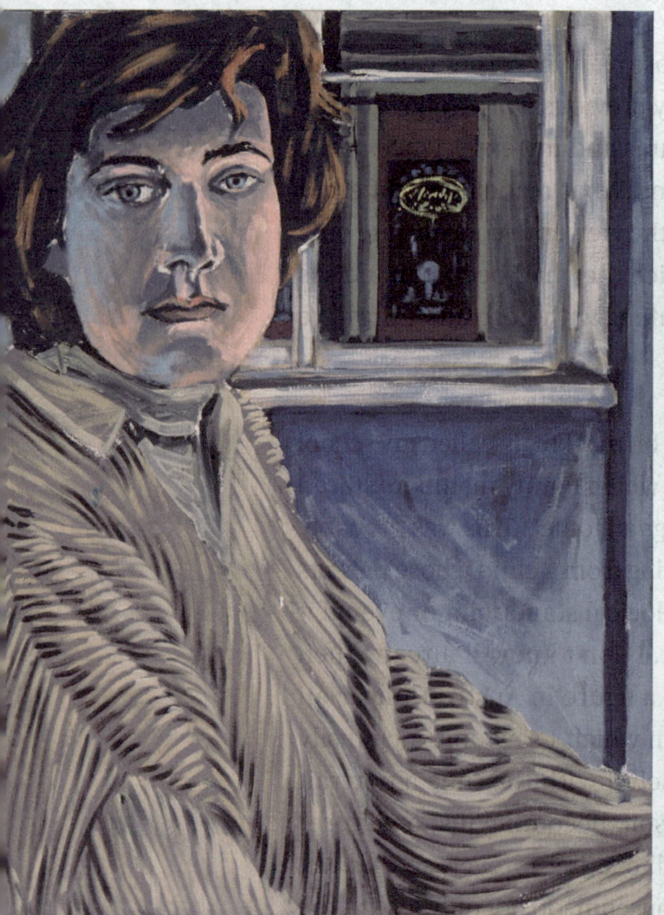

84

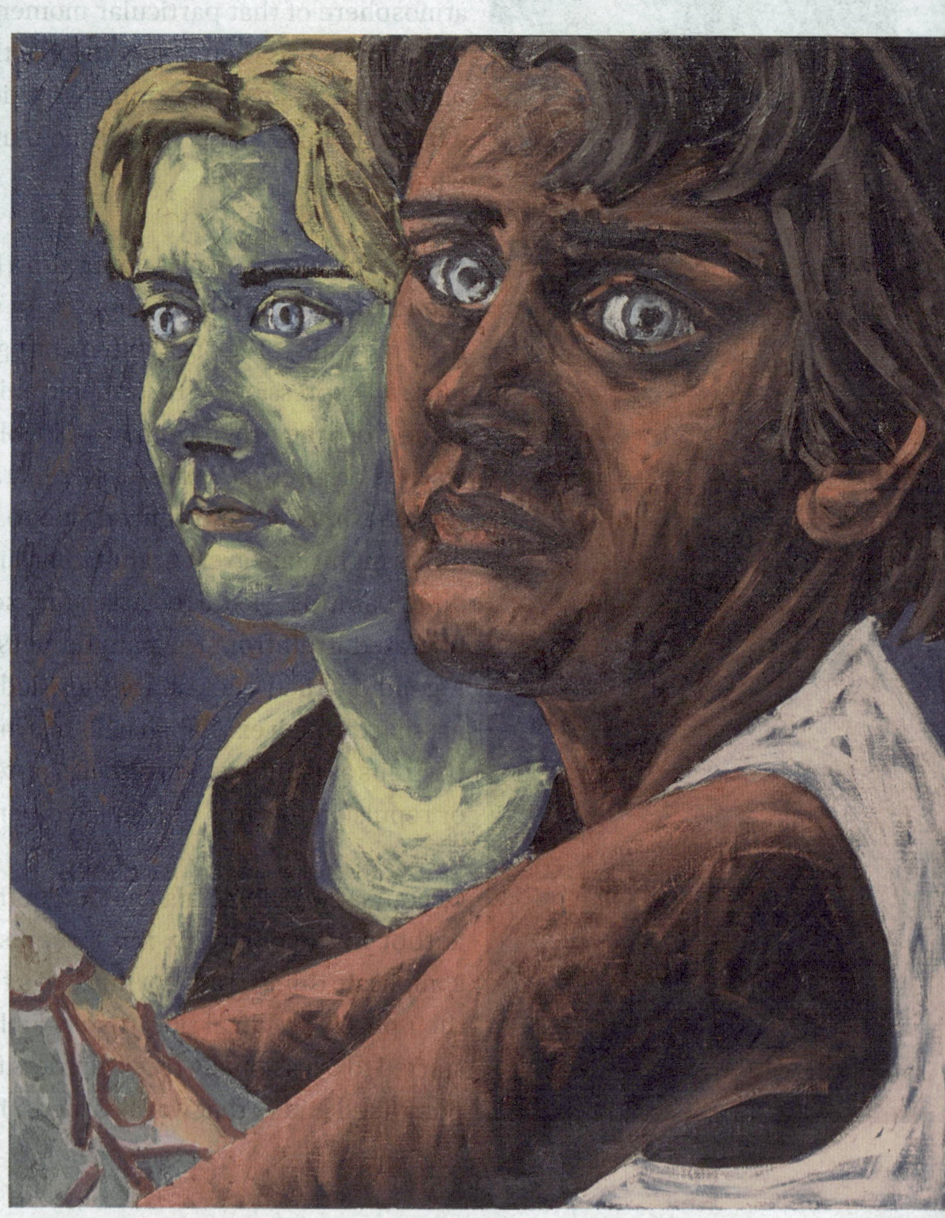

85

86

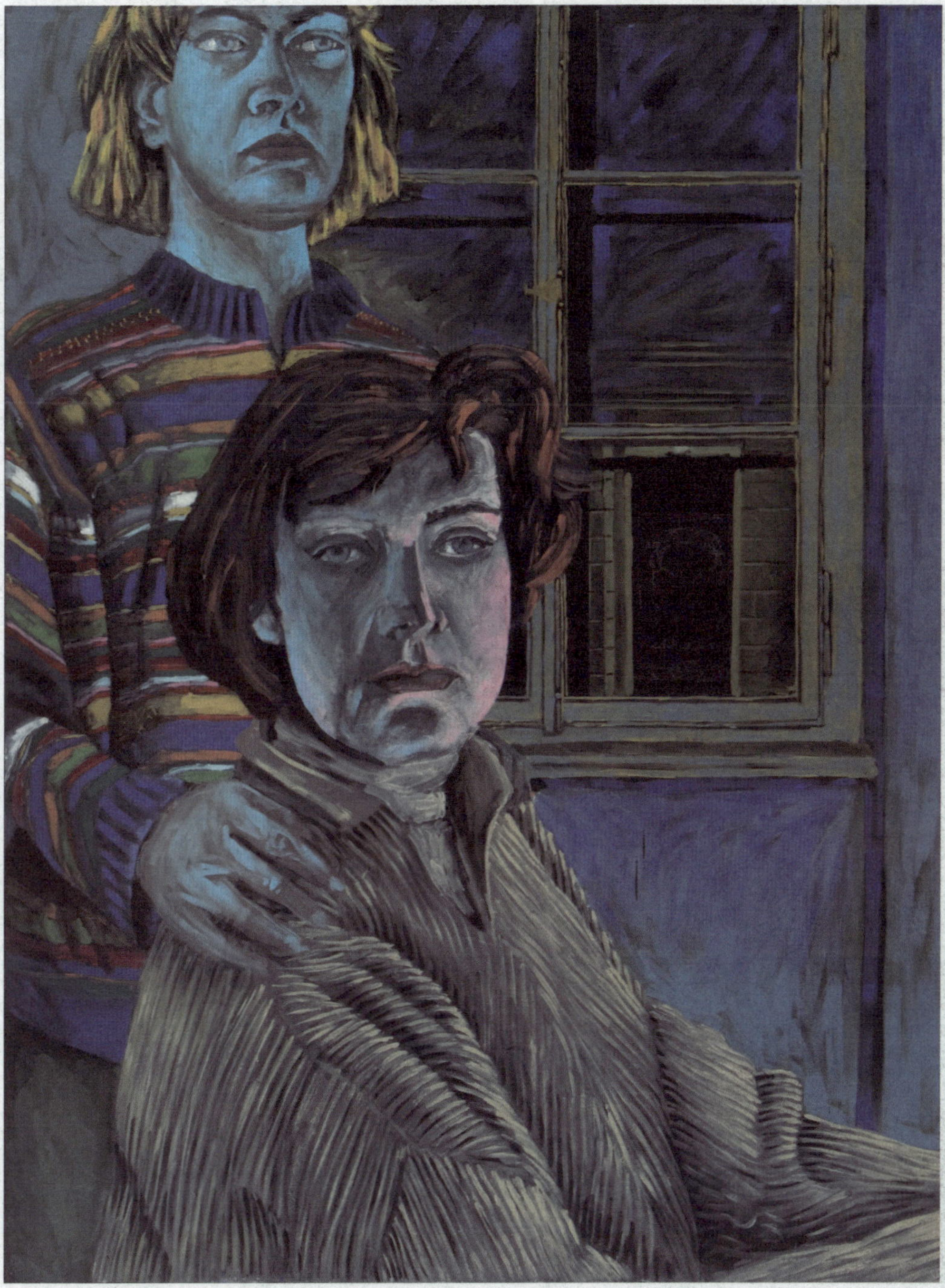

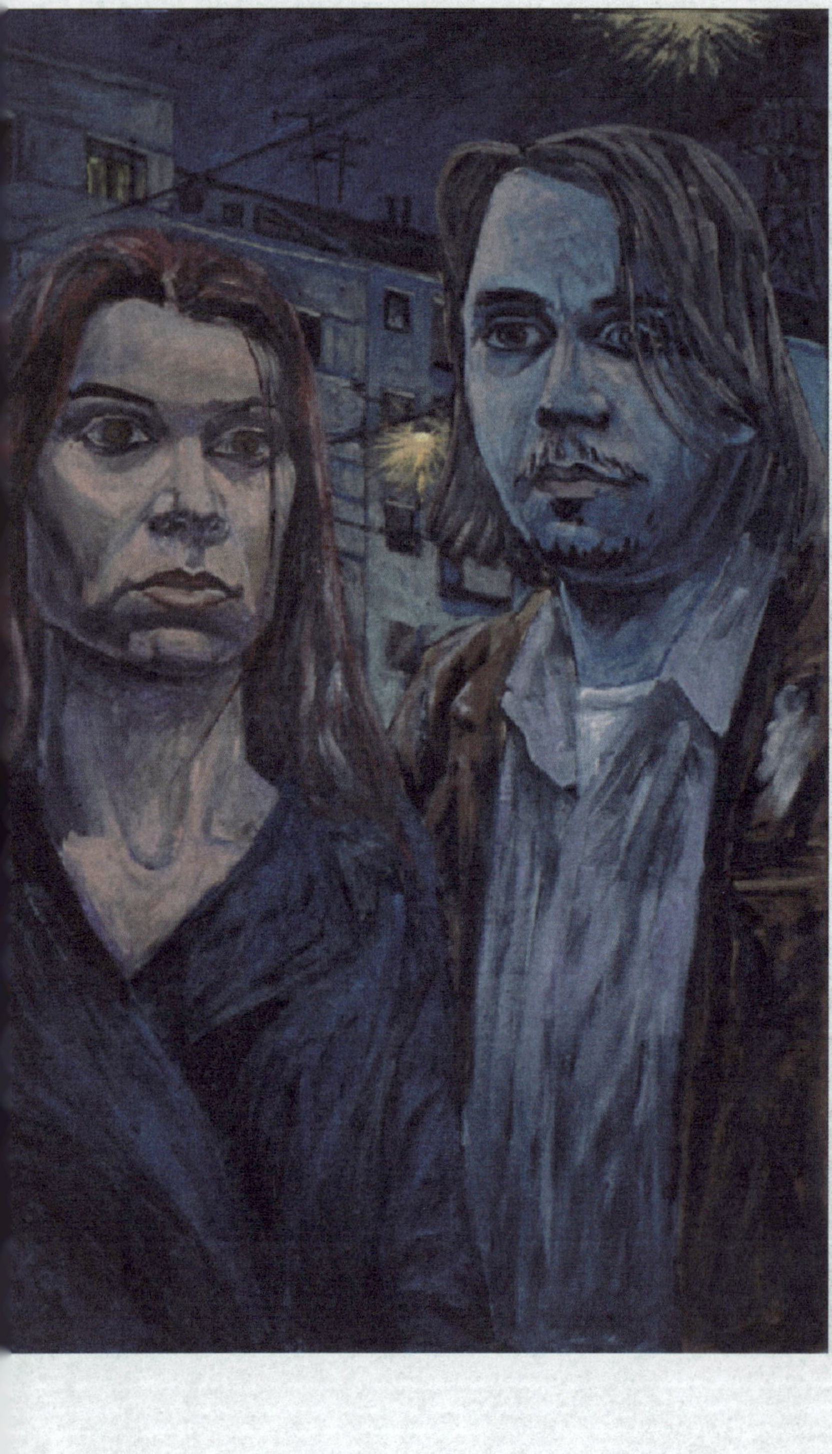

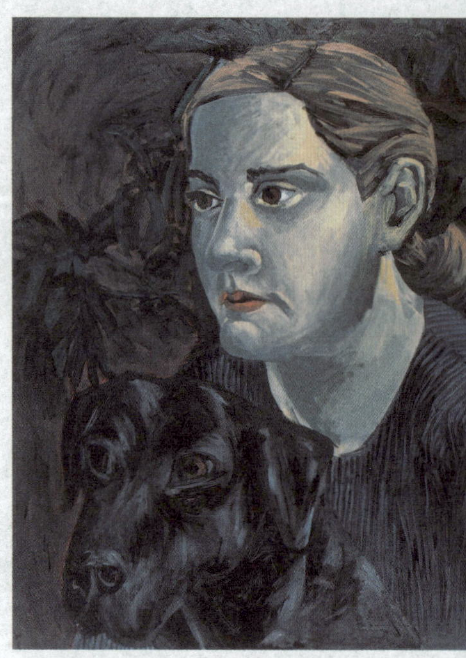

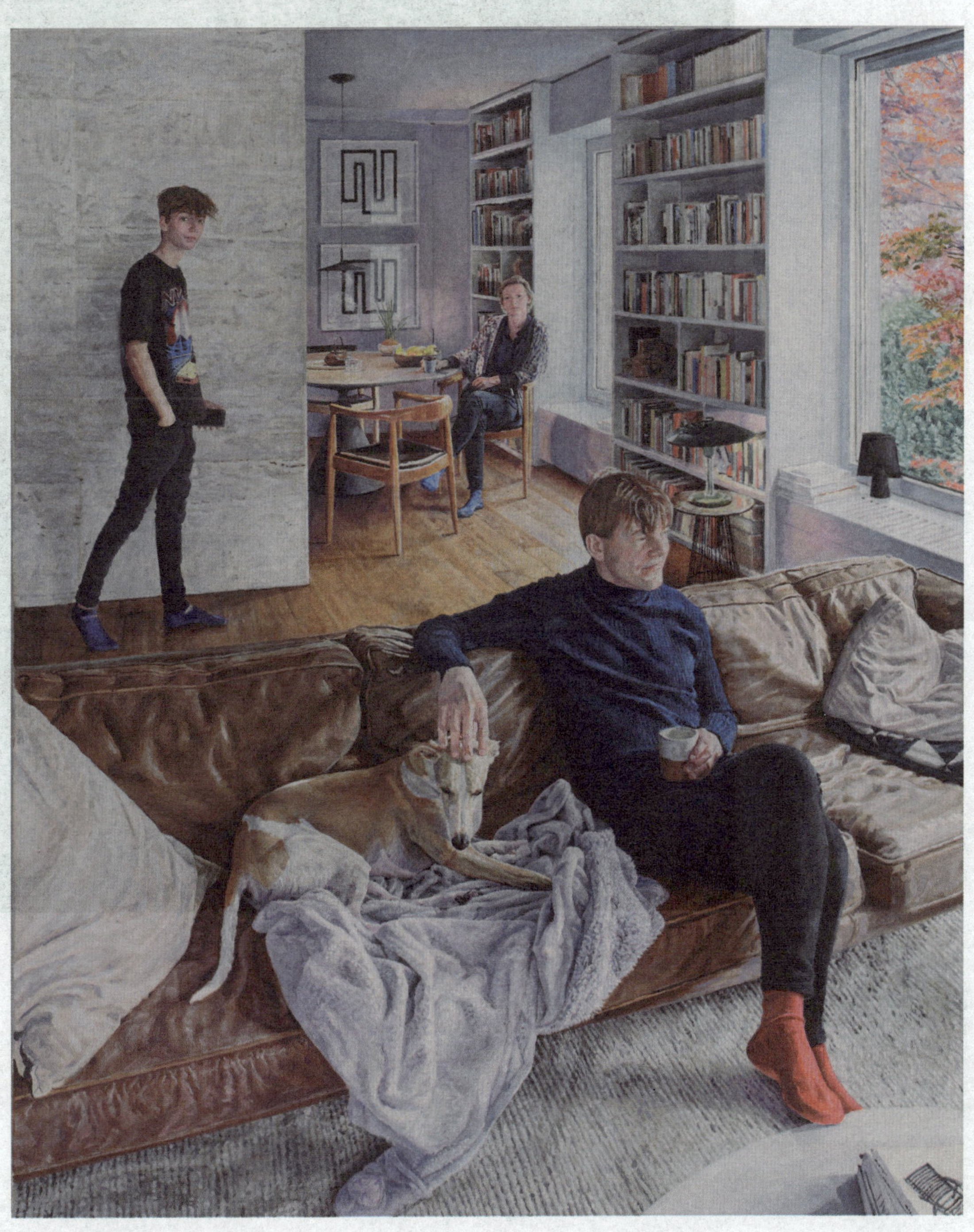

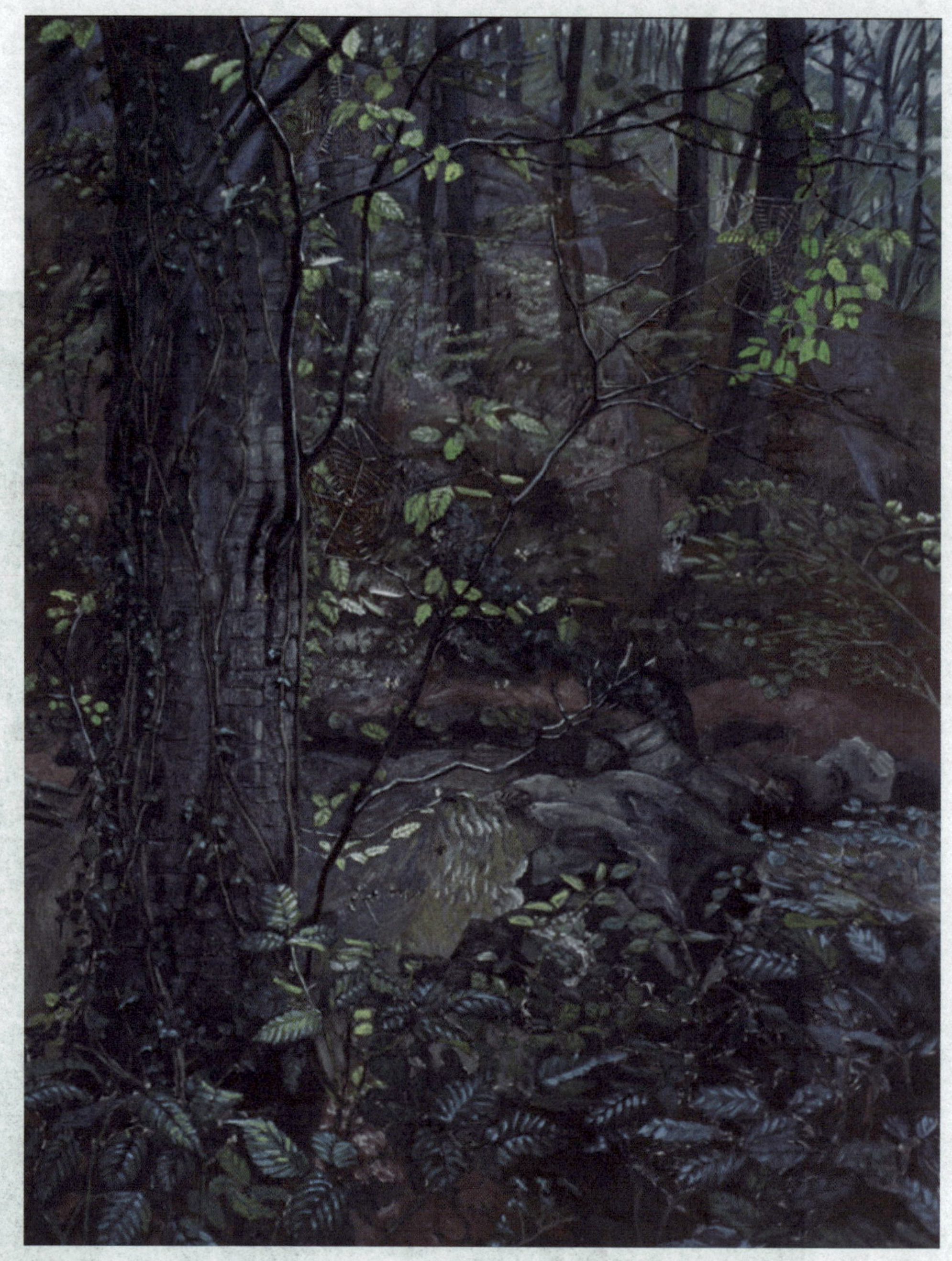

90

Forests

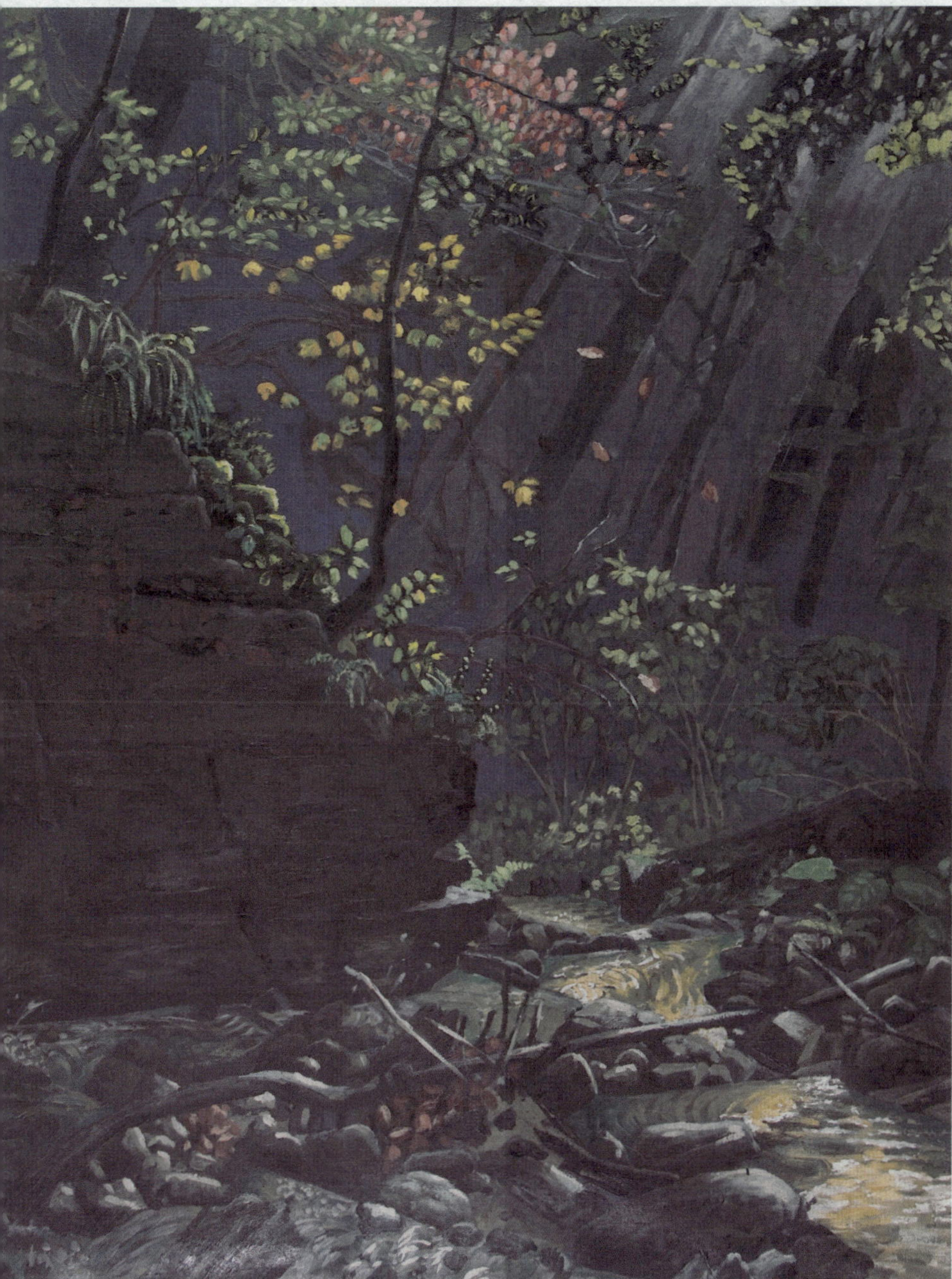

The cameraman, the lighting and the sound technician pointed their weapons at me. I felt uncomfortable, the glare of the spotlight blinded me. Next to me was the journalist. When we got the signal that we could start our conversation, she looked at me with her eyes shining with enthusiasm and said: "So you paint. Is painting not dead?"

Oh, nooo! What does she want from me now? Should I confirm that? Or should I make a plea in defense of painting? I don't give a damn, let me paint in peace. I was annoyed with myself, I could have expected such a question and prepared myself, I knew that the thesis about the death of painting had spooked through the local press for months (while it had been present in the art literature for decades). I was also annoyed with the journalist, of course. Why must everyone always repeat the same things like parrots? She has no eyes to look around a bit and ask me something about the paintings? I started stammering about how I am still alive and painting, and how the brook painted in the picture behind us (I pointed in that direction so that she might pay attention to it) is still lively flowing down the slope in the forest. I don't know what other nonsense I was spouting; it was probably totally disastrous. I really needed a drink.

91

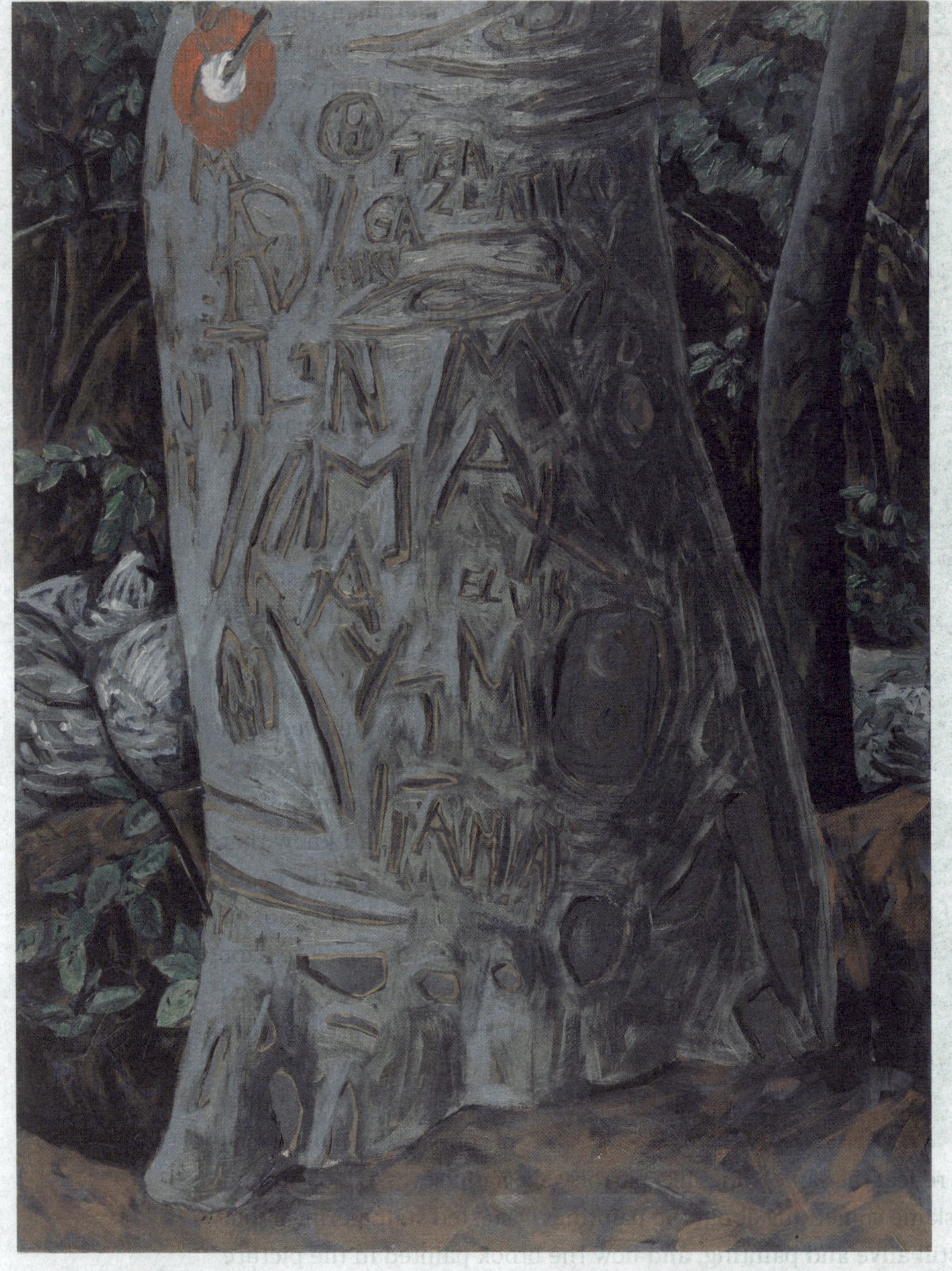

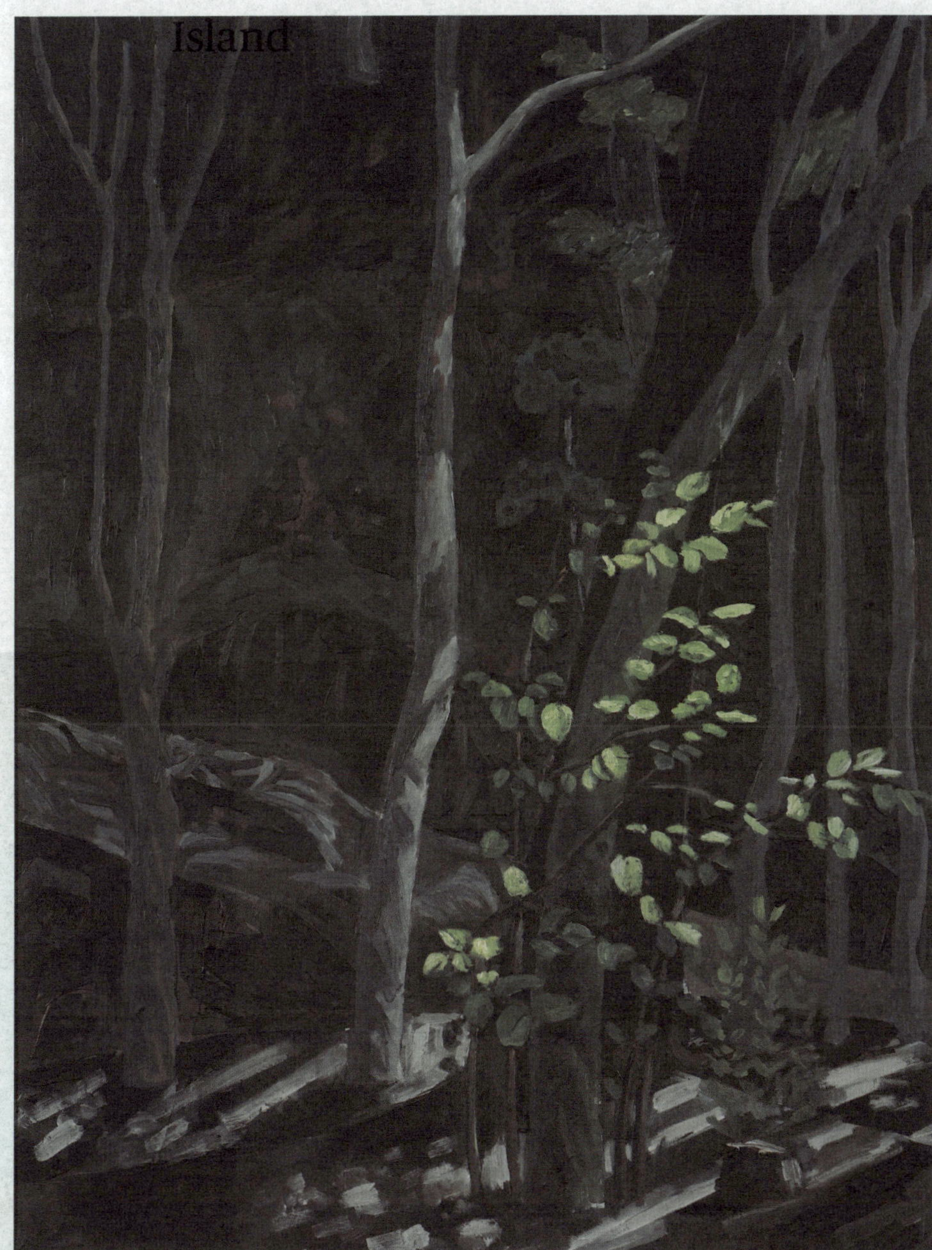


92

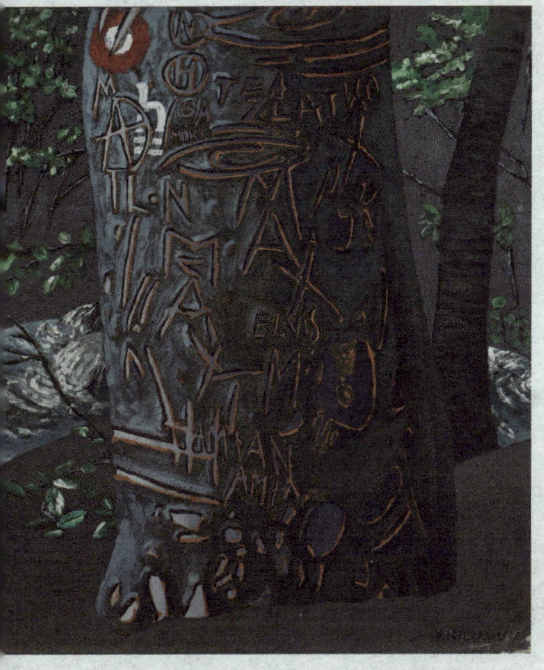

21

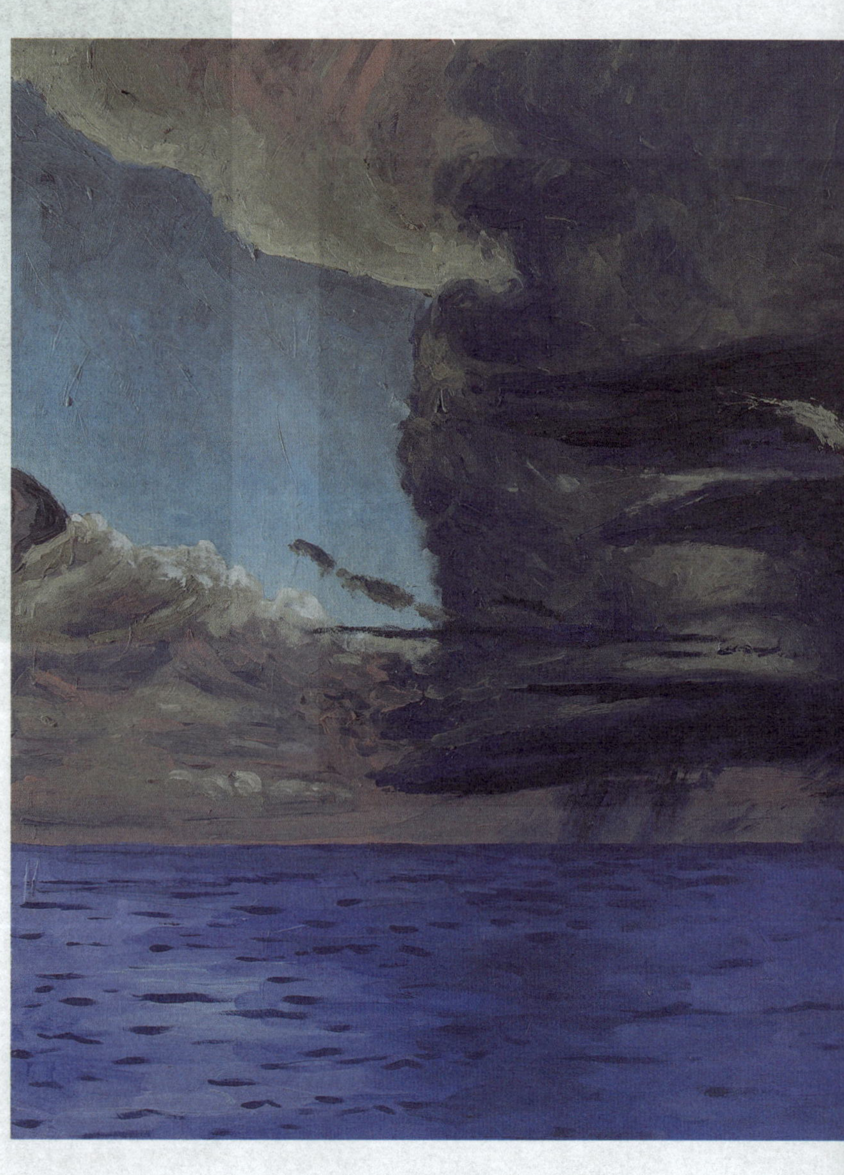

Dear friend,

we have never been able to clarify what your frequently expressed remark that you needed to ride a bike for several hours a day in order to sweat everything out and "stand purified in front of a painting" actually meant. As I understood it, you did not mean that the purpose of this ritual was to sweat out the toxins accumulated in your body, but rather the purification from everyday life, so that you could create "pure paintings" (peinture pure), liberated from the painful traces of ordinary life.

I assume that I have interpreted your words correctly (although we could never clarify their meaning), because I am familiar with this esoteric story from texts about the painting of the last century, which we still anachronistically call modernist. I must confess that somehow this story didn't strike me as particularly appealing. I hope you do not resent me for taking the opposite path, allowing that which I live, think and feel to show in my paintings. In our time, painting seems to be one of the few remaining islands where individuality is still possible.

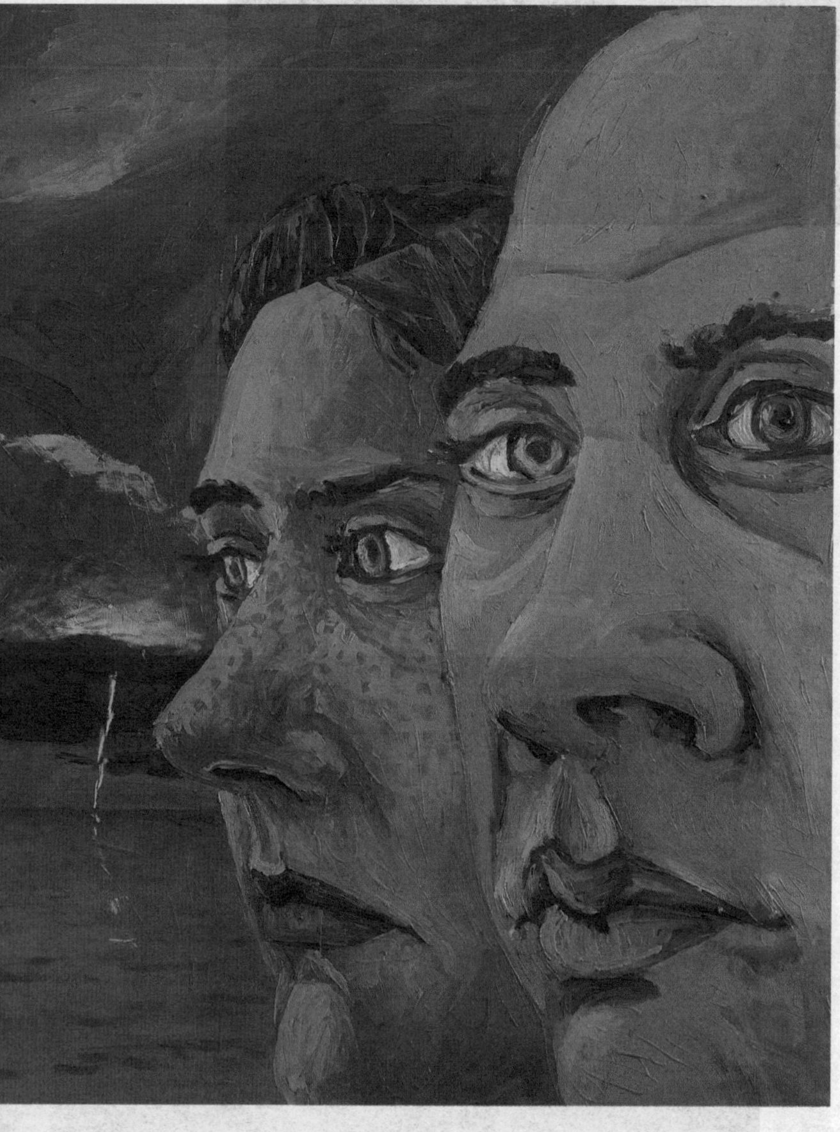

And therefore: if at some point I get the feeling of being alone, isolated, surrounded by the horizon like a prison wall, resembling an island where life is gradually becoming extinct, this will certainly find expression in my paintings, whether I want it or not. It may not be great painting (grande peinture), but unfortunately, we never got the opportunity to elucidate what it was supposed to be.

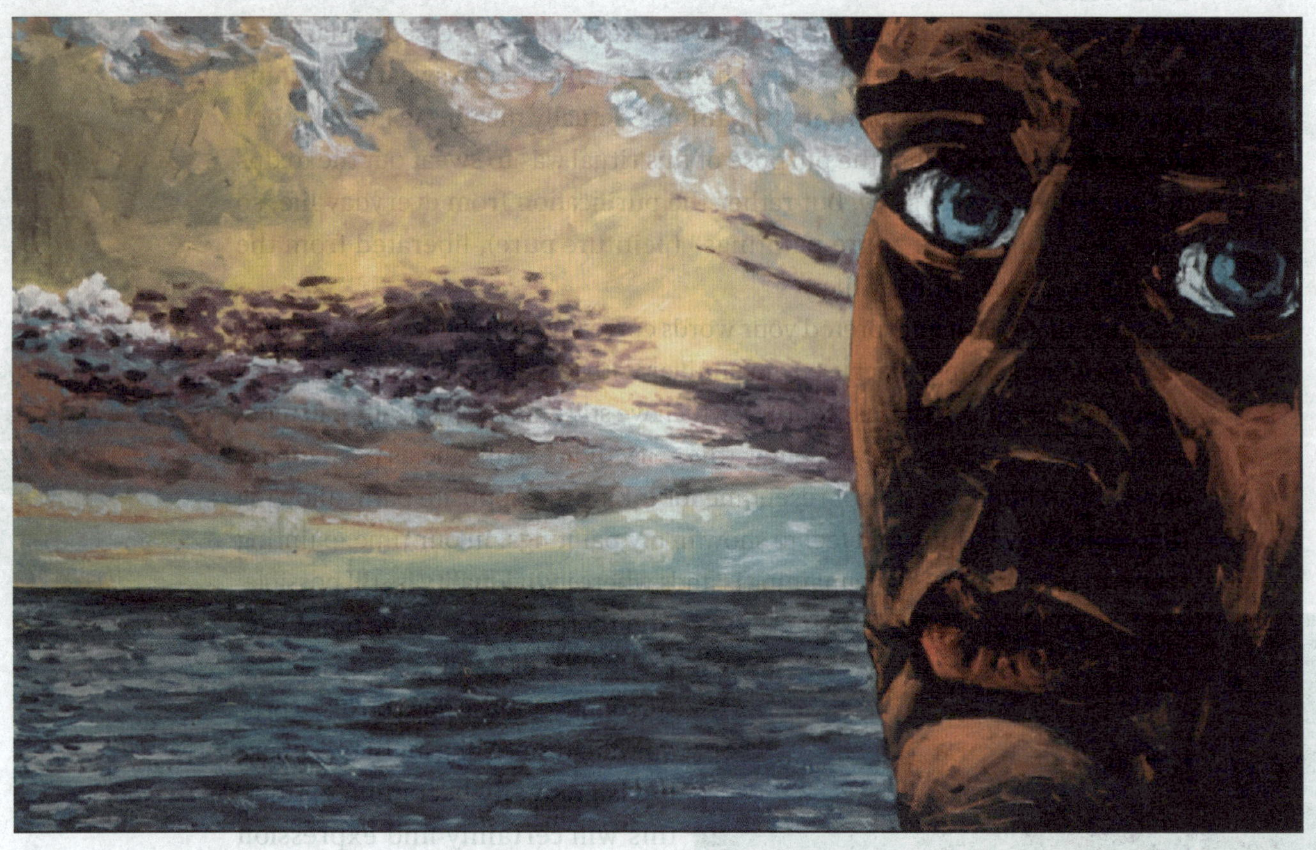

94

95

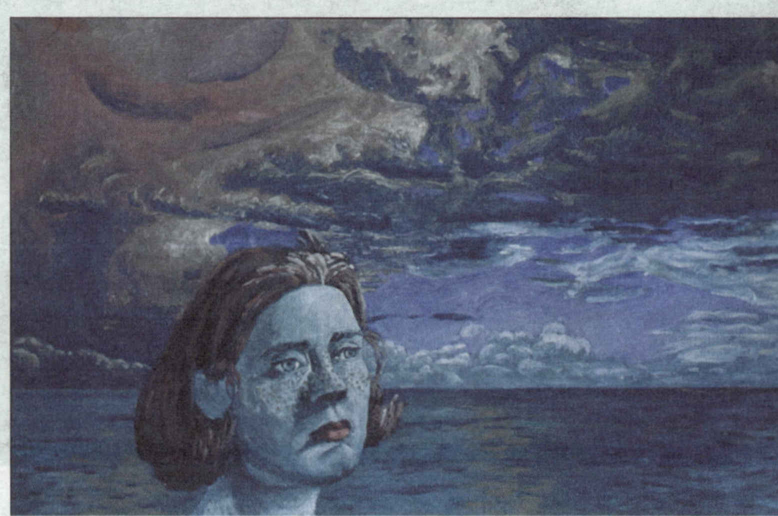

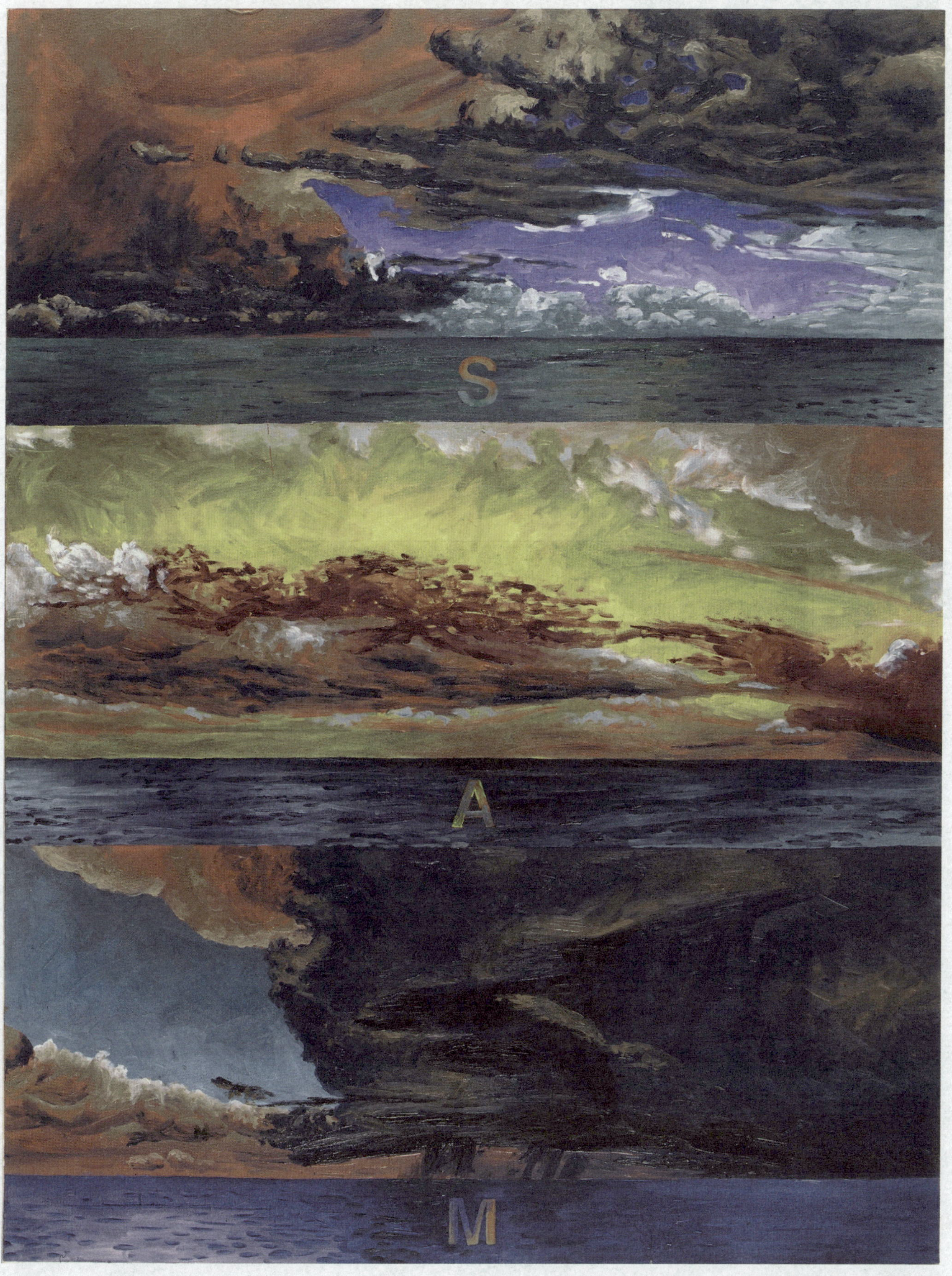
S
A
M

97

Septic

We passed and greeted each other at the entrance to the cafe. We knew each other superficially, from various exhibition openings. He congratulated me on my exhibition. I don't know if he was a doctor, but when I asked him how he liked it, he replied that it seemed "a little septic" to him. I didn't quite understand this answer, so I replied that this might be due to my fondness for the band Septica. I could read in his eyes that he didn't understand what I was saying either. We parted with a warm smile.

Septica came to my mind because I had been to their concert a few days earlier. At that moment I felt a childish satisfaction because I had answered so glibly (this is not typical for me). Instead, however, I should have asked him what he actually meant by that, because I couldn't get that remark out of my mind. But it was too late for that, so I reached for the foreign words dictionary to find out its meaning. Septic is something that is "contaminated by disease agents," "germ-infested," "infected," "poisoned," etc., so I can only assume that he found the exhibition, my work as a whole, or one of its components "unclean".

I would be lying if I said it left me completely indifferent, but I certainly would have been much more upset had he found the exhibition "a bit aseptic".

# BEECH CRUST

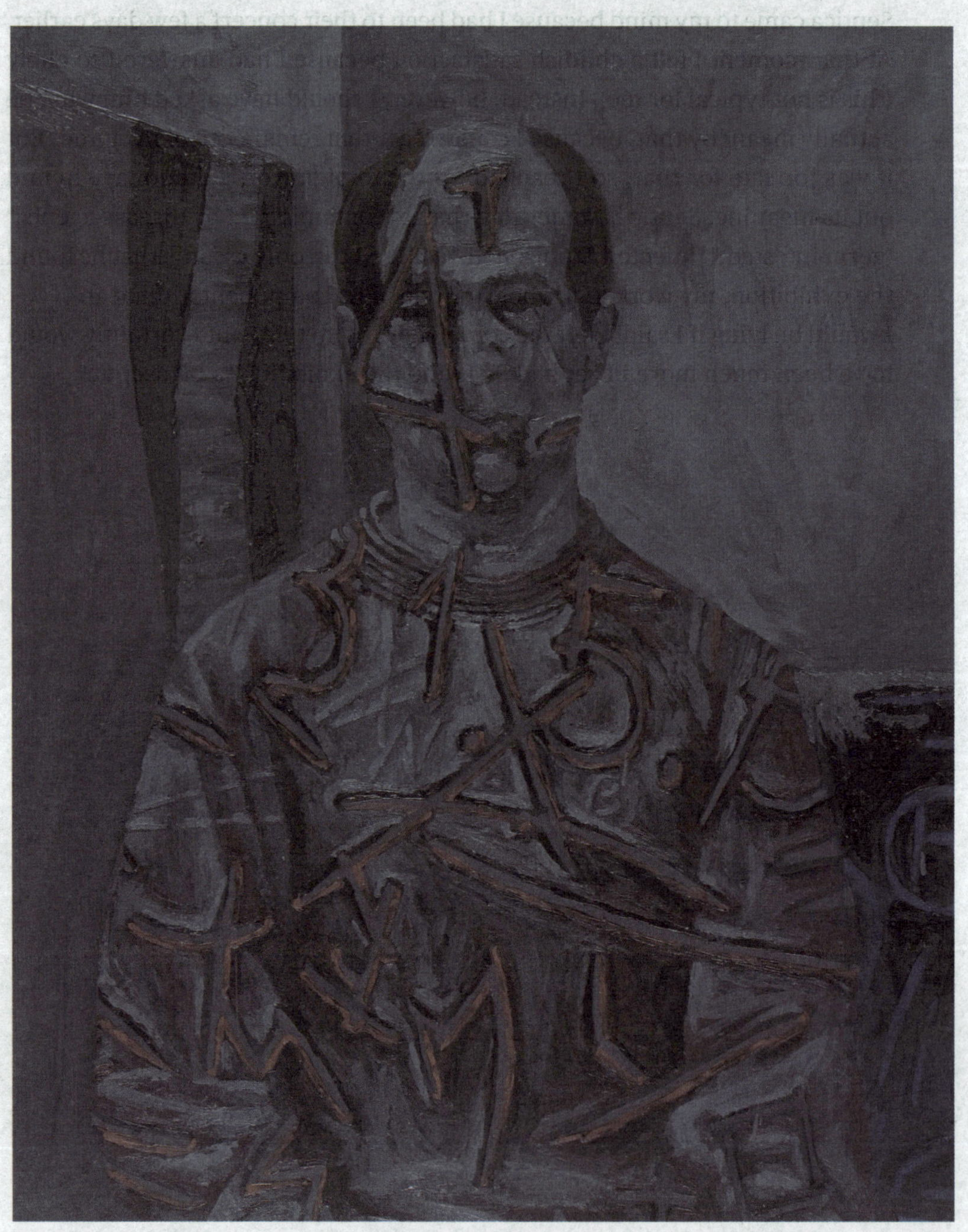

23

Scar

From the window, I saw someone hugging a birch tree, the only tree in our concrete courtyard enclosed from all sides. This person clung to the trunk so sensuously that watching this scene made me feel a similar discomfort as if I had accidentally caught two beings in an intimate exchange of affection. Later I read on the Internet that the ritual of "tree hugging" originated in Japan, that it is called dendrotherapy and is supposed to be very healing.

At that time, I also had a rather close relationship with trees. I did not hug tree trunks, but I drew them, and these three or four years spent in frequent visits to the forest were undoubtedly beneficial to my physical health. Thanks to the exercise and the fresh air, I was in good shape, while drawing in the silence of the forest, carefully observing the chosen motif and its almost imperceptible but constant changes, was a form of contemplation that benefited my mental health.

I drew various trees, young and old, ashes, oaks and chestnuts; but I write all this because of a beech. It grew along a hiking trail and, judging by the girth of its trunk, it was quite old. Its otherwise smooth bark, crisscrossed with gentle horizontal ripples, was littered with wide-open scars, carved names and initials, simple scratches and marks. Fresh scuffs stood out through their intense orange on the gray bark. In places where her branches broke or were sawed off, it had the so-called "tree eyes." It also bore a climber's mark and other markings - I assume they had to do something with forestry. I painted it several times, and in these repetitions my painting style gradually changed. Thanks to this new experience, I began to think differently about the surface of the painting and about the painting as such, and for that I am infinitely grateful to the Beech. If I ever take that hiking trail again, and if she is still standing there, I will hug her tightly.

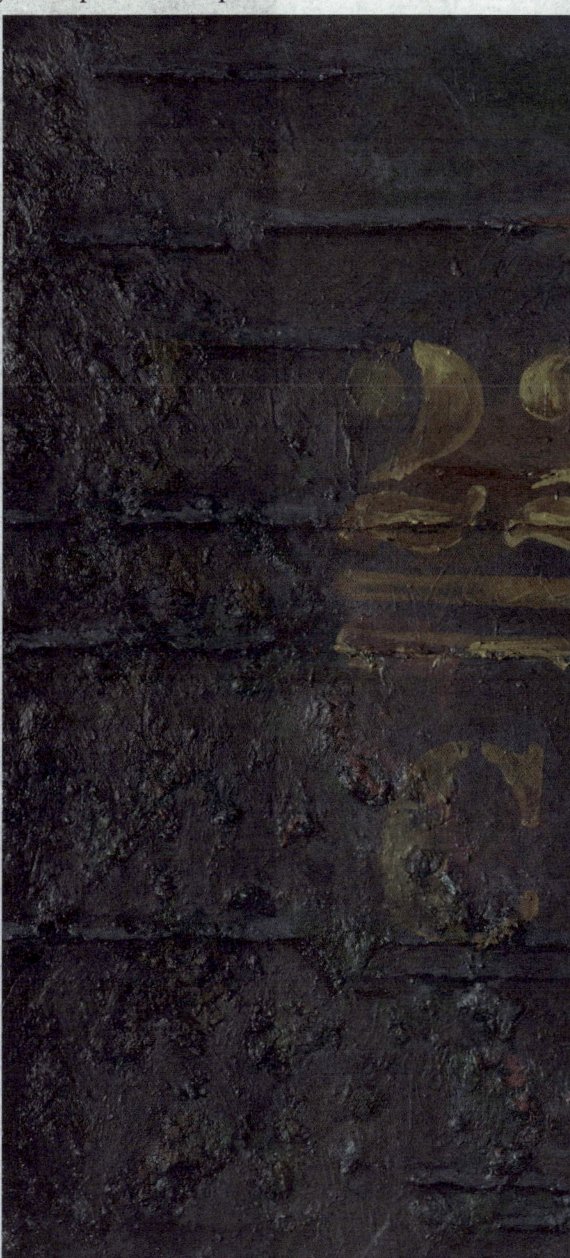

98

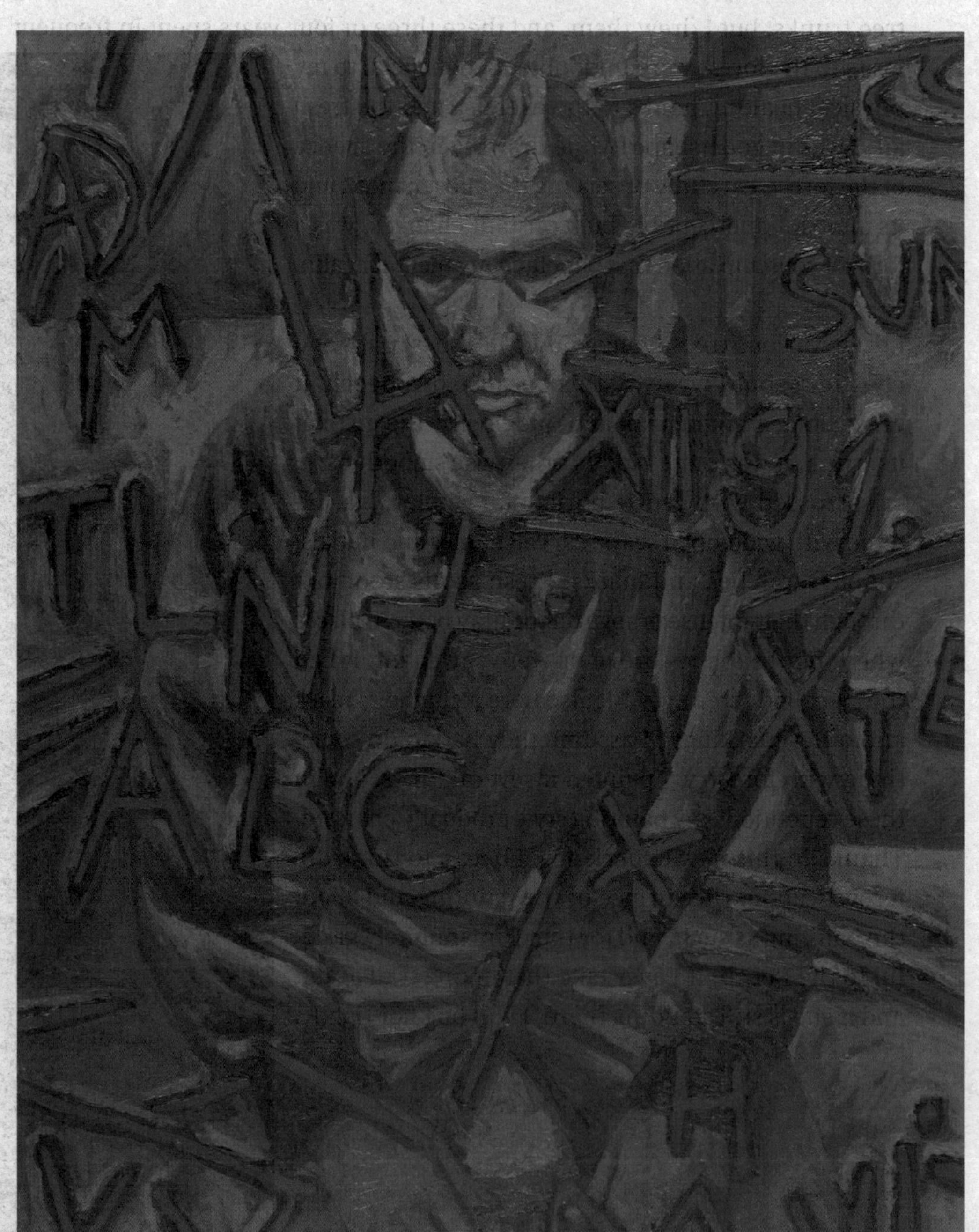
M
A
SUN
M
9
TLN
N+
XT E
ABC
H

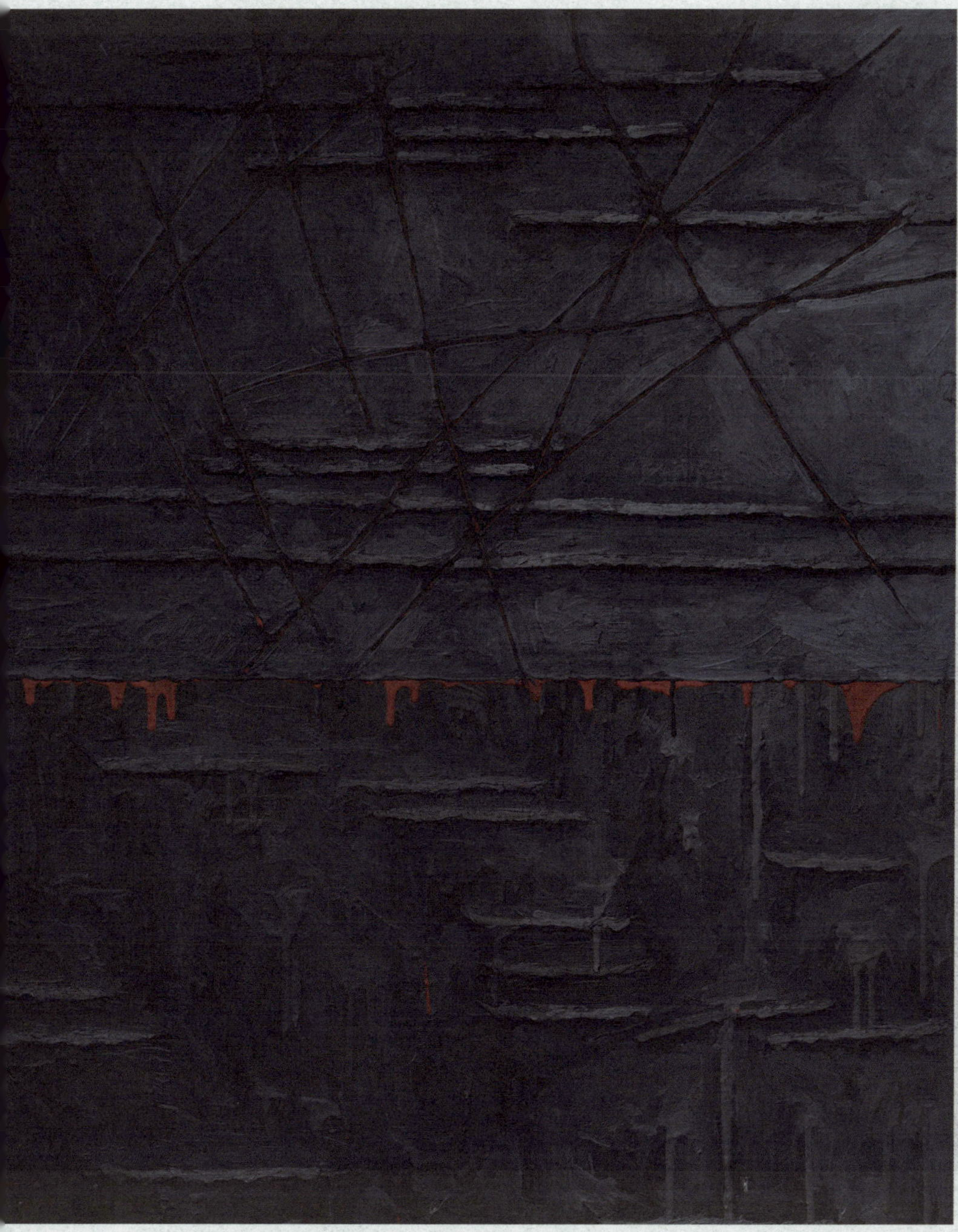

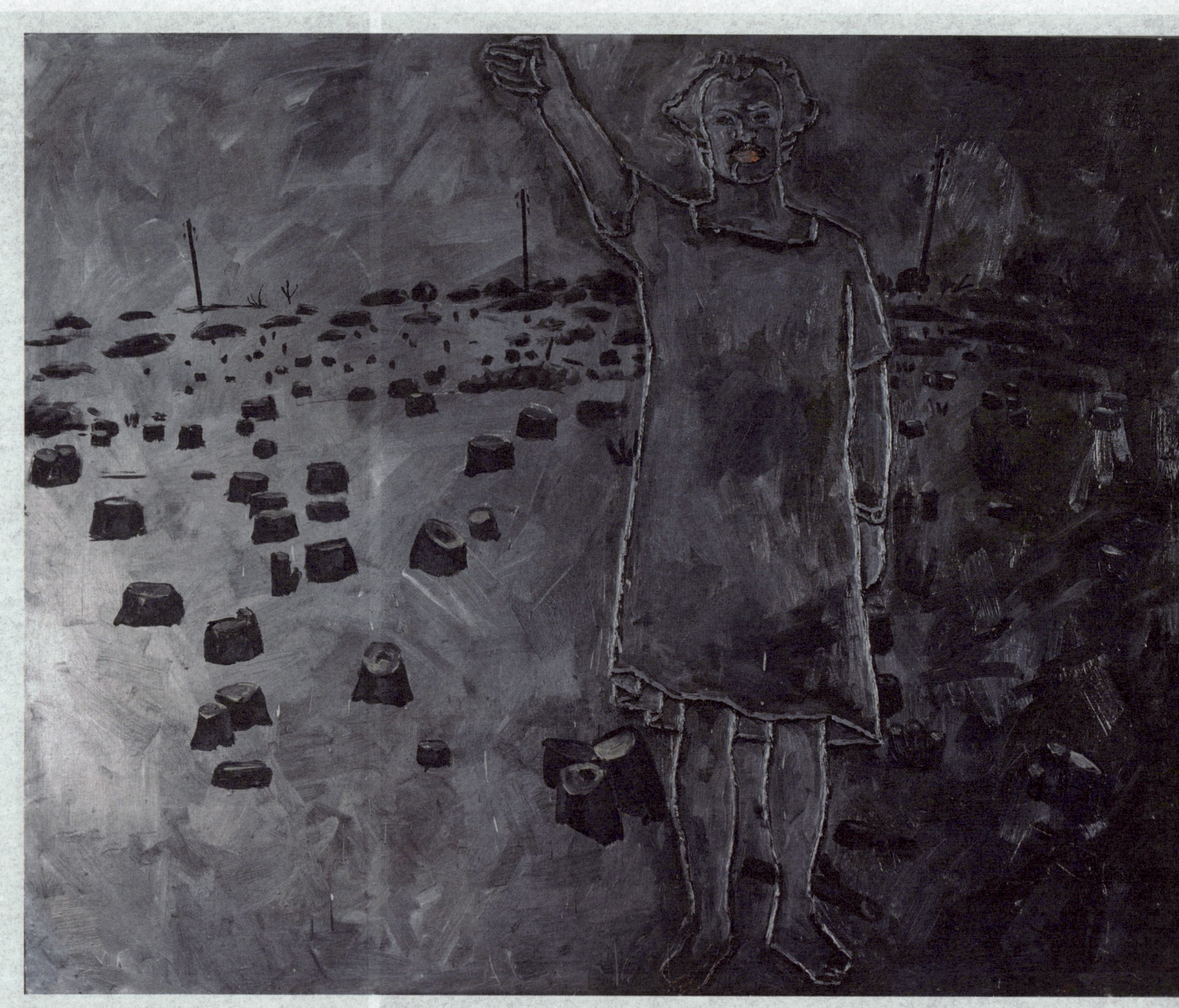

(1)


I painted the canvas as if
its one side were illuminated, the other
in the shadow. I painted slowly, meticulously,
with colors I mixed so that
the painting radiated heaviness and felt
like a leaden plate, from the one side
lit by weak light. With the same
colors I simultaneously made a drawing
that rose from the surface like a relief.



(2)


Along the forest path that I passed
almost every day for months lay
a clumsily felled young oak.
The obvious futility of this death
upset me - I could in no way figure out
why someone would cut a young tree
and then leave it like that. For days
I spun different stories in my head,
looking for a possible reason for this
senseless act. About that time
I saw the self-portrait of painter
Igor Rončević, who depicted himself
holding an axe.



(3)


A relief line on the painted surface
of the canvas highlights the uniqueness
both of the painted subject and the surface,
while the surface creates mood and
determines the emotional experience
of the drawing. It depicts painter
Igor Rončević with an axe.
On a ground prepared in this manner
I painted the felled young oak.

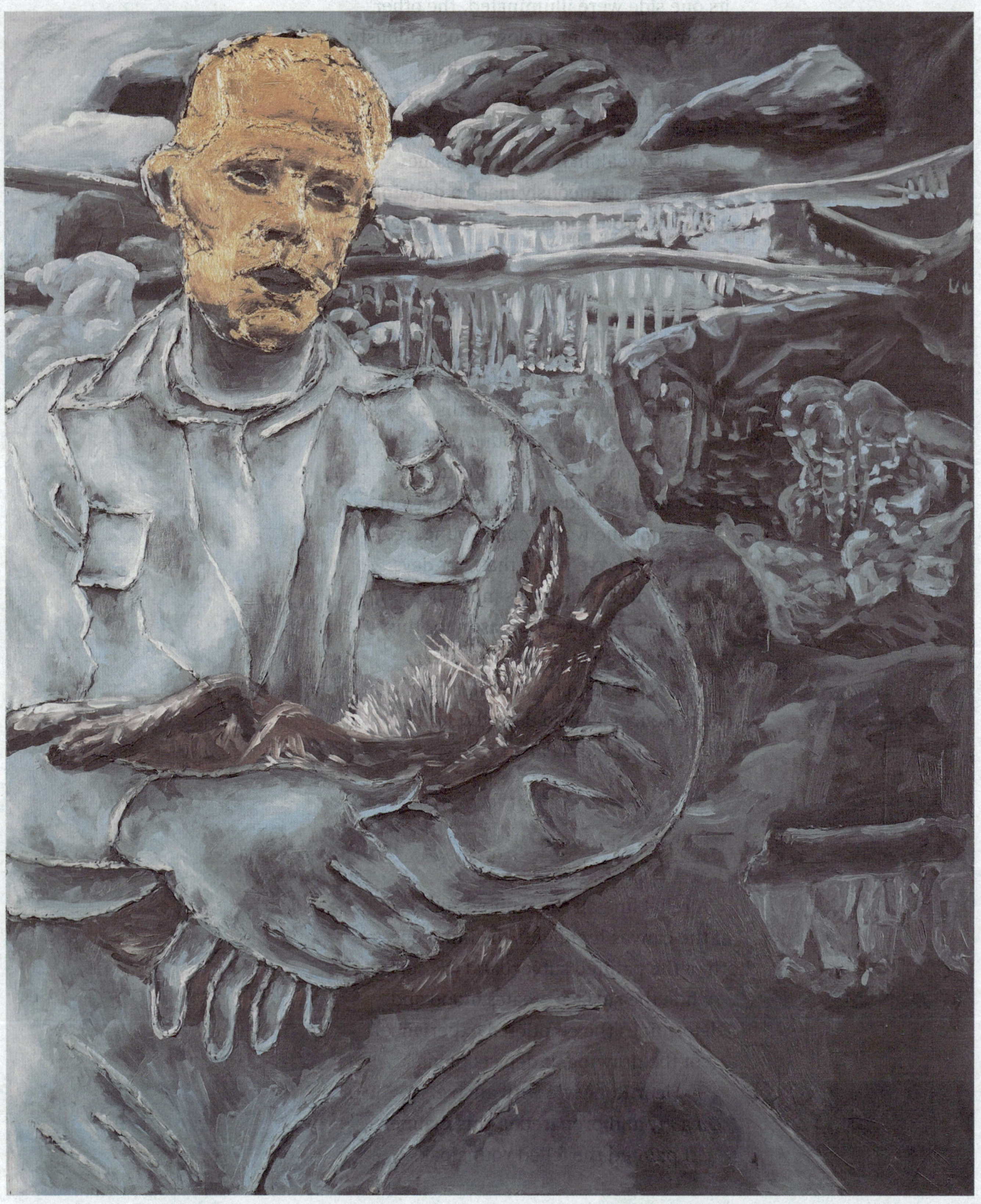

The Rabbit and the Rivulet

At night one cruel winter
When winds severely blow
A rivulet gets frozen
And covered by the snow.


One tiny, lonely bunny
Seeks the rivulet's bed
Where did it only go
The little bunny's sad.


The tiny rabbit cries and cries
For his beloved brook
He thinks he wasn't nice
That rivulet who took.


In sorrow the rabbit thinks
Where the brook now might be
Perhaps it went with swallows
To distant southern sea.

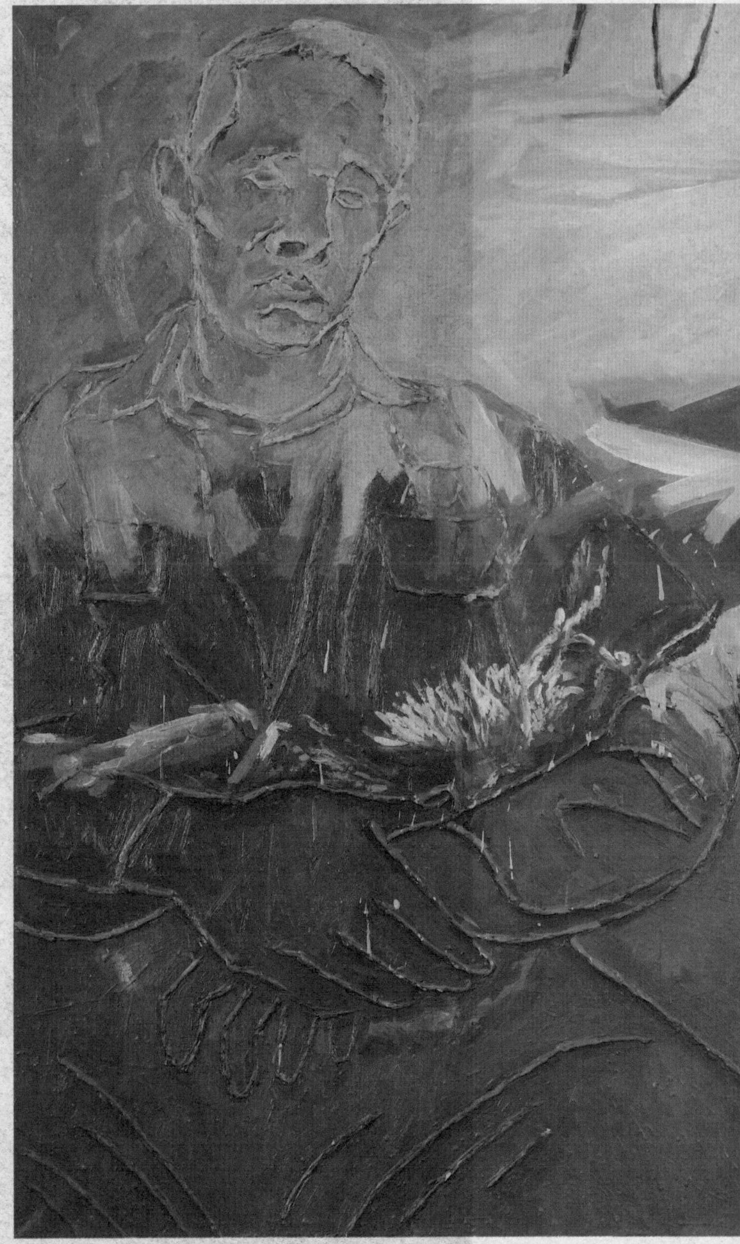

103

Croatian children's song by Branko Mihaljević.
Recast by Andy Jelčić.

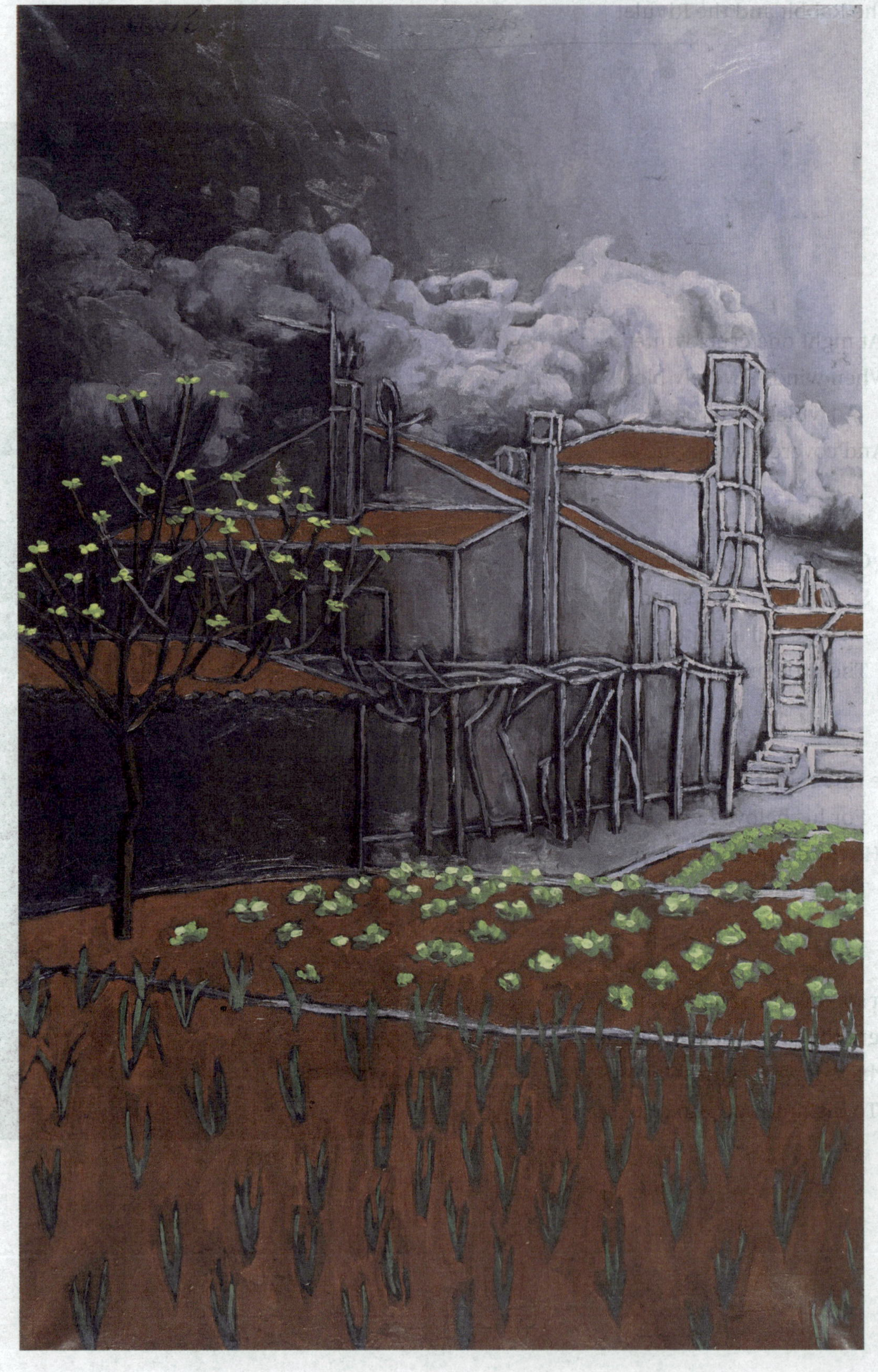



Stillness

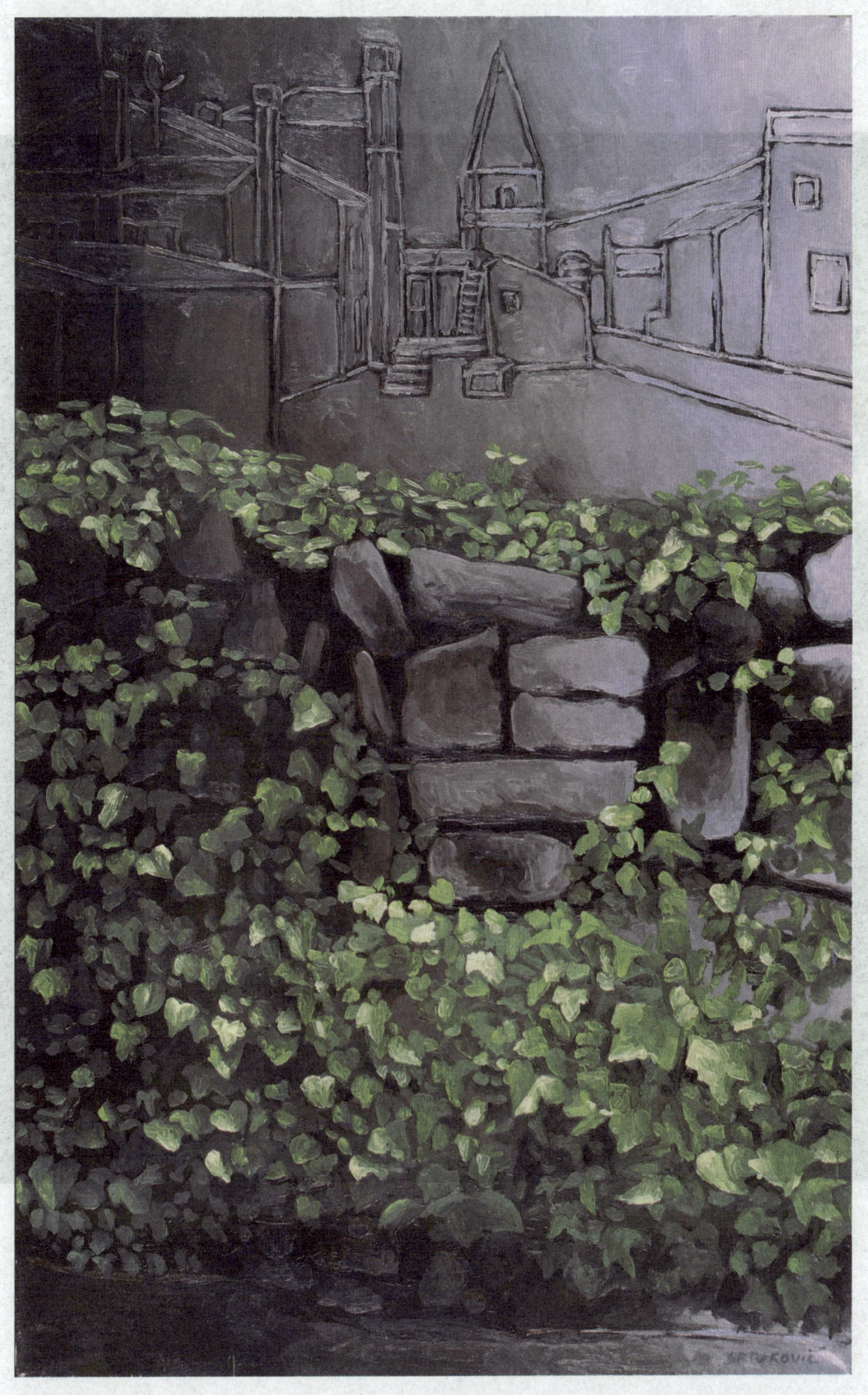

Pictures seen by someone else

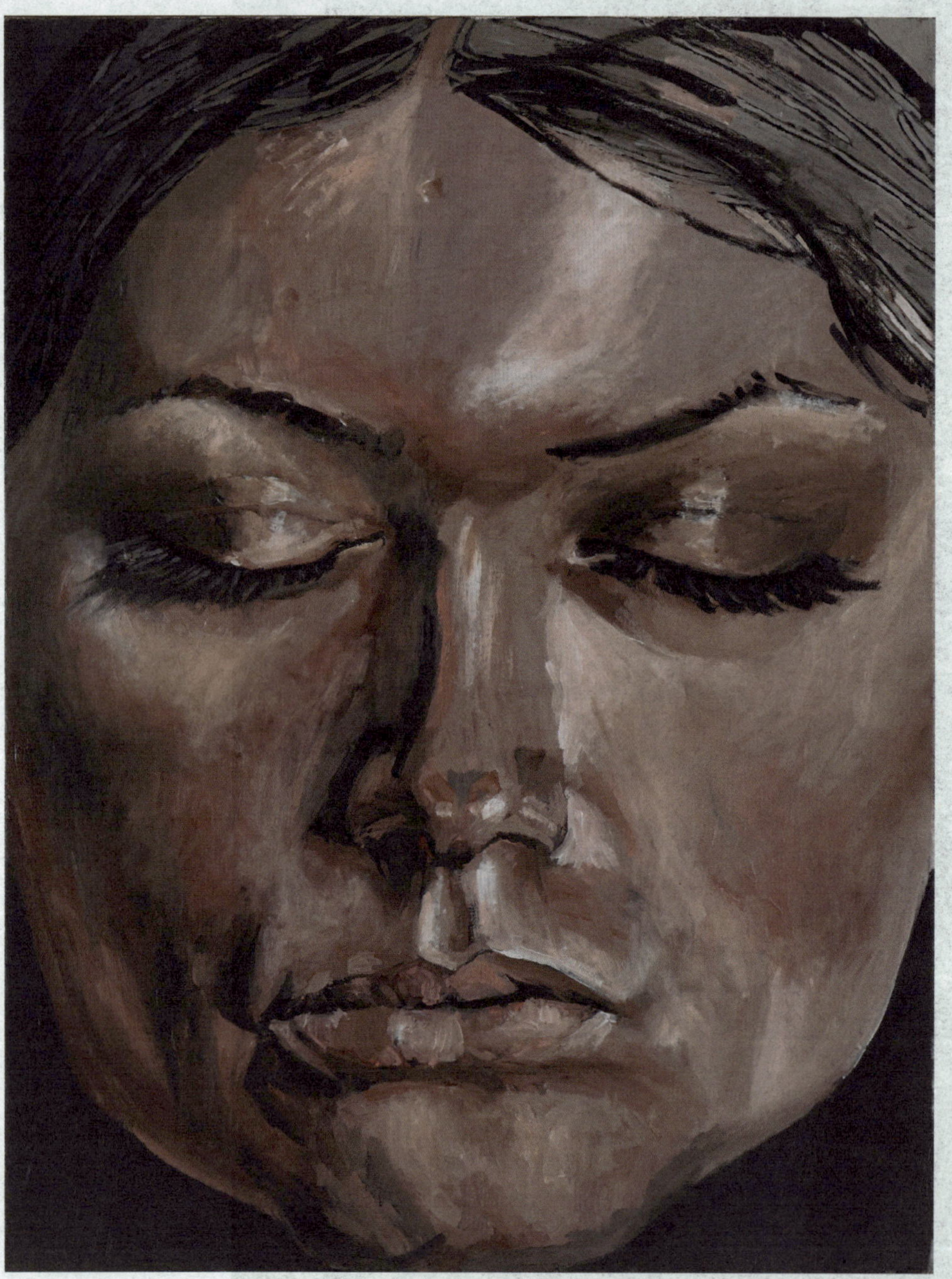

I got up at the break of dawn. There were only a few days left until the opening of my exhibition, but it seemed to me that the paintings needed many finishing touches. I put on the T-shirt worn by a model for the painting I had been working on already for months, supposed to be the mainstay of the entire exhibition, and set off for the studio. The T-shirt was printed with the words: "God, how I love Botticelli."

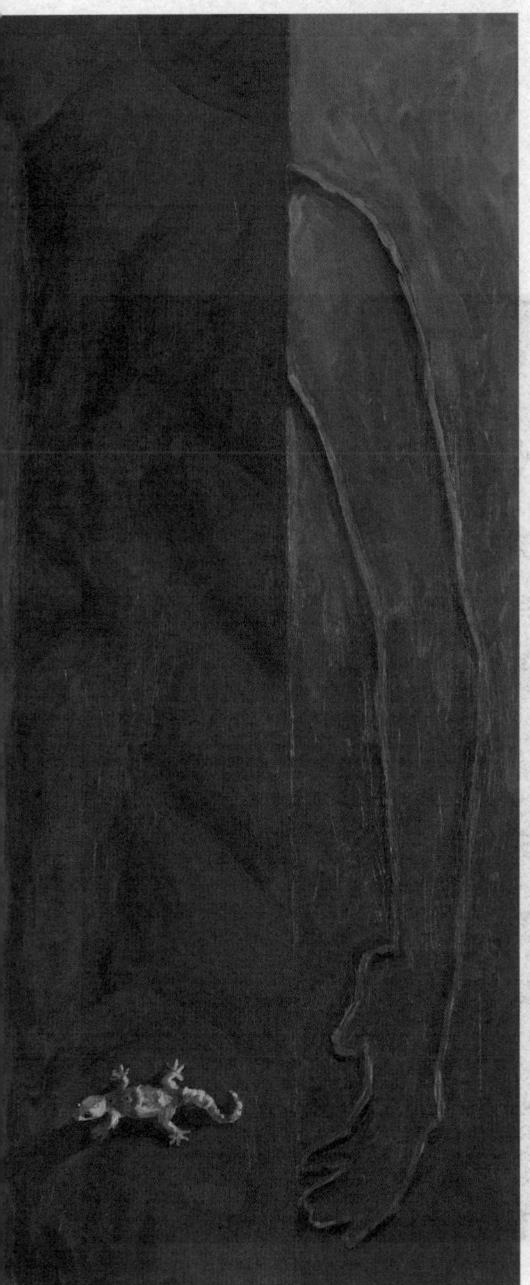

It was a beautiful morning in June, the sun was just rising. Large, glowing, it shone down on the roofs under the cloudless, royal blue sky. Apart from the chirping of birds, there was almost no other sound. At the roundabout encircling the so-called Džamija Square, a cyclist suddenly appeared, focused in my direction as I descended the stairs from the fountain to the roadway. It was a newspaper delivery man who had also gotten up early as I did. I think he was trying to figure out what was written on my T-shirt, but either the sun was blinding him or he was just nearsighted. He wasn't looking where he was driving, so his front wheel slid into the streetcar track. Together with the newspapers on the luggage rack, he landed on the roadway directly in front of me.

Fortunately, there was no traffic, and the cyclist did not appear to be injured. I rushed over to help him get up and pick up the scattered newspapers. I felt a bit guilty for the accident because of my T-shirt. I tried to explain why I was wearing it, namely to draw attention to my exhibition. And further, that this sign of my fondness for Botticelli in the painting suggested to the viewer that he had found the key to its interpretation, when in fact he was only misled by it. But the cyclist firmly refused my help. His look and attitude suggested not only discomfort and annoyance at his stupid position, but also a certain dislike for me. Therefore, I left him alone and continued my walk. Somehow it seemed to me that he thought I was gay.

109

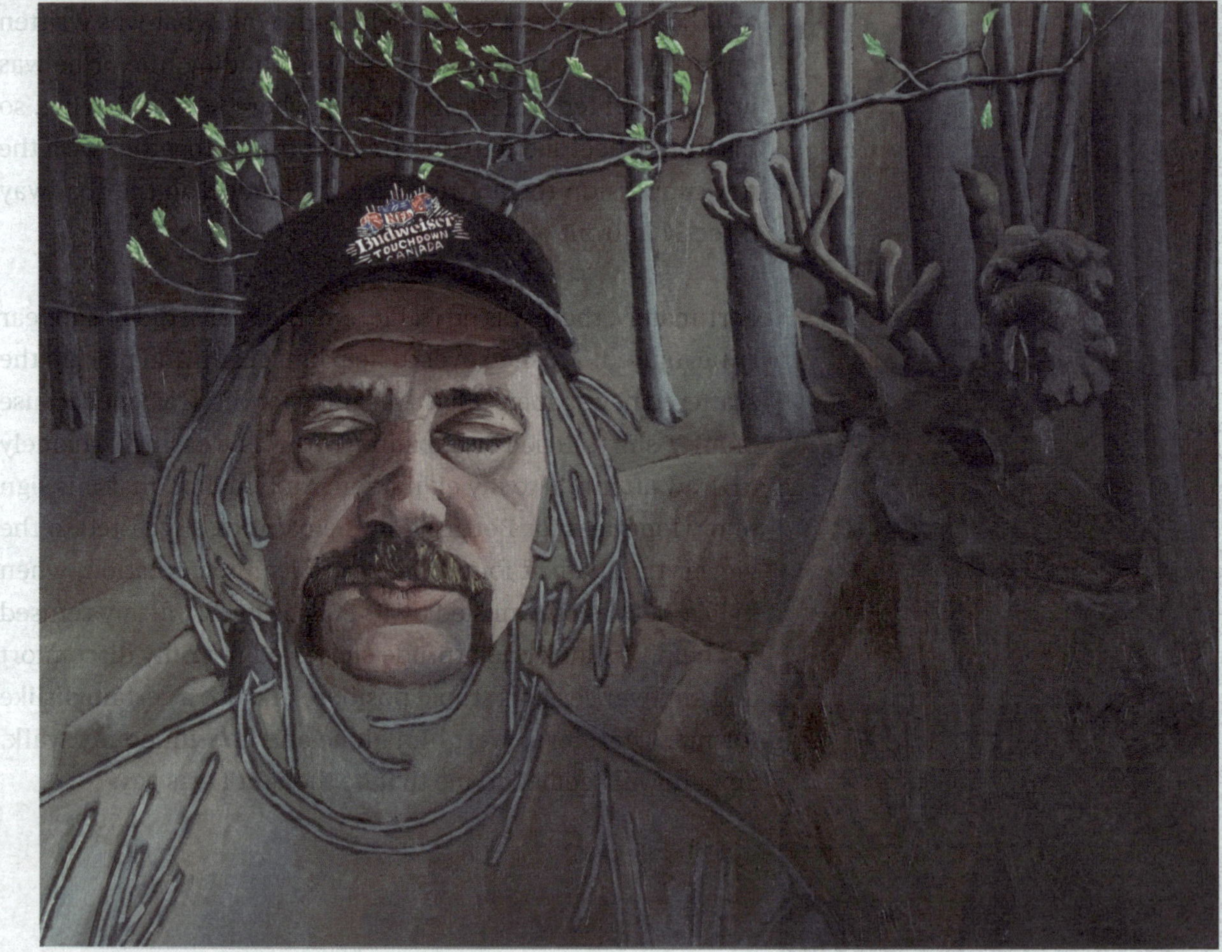

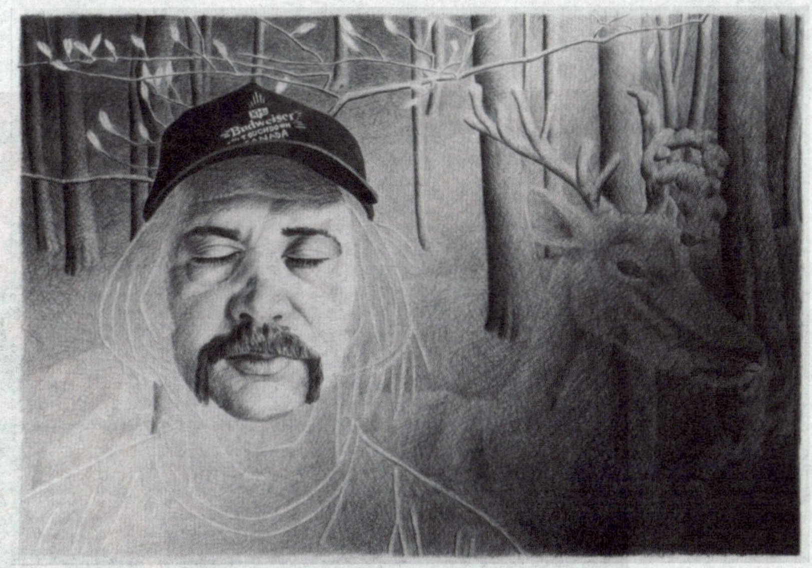

108

19

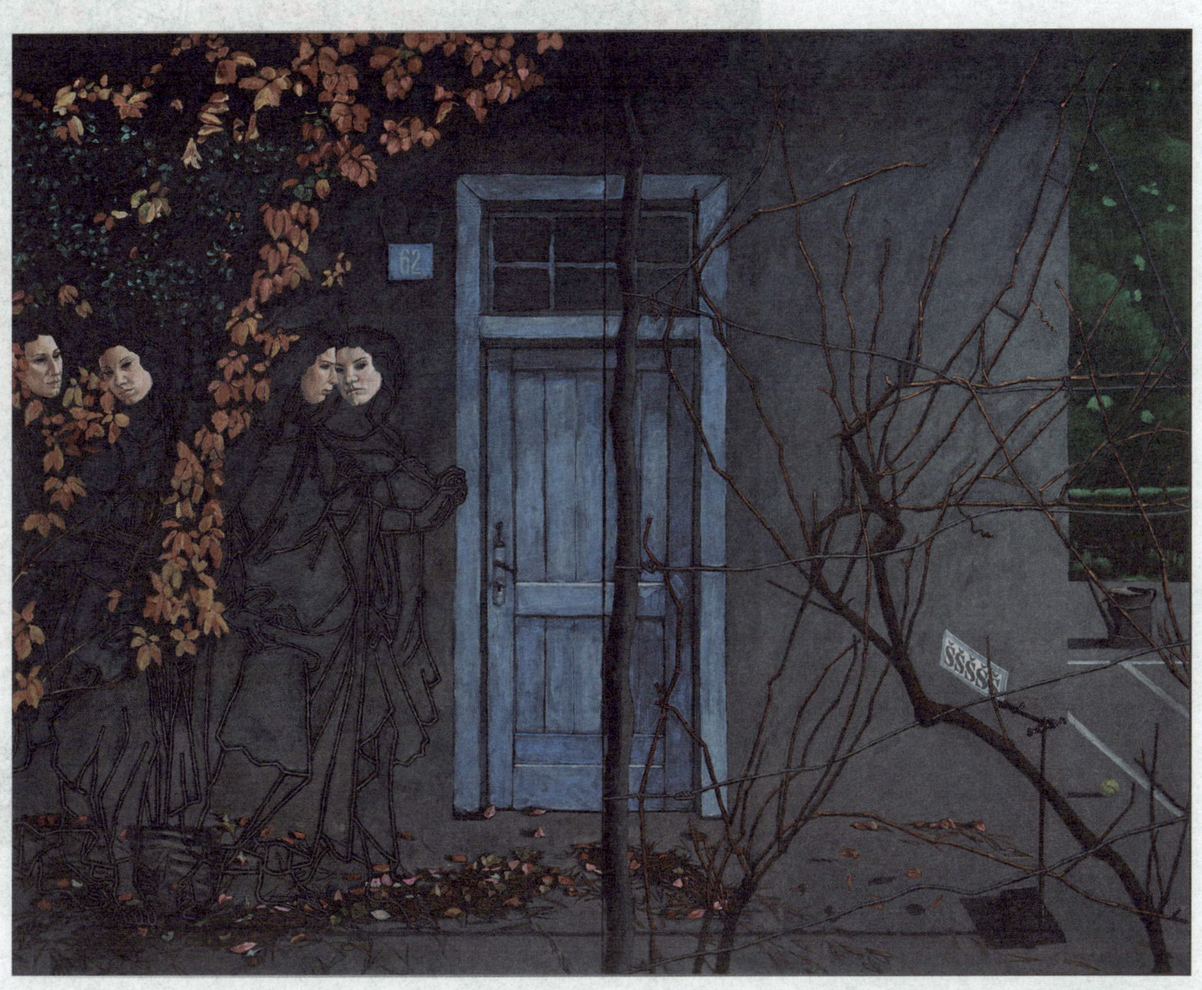

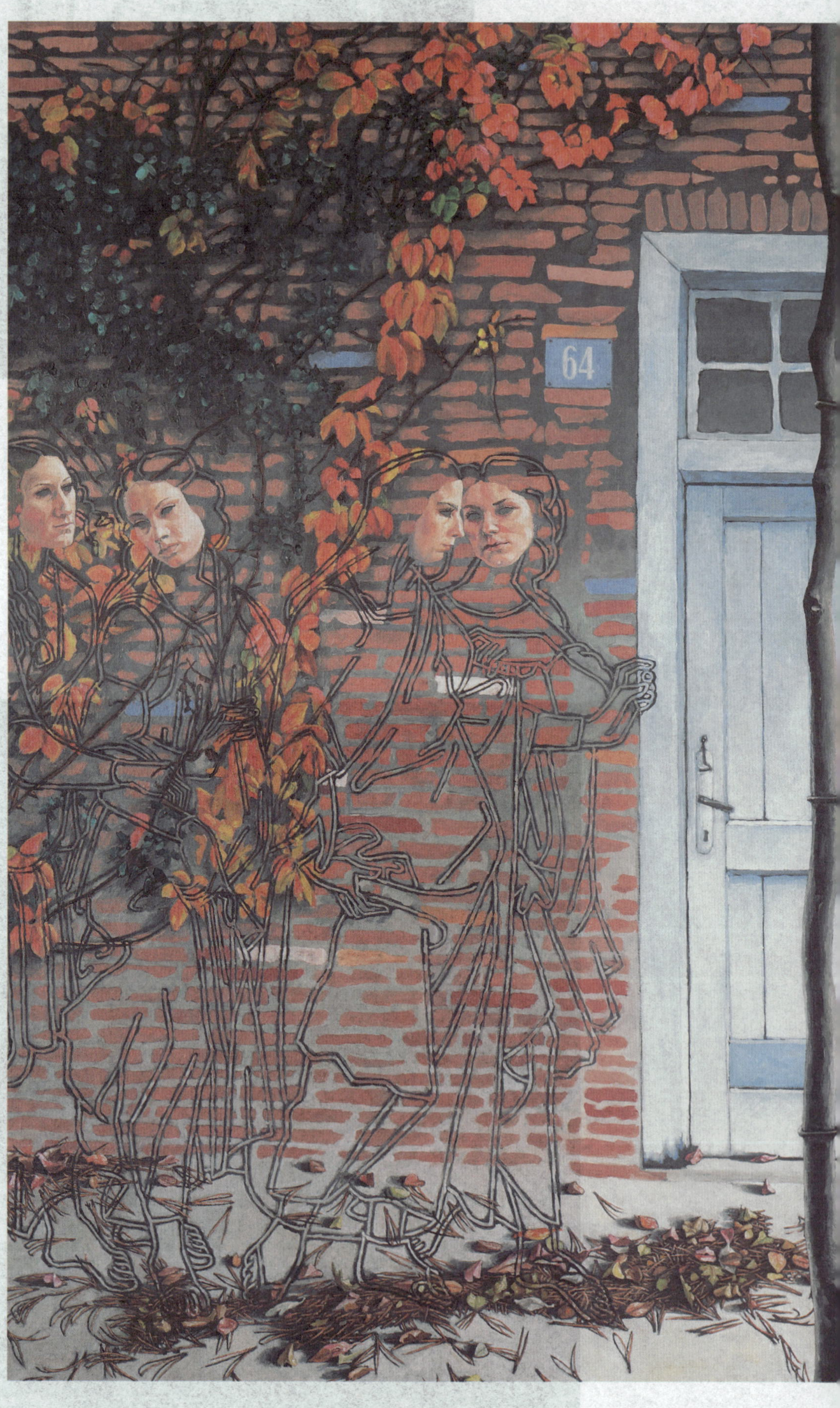
64

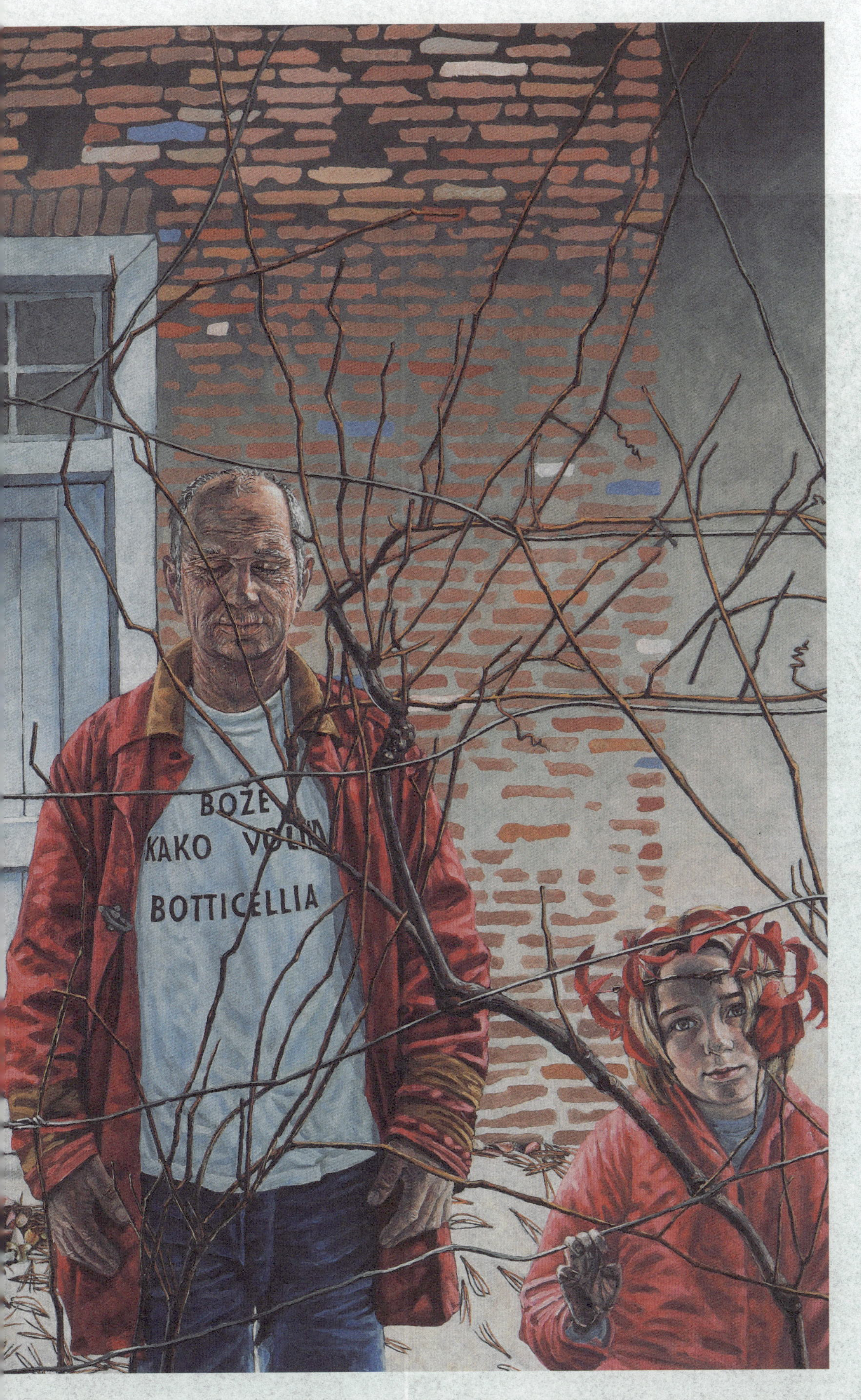

BOŽE
KAKO VOLIM
BOTTICELLIA

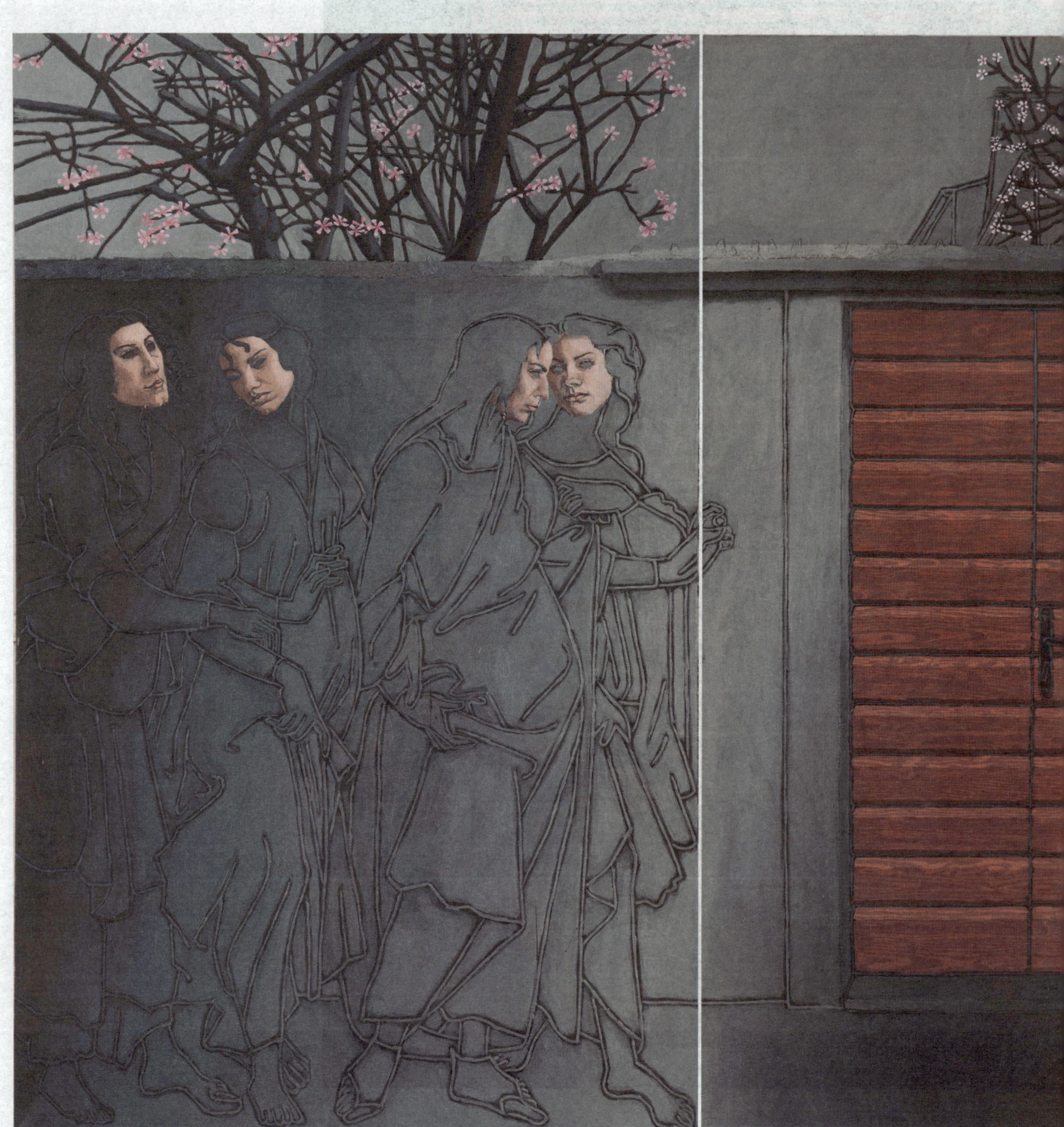

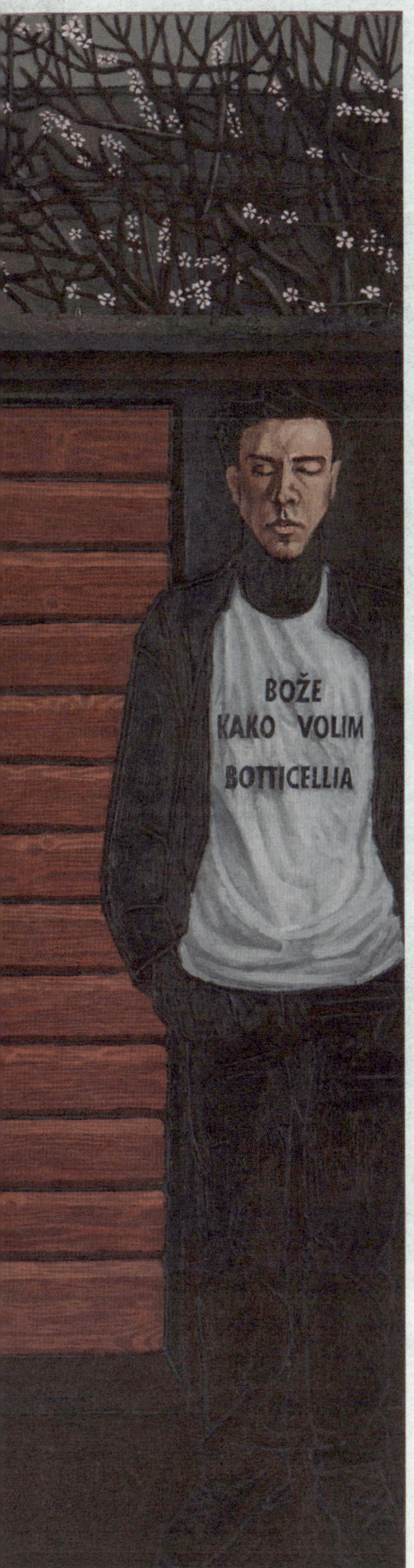


111

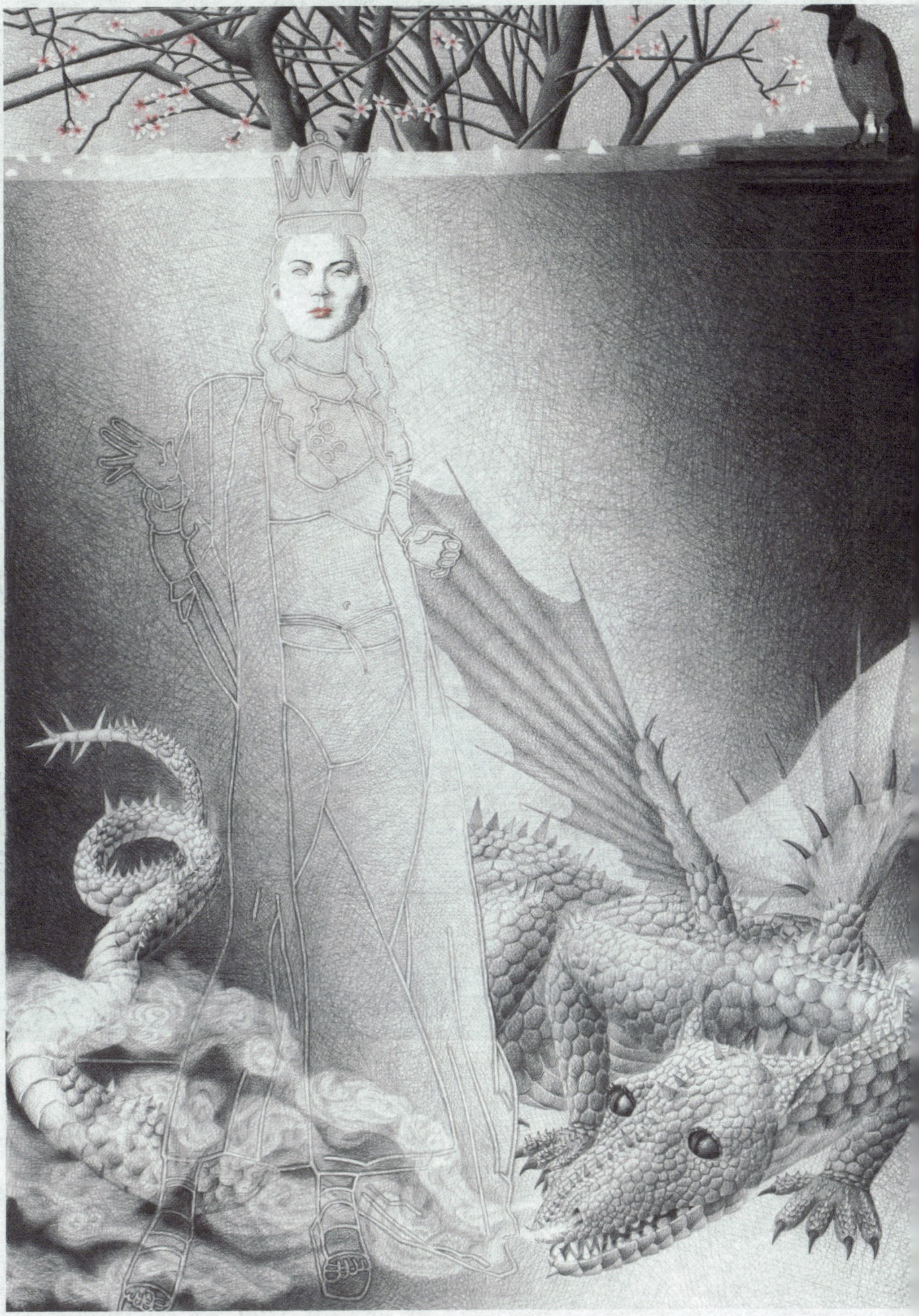

113

112

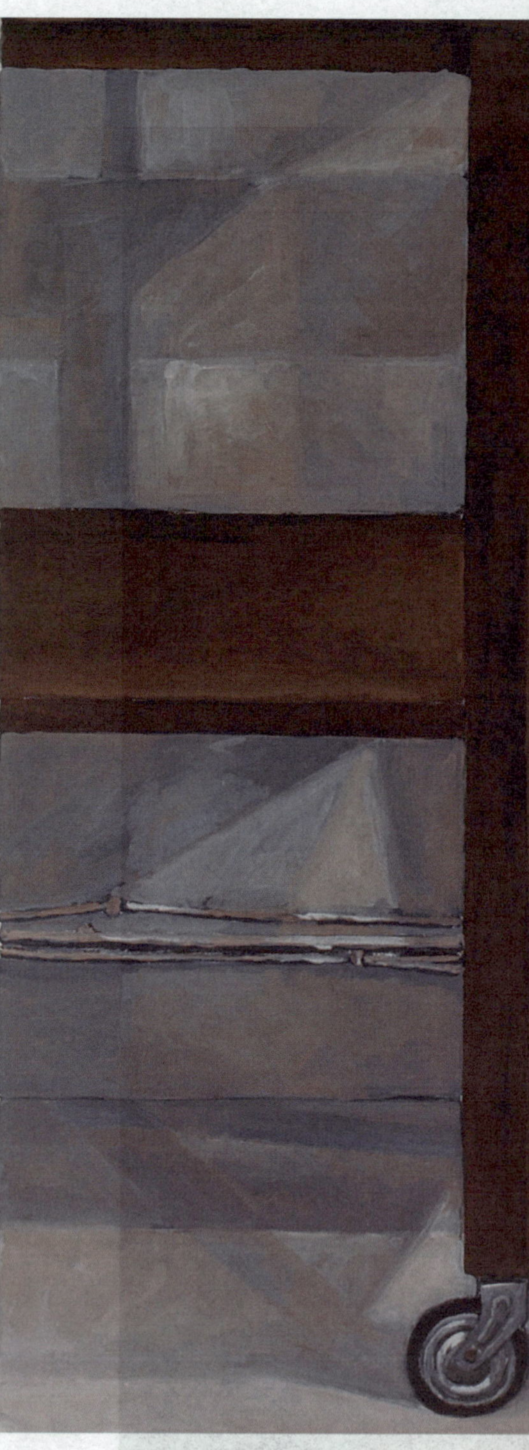

Storage-Room

102

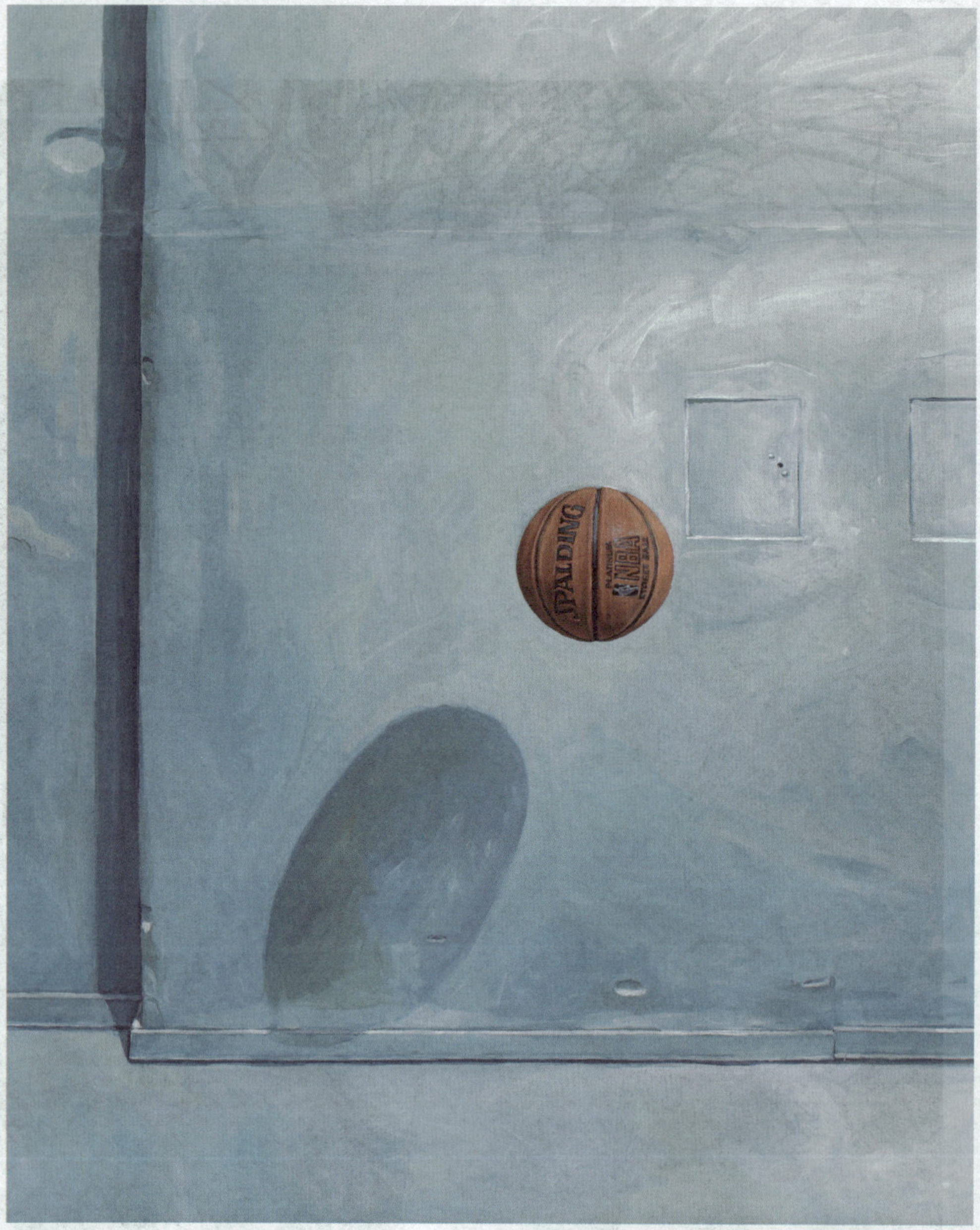

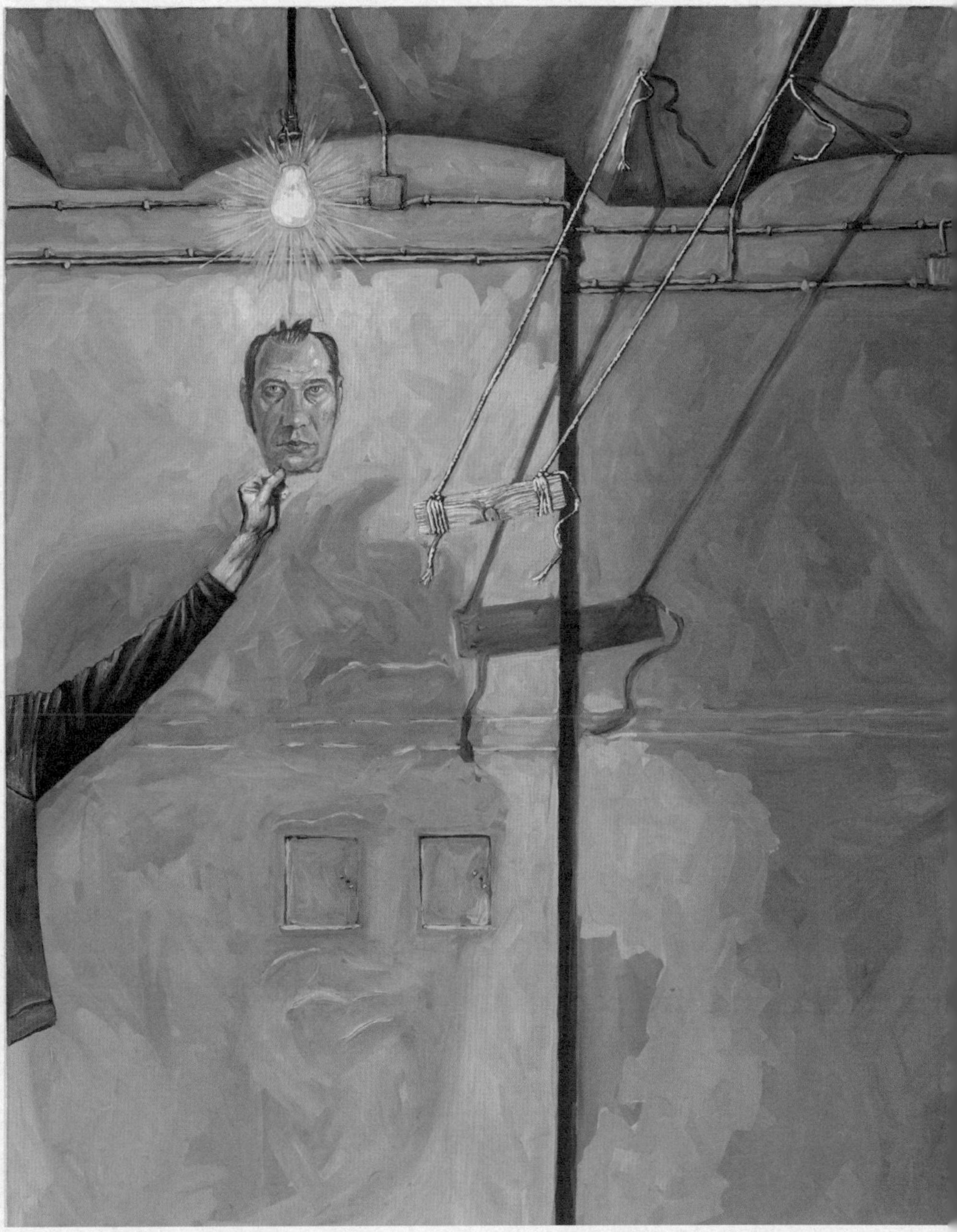

Painting is kept in a storage-room in our common universal soul. All ways of applying paint, all tricks of the trade, everything "new" and "old" exists in this storage-room since time immemorial and forever, timelessly, and will remain there as long as this common universal soul, i.e. mankind, exists. The first painter already contained all painters who came after him, just as the one born at this moment contains all those who preceded him. The painter takes from the storage-room what he needs, or what he is able to take from it, and brings it to the light of the unique moment in which he lives. On this unique moment and on him it depends what will emerge from the storage-room and how that will be used, what shape it will take in the painting.

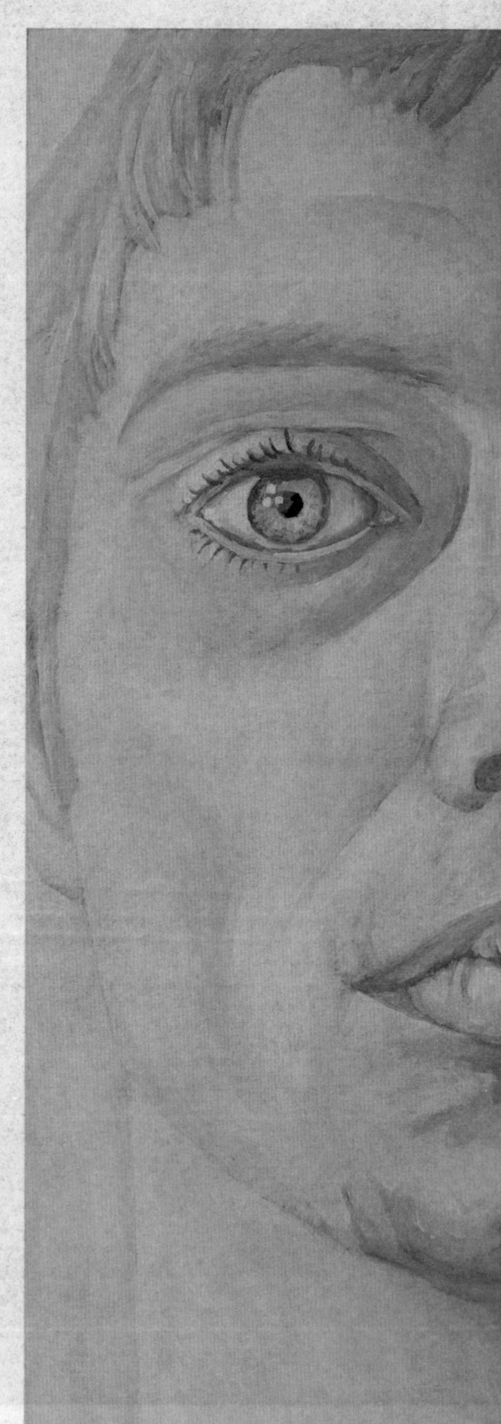

Scene

Deep within ourselves we have the need for our mirror-image, which includes
everything that surrounds us. Looking at this image, we strive to position our
existence in the Totality, which seems insuperable without this gaze directed
at ourselves. We also feel the need to envelop our mirror-image in the specific
atmosphere of the moment in which we live, in order to harmonize it with what
we feel and think about ourselves. Such an image, wrapped in the
peculiar atmosphere of the moment of its creation, I call a Scene.

116

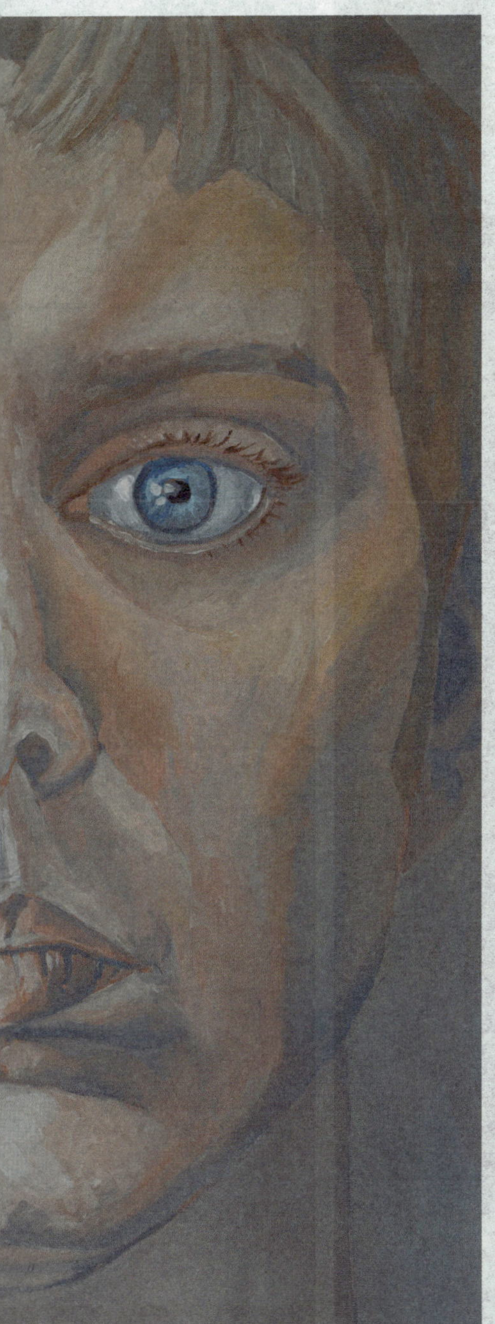

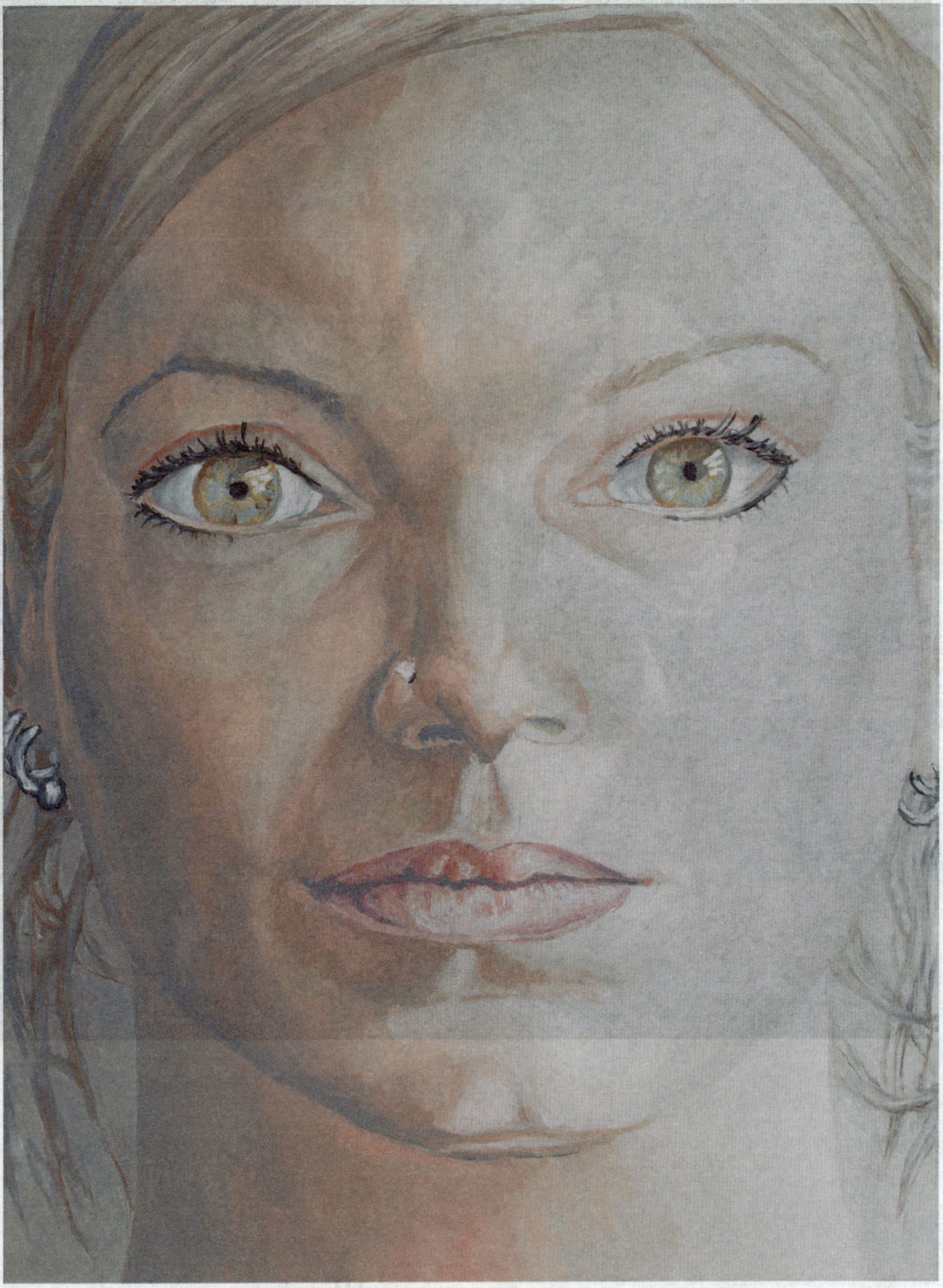

Illusion

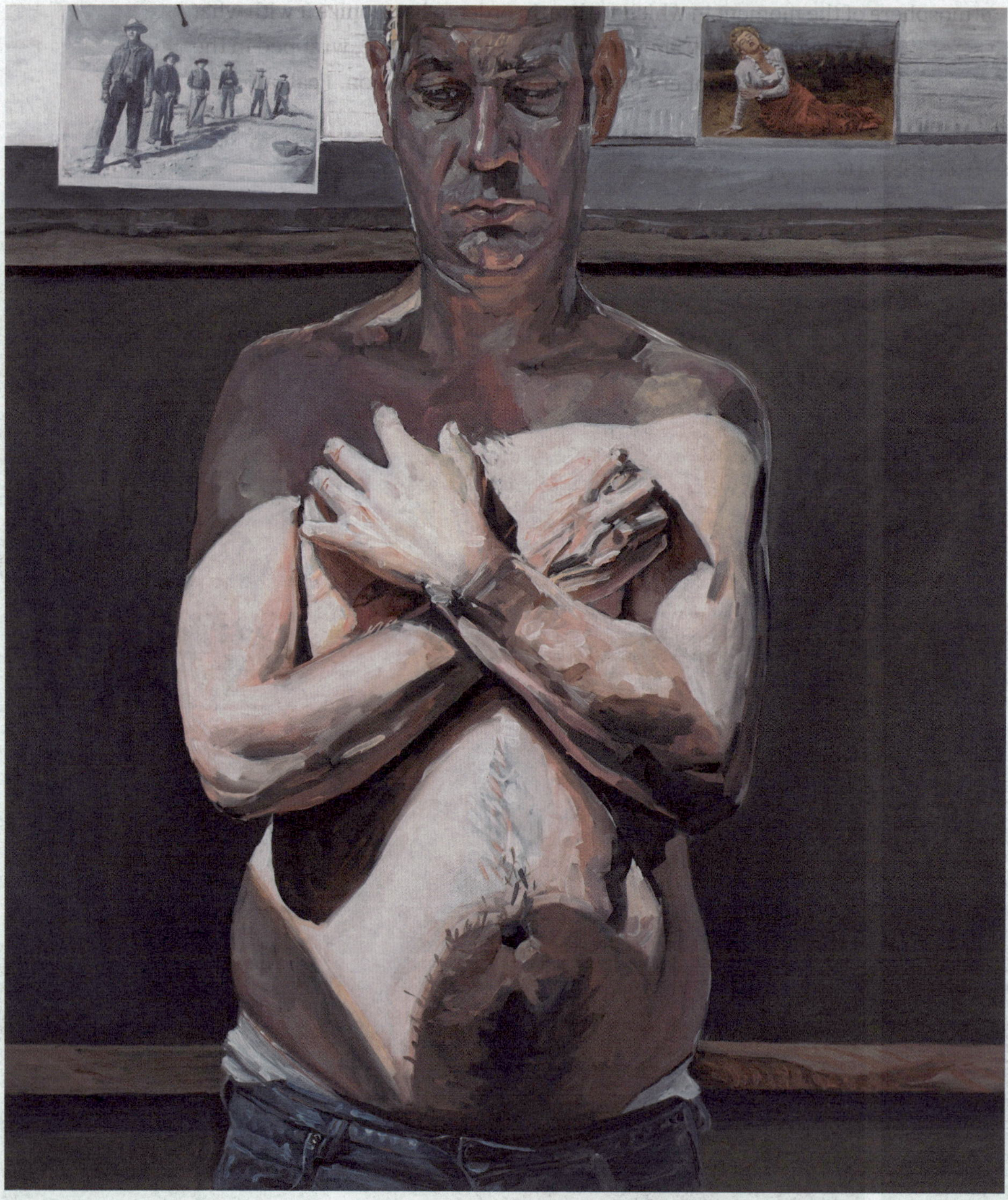

Illusion

A painting is a simple, usually square object that occupies a certain space in the real world. But what is painted on its surface represents the entrance into a space that exists simultaneously to the real one, a space built by our will to create our own world in spite of the real one. All the material values and spiritual meanings that this simple object may have for us exist only in our parallel, artificial space. The highlighting of this artificial nature of a painting is what I call Illusion.

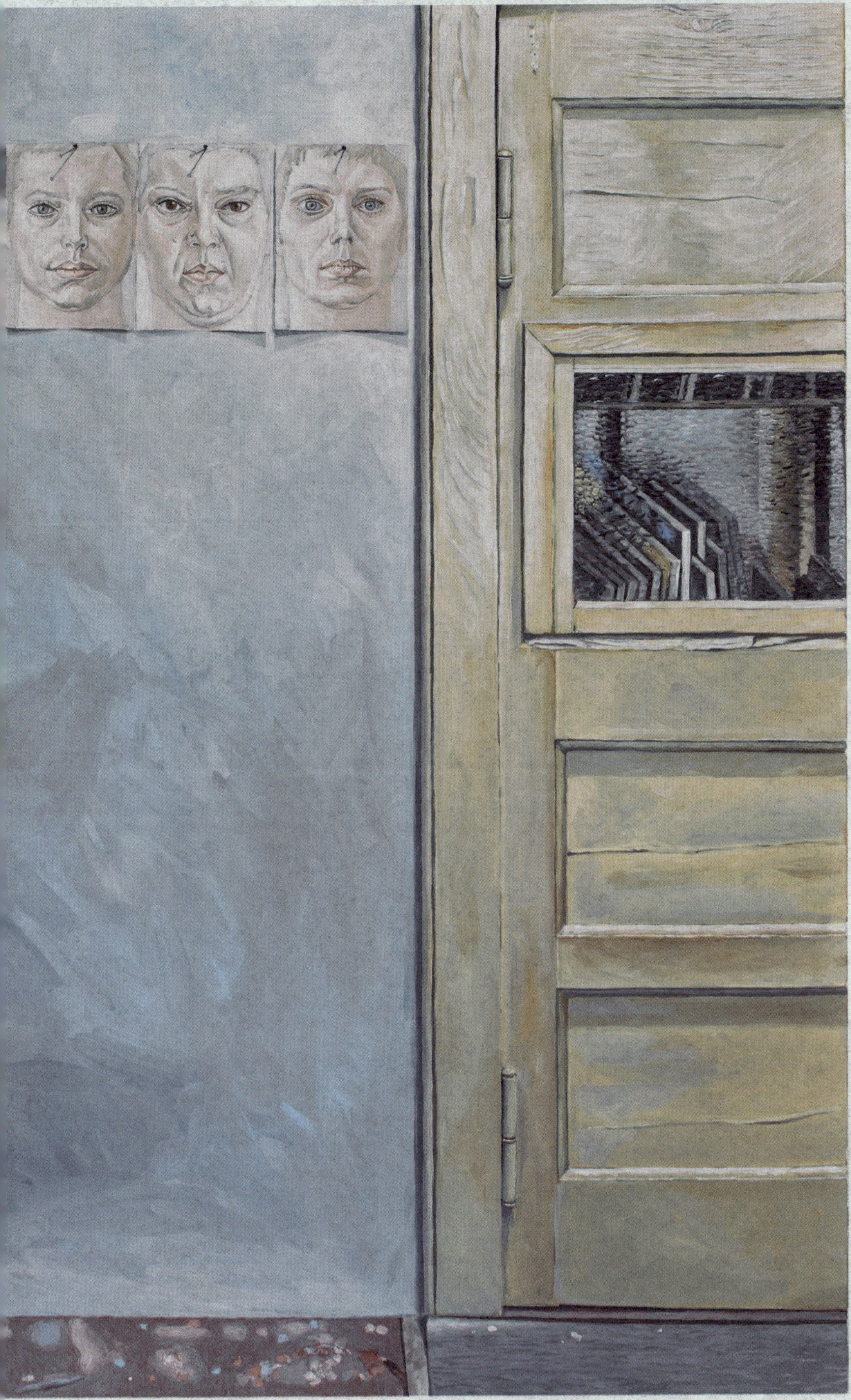

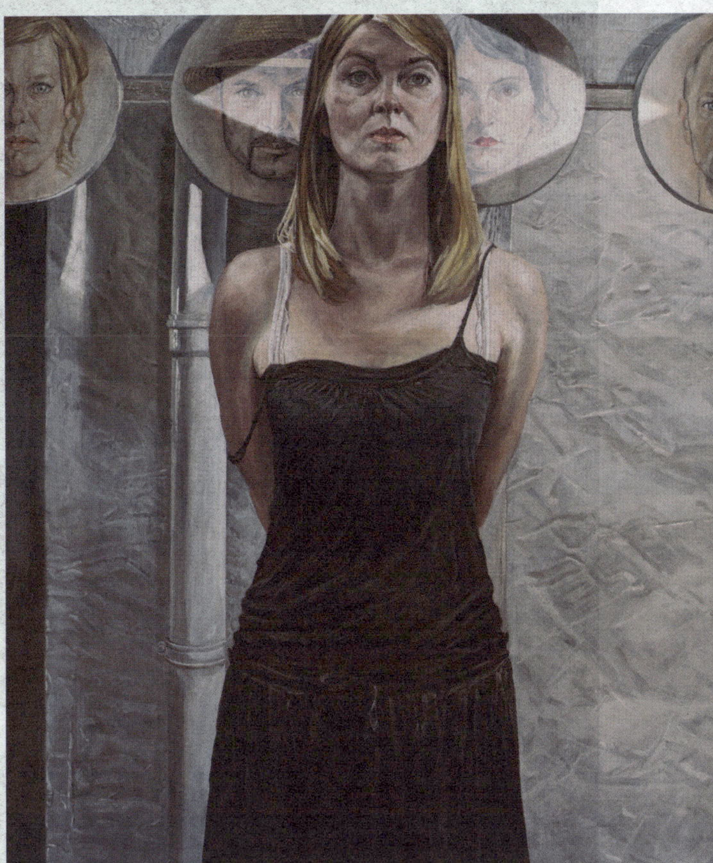

118

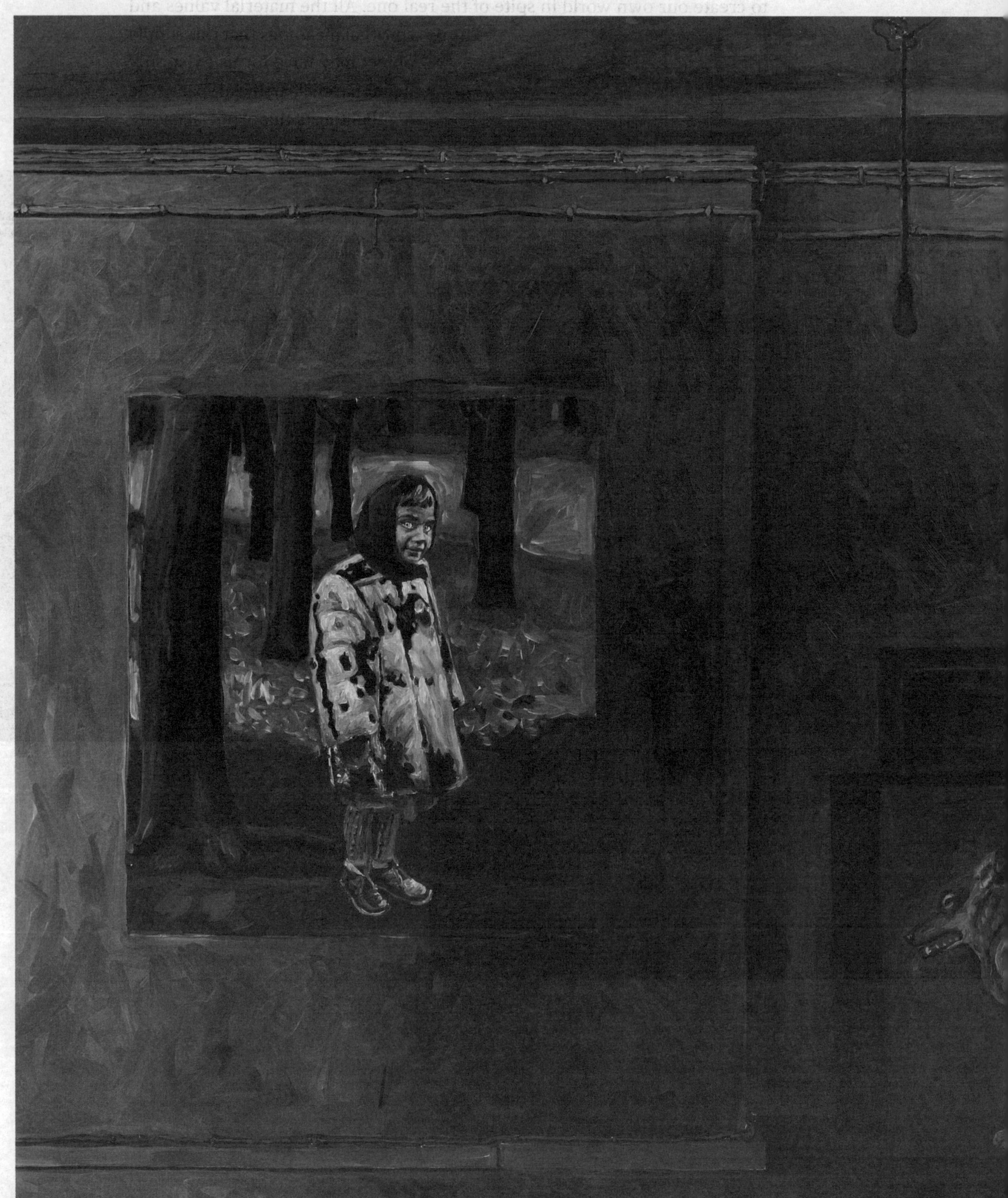

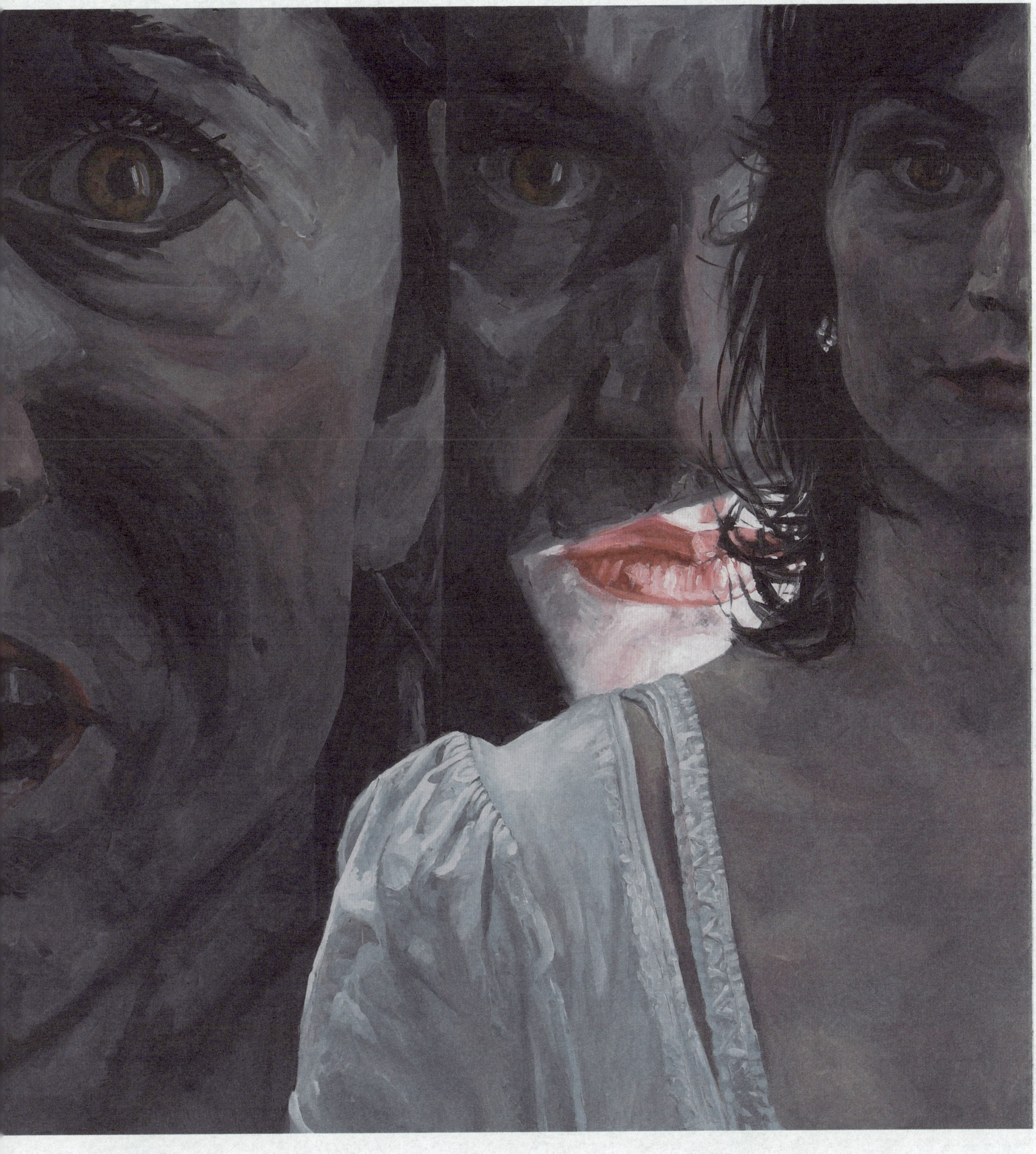

OBSERVATION

I have made drawings of Alex, Christian, Constanze, Consuelo, Giacomo, Giuliano, Ernestine, Ero, Fabienne, Irma, Jeremy, Jörg, Karin, Karsten, Katja, Lara, Manuela, Michele, Miriam, Sabine, Stefano, Thorsten and will make some more. Those have sat model form me and the others will also do so.

Before them I made drawings of Marijana and Matea, Mia and Dolina, Fijolić and Švabo, Ivana and Marko, Miranda and Stanko, Barbara and Lucija, Deša, Ivana, Jelena and Zdravka, Igor and that other Igor, Sanja and Nera. Nera is a dog, but I also drew the Beech-tree and the Brook glistening in the sun,

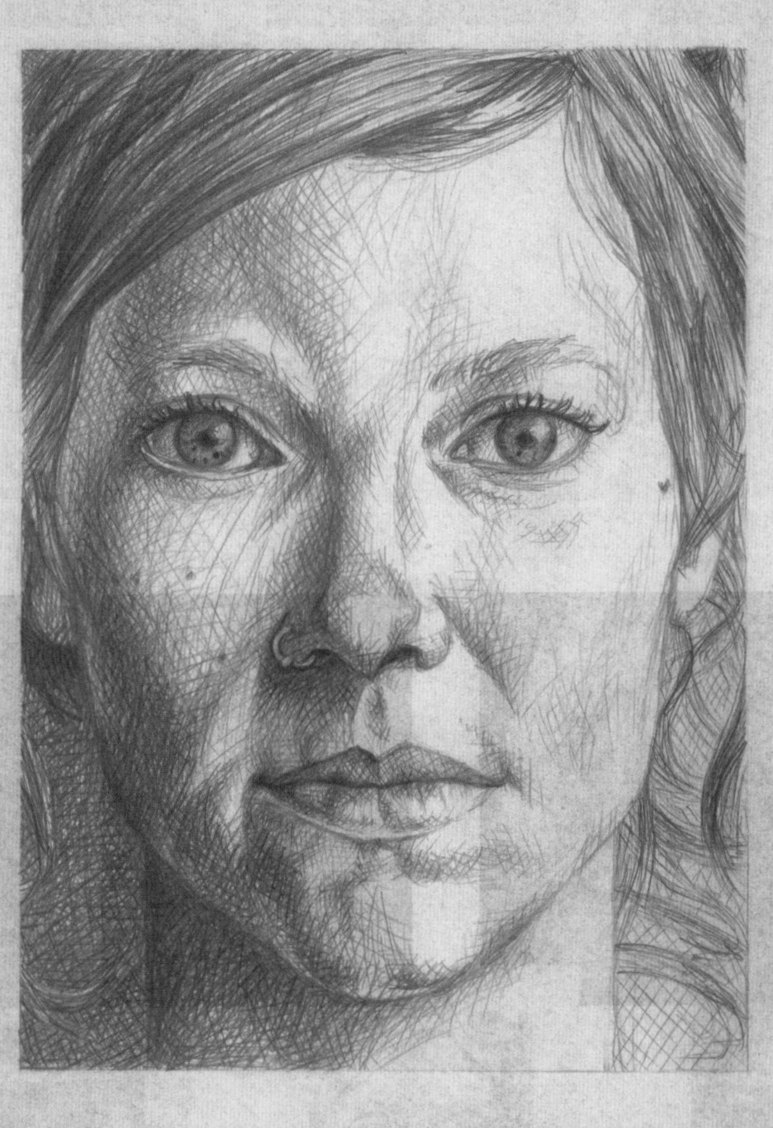

and the Young Tree and the Old Chestnut and the Red Rocks, which were also my models. But this was somehow different, I made these drawings because they served me as models for paintings (like the photos after which I painted some people and objects). What do I actually want to achieve when I strive to faithfully reproduce a face I see before me? I really cannot give a reasonable answer to this question. Perhaps it is important to me to be with these people, to sit across them for hours day in day out, and feel that slight uneasiness, that brief excitement when our gazes meet.

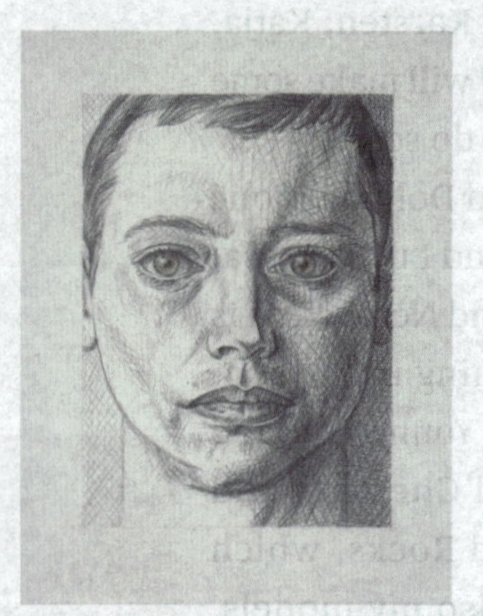 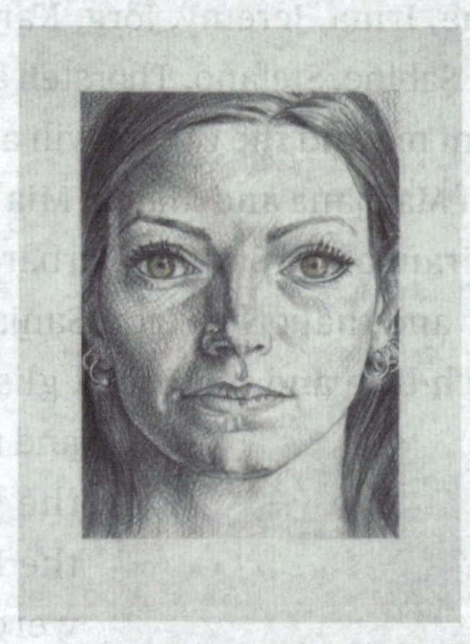 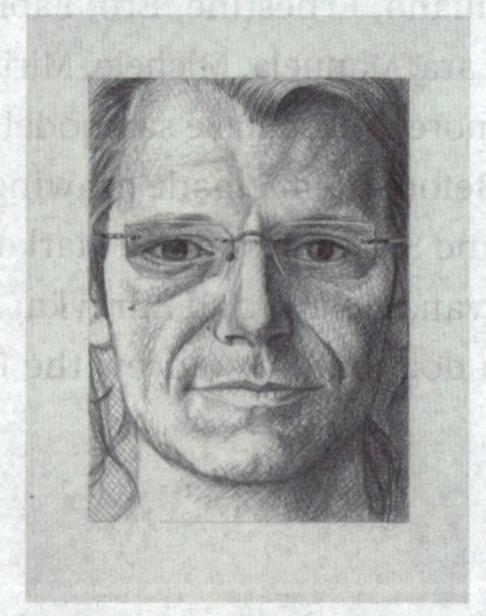 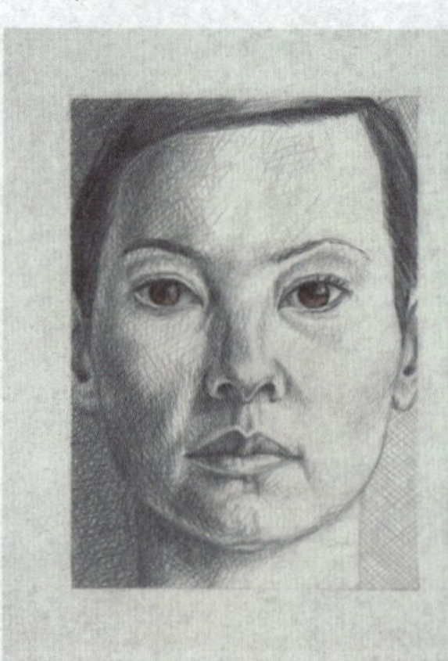

123

124

125

126

131

132

133

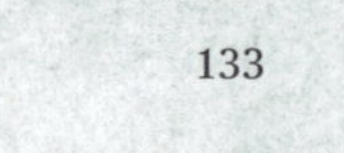

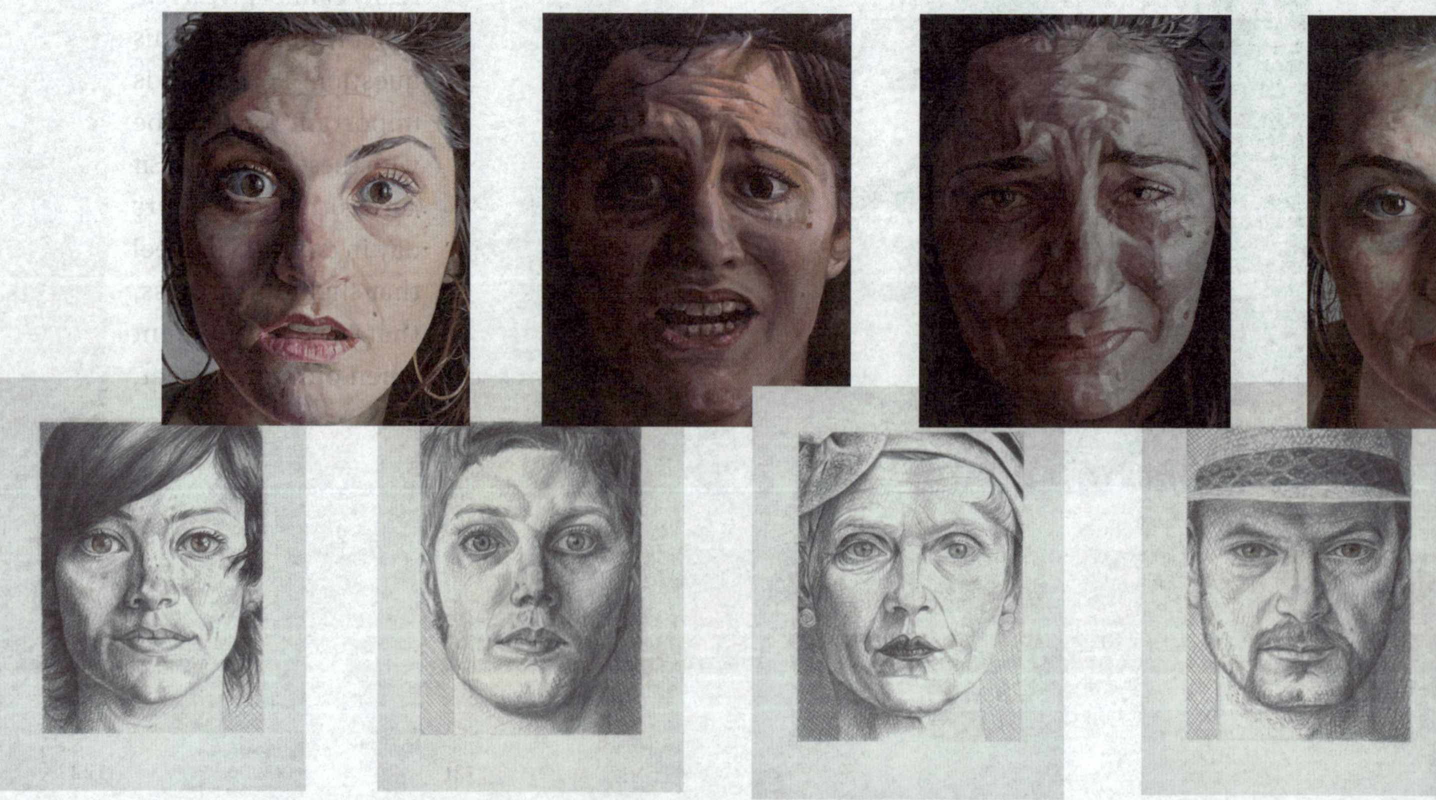

137

138

139

140

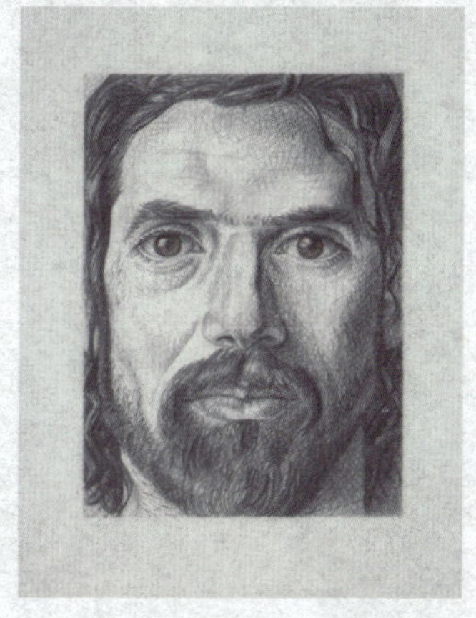

127

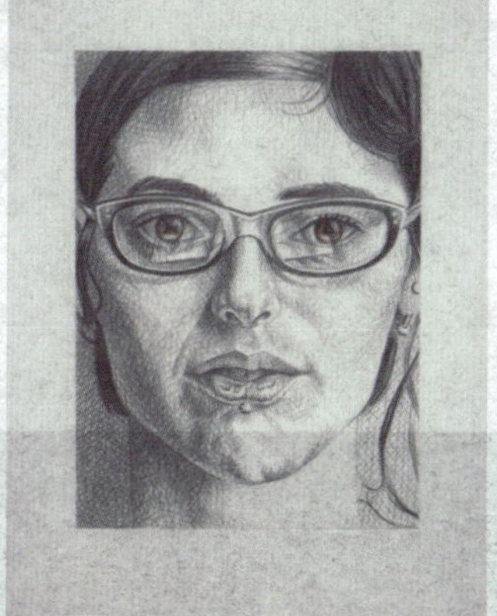

128

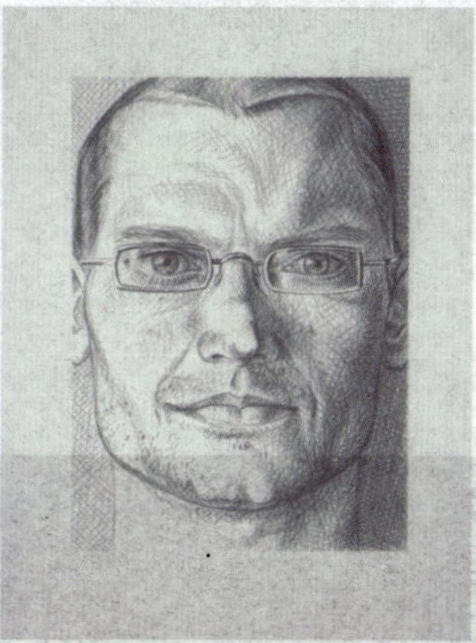

129

134 135 136 25

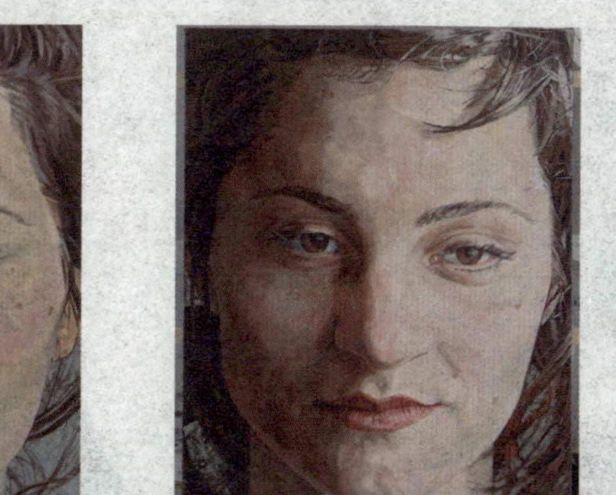

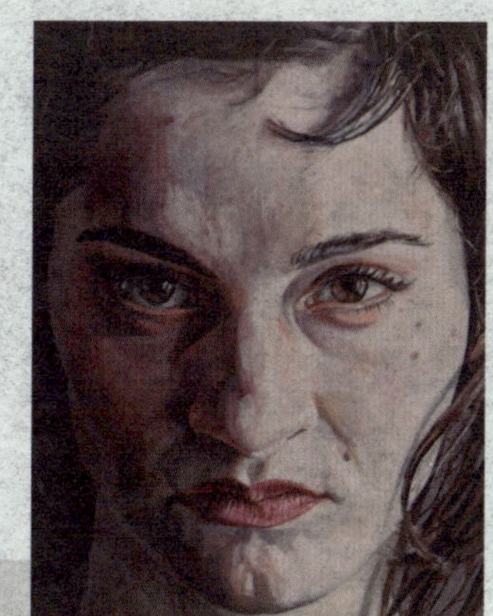

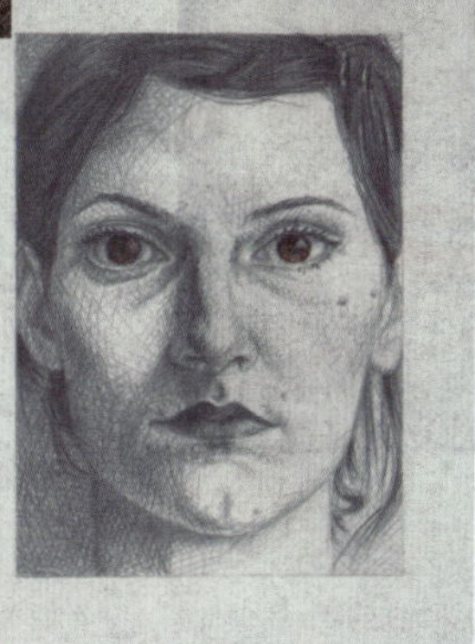

141

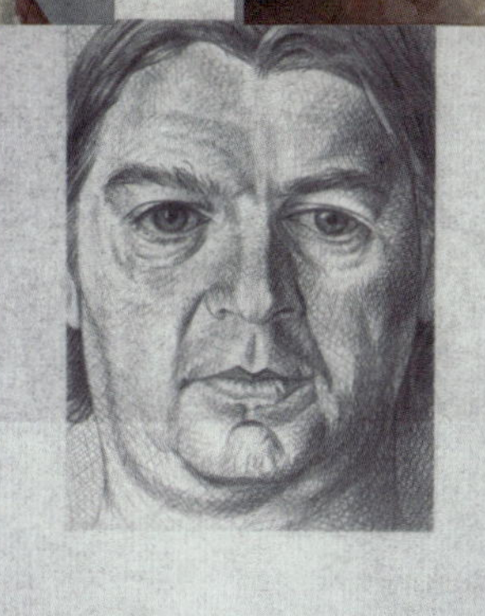

142

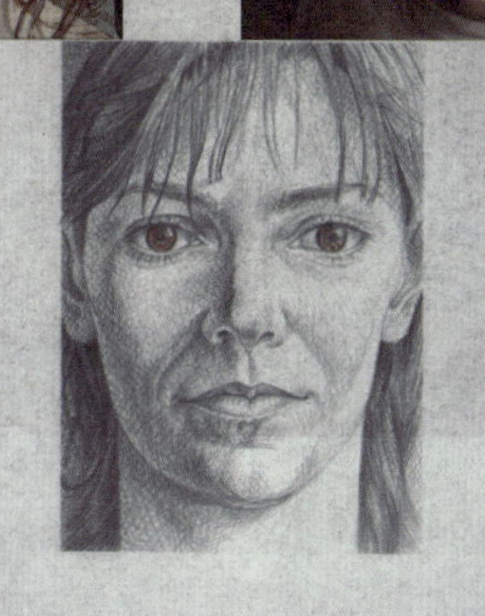

143

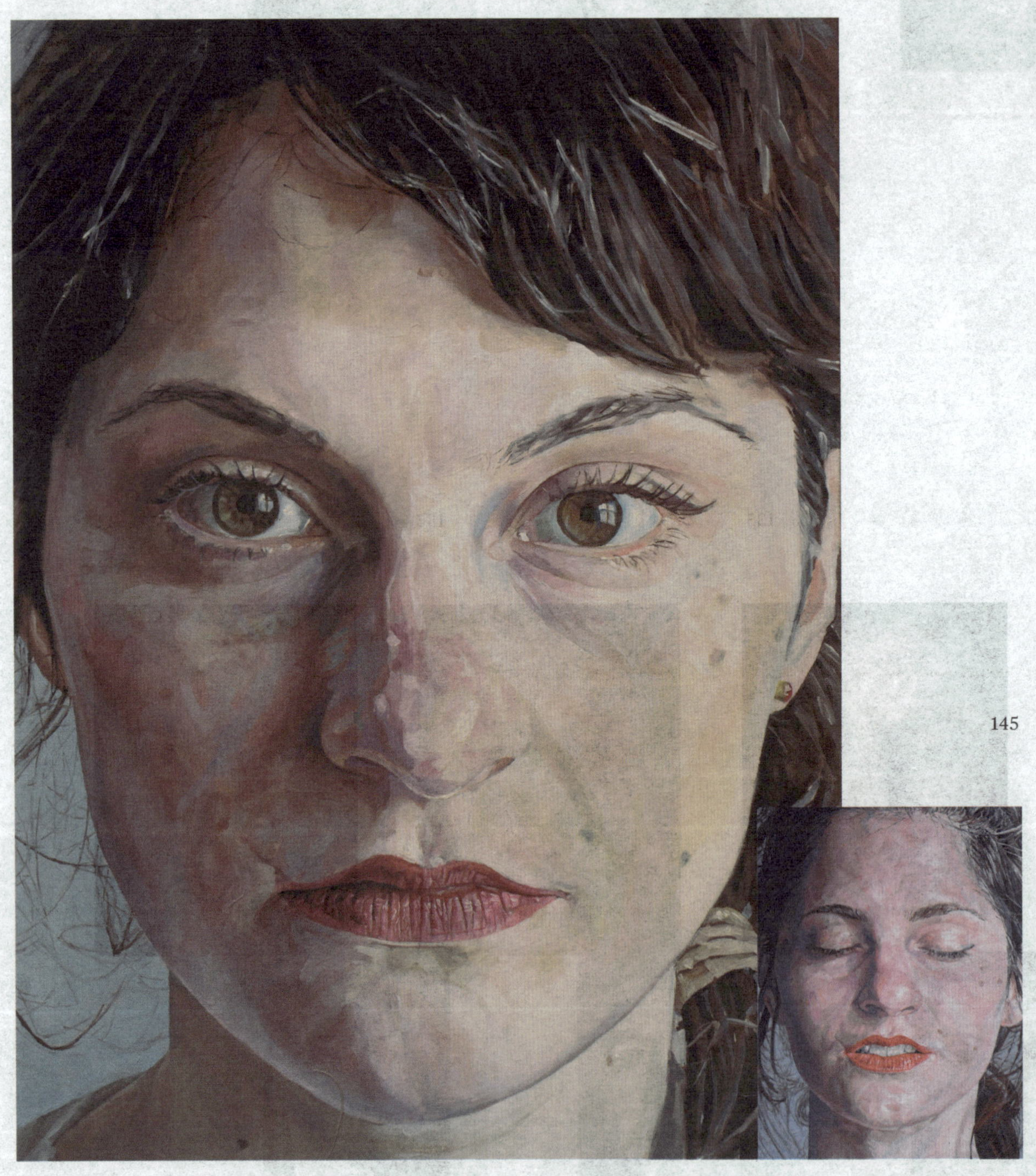

145

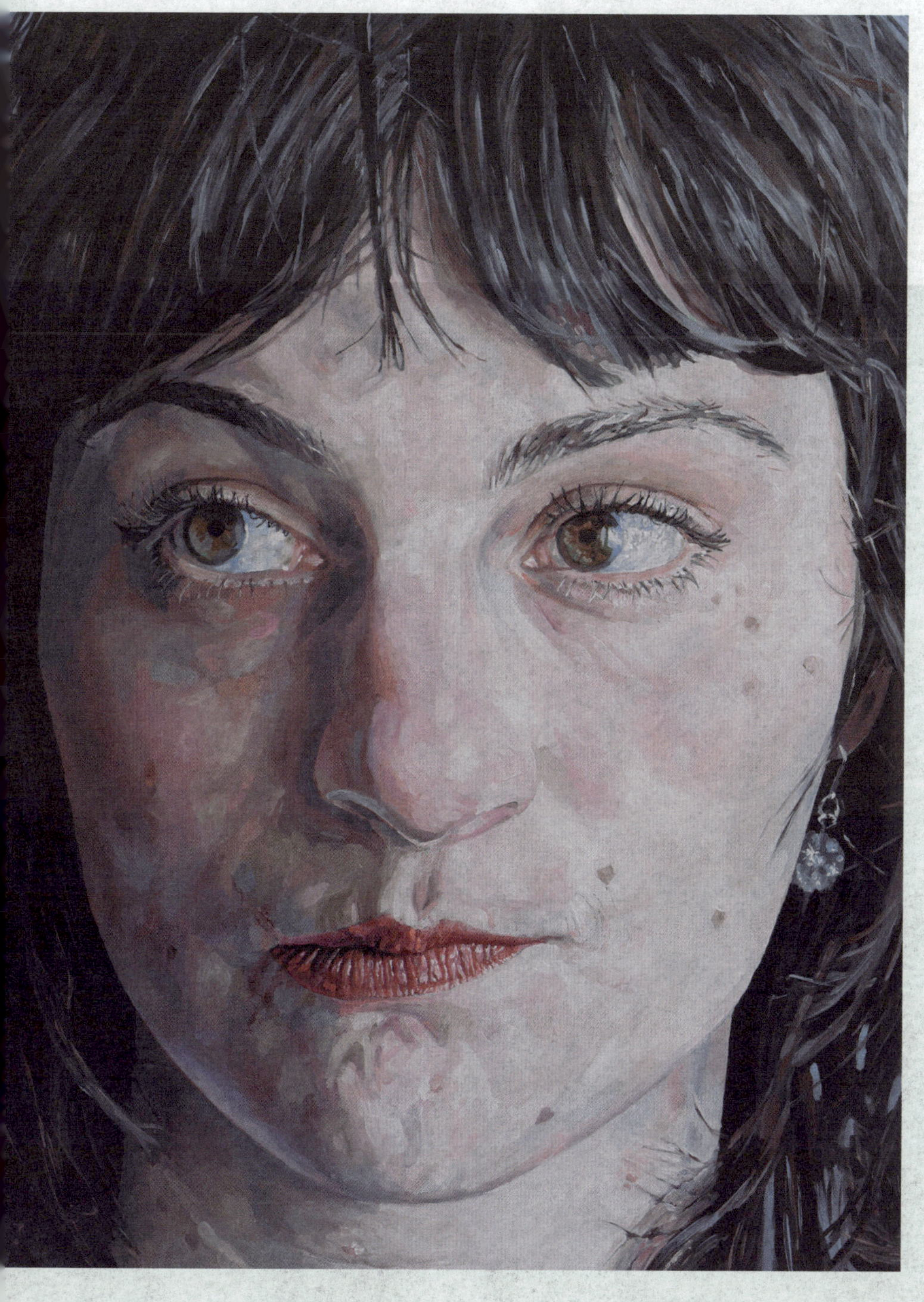

# AS IF



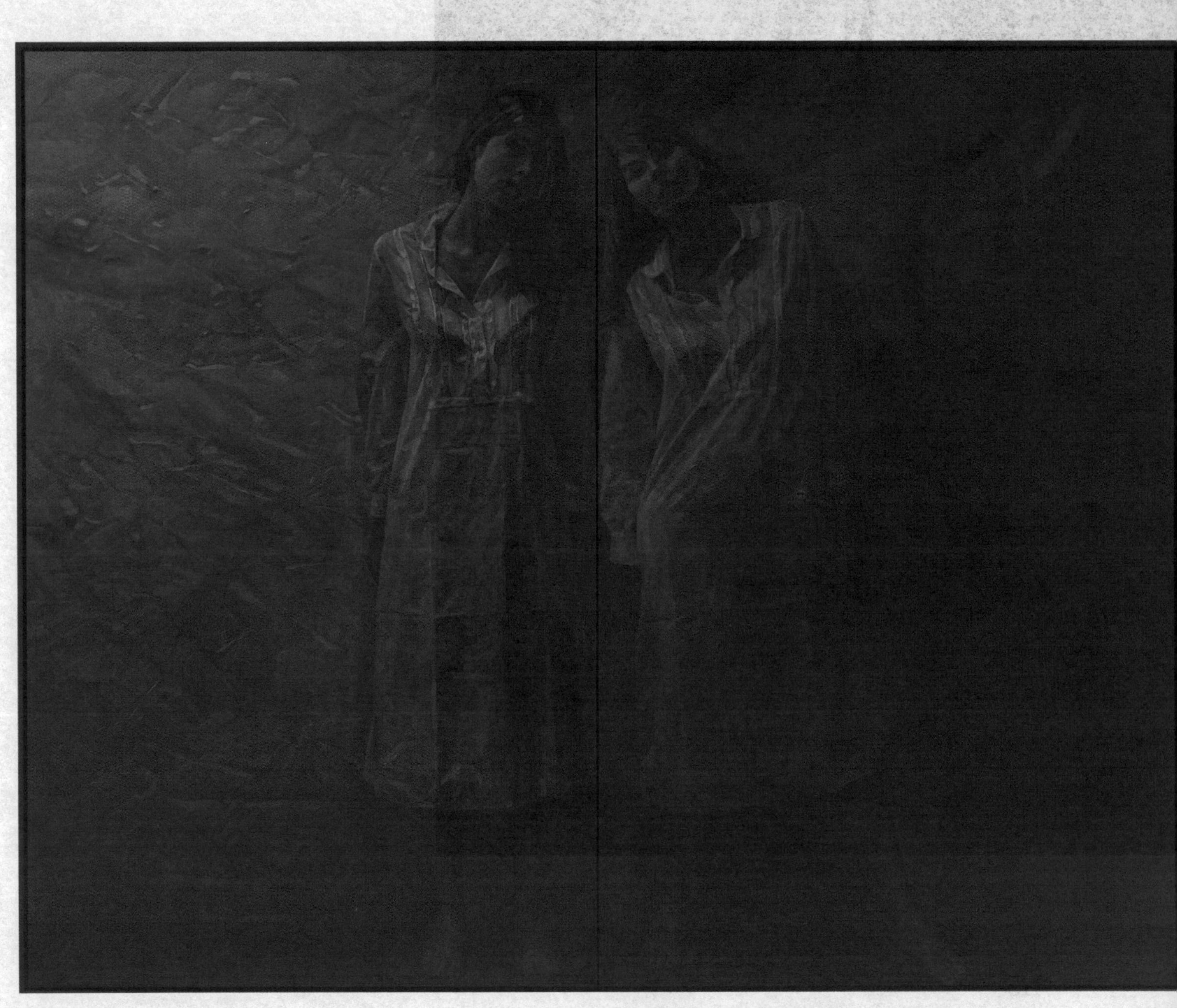

I thought I had grasped the characteristics of my occupation. Illusion and Scene seemed to me more or less fitting names for what I do when I paint. I must now confess - quite willingly, because one is naturally happy when he discovers something new - that I have reached the insight that Concept and Procedure are the principal characteristics of painting. However, I do feel certain uneasiness because of the fact that time flies. The other day I had to go to the optician because I can no longer clearly see what I'm drawing and have long since given up reading; I have had porcelain teeth for some time now, and I'm slowly beginning to detect a foul odor about myself. But even without glasses, I can see that my paintings are getting better. I don't know if this is because I've prioritized Concept and Process over Illusion and Scene, or maybe even because of their interplay. However this is, if I'm lucky enough to stay strong and in good health for a few more years, I should paint some really good pictures.

Maybe I should have put it this way after all:

Once upon a time there was a white nightgown at Humana. Humana is a second-hand store at Frankfurter Tor. I sent Ernestine there with 20 euros to buy a white garment that she would wear while I project a star map onto her. I wanted it to look like it was night, but at the same time I wanted it to be visible that it was just a projection of the starry sky onto a model. I like to move in that space between the painted image and the inner one evoked by it. Perhaps this is the space Luc Tuymans was thinking of when he said he saw "this small space between the image and its interpretation as the only possibility." Although this is nothing new. In Caravaggio's *Entombment,* for example, you can clearly see that the whole scene is just a pose, an illusion meant to awaken in us the real image of that tragic moment. To make a long story short, Ernestine bought exactly that nightgown at Humana for 5 euros.

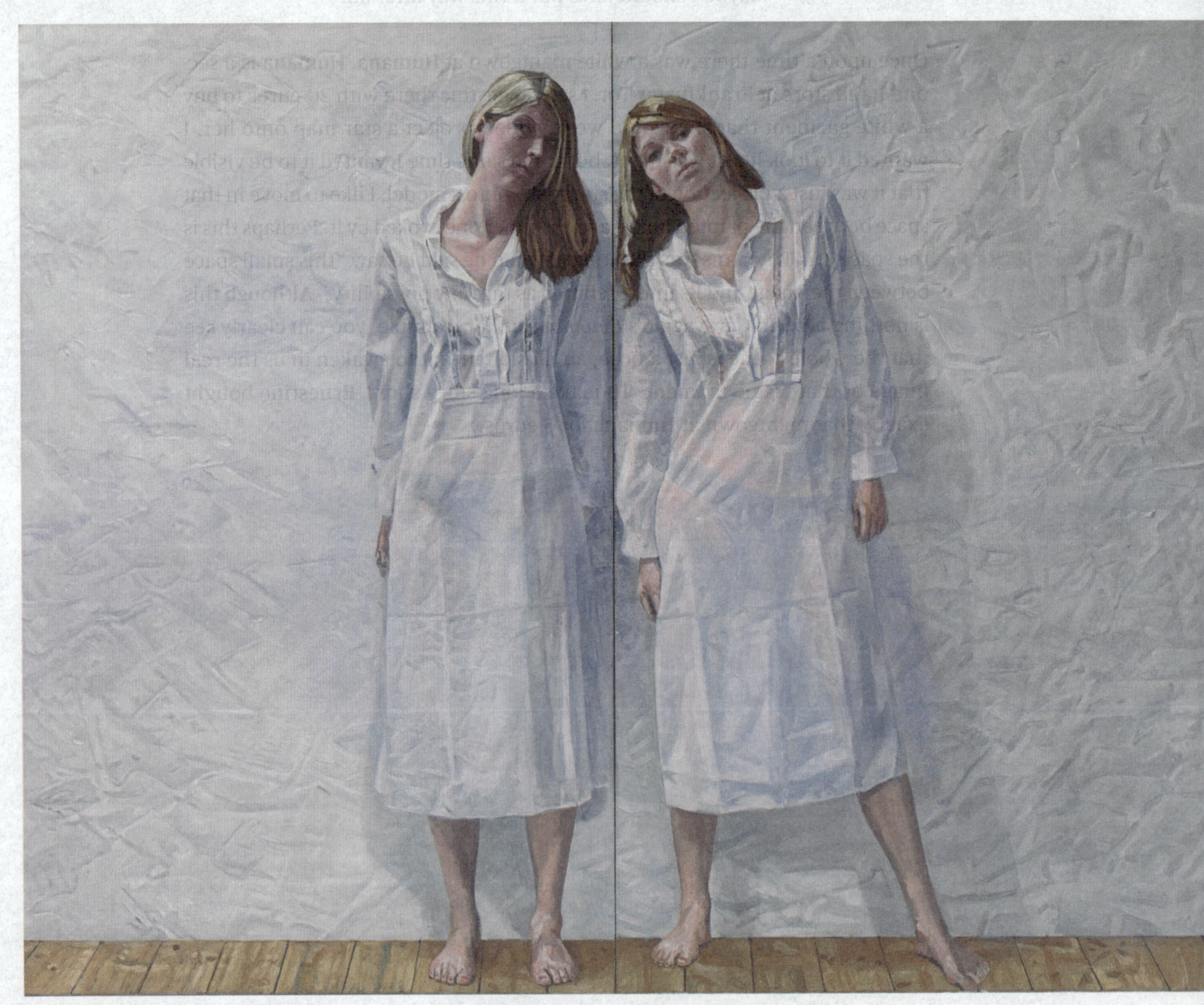

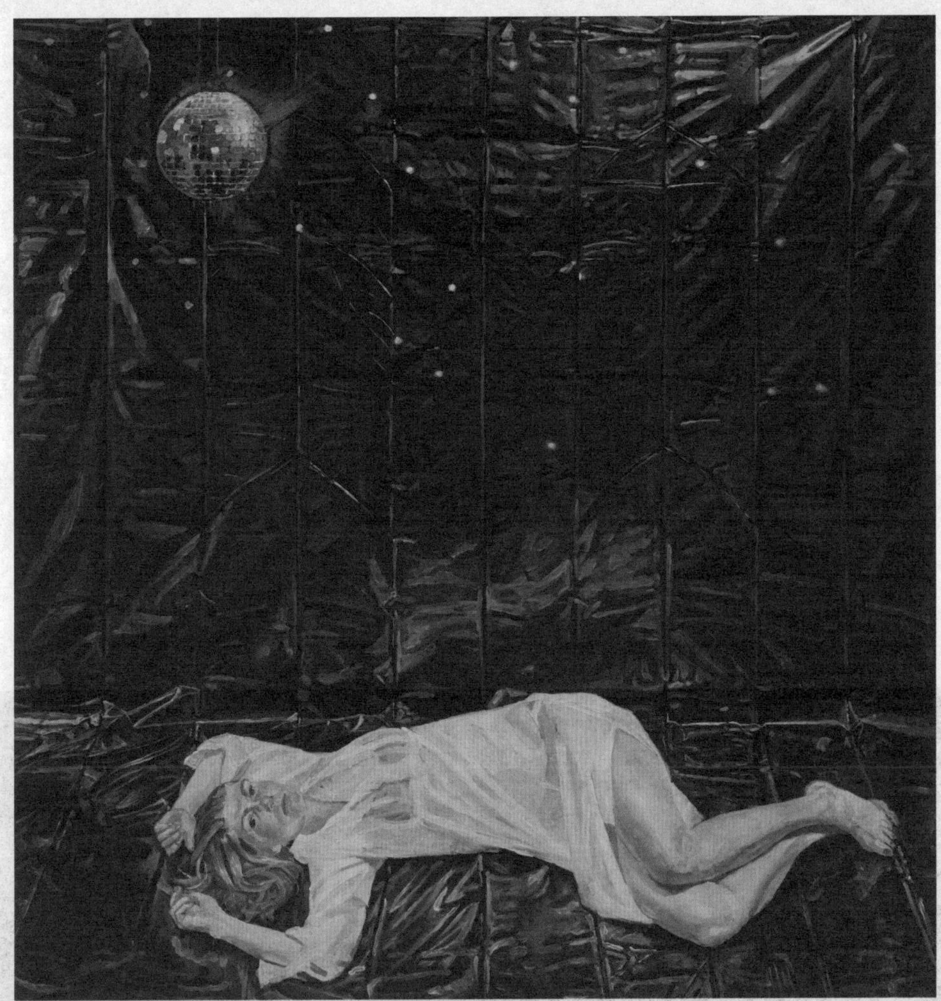



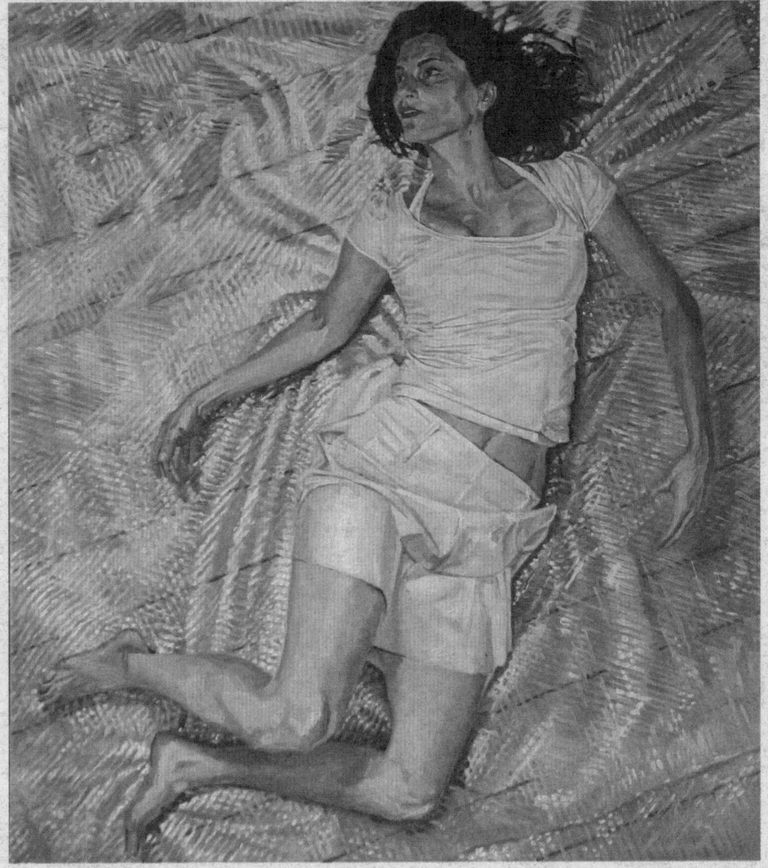

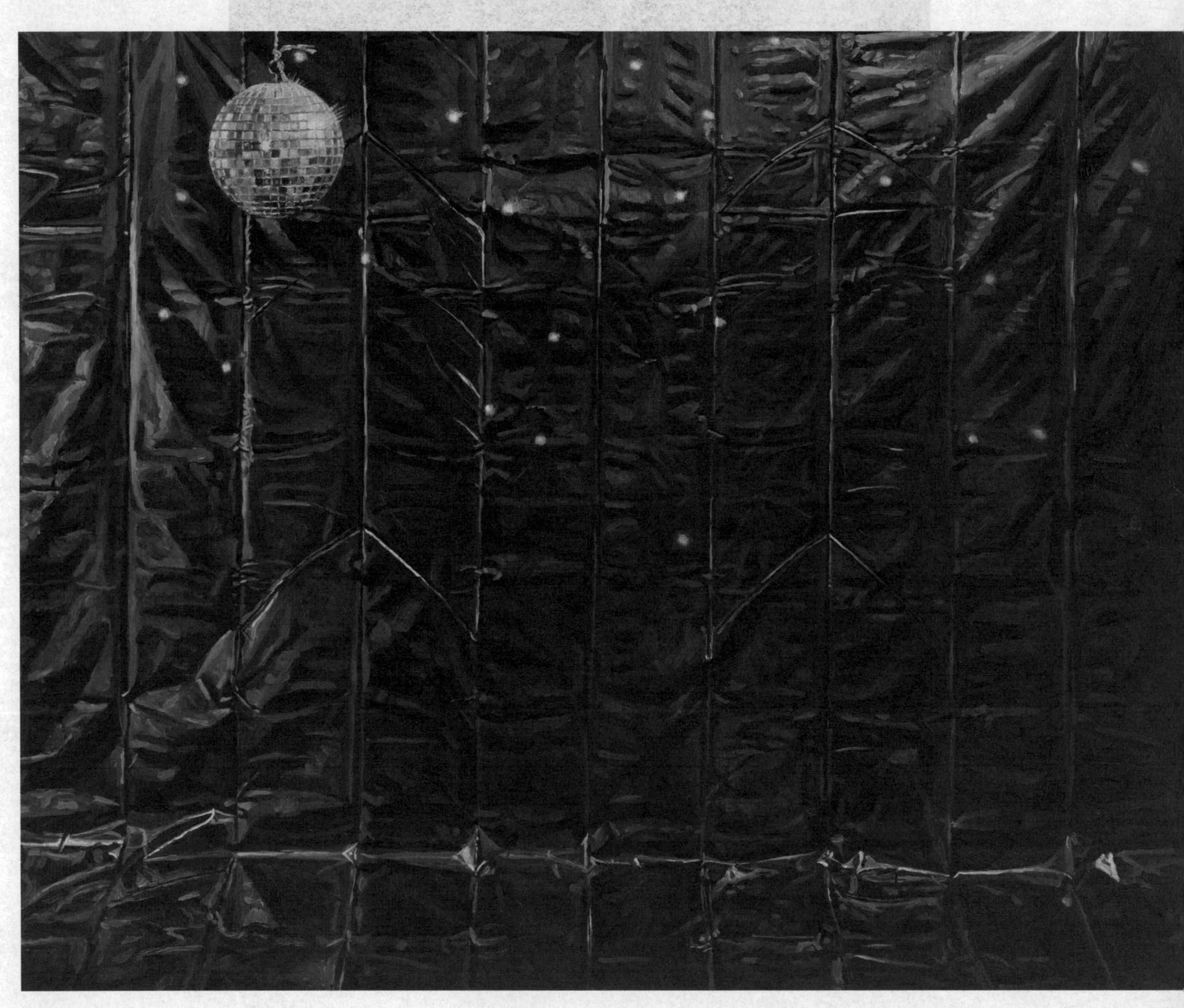

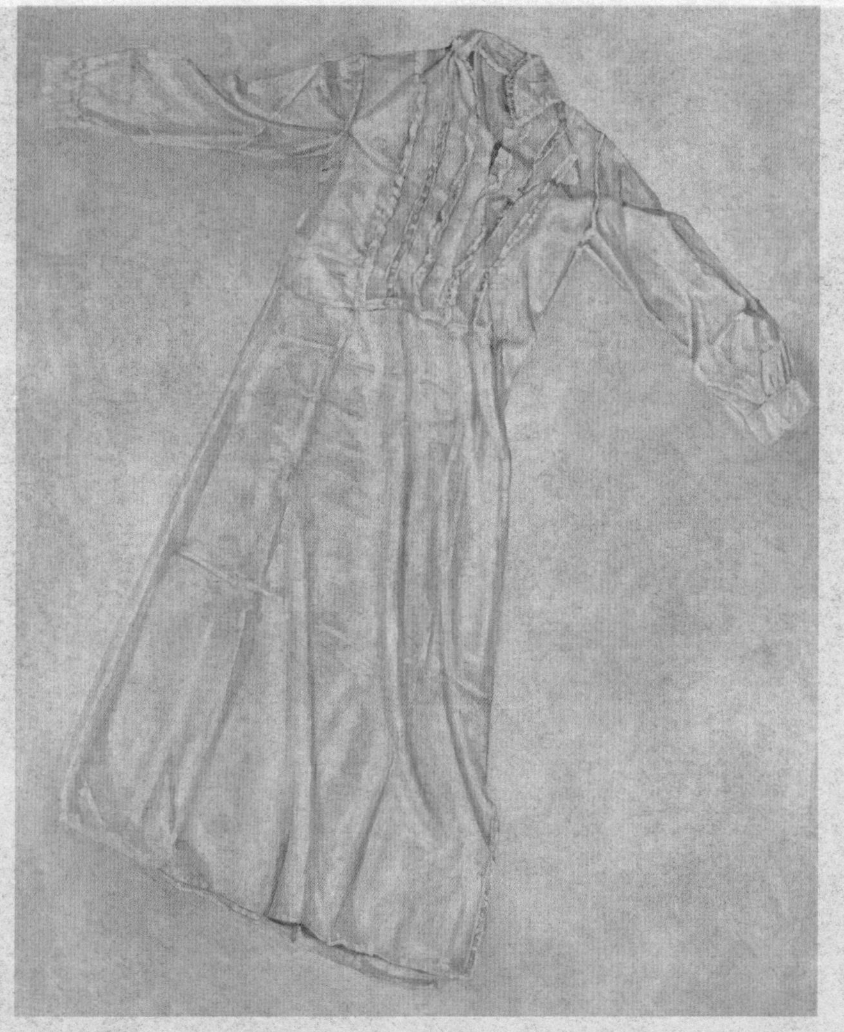

149

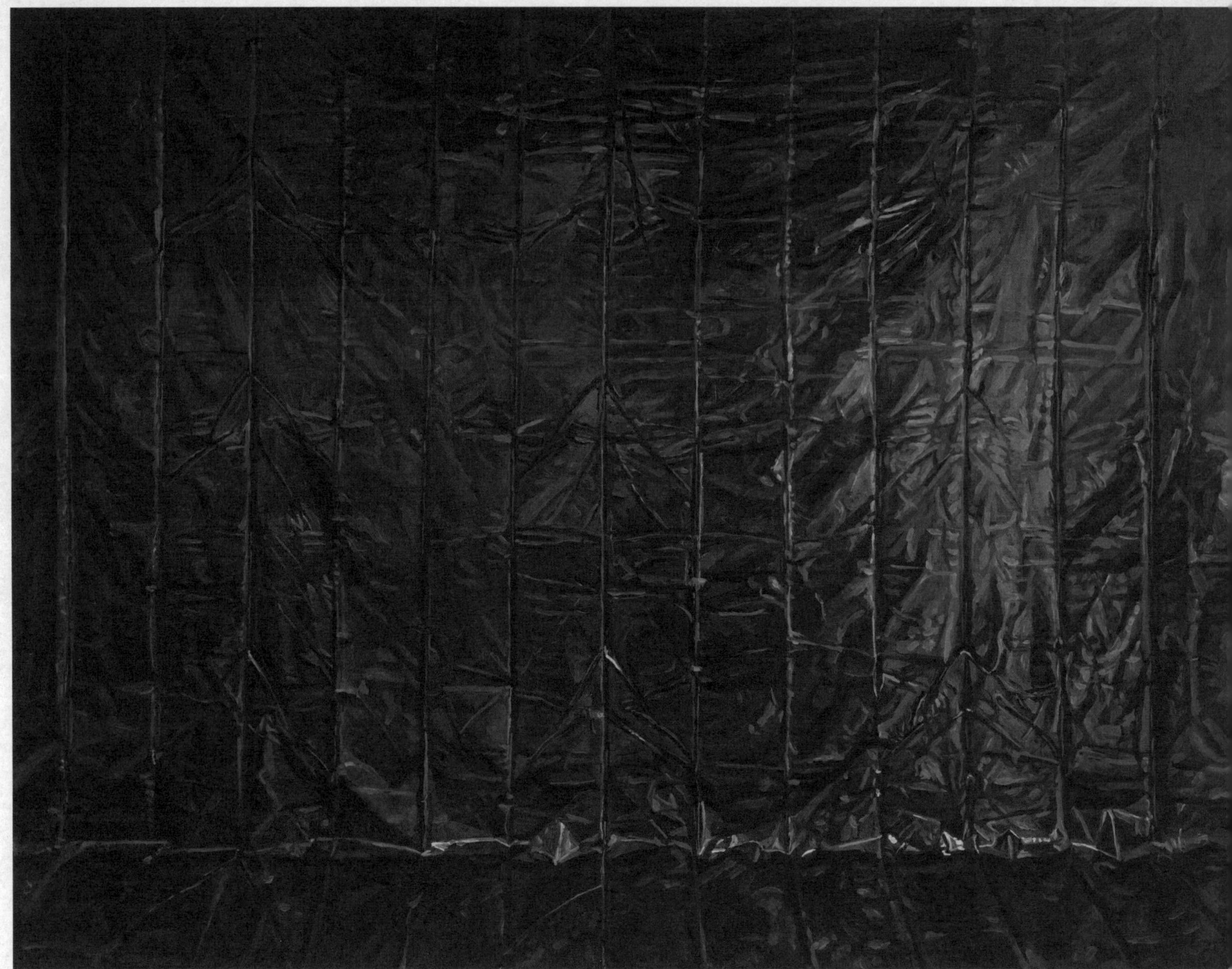



Place

She said she felt the potential that was in me and could see exactly what my future paintings would look like. To reinforce this, she said that in the painting *Place* I should get rid of "that stupid socket" and reduce the floor area to only 7 cm. I took her advice and painted the picture *White Square*. Hmm, not bad, I thought, it looked serious, so much in the style of the patent artists of the last century. Maybe I could also secure a place in art history this way; on the canvas a large wall surface, neatly executed, with 7 to 10 cm of floor underneath. But damn, I was missing my "stupid socket" and all the pleasure of painting this little diversion from the real world.

Actually, it was a typical women's "bait and switch" game: either you are with me, and then you're great, or you are not, in which case you are a piece of shit. I opted for the latter and just ran away.

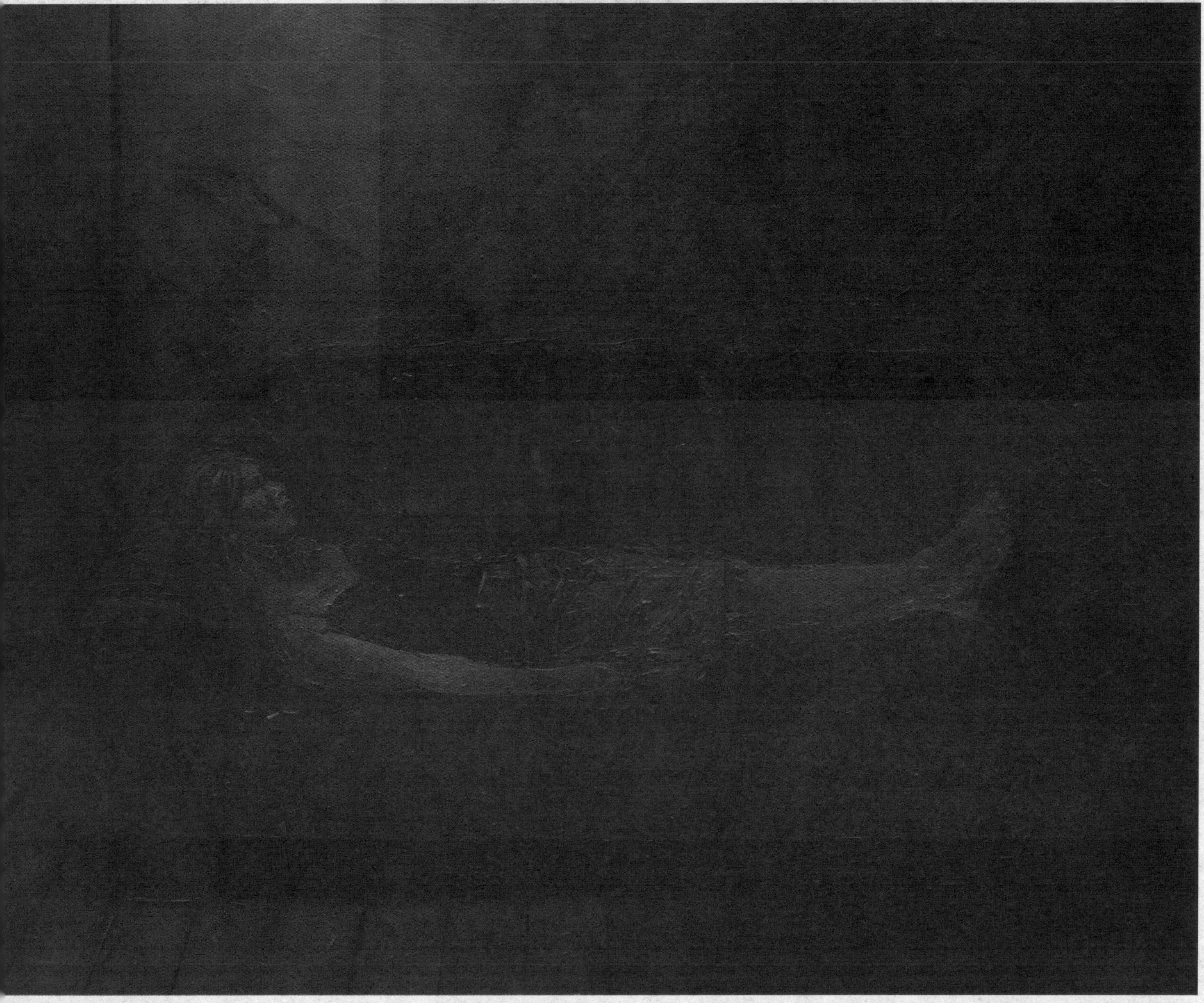

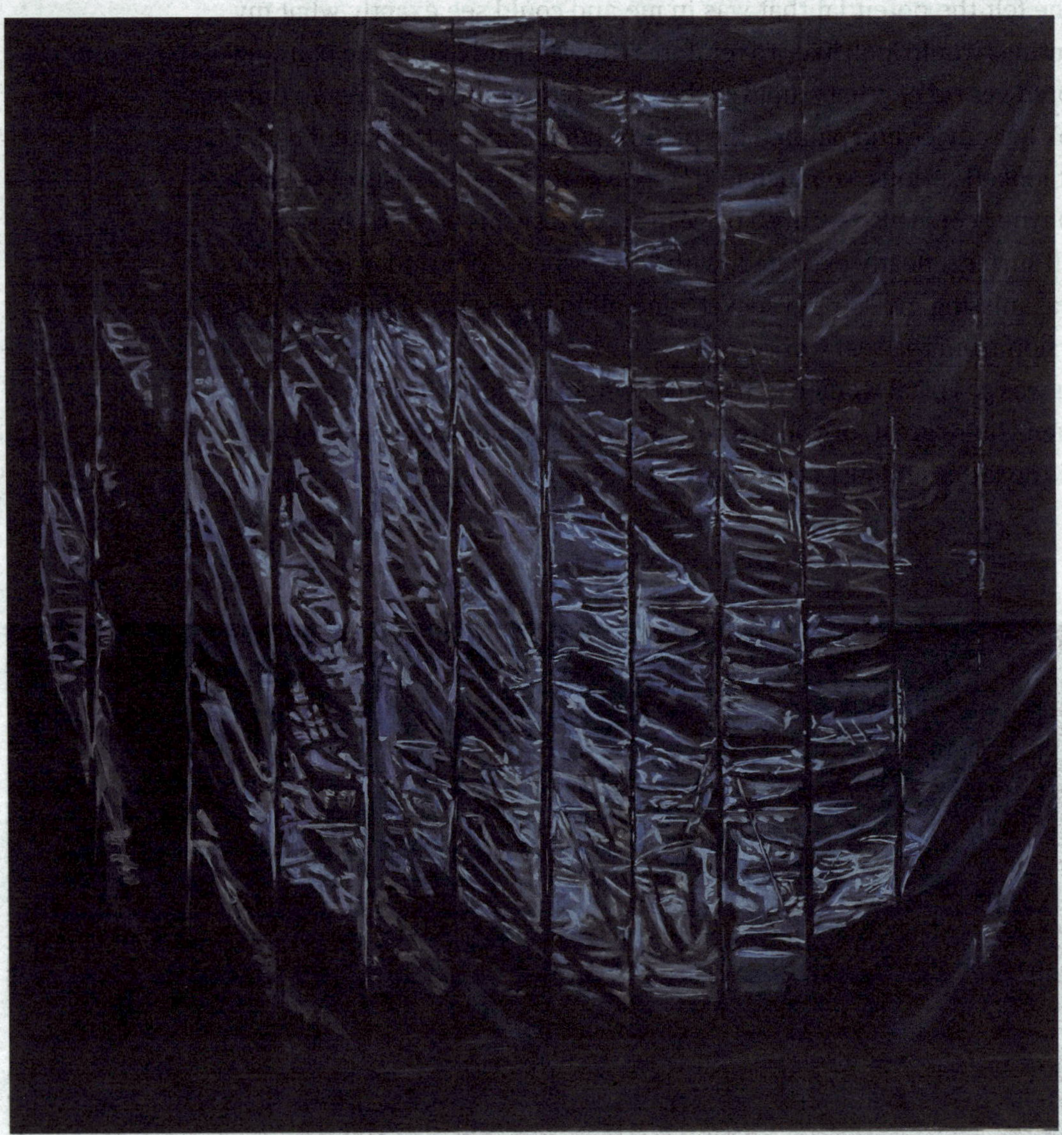

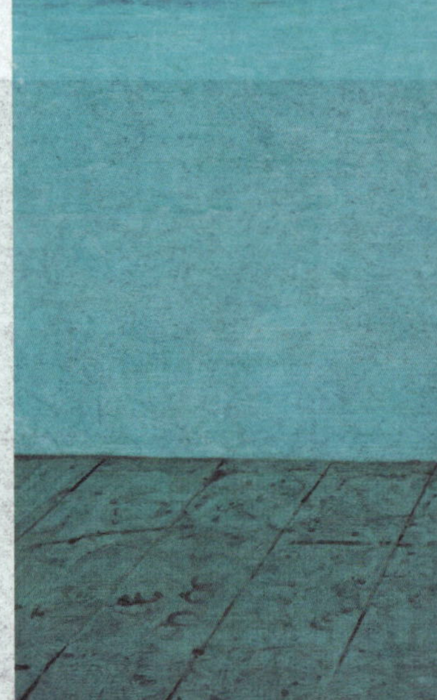

152

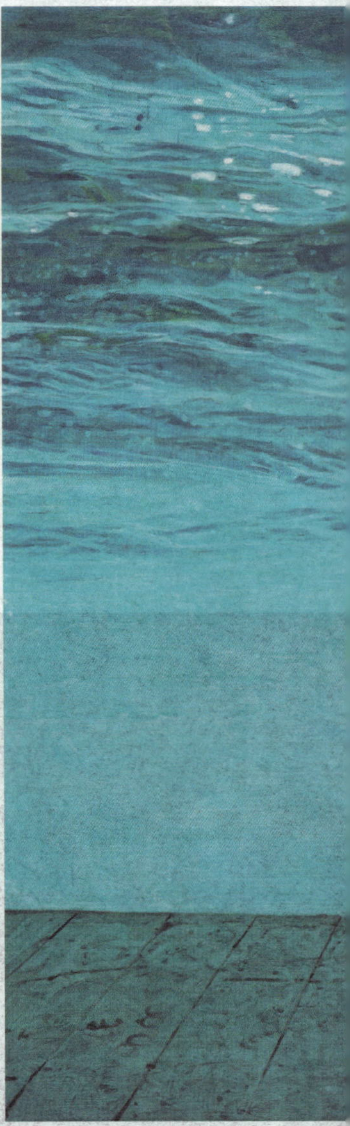

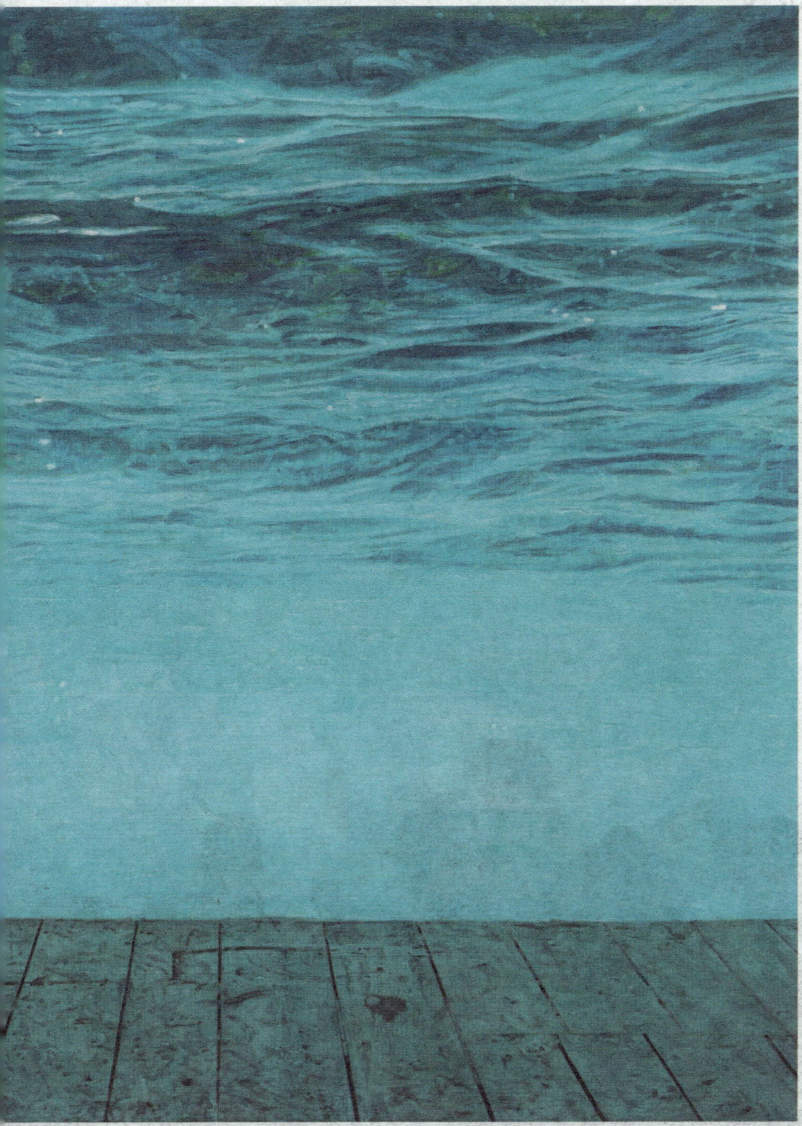

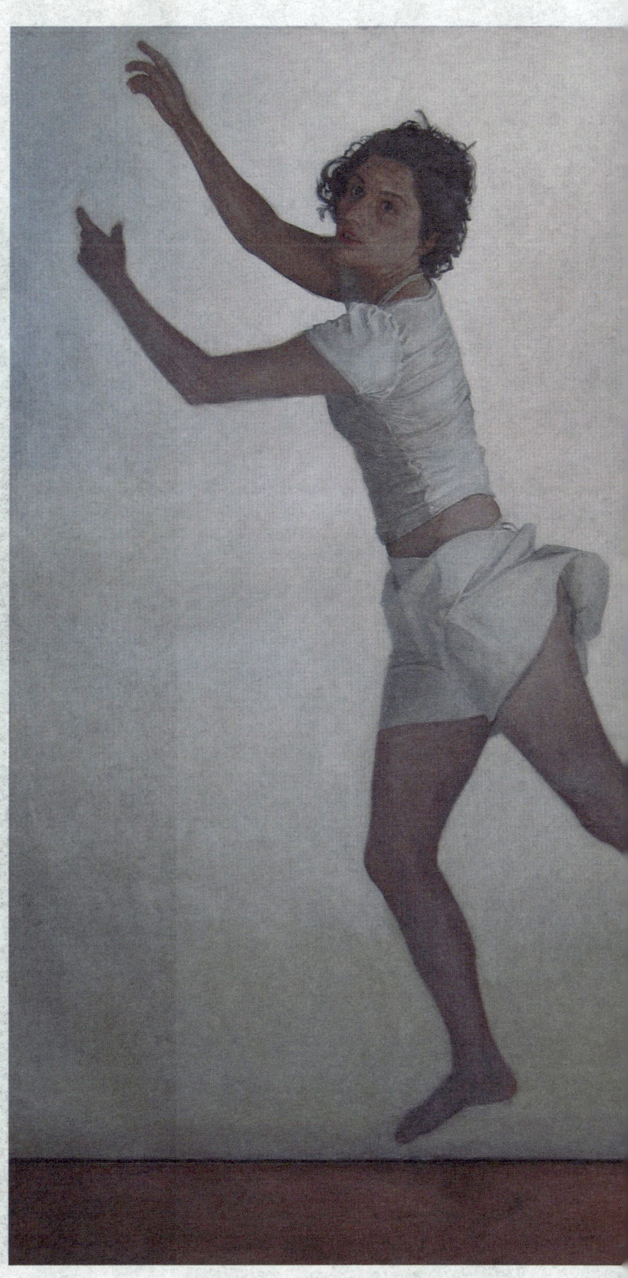

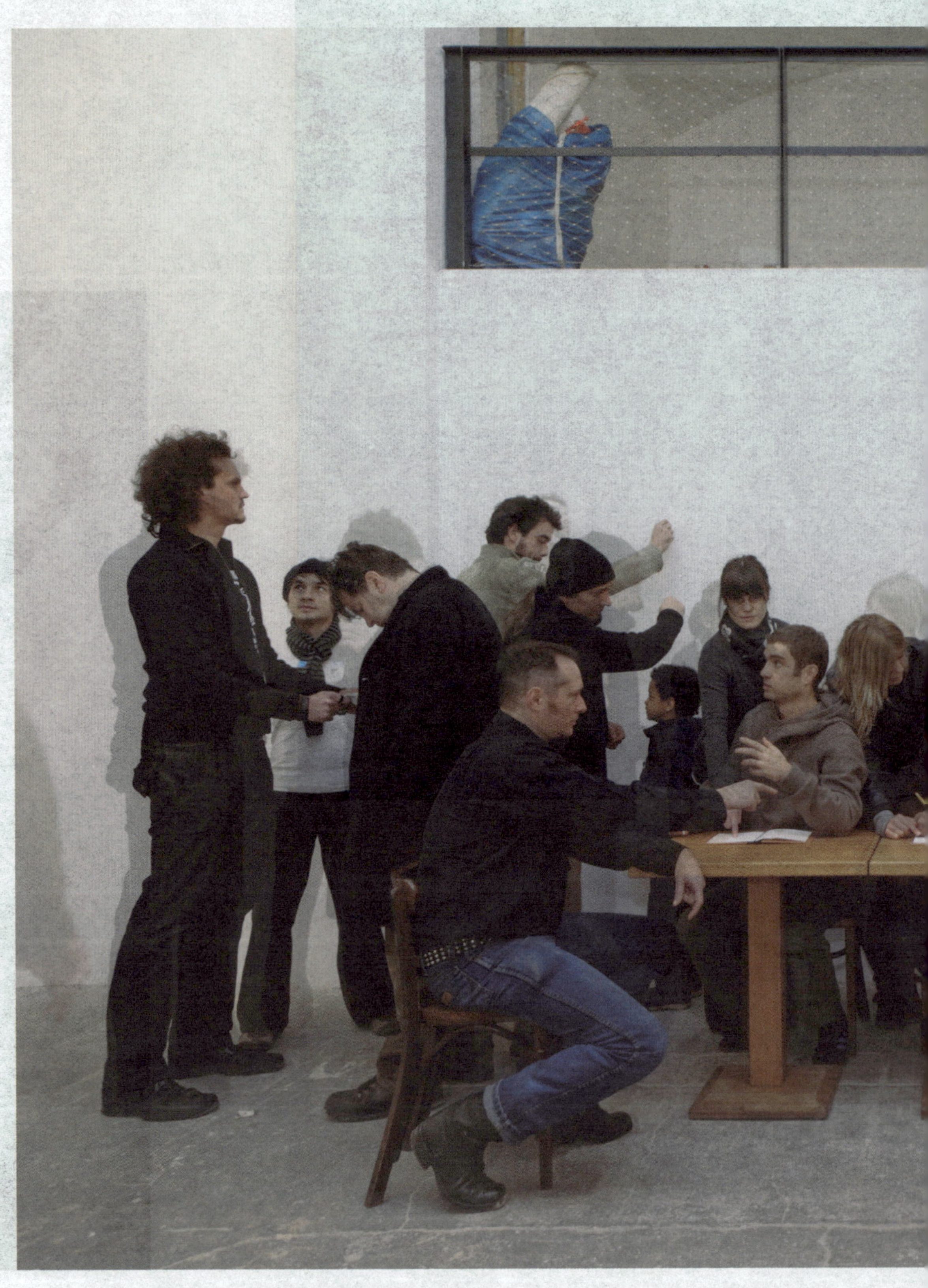

STAGINGS

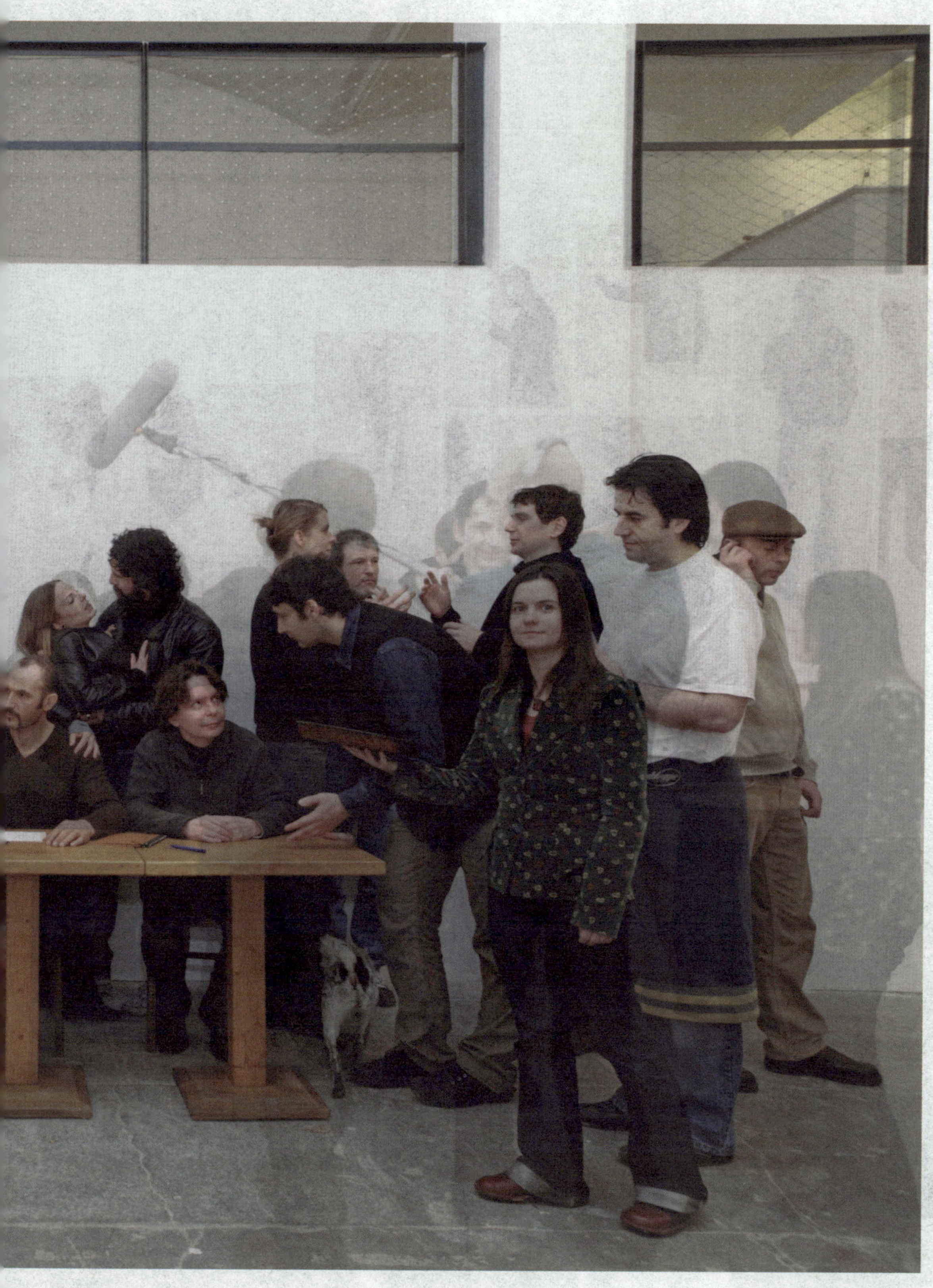

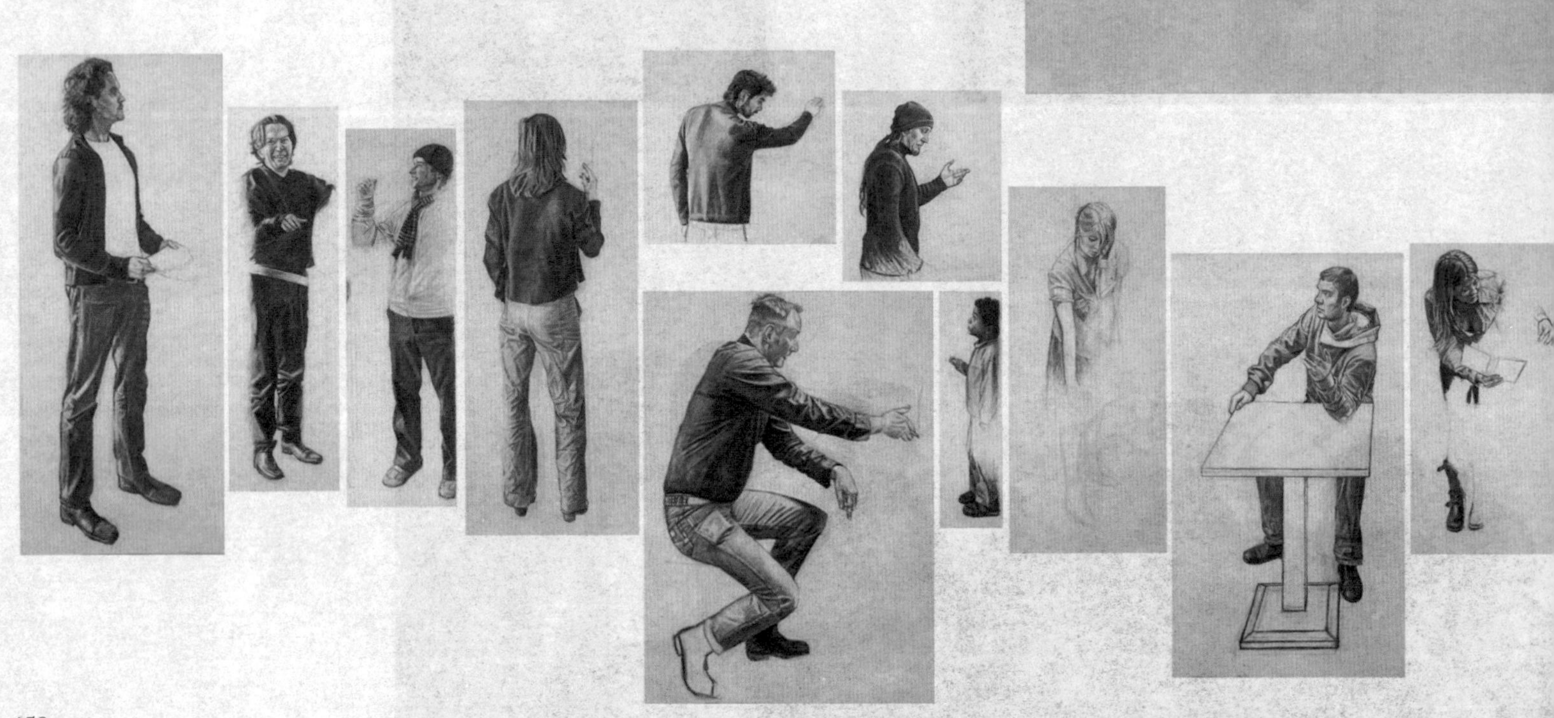

158

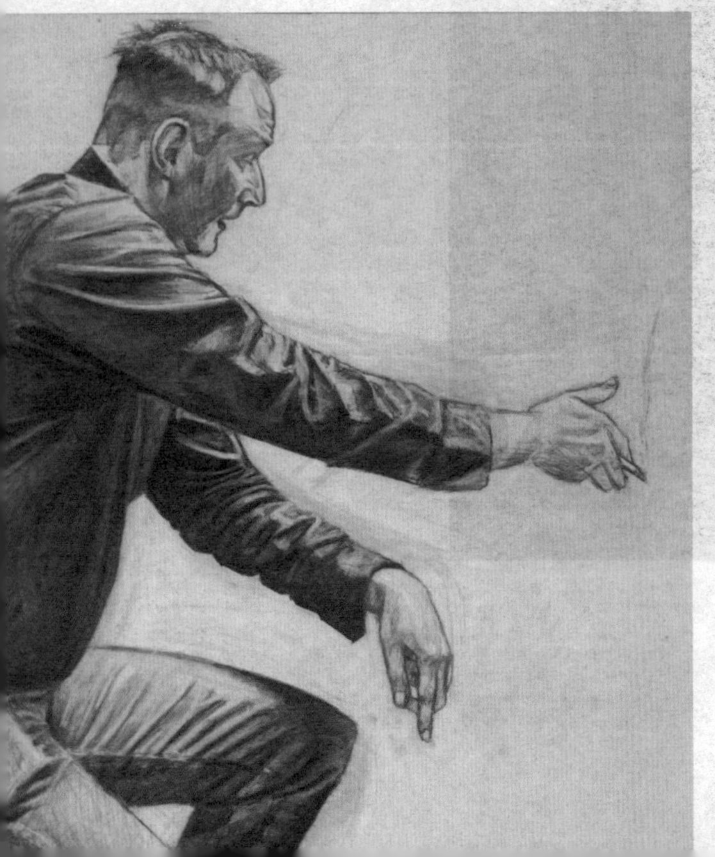



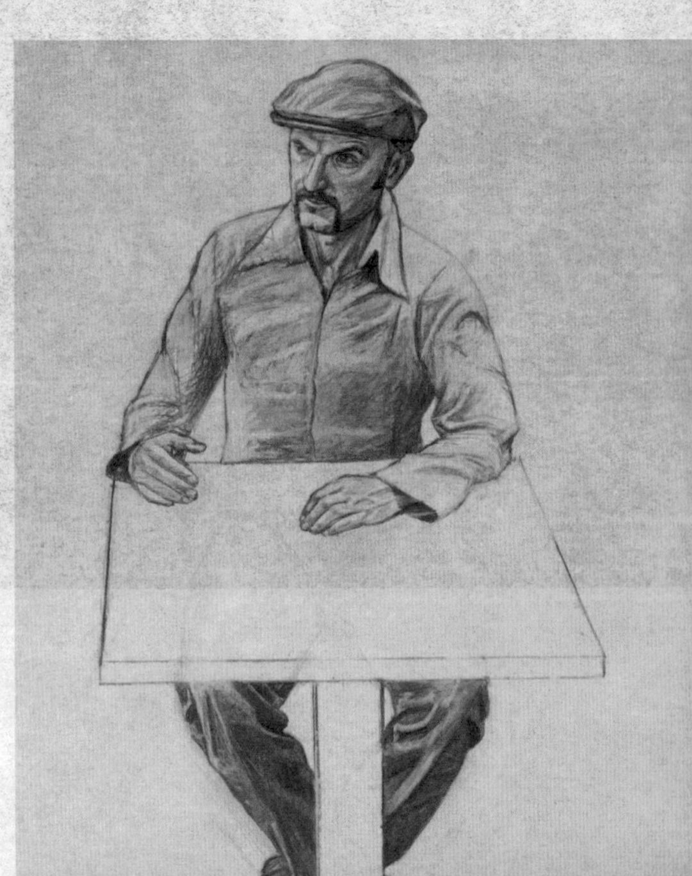

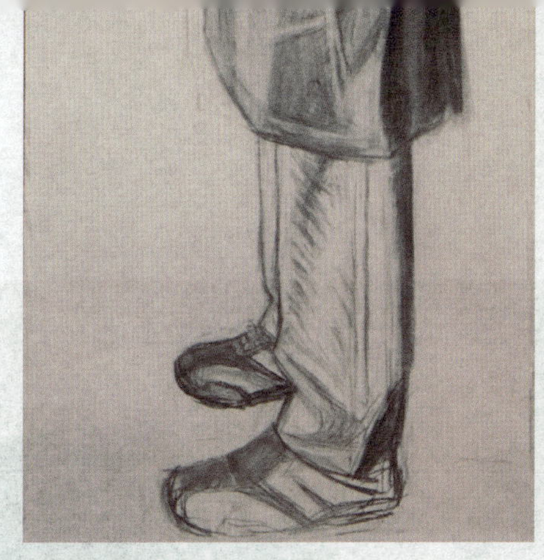
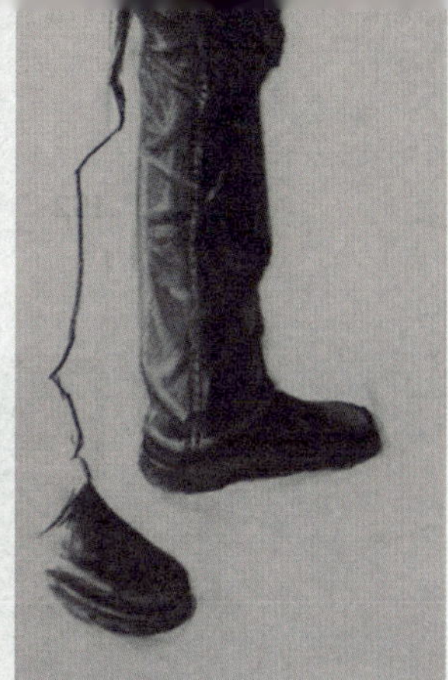

156

157

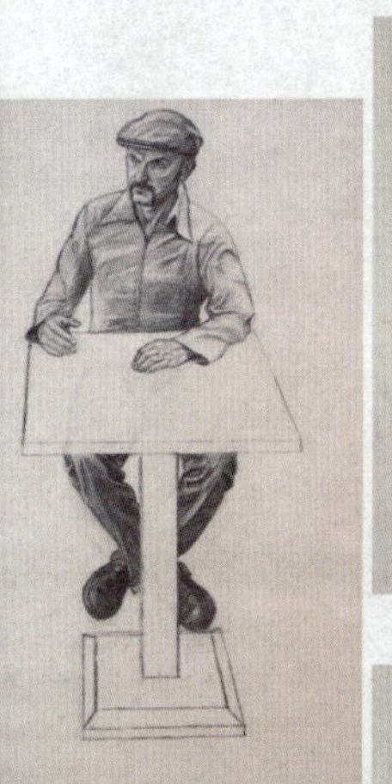
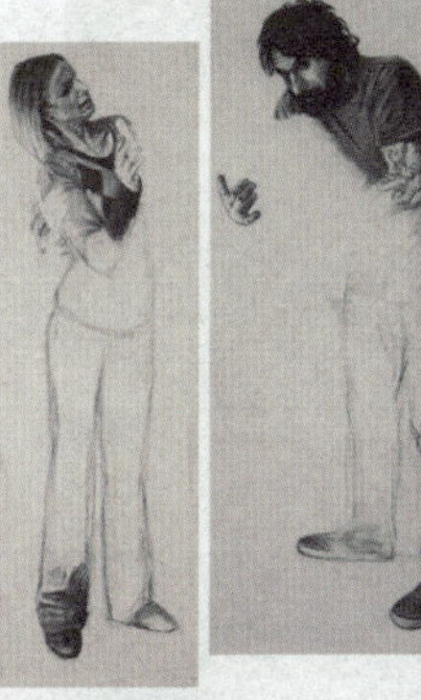
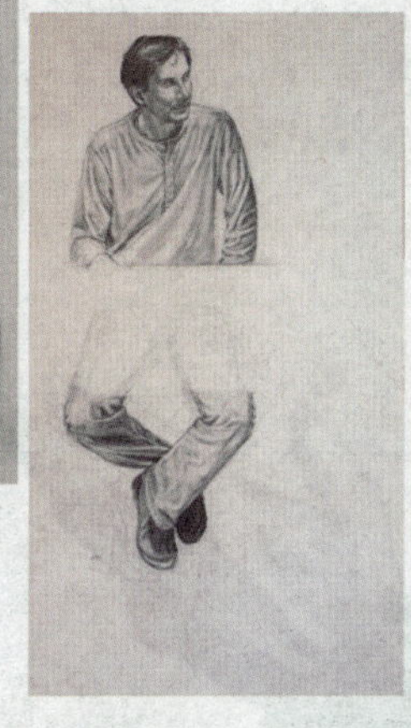
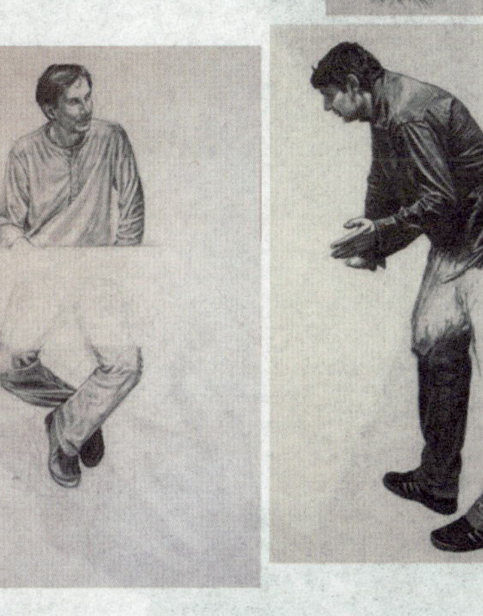
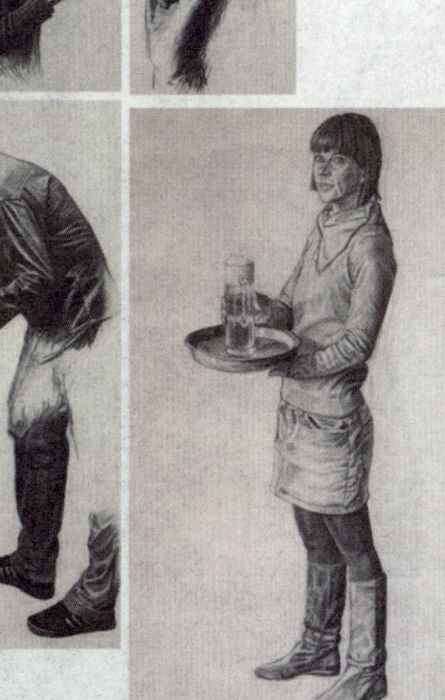
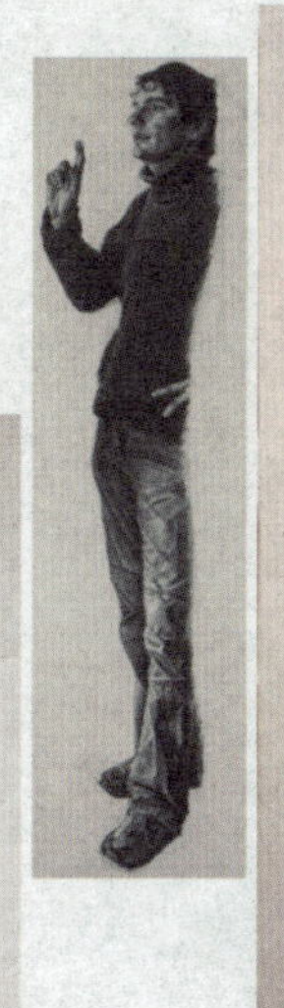
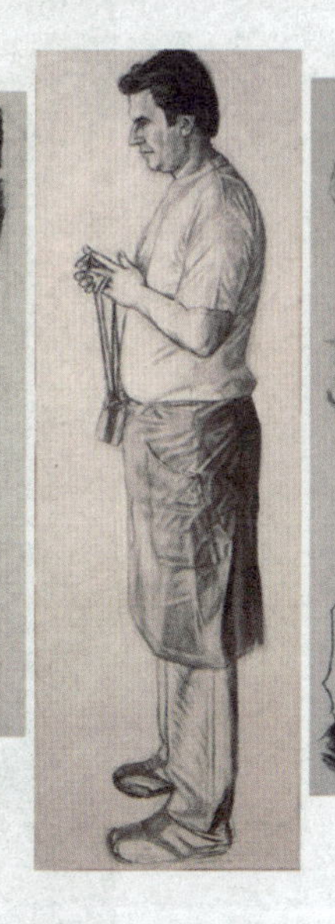
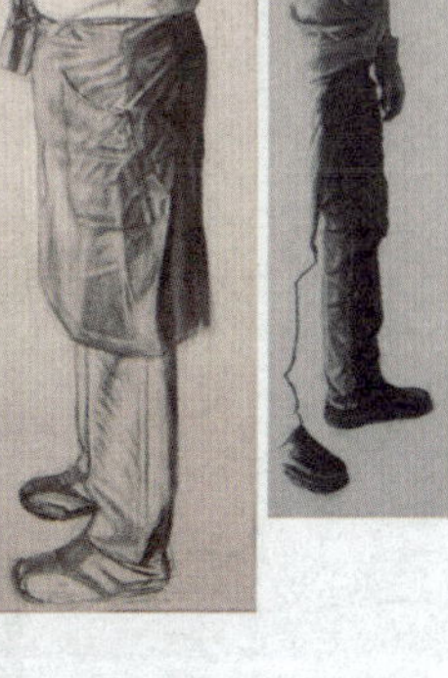
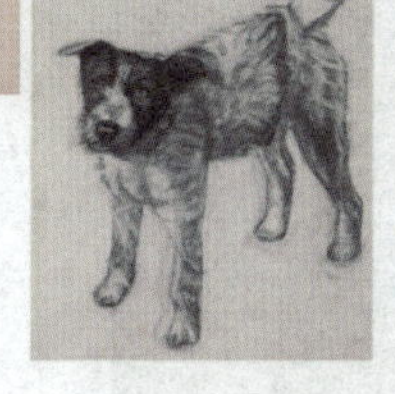
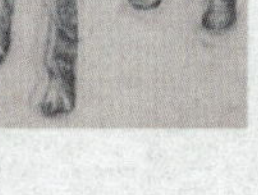
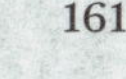

160

161

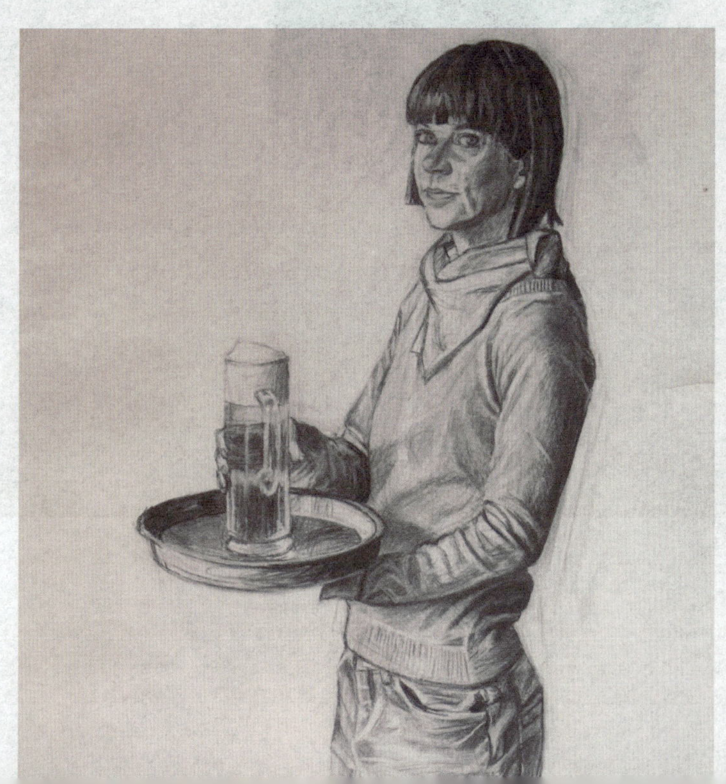
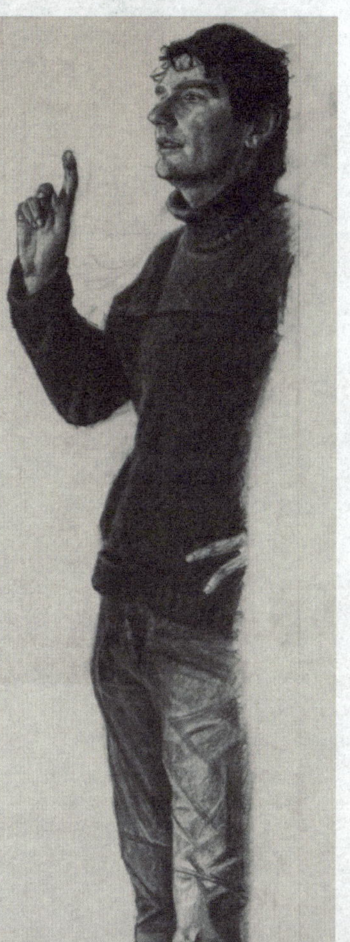

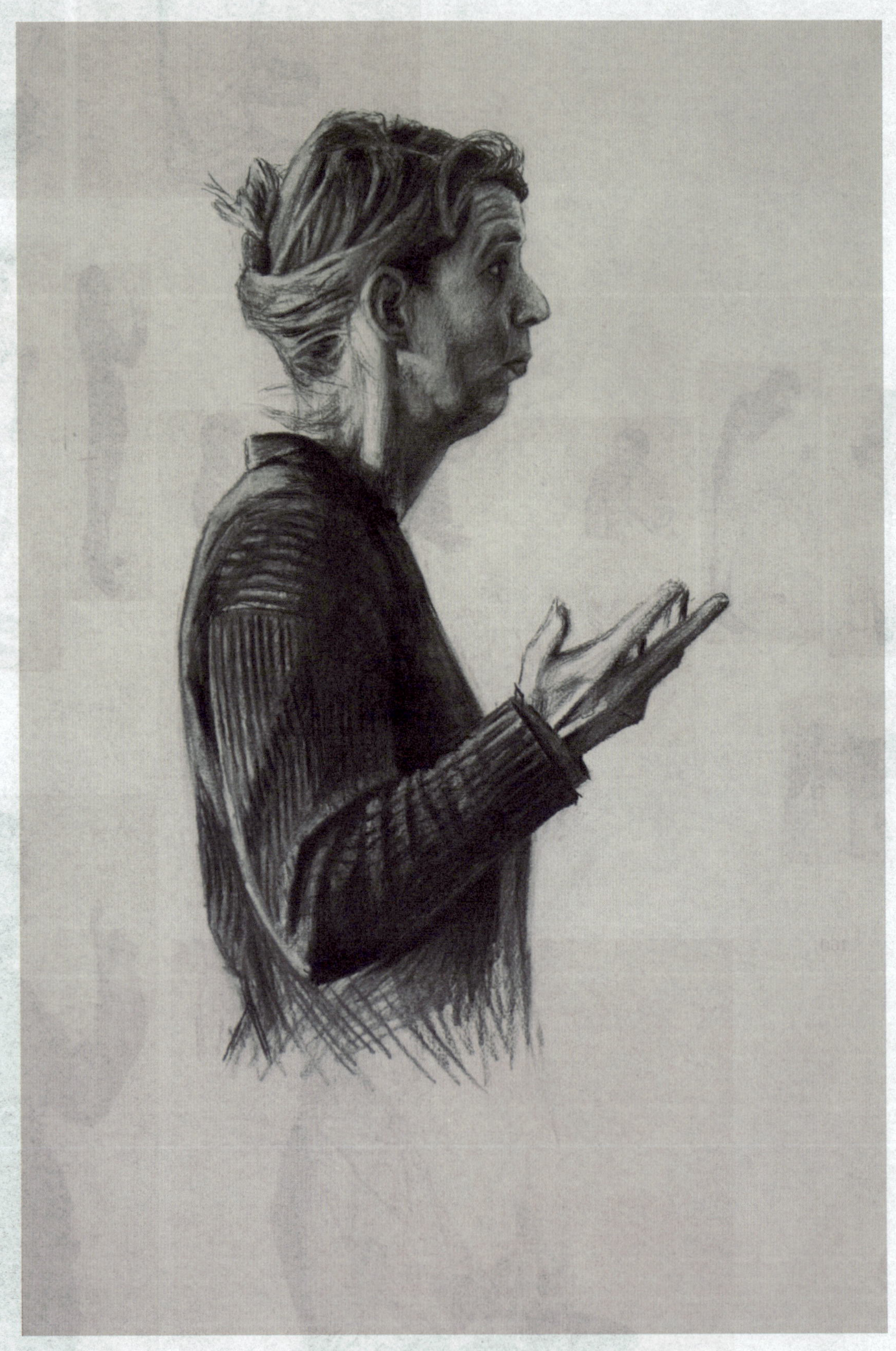

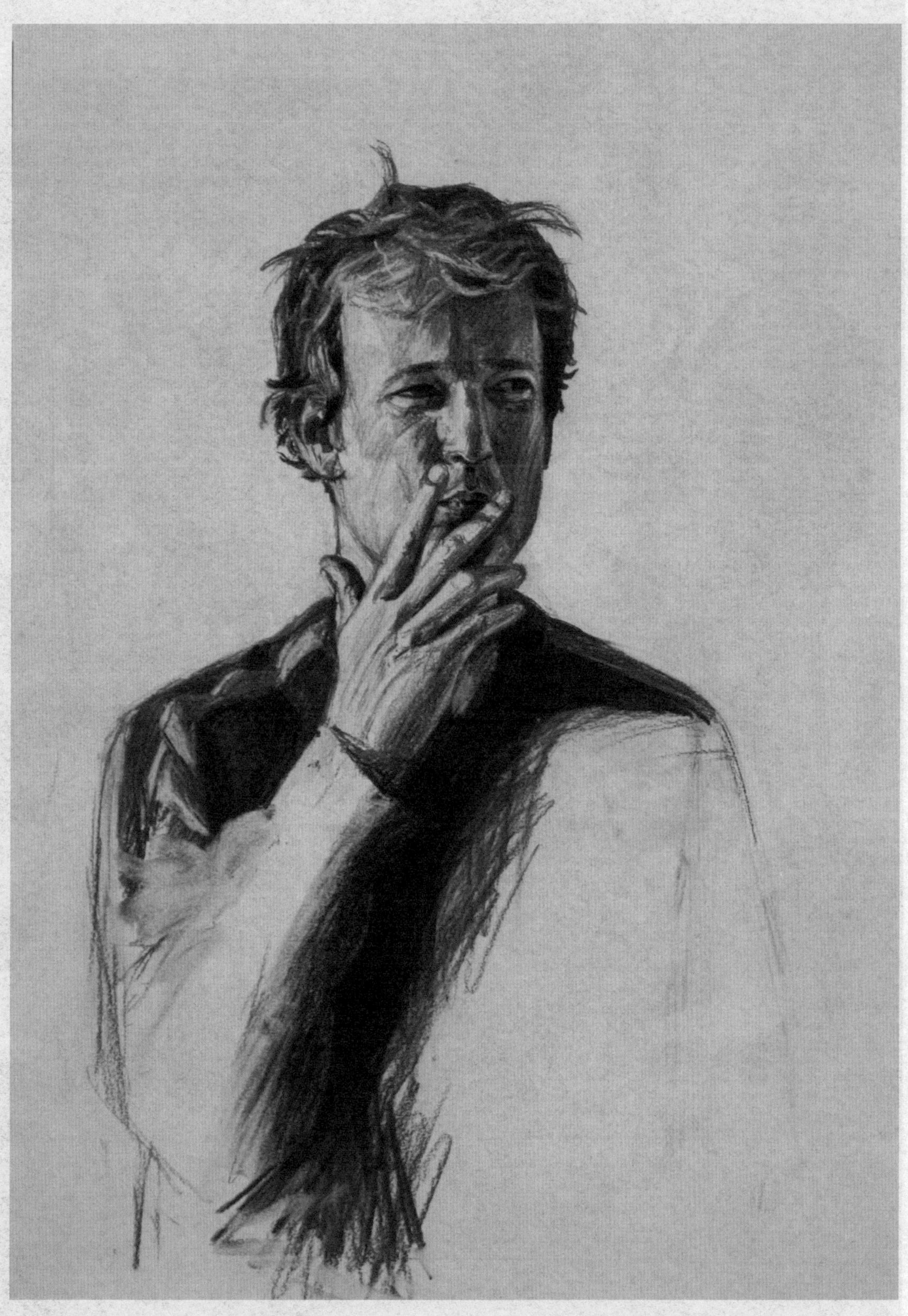

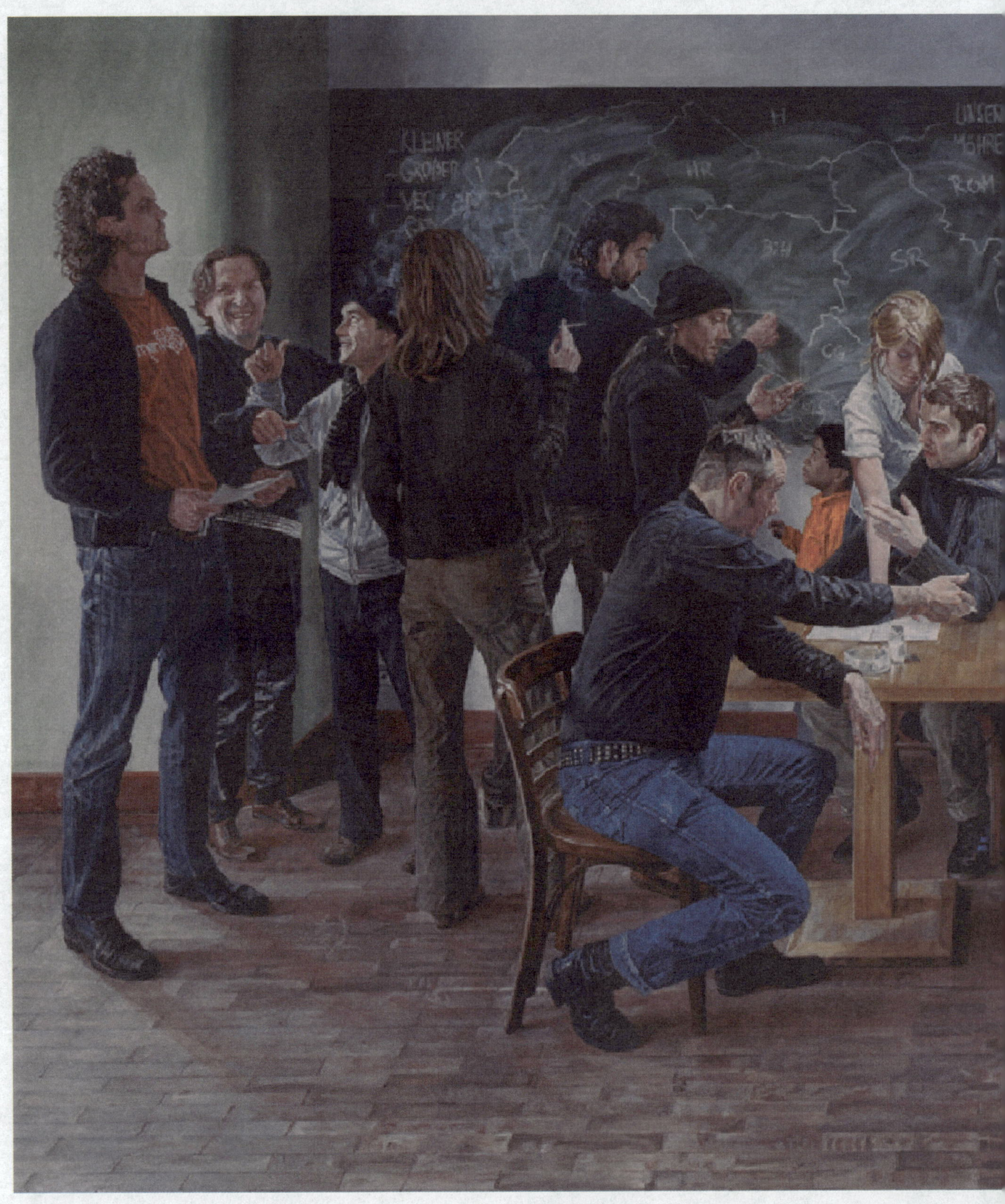

KLEINER
GROßER
VEG
H
UNSER
MÖHR
ROM
HR
BIH
SR

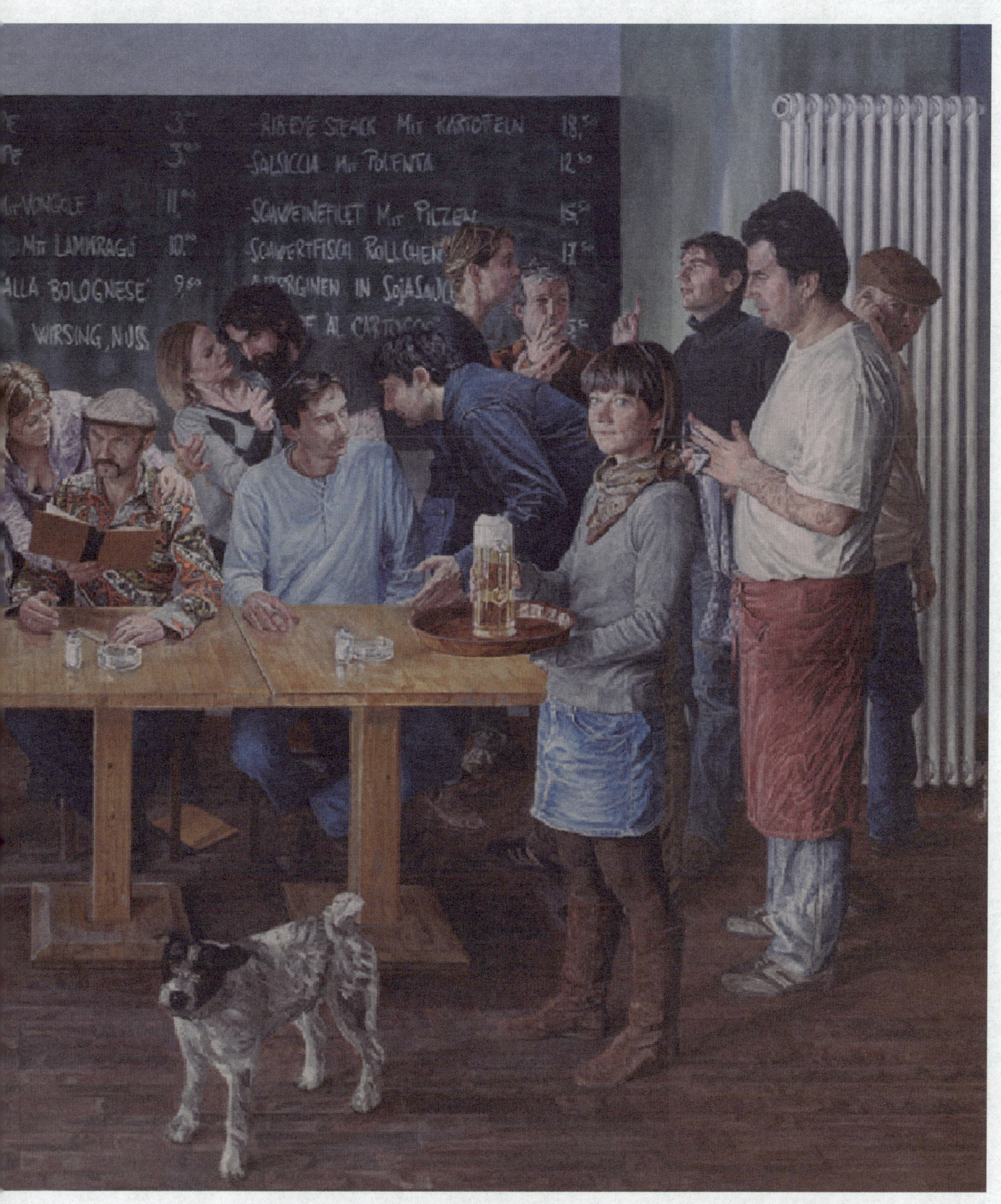

RIB-EYE STEAK MIT KARTOFELN    18,°
SALSICCIA MIT POLENTA    12,°
SCHWEINEFILET MIT PILZEN    15,°
SCHWERTFISCH RÖLLCHEN    17,°
AUBERGINEN IN SOJASAUCE
AL CARTOCCIO
WIRSING, NUSS
ALLA BOLOGNESE    9,°
MIT LAMRAGÙ    10,°
VONGLE    11,°

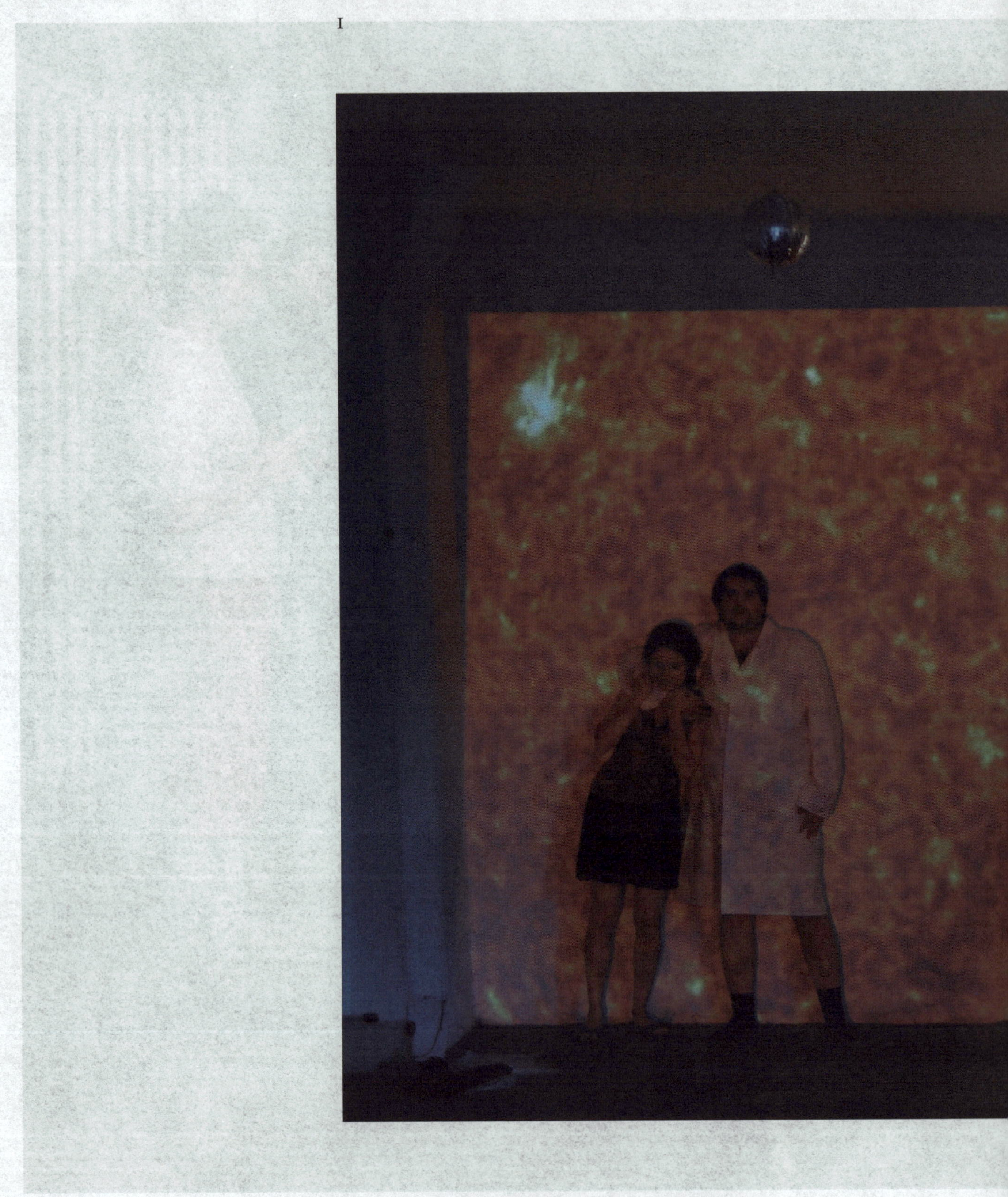

Studio Performances 

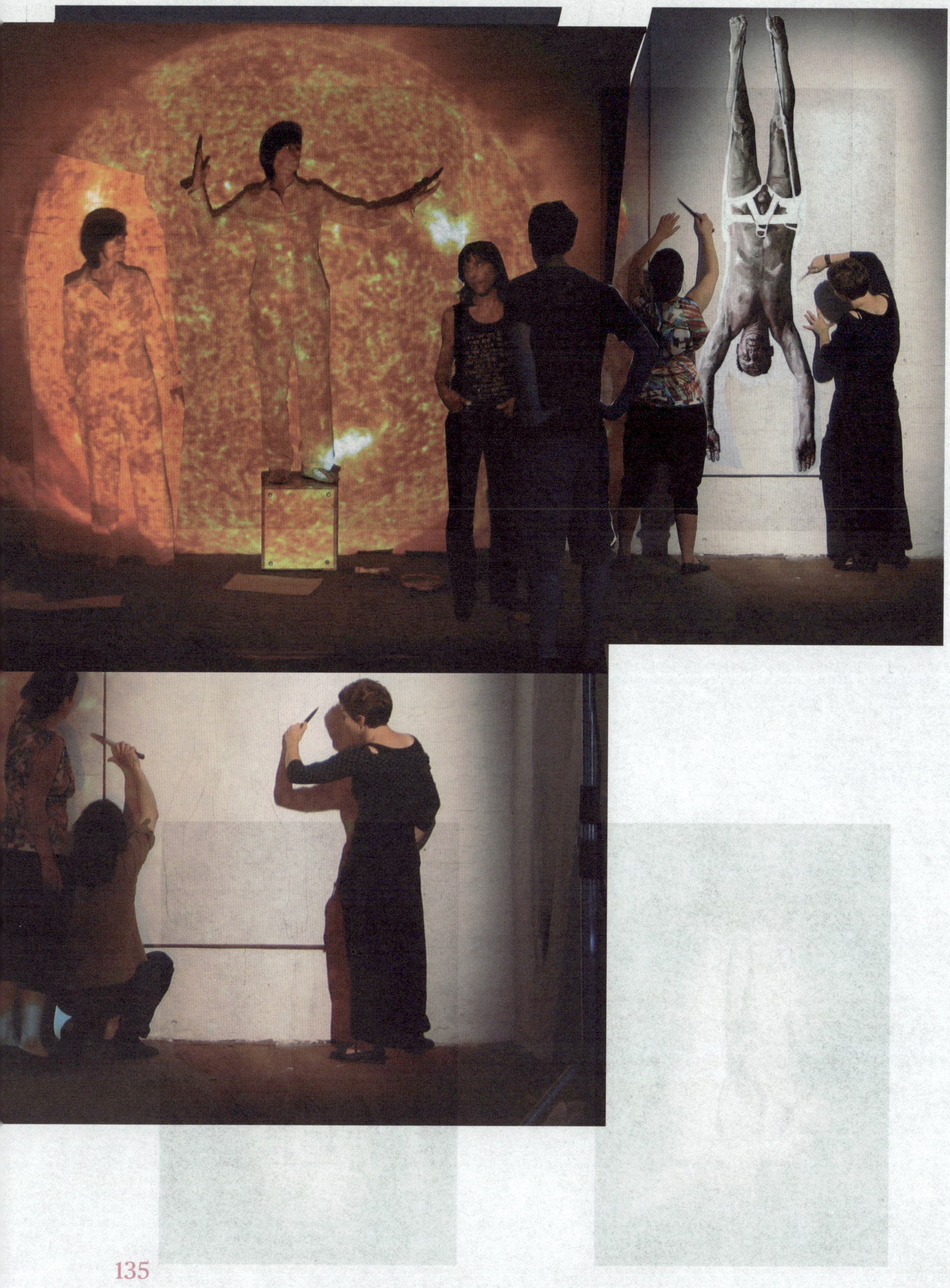

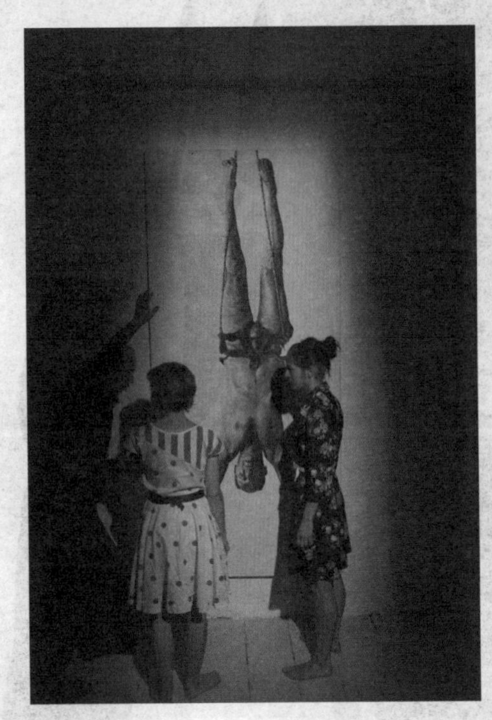
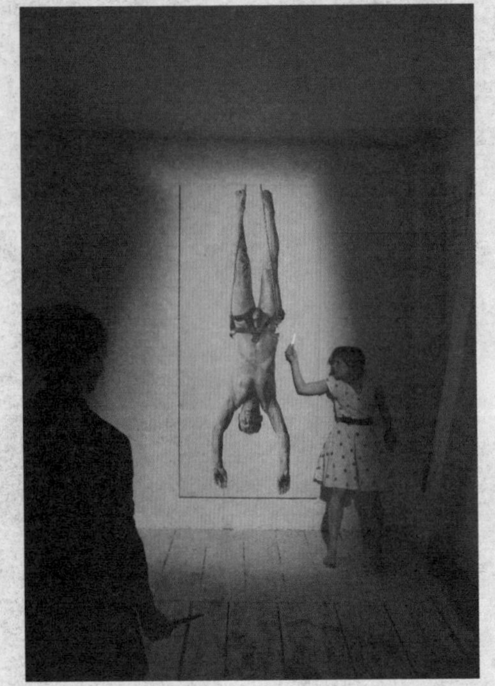

J

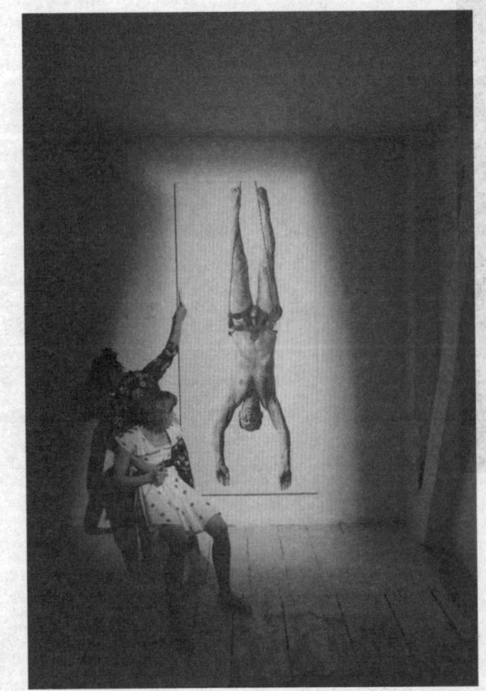
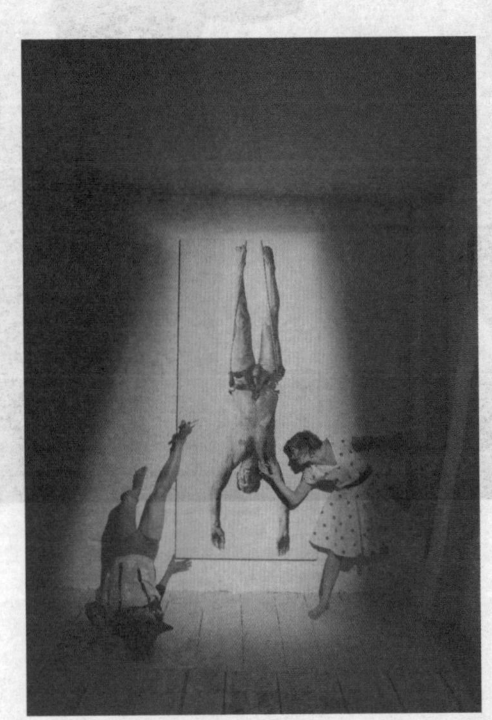

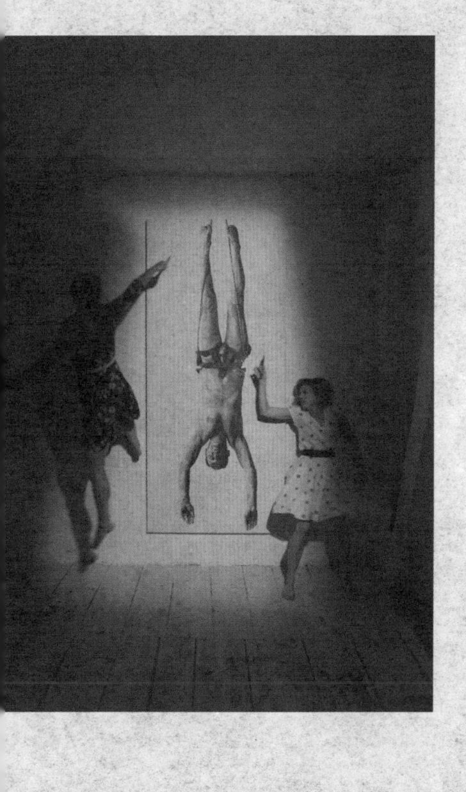
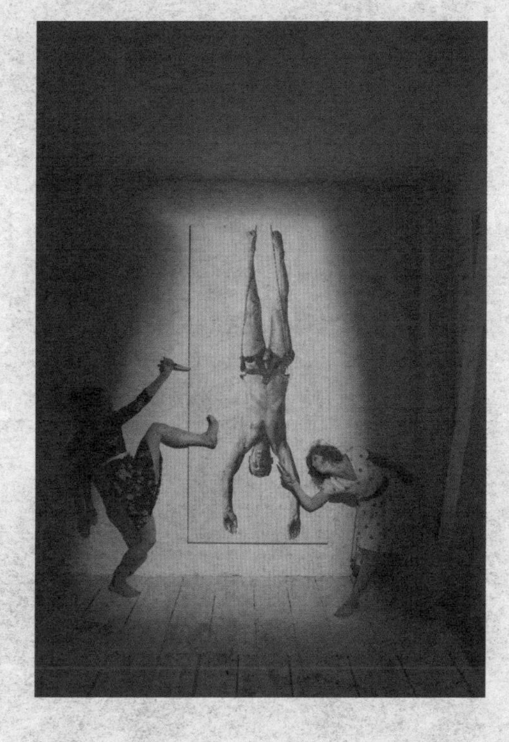
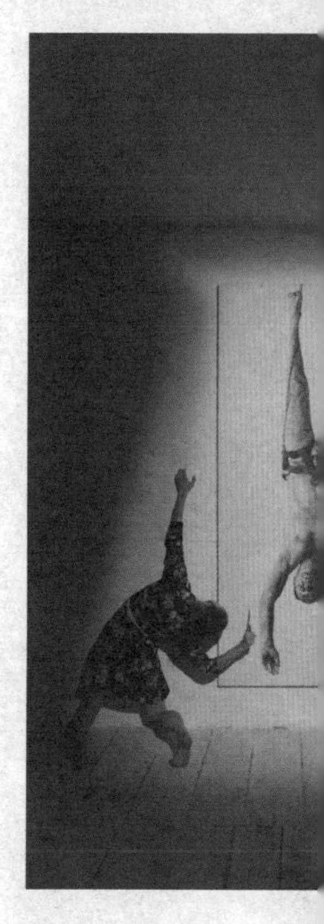
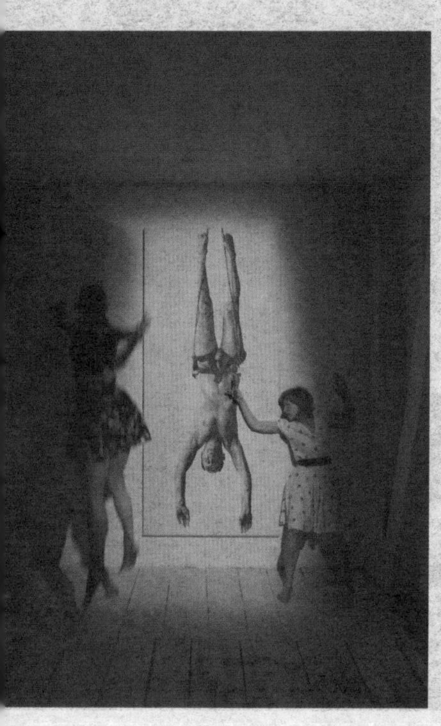
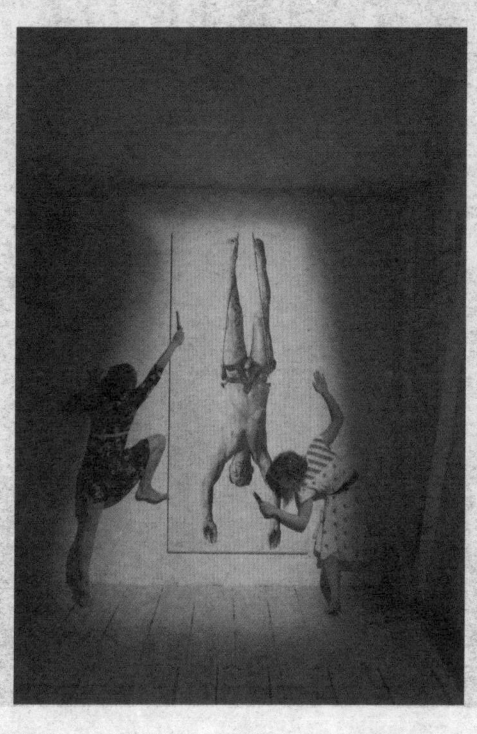
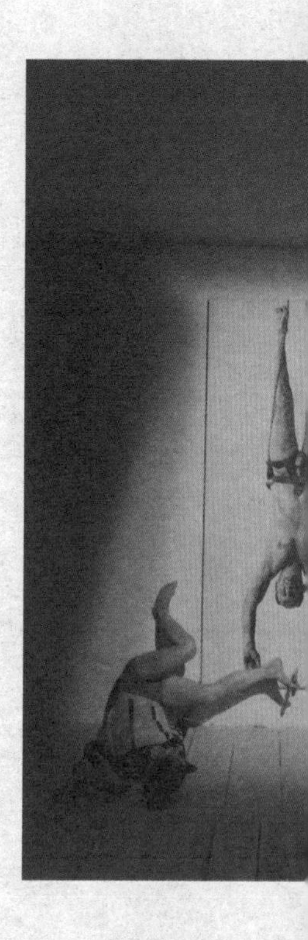

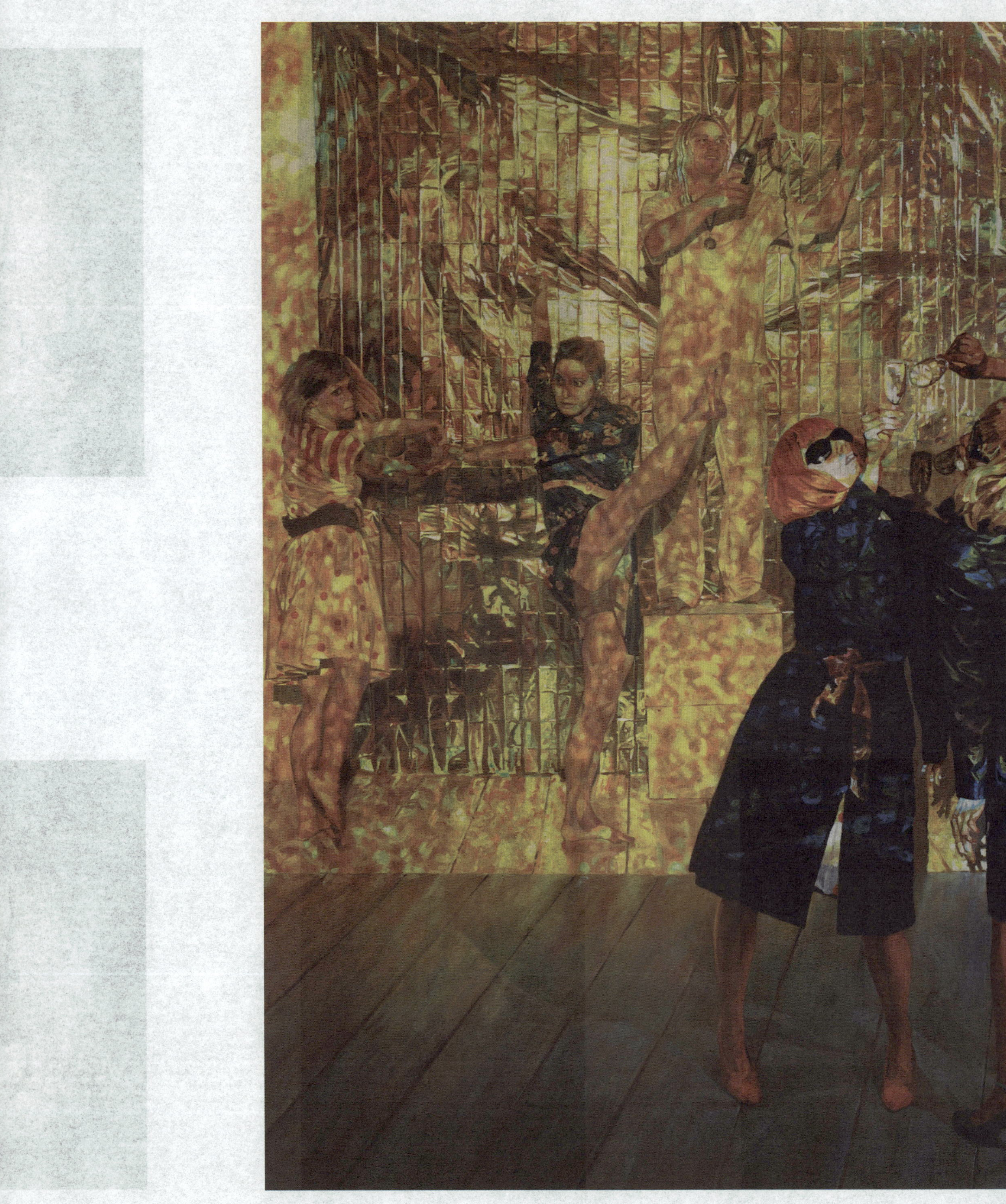

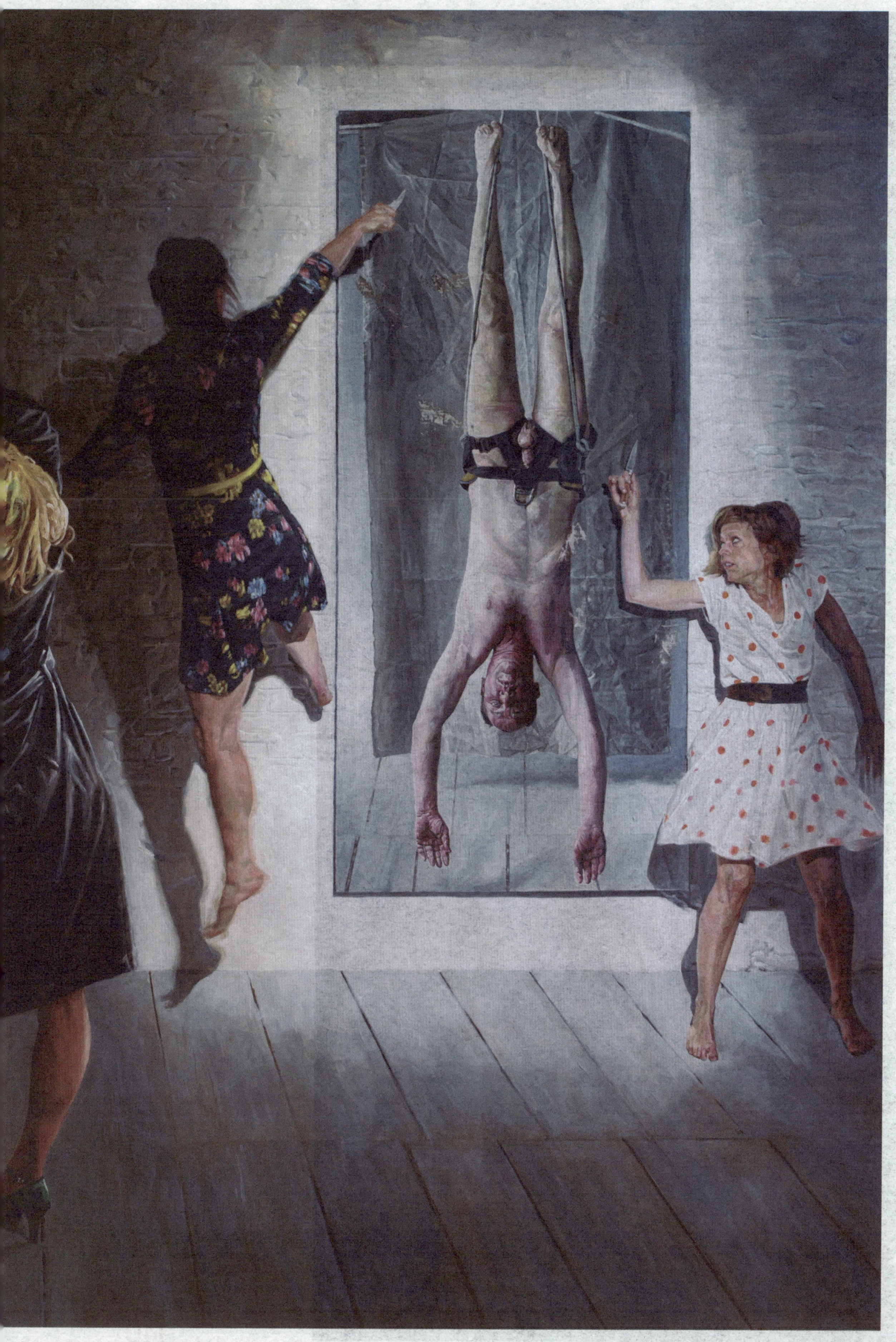

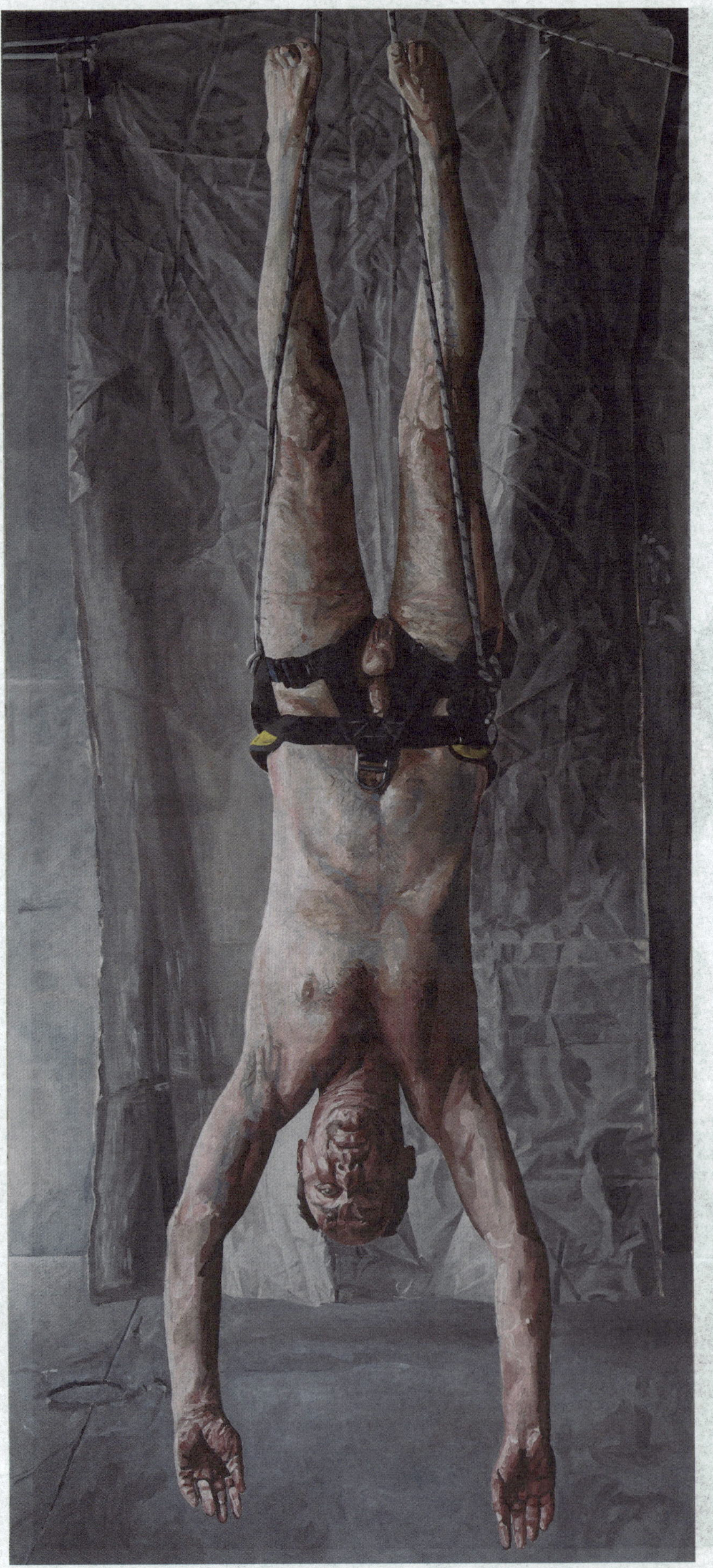

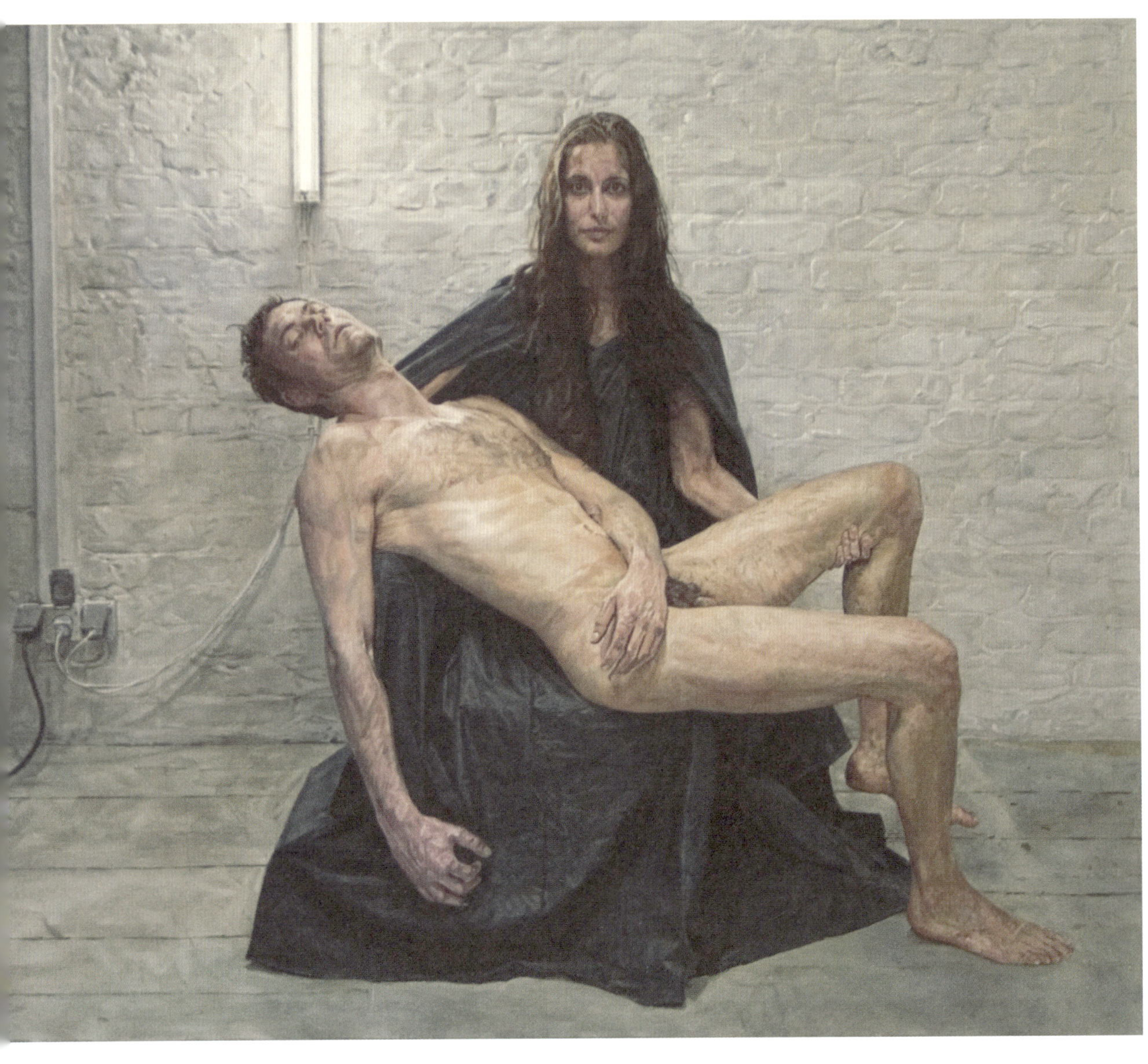

34

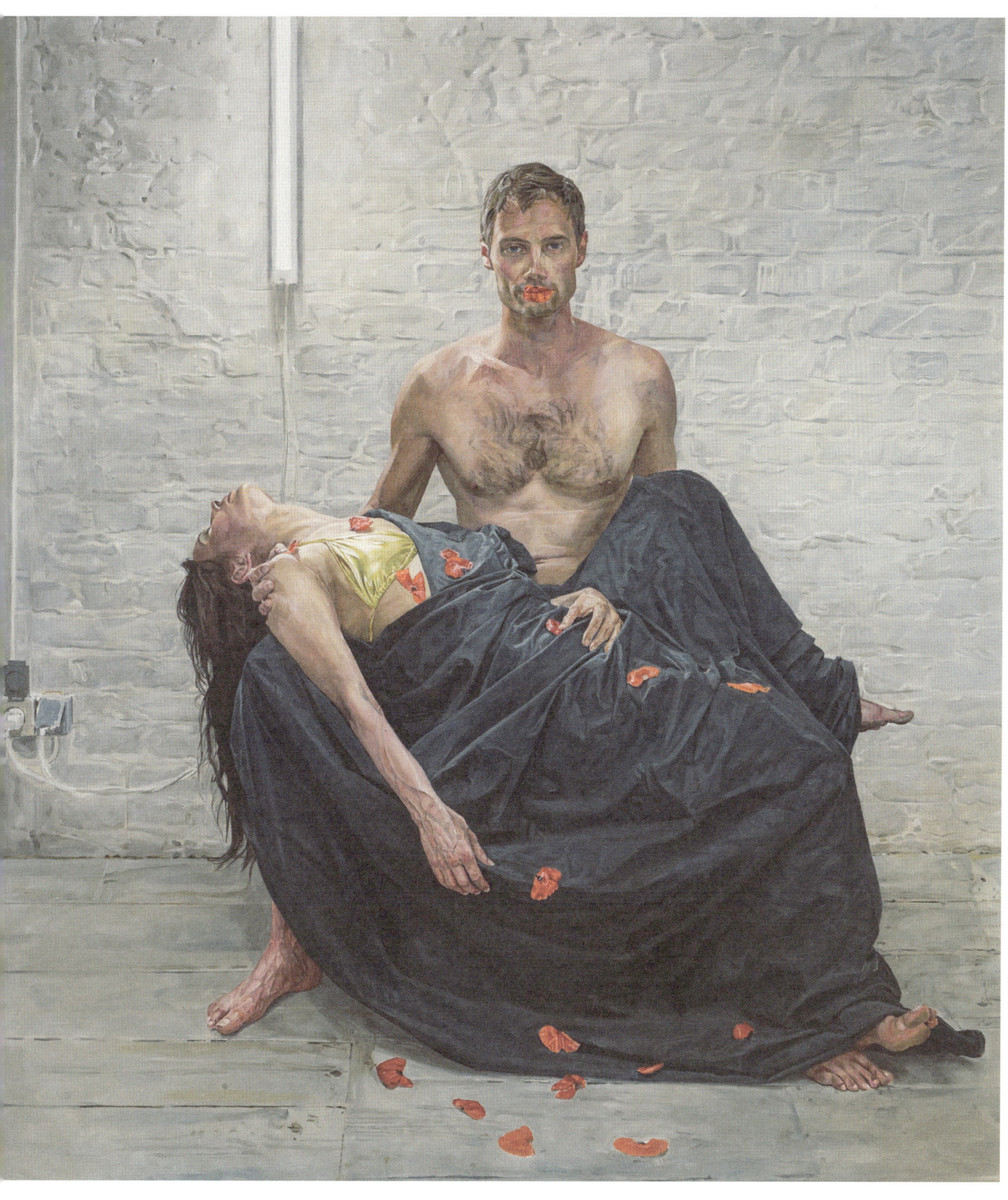

33

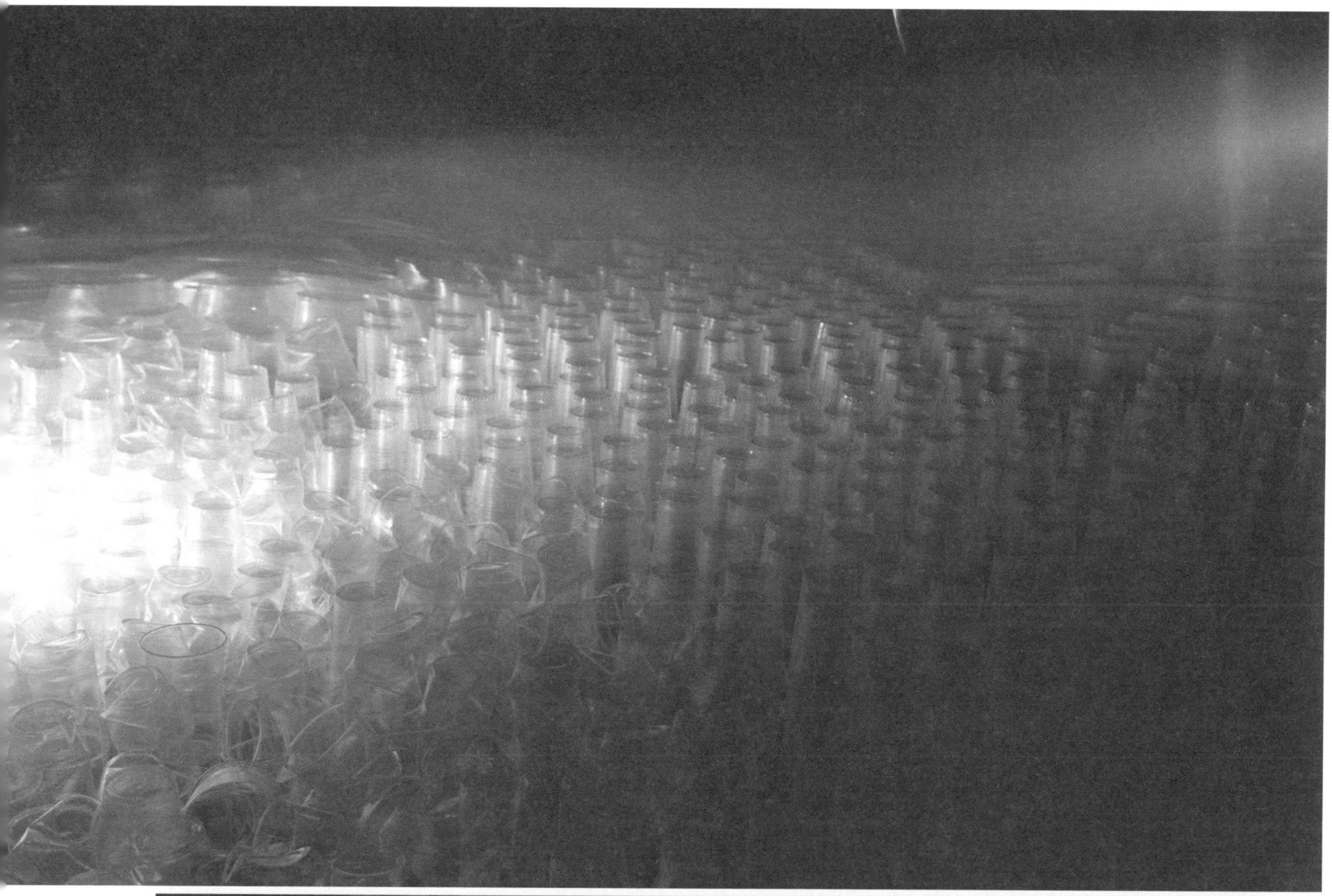

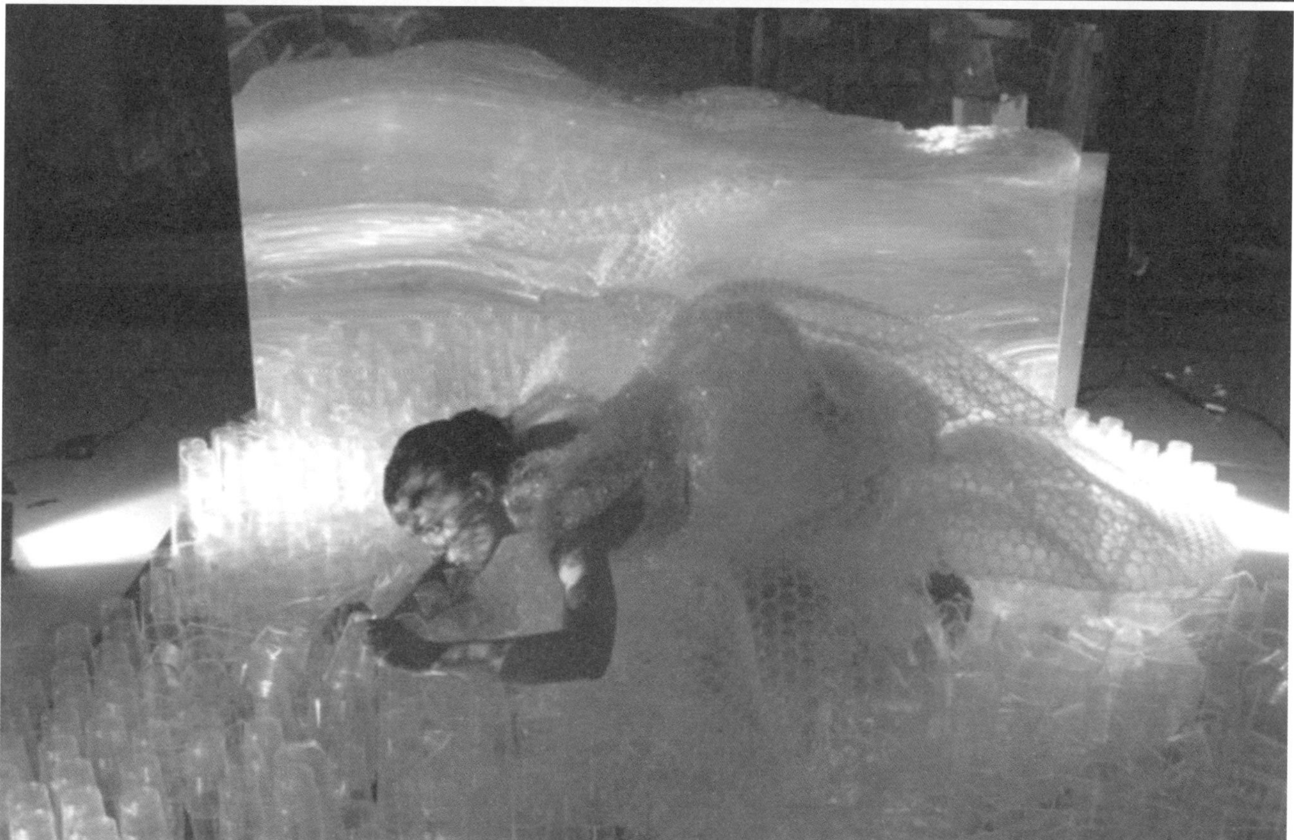

K

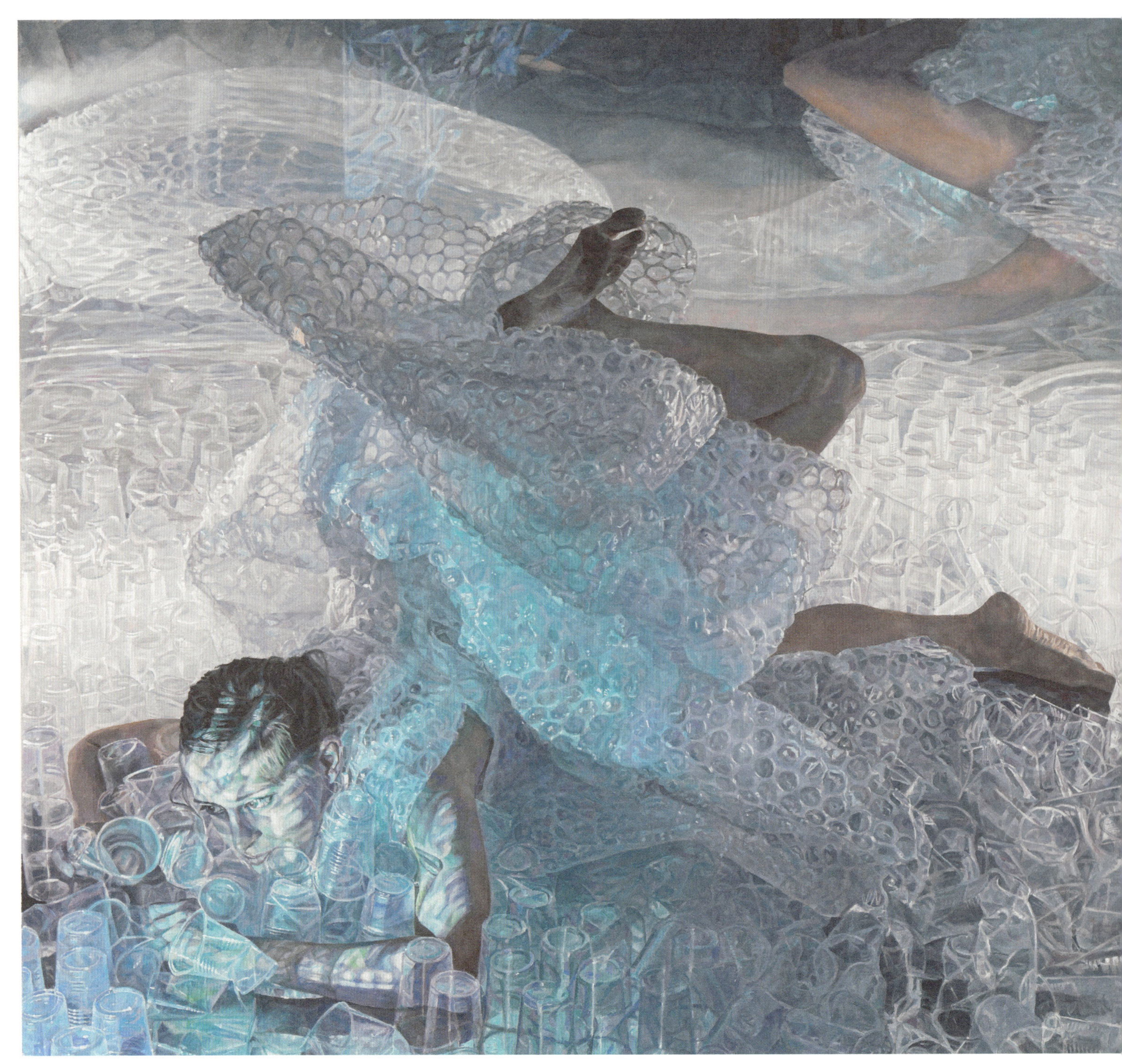

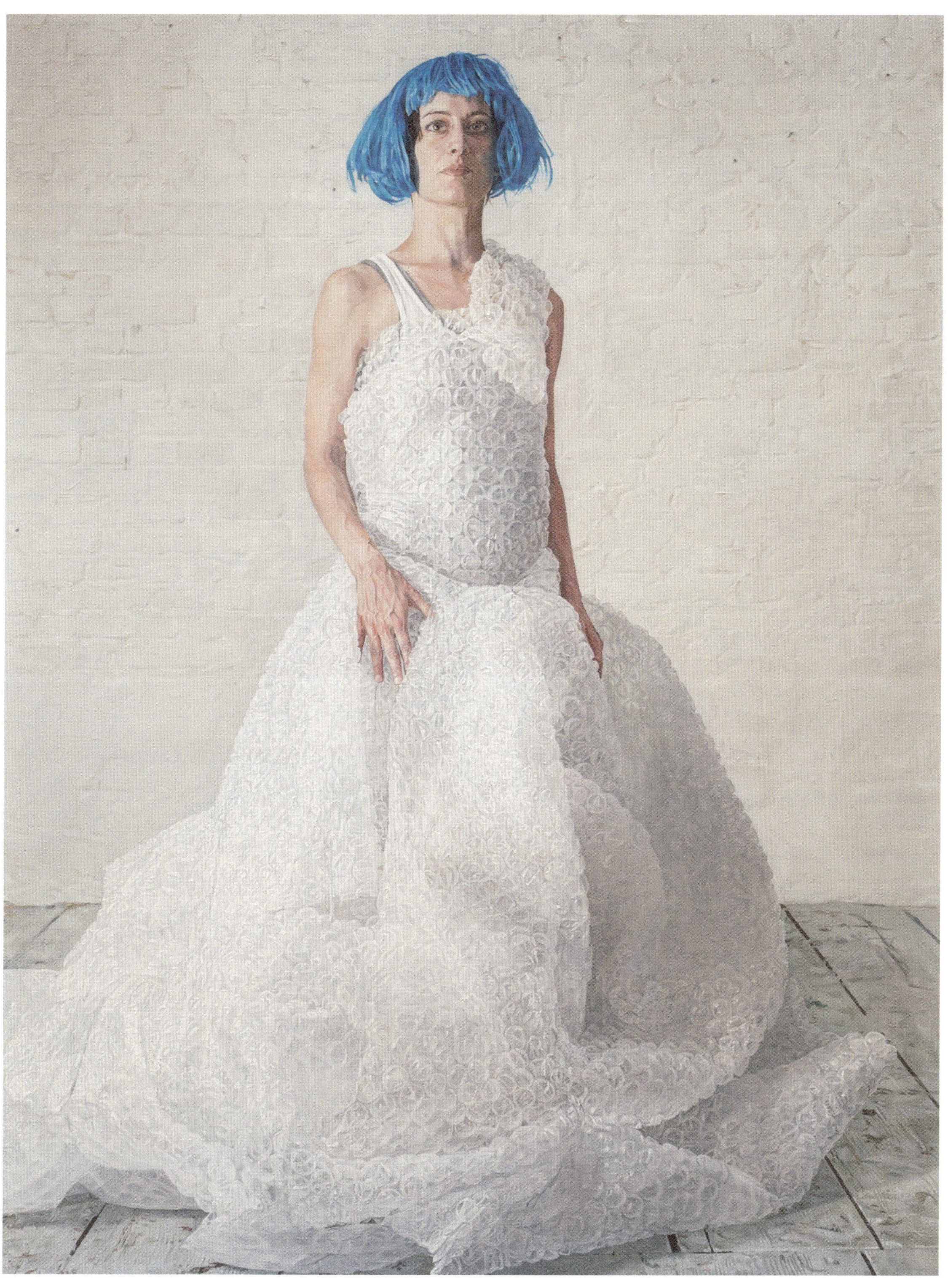

165

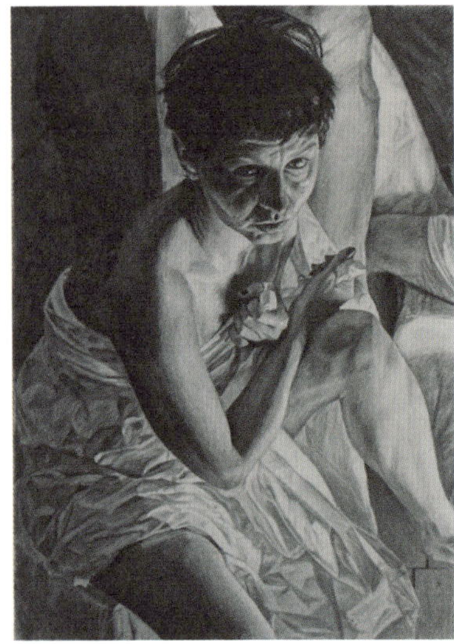

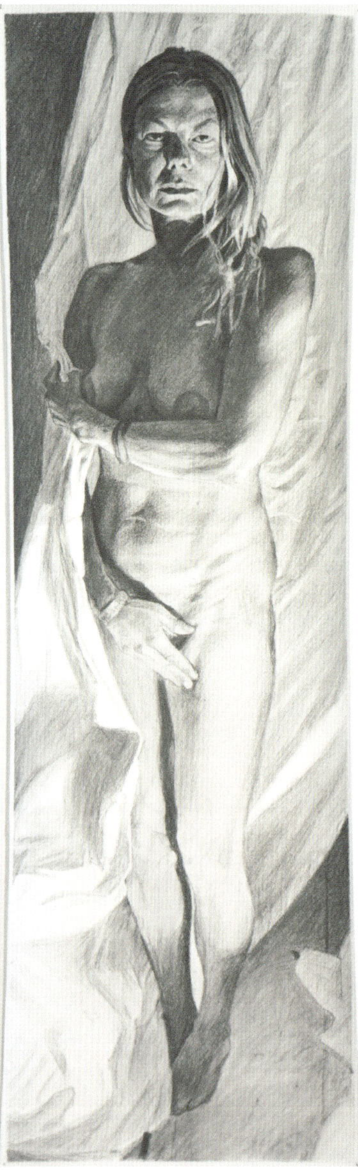

167

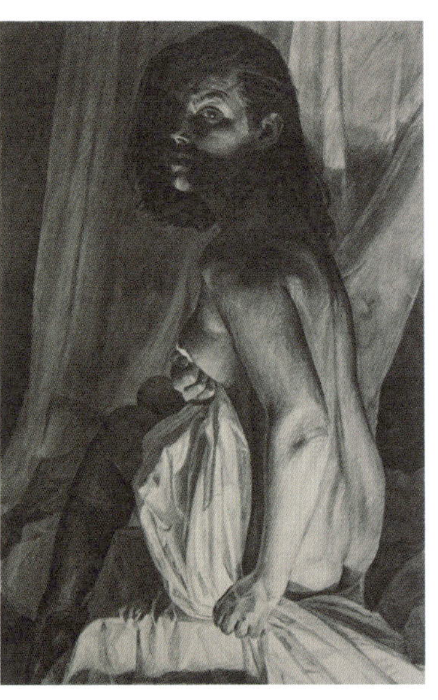

Women's Bath

169

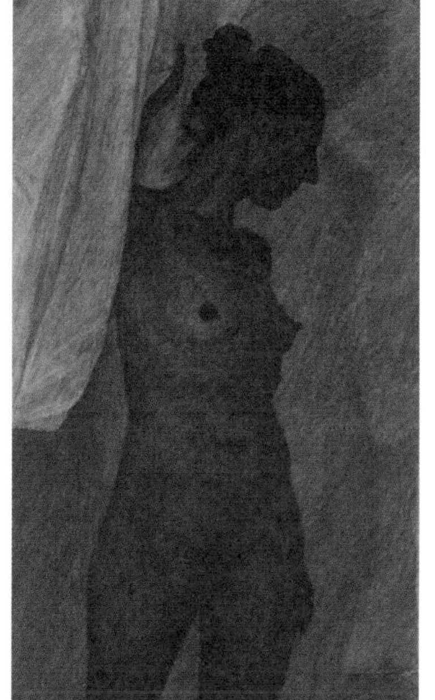

170

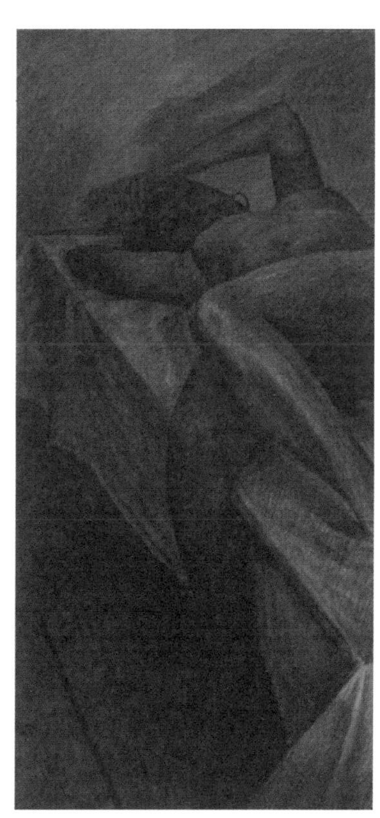

171

172

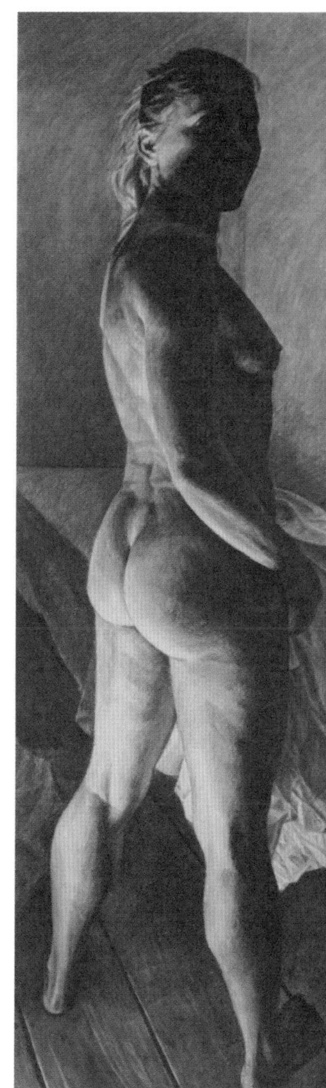

168

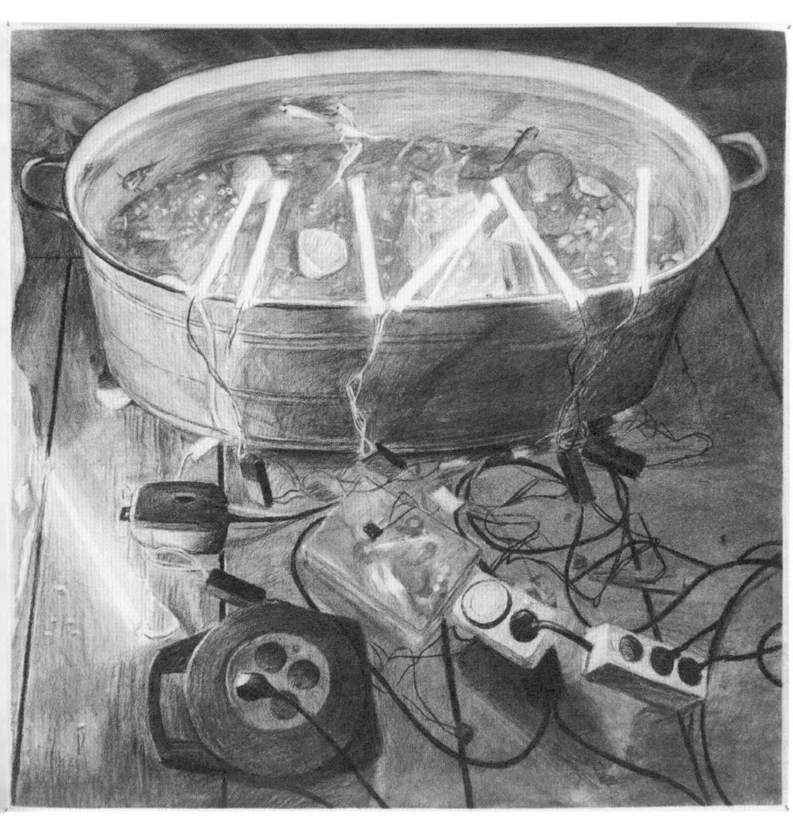

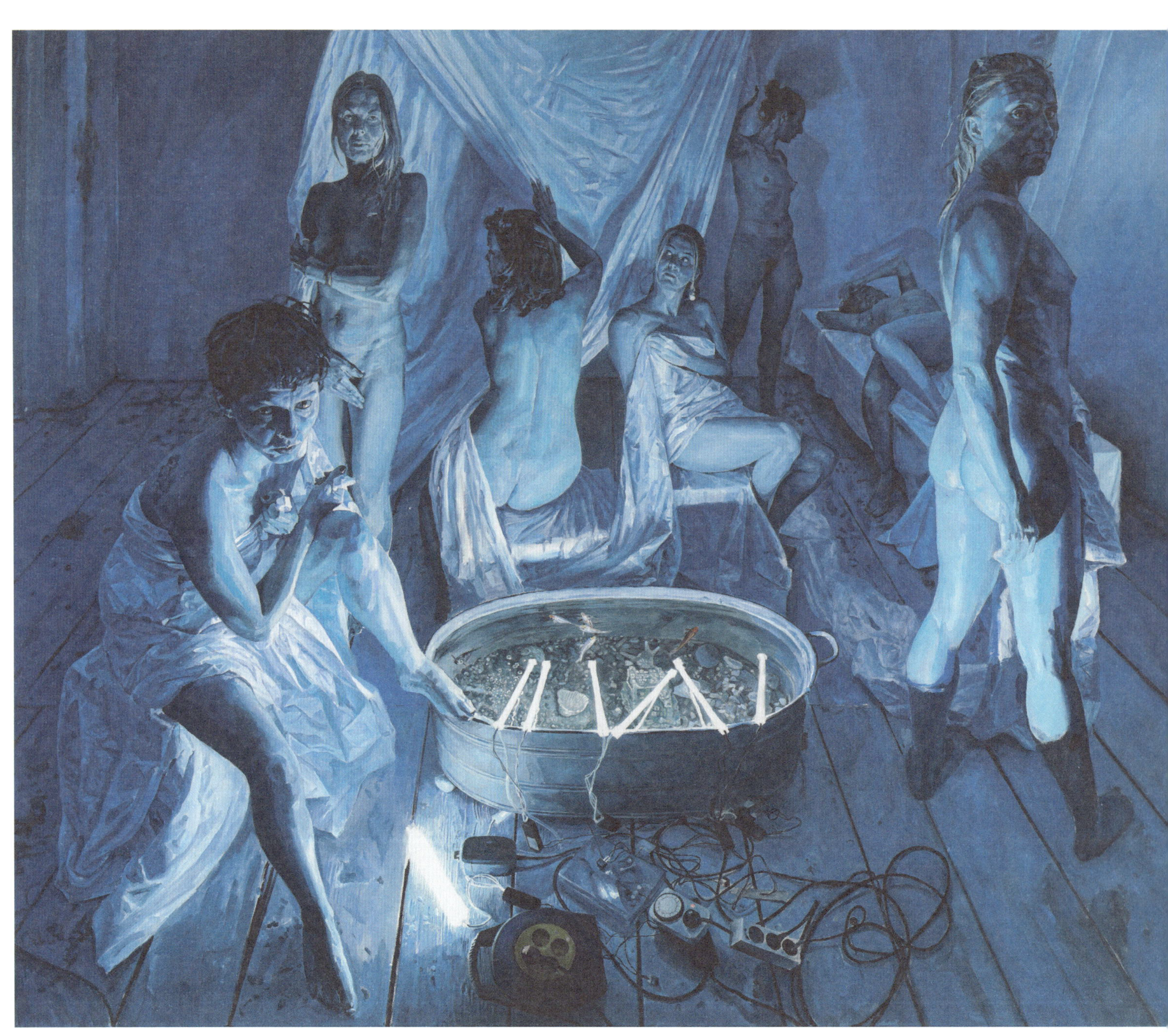

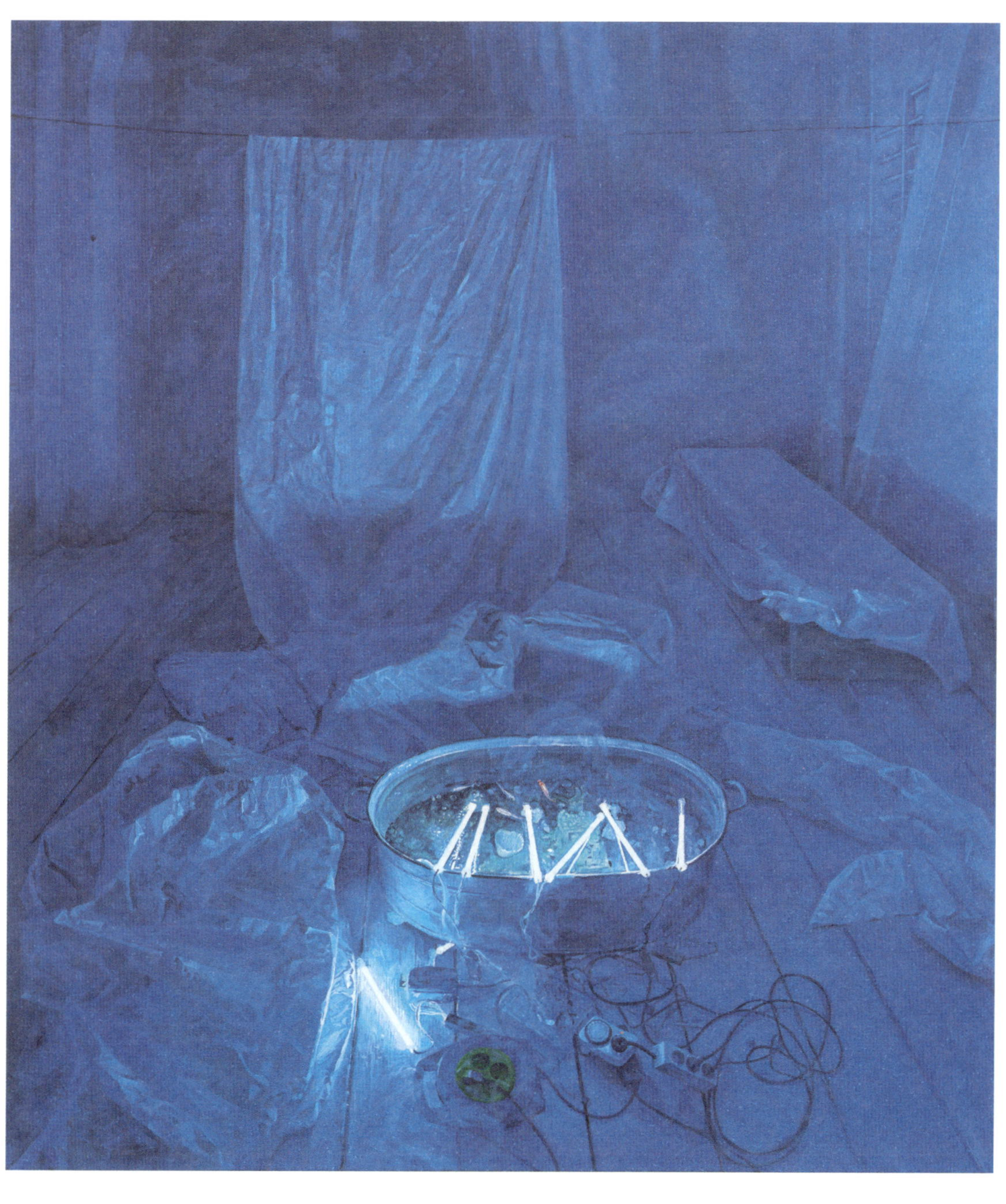

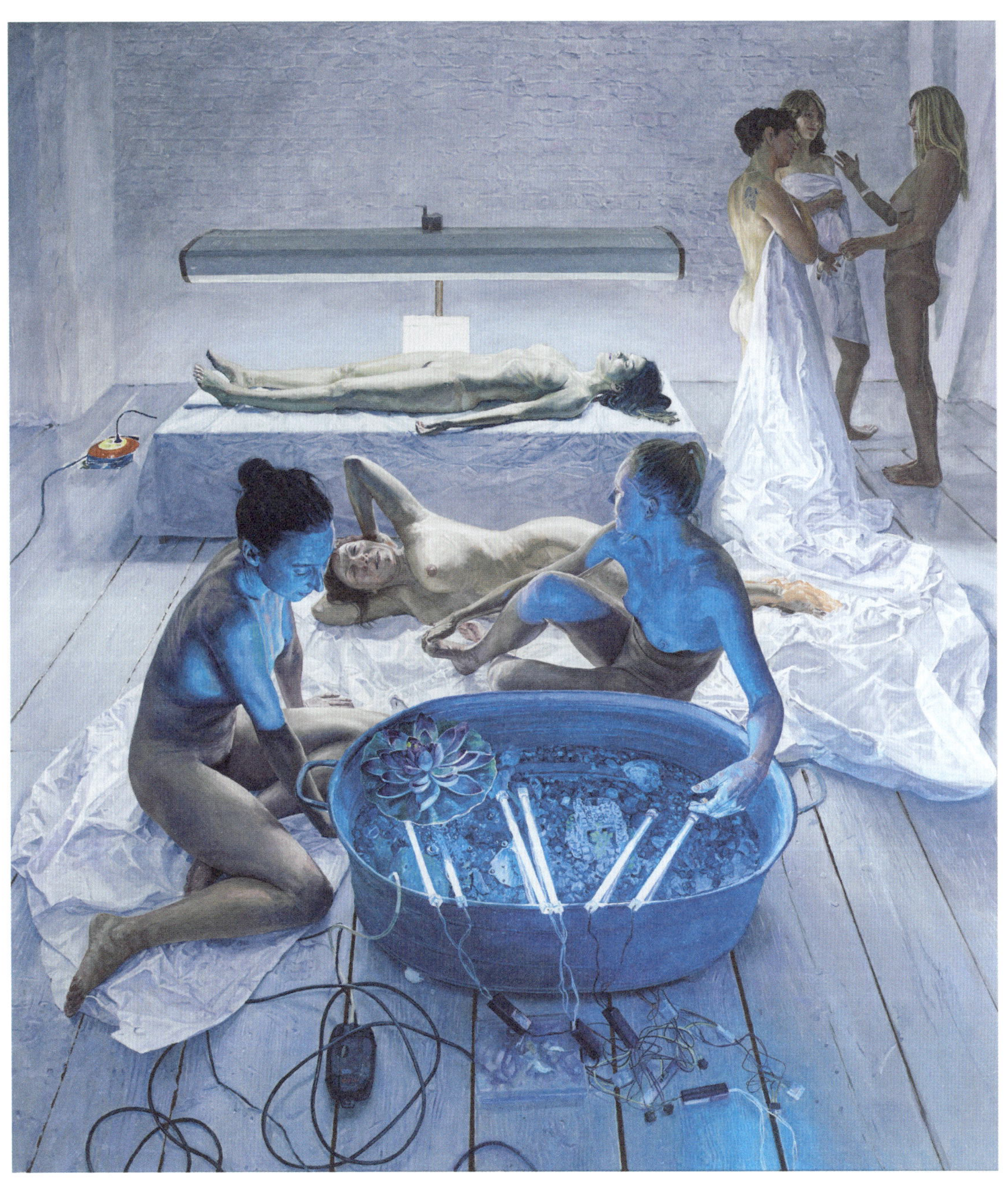

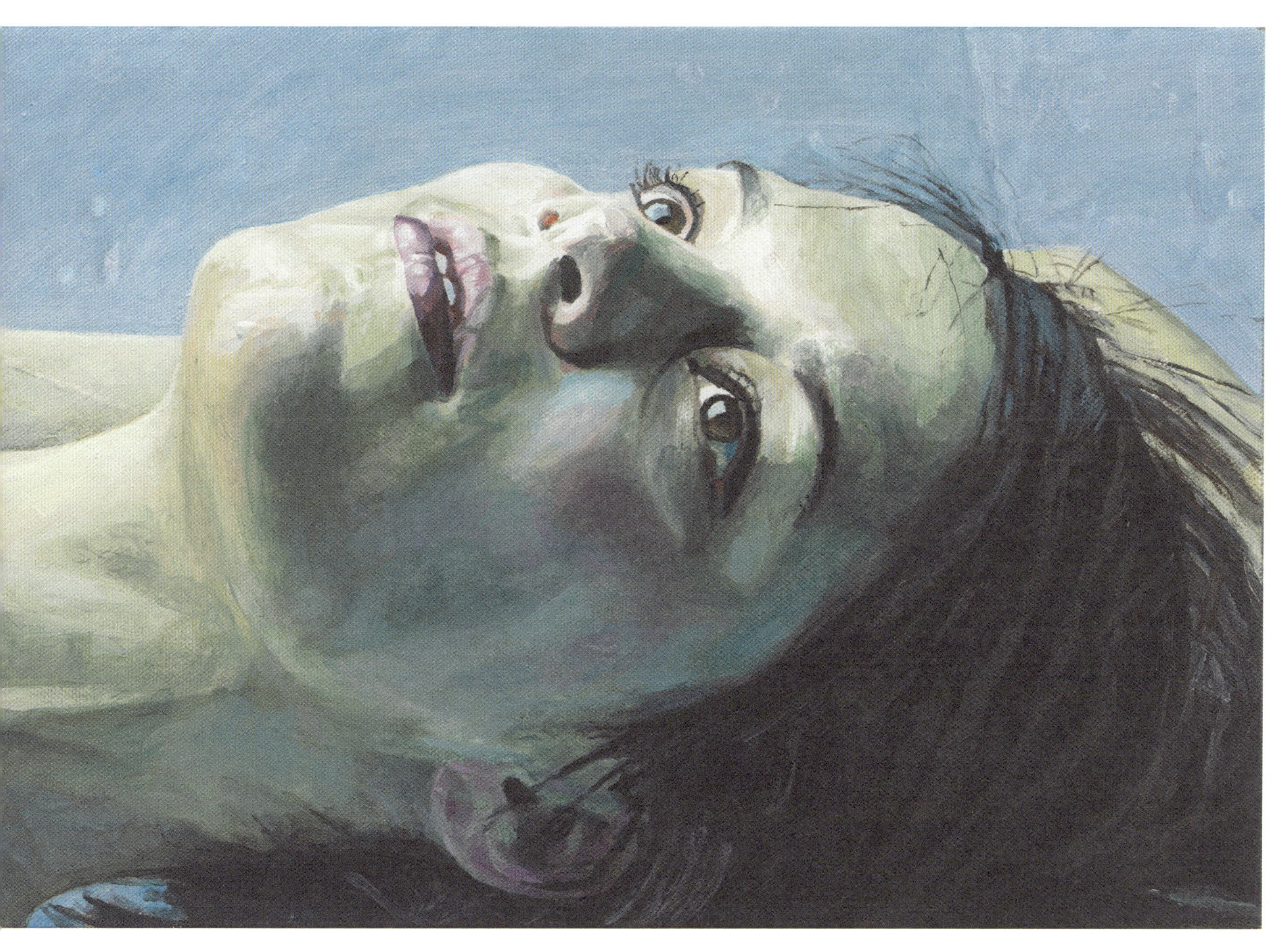

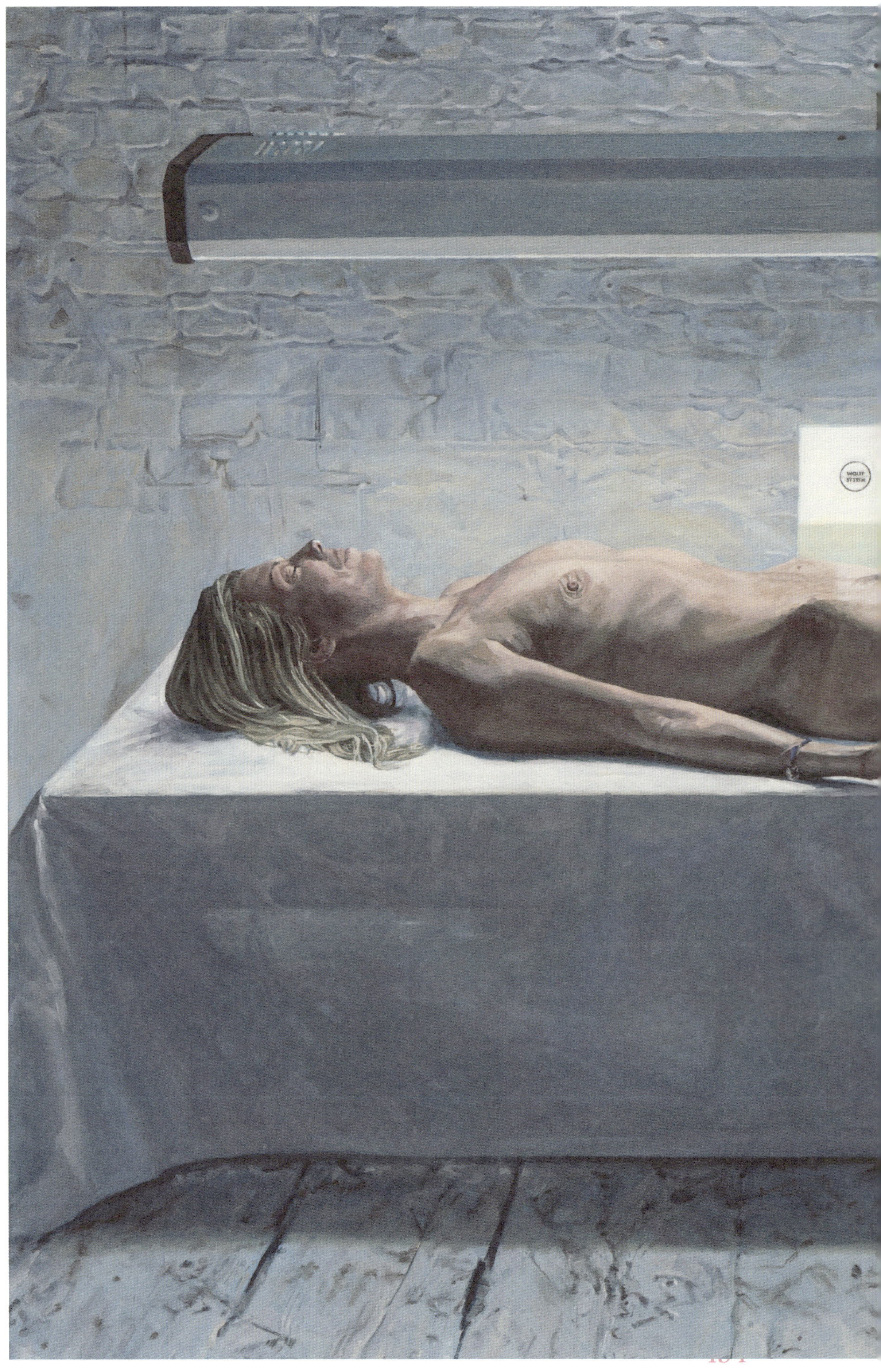
WOUT
SYSTEM

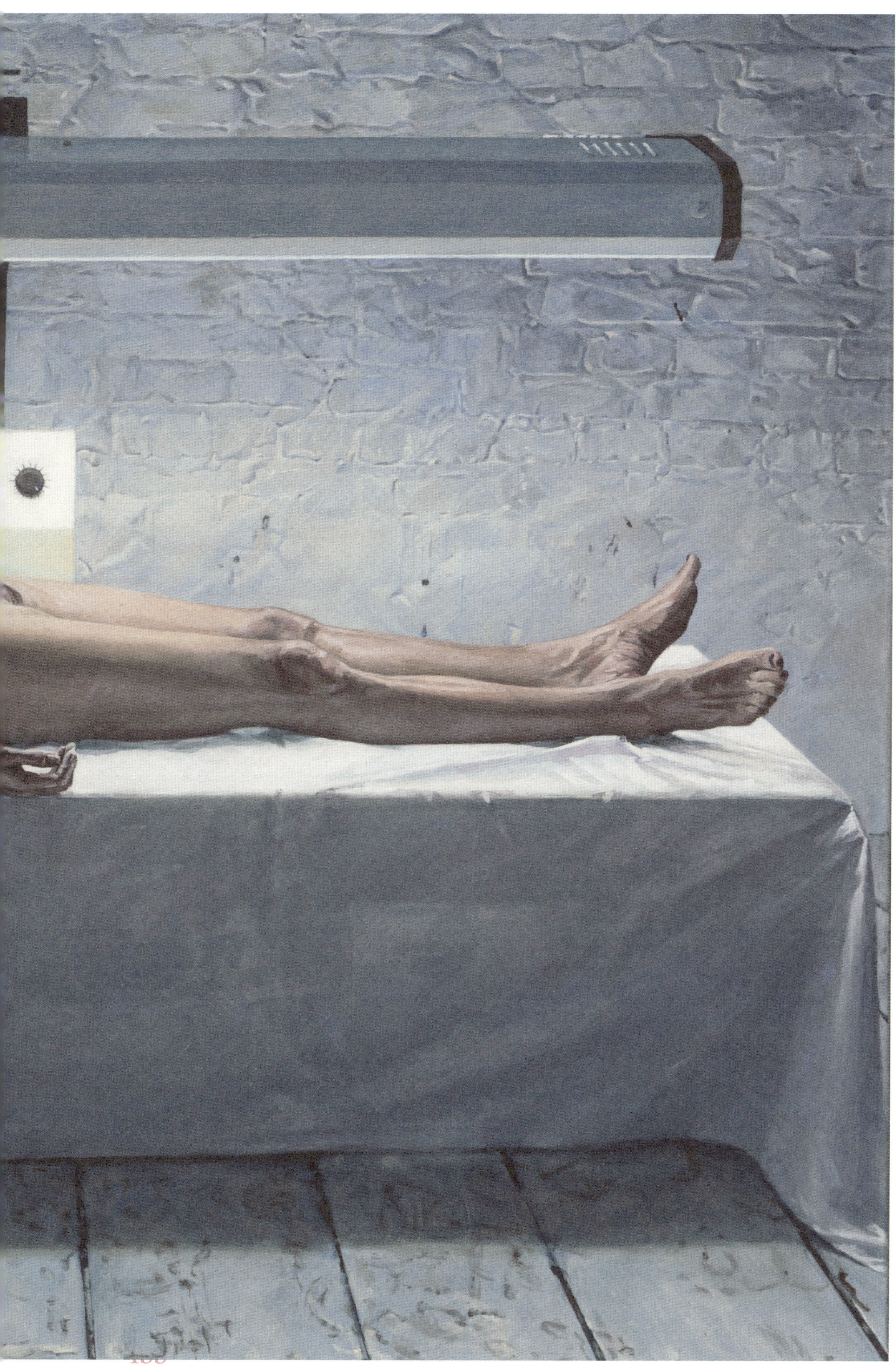

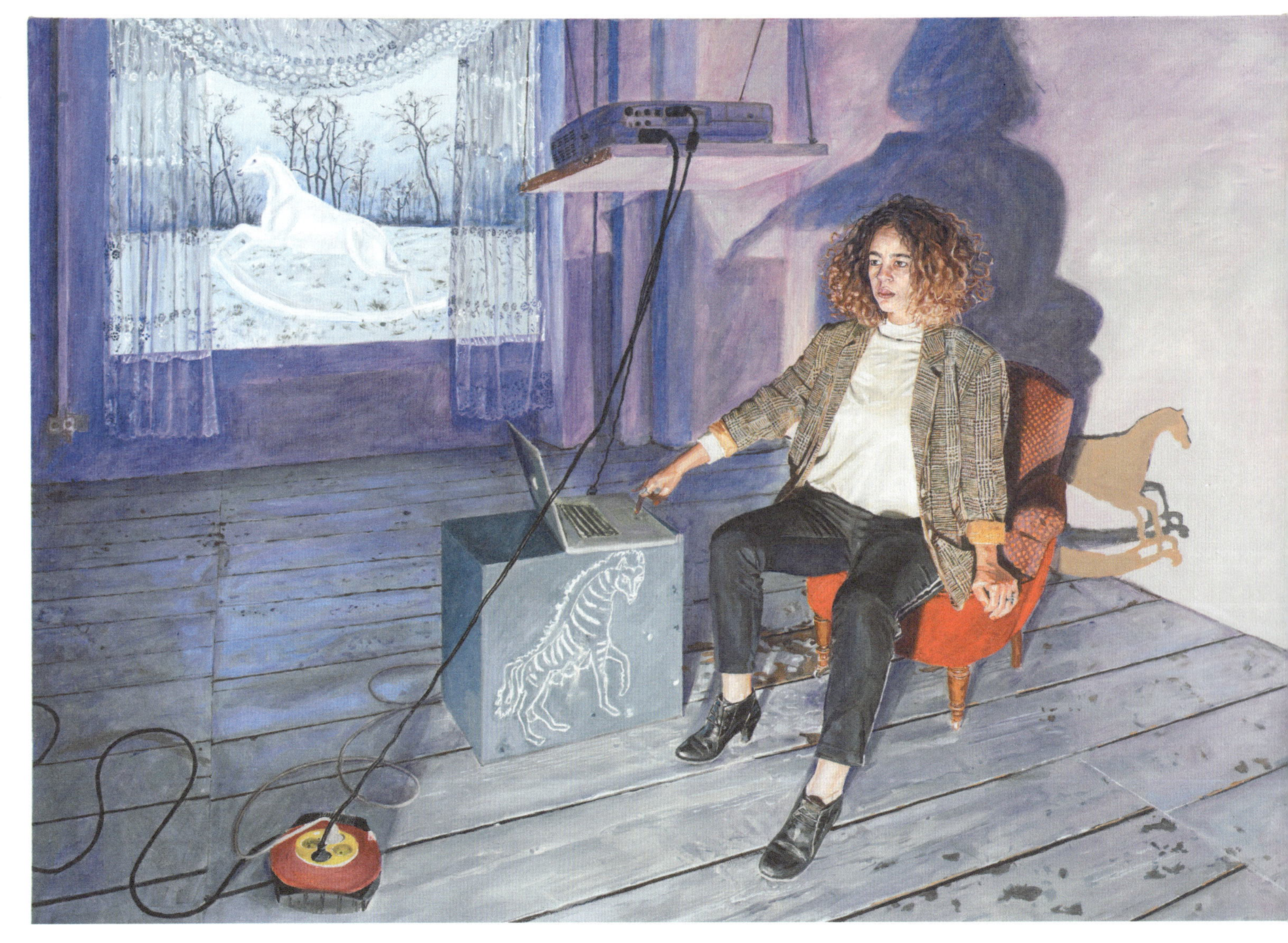



Let Me Show You My Dream

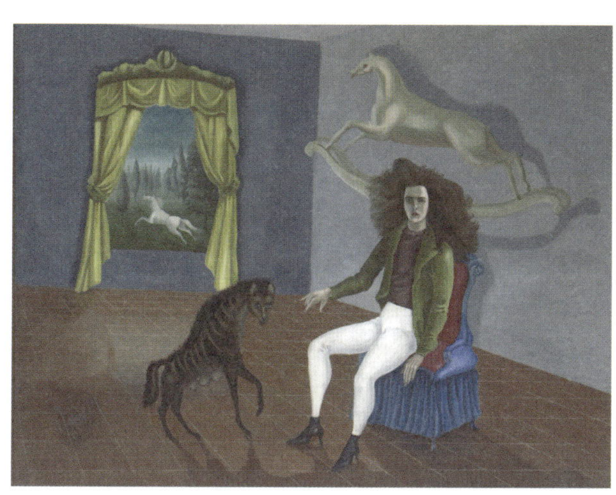

Leonora Carrington, Self-Portrait
New York, bpk | The Metropolitan Museum
of Art, The Pierre and Maria-Gaetana
Matisse Collection, New York

# SLOWING DOWN

In recent years I have been living in a constant inner struggle. My paintings, namely - or what I try to capture through them - demand more and more time. I believe that the reason for this is not that I am getting older and generally slower, but rather in the fact that more and more details accumulate in my paintings and that my way of painting, this endless glazing of one and the same spot to achieve the desired presence and density of the object, takes me hours upon hours that somehow pass imperceptibly. Sitting for days before the same painting, held captive by a single detail, I often think that I should speed up the painting process, become more productive and work in concord with our time when everything is happening at breakneck speed and when - alas! - no one will anyway have either the patience or the concentration to engage in the old-fashioned slow pleasure of looking at my paintings.

Actually, I got myself into this trap, as it sometimes seems to me. I have let myself be guided by life circumstances in the selection of a motif instead of a plan or system. When I look at what I have produced, I however realize that it is painted in the right way. Because of the energy, the atmosphere and everything I wanted to achieve consciously and unconsciously with each of those paintings. Since I could not invent (until now) a patent to paint quickly and simply, and at the same time be satisfied with the result, each time I humbly accept that this slow and laborious, sometimes frustrating way of painting, is just my own recognizable way. That is why I decided to present the paintings created in recent years under the title *Slowing Down*.

The paintings shown here are perhaps not most accurately described by the title *Gold Foil*. The golden colour of the foil was not the main reason that prompted me to paint it, but rather its property of reflecting the surroundings in a distorted way. This gave me a template that, depending on the particular distance of the models or objects from the foil, makes space and figures appear more or less fragmented, so that one rather senses than recognizes them. This sensing of what might be represented gives the impression that the painting is liberated from the strongly narrative representationalism and that the painting process is freer, more autonomous, thus acquiring advance over the represented object. But actually, the approach and painting method here are completely the same as in my other paintings described by some as "classical, pronouncedly figurative". If you look at the foils from this point of view, it becomes clear that the real object of the paintings is the clearly figuratively depicted gold foil and everything else is only reflected in it.

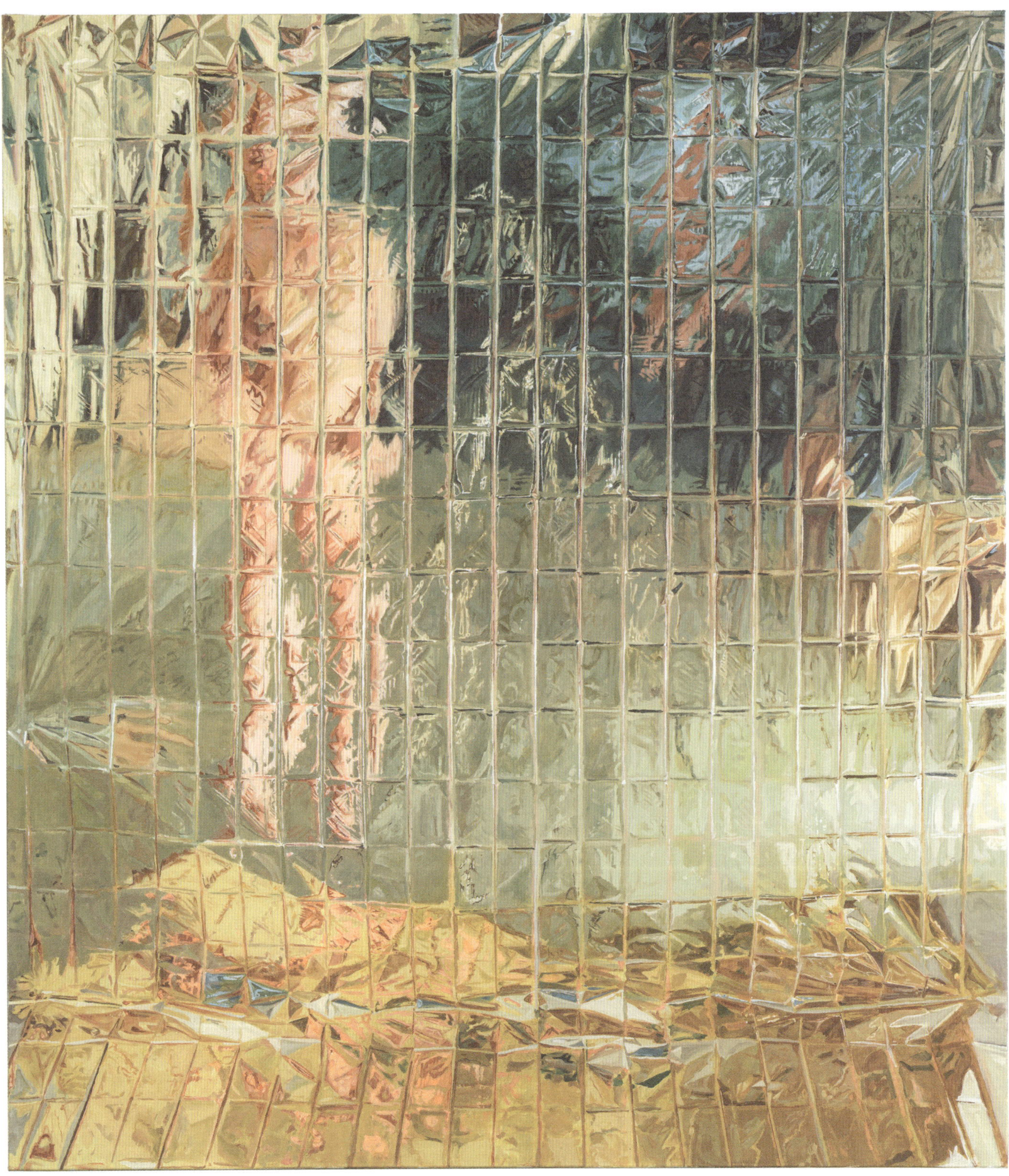

Reflections 

My friend Leonida counted 432 rectangles in the picture *Reflection of the Studio on Gold Foil*. I did not recount, because if she says so, it must be right. The rectangles on foil were created by folding them for wrapping. I painted them as I saw them. The geometric structure of these "tiles" and the distorted reflections that emerge from them, give the painting a modernist impression. Especially if you look at individual "tiles", you might think that the picture is a puzzle of paintings from the modernist period. As they were created using the same procedure I normally use, I firmly assert that this was not my intention; I did not try to ironize modernism or comment on it at all (at least not consciously). Nevertheless, it is entertaining to discover and observe these fragments.

44

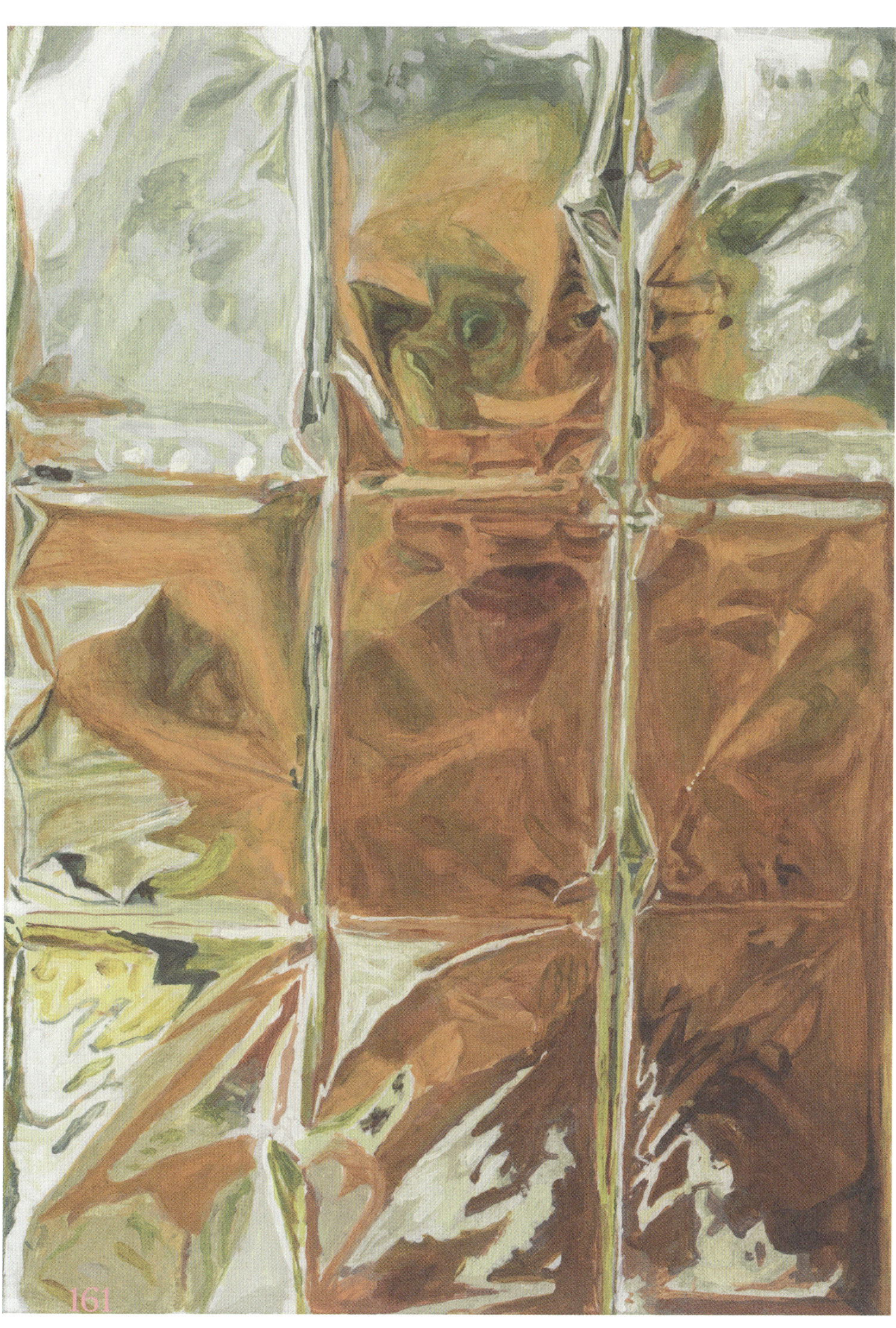

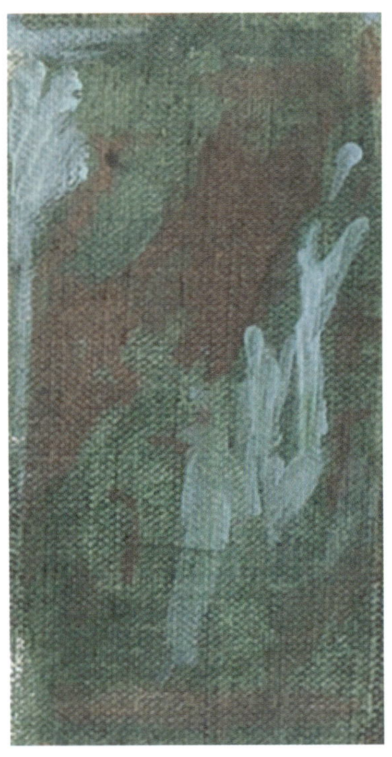

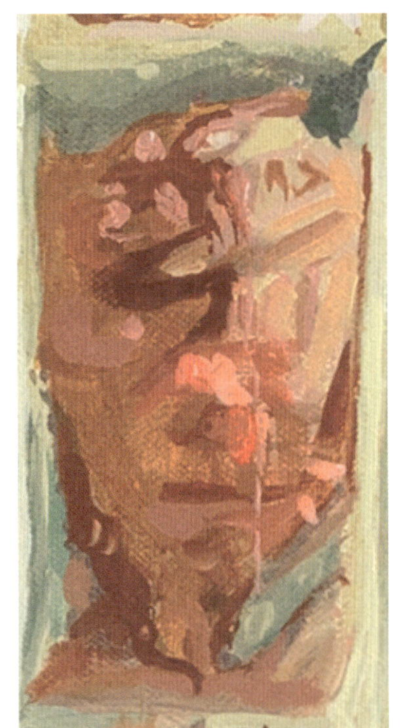

L

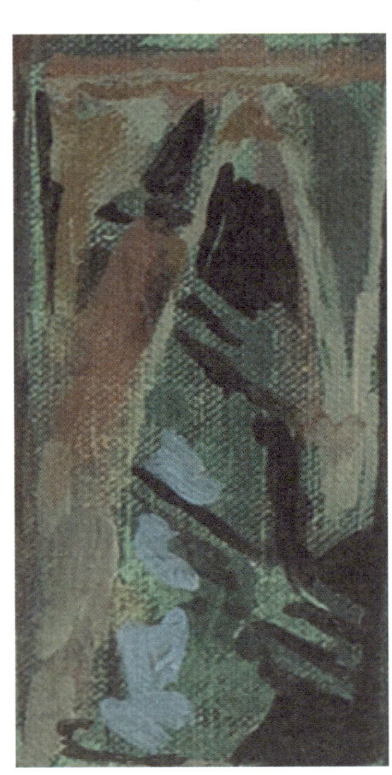

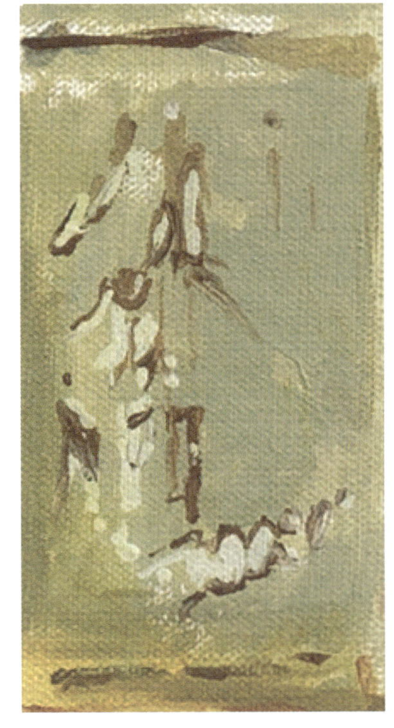

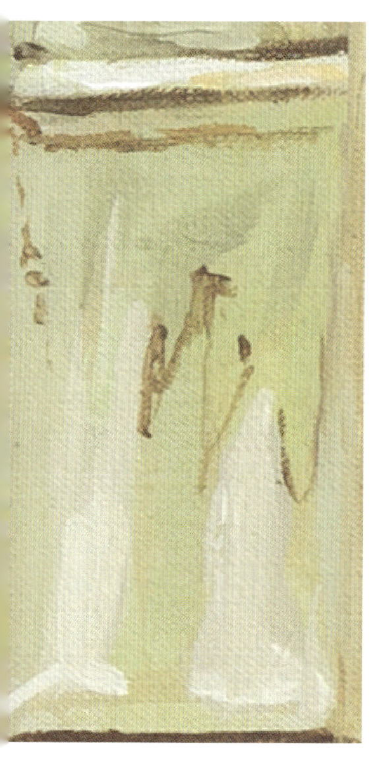

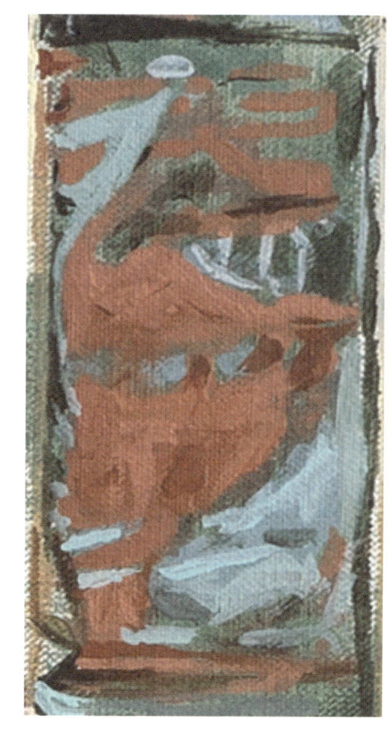

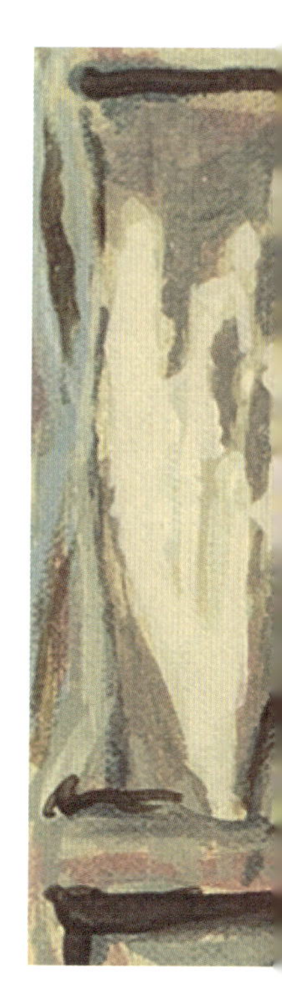

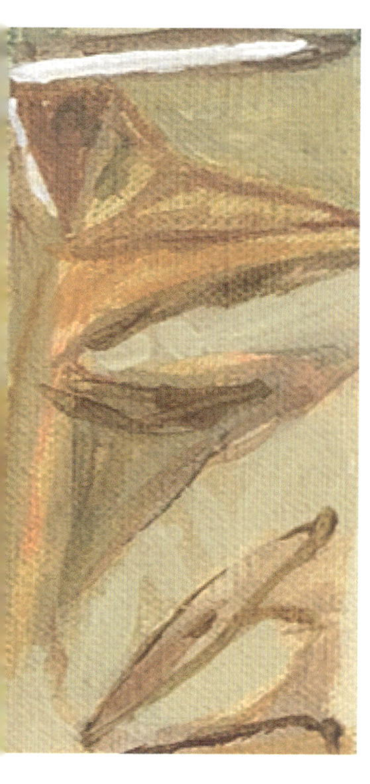

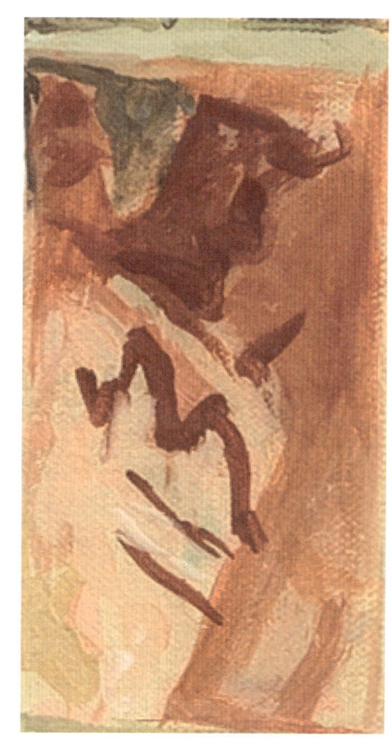

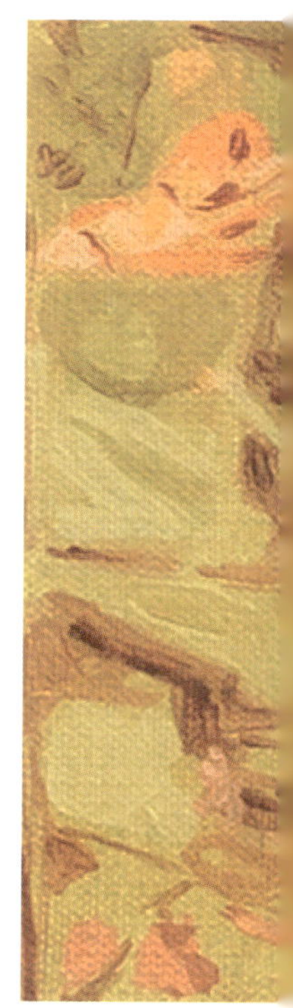

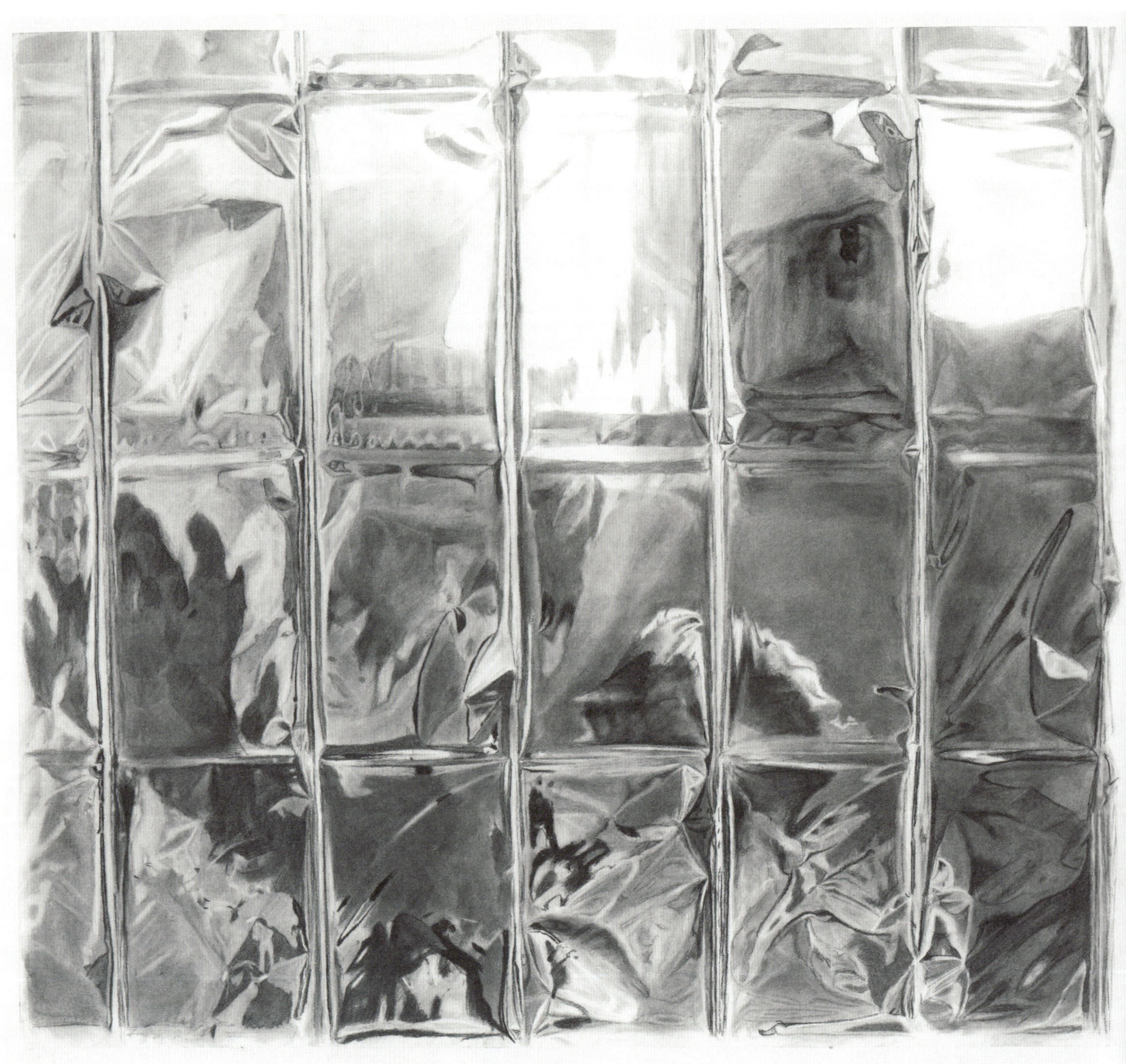

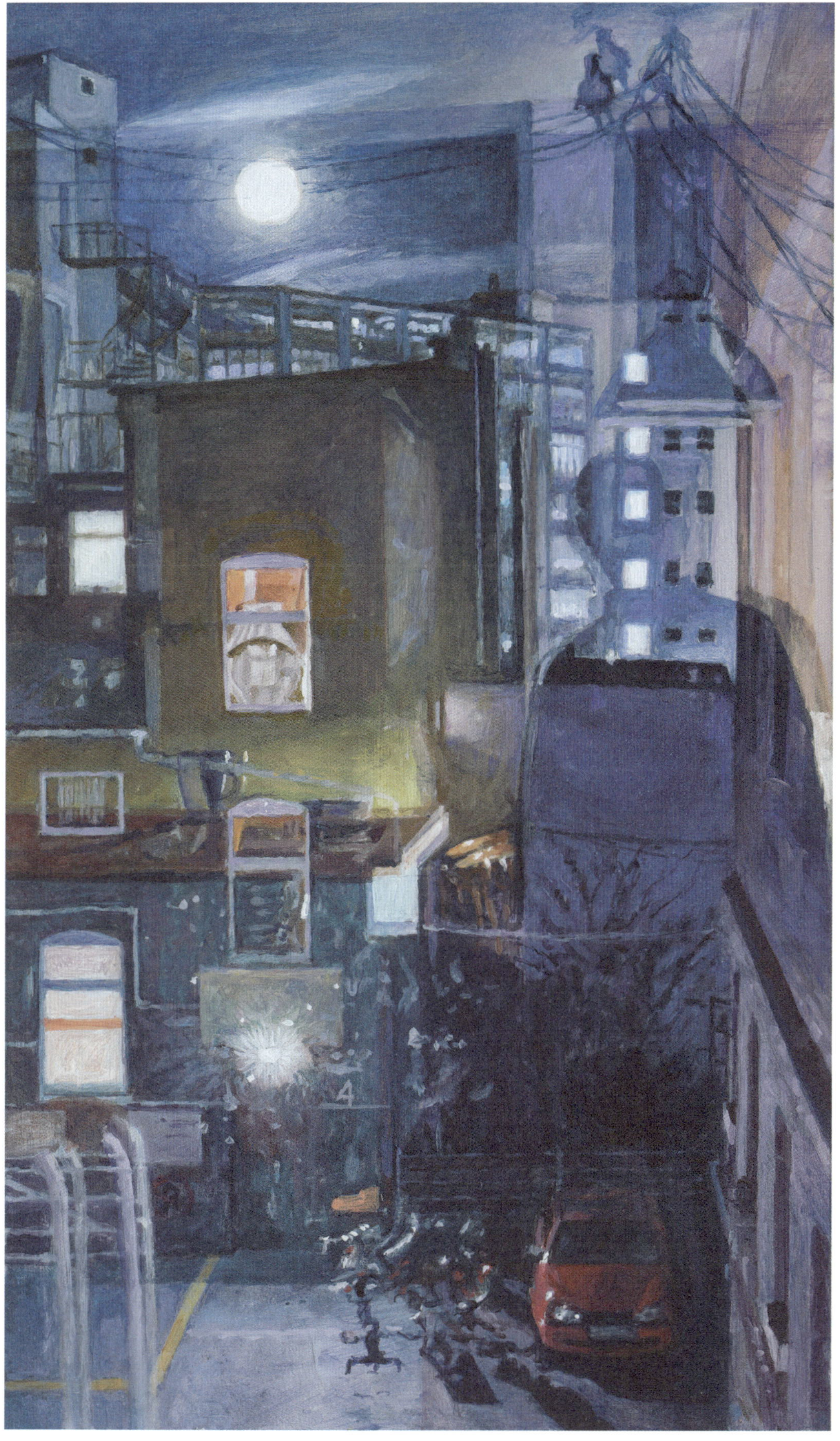

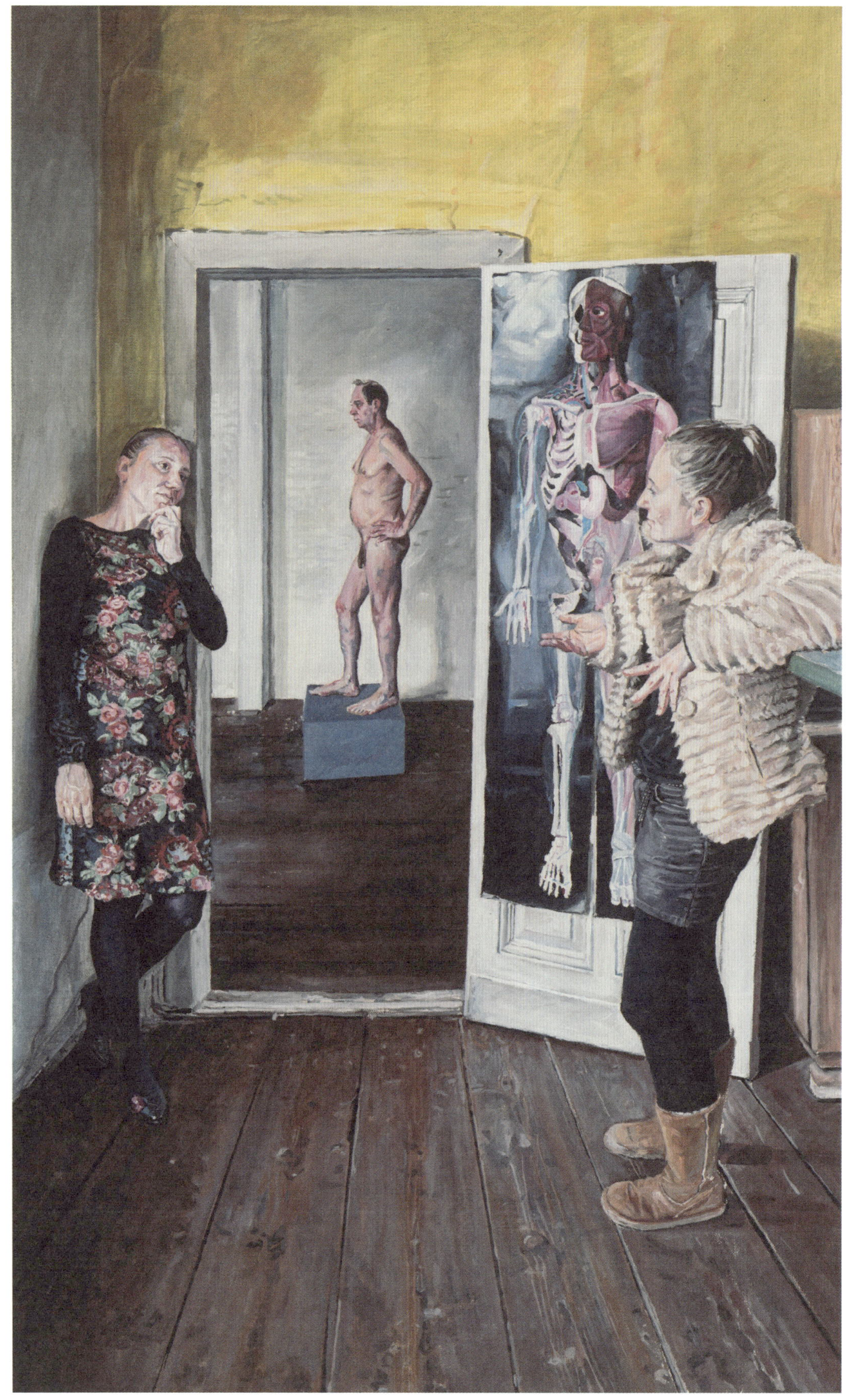

## 45

Studio Visit

It can be said without exaggeration that almost all visits to my studio are neatly registered in my paintings. For very few friends and acquaintances a role has not yet been found, a reason to be painted. But this does not mean that one day also those people will not be painted after all. Painting is a solitary occupation, and my paintings need people. Therefore, a social gathering at the studio, even if it's just a boozy evening, can be seen as part of the creative process. To use an analogy with the natural world, I sometimes feel like a flytrap symbiotically connected with the studio. Visitors like to come, attracted by the atmosphere of the space, without suspecting that sooner or later they will have to pose. Sometimes this lasts only a short time, sometimes it drags on for months. Of course, everyone leaves the studio alive, healthy and lively, so that the comparison with the flytrap might be unfounded after all.

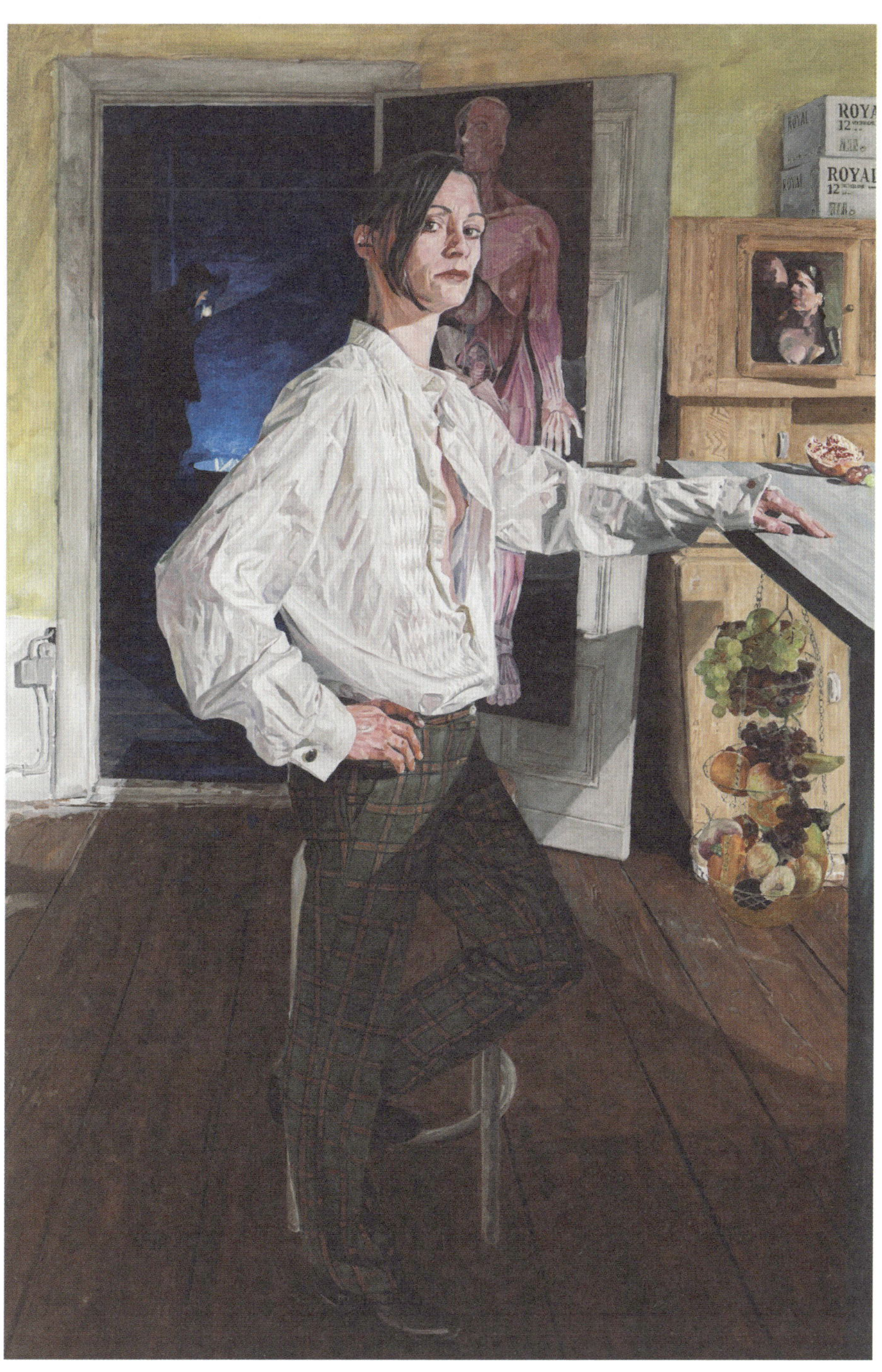

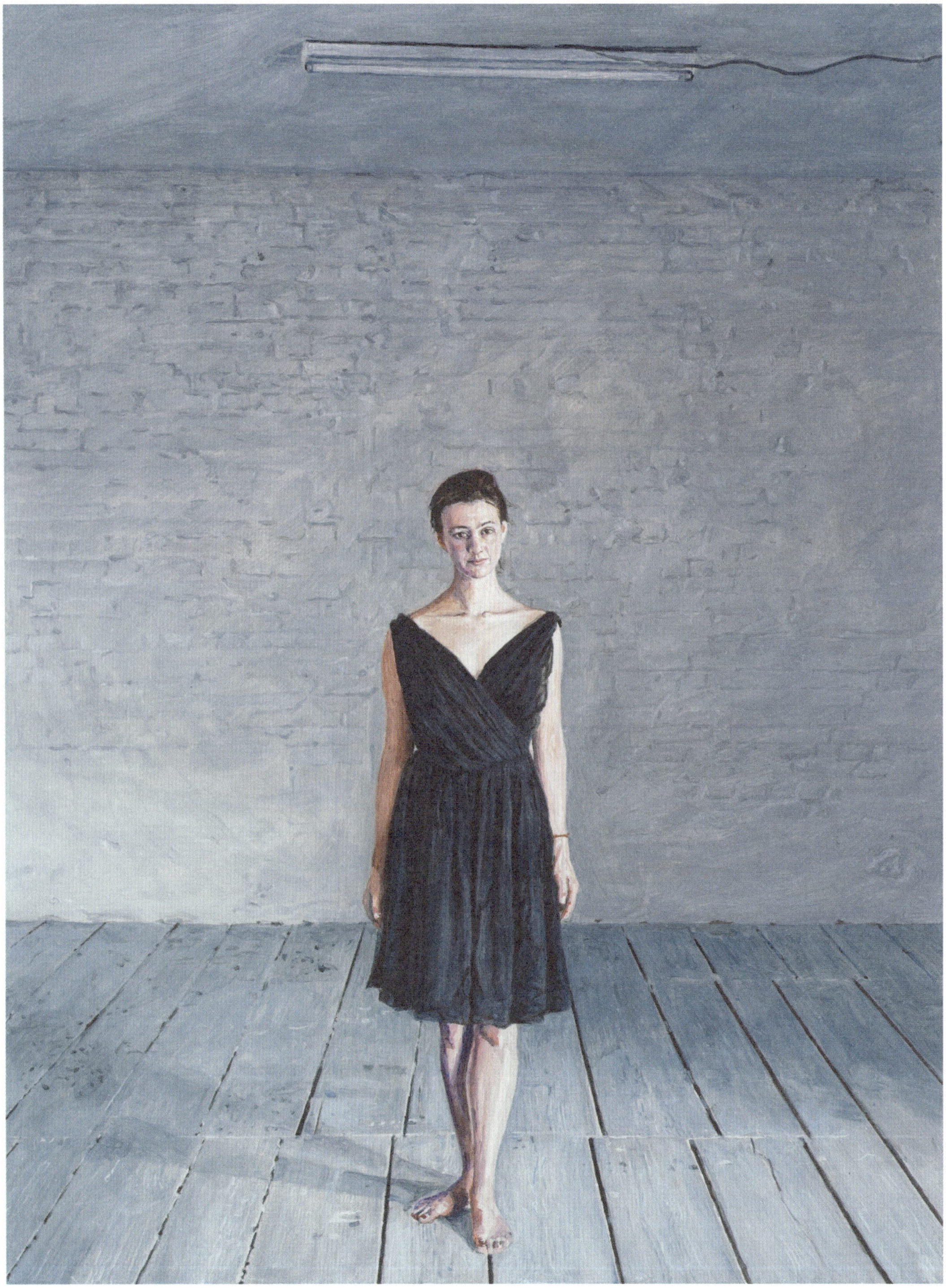

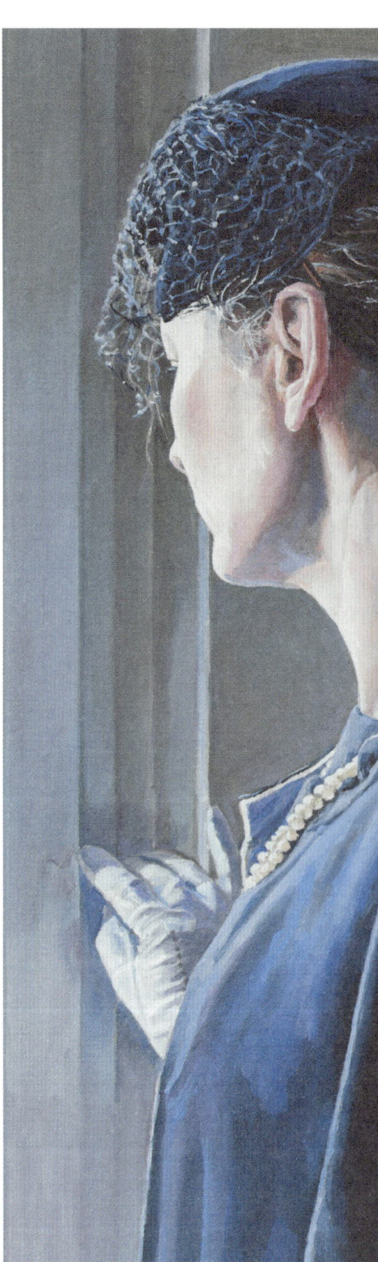

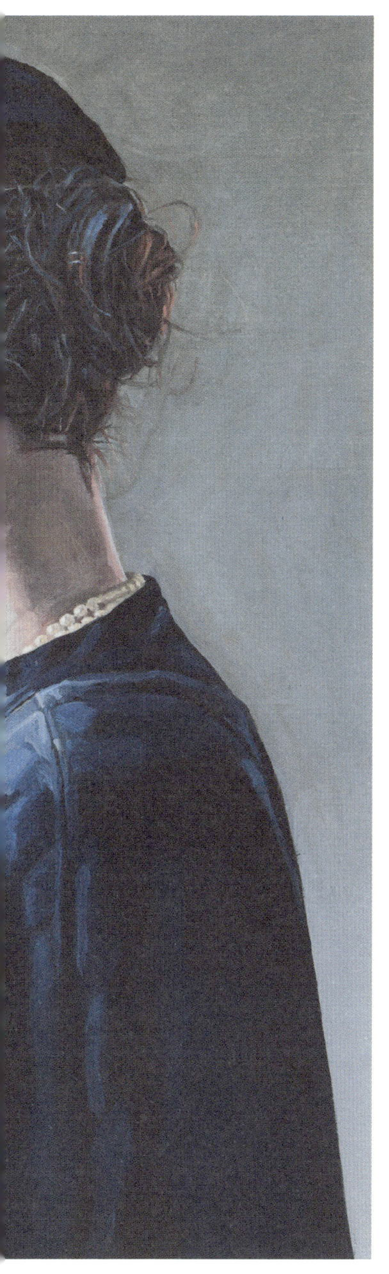

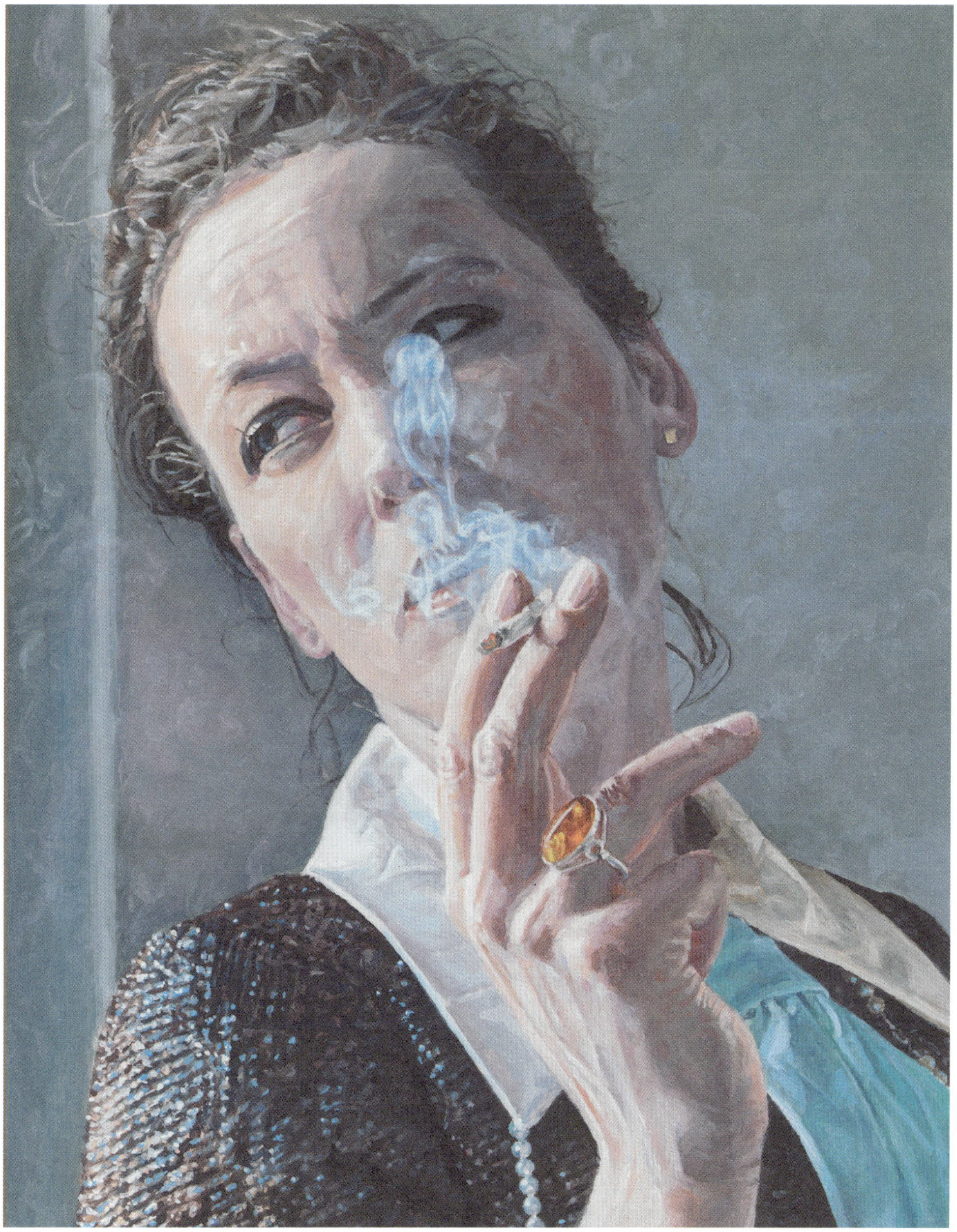

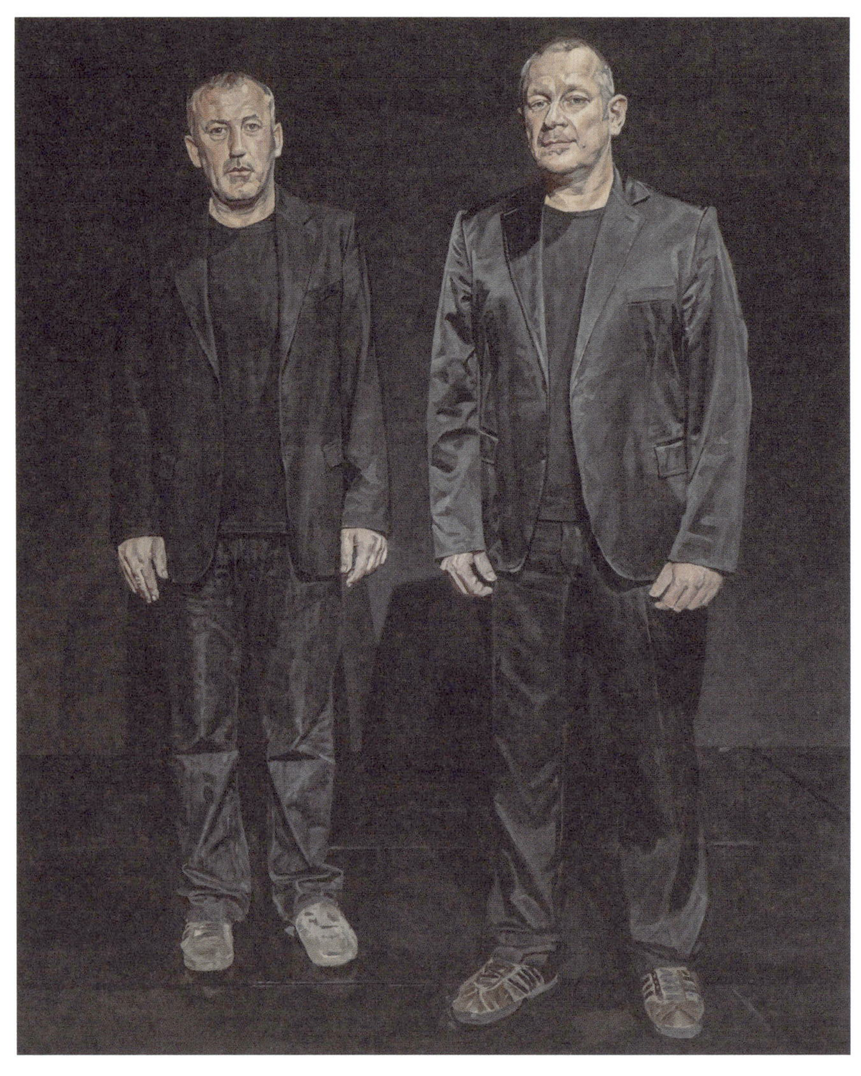

180

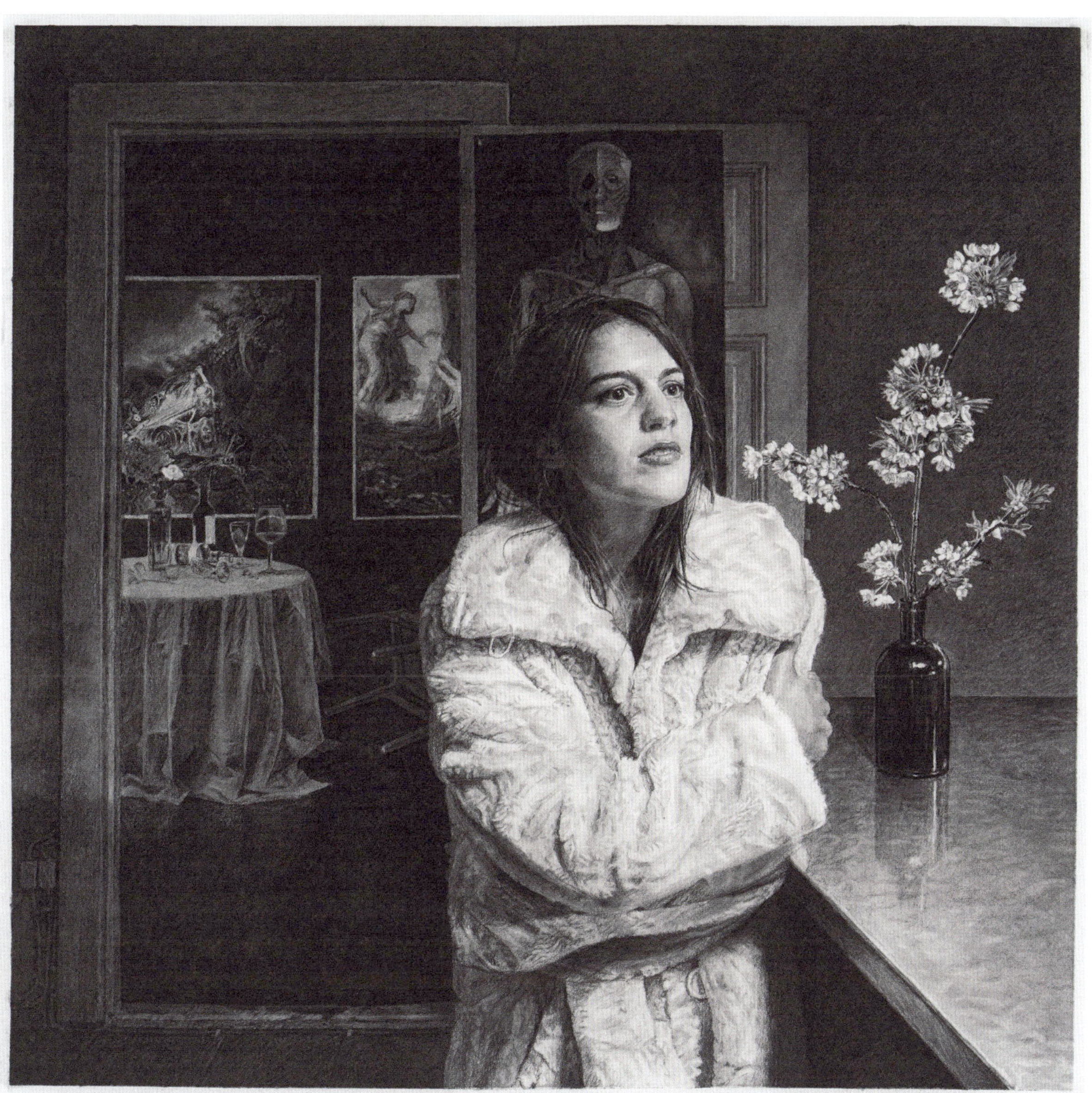

10

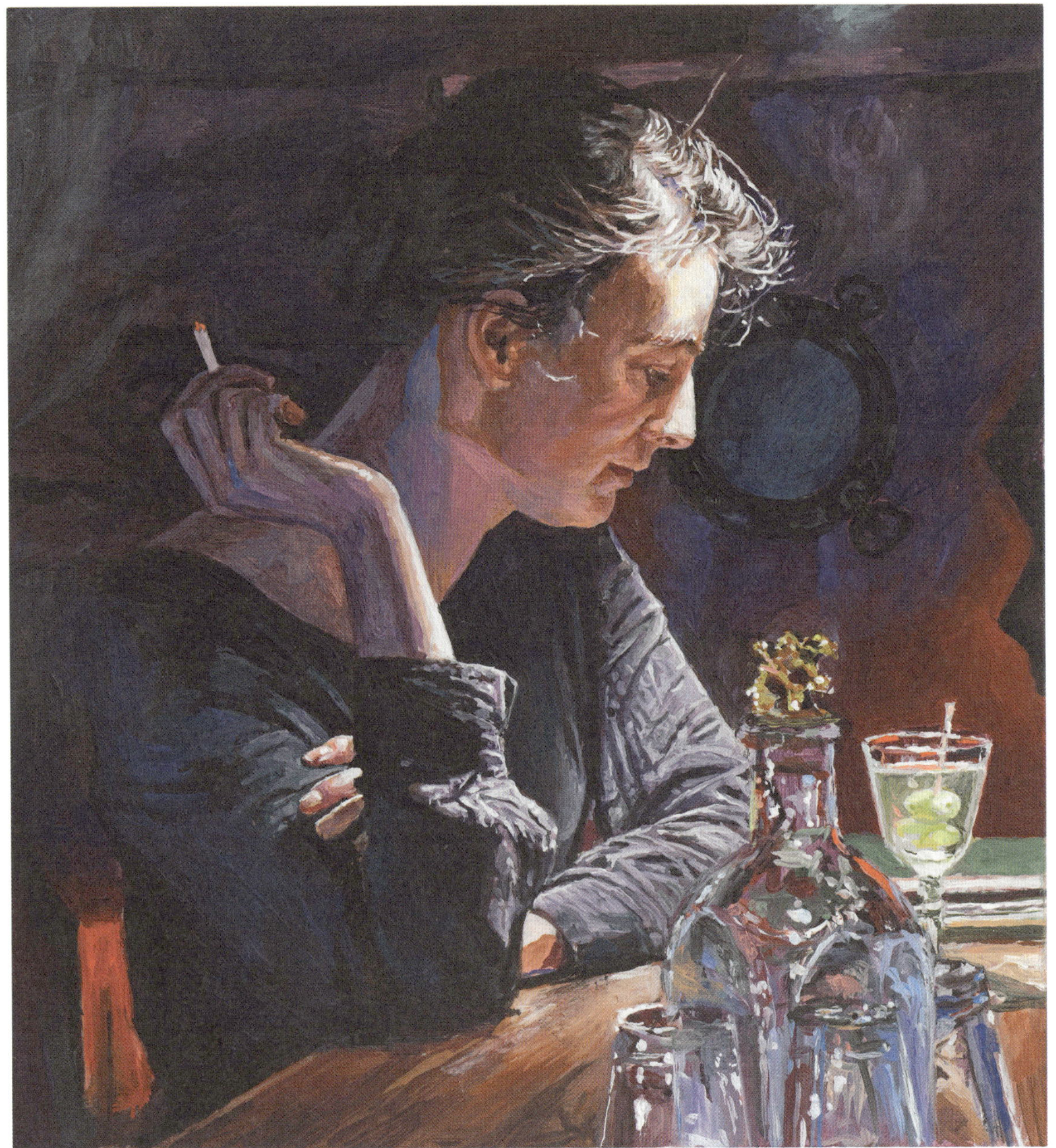

181

The Bar

In the twilight, thousands of tiny reflections flicker like stars in a reddish universe. On glasses and bottles, on shakers and jiggers, on spouts of the liqueur bottles neatly lined up on the counter, on the rest of the metal and glassware used by the supremely trained bar staff as they measure, shake, mix, decant and pour out liquids in different colours (some of them steaming, some of them flickering with bluish flames). The bottles with intoxicating contents on the shelf beyond the counter radiate earthy hues. Amid all these shimmering highlights, lazy cigarette smoke floats and meanders like cosmic fog in a photo from the Hubble Telescope. Beneath the lights, hovering low over the counter, the wisps of smoke shine up and obscure, as if with a veil, the beautiful face I'm watching. Faces change from evening to evening, from glass to glass, which mostly inspires me to melancholically meditate on transience.

54

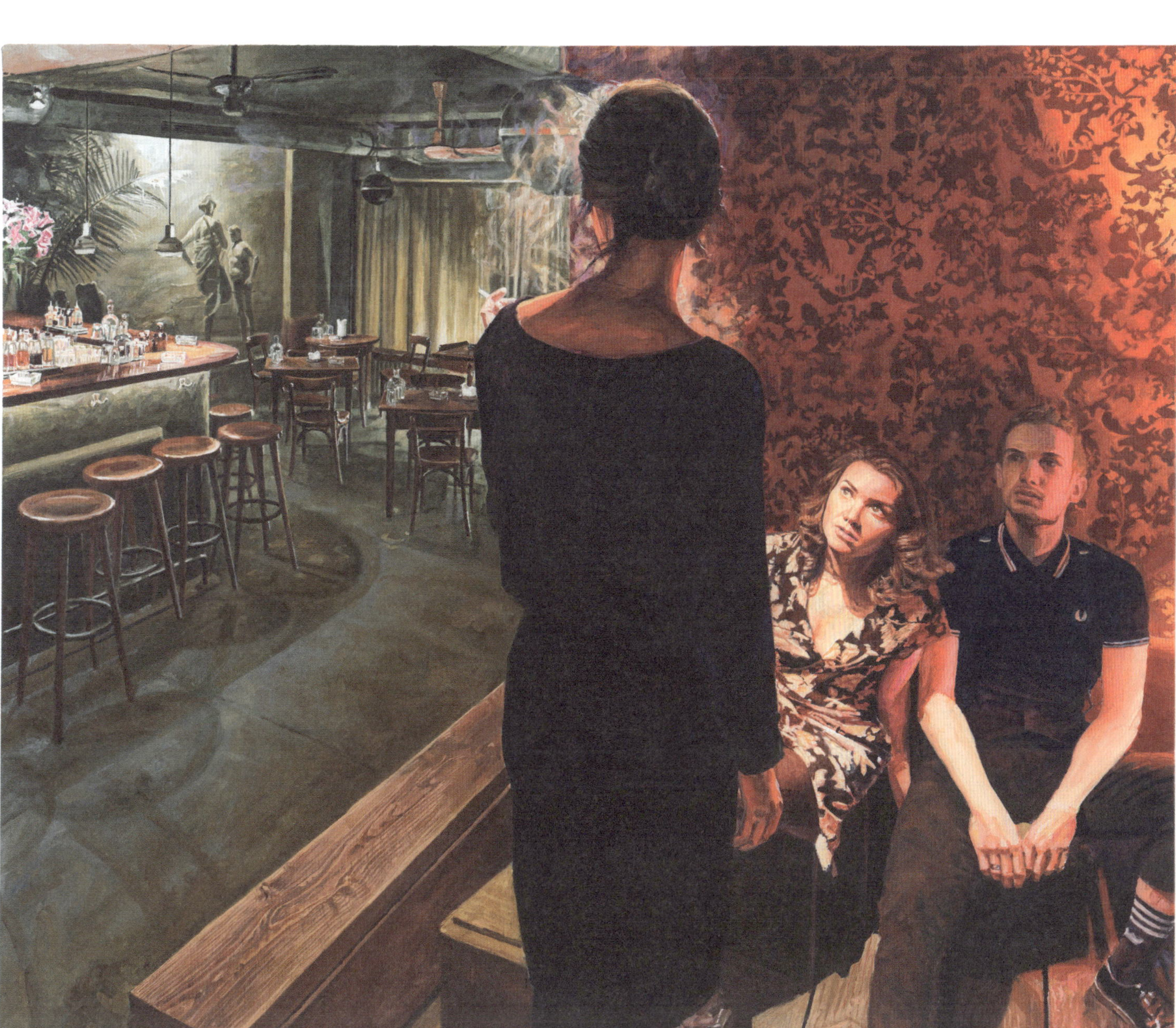

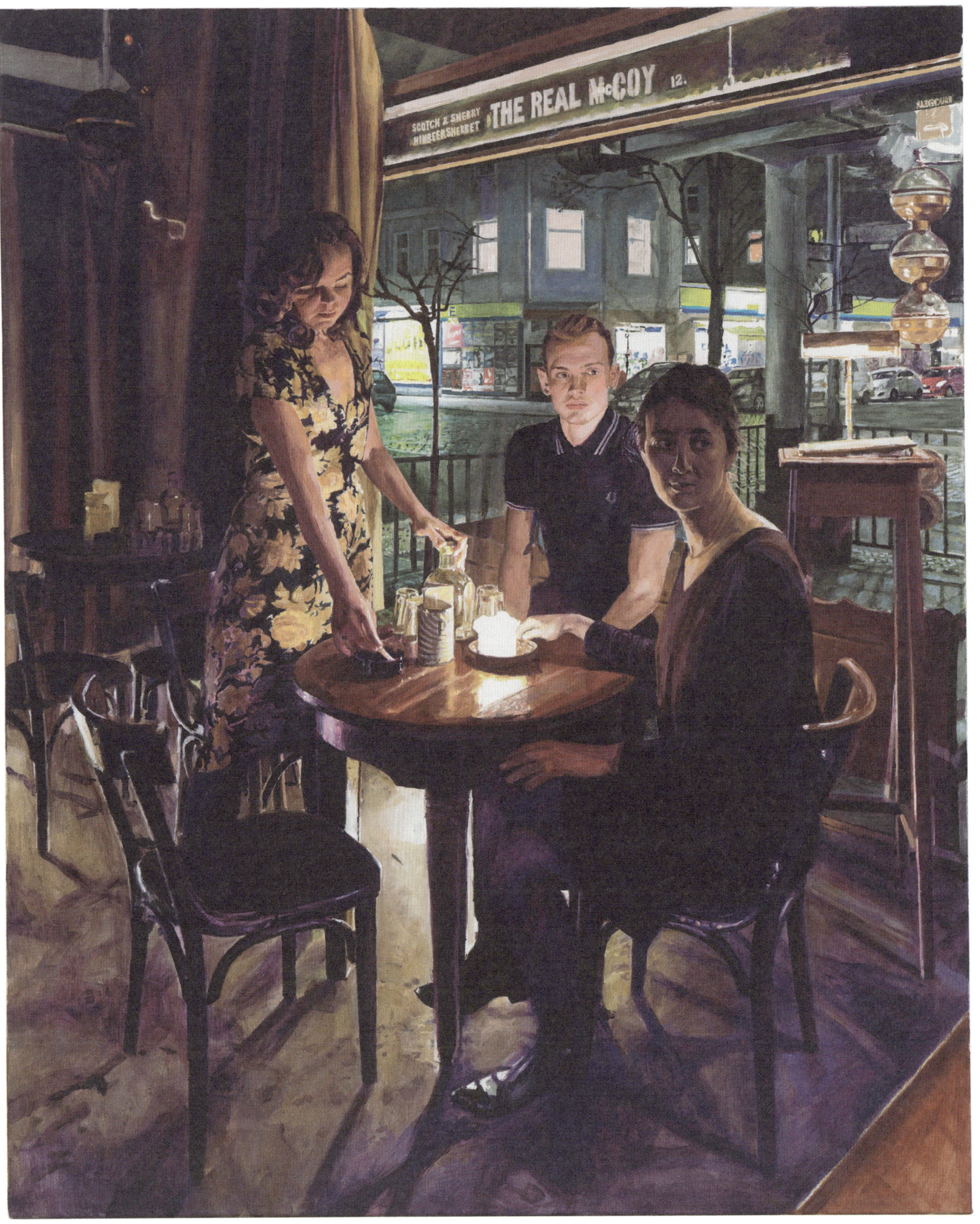
SCOTCH & SHERRY
HIMBEERSHERBET
THE REAL McCOY 12.

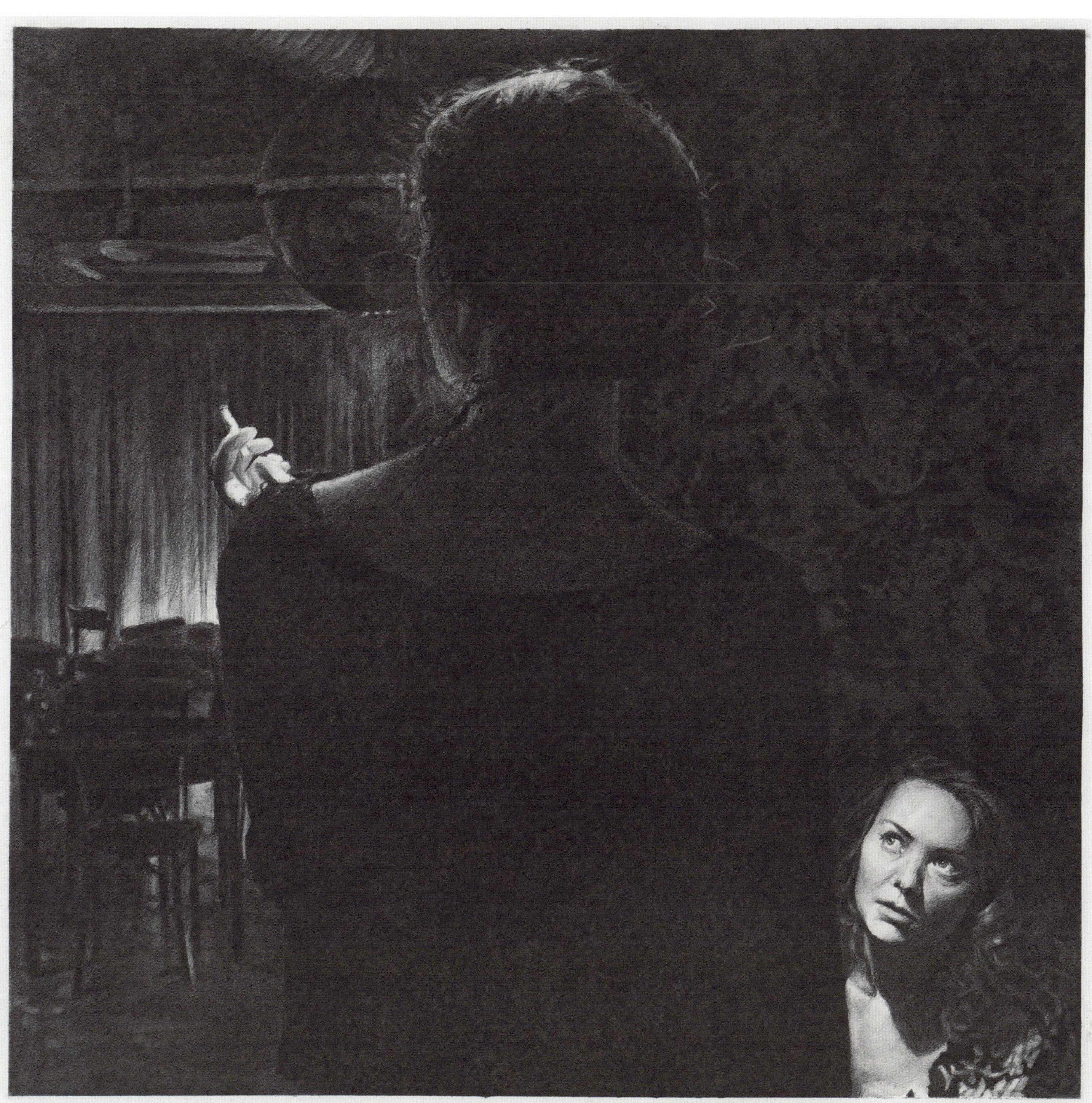

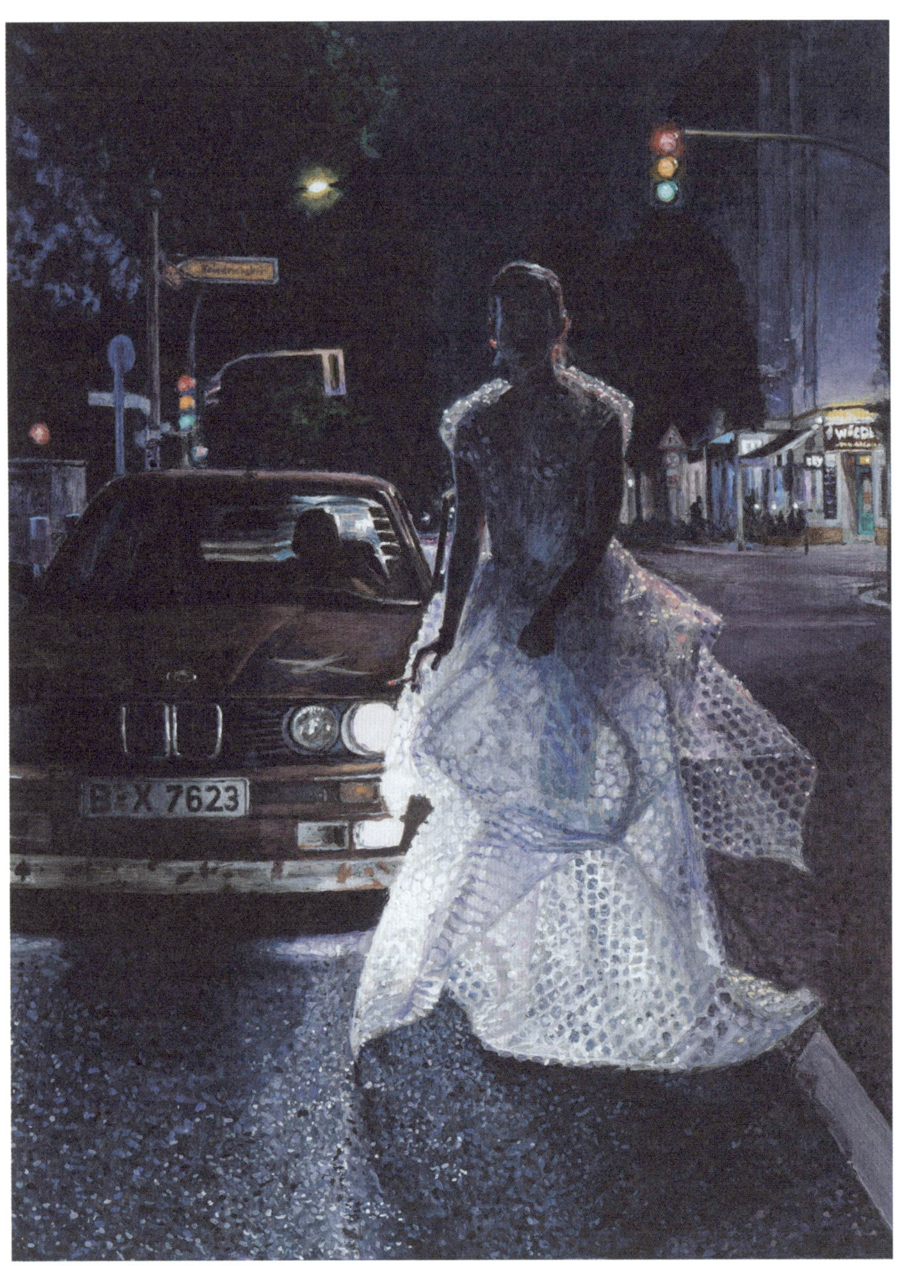



183

Night Light Melancholy

Night lights fascinated me even before I started hanging around the city at night as a teenager. The city was where I discovered life. And movies. Movies in which it is night and raining and neon lights spread over the wet asphalt in endless shades. In contrast to the darkness of the night, the colors of these lights are intense. Terribly cool movie characters, only partially illuminated, emerge from the darkness. Yes, that's what I always wanted to paint, and I don't know why it took so long for that desire to surface. Certainly, there were other things I wanted to paint. And I also felt that I was not yet up to the task as a painter. For a long time, I hesitated. But now I believe I am capable of painting a night scene of an intersection in the rain, where the headlights of cars and traffic lights are reflected in the wet asphalt.

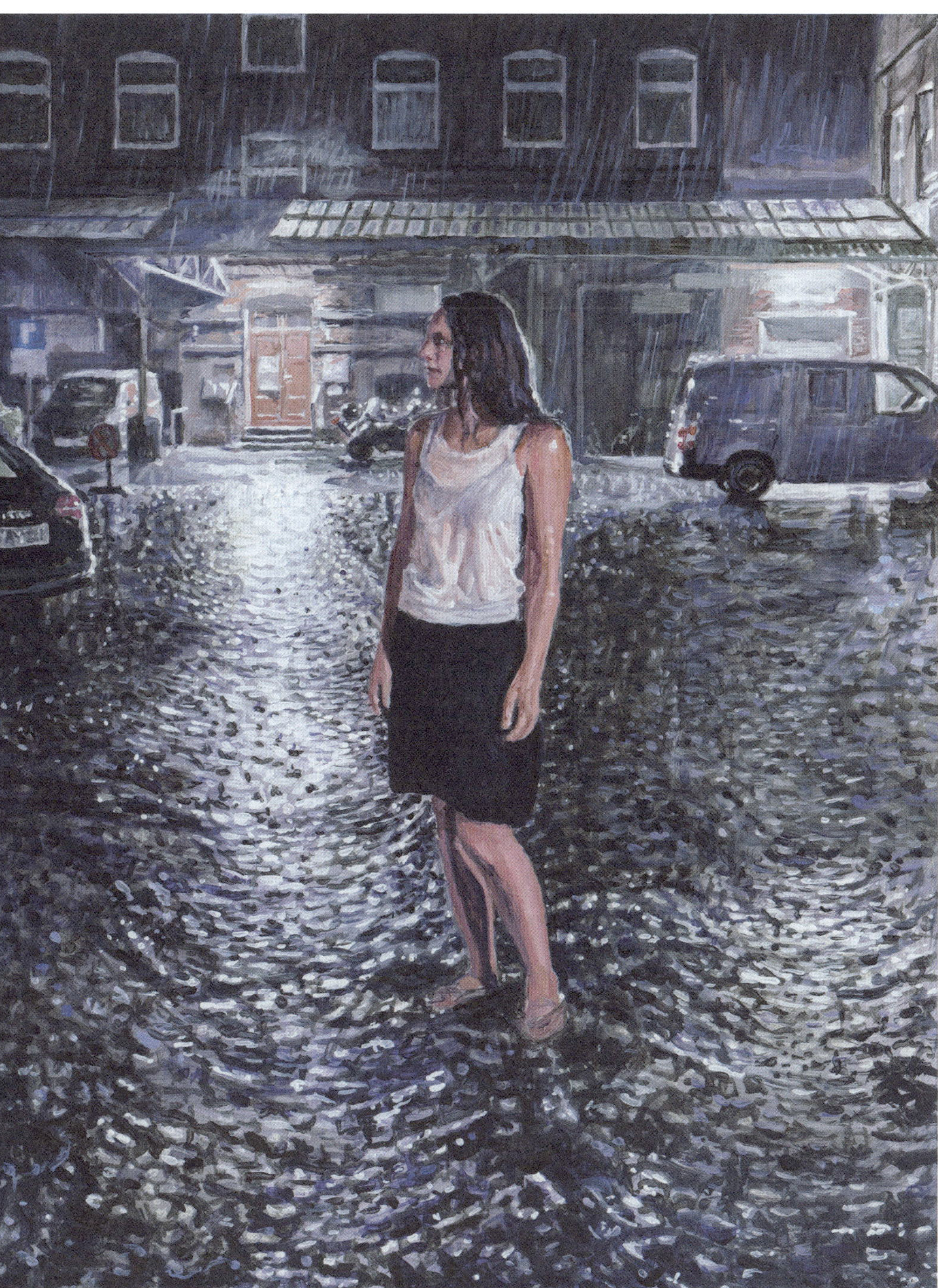

49

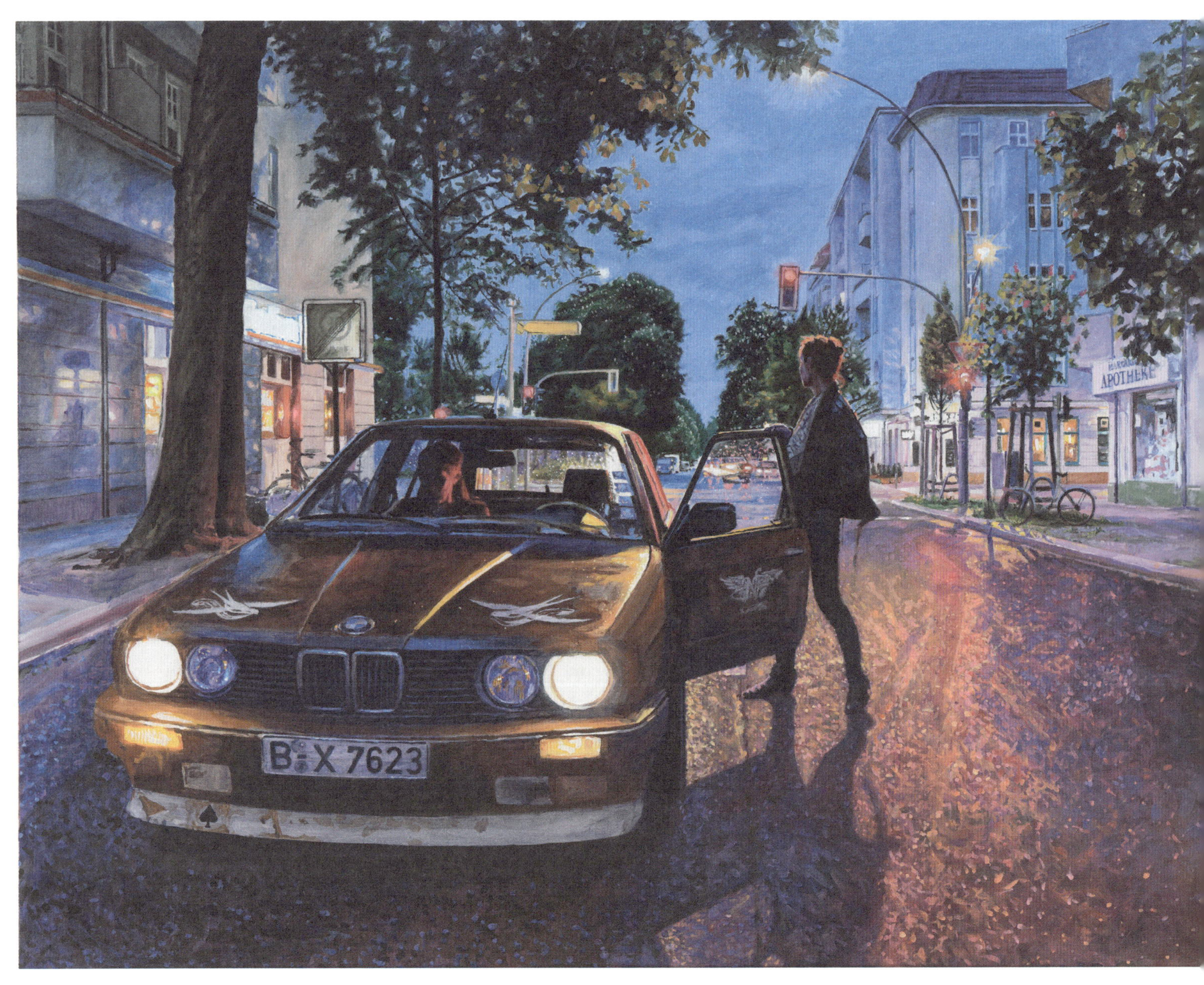
APOTHEKE
B X 7623

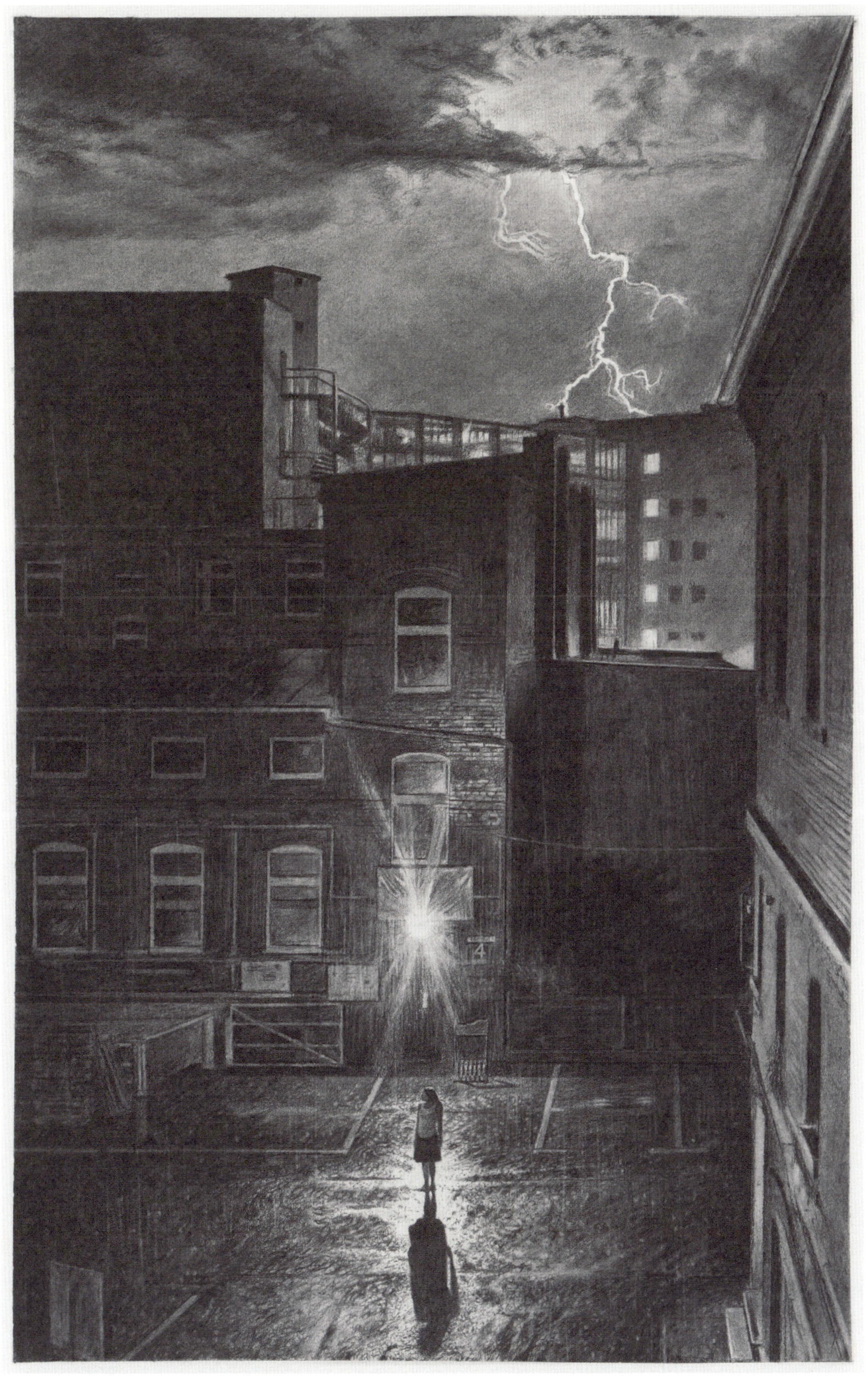



179

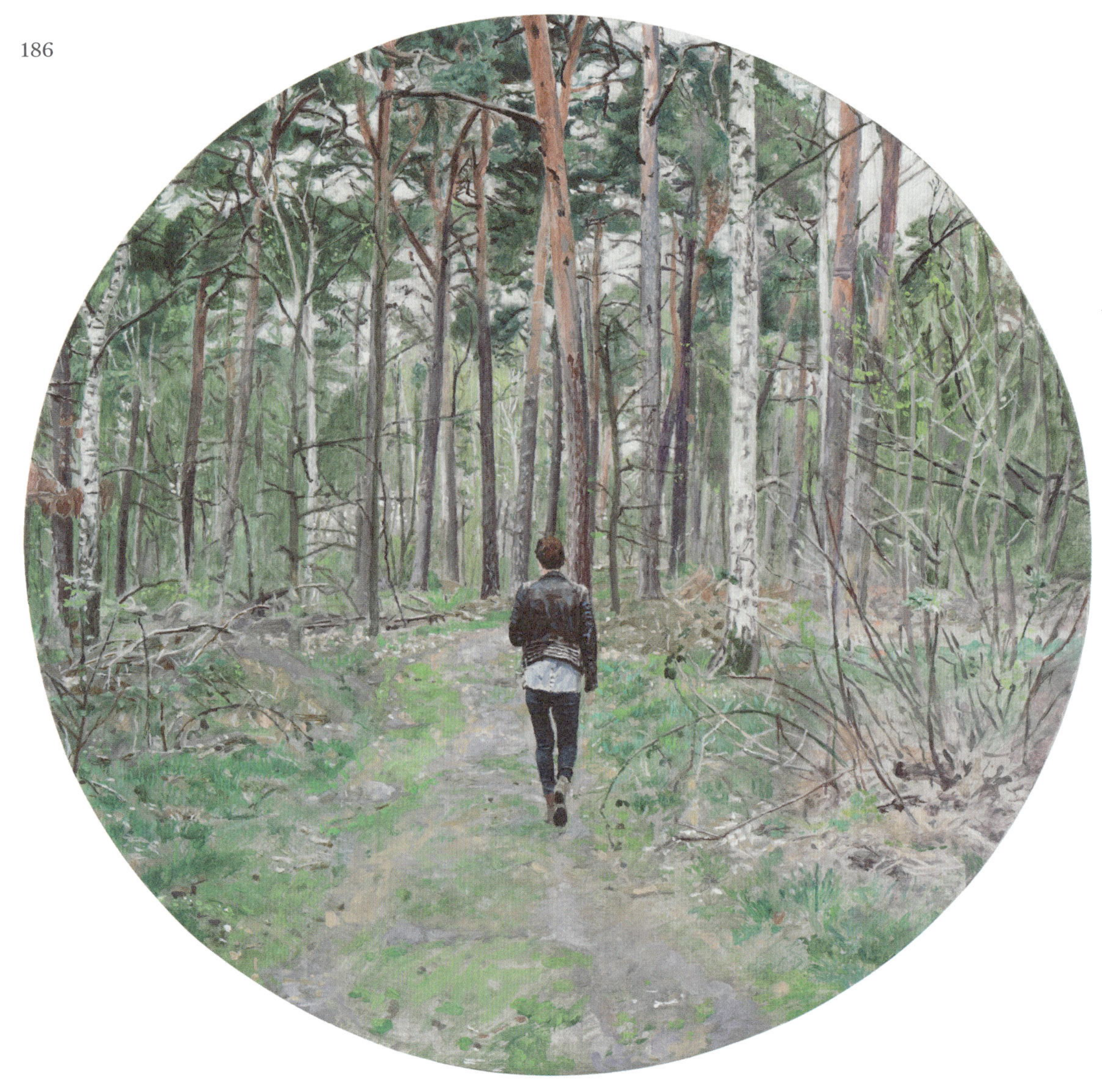

Excursion

I dreamed that I was on a road trip through Brandenburg with the singer of the band Victims of Women Intolerance. I do not know where this name came from, the Internet could not confirm the existence of such a band. Possibly it has to do with something deeper, which I would rather not go into now. And the singer didn't look like any of the few I know either. Actually, he had no particular features. We drove off from his weekend cottage, on narrow, tree-lined country roads so typical of Brandenburg. As we drove - partly through the effect of movement and partly because this simply occurs in dreams - the shapes I perceived began to merge and flow into each other. For example, a part of the landscape overgrown with trees would suddenly take on the shape of a house or a car, clearly recognizable, as if these shapes were wrapped in something with a printed landscape image. I am telling all this because it reminded me very much of the reflection of the forest on the polished body of the Mercedes in my picture *Autumn Excursion*.



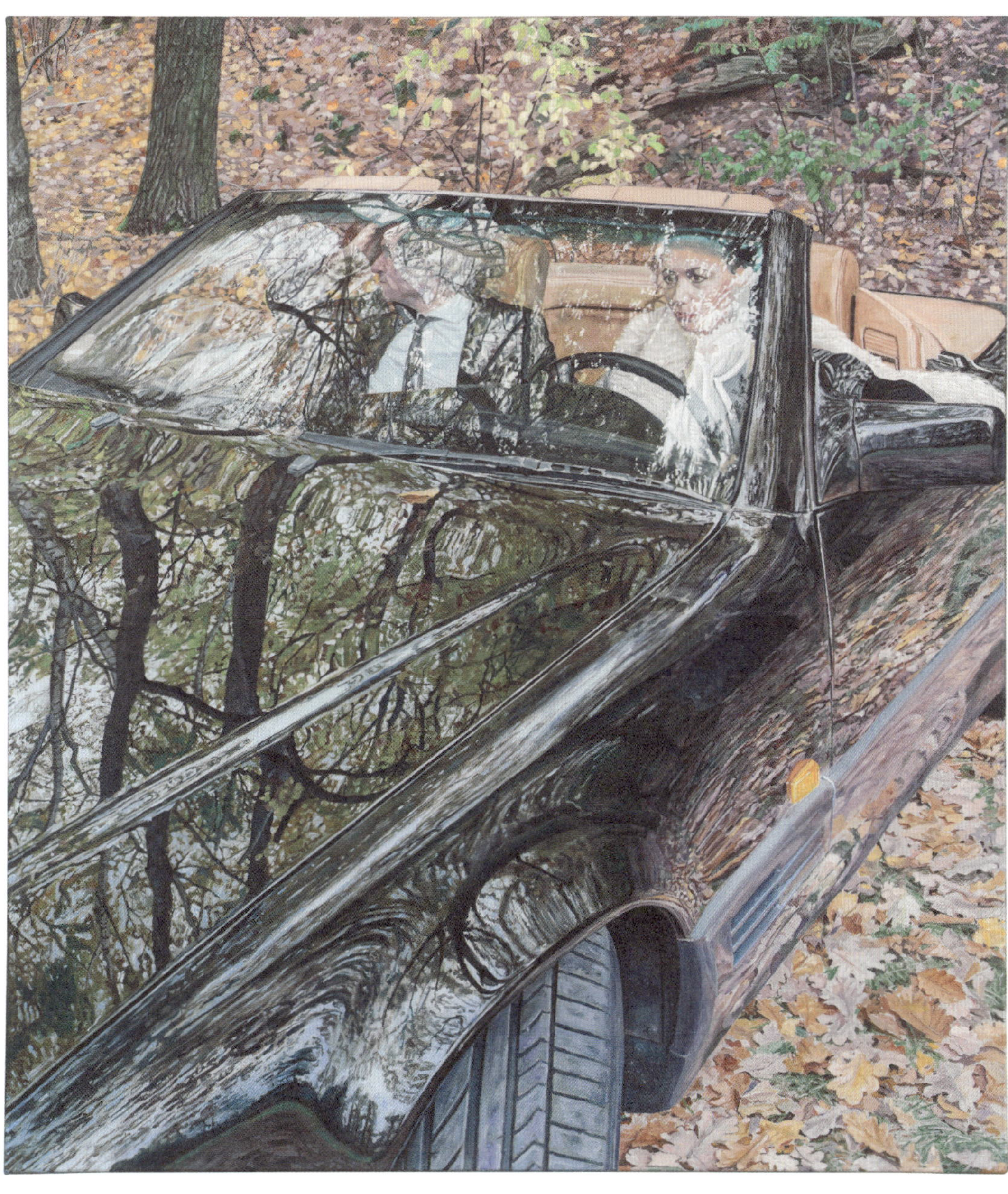

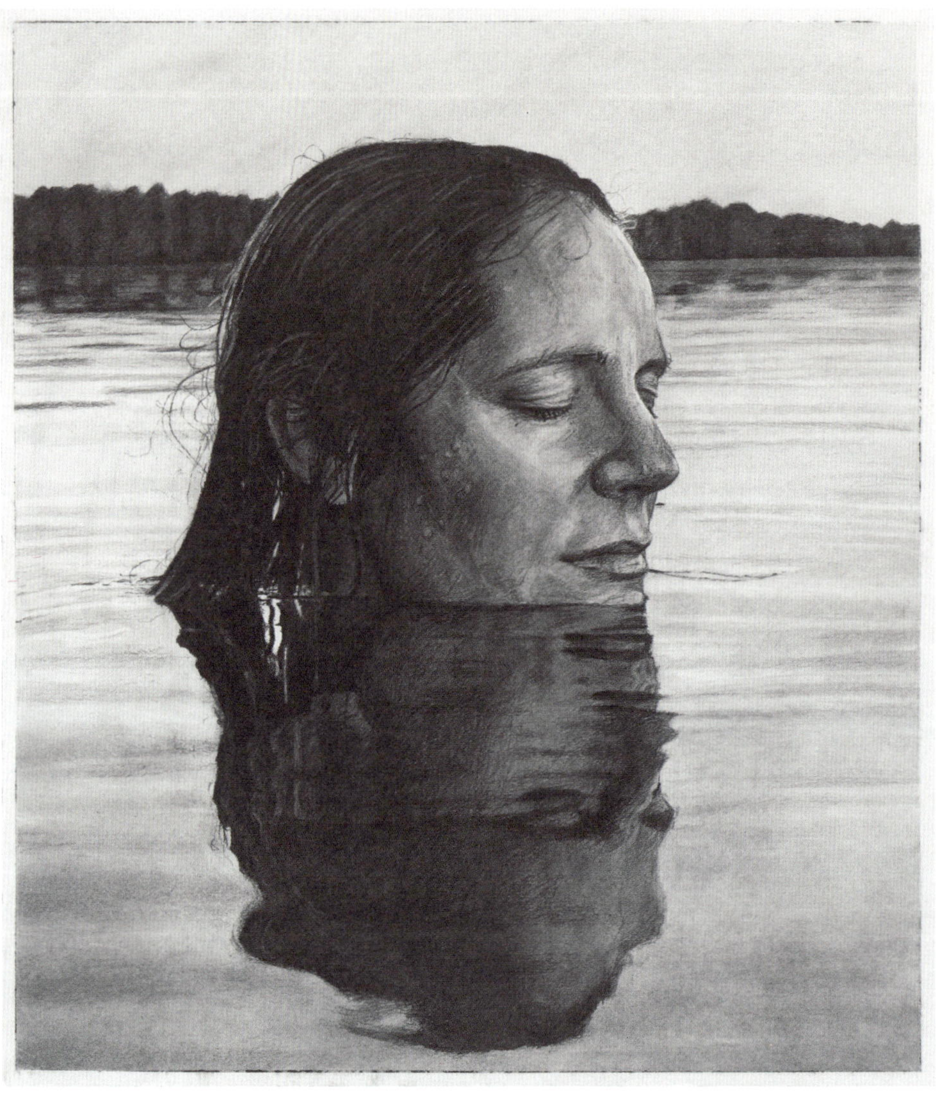

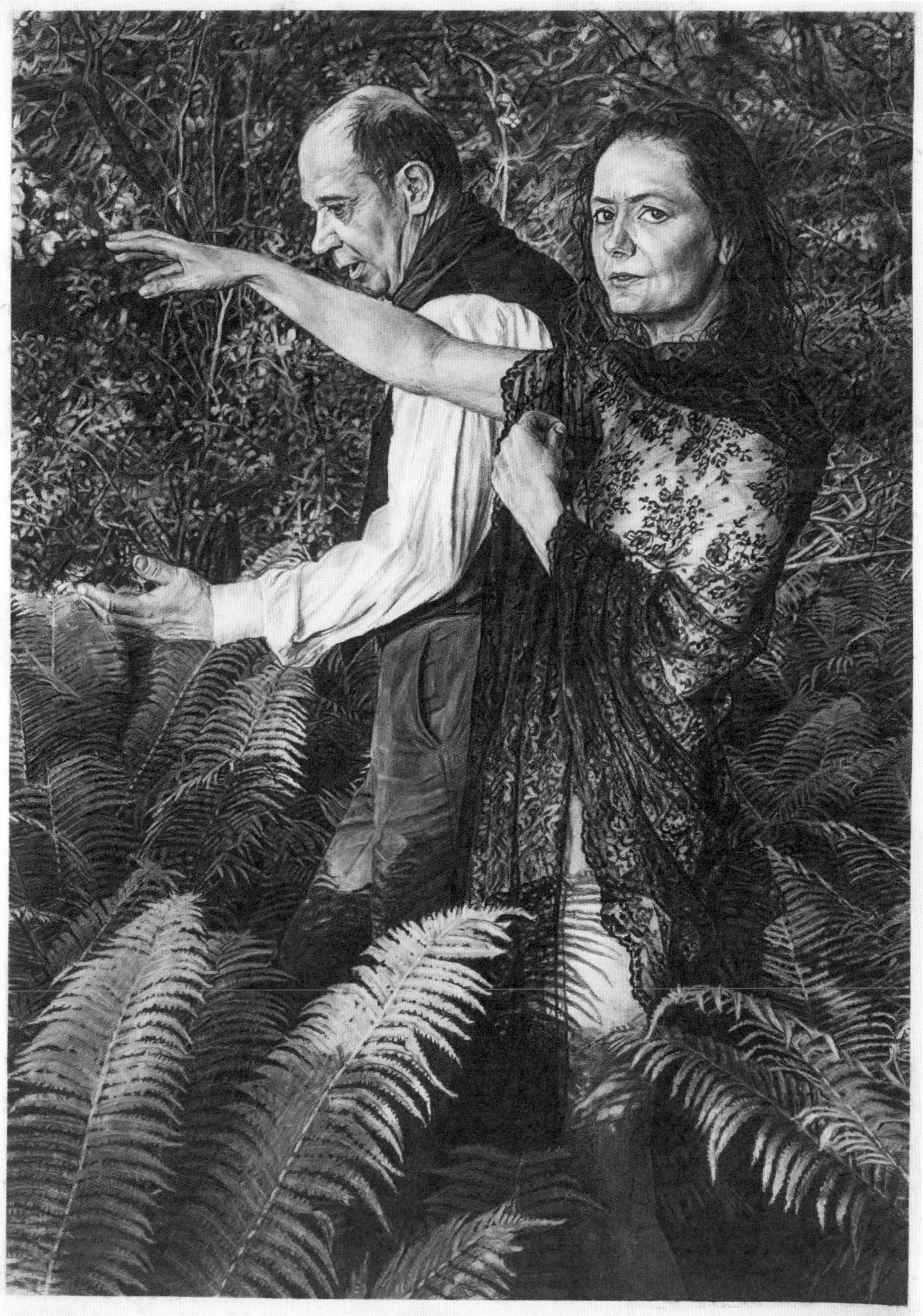

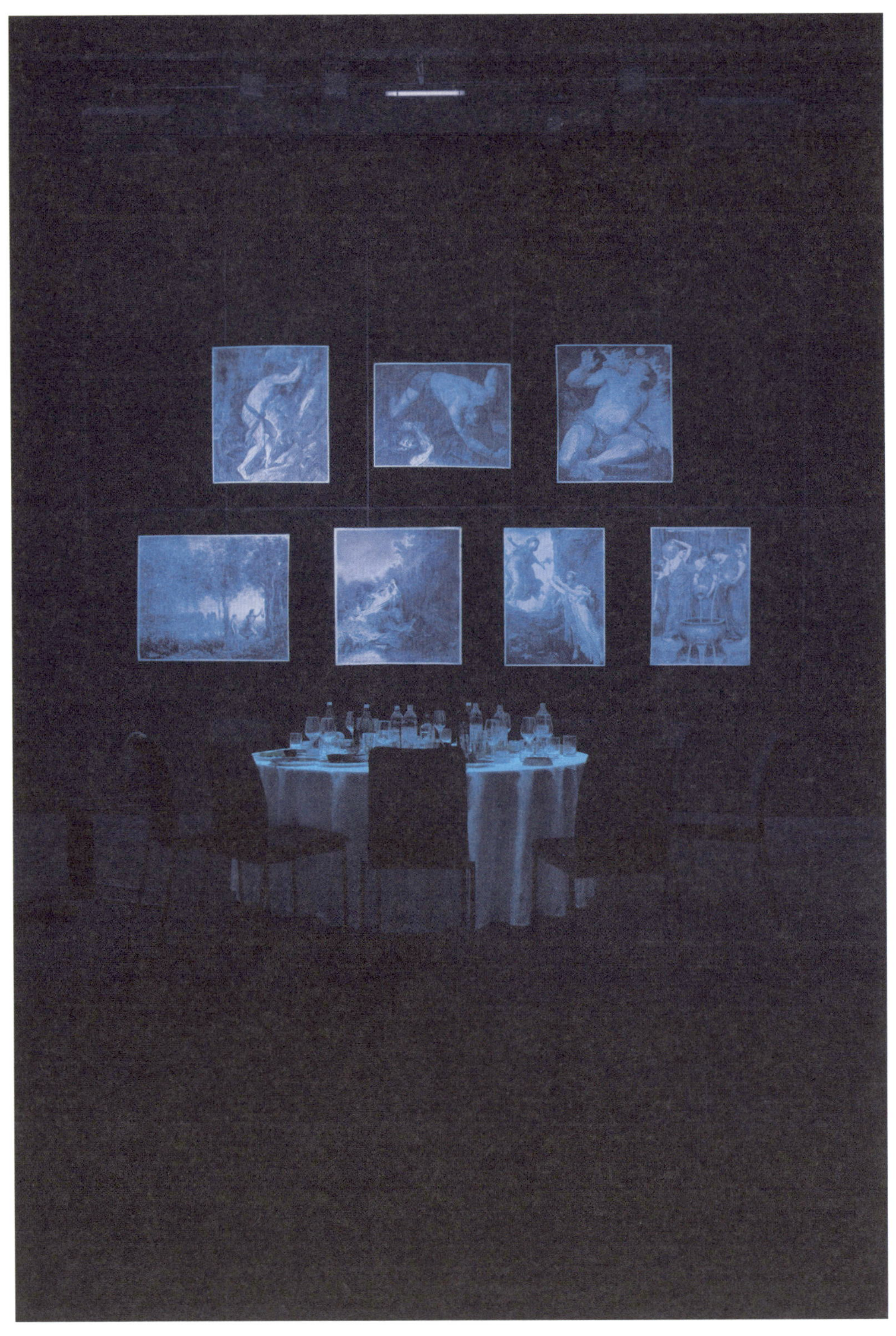

I wanted to have a party in my studio titled *Underworld*. I planned to illuminate the room with the ultraviolet, so-called black light. On the walls, charcoal drawings on paper with white areas radiating a bluish, unnatural glow in the dark under the ultraviolet light. The drawings were supposed to be copies of paintings by Old Masters with scenes of the underworld from the Greek mythology. I imagined how the party guests, dressed only in white or black, obligatory for this evening, would move through the studio in the cigarette smoke mist like flickering ghosts. That was actually a banal club or disco scene, but it still seemed to me that it could be somehow mystical.

But when I started the first drawing, I realized that despite my presumption that I had enough experience in my profession, I was still childishly naive. The time that had to be invested into making of a faithful copy indefinitely postponed the date of the planned party into the future. The desire to organize it also slowly waned. Nevertheless, I continued the work, even though I had a feeling I was doing something totally absurd. Why on Earth am I wasting time on copies? To have someone nickname me "Rembrandt"? And will this concept survive if there is no party? I know that a "real professional artist" would leave this tedious job to someone else to do it for him, and he would take up something more important during that time.

But working on these copies I began to enjoy the lack of sense and purpose of this enterprise. Moreover, I did not want to give up the pleasure: first, the work with charcoal, and second, the gradual "entering" into the original work used as a template. In the end, this experience has been like a descent into the underworld; if not a raucous party, it is still a way of conversing with those who no longer walk the surface of the Earth.

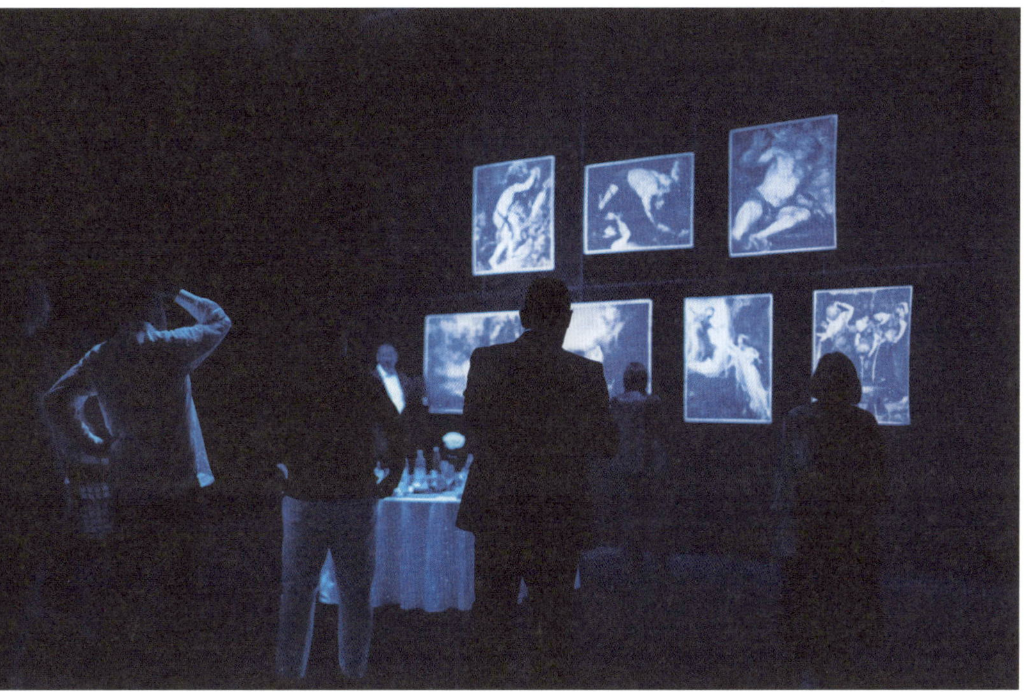

M

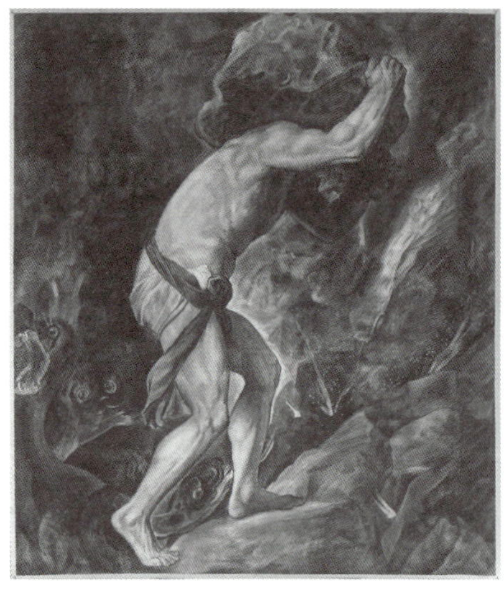

Sisyphus (after Titian),
charcoal drawing on paper,
110 x 95 cm, 2020
Original housed at
the Museodel Prado, Madrid

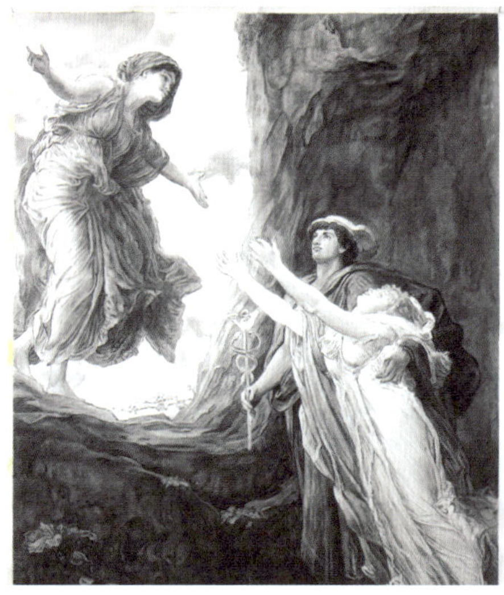

Return from Persephone
(after Frederic Leighton),
charcoal drawing on paper
110 x 80 cm, 2020
Original housed at Leeds
Art Gallery

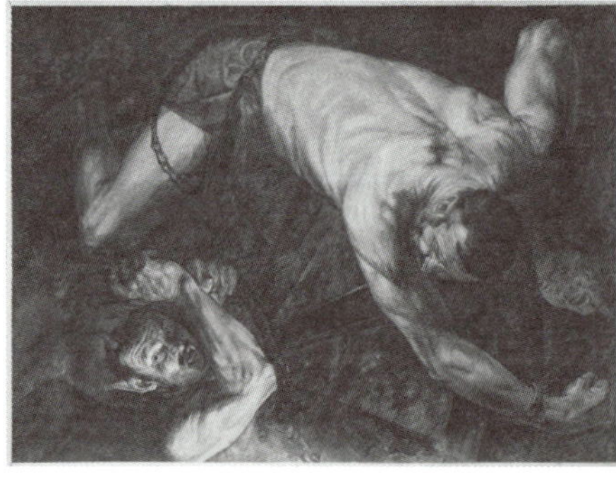

Ixion (after Jusepe de Ribera),
charcoal drawing on paper,
83 x 110 cm, 2020
Original housed at
Museo del Prado, Madrid

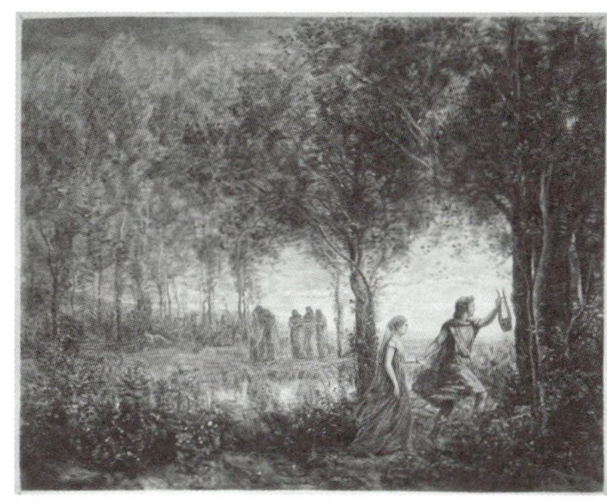

Orpheus leads Eurydice
out of the underworld,
charcoal drawing on paper,
102 x 125 cm, 2020
Original housed at the
Museum of Fine Arts, Houston

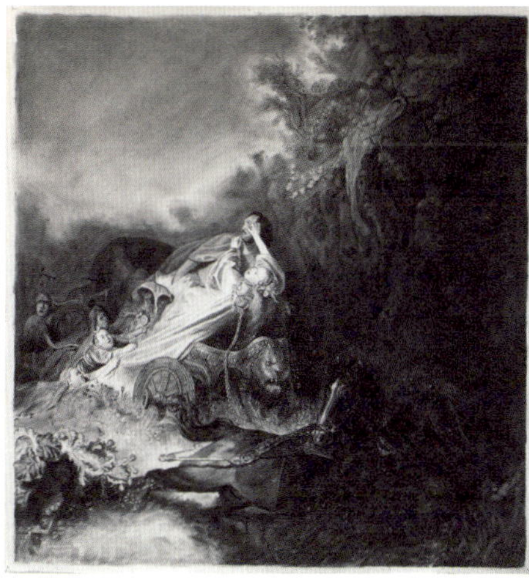

Rape of Proserpina
(after Rembrandt),
charcoal drawing on paper,
110 x 102.5 cm, 2019
Original located at the
Gemäldegalerie, Berlin

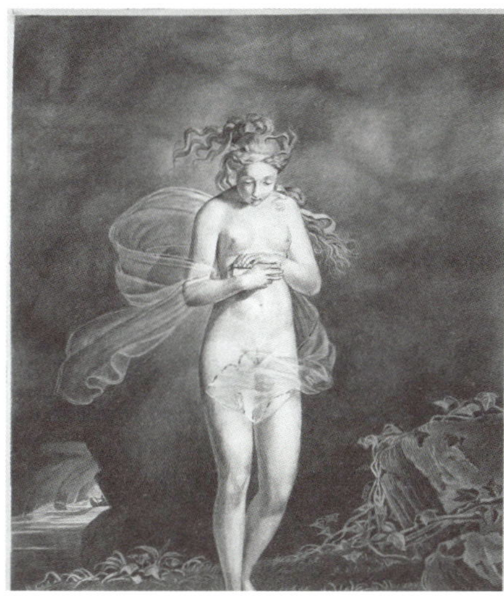

Psyche
(after a lithograph by
Antoine Maurin based
on a painting by
Claude-Marie Dubufe),
charcoal drawing on paper,
110 x 82 cm, 2020

# LOVRO ARTUKOVIĆ

## Plates

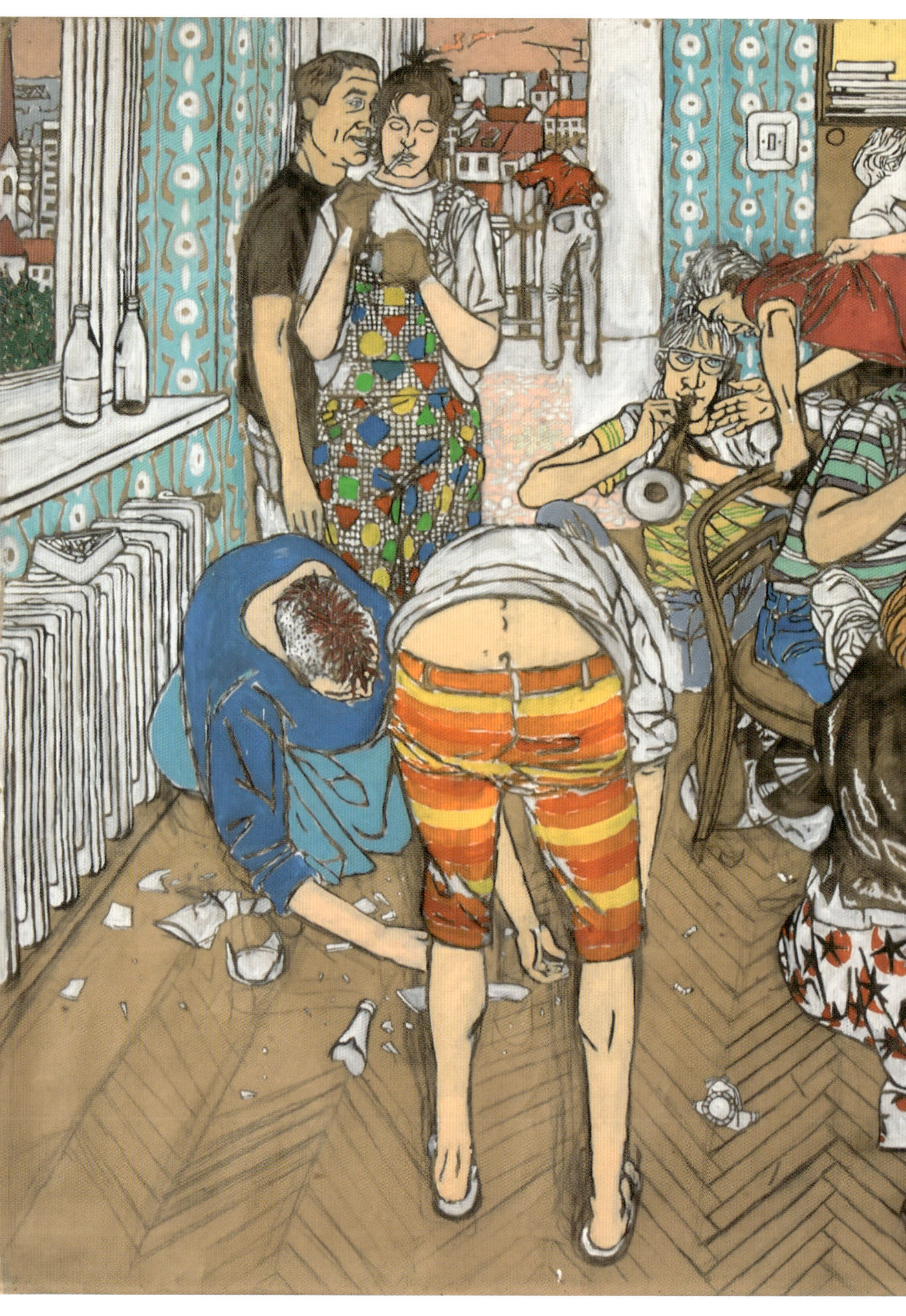

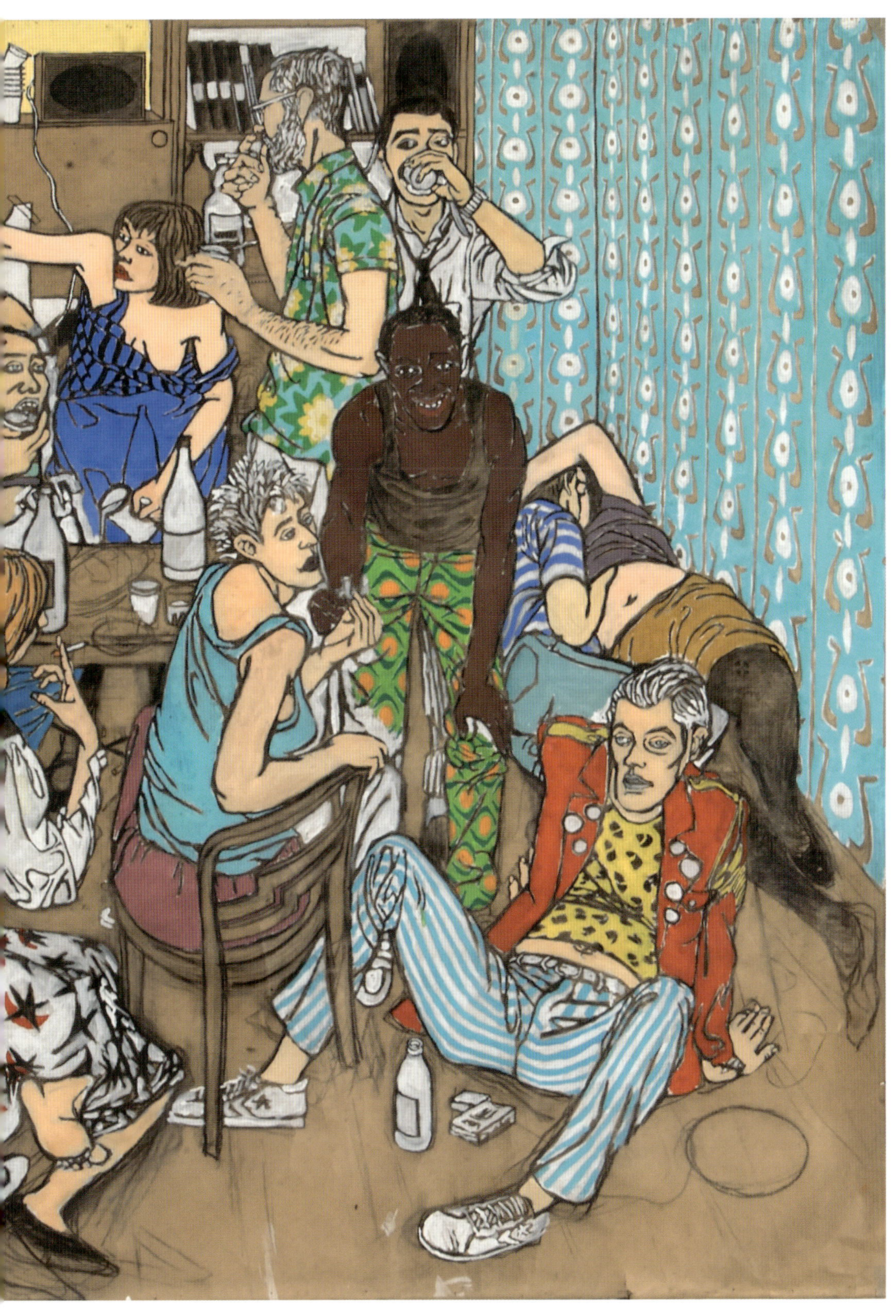

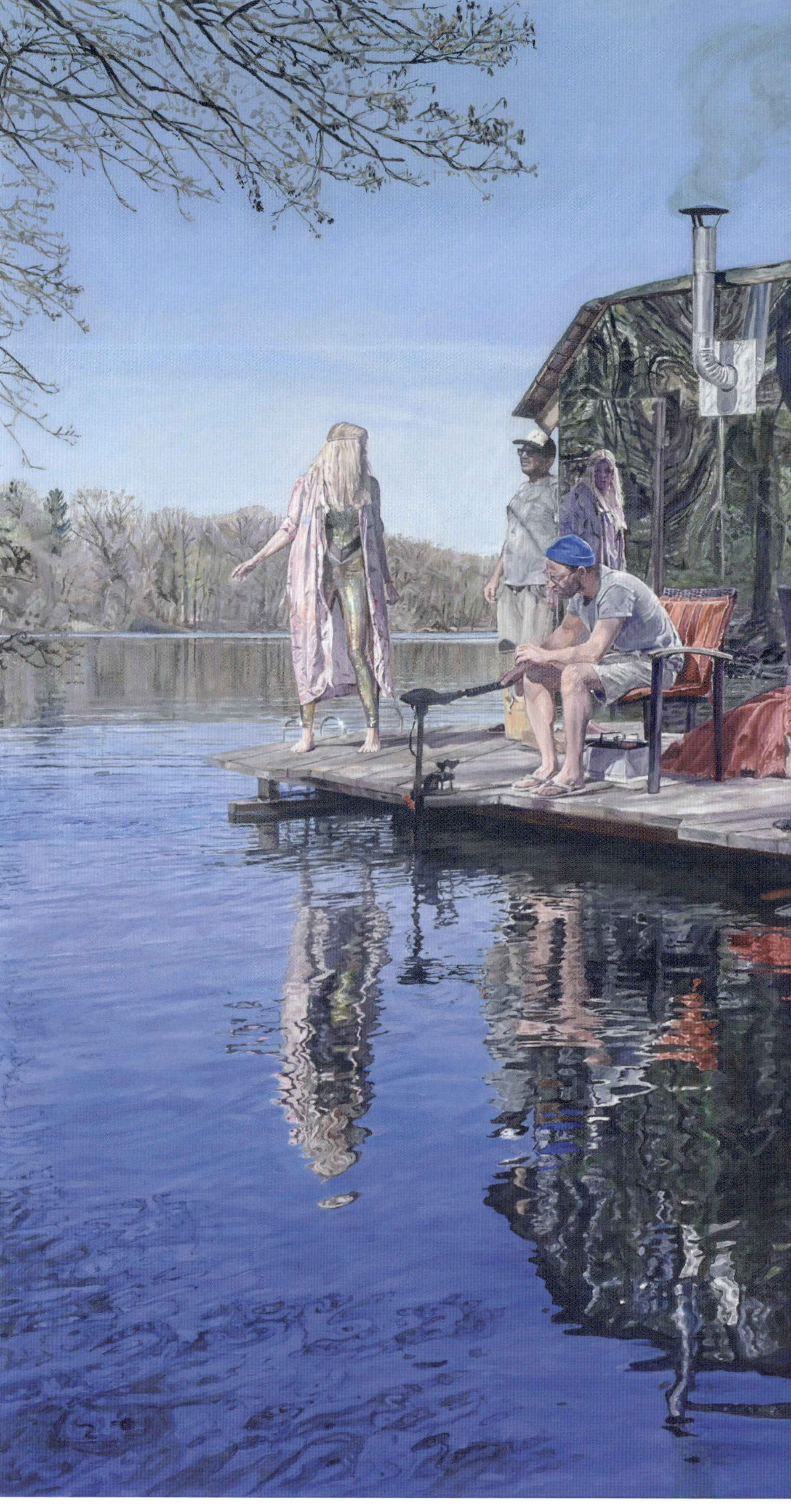

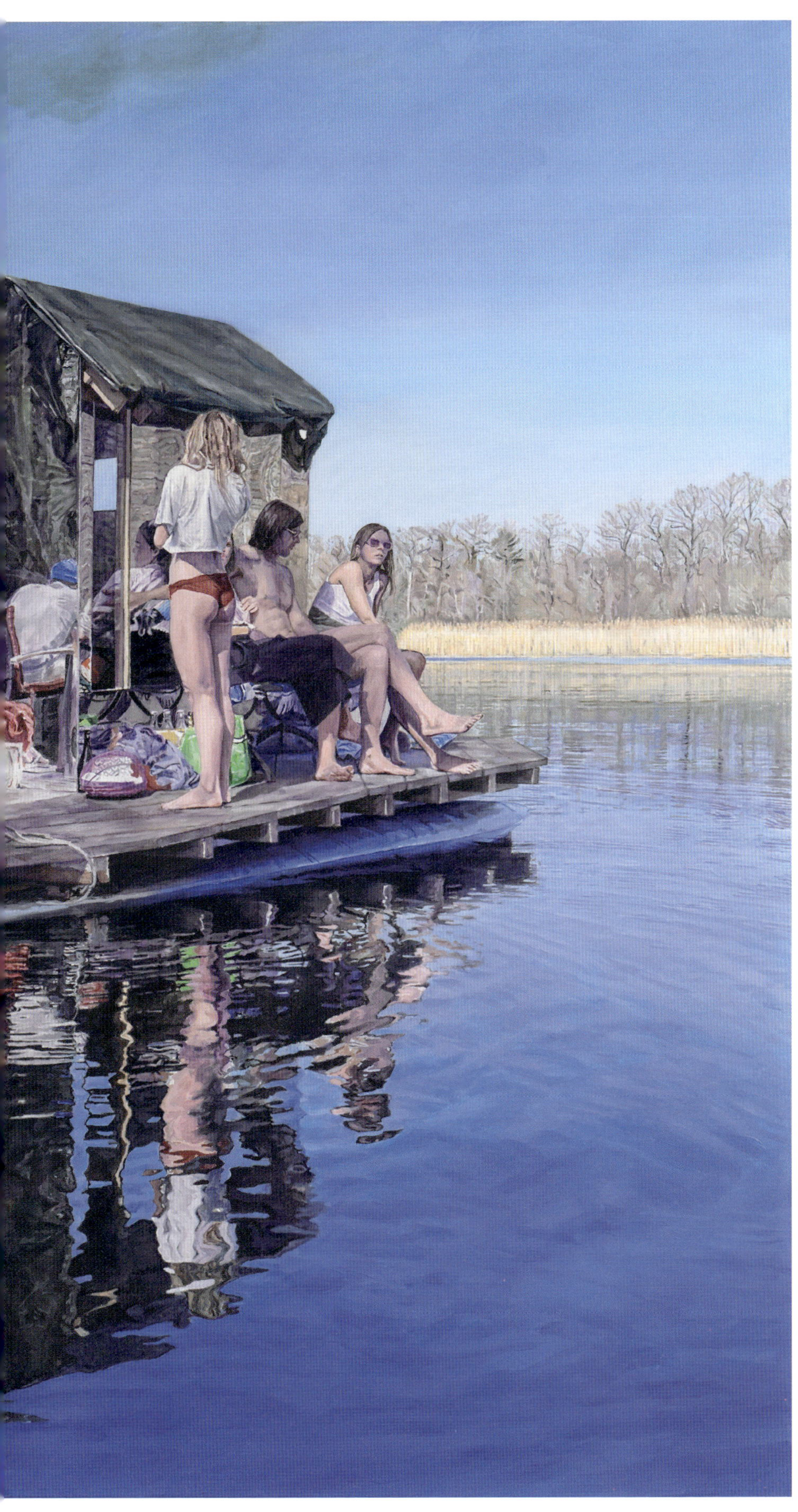

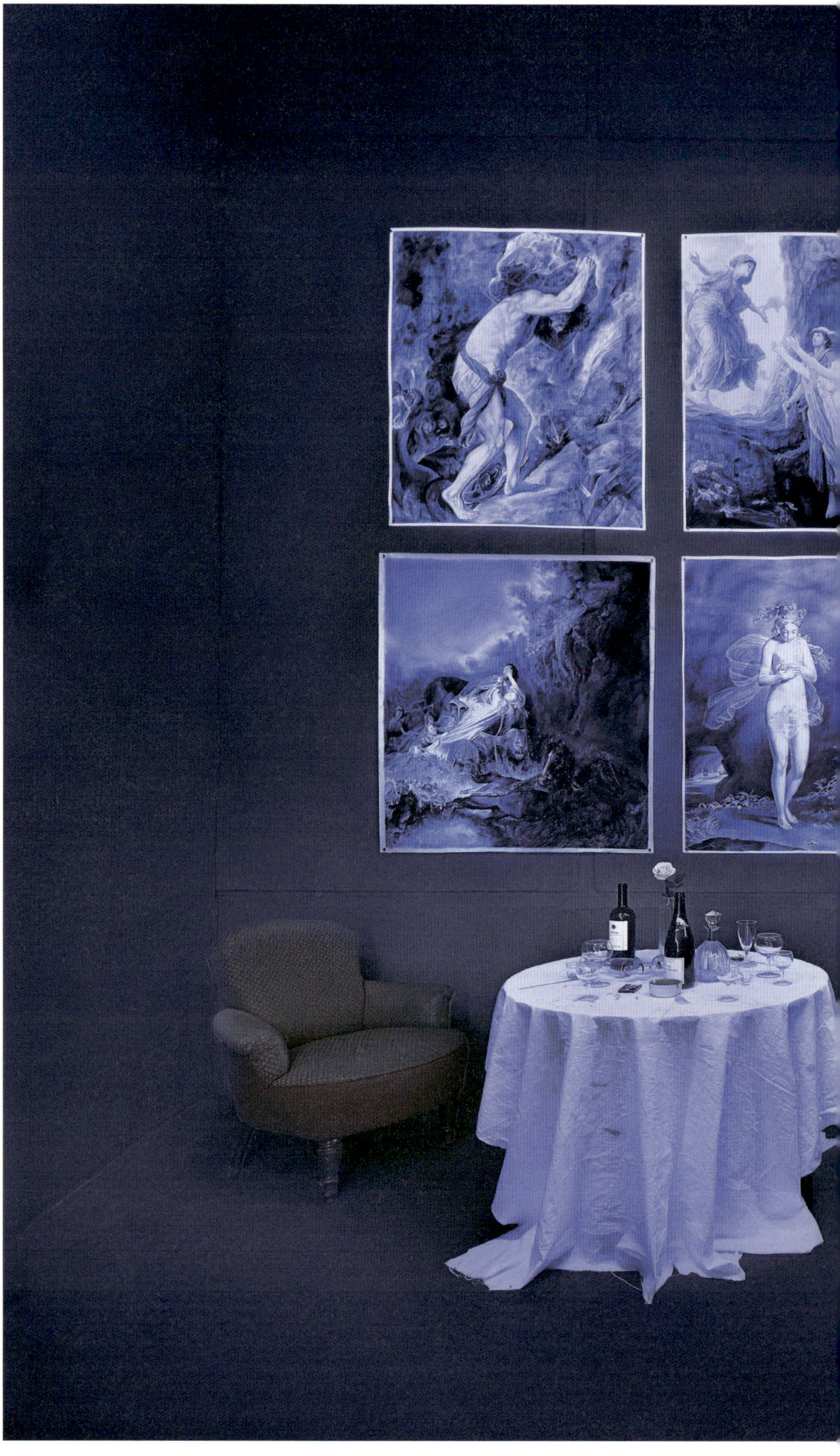

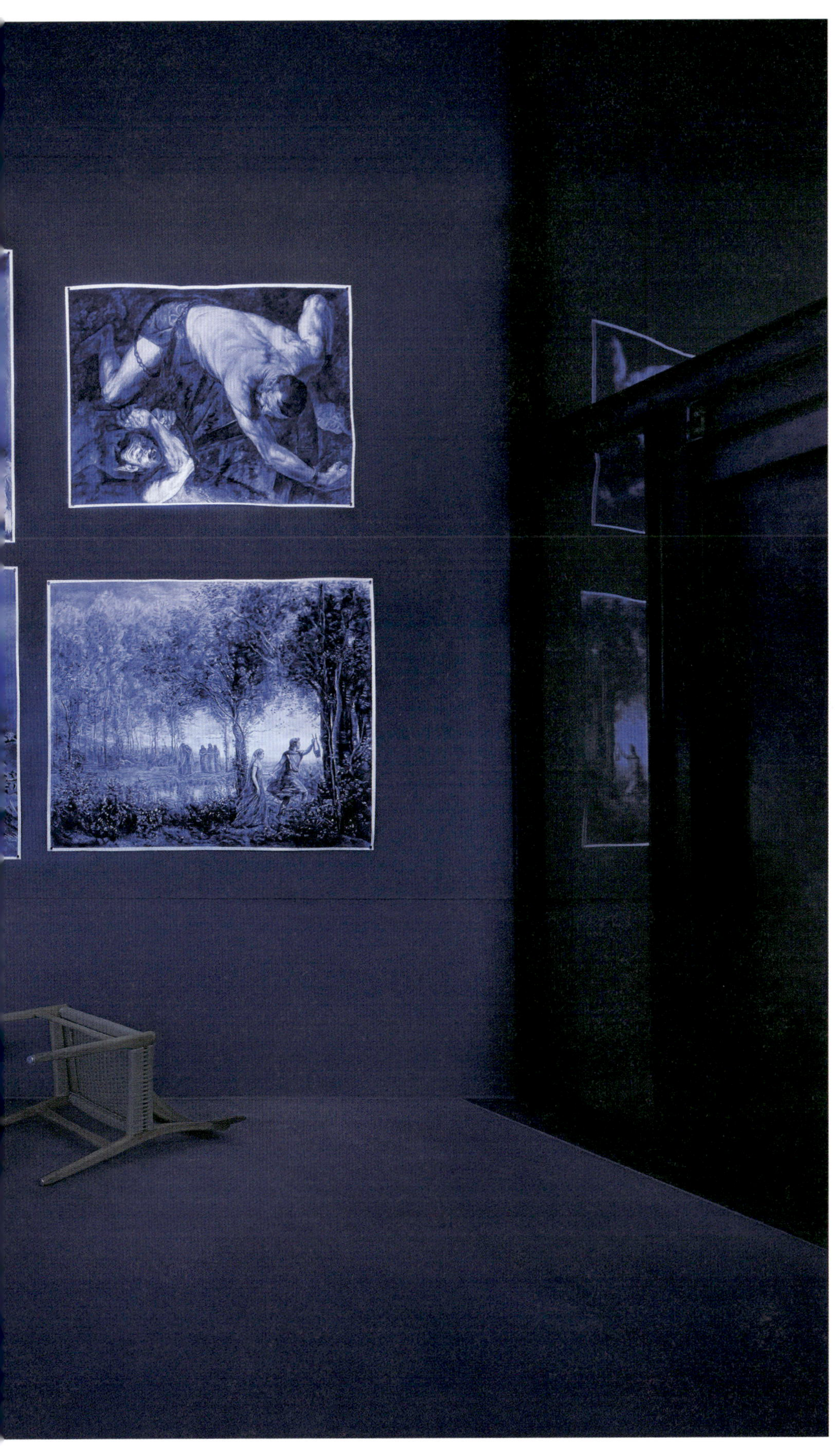

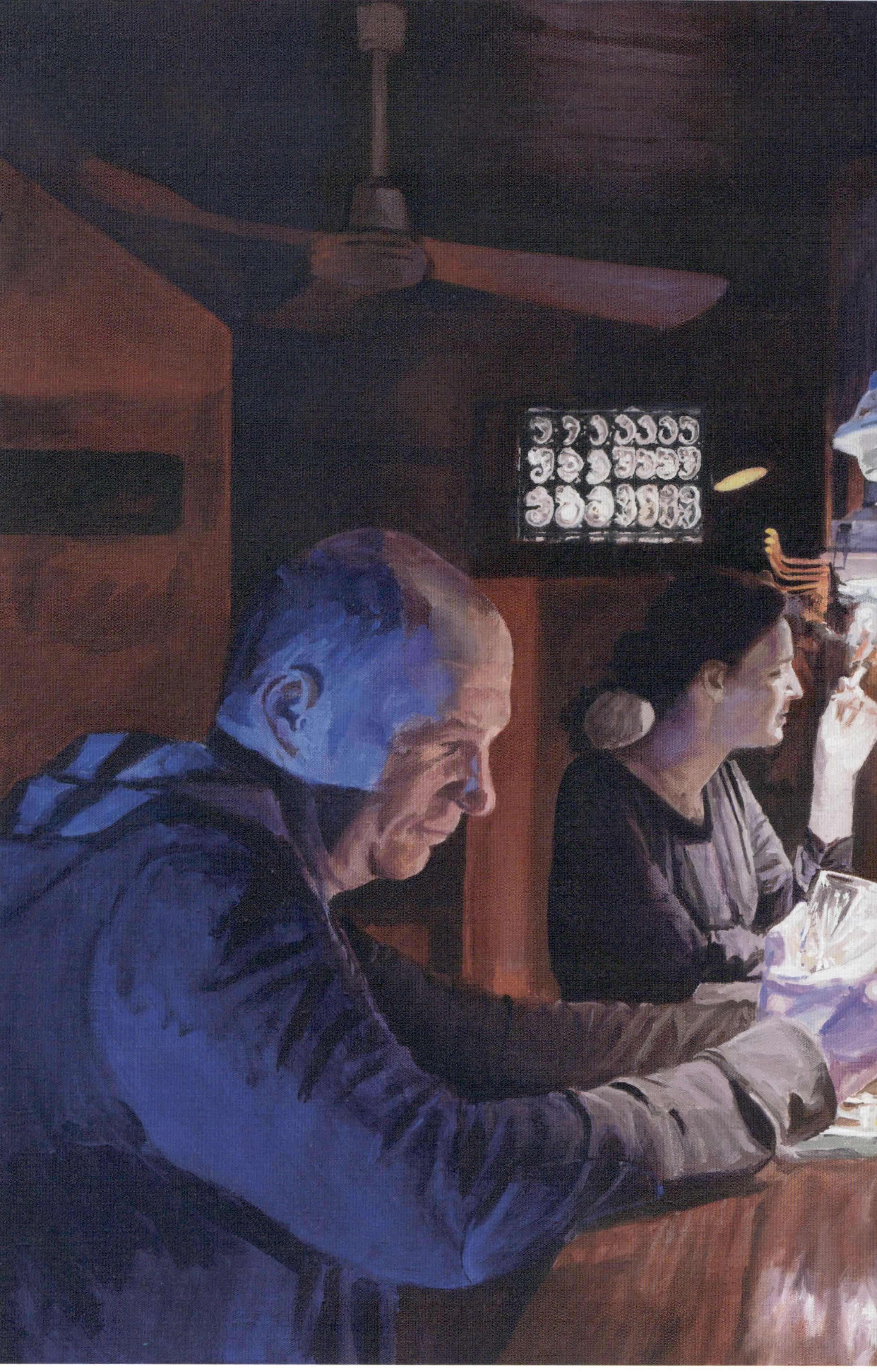

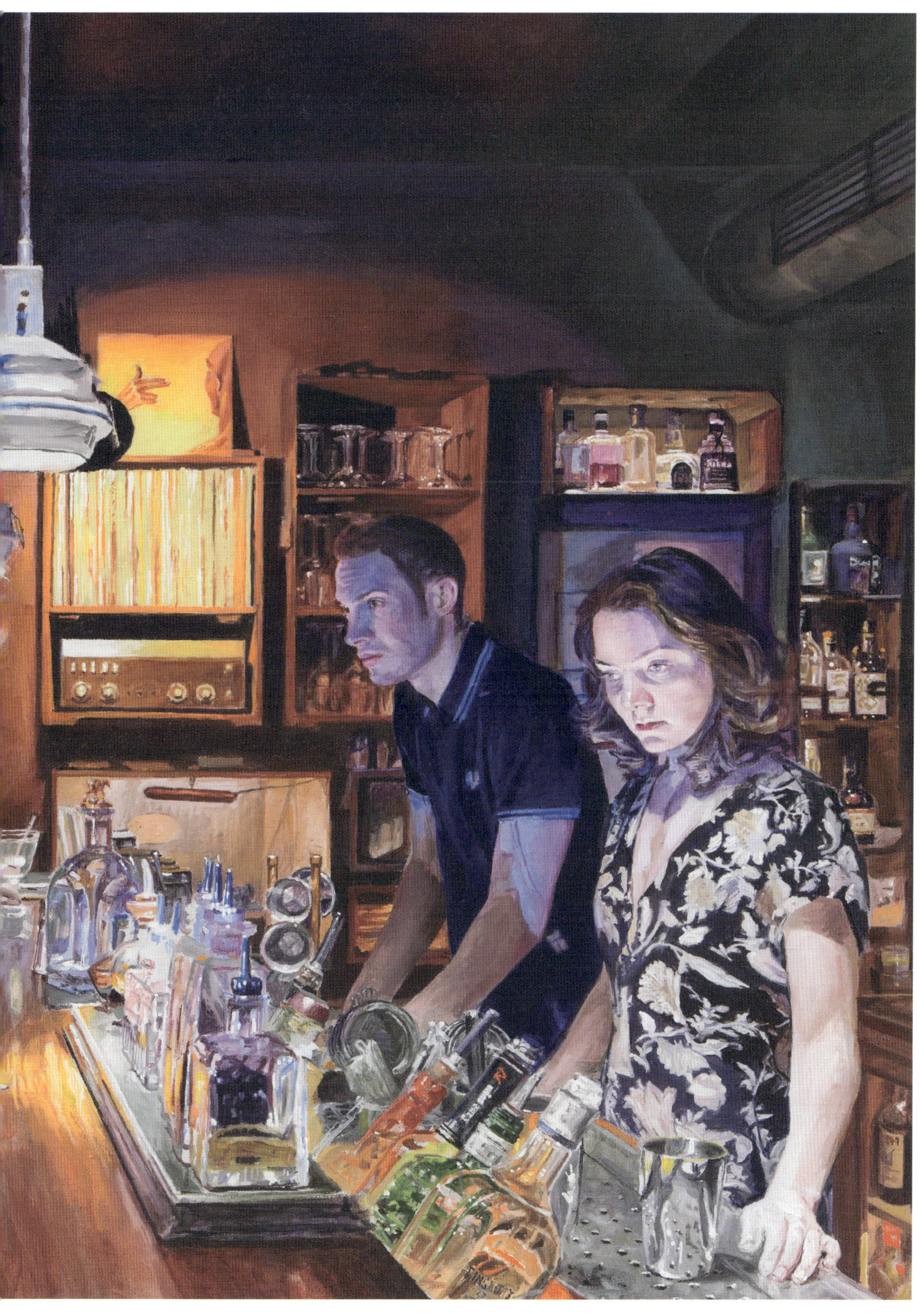

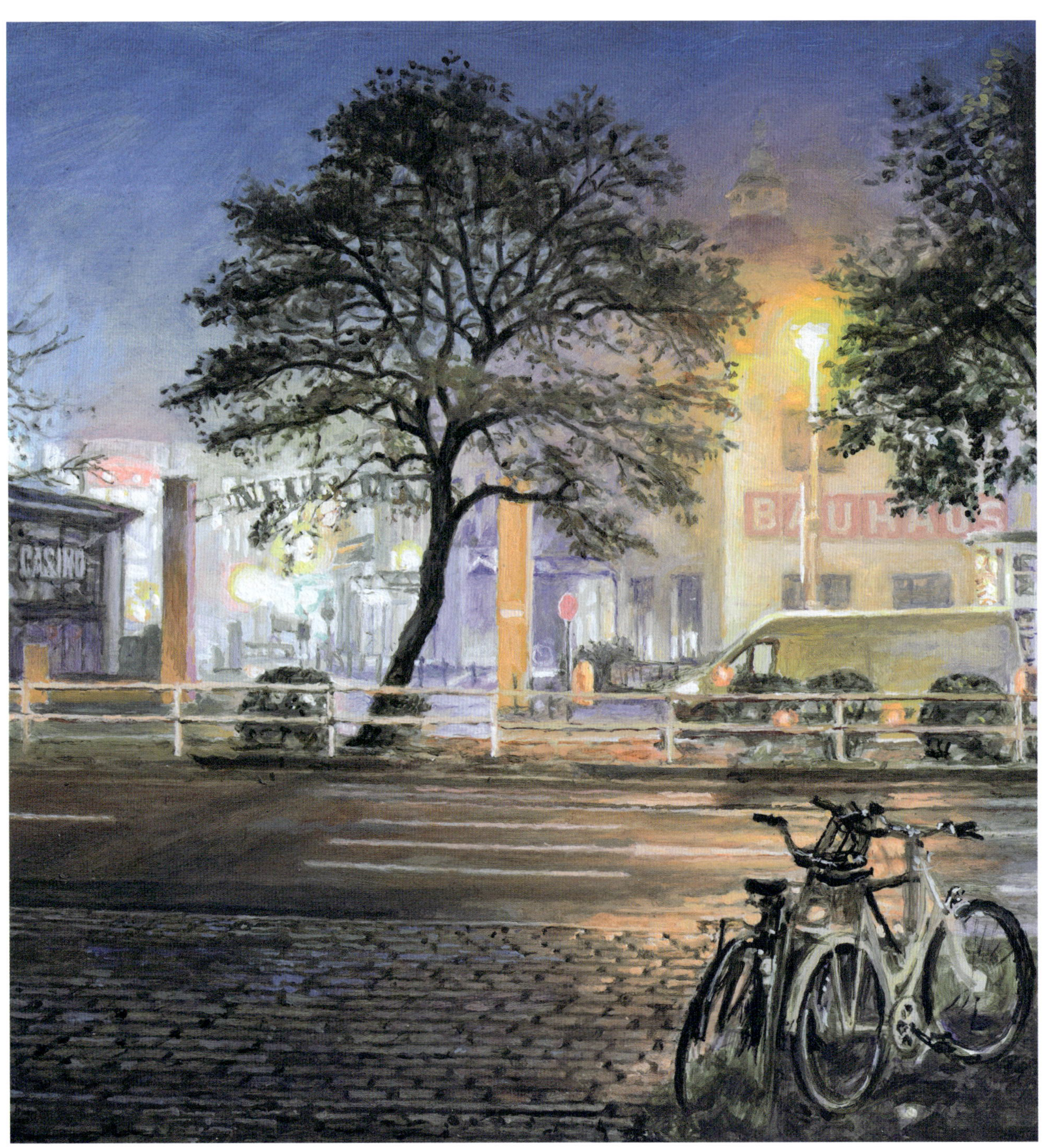
CASINO
BAUHAUS

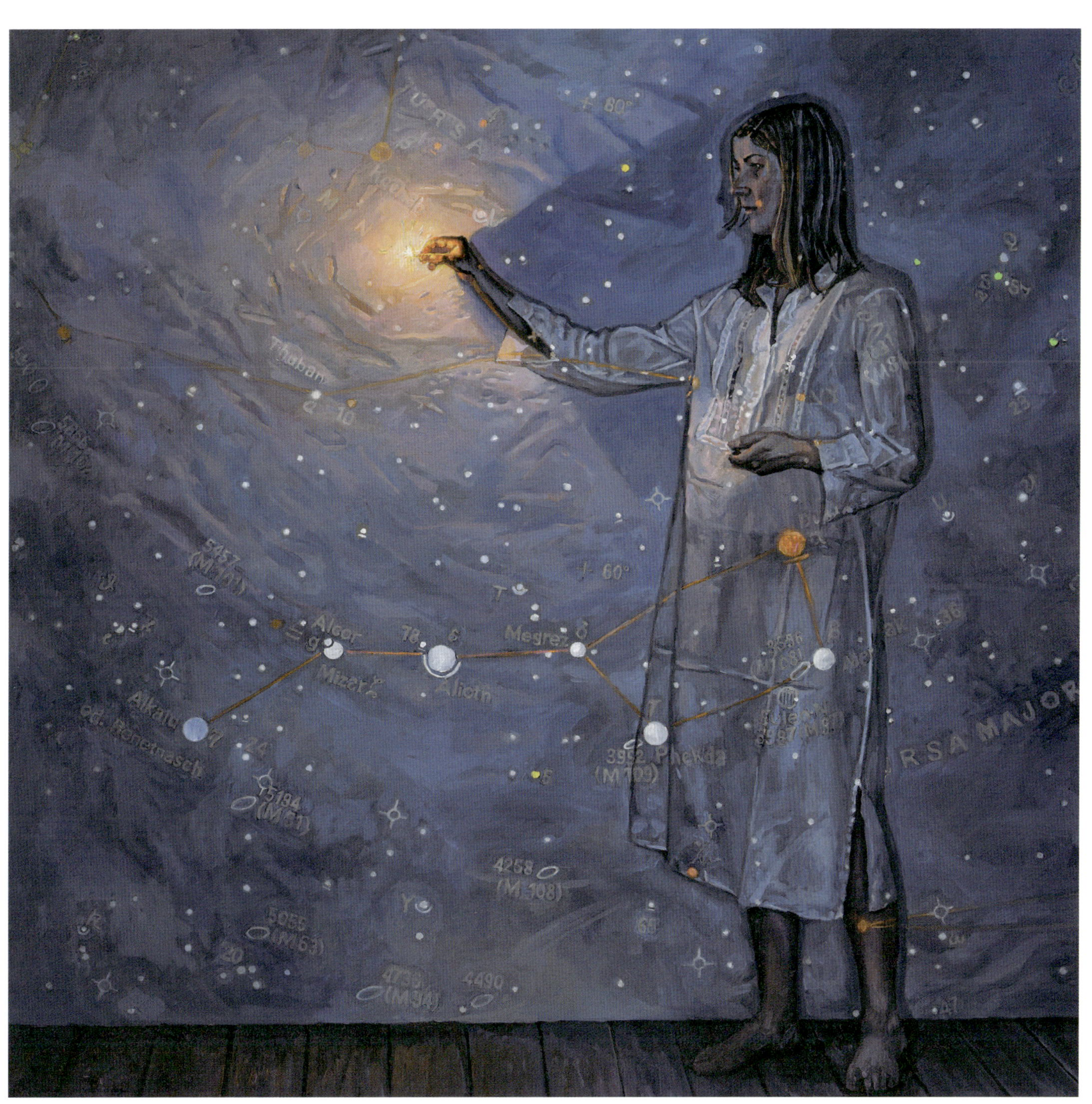

URSA
+ 80°
Thuban
10
+ 60°
5457
(M 101)
Alcor
78
Megrez
Mizar
Alioth
Alkaid
od. Benetnasch
24
5194
(M 51)
3992 Phecda
(M 109)
4258
(M 108)
5055
(M 63)
4736
(M 94)
4490
URSA MAJOR

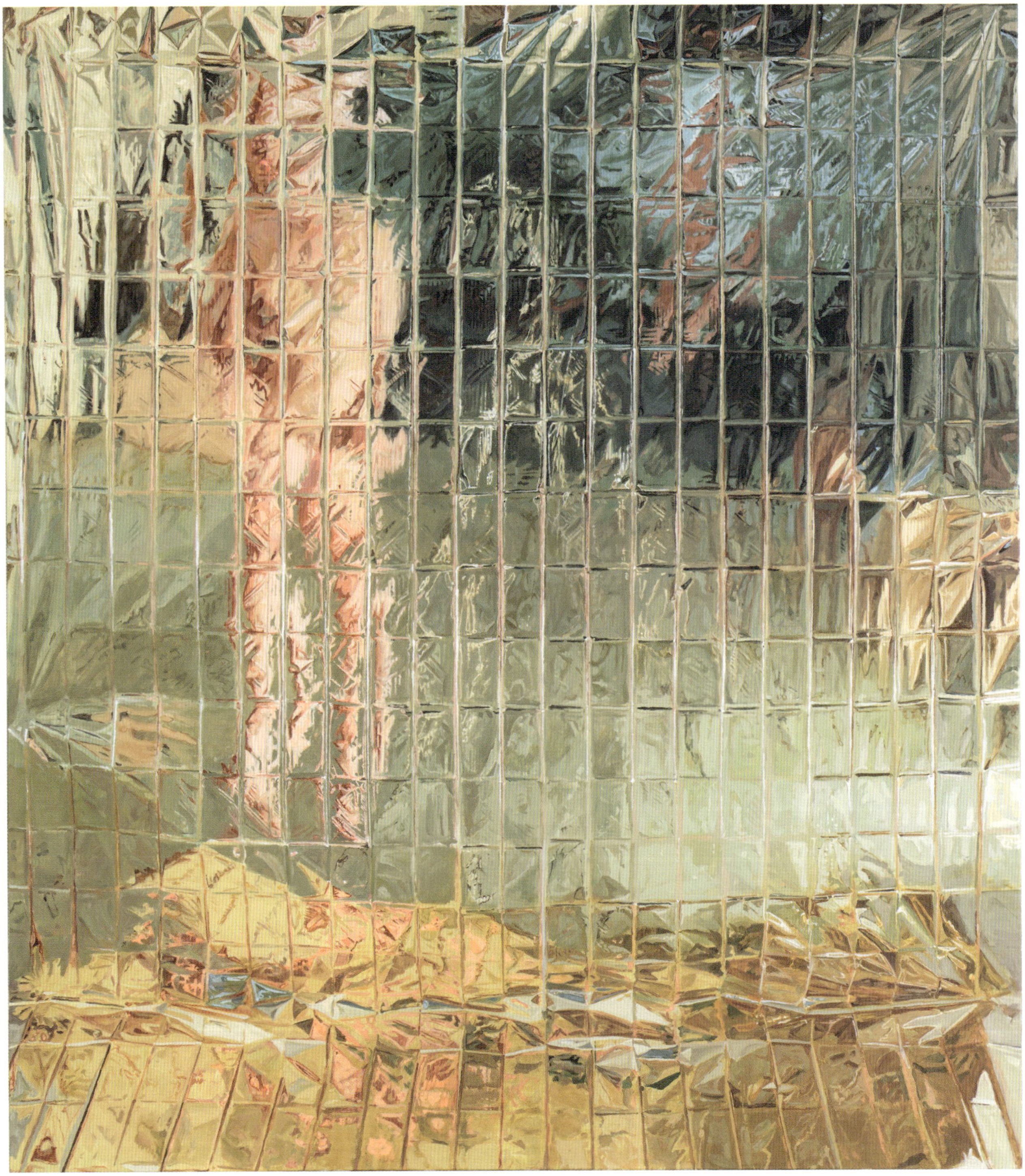

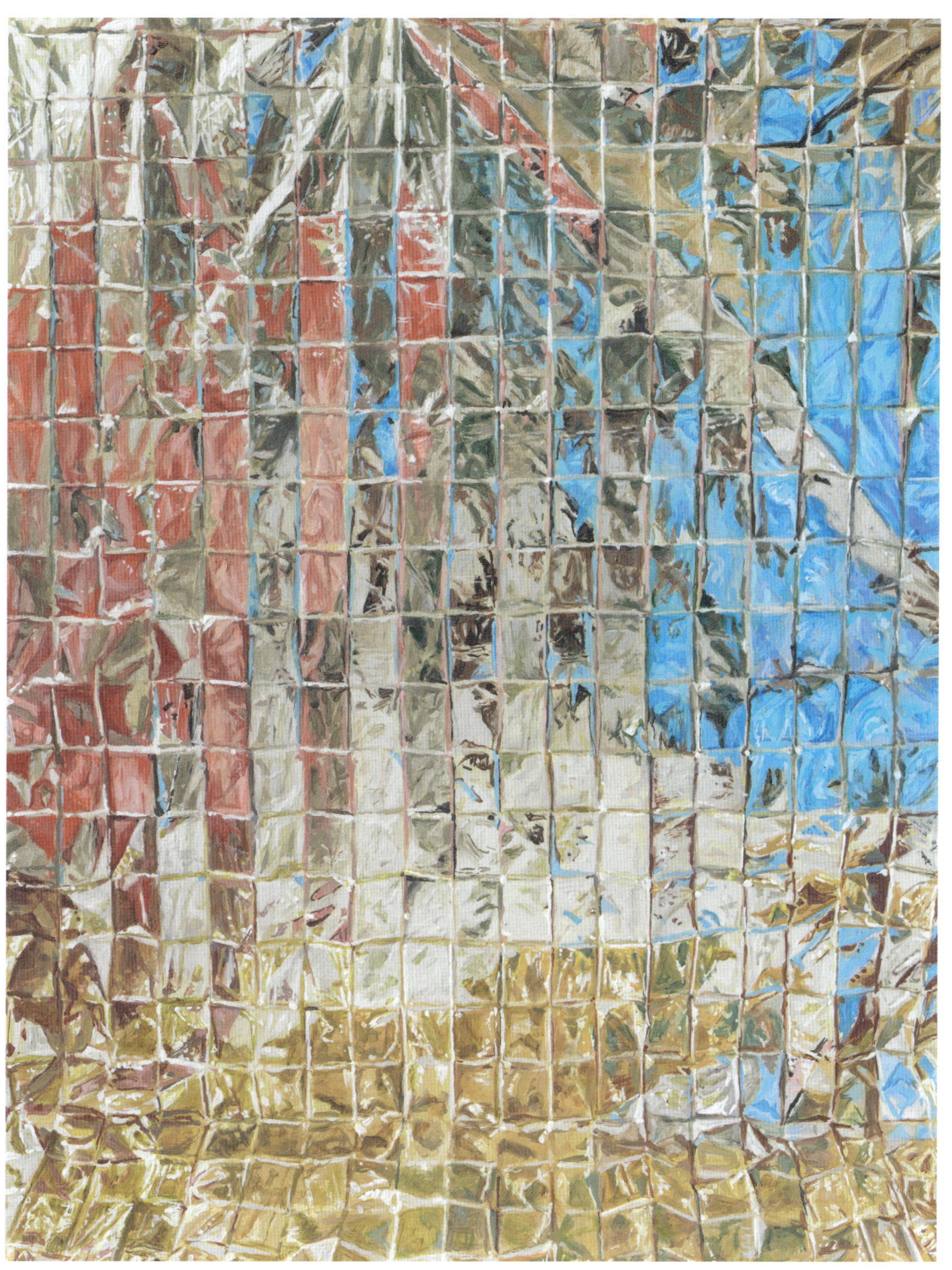

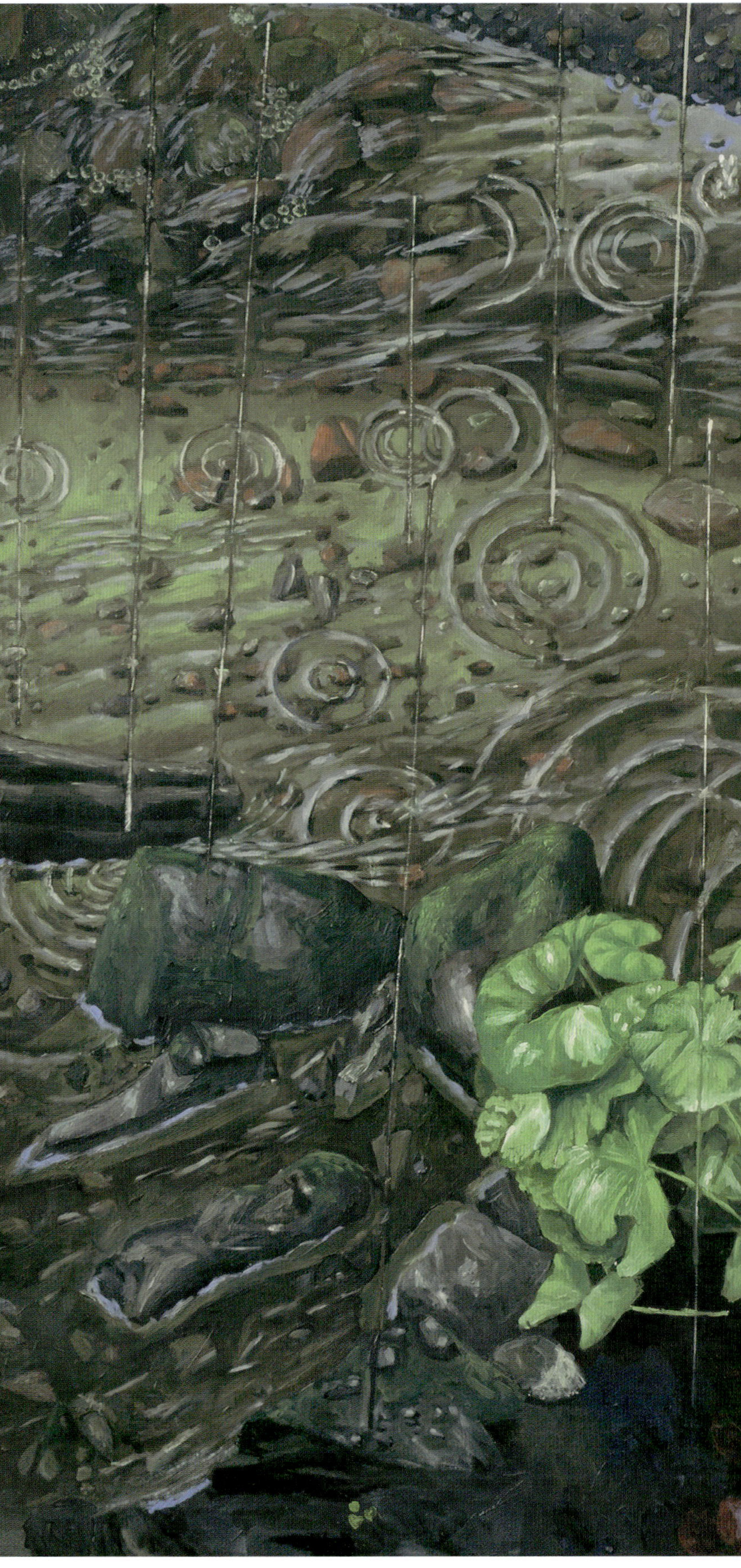

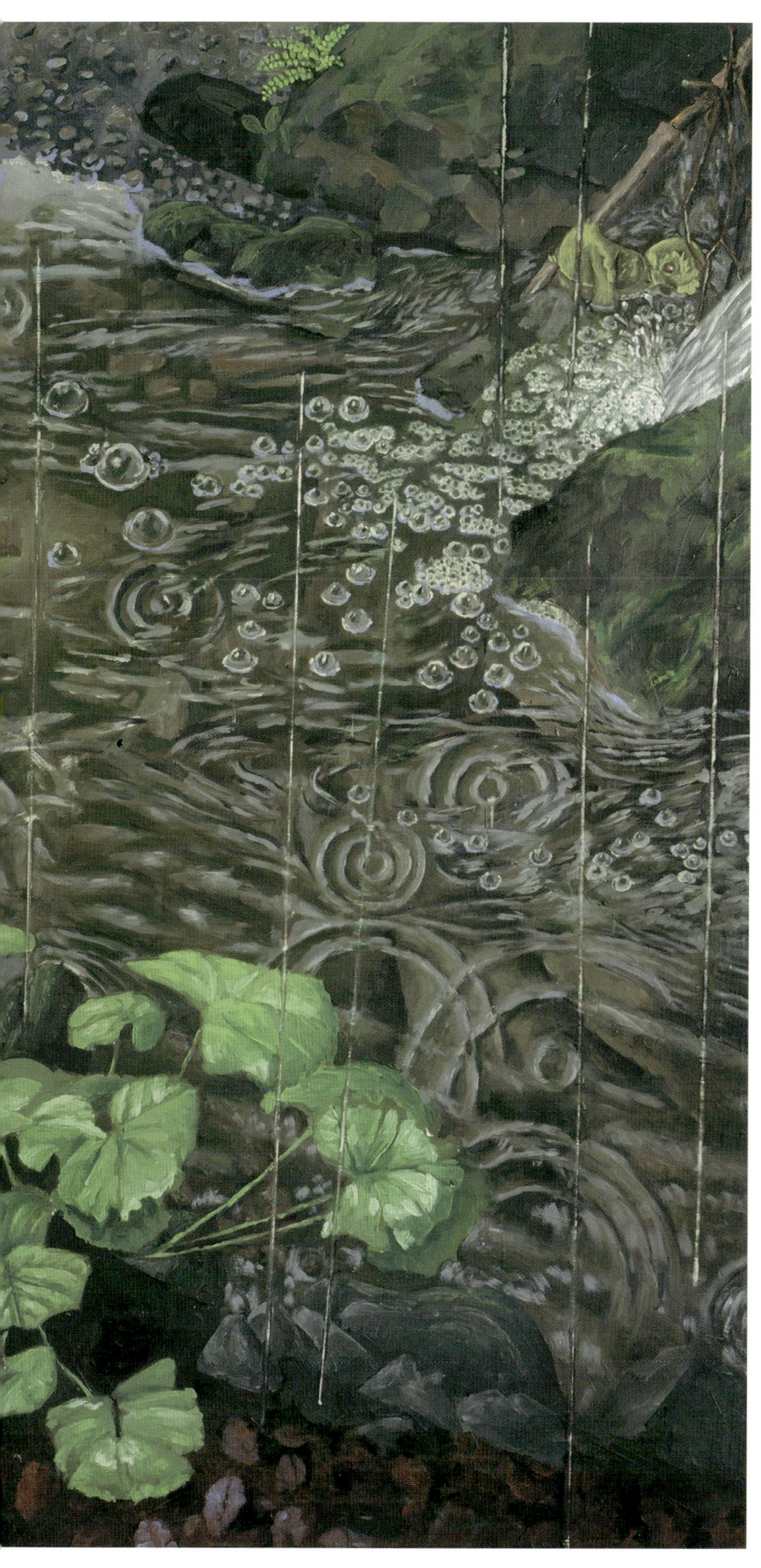

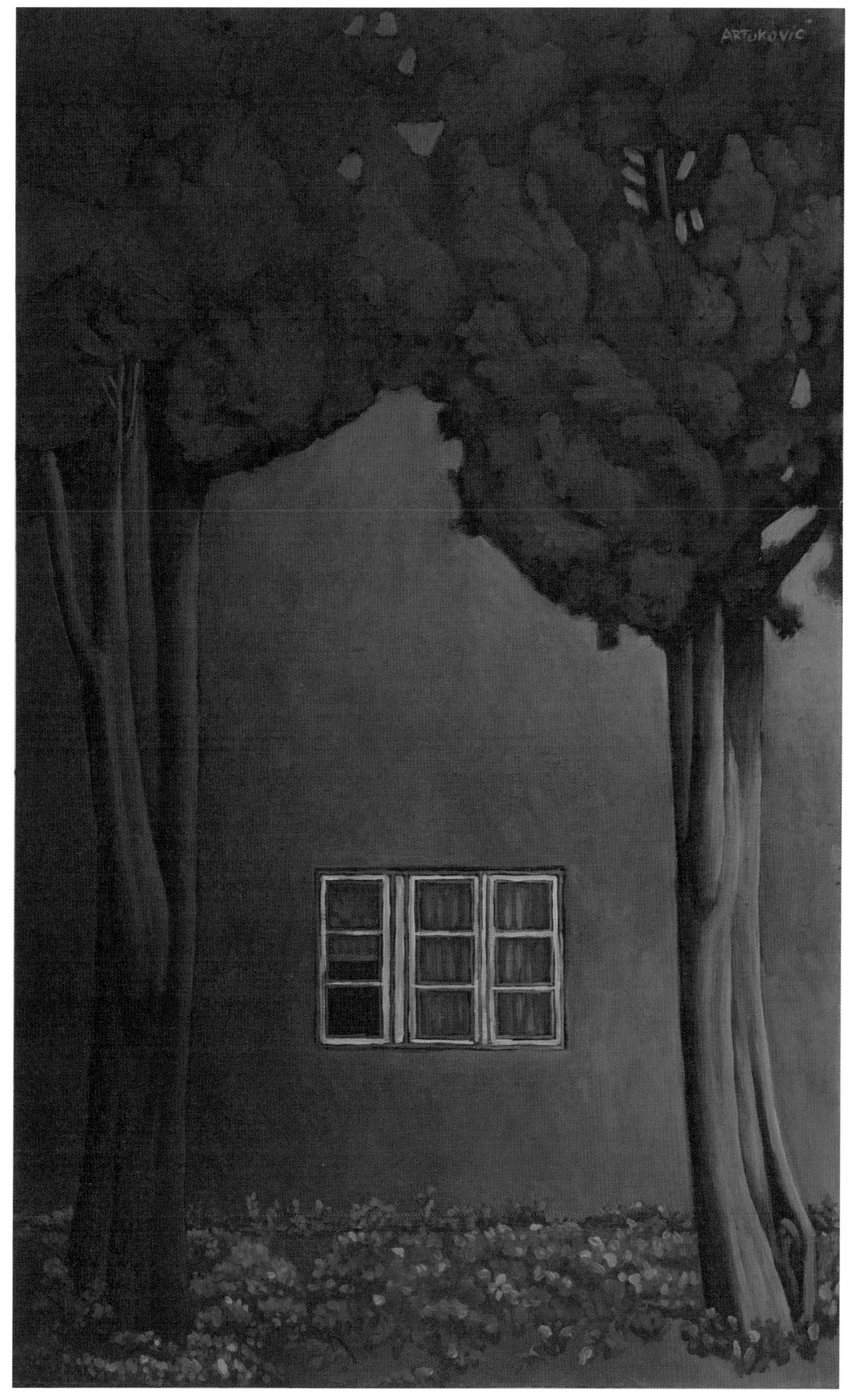

ARTUKOVIC

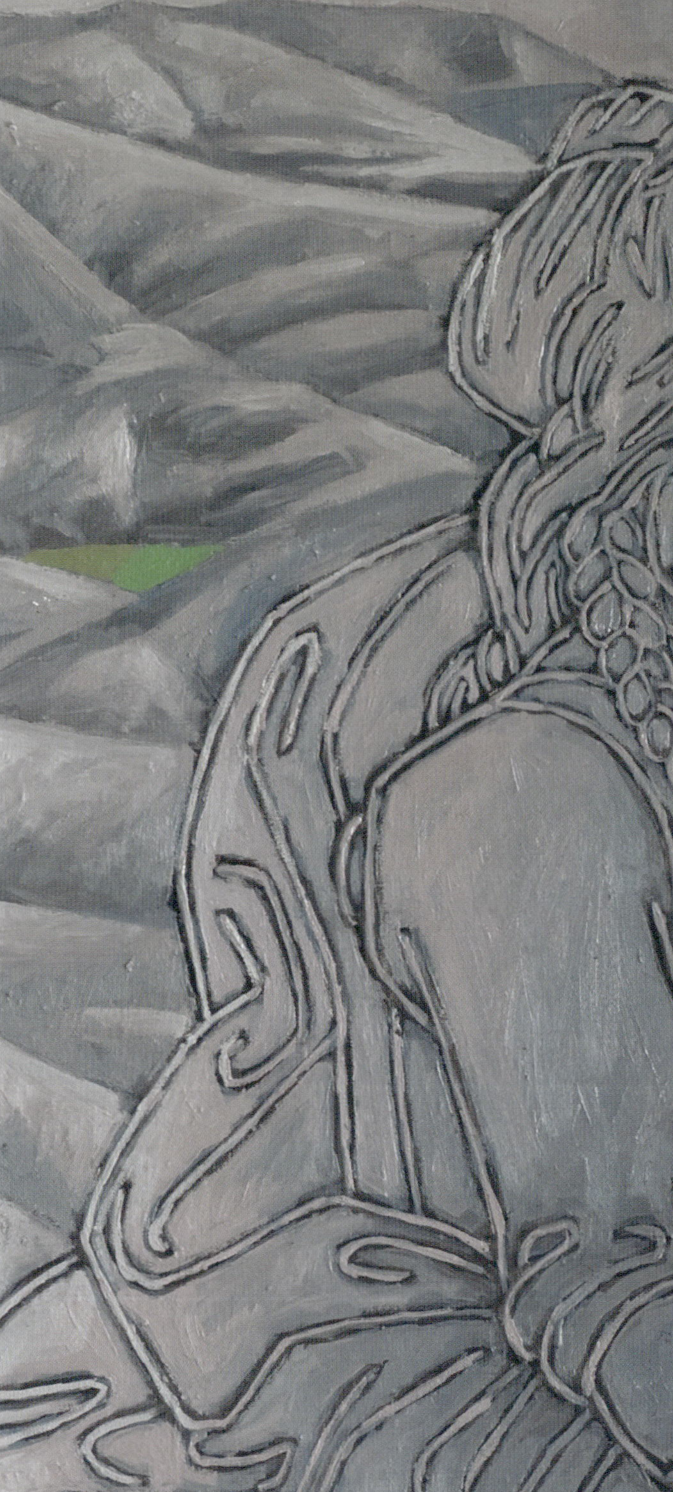

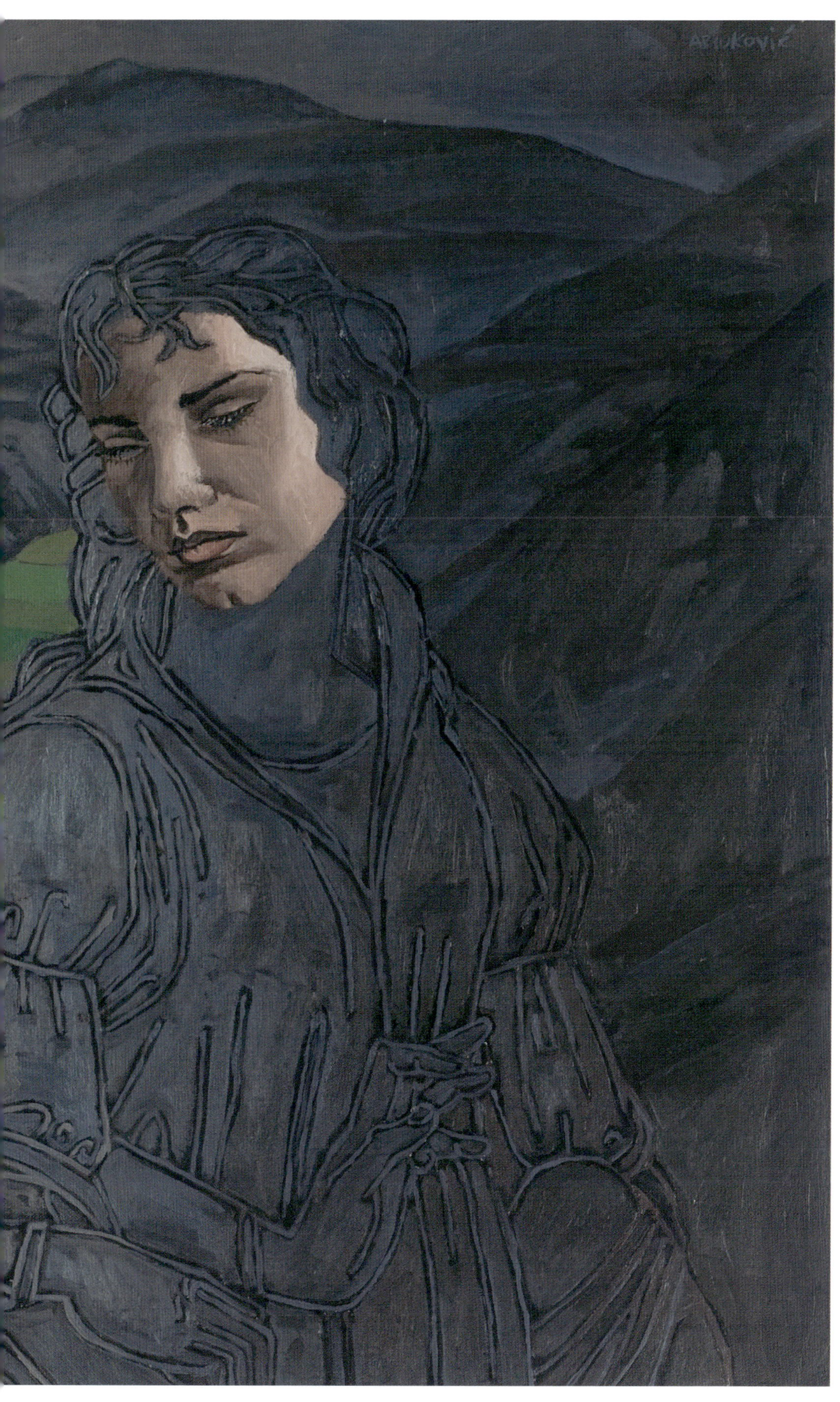

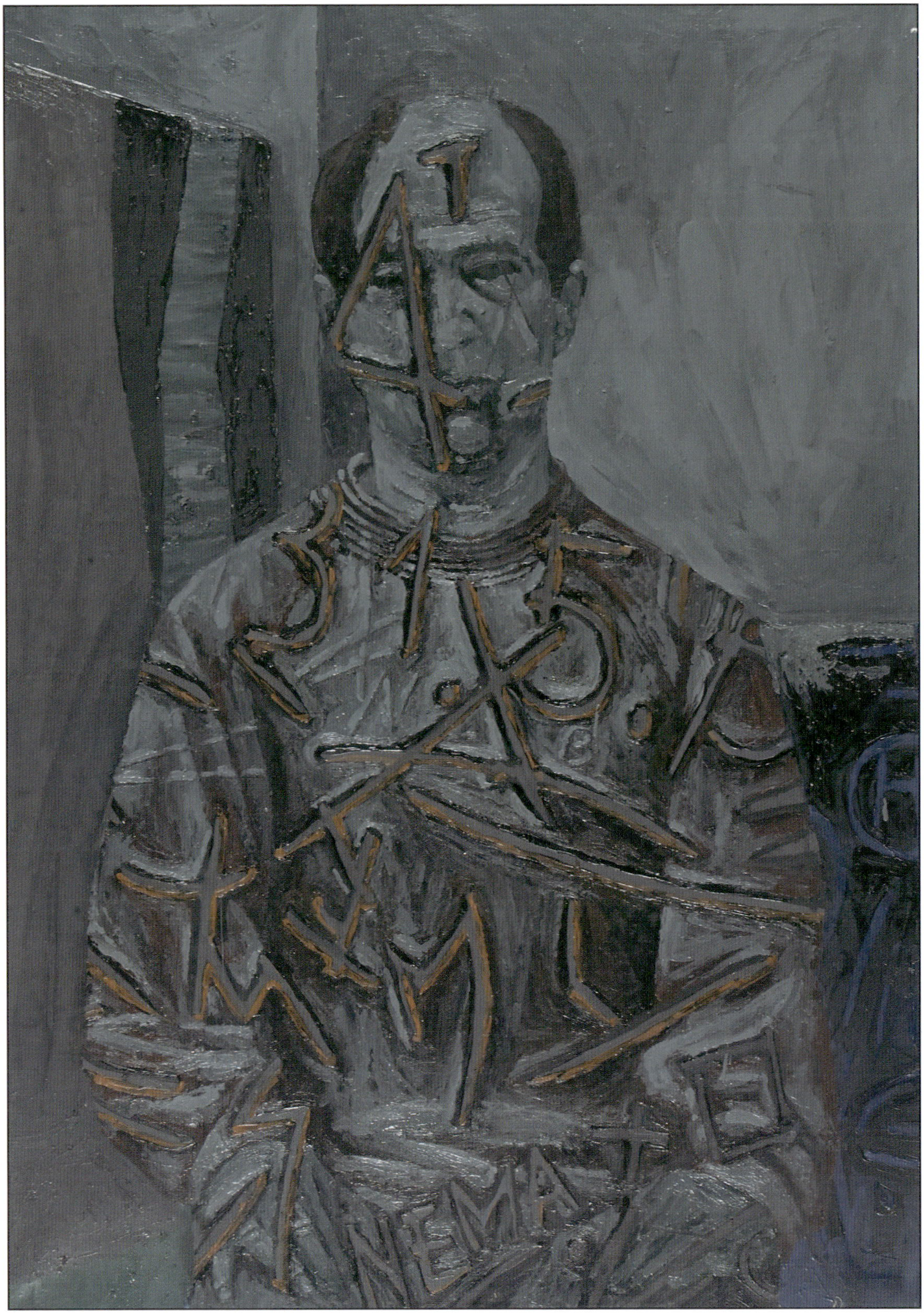

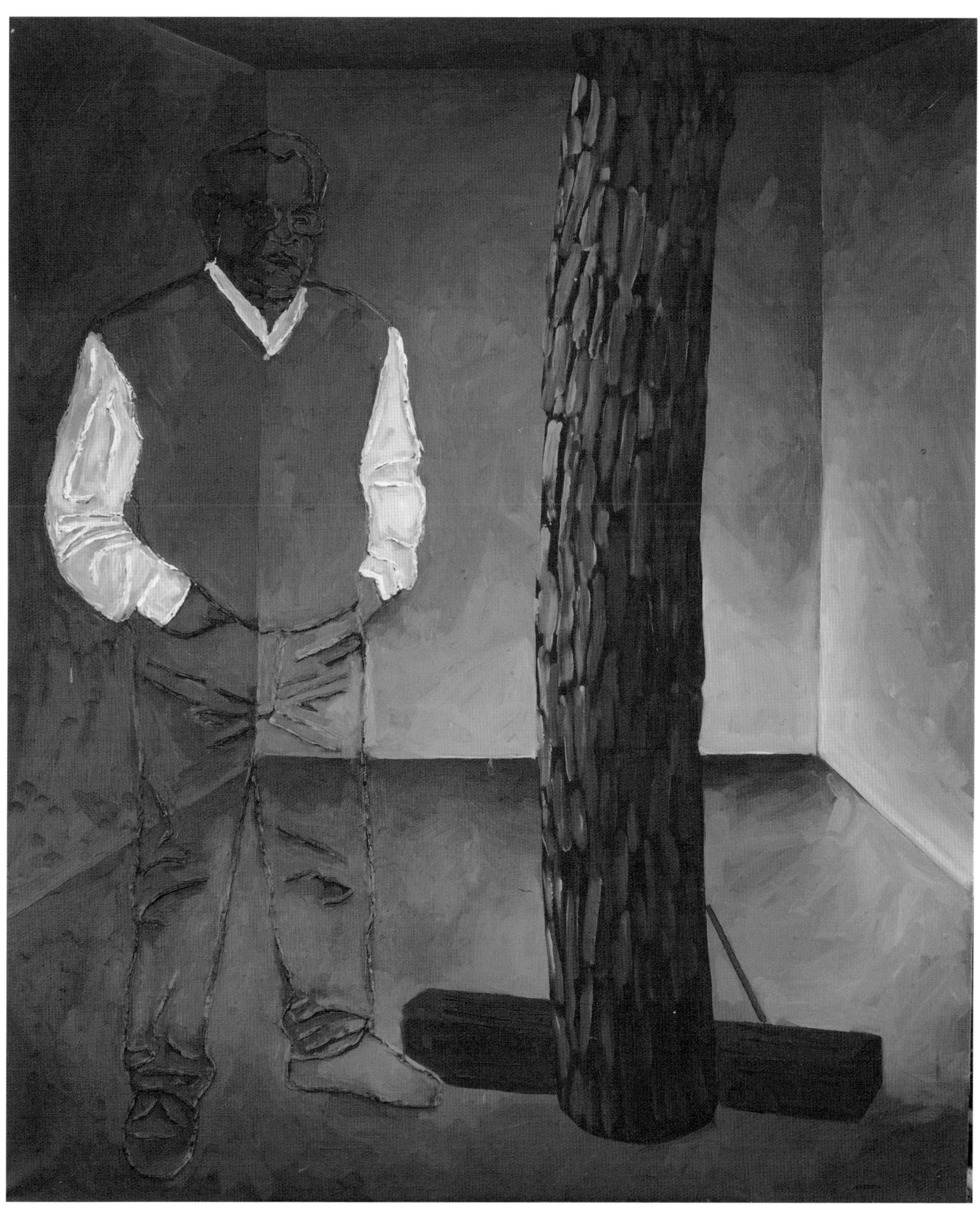

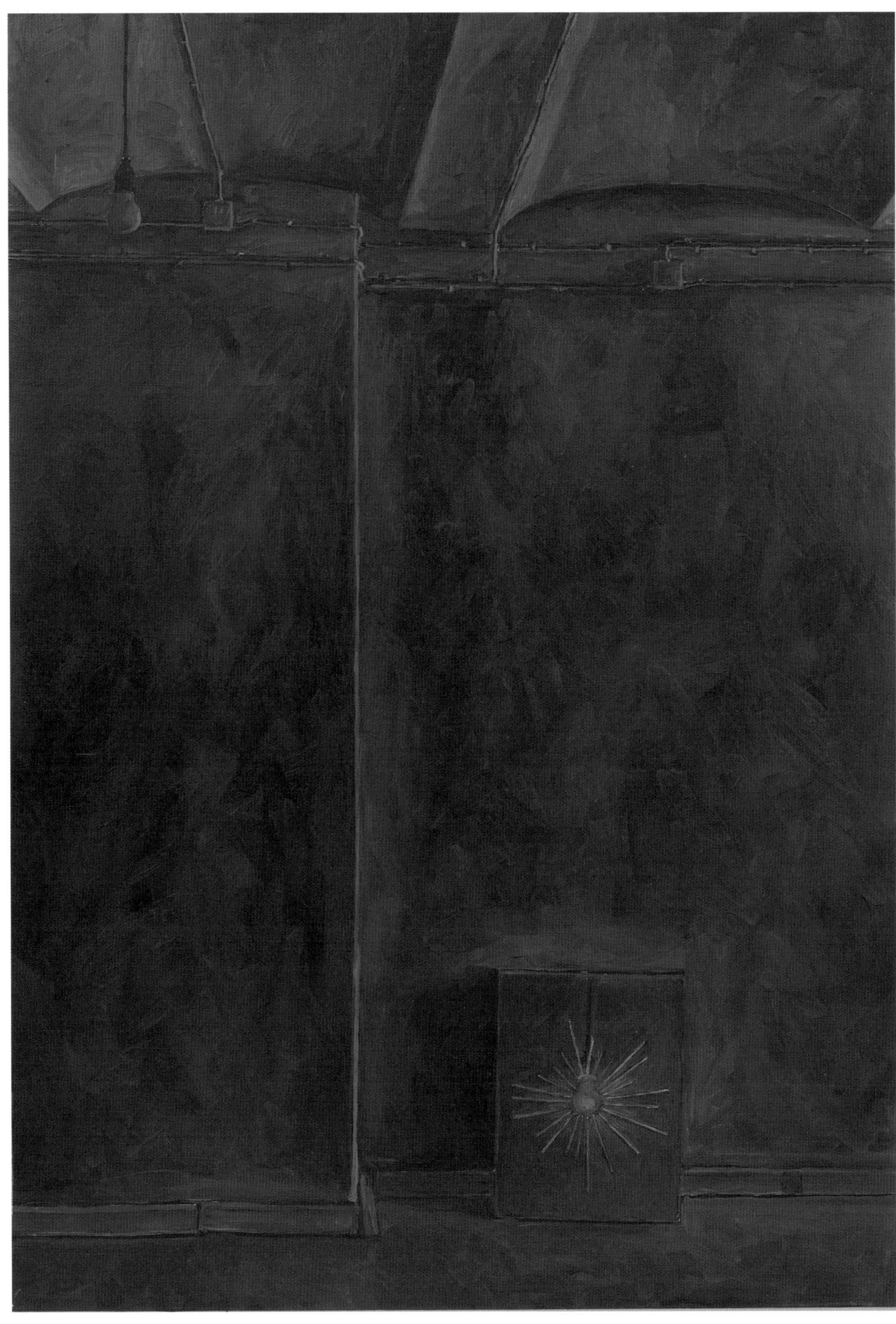

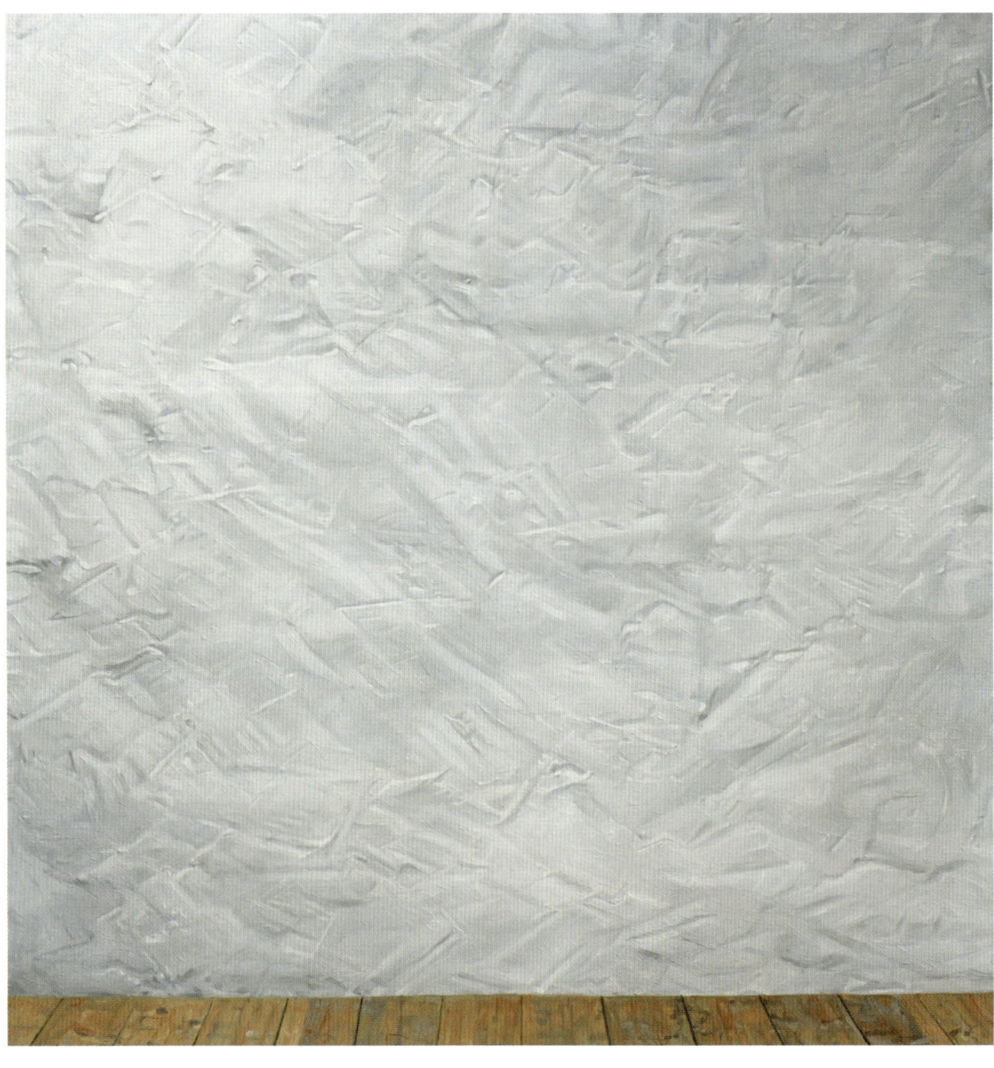

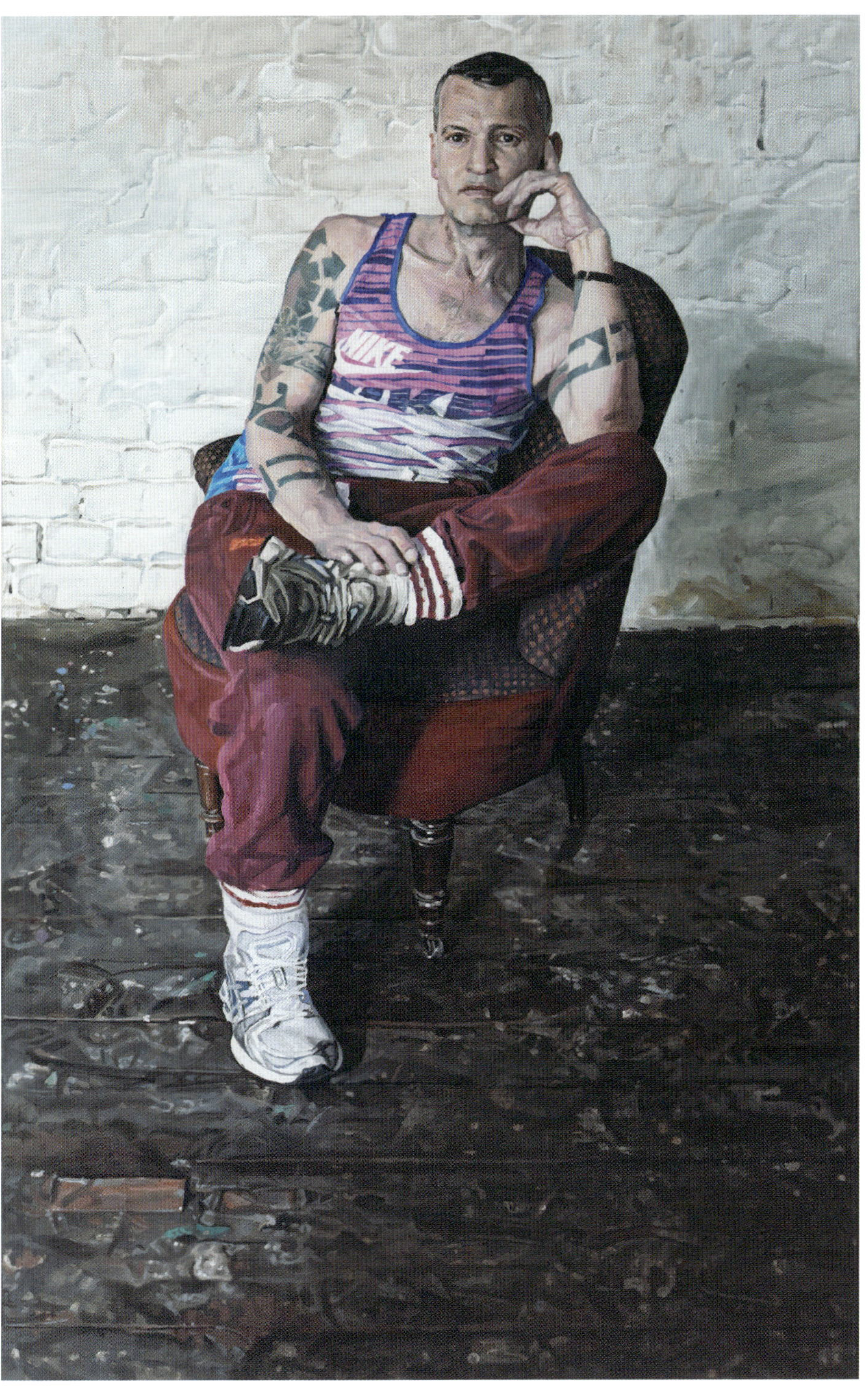

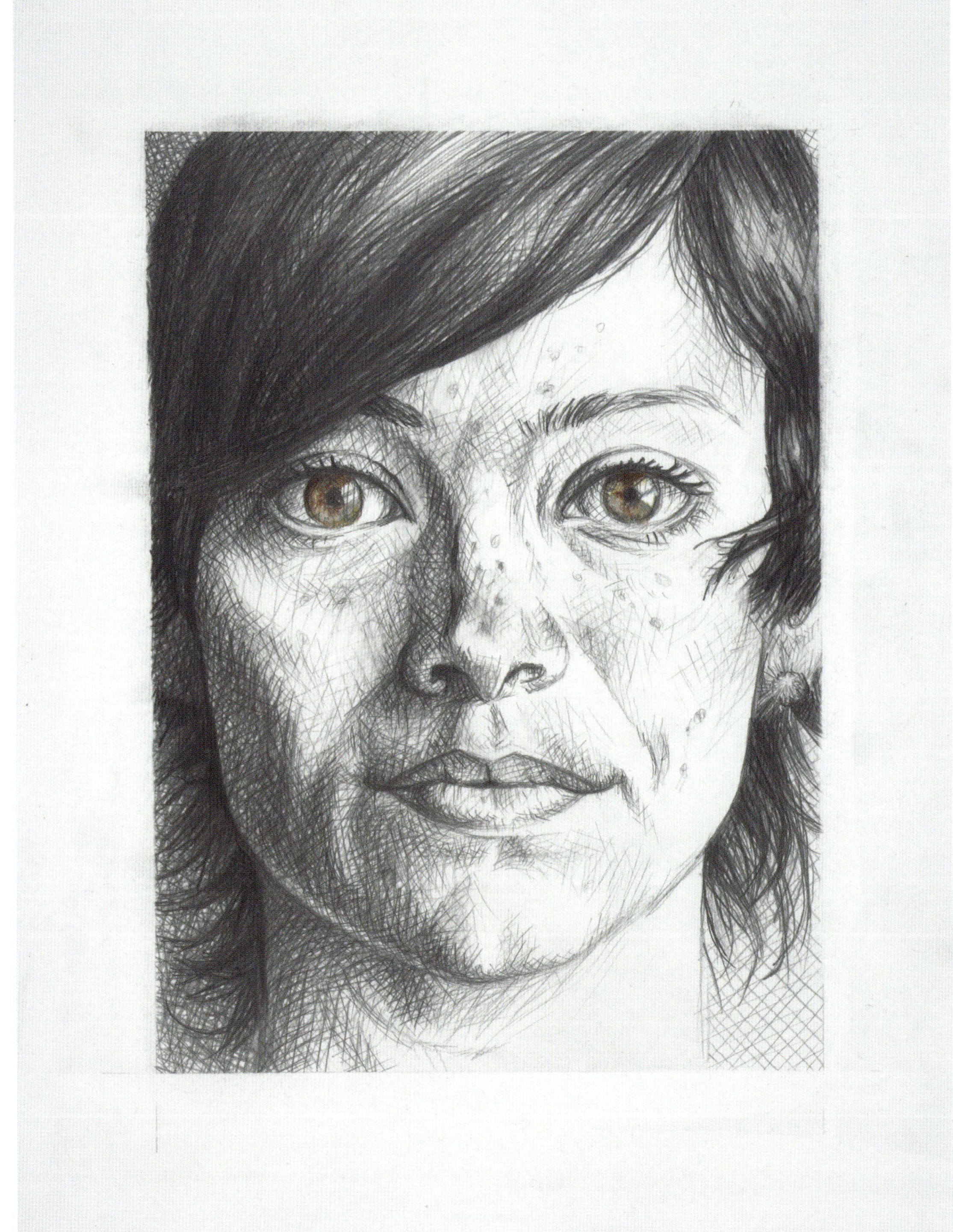

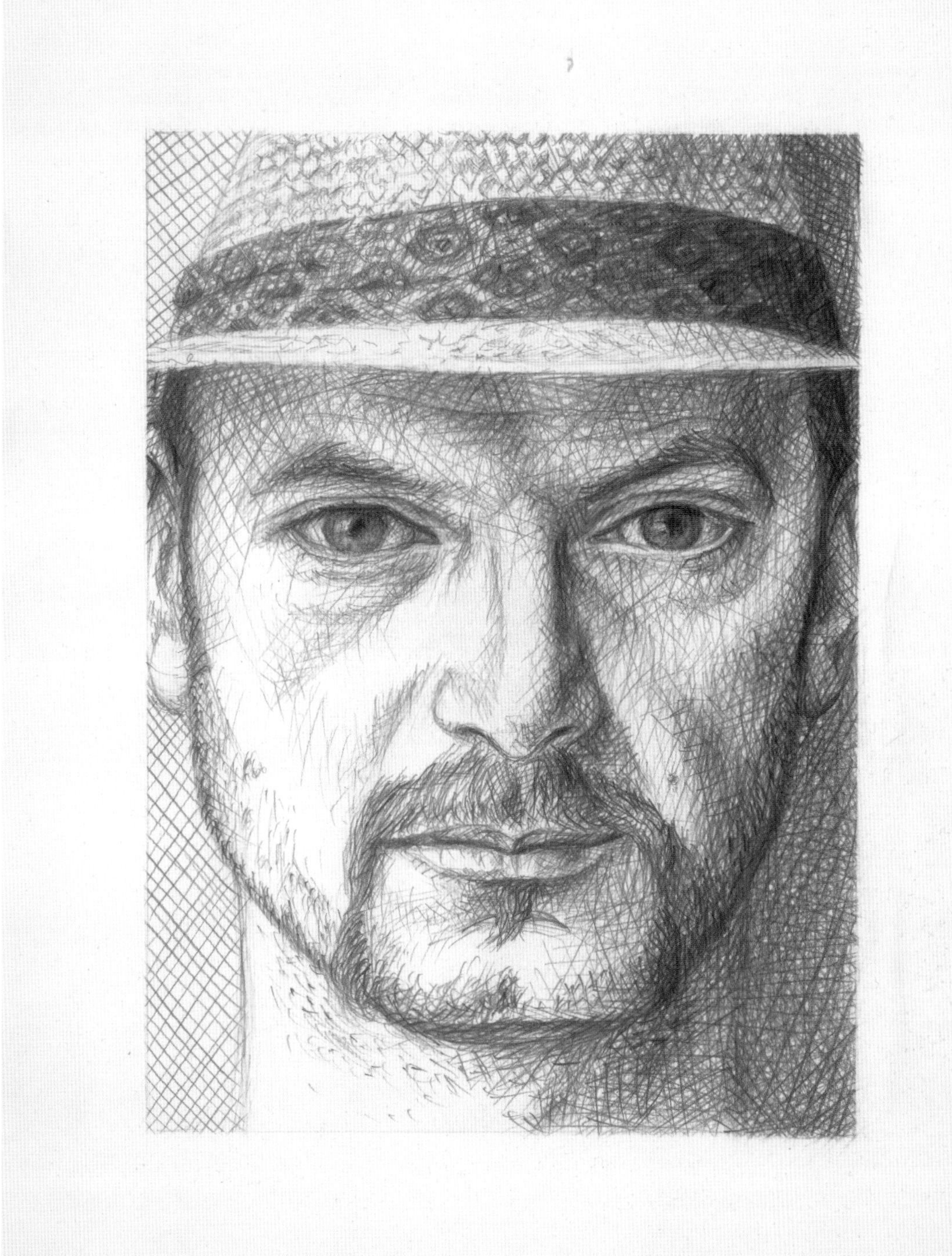

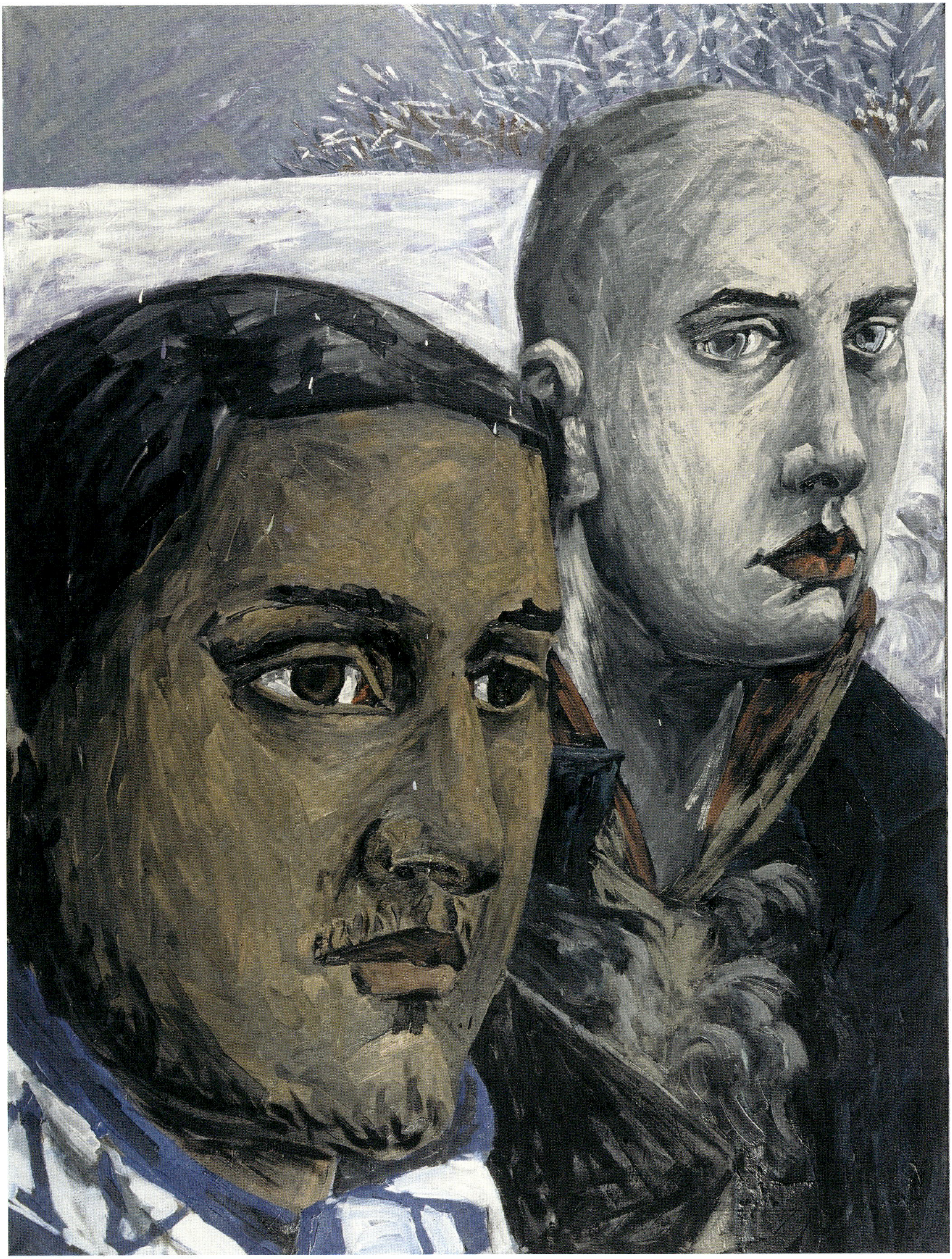

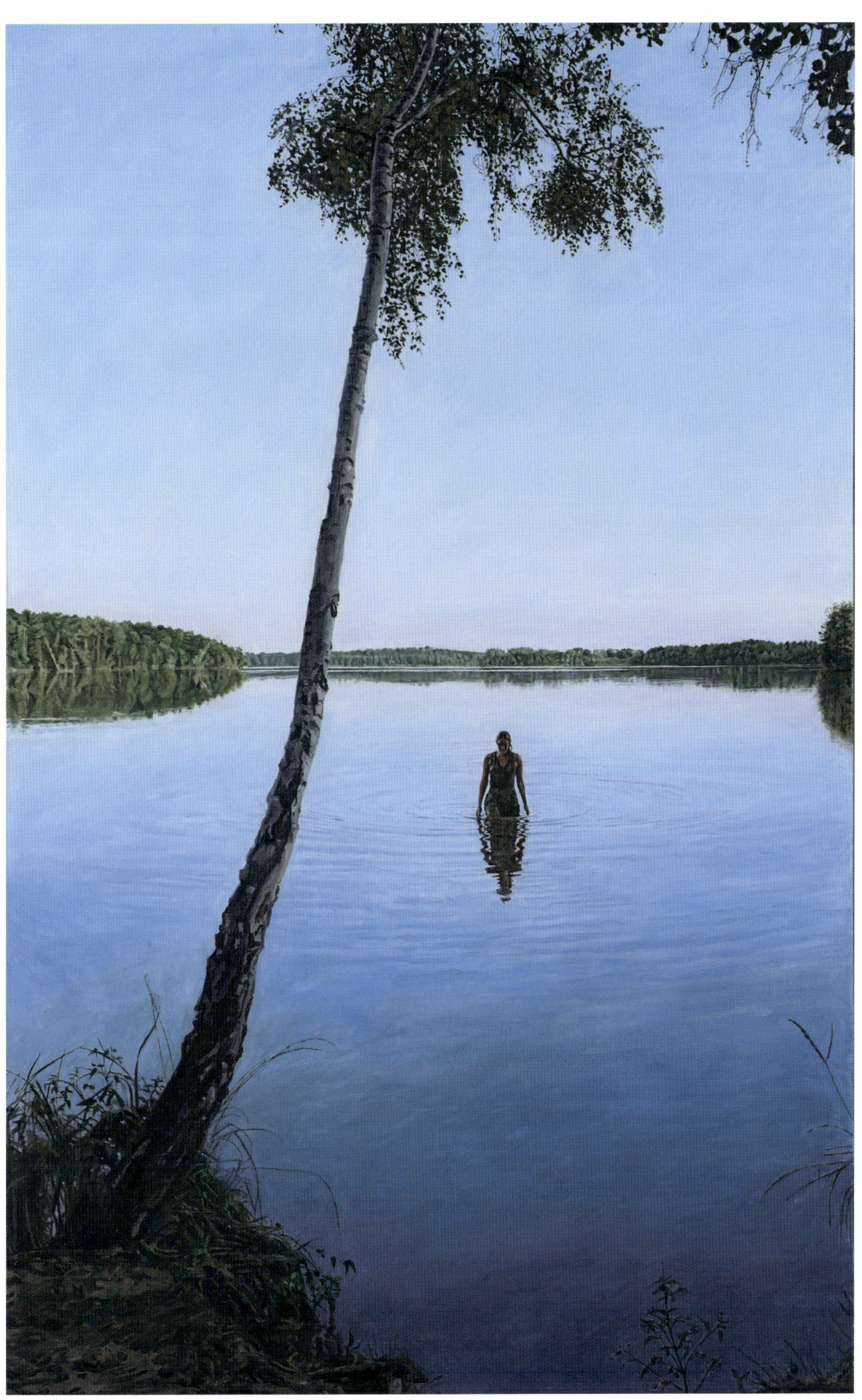

SUMMARY


SAŽETAK

10
**BORIS VON BRAUCHITSCH**
**SIZIF S CIGARETOM**
**RAZMIŠLJANJA O SLIKAMA LOVRE ARTUKOVIĆA**

Kad je Correggio slikao Ganimeda kojega odnosi orao ili kad je Rubens portretirao Cezara, tim su slikarima vjerojatno pozirale osobe iz njihova okruženja, utjelovljujući u ateljeu mitološke ili povijesne ličnosti. Zašto bi onda, kaže Lovro Artuković, on postupao drukčije pri kompoziciji velike povijesne slike koja prikazuje važan trenutak u povijesti njegova nekadašnjeg zavičaja? Bez mnogo pompe, s prijateljima je u berlinskoj gostionici postavio prizor potpisivanja Dejtonskog sporazuma kojim je 1995. trebao biti okončan rat i politički raskoli u Bosni i Hercegovini, a tom je prigodom politički ritual pretvorio u vjerski. Iz svečano inscenihranog, ali u konačnici dramaturški dosadnog stvarnog pariškog događaja - ondje su tri sumnjive osobe potpisale ugovor praćene kritičkim pogledima zapadnih kolega - u Berlinu je upriličena etnički šarena Posljednja večera s jasnim referencijama na Leonarda da Vincija i Veronesea (kojemu se Posljednja večera bez psa činila nezamislivom).

No poticaj za ovu sliku došao je više iz njemačkih, nego iz hrvatskih odnosa: od umjetnika s područja bivše Jugoslavije „na Zapadu" - točnije u Berlinu - očekuje se da svojom umjetnošću iskažu politički stav. Hrvatski bi umjetnik dakle trebao biti politički umjetnik, pa stoga monumentalnu sliku Lovre Artukovića treba u prvome redu shvatiti kao komentar toga očekivanja, koje ironično potkopava.

*Potpisivanje deklaracije o priključenju Zapadne Hercegovine i Popova Polja Republici Hrvatskoj (Tko je naručio pivo?)* glasi točan naslov djela, pri čemu je najvažniji dio u zagradi. Kao što znamo, umjetnost bi trebala postavljati pitanja.

Politički sukob, težak za proniknuti i razriješiti, svodi se na jednostavno pitanje na koje svi nazočni mogu lako dati odgovor, pa se ono iznenada učini najvažnijim, zapravo elementarnim s obzirom na bezumlje koje je Jugoslavija u raspadu doživjela tijekom godina nakon 1991.

Pitanje o tome tko je naručio pivo moglo bi se s obzirom na jeziva ratna događanja učiniti nekorektnim i apsurdnim, no ono otkriva stvarni apsurd - onaj povijesne zbilje. Tako što 22 prijatelja najrazličitijeg podrijetla okuplja za stolom ispod ploče na kojoj granice država postaju nevažnima u odnosu na jelovnik koji najrazličitijim ukusima nudi ponešto primamljivo, slika Lovre Artukovića izgleda kao vrlo neposredan poziv na miran suživot ili barem supostojanje s poštovanjem, što hrvatskome slikaru nudi njegov novi berlinski zavičaj. Imamo li pred sobom umjesto zakučastih dokumenata pepeljaru, a umjesto pera u ruci cigaretu, i način rasprave doima se ugodnijim čak i onda kada potreba za njom izgleda velika, a zbunjenost povremeno znatna.

Kad se Lovro Artuković iznimno upušta u kopiranje starih majstora, tada to ne čini zato da bi sebi ili drugima dokazao spretnost baratanja kistom, nego zato što zamišlja živo umjetničko djelo, primjerice zabavu na kojoj se gosti, uronjeni u ultraljubičastu svjetlost, kreću između podzemlja prizora iz povijesti umjetnosti. Ne plešu po vulkanu, nego ispod njega, između Iksiona i Sizifa, Perzefone i Prozerpine. No te kopije ostaju slikarevim rubnim primjedbama. Štoviše, one su nove interpretacije mitova i bajki koje ga zanimaju godinama, drevne priče o sreći i vječitoj ljubavi, izdaji, gubitku i zabludi, koje postoje u svim kulturama. Naposljetku umjetnik sam postaje Orfejem koji nakani svoju Euridiku izvesti iz Hada, pri čemu se on i djevojka pretvore u Ivicu i Maricu, zalutale u šumi, očito bez prostornog i vremenskog kraja, jer od izgubljene djece odavno je nastao par u dobi bake i djeda koji se oprezno probijaju šumom, ne nailazeći na spasonosnu vještičinu kućicu. Ultraljubičasto svjetlo, što ga je Artuković zamislio kao rasvjetu ateljea za svoj podzemni performans, dočekuje nas opetovano na njegovim slikama, kao da su ga takvog sablasnog platna upila. Tako je to primjerice u Ženskoj kupelji sa sedam ženskih likova, koji umotani u samo jednu dugu tkaninu okružuju limenu kadu s neonskim cijevima, a u njoj se praćakaju zlatne ribice. I ovdje je naslovu dodana napomena u zagradi, ponovno je riječ o pitanju i čini se da je to najvažniji putokaz: (Diana i Akteon?).

Promatrač može sam odgovoriti na to pitanje, zamislivši mit o mladome lovcu Akteonu, koji je boginju lova iznenadio dok se kupala, a ona ga je za kaznu pretvorila u jelena, pa su ga, ne prepoznavši ga, rastrgali vlastiti psi.

S obzirom na to da na slici nema ni jednog muškarca, muški promatrači mogu pretpostaviti da su pred slikom preuzeli Akteonovu ulogu i sada, nakon što ih je Diana takoreći u sedam stupnjeva reakcije na njihove poglede otkrila, postaju žrtvama vlastita promatranja slike. Sablasno svjetlo odavno je improviziranu idilu zajedno s dražesnom boginjom pretvorilo u tunel strave, tako da je još samo pitanje vremena kad će osveta s Olimpa sustići promatrača.

Svjetlo je ionako konstitutivni element. Za gledanje i slikarstvo u cjelini, a posebno na slikama Lovre Artukovića. Primjerice kad triput slika isti prizor uz različitu rasvjetu - ženu u spavaćici podvostručenu u par blizanki - jednom pred svijetlim, grubo ožbukanim zidom, jednom pri ugašenom svjetlu, a jednom sa zvjezdanom kartom i prikazom sazviježđa Blizanaca projiciranima na nju. Dvojica junaka, Kastor i Poluks, izbačena na nebeski svod kao glavne zvijezde, pojavljuju se kao dvije svijetle, odnosno obojene mrlje na licima dvostrukog ženskog lika. Atelje s daščanim podom, svemir, antička mitologija krotitelja konja i prizor mlade žene u spavaćici iz trgovine rabljenom odjećom pretapaju se, ili točnije rečeno naslaguju, u višeslojnu priču.

No onda je sablasnosti nestalo, ostao je goli zid. Taj zid nad daščanim podom poznat je s mnogih Artukovićevih slika, nalazi se u dvorištu na 52°29'11" sjeverne širine i 13°25'30" zapadne duljine. Da je učestalost te pojave mjerodavan kriterij, u slikarovu bi opusu imala najvažniju ulogu. I zaista se ta pozadina opetovano pojavljuje u prvome planu, glatko platno pretvara se u ožbukani zid usporedan sa slikom, posve samodostatan, u najboljemu slučaju naglašen utičnicom ili uronjen u plavičasto svjetlo noći.

Onda je netko ispred njega postavio trosjed, prikazan kao grubo sklepan i zgužvan, sa svim znakovima raspadanja, kao da je posve svejedno i time jednako vrijedno slike, što se događa na ovoj pozornici ateljea.

Lovro Artuković ne slika vatru, vodu ili zvjezdano nebo, nego projekcije vatre ili vode na zidu ateljea ili projekciju karte zvjezdanoga neba na gruboj žbuci. Elementi prirode, svemir i svijet gostuju u njegovu ateljeu. Moguće je napustiti taj prostor, ali to za umjetnost nije nužno. Tako prostor ateljea uvijek ostaje dijelom slika.

Ponekad Lovro Artuković djeluje poput druželjubiva usamljenika. Naoružan šarmantnim otporom prema odbojnostima vanjskoga svijeta koji se pravi da je stvarnost, razvija dimenzije i slojeve vlastite percepcije pred onim zidom i na onom zidu koji mu opetovano i iznova postaje platnom, da bi one onda kao takve napustile atelje i vani pronijele vijest o intimnome univerzumu. Samotnjaku u njegovoj pustinji odgovara proces umjetničkoga rada koji slikar opisuje kao usporenje. Dok se vani stvari odvijaju sve brže, on sebi uzima sve više vremena. On to objašnjava sve većom opsjednutošću pojedinostima i mogao bi biti u pravu. Pristaje uz njega da je upravo u nepredmetnosti bogatstvo detalja najveće. U zrcalnim folijama, koje od 2018. nadalje opetovano uzima kao motiv, odrazi se fragmentiraju, iskrivljavaju, zamućuju i rasipaju, ne apstrakcijom, nego promišljanjem.

Više pojedinosti jamči dulje vrijeme nastanka, također i više vremena za razmišljanje i uranjanje u slike. Fizičkome odrazu odgovara duhovni. Nabori zrcalne folije razbijaju ono što je pred njima kao u kaleidoskopu. A pred njima su pak stari majstori, motivi iz vjerskoga fundusa povijesti umjetnosti, vlastita djela, rastrgani likovi i prostori. Iza njih je, što u međuvremenu znamo, zid, goli zid ateljea. A između je folija: posve tanka, krhka, zlatna pozadina kao sa srednjovjekovne slike na dasci. No ovaj put u obliku najfinijeg materijala u kakav se umata unesrećene u prometu ili izbjeglice iz čamaca nakon spašavanja.

Tanašni sloj između običnog, tvrdog, bjelkastog zida i odraza u mašti postaje folijom za spašavanje. Umjetniku, promatraču, možda i općenito pri opažaju svijeta.

16

LEONIDA KOVAČ
DOGAĐAJ SLIKE

Postoji jedna crno-bijela, evidentno, precizno režirana fotografija s koje tri para očiju netremice gledaju u pogled koji ih promatra. Te oči koje uzvraćaju pogled pogledu koji ih pretvara u sliku pripadaju dvjema živim osobama i slici ovješenoj na zidu pred kojim sjede. Slika sa zida frontalni je prikaz krupnog plana lica mladog muškarca. Naslovljena je *Giacomo* i naslikana 2019. godine. Razmakom između njegovih širom otvorenih očiju jasno je definirana, kao u kakvoj renesansnoj *sacra conversazione*, vertikalna os simetrije fotografske slike o kojoj je riječ. Taj razmak između očiju lica naslikanog uljem na platnu odgovara razmaku između glava dvaju fizičkih tijela osoba koja sjede pred zidom na kojemu se vidi slika. Naslikana slika, doslovce, gleda preko njihovih ramena u pogled koji ih sve zajedno pretvara u sliku. Fotografija koju spominjem snimka je uprizorenja fotografskog portreta dviju nadrealističkih slikarica Leonore Carrington i Leonor Fini, koji je 1952. u Parizu snimila Denise Colomb. U tom *re-enactmentu* fotografske slike Leonoru Carrington i Leonor Fini, koje fotografkinji poziraju opremljene čudnovatim animalnim oglavljima, impersoniraju Lovro Artuković i Natascha Schönaich, a pogled sa slike ovješene iza njihovih leđa pripada licu koje se pojavljuje u Artukovićevoj slici *Tko tu koga gleda,* koja je 2004. bila izložena na njegovoj izložbi *Spremište*. Za razliku od te izložbe postavljene u javnom prostoru i namijenjene mnogobrojnoj publici, fotografija snimljena u umjetnikovu atelijeru reproducirana je na letku kojim je oglašena izložba *Some Things Just Stick in Your Mind,* održana u istome tom atelijeru 2019., izložba kojom je Lovro Artuković prijateljima i suradnicima predstavio svoju netom dovršenu sliku *Da vam pokažem svoj san (prema Leonori Carrington) - re-enactment* umjetnična *Autoportreta* nastalog 1937./38., koji se danas čuva u Metropolitan Museumu u New Yorku. Naslov te "komorne" izložbe - koji je također citat (naslova pjesme koju su 1965. napisali Mick Jagger i Keith Richards) - upućuje na brojna pitanja artikulirana radovima Lovre Artukovića tijekom zadnjih četiriju desetljeća.

Lovro Artuković kategorički tvrdi da se bavi slikama, a ne slikarstvom, premda povijest slikarstva počiva u svakoj čestici njegove slike, ili barem ja to tako vidim. Njegove me slike suočavaju s istim onim pitanjem Georgesa Didi-Hubermana postavljenim na početku njegove prevratničke knjige *Devant l'image* (1990.) koja "propituje *ton sigurnosti* koji često prevladava u lijepoj disciplini povijesti umjetnosti."[1] On pita: "[...] koji su to opskurni ili trijumfalni razlozi, koji morbidni strahovi ili manijakalne egzaltacije, doveli do toga da povijest umjetnosti poprimi takav ton, takvu retoriku sigurnosti? Kako je takvo *zatvaranje* vidljivoga u čitljivo, i svega toga u shvatljivo znanje, uspjelo i s takvom naoko samorazumljivošću, konstituirati samo sebe? [...] Ukratko, dotično 'specifično znanje o umjetnosti' završilo je u nametanju svoje vlastite *specifične forme diskursa* svom predmetu interesa po cijeni izmišljanja umjetnih granica tom predmetu interesa - predmetu lišenom njegove vlastite protežitosti ili razvoja. Tako prividna samo-očitost i ton sigurnosti koje to znanje nameće postaju razumljivi: sve što ono traži u umjetnosti odgovori su *već dani* njegovom diskurzivnom problematikom."[2]

Slike s izložbe *Spremište* Lovro Artuković popratio je 2004. komentarom posve suprotnim tom "specifičnom znanju o umjetnosti" koje je predmet Didi-Hubermanove kritike: "Slikarstvo

1  Georges Didi-Huberman, *Confronting Images: Questioning the Ends of Certain History of Art*, (prev. John Goodman), The Pennsylvania State University Press, 2005., str. 2.

2  Ibid., str. 3-4.

je pohranjeno u Spremištu koje se nalazi u našoj zajedničkoj, ukupnoj duši. Svi načini nanošenja boje, svi zanatski trikovi, sve 'novo' i sve 'staro' postoji u tom Spremištu oduvijek i zauvijek, bezvremeno, i postojat će sve dok je te zajedničke, ukupne duše, tj. čovječanstva. Prvi slikar sadržavao je već u sebi sve slikare koji će se pojaviti nakon njega, baš kao što onaj koji se ovaj čas rađa sadrži u sebi sve one koji su mu prethodili. Slikar uzima iz Spremišta ono što mu treba ili ono do čega svojom sposobnošću može doći i to iznosi na svjetlo jedinstvenog trenutka u kojemu živi. O tome jedinstvenome isječku vremena i o samom slikaru ovisi što će iz Spremišta izaći i kako će biti upotrijebljeno, kako će se materijalizirati u Slici.”

Kako se to, primjerice, *Autoportret* Leonore Carrington materijalizirao 2019. u ateljeru Lovre Artukovića, postavši slikom *Da vam pokažem svoj san*? Od početka 2000-tih taj atelijer u njegovim slikama učestalo biva denotiran kao mjesto radnje, međutim, mjesto radnje nije istovjetno mjestu događaja slike. To naslikano mjesto u dramaturgiji slike ne funkcionira kao *mise en scène* nekog događaja. Slika atelijera postoji da bi pokazala insceniranost prizora, a insceniranost prizora nije istovjetna insceniranosti slike, zato što slika ne može biti inscenirana: ona se događa i u tom je događanju ekscesna: ne na formalnoj nego na molekularnoj razini. U slici *Da vam pokažem svoj san* koja naslovom implicira dijalektiku intimnog i ekstimnog, gdje se *Autoportret* Leonore Carrington događa u atelijeru Lovre Artukovića, za razliku od umjetnice koja sjedeći u naslonjaču odjevena u jahaće hlače kažiprstom desne ruke pokazuje prazninu između sebe i hijene koja joj se približava gledajući u nešto izvan slike, žena s Artukovićeve slike kažiprstom pritišće tipku laptopa smještenog na postament s čije je prednje strane nacrtana hijena. Laptop je kablovima spojen s projektorom koji na mjesto prozora sa zavjesama, kroz koji se u slici Leonore Carrington vidi galopirajući bijeli konj, projicira sliku prozora sa zavjesama kroz koji se vidi bijeli drveni konjić za njihanje. Takav konjić u izvorniku lebdi pred zidom iza umjetničinih leđa, dok se na zidu vidi njegova tamna sjena. U Artukovićevoj je slici ta sjena zamijenjena velikom sjenom sjedeće žene, a drveni konjić plošnim, kartonskim što proviruje iza naslonjača. U slici *Da vam pokažem svoj san* rasprizorujuća aproprijacija autoportreta jedne bjegunice ne konotira pojam nadrealizma u terminima u kojima ga opisuje “lijepa disciplina povijesti umjetnosti”. Sklonija sam taj *re-enactment* shvatiti u smislu pitanja postavljenog u jednomu Sebaldovom romanu: “I zar ne bi bilo zamislivo, nastavio je Austerlitz, da mi i u prošlosti, u onome što se već odigralo i što je najvećim dijelom nestalo, imamo dogovore i moramo tamo pronaći mjesta i osobe, koji su, takoreći s onu stranu vremena, s nama nekako povezani?”[3] U toj atopičnoj lokaciji “s onu stranu vremena” prepoznajem događaj slike koji se u slikarstvu Lovre Artukovića manifestira kao *mise en abîme*. Bezdanost.

Godinu dana poslije, 2020. Lovro Artuković postavio je u berlinskoj Kewenig Galerie instalaciju *Tulum u podzemnom svijetu*. U sobu osvijetljenu ultraljubičastim svjetlom postavio je okrugao stolić prekriven bijelim stolnjakom na kojemu su se nalazile dvije neotvorene boce vina, nekoliko čaša, pepeljara i cvijet u vazi, a uz njega fotelju i jednu prevrnutu drvenu stolicu. Taj se aranžman nalazio pred zidom na koji je čavlićima u dva reda zakucao šest crteža izvedenih ugljenom na papiru tijekom 2019. i 2020. godine. Posrijedi su prizori iz grčke mitologije koji se zbivaju u podzemnom svijetu, a Artuković ih je nacrtao prema slikama nastalim u razdoblju između 16. i 19. stoljeća. Konkretno, to su Tizianov *Sizif*, *Povratak Perzefone* Frederica Leightona, Riberin *Ixion*, Corotov *Orfej vodi Euridiku iz podzemnog svijeta*, Rembrandtova *Otmica Perzefone* i *Psiha koja Veneri vraća kutijicu s ljepotom* nacrtana prema litografiji Antoinea Maurina, nastaloj prema slici Claudea-Marie Dubufea.

U zapisu o inscenaciji tuluma u podzemnom svijetu slikar kaže:

“Htio sam u svojem atelieru prirediti tulum pod naslovom 'Podzemni svijet'. Zamislio sam da prostor bude osvijetljen ultraljubičastim, takozvanim 'crnim svjetlom'. Na zidovima crteži ugljenom na papiru, čije bjeline pod UV-osvjetljenjem zrače neprirodnim plavičastim sjajem. Crteži su trebali biti kopije slika starih majstora koje prikazuju scene iz podzemnog svijeta grčke mitologije. Zamišljao sam kako gosti, za tu prigodu odjeveni samo u propisano bijelo ili crno, poput svjetlucavih duhova tumaraju ateljeom u maglici duhanskog dima. Po sebi je to zapravo banalan prizor, kao iz kakva kluba ili diska, ali činilo mi se da bi ipak mogao imati nešto mistično.

Kad sam počeo raditi na prvom crtežu, uvidio sam, međutim, da sam, premda umišljam da sam nakupio dovoljno iskustva u svojem poslu, još uvijek djetinjasto naivan. Vrijeme koje je trebalo uložiti u izradu vjerne kopije pomicalo je, naime, termin planiranog tuluma sve dalje u neodređenu budućnost. A i želja da ga priredim polako je jenjavala. Ipak sam nastavio raditi, unatoč osjećaju da činim nešto posve apsurdno. Zašto, zaboga, trošim vrijeme na nekakve kopije? Da bi mi netko nadjenuo nadimak 'Rembrandt'? I stoji li koncept ako tuluma ne bude? Pritom znam da bi 'pravi profi-umjetnik' prepustio taj mukotrpni posao nekome drugom, a sâm se posvetio pametnijem poslu.

No kako je rad na kopijama tekao, tako je u meni rasla stanovita radost zbog toga što moj pothvat nije imao nikakva smisla ni svrhe. A osim toga se nisam htio odreći užitka: kao prvo u crtanju ugljenom, a kao drugo u postupnom 'ulaženju' u orginalno djelo koje mi je služilo kao predložak. Na kraju krajeva, to je iskustvo ipak bilo poput silaska u podzemni svijet - ako već ne razuzdan tulum, onda ipak neka vrst druženja s onima koji više ne kroče Zemljom.”

Čitajući ovaj umjetnikov iskaz. nameće mi se nekoliko pitanja. Prije svega, može li se izvedbeni postupak koji opisuje svesti na puko kopiranje ili je posrijedi nešto drugo? Nadalje, je li taj pothvat prijevoda slika autora iz minulih stoljeća u minuciozne crteže ugljenom na papiru doista besmislen i nesvrhovit? Naime, 2022. Lovro Artuković je ugljenom na papiru nacrtao prizor iz vlastita

3   W. G. Sebald, *Austerlitz*, prev. Andy Jelčić, (Zagreb: Vuković & Runjić, 2006.), str. 273.

ateliera i naslovio ga *Perzefona*. U prednjem planu prikazana je mlada djevojka odjevena u kaput od umjetnog krzna koji grčevito stišće uz svoje tijelo kao da joj je hladno. Pogled joj je usmjeren u daljinu, u nekoga ili nešto što se u slici ne vidi. Na kuhinjskom šanku na koji se blago naslanja, nalazi se staklena boca u koju je uronjena grana procvjetale voćke. Iza djevojčinih leđa su otvorena vrata umjetnikova ateliera na koja je priku-can papirnati anatomski model muškog tijela koji se također često pojavljuje u njegovim slikama. Kroz ta se vrata nazire inscenacija *Tuluma u podzemnom svijetu* s jasno prepoznatljivim crtežima Rembrandtove *Otmice Perzefone* i Leightonova *Povratka Perzefone*. Pitanje koje se ovdje nameće glasilo bi što je u Artu-kovićevoj slici označeno pojmom Perzefona? Mlada djevojka u prvom planu slike? Seksualno nasilje normalizirano narativom grčkog mita i diskursom njegovih bezbrojnih slikovnih repre-zentacija? Povratak potisnutoga? Sve to zajedno? Ili nešto peto?

Lovro Artuković je 2020. ugljenom na papiru izveo *re-enactment* crteža simbolističkog slikara Odilona Redona *Orfejeva glava na vodi ili Mistik* (1880.). Dva crteža, ne-identična prikaza istog motiva, naslovio je *U vodi*. Format svakog od tih crteža približno je dvostruko veći od Redonova, a gotovo fotografski realistična glava, za razliku od skicozne Redonove, zrcali se na površini vode pokazujući tako svog iz-obličenog dvojnika. I nije posrijedi muška nego ženska glava čije potpuno opušteno lice "pluta" od profilnog prikaza u jednom do gotovo frontalnog u drugom crtežu. Ona se okreće, i u tom blagom, jedva primjetnom okre-tanju vizualiziranom kroz dva slikarska kadra prepoznajem artikulaciju Orfejeve transgresije zabrane okretanja, koja će rezultirati nepovratnim gubitkom. Rodna inverzija koja se do-gađa u ovome vizualnom prijevodu grčkog mita inducira pitanje koje bi, parafrazirajući naslov ranije spomenute Artukovićeve slike iz 2004., glasilo tko tu koga vodi iz podzemnog (ili možda podvodnog) svijeta? I nadalje, zašto se ona okreće? Ona, a ne on, okreće se i u crtežu iz 2021. naslovljenom *Orfej i Euridika (iliti Ivica i Marica - svejedno)* u kojem Orfeja i Euridiku (ili Ivicu i Maricu), krećući se opernom gestikulacijom kroz gustu paprat, impersoniraju Lovro Artuković i Jeannine Simon. Dok on nešto govori, ili možda pjeva, njezina ispružena desna ruka hvata nešto nevidljivo dok se ona pogledom direktno obraća promatračima slike. Ili, možda, sudionicima tuluma u podzemnom svijetu?

*Tulum u podzemnom svijetu* Lovre Artukovića odmah mi u sje-ćanje priziva jedan filmski tulum, raskošni i razvratni tulum koji u Jarmanovu filmu *Caravaggio* (1986.) u vatikanskome pod-zemnom svijetu priređuje kardinal Scipione Borghese, pokrovi-telj i kolekcionar umjetnosti, koji je, među ostalim, od mladog Berninija naručio skulpturalnu kompoziciju *Otmica Perzefone* (1621.). Derek Jarman je osobitu pažnju posvetio rekonstrukciji Caravaggiova svjetla i slikaru svojstvenim verističkim detaljima u prikazu ljudskih likova. U vrijeme kada je snimljen, film je efekt začudnosti postigao interferencijom povijesnog i aktual-nog vremena artikuliranom scenografijom i kostimografijom. Naime, u pojedinim epizodama situacije iz Caravaggiova života inscenirane su u dvadesetostoljetnim ambijentima vidljivo osvi-jetljenim električnim žaruljama. Električna žarulja redoviti je motiv, preciznije rečeno, protagonist radova Lovre Artukovića,

od onih ranih iz serija *Abeceda narcisoidnosti* i *Konstruirana svakodnevica* s početka 1990-ih, preko slika koje je početkom 2000-tih predstavio izložbom *Spremište*, do njezinih varijacija u formi neonskih cijevi u slikama iz serije *Ženska kupelj* (2014. - 2017.) ili svjetala ulične rasvjete, semafora, automobilskih farova, ili barskih svjetala nezaobilaznih u radovima iz serije *Noćna svjetla* (2019. - 2020.).

Otprilike u isto vrijeme kad Derek Jarman snima film *Caravaggio*, Lovro Artuković počinje u zagrebačkim galerijama izlagati ra-dove u kojima su, usprkos svojevrsnoj stripovsko-popartističkoj artikulaciji slikarskog polja, postojale jasne reminiscencije na teme iz povijesti slikarstva. Jedna od tih slika je *Tulum* (1985.), izvedena jajčanom temperom i ugljenom na papiru dimenzija 180 x 260 cm. Reprezentirani prostor privatnog stana u kojemu se sredinom 1980-ih zabavlja mnoštvo djevojaka i mladića struk-turalno je analogan reprezentiranom prostoru Artukovićeva berlinskog ateliera koji će se od 2010-ih do danas pojavljivati kao permanentni motiv njegovih slika, od kojih ovdje ističem već ranije spomenuti crtež *Perzefona* (2022.), te ulja na platnu *Disput o smislenosti figurativnog prikaza* (2015.), *Disput u ateljeu* (2015. - 2020.), *Anne (Royal)* (2015.) i *Djevojka s jabukom* (2017.). U oba slučaja posrijedi je reprezentacija zatvorenog prostora, sobe s vratima smještenim na stražnjem zidu kroz koja se vidi naoko sporedno zbivanje u drugoj prostoriji, i prozorom s lijeve strane koji u sliku propušta atmosferu izvanjskoga. Za razliku od prikaza berlinskog ateliera, soba iz slike *Tulum* naslikana je shematski, poput kutije s koje je odstranjena prednja stranica. Njezini su zidovi ornamentirani uzorkom koji podsjeća na stili-zirani firentinski ljiljan. I ne, nije posrijedi prikaz zidne tapete. Jer, isti će se ornamentalni uzorak pojaviti u Artukovićevu gvašu *Primavera* (1985.), koji je evidentna resemantizacija Botticellijeve slike koja se danas, s četrdesetogodišnje distance, u vremenu obi-lježenom hegemonijom informatičkih tehnologija, doima poput UV mappinga za teksturiranje u procesu kompjutorskog 3D mo-deliranja. Lovro Artuković prikazao je virtualni prostor, kocku ornamentiranih zidova nastanjenu siluetama likova s Botticellije-ve slike čija su tijela ispunjena istim ornamentalnim uzorkom koji se nalazi na zidovima unutar kojih su zatočeni. Takvi, doimajući se poput duhova, oni precizno vizualiziraju smisao naslova komorne izložbe iz 2019. - *Some Things Just Stick in Your Mind*.

Na to da je podzemni svijet u kojemu se 2020. događa Artukovi-ćev tulum područje nesvjesnoga ukazuje još jedna njegova rana varijacija na Botticellijevu temu, slika *Privođenje* iz 1986. godine. Kao predložak mu je poslužio fragment freske tog renesansnog majstora koji se danas, pod nazivom *Mladić kojeg se upoznaje sa Sedam slobodnih umijeća* čuva u pariškom muzeju Louvre. Na Botticellijevoj fresci ženski lik vodi mladića za ruku do grupe od sedam žena, koja alegorijski prikazuje Sedam slobodnih umijeća. U slici *Privođenje* Lovro Artuković svoju repliku Botticellijeve kompozicije jasno označuje kao fantazam. Jer, muškarac koji se uspinje stubištem i žena koja ga vodi za ruku naslikani su odje-veni, dok je sedam žena koje sjede u pozama istovjetnim Botti-cellijevim Slobodnim umijećima naslikano golo, bivajući tako prije nalik erotiziranim tijelima reprezentiranim u brojnim sli-karskim prikazima ženskih kupelji negoli alegorijama Gramatike,

Retorike, Logike, Aritmetike, Geometrije, Astronomije i Muzike. U Artukovićevoj slikarskoj izvedbi hibridizacija dviju ikonografskih tema popraćena je otapanjem granice između reprezentacije fizičkog i fantazmatskog prostora. Njegove su kupačice, ili ako hoćemo, Slobodna umijeća, smještene na pozornicu - u kutiju čije su stjenke također oslikane ornamentom koji se ponavlja po načelu beskonačnog uzorka. Nije li i mit svojevrsni beskonačni uzorak? Freska Sandra Botticellija nastala krajem 15. stoljeća, koju Lovro Artuković resemantizira slikom *Privođenje*, naslikana je na zidu Vile Lemmi čiji je vlasnik bio Giovanni Tornabuoni, ujak Lorenza Medicija. Uz nju se nalazila još jedna freska, *Tri gracije donose darove mladoj ženi*. Obje su naslikane u povodu vjenčanja Tornabuonijeva sina Lorenza s Giovannom Albizzi. Citat ove druge freske pojavio se 2001. u slici izvedenoj uljem na platnu i krhotinama stakla, koju je Lovro Artuković naslovio *Bože kako volim Botticellia*. Dijalektika boje i neboje - koja u toj slici funkcionira kao temeljni kompozicijski postulat - artikulira specifičnu vrstu vremenitosti, ne-kronoško vrijeme, odnosno simultanost različitih vremena u istomu mjestu događaja slike. To djelatno nekronološko vrijeme briše granicu između činjeničnog viđenja i fantazma. Kao i u Botticellijevoj fresci radnja se i ovdje zbiva pred zidom, međutim, na Artukovićevoj je slici taj zid jasno označen kao ogradni zid kuće u čijem vrtu cvjetaju voćke. U zidu su zatvorena vrata, a pred njim stoji mladi muškarac sklopljenih očiju na čijoj bijeloj majici piše "Bože kako volim Botticellia". Njegova frontalna impostacija u kadru odgovara mjestu na kojemu se u Botticellijevoj fresci nalazi profilni prikaz mlade žene kojoj Gracije donose darove. Četiri ženska lika ocrtana reljefnim konturama guste sive boje, identične boji naslikanog zida, koje mu se graciozním koracima približavaju s lijeve strane slike, doslovni su citat pokreta likova s Botticellijeve freske. One dolaze. Konturiranost prozirnih tijela denotira njihov status ukazanja. Sivu monokromiju ove slike probijaju jedino lica svih pet ljudskih figura, naslikana u boji ljudske puti, ciglenocrvena vrata u ogradnom zidu, te ružičasti i bijeli cvjetovi voćki. Indikativno je to što oči Artukovićevih Gracija nisu naslikane, doimaju se poput proreza na maskama, tako da se promatrač/ica umjesto s njihovim pogledima susreće sa sivilom zida, koje se kroz njih nazire.

Botticellijeve Gracije prozirnih tijela, konturirane poput utvara, pojavit će se u još nekoliko slika koje je Lovro Artuković naslikao u prvom desetljeću 21. stoljeća, objedinivši ih zajedničkim naslovom *Vidim slike koje netko drugi gleda*. Spomenut ću ovdje platno naslovljeno *Slika za zube* (ŠŠŠŠ) na kojem se Gracije kreću ispred kuće s plavim drvenim ulaznim vratima, označene kućnim brojem 62, te sliku iz 2006. naslovljenu *64*, koja je zapravo slikarev autoportret s kćeri. Broj 64 naslikan je kao kućni broj ciglene građevine pred kojom se ukazuju prozirne Botticellijeve Gracije, ali zapravo označuje pojam budućnosti. Naime, slika je nastala u vrijeme kada je Lovro Artuković imao četrdeset i sedam godina, ali je sebe frontalno prikazao kao šezdesetčetverogodišnjaka, sijede kose, zatvorenih očiju, odjevenog u crvenu raskopčanu jaknu ispod koje je bijela majica s natpisom "Bože kako volim Botticellia". Lik djevojčice koja stoji uz njega i gleda iz slike, odjevena također u crvenu jaknu, s nekoliko jesenskih listova u kosi, prikazan je u dobi u kojoj je slikareva kći tada doista bila.

U seriji *Vidim slike koje netko drugi gleda* - čiji naslov implicirajući

pitanje "tko je taj drugi?", ponovo upućuje na područje nesvjesnog, odnosno na Lacanovo (nedostupno) Realno - učestalo se pojavljuju frontalno prikazani likovi žene, muškarca i djevojčice zatvorenih očiju, čija se minuciozno naslikana kolorirana lica ističu spram njihovih prozirnih konturiranih tijela koja ih stapaju sa sivim okružjem. Među tim slikama je i umjetnikov autoportret naslovljen *San lovca na jelene* (2001.) koji ovaj ciklus ne povezuje samo s ciklusima *Šumski prizori* i *Umjetnici u prirodi*, nastalima u drugoj polovini 1990-ih, nego i s nizom insceniranih i pomno režiranih prizora koje je Lovro Artuković naslikao između 2015. i 2021. objedinivši ih naslovom *Izlet*.

Seriji *Šumski prizori* pripadaju i slike *Bukva* (1996.) i *Bukva s ožiljcima* (1997.), koje će autor puno godina poslije spomenuti u tekstu *Zahvala Bukvi*:

"[...] Svojedobno sam i ja bio u prilično intenzivnom kontaktu s drvećem. Nisam grlio stabla, ali sam ih crtao, a te tri-četiri godine čestih odlazaka u šumu nedvojbeno su bile vrlo dobre za moje tjelesno zdravlje. Zbog kretanja na čistom zraku bio sam u dobroj kondiciji, dok je crtanje u tišini šume, pažljivo promatranje izabranog motiva i njegovih gotovo neprimjetnih, ali neprestanih mijena bilo oblik kontemplacije, koji je godio mojem duševnom zdravlju.

Crtao sam različita stabla, mlada i stara, hrast, kesten i grab; ali pišem sve ovo zbog jedne bukve. Rasla je uz planinarsku stazu, a sudeći po opsegu debla bila je prilično stara. Kora joj je bila prepuna široko razjapljenih ožiljaka, urezanih imena i inicijala, jednostavnih recki i znakova. Svježe ogrebotine iskakale su intenzivnom narančastom na sivoj boji kore. Imala je takozvane „oči drveta" na mjestima gdje su joj otpale ili odsječene grane i vodoravne ispupčene ožiljke koji su podsjećali na tetovažu. Bila je na njoj također naličena planinarska markacija i još neke oznake - pretpostavljam, šumarske. Naslikao sam je više puta i u  tom se ponavljanju postupno mijenjao način na koji sam slikao. Zahvaljujući tom novom iskustvu počeo sam drugačije razmišljati o površini slike i o slici kao takvoj, i za to sam joj beskrajno zahvalan. Ako ikad budem opet planinario tim putem i ako ona još bude ondje stajala, čvrsto ću je zagrliti."

U isto vrijeme kad Lovro Artuković slika *Bukvu* i *Bukvu s ožiljcima* nastaje i serija gotovo monokromnih sivih slika čiji se krupni planovi koji artikuliraju dramatiku same slikarske tvari razlikuju od svega što je naslikao prije i poslije. Riječ je o seriji *Ožiljak* koja sadrži i dva njegova autoportreta - prikaza vlastite sjedeće figure viđene kroz svojevrsni predplan slike nalik kopreni načinjenoj od ožiljaka prepisanih s tijela bukve. Naslovljeni su *Autoportret* (1996.) i *Autoportret (kao bukva)* (1997.). Ožiljak, dakako, upućuje na pojam traume, a rad traume (koja je po definiciji nijema; poput bukve?) neodvojiv je od onoga što Sigmund Freud označuje terminom *Nachträglichkeit* - naknadnost. Premda Freud ne daje definiciju ni cjelovitu teoriju naknadnosti, taj je pojam iznimno važan u njegovu pojmovnom aparatu. U pismu Fliessu od 6. prosinca 1896. on kaže: "[...] radim s pretpostavkom da je naš psihički mehanizam nastao nanošenjem slojeva jedan na drugi, tako što je s vremena na vrijeme postojeća građa, sastavljena od tragova sjećanja, doživljavala *prepravke* u skladu s novim odnosima, neku vrstu *prijepisa*."[4] Sažimajući glavne crte tog Freudova pojma, Laplanche i Pontalis zaključuju: "Naknadno ne biva prepravljeno ukupno doživljajno iskustvo, nego se odabiru dijelovi koji se, u trenutku doživljaja, nisu mogli uklopiti u neku značenjsku cjelinu. Obrazac za to je traumatični događaj. Naknadno prepravljanje potiču novi događaji i situacije ili organsko sazrijevanje, što subjektu omogućuje pristupanje novom tipu značenja i ponovnu obradu ranijih doživljaja."[5]

Artukovićeva tvrdnja prema kojoj "Slikar uzima iz Spremišta ono što mu treba ili ono do čega svojom sposobnošću može doći i to iznosi na svjetlo jedinstvenog trenutka u kojemu živi", analogna je ovoj psihoanalitičkoj elaboraciji jednog od Freudovih ključnih pojmova. No, potrebno je vratiti se samom pojmu slike. U hrvatskom jeziku ne postoji terminološka distinkcija u označavanju različitih značenja pojma slike za što u engleskom postoje riječi *picture*, *painting* i *image*. W. J. T. Mitchell razlike između tih termina objašnjava krajnjim ambigvitetom same riječi slika (*image*) koja denotira fizički predmet - sliku ili skulpturu, ali i mentalni, imaginarni entitet, psihološku *imago*, vizualni sadržaj snova, sjećanja i opažaja. On napominje da slika svoju ulogu igra i u verbalnim i u vizualnim umjetnostima, a može čak i prijeći preko granice između viđenja i čujnosti u pojmu akustičke slike.[6] U psihoanalitičkim teorijama *imago* se definira kao "nesvjesna predodžba", no prije negoli slika, posrijedi je stečena imaginarna shema, statični obrazac kroz koji subjekt promatra drugu osobu.[7] Disolucija takvih imaginarnih shema u slikama Lovre Artukovića događa se u postupku inscenacije. Stoga ne začuđuje da je izložbu održanu 2014. u zagrebačkoj Laubi, na kojoj je pokazao slike koje su nastajale od 2006., naslovio *Uprizorenja*. U tim je slikama do vrhunca doveo umijeće slikanja inkarnata.

Slikanje inkarnata ovdje ne znači reprezentaciju puti jer mimezis nije posrijedi. Ljubičasti pigment koji Lovro Artuković koristi zove se *caput mortuum*. Prisutan je u djelima starih majstora. I alkemijska praksa poznaje *caput mortuum* koji se naziva i *nigredo*, a označuje beskorisnu otpadnu tvar koja nastaje u procesu sublimacije i sinonim je raspada i truljenja, pa su stoga alkemičari taj talog označavali simbolom stilizirane ljudske lubanje. Impresionisti su *caput mortuum* prognali iz slikarstva koje je u nadolazećem razdoblju definitivno svjedočilo vlastitoj sekularizaciji.

Termin *inkarnat* opće je mjesto diskursa discipline povijesti umjetnosti. U hrvatskom je jeziku preuzet iz njemačkog gdje označuje materične sklopove koji iluzioniraju boju ljudske puti. U njemačkom je jeziku u upotrebi i termin *Fleischfarbe* - što doslovce znači "boja mesa". Engleski jezik isti pojam denotira imenicom *incarnadine* koja ujedno označuje i svijetlogrimiznu ili ružičastocrvenu boju. Imenica je u 16. stoljeću u engleski stigla iz francuskog i talijanskog jezika u kojemu riječ *incarnatino* podrijetlo vuče iz latinskog *incarni*, što dakako vodi do pojma inkarnacije, a time i do zaključka da slikajući inkarnat Lovro Artuković ne reprezentira površinu tijela. Premda nas modernistička retorika uvjerava da slika nije ništa drugo doli ravna površina pokrivena bojom.

Na izložbi *Uprizorenja* izložio je i nekoliko nedovršenih slika. Nedovršenost u ovom slučaju ne znači da određenoj slici nešto nedostaje, već bi se prije moglo reći da u svim aspektima izvedbe Lovro Artuković izbjegava ono što se u filmskom žargonu naziva *closure* - zatvoreni kraj. On, naime, istu sliku na istom platnu nikada ne prestaje slikati, tako da ponekad nastavlja čak i onda kada slika, zadobivši "vlasnika" napusti njegov atelijer. Temporalnost tih nedovršivih platana pokazuje da isto nikada nije isto, te da to što se na površini platna vidi nije ono što slika jest. Slika nije i ne može biti dovršena zato jer ona nije reprezentacija (nečega) nego (trans)figuracija koja pričinjajući se realističkim prikazom odlazi s onu stranu realizma gdje uspostavlja odnos s Realnim. Ovdje, dakako, mislim na Lacanovo Realno. I baš zato je to što postoji na Artukovićevim platnima bliskije permanentnom performansu koji se događa ispod praga percepcije, negoli kategoriji slike. Riječ je o živućoj izvedbi u kojoj mimezis postaje scenska rekvizita. To događanje, zamućujući granicu između živog i neživog, generira nelagodu u slici, ili preciznije, nelagodu bivanja pred slikom koja promatrače iz prostora izvanjskosti transportira u vlastito prizorište.

U slici *Solarij* (2013. - 2014.) iz serije *Ženska kupelj*, čitavom širinom slikarskog kadra proteže se golo žensko tijelo. Poput Holbeinova mrtvog Krista u plitkom, tijesnom grobu.

Jednu od svojih refleksija o depresiji i melankoliji objavljenih u knjizi *Crno Sunce* Julia Kristeva ispisuje pristupajući Holbeinovu *Mrtvom Kristu u grobu* posredstvom zaključka kneza Miškina, lika iz romana Fjodora Mihajloviča Dostojevskog, prema kojemu "neki ljudi mogu izgubiti vjeru gledajući tu sliku"[8]. U licu tog mrtvog Isusa Nazarećanina ona prepoznaje "izraz beznadne boli", a u njegovoj plavičasto-zelenkastoj puti, čovjeka koji je "doista mrtav, napušten od Oca i bez obećanja u Uskrsnuće"[9]. Kristeva ukazuje na Holbeinov radikalni otklon od talijanske renesansne i manirističke ikonografije Pasije. Talijanska ikonografija - piše ona - "uljepšava i oplemenjuje Kristovo lice u muci okružujući ga likovima koji su uronjeni u bol, ali i uvjereni u izvjesnost Uskrsnuća, sugerirajući time i nama stav koji bismo trebali zauzeti suočavajući se s Pasijom.

4    Freudovo pismo Fliessu citirano je prema J. Laplanche – J.-B. Pontalis, *Rječnik psihoanalize*, prev. Radmila Zdjelar i Boris Buden, (Zagreb: August Cesarec i Naprijed, 1992.) , str. 245.

5    Ibid., str. 246.

6    W. J. T. Mitchell, *What do Pictures Want?: The Lives and Loves of Images* (Chicago and London: The University of Chicago Press, 2005.) str. 2.

7    J. Laplanche – J.-B. Pontalis, *Rječnik psihoanalize*.

8    Julia Kristeva, "Holbein's Dead Christ", u *Black Sun: Depression and Melancholia*, trans. Leon S. Roudiez (New York: Columbia University Press, 1989.), str. 107.

9    Ibid., str. 110.

Nasuprot tome, Holbein ostavlja leš čudno usamljenim." Prije negoli u crtežu i koloritu, Kristeva u tom *kompozicijskom činu* prepoznaje "obremenjivanje slike melankolijom". Zaključujući da je umjetnik Krista prikazao u najgoroj vrsti napuštenosti - ostavljenog od Oca i odvojenog od svih nas - ona postavlja pitanje je li nas možda Holbein pozvao da kristovski grob zamijenimo živućim grobom, da "sudjelujemo u naslikanoj smrti i tako je uključimo u naš vlastiti život da bismo s njom živjeli i učinili da ona zaživi? Jer, ako je živo tijelo, nasuprot krutom lešu, plešuće tijelo, ne postaje li onda naš život, kroz identifikaciju sa smrću 'danse macabre'?"[10]

U Artukovićevoj slici golo žensko tijelo leži na stolu prekriveno bijelom plahtom koja se uslijed svjetla koje ju odozgo obasjava doima plavom. Za razliku od Holbeinova Nazarećanina, njezine su oči i usta zatvoreni, a šaka, uz tijelo ispružene desne ruke, blago savijenih prstiju otvara se dlanom prema izduženom, horizontalnom rasvjetnom tijelu smještenom nad stolom. Dimenzije toga uzdignutog predmeta odgovaraju dimenzijama tijela koje pod njim leži. Međutim, nimalo nalik Holbeinovoj prostornoj restrikciji gdje *tableau* dopušta vidjeti jedino sadržaj grobne niše, Artuković portretira i prostor u kojemu to golo žensko tijelo nepomično leži pod nečim što se doima kao metalni poklopac kakvog sanduka. Kadar slike *Solarij* nalik je filmskom kadru snimljenom u dva plana. U njemu je istaknuta mizanscena: vidi se da stol stoji na daščanom podu i da se iza njega nalazi cigleni zid obojen u bijelo, pri čemu je ta bjelina zbog odsjaja "umjetnog sunca" - svjetla ultraljubičaste solarijske lampe - naslikana u plavim i ljubičastim tonovima. Da naslov slike ne upućuje na nešto drugo, scenu na čijem pragu stojim pred platnom velikih dimenzija mogla bih odčitati kao prizor iz obdukcijske sale, prostorije koja od kraja 20. stoljeća postaje neizostavnim, a nerijetko i glavnim mjestom radnje televizijskih serijala - prostor namijenjen ispitivanju "nijemih svjedoka". Ako je u današnjoj vizualnoj kulturi učinak masmedijskih pokretnih slika analogan učinku koji su sredinom drugog milenija imale slikarske kompozicije sakralnog sadržaja, onda nas te slike pozivaju na identifikaciju sebe samih s beživotnom materijom koja je nekad bila ljudsko biće. U suživotu sa sveprisutnim monitorima i projektorima, u vremenu disolucije granice između biološkog i tehnološkog tijela pri čemu nestaje razlika između stvarnog i virtualnog, sama praksa življenja, upogonjena imperativom konzumacije užitaka, postaje "danse macabre" koji Julia Kristeva, pišući o Holbeinovoj slici, apostrofira razmatrajući genezu i učinke melankolije. Možda baš zato nepomično tijelo koje se proteže čitavom širinom Artukovićeve slike - prikazano u stazi "poljepšavanja", u indukciji kemijske reakcije tijela na umjetno sunce, u preobrazbi koja će se najprije očitovati na koži - neodoljivo podsjeća i na Holbeinova Krista u grobu i na junake filma *Prometheus* Ridleyja Scotta - Kanea na ambulantnom ležaju svemirskog broda Nostromo i arheologinju Elizabeth Shaw koja usprkos svemu ipak vjeruje u Boga i koja u hermetički zatvorenomu medicinskom uređaju (proporcijama analognomu tijesnom grobu s Holbeinove slike) izvodi kirurški zahvat na samoj sebi: pobacuje čudovište.

Jean-Luc Nancy tvrdi da je svaka slika esencijalno "monstrativna" ili "monstrantna" i kao takva ona jest monstranca (ili uzorak), ono što se u francuskom naziva *ostensoir*. Zaključuje, nadalje, da slika pripada poretku čudovišta jer je *monstrum* čudnovati znak koji upozorava (*moneo, monstrum*) na božansku prijetnju: "Ono što je monstruozno pokazano (*monstré*) nije aspekt stvari; nego, posredstvom aspekta ili pojavljujući se iz njega (izvlačeći iz dubina, otvarajući i gurajući naprijed), jedinstvo i silina te stvari. Sama sila nije ništa drugo nego jedinstvo istkano iz osjetilne raznolikosti. Aspekt se nalazi u toj raznolikosti, on je odnos koji se proteže među dijelovima figure, međutim, sila počiva u jedinstvu koje ih spaja da bi ih iznijela na svjetlo dana. To je ono što nam sve slike pokazuju, neumorno i stalno na novi način: rad te sile ili potragu za njom. Slikar ne slika formu osim ako, nadasve, ne slika silu koja zahvaća forme, odvodeći ih u prezentnost. Pod tom se silom forme deformiraju i transformiraju. Slika je uvijek dinamička ili energetska metamorfoza. Ona počinje prije formi i odlazi s onu stranu formi. Svaka je slika ova vrsta metamorfičke sile, čak i ona najnaturalističkija."[11]

U razdoblju između 2006. i 2012. Lovro Artuković stvara niz od dvanaest slika koji naziva *Lice slike*. Posrijedi su kadrovi dimenzija 145 x 105 cm izvedeni uljem na platnu gdje se pojavljuje žensko lice naslikano u ekstremnomu krupnom planu. Ne radi se o portretima osoba jer odnos slikara i modela u procesu nastanka slike ovdje biva odnosom režisera i glumice (Karin Enzler), čiji zadatak postaje mimikom lica iskazati određeno emotivno stanje. Utjeloviti dramaturški zahtjev. Slikarski će postupak potom to stanje transformirati u energiju materije, a ta će eksplicirati prezentnost sile iskazavši je na površini lica kao trajnopulsirajuću boju nezaustavljivu granicama obrisa. Živuću boju koja jest raz-obličujuća i trans-formativna sila. Moglo bi se reći da svaki pojedini kadar Artukovićeva *Lica slike* u kojemu isto lice prestaje biti identično samome sebi, artikulira pojedini aspekt te metamorfičke sile o kojoj piše Nancy, jer ono što se tu događa s pikturalnom tvari doista treba razmatrati u terminima *de-formirajućih* transformacija. Materija upogonjena tom neimenjivom silom, ovdje doista *iz-obličuje*. Lice izlazi iz vlastitih kontura, njegova ih tvarnost probija. Koža, u preobrazbi lišena epiderme, postaje drugo ime za portretiranu metamorfičku karnalnu silu koja se doista *u-tjelovila* i postala inkarnatom. Njezin se izboj na površini lica slike pokazuje kao *caput mortuum* - pulsacija živog tkiva u neživoj slici.

Nancy tvrdi da u podlozi svake slike postoji nezamislivo imaginiranje: umiranje kao pokret samoprezentacije: "Na krajnjem završetku svekolike imaginacije postoji pristup bez pristupa onome nikad-još-poslikovljenome, i beskonačnoj u-figuraciji svake konačne figure. Slika uvijek obećaje više od slike, i ona uvijek održava obećanje otvarajući svoju imaginaciju u svoje vlastito nezamislivo. U podlozi slike je imaginacija, a u podlozi imaginacije je drugo, pogled drugoga, odnosno pogled na drugo i drugo kao pogled koje se, sljedno tome, otvara kao drugo pogleda, pred-videći ne-pogled."[12]

10   Ibid., str. 112-114.

11   Jean-Luc Nancy, "Image and Violence", u: *The Ground of the Image*, trans. Jeff Fort, (New York: Fordham University Press, 2005.), str. 21-22.

12   Nancy, "Masked Imagination", u: *The Ground of the Image*, str. 97.

To Nancyjevo "drugo", koje razumijevam u tangencijalnom odnosu s Lacanovim Drugim, odnosno Realnim, vodi me *Blizankama* koje se na Artukovićevim platnima pojavljuju od 2006. do 2014. godine. Postoji crna i bijela varijanta *Blizanki*; postoji jedna Blizanka kojoj pred slikom sazviježđa Blizanaca odnekud dolijeće nogometna lopta s brojem 90; postoji djevojčica u Blizankinoj spavaćici koja paleći šibicu dovodi jedan segment projicirane galaksije u stanje vidljivosti, i konačno, postoji spavaćica sama (kao da lebdi) - bijela noćna košulja (na bijeloj podlozi) koju je tijelo napustilo. Da bi postalo - što?

Melankolija *Blizanki* generirana je prije svega Artukovićevim kompozicijskim činom koji deiluzionira bajku time što pokazuje da se radi o naslikanoj slici - o dva zasebna slikarska platna montirana zajedno tako se dodiruju vertikalnim bridom čija vidljivost u tkivu slike artikulira pojam reza. Taj rez nije isto što i filmski rez. Bilo bi ga uputno razmotriti u kontekstu Freudova, odnosno Lacanova termina *Spaltung*, jer Lovro Artuković slika prizor rascijepljen u vlastitoj koherenciji. Posrijedi je koherencija projekcije, pri čemu je *projekcija* pojam koji se nalazi u referencijalnom polju svake njegove slike. Bilo da je doslovce naslikana ili ne, projekcija postaje protagonist slike - medij: ni novi ni stari nego nekronološka djelatna sila kojom je inducirana dramaturgija permanentnog performansa u Realnome.

*Blizanke* (2009.) poziraju (pričinjajući se da to ne čine) pred bijelim zidom, odjevene u bijele noćne košulje, stojeći bosim nogama na daščanom podu. Zid i daščani pod svojevrsni su zaštitni znak svih Artukovićevih slika nastalih u 21. stoljeću. Naslikani, oni denotiraju da je promatrani prizor insceniran u atelijeru, i da će ono što jednom postane vidljivo kao realistička slika uvijek ostati projekcija sposobna za indukciju daljnjih projekcija. Što je projicirano u to što vidim? I što slika u mene, povratno projicira? *Blizanke* (2009.) pokazuju upravo taj povratni pogled; inklinirajući jedna prema drugoj, različite i paradoksalno iste, one gledaju u nas mimo nas, pozivajući naš pogled da se zaputi s onu stranu njih samih. Do bijelog zida pred kojim stoje i koji se doima poput čistog, ali zgužvanog papira. Na njihovim bijelim noćnim košuljama još bjeljom su bojom naslikani pregibi što denotiraju da je ta odjeća bila izglačana i uredno složena prije odijevanja za prizor koji se vidi u slici. Tekstura tkanine gotovo je identična teksturi zida na koji se projiciraju naslikane, jedva vidljive, sjene tijela Blizanki. Na slici nastaloj dvije godine prije i naslovljenoj *Blizanci* (2007.) Blizanke, odjevene u iste noćne košulje, u istom inklinirajućem položaju stoje pred zidom na koji se projicira slika indigo-plavoga zvjezdanog neba s bijelim slovima ispisanim imenima sazviježđa. Tijela tih dviju djevojaka postaju ovdje, zajedno sa zidom pred kojim stoje, ekran za projekciju. Narančastom bojom istaknuto sazviježđe Blizanca postaje pritom rascijepljeno nespojivim ostatkom, procjepom koji nastaje u dodiru dvaju slikarskih platna koja nisu diptih nego figuracija totalnog prostora slike.

Pojam totalnog prostora pojavljuje se u diskursu o modernom slikarstvu sredinom dvadesetog stoljeća, a u rascjepljivanju "totalnog prostora" slike kakvo se pojavljuje u radovima Lovre Artukovića prepoznajem upravo repliku zahtjevu koji Clement Greenberg postavlja slikarstvu. Inzistiranjem na "normi medija", odnosno na plošnosti kao svojstvu koje slikarstvo ne dijeli ni s jednom drugom umjetnošću, na čistoći medija, Greenbergova racionalizacija implicite normira i želju: "Prostor kao neprekinuti kontinuum koji spaja umjesto da razdvaja stvari, daleko je shvatljiviji pogledu negoli dodiru (i to je još jedan razlog za isključivi naglasak na vizualnom). Ali prostor kao ono što spaja, umjesto da razdvaja, također znači i prostor kao totalni objekt, i upravo je taj totalni prostor ono što apstraktno slikarstvo sa svojom manje-više nepropusnom površinom 'portretira'."[13] Greenberg će ubrzo pojasniti i razloge za progon naracije iz slikarstva: "Slikovni je prostor izgubio svoje 'unutra' i sav postao 'izvan'. Promatrač više ne može pobjeći u njega iz prostora u kojemu on sâm stoji. Ako tu uopće postoji obmana oka, ona se prije postiže optičkim negoli slikovnim sredstvima: odnosom boja i oblika koji su naširoko razdvojeni od deskriptivnih konotacija, a često i manipulacijama u kojima vrh i dno, kao i prednji plan i pozadina postaju međusobno zamjenjivi. Apstraktna slika, čini se, ne nudi samo užu, više fizičku a manje imaginativnu vrstu iskustva negoli iluzionistička slika, nego se pokazuje da je ona za to sposobna bez imenica i prijelaznih glagola, dakle, jezikom slikarstva."[14] Međutim, ovakvom se institucionalnom normiranju iskustva suprotstavio možda najradikalniji od svih apstraktnih slikara, Marc Rothko, izjavivši sljedeće: "Ako vas u mojim slikama pokreću samo odnosi boje, promašili ste njihov smisao. Mene zanima izražavanje snažnih emocija - tragedije, ekstaze, prokletstva."

Tragedija, ekstaza i prokletstvo imenice su koje svoj učinak ostvaruju u sprezi s prijelaznim glagolima. Taj učinak površinu slike čini propusnom (onako kako se to događa u pokretu Rothkovih elementarnih čestica boje), a ta propusnost vodi do opipljivosti sile što djeluje iz podloge slike.

Riječi "površina" i "podloga" također su imenice i kao takve postaju prikazanim motivima, štoviše, dramaturškom okosnicom a ujedno i mizanscenom događanja u slikama Lovre Artukovića. Najočitije je to u slikama čija je tema eksplicirana odnosom dviju riječi koje autor smješta u njihov naslov: *kao da*. To *"kao da"* denotira privid kao supstancu onoga što realistička slika daje da bude viđeno. *Kao da* sriče vlastitu uprizorenost. Kao da su *Lažne blizanke u noći* (2013.), *Kao da je zvjezdana noć* (2007.), a radi se zapravo o nepropusnoj crnoj plastičnoj foliji (poput one što u Fellinijevu *Casanov*i glumi more) i rotirajućoj srebrnoj disco kugli. A sve je to naslikano tako da se čini kako nas prostor dodiruje, premda nam *kompozicijski čin* jasno pokazuje da stojimo izvan slike. Na njezinom pragu.

Za razliku od Greenberga koji, čini se, ne dvoji o mogućnosti slikarstva da načini portret totalnog prostora, koji bi trebao biti i totalni objekt, Nancy implicite poriče mogućnost portreta, jer "slikar ne slika formu osim ako, na-

13   Cement Greenberg, "On the Role of Nature in Modernist Painting", u: *Art and Culture* (London: Thames & Hudson, 1973.), str. 173. Tekst je prvi put objavljen 1949. godine.

14   Greenberg, "Abstract, Representational and so forth", u: *Art and Culture*, str. 136-137. Tekst je prvi put objavljen 1954. godine.

dasve, ne slika silu koja zahvaća forme odvodeći ih u prezentnost". A plošnost i prezentnost uzajamno se isključuju. U knjizi *Corpus*, koja je zapravo refleksija o inkorporirajućoj rečenici - *Hoc est enim corpus meum* - Nancy konstatira da "tjeskoba, želja da se vidi, dotakne i jede tijelo Boga, da se *bude* to tijelo, *da se bude ništa drugo doli to,* formira načelo Zapadnog (ne)razuma. To je razlog zašto se tijelo, tjelesno, nikada ne događa, ponajmanje onda kada je imenovano i sazvano. Za nas je tijelo uvijek žrtvovano: euharistija."[15] Konstatirajući da tijelo jest težina i da zakoni gravitacije uključuju *tijela* u prostoru, on se pita nismo li izmislili nebo samo zato da bismo učinili da tijela padnu s njega. Pritom tvrdi da je "Tijelo" naša ogoljena agonija i može služiti kao drugo ime za Stranca. Podsjećajući kako se jednom program modernosti sastojao u tome da se ne piše *o tijelu*, već da se piše samo tijelo, Nancy apostrofira dodir, a izvedbu pisanja tumači kao dodirivanje.[16] On nadalje zaključuje da je slikarstvo umjetnost tijela u tome što ono poznaje jedino kožu, bivanje kožom skroz i naskroz: "Drugo ime za lokalnu boju je *karnacija*. Karnacija je ogromni izazov koji su postavili svi oni milijuni tijela u slikama; ne *in*karnacija gdje Duh natapa tijelo, nego čista i jednostavna karnacija, koja upućuje na vibraciju, boju, frekvenciju, nijansu mjesta, događaja egzistencije."[17] Tijela se ne događaju u diskurzu ili u tvari, tvrdi Nancy. Ona se ne nastanjuju "um" ili "tijelo" već se događaju na limitu - vanjskoj granici, prijelomu i presjeku svega što je strano u kontinuumu smisla i kontinuumu materije.[18]

Poput Nancijevog pisanja, Artukovićevo je slikanje dodirivanje. U njegovim platnima nebo nije ništa drugo doli projekcija; tijela s njega ne padaju. *Kao da lebde* - i ne čini se nimalo slučajnim da je podloga pred kojom lebde - uvijek monokrom - jednom plav, drugi put bijel, treći put crven: poput boja kojima je naslovljena melankolična trilogija Krzysztofa Kieślowskog.

U slikama Lovre Artukovića nema ni traga iluzionizmu; one namjerno otkrivaju svoje "specijalne efekte". U slici *Na krilima* slikarska izvedba proizvodi dojam čujnosti zvuka naslikane aluminijske folije koja tu postoji u funkciji neprozirne, ali zato reflektirajuće pozadine pred kojom se lik djevojke u bijeloj haljini doima kao da leti. Krila, još bjelja od prebijele haljine, naramenicama pričvršćena za leđa, naslikana su takvom verističkom preciznošću da je gotovo moguće osjetiti mekani dodir njihovog perja na vlastitoj koži. Artuković ne slika let, ni pravi ni fingirani nego osjetilnu senzaciju, transformativnu silu - to "jedinstvo istkano iz osjetilne raznolikosti" koje pogled, odnosno mrežnica oka, ne može verificirati. I utoliko još jednom potvrđuje Nancyjevu tezu da je slika očitost nevidljivoga[19]. Stoga je posve irelevantno konotiraju li naslikana krila anđela ili Ikara, jer radi se o padu, o tijelu u ponoru vlastite karnalnosti, o bezdanu koji Artukovićeve slike, resemantizirajući aspekte dobro poznatih mitova, dovode do prezentnosti.

Resemantizacija je izrijekom učinjena slikom *Pietà obrnuto* (2011.), koja ima i svog "dvojnika" - sliku naslovljenu *Modeli poziraju za Pietu* (2011.). Nedvojbeno je da obje slike referiraju na najslavniji prikaz Djevice Marije s tijelom mrtvog Krista u naručju, onaj Michelangelov. Međutim, Artukovićev kompozicijski čin u kojemu protagoniste Pasije smješta pred isti onaj bijeli cigleni zid koji je zapravo glavni akter mnogih njegovih slika, jasno pokazuje da se radi o teatričnom uprizorenju u kojemu Pasija, prije negoli Kristovu muku, označuje tjelesnu strast. Prizor je artikuliran u dva plana. U stražnjem je istaknuta "scenska rasvjeta", prikaz vertikalno postavljene blješteće neonske cijevi pričvršćene za zid i strujnim kabelom spojene s minuciozno naslikanom utičnicom na istome tom zidu. U prednjem je planu erotizirani prizor u kojemu žena odjevena u široku crnu halju u krilu drži otežalo tijelo posve golog muškarca, čije su genitalije nepokrivene perizomom koja u kršćanskoj ikonografiji funkcionira kao označitelj Raspeća. Za razliku od Michelangelove Madonne, ona ne spušta pogled na položeni "teret" nego iz slike direktno gleda u promatrače. Težina ležećeg tijela postavljena je ovdje u direktan odnos s dodirom: slikar ističe napete mišiće ženine lijeve ruke kojom ona pridržava otežalu nogu onoga koji joj leži u krilu. U drugoj slici, *Pietà obrnuto*, mizanscena ostaje ista, a muškarac i žena zamjenjuju mjesta. On je i dalje gol do pasa i sjedeći, čvrsto se stopalima upire o daščani pod, dok ona zavijena u istu crnu draperiju, zabačene glave i uzdignute, u koljenu savijene lijeve noge, leži u njegovu naručju. U spuznuću s njezina desnog ramena koje muškarac obgrljuje, draperija otkriva da ona na sebi ima grudnjak kupaćeg kostima. Ovakva impostacija ležećega ženskog lika u kompoziciji *Pietà*, prije negoli mrtvog Krista u sjećanje priziva Berninijevu *Svetu Terezu u ekstazi*. Erotizacija prizora pojačana je naslikanim crvenim cvjetnim laticama posutim po drapiranom tijelu žene, i jednom laticom zalijepljenom na usne muškarca.

Čitajući *Mrtvog Krista u grobu* u kontekstu melankolije koju karakterizira identifikacija s napuštenim objektom[20], Kristeva se osvrće na jednu drugu Holbeinovu sliku, na gotovo monokromni diptih s prikazima Krista kao Čovjeka boli i Djevice Marije kao Mater Dolorosa[21]. Analizirajući sliku ona primjećuje da se "tijelo Čovjeka boli, neobično atletsko, mišićavo i napeto, prikazano kako sjedi pod kolonadom, desne ruke svinute pred spolnim organom, doima spazmičkim; sama glava okrunjena trnovom krunom s bolnim licem razjapljenih usta, izražava mračnu patnju nejasnog erotizma". Konstatirajući to, Kristeva postavlja sljedeća pitanja: "Iz koje muke izvire takva bol? Nije li Bogočovjek čemeran, odnosno progonjen

<br>

15  Jean-Luc Nancy, *Corpus*, trans. Richard A. Rand (New York: Fordham University Press, 2008.), str. 5.

16  Ibid., str. 8-11.

17  Ibid., str. 15-17.

18  Ibid., str. 17.

19  Jean-Luc Nancy, "The Image – the Distinct", u: *The Ground of the Image*, str. 12.

20  Sigmund Freud melankoliju povezuje s gubitkom, a kao njezina obilježja navodi "bolnu potištenost, prestanak interesa za vanjski svijet, gubitak sposobnosti za voljenje, inhibiciju svih aktivnosti, slabljenje osjećaja samopoštovanja koje se manifestira u samoponižavanju i samopovređivanju koje kulminira u iluzornom očekivanju kažnjavanja". Za razliku od žalovanja, piše on, "gdje svijet postaje jadan i prazan, u melankoliji to postaje sam *ego*. Slobodni libido ne premiješta se na drugi objekt, već se povlači u *ego*. U tom se procesu *ego* identificira s napuštenim objektom, te se tako gubitak objekta transformira u gubitak *ega*, a konflikt između *ega* i voljene osobe u rascjep između kritičke aktivnosti *ega* i *ega* izmijenjenog identifikacijom". Sigmund Freud, *Mourning and Melancholia*, (trans. James Strachey), SE, vol. XIV (London: Hogarth Press and The Institute of Psychoanalysis), str. 244 i 249.

21  Diptih datiran oko 1520. godine nalazi se u zbirci baselskog Kunstmuseuma.

smrću, *zato* što je seksualan, žrtva seksualne strasti?"[22] Isto sam pitanje sklona prepoznati u Artukovićevim varijacijama na temu *Pietà* u kojima lica protagonista koji uprizoruju klasični prizor kršćanske ikonografije bezbroj puta citiran u djelima moderne i suvremene umjetnosti - od Eisensteina, preko Picassa do Sam Taylor Wood - ne odaju ni najmanji trag ojađenosti.

Eksplicitni prikaz "tormentuma" pojavit će se, međutim, u Artukovićevu *Visećem autoportretu* (2009. - 2013.), koji će i sâm postati slika u slici na platnu dimenzija 270 x 360 cm, nastalom u razdoblju između 2009. i 2011. godine, naslovljenom *Apolon i Marsija (Trijumf novih medija nad slikarstvom)*. U *Visećem autoportretu* naslikanom u prirodnoj veličini (250 x 110 cm) tijelo se događa na granici: teatričke inscenacije i medijske slike, konkretno snimki sadističkih iživljavanja načinjenih iz razonode mučitelja u izolacijskim logorima, otvorenima početkom nikad objavljenog svjetskog rata započetog nakon famoznog 11. rujna, s kojim smo kročili u epohu nekropolitike i totalne (medijske) kontrole. Slikar se u ovom platnu portretira doslovce kao meso obješeno, recimo, u unutrašnjosti kakve hladnjače. Ono na čemu visi su konopi pričvršćeni na alpinistički remen zategnut oko golog tijela. Taj remen istodobno konotira ekstremni sport, težnju usponu - dosezanju mjesta gdje još nijedno ljudsko biće nije kročilo, ali i sadomazohističku opremu. U drugom planu slike, viseći paralelno s tijelom slikara pred zidom koji zaklanja, naslikana je zgužvana, prljavobijela platnena zavjesa. Slikarsko platno iz kojeg je tijelo umaknulo? Ili možda, Torinsko platno s inkarnacijom jedne posve drukčije slike? *Caput mortuum* obitava na glavi u koju se slila krv, na prsima i dlanovima koji se otvaraju prema promatraču čije je tijelo pripušteno do ruba slike.

U *Trijumfu novih medija nad slikarstvom,* koju sâm autor naziva "glomaznom slikom" podsjećajući time na sve one primjerke takozvanoga historijskog slikarstva, na platna enormih dimenzija kojima su napučene sale muzeja europskih metropola, *Viseći Autoportret* odigrat će ulogu satira Marsije kojemu je bog Apolon oderao kožu pobijedivši ga, na prevaru, u natjecanju u sviranju. Marsija je, naime, naivno dograbio dvostruku sviralu od jelenje kosti koju je božica Atena odbacila ugledavši svoj lik u vodi i shvativši da joj izobličeni obrazi, poplavili od puhanja (*caput mortuum*?), kvare ljepotu. Marsijina je svirka izazivala udivljenje dok je u pratnji Kibele - Velike Majke Bogova - putovao Frigijom, stoga ga je zavidni Apolon izazvao predloživši mu da se natječu svirajući svaki svoj instrument naopako, te da pobjednik može s pobijeđenim učiniti što hoće. Budući da flautu, za razliku od Apolonove lire nije bilo moguće svirati naopako, Muze su presudile u Apolonovu korist, a Marsijina se odrana koža našla prikovana za bor.

Ova me mitska pripovijest ponovno vodi terminima u kojima sredinom 20. stoljeća Clement Greenberg, najutjecajniji američki kritičar toga razdoblja, stvara modernistički mit o mogućnosti čistoće pojedinog umjetničkog medija i argumentira prohibiciju naracije iz slikarstva. On piše: "Kubizam je poduzeo potpuno dvodimenzionalnu transkripciju trodimenzionalnih fenomena za inat svemu što su impresionisti naučavali o svjetlu i sličnosti;

bivajući *skulpturalno* iscrpnim, pokazujući u osjenčanom reljefu stražnju, bočnu, kao i prednju stranu predmeta, kubizam je završio u još radikalnijem poricanju svakog iskustva koje nije doslovce dostupno oku.  Sa svijeta je bila svučena površina, koža, i ta se oplošnjena koža protegnula na plošnost plana slike. Slikarska se umjetnost u cijelosti reducirala na ono što je bilo vizualno provjerljivo, a Zapadno je slikarstvo konačno odustalo od petstogodišnjeg rivalstva s kiparstvom u nastojanjima da bi se evociralo taktilno. A skupa s taktilnim trebalo se odreći repertoara slika i poslikovljenja, utoliko i svega što je iz svijeta neslikarskog prostora donosilo konotacije i asocijacije koje mrežnica sama od sebe nije mogla verificirati."[23]

Dovodeći u odnos greenbergovsku "čistku", odnosno metaforu napinjanja oderane kože na mjesto jedinstvenoga slikarskog plana s Artukovićevim narativom, konkretno s *Visećim autoportretom* s eksplicitnim prikazom naopako visećeg penisa, te obj.ešenom tkaninom koja bi mogla biti i ta sa svijeta oderana koža koja je mističnom diskurzivnom transfiguracijom odjednom postala slikarsko platno, ne mogu se ne prisjetiti konteksta u kojemu Lovro Artuković započinje slikarsku karijeru. Naime, danas je posve jasno da je retorika visokog modernizma imala vrlo jasan cilj - depolitizaciju umjetnosti. Depolitizirana, "apstraktna" umjetnost tijekom druge polovine 20. stoljeća postala je *mainstream* u Hrvatskoj, tada jednoj od jugoslavenskih republika. Lovro Artuković, koji se na hrvatskoj umjetničkoj sceni pojavljuje početkom 1980-ih, nikada nije bio zainteresiran za modernistički formalizam; u njegovim je radovima uvijek postojala "priča" koja je vodila drugim pričama. Podsjećam ovdje na ironičnu, i zapravo kritičku sliku naslovljenu *Kičer u sjeni* (1999.) iz serije *Umjetnici u prirodi*, koja nedvojbeno konotira greenbergovsku binarnu opoziciju avangarde i kiča[24], gdje je takozvana "figurativna umjetnost" implicite bila gotovo izjednačena s kičem. Sličnim površnim binarnim opozicijama i predrasudama koje one generiraju svjedočimo i danas. Jedna od njih je i podjela na takozvane "tradicionalne" i "nove medije". Slika *Apolon i Marsija* referira upravo na to i zato je u multimedijskom performansu koji se uprizoruje na slikarskom platnu poraženi Marsija zapravo slikarska slika - autoportret (samo) obješenog slikara. Međutim, kompozicijski čin počinjen u obje slike uskraćuje mogućnost nedvojbenog zaključka radi li se tu o kazni ili o erotskom užitku.

Kadar slike *Apolon i Marsija (Trijumf novih medija nad slikarstvom)* podijeljen je na tri usporedna plana od kojih niti jedan nije ni prednji, ni srednji, ni stražnji. Cijela je slika zapravo međuplan u kojemu se događa nekoliko simultanih scenskih izvedbi, koje su ujedno i slikarske izvedbe. Lovro Artuković ovdje slika razine performansa u kojemu stvarno nije moguće razlučiti od virtualnog, ili ako hoćemo istinito od lažnog, a ta irelevantnost istinitosti vodi prema pojmu performativa. Spominjući performativ od kojega je pojam performansa neodvojiv, smatram potrebnim podsjetiti da Shoshana Felman

23  Greenberg, "On the Role of Nature in Modernist Painting", u: *Art and Culture,* str. 172.

24  Greenbergov tekst "Avagarda i kič" prvi je put objavljen 1939. godine.

22  Kristeva, op. cit., str. 112.

razlikuje tri značenjske konotacije engleske riječi performance: lingvističku, teatričku i erotičku[25], a sve su te konotacije sadržane u Artukovićevoj "lažnoj povijesnoj slici"[26]. I slika *Apolon i Marsija (Trijumf novih medija nad slikarstvom)* izrijekom pokazuje vlastitu in


 insceniranost na istoj pozornici gdje se zbivaju svi Artukovićevi "događaji tijela" - u atelijeru s bijelim ciglenim zidom i daščanim podom. Ono što slika daje da bude viđeno jest *re-enactment* jedne kazališne izvedbe, a u tom slikarskom *re-enactmentu* događa se poništavanje binarne opozicije između slikarske, naslikane slike i digitalne, elektroničke slike projicirane na plohu ekrana naslikanog unutar slike. Ono što predstavu koja se dogodila u jednome drugom prostoru i u jednome drugom trenutku spaja sa slikarskim platnom koje tu izvedbu resemantizira jest motiv zida. Jer modeli koji poziraju za *Apolona i Marsiju* plesačice su iz skupine *Nightmare before Valentine* koje u teatru izvode predstavu *Früchte im Koma* čija se koreografija temelji na njihovim skokovima pri čemu vlastitim tijelima udaraju o zid. S desne strane tog Artukovićeva platna naslikana je slika *Viseći Autopotret* koja u novoj slikarskoj dramaturgiji igra ulogu satira Marsije, prema kojemu se, s noževima u rukama, zaljeću dvije plesačice, istim onakvim skokovima kakve izvode u predstavi *Früchte im Koma*. Impersoniraju li one ovdje likove Muza koje su proglasile pobjednika i time omogućile Apolonu da odere Marsijinu kožu? S druge, lijeve strane Artukovićeva platna, Apolon na "pobjedničkom postolju" otvara šampanjac. Međutim, prostor u kojemu Apolon slavi, virtualni je prostor projekcije. Njegov "trijumf" projicira se na zlatnu ispresavijanu, zrcaleću foliju koja služi kao ekran. Na isti se ekran projicira fotografija teleskopske snimke eksplozija na sunčevoj površini, pa se pobjednikova figura, kao i figure istih onih dviju plesačica koje tu pred "Apolonom" izvode svoj performans, gubi u nejasnoći. Pjenušac koji pobjednik otvara u prostoru ekrana ispija se u prostoru slikareva atelijera gdje traje izvedba "zlostavljanja slike". Ispijaju ga, također u koreografiranom pokretu nazdravljajući staklenim čašama, dvije žene u elegantnim crnim kožnim mantilima, pogleda zaklonjenih tamnim naočalama, smještene gotovo u geometrijsko središte slike, u međuprostor trijumfa i kazne. Nancy na jednome mjestu konstatira da umjetnost "nije simulakrum ni apotropejska forma koja će nas zaštititi od neopravdanog nasilja. Ona je egzaktna spoznaja da se nema što obznaniti, pa čak ni ponor, te da bezpodložnost nije vatreni bezdan nego neizbježnost koja beskonačno visi sama nad sobom."[27] U Artukovićevim kostimiranim i koreografiranim "izvedbama" slike postoji osebujan odnos između tijela i ruha. Ili možda točnije, metamorfičke sile i njezinog uvijek novog ruha. Pojam ruha slike (koja uvijek održava obećanje) u njegovim je radovima konotiran prikazom pakirnog materijala kojim se umjetnina zaštićuje od mehaničkih oštećenja - plastične folije sa zračnim mjehurićima. U takvo je ruho odjevena djevojka s plavom perikom u slici *Ari u trash kostimu* (2012.). Istim je materijalom omotana i u kompoziciji *Ari*


25  Shoshana Felman, *Skandal tijela u govoru: Don Juan s Austinom ili zavođenje na dva jezika* (Zagreb: Naklada MD, 1993.), str. 24.

26  Artuković sliku *Apolon i Marsija* naziva lažna "povijesna slika". Vidjeti intervju s Patricijom Kiš, Jutarnji list, 21. 02. 2011., http://www.jutarnji.hr/lovro-artukovic--ovo-sam-ja-sa-64--htio-sam-znati-kako-cu-izgledati-kad-ostarim--plasi-me-prolaznost-vremena--i-smrt/926802/ (pristup 20. 7. 2014.)

27  Nancy, "Image and Violence", u: *The Ground of the Image*, str. 26.


*pleše s plastičnim čašama* (2012. - 2013.). Tijelo kao slika? Ovojnica kao pigment? Slika kao kostim? Ili, tijelo kao kostim? Strano sebi samom. Kao da je melankolični *Alien*, ili *Sramežljivi kauboj* (2005. -2010.), što je naslov jednog od Artukovićevih autoportreta. U tom se autoportretu prikazao frontalno, oborenog pogleda. Gol do pasa, skrivajući obnažene grudi prekriženim rukama, on stoji pred slikarskim platnom koje je licem okrenuto prema zidu tako da se ono što je naslikano ne vidi. Nad tom su slikom naslikane dvije fotografije s jasno prepoznatljivim prizorima iz westerna. Dva posve drukčija autoportreta naslikat će 2022. godine. Prvi, naslovljen *Autoportret - misleći na Marina Tartagliju*, re-enactment je jedne od najvažnijih slika u povijesti hrvatskoga modernog slikarstva, ekspresionističkog autoportreta koji je u vrlo malom formatu Marino Tartaglia naslikao 1917. godine. Taj je *Autoportret* prvi put bio izložen 1918. na *Mostra d'arte indepedente* u rimskoj galeriji L'Epoca, zajedno s djelima Giorgia de Chirica, Carla Carràa i Enrica Prampolinija. Drugi Artukovićev autoportret koji doslovce vizualizira futuristički pojam vrtoglave brzine, koloristički je srodan onom prvome, a naslovljen je *Autoportret - u trenutku kada se pokušavam nečega sjetiti*. Pokušaj prisjećanja vizualiziran je prikazom rasprskavajuće glave. Oba autoportreta izvedbeno su srodna nekoliko godina ranije nastalim slikama iz ciklusa *Odrazi*, koje je Lovro Artuković, zajedno s onima iz serija *Posjet atelijeru, Noćna svjetla* i *Izlet*, pokazao 2020. na izložbi naslovljenoj *Usporavanje*, postavljenoj u Nacionalnom muzeju moderne umjetnosti u Zagrebu.

Govoreći o tim radovima on kaže da to što slikama namjerava doseći zahtijeva sve više vremena: "Slike bivaju sve napučenije detaljima a način slikanja, bezbrojna prelaženja jednog te istog mjesta na slici lazurama da bih dobio željenu prisutnost i gustoću naslikanog, uzima sate i sate koji nekako neprimjetno prolaze. Često, sjedeći zarobljen danima na jednom detalju slike, mislim kako bih trebao ubrzati postupak slikanja, biti produktivniji, raditi adekvatnije vremenu u kojem se sve odvija sumanutom brzinom i u kojem, ajoj, ionako nitko neće imati ni strpljenja niti koncentracije da se staromodnim užitkom gledanja upusti u promatranje moje slike."

Moj vlastiti, možda i staromodni užitak gledanja njegovih slika, koje prikazuju odraze na poliesterskoj metaliziranoj foliji koja se kao obvezni sadržaj nalazi u automobilskoj kutiji prve pomoći, vodi me pitanju o razlici, odnosno o enigmi toga nečega neimenovanog što Lovro Artuković slikajući "namjerava doseći". Poliesterska folija, poznata pod nazivima Rettungsdecke, emergency blanket, space blanket ili pokrivač za preživljavanje, standardnih dimenzija 210 x 160 cm, izumljena 1964. u okviru NASA-inoga svemirskog programa, višenamjenski je proizvod. Taj vodootporni i vjetronepropusni pokrivač s jedne strane zlatne, a s druge srebrne boje održava tjelesnu temperaturu stabilnom, a njegova sjajeća površina spasiocima olakšava potragu za unesrećenim osobama. U Artukovićevom se slikarstvu njegov portret prvi put pojavljuje 2009. u slici iz serije *Mjesto*, naslovljenoj *Zlato (pokrivač prve pomoći)*. Mjesto je, dakako, umjetnikov atelijer, a zlato poliesterna folija pričvršćena za zid, koja seže do poda atelijera. Površina joj je raščlanjena pravilnim rasterom četvrtastih faseta nastalih zbog presavijanja, odnosno ambalažiranja prekrivača. U toj slici motiv reflektirajućega lažnog zlata zauzima puni kadar dimenzija 145 x 125 cm. Iste godine pokrivač prve pomoći pojavit će se u slici *Novogodišnja haljina* u funkciji zlatne pozadine pred kojom lebdi zelena haljina iz serije *Kao da*. Naslikani motivi iz te serije, kao i sâm njezin naziv, reprezentirajući prizore u stanju insceniranosti, konotiraju pojam privida. Ili varke za oko. Privid u svojim mnogostrukostima postat će jednom od glavnih tema slika na kojima Lovro Artuković radi od 2018. do danas. U njima naslikani odrazi - vidljivi na površini zlatnog pokrivača prve pomoći - defiguriraju prizore iz umjetnikova atelijera. Ta se defiguracija manifestira kao beskonačno umnažanje različitih slika unutar jedne te iste slike. *Mise en abîme?*

Kad spominjem razliku pomišljam na instalaciju *Tragedia civile* koju je Jannis Kounellis izveo u svibnju 1975. u napuljskoj galeriji Lucio Amelio. Galerijski zid na čijem se lijevom dijelu nalaze ulazna vrata u prostoriju u cijelosti je obložio kvadratičnim zlatnim listićima. Uza nj je postavio starinsku drvenu, takozvanu bečku vješalicu, i na nju ovjesio iznošeni crni muški kaput i šešir. Na desni bočni zid pričvrstio je petrolejsku lampu čije će svjetlo diskretno oponirati dominantnome neonskom osvjetljenju galerije. Zlatni će zid isijavati specifičnu svjetlost i ujedno inkorporirati tamne sjene stalka i odložene odjeće. Postoje brojne interpretacije Kounellisove instalacije u kojima se, među ostalim, reference za upotrebu zlatnih listića pronalaze u antičkim mitologijama, tradiciji srednjovjekovnog slikarstva i u umjetnikovu udivljenju djelom Andreja Rubljova. Nadalje, naslov i impostacija predmeta u tom enigmatičnom radu dovode se u vezu s teatričnošću pri čemu historijska transverzala seže od grčke tragedije do Brechtova epskog teatra. U tim se interpretacijama *Tragedia civile* kontekstualizira i upotrebom zlata u konceptualnim umjetničkim praksama 20. stoljeća s posebnim naglaskom na zlatne listiće kojima je Beuys obložio lice dok je razmišljao kako mrtvom zecu objasniti slike.[28]

Za razliku od Kounellisa koji zid pokriva pravim zlatom, Lovro Artuković na zid atelijera postavlja jeftinu poliestersku foliju zlatne boje koja tu postaje svojevrsnim ekranom na kojemu se događa defigurirajuće zrcaljenje koje postaje predmetom slikarske reprezentacije.

Međutim, pravi zlatni listići pojavili su se u njegovom radu dvadeset godina prije, u slikama iz serije *Umjetnici u prirodi*. Posrijedi su slike *Zeko i potočić* (1999.) i *Zeko i smrznuti potočić* (2000.) u kojima je lik Josepha Beuysa s mrtvim zecom u naručju naslikan prema fotografijama snimljenim 26. studenog 1965. za vrijeme tog čuvenog performansa u Galeriji Schmela u Düsseldorfu, smješten u krajolik koji konotira mjesto radnje najtužnije hrvatske pjesme za djecu evocirane naslovima Artukovićevih slika. Beuysovo je lice na tim slikama izvedenim uljem na platnu uobličeno zlatnim listićima. Slika *Zeko i smrznuti potočić* netragom je nestala kada je 2002. ukradeno transportno vozilo kojim su slike Lovre Artukovića s izložbe u Lisabonu putovale prema Zagrebu.

Danas, gledajući slike čiji je protagonist fasetirana reflektirajuća površina pokrivača za preživljavanje, pitam se je li to što Lovro Artuković nastoji dosegnuti slikajući analogno Beuysovome nijemom nastojanju da objasni slike mrtvom zecu? Ili, možda preciznije, je li uopće moguće objasniti slike? Povijest slikarstva prepuna je mrtvih zečeva, a Lovro Artuković uporno mi ponavlja da se on bavi slikama, a ne slikarstvom. Defigurirajuće zrcaljenje koje se događa u njegovim slikama kristalizira pitanje o prevodivosti; o odnosu između vidljivog i viđenog artikuliranom dinamikom makro i mikro plana slike. Iz samog čina slikanja ishodi nesvodiva razlika između viđenja slike (zbivanja *pred slikom*) i događaja slike; rascjep u kojemu obitava to što Artukovićevo djelo čini teatričnim. Jer, kolikogod iluzioniranje bilo uspješno, mimezis nastupa samo zato da bi sliku izložio nezaustavljivom vihoru trans(re)lacija. Nije slučajno da zlatna, reflektirajuća površina pokrivača prve pomoći biva naslikana u različitim formatima i na različitim materijalnim podlogama, konkretno, uljem na drvu i uljem na platnu. Mogla bih u toj činjenici detektirati referencu na povijest slikarstva, na putanju slika od srednjovjekovlja do modernosti. Primjerice, slika naslovljena *Biće iz bajke - kubističko* (2018.) izvedena je uljem na drvu dimenzija 33,5 x 22,5 cm pri čemu joj je površina podijeljena na devet pravokutnih faseta posredstvom kojih se u slici događa fragmentacija te se, posljedično, prikazani lik izobličuje. Njegova iz-obličenost onemogućuje da se sa sigurnošću ustvrdi radi li se tu o odrazu nekoga tko stoji pred slikom ili o nekome tko se iz dubine prostora unutar slike (odvojenog od izvanjskog prostora svojevrsnom prozirnom pregradom) primiče onome tko sliku promatra. *Zarobljeni duh* (2019.) - crtež ugljenom na papiru izveden u nešto većem formatu - prividno rješava tu nedoumicu jer je u tamnoj konfiguraciji s lijeve strane papira moguće prepoznati (ili izmaštati) nešto nalik dlanu kojim se reprezentirani duh oslonio na fasetiranu membranu koja ga dijeli od promatrača, a taj je možda istovjetan njemu samome. Čin ekstremnog približavanja izobličenog lica tog duha licu pretpostavljenog promatrača neodoljivo me podsjeća na suspenziju granice između intimnog i ekstimnog, izvedenu Courbetovim mladenačkim autoportretom *Le Désespéré* (*Očajnik*) naslikanim između 1843. i 1845. godine. Historiografija umjetnosti kaže da se umjetnik od te slike nije odvajao do kraja života, kao ni da Vinci od Mona Lise. Courbet je naslovom svoje najslavnije slike, koja je formatom prisvojila prerogative tada najcjenjenijeg žanra - historijskog slikarstva, do krajnosti zakomplicirao definiciju realizma. Puni naslov glasi: *L'Atelier du peintre. Allégorie Réelle déterminant une phase de sept années de ma vie artistique (et morale)*. *U slobodnom prijevodu: Slikarov atelijer: Stvarna alegorija koja sažima sedam godina mog umjetničkog (i moralnog) života*. Stvarna alegorija bila bi, po definiciji, oksimoron. No, što ako se pokuša postaviti pitanje kakvu stvarnost definicije stvaraju? I nadalje, u kakvom je odnosu tako stvorena stvarnost s onim što Courbet naziva moralnim životom?

Za razliku od Courbeta Lovro Artuković će sliku izvedenu uljem na platnu dimenzija 220 x 190 cm nasloviti *Odraz ateljea u zlatnoj foliji* (2018.). To što je odraženo neka su gola tijela. Ili se odraženi oblici takvima samo pričinjaju. Pravilnim rasterom reprezentiranih linija tragova ambalažiranja, odnosno presavijanja folije,

28   Giorgio di Domenico, „'Una partecipazione che va trovata': Jannis Kounellis, Tragedia civile, 1975", u: *Studi di Memofonte*, br. 21/2018., Fondazione Memofonte, str. 216-242. https://www.academia.edu/38567354/_Una_partecipazione_che_va_trovata_Jannis_Kounellis_Tragedia_civile_1975 (pristup 18. 2. 2020.)

slika je podijeljena na 432 pravokutna polja, a u svakom od njih događa se druga slika. Neke od njih nalik su onome što diskurs discipline povijesti umjetnosti kategorizira kao monokromno slikarstvo, ili apstraktni ekspresionizam, ili cézanneovski pejzaž, a druge pak podsjećaju na scenografiju njemačkog ekspresionističkog filma. U slici naslovljenoj *Io i Jupiter* (2019. - 2020.) pokrivač prve pomoći zrcali likove čija me tjelesna mimika podsjeća na Picassove *Gospođice iz Avignona*, a u pojedinim fasetama slike *Crna silueta* (2019.) vidim prizore nalik vedutama grada. Jednu od slika iz serije *Odrazi* umjetnik naslovljuje *Navještenje* (2019. - 2020.). Taj mi naslov, kao i posve evidentni slikarski postupak disolucije slike u sjećanje prizva seriju *Verkündigung nach Tizian* (1973.) Gerharda Richtera u kojoj će izvedbena gesta paradoksalnog brisanja površine slike sukcesivno, iz platna u platno, defigurirati jednu od središnjih tema kršćanskog mita, privodeći je samoj njeznoj suštini artikuliranoj prevođenjem crvene boje kojom Tizian figurira arkanđelovo uskovitlano ruho u maglovitu čestičnost. U toj se haptičnoj, a istodobno neuhvatljivoj izmaglici događa otapanje obrisa koje sve boje i nijanse stapa onako kako se to događa u Rothkovim monokromnim poljima. Usput budi rečeno, u geometrijskom središtu Artukovićeva *Navještenja* smjestilo se nepoznato nešto, koloristički dvokomponentno, naslikano jarkim i muklim tonom crvene. Naslonjač u atelijeru? Iza toga nečeg otvara se zelena dubina. U rasapu kompaktne slike, po učinku analognom Richterovoj i Rothkovoj osmozi, čestičnost artikulirana radovima Lovre Artukovića postavlja pitanje o slici i njezinim višerazinskim interferencijama sa živim tijelom. Pitanje je to o enigmi slike, a ne o njezinim definicijama, jer ono se ne odnosi na to što i kako vidim nego na supstance koje obitavaju u sedimentima podloge mog viđenja. Podloga viđenja jest *mise en abîme* i ona u slikarstvu Lovre Artukovića igra ključnu ulogu u događaju slike.

*Mise en abîme* se kao načelo beskonačnog umnažanja mikronarativa unutar slikanjem zasićenog formata platna pojavljuje i u naoko formalno posve drukčijim, "kompaktnim" slikama u kojima se događa kondenzacija mimetičkog i dijegetičkog registra prizora. Tako se u slici *Pun mjesec u mojoj kuhinji* (2019.) na nevidljivom staklu kroz koje se pruža pogled s prozora atelijera zrcali tamna sjena umjetnikova tijela. Za razliku od neprozirne *Crne siluete*, kroz ovu se sjenu vide prozori okolnih zgrada, koji svijetle u tami. Isti će se prozori vidljivi iz kuhinje umjetnikova atelijera pojaviti u slikama *U dvorištu* (2019.) i *Lene u potopu* (2019.). Možda baš te tri slike sagledane zajedno, slike u kojima se očište sukcesivno spušta da bi fokusiralo pojam varijabilne pozicije viđenja, postavljaju pitanje o mjestu događaja slike, o topografiji što obitava s onu stranu ikonografije. Pozicija "s onu stranu vremena", koju sam pri početku ovog teksta identificirala kao prostor ekscesnog događaja slike, koji se u slikarstvu Lovre Artukovića manifestira kao *mise en abîme*, kriptografirana je i slikom *Raspra u atelieu* (2019. - 2020.). U njoj se, jedva vidljiva u odrazu prozorskog stakla, nazire sićušna prozirna figura koja s druge strane odraza prekriženih ruku promatra prizor. Radi li se o autoru slike ili o nekome drugome? Za razliku od Courbetove "stvarne alegorije" u Artukovićevoj slici pojam umjetnost ne podliježe simbolizaciji. Umjetnost ovdje nije označena likom gole žene - nijemim označiteljem koji konotira sve drugo osim sebe same, pasivnim tijelom pred moćnim pogledom umjetnika. Traži li možda šest ženskih likova prikazanih u slici umjetnikova

atelijera autora? I Pirandellova je drama svojevrsni *mise en abîme*, predstava unutar predstave. Pretpostavljenog autora čiju poziciju u prostoru prikazanog prizora, ali smještenog izvan slike, možda odaje odraz u prozorskom staklu naslikanom u stražnjem planu, pronalazi, čini se, jedino psić koji mu se pogledom obraća iz prednjeg plana. Taj pseći pogled priziva mi u sjećanje dramaturgiju žanr-scena nizozemskog baroka u kojoj, ne bez razloga, važnu ulogu igraju životinje. Šest Artukovićevih ljudskih likova - žena koje šutke "raspravljaju" u kuhinji njegova atelijera, portreti su jedne te iste glumice, Jeannine Simon, koja za potrebe izvedbe slike mijenja odjeću, položaj u prostoru, gestikulaciju i izraze lica. Ta istost modela koja nije identičnost prikazanog lika, uvodi u sliku dimenziju simultanog, nekronološkog vremena, koja se manifestira kao usporavanje. Usporavanje, koje u Artukovićevu slikarstvu djeluje poput filmskog raskadriranja, u slici umnaža prividno sporedne prizore. Tako se u jednom od tih prizora kroz otvorena kuhinjska vrata vidi radni prostor atelijera s nedovršenim portretom muškarca (poznatog sa slike *Runar*, 2015.), a u drugome se - kroz prozor naslikan iza leđa žene postavljene u prednji plan - otvara pogled na ulicu gdje grupa ljudi također o nečemu žustro raspravlja. U prizoru tučnjave njihove sićušne, ali minuciozno izrađene figure podsjećaju me na narativnu strukturu renesansne slike u kojoj neimenovana priča u stražnjem planu privlači pozornost snažnije od naslovne teme slike. Što se to događa na ulici?

Ima nečeg fassbinderovski bolnog u timbru Artukovićevih slika berlinskih ulica i barova. U nježnosti teksturizacije likova i bešumnosti kojom oni nastanjuju prizore, u muklim svjetlima razornog intenziteta, koja im tijela izvlače iz nevidljivosti. Kažem teksturizacije, a ne tekstualizacije (jer teksturu shvaćam divergentnom tekstu), pozivajući se pritom na Proustovu distinkciju po kojoj je pisanje nešto potpuno suprotno opisivanju. Analogno tome, slikanje Lovre Artukovića nije prikazivanje; zato ne kažem prizorima s berlinskih ulica i iz berlinskih barova, nego slikama ulica i barova. À propos Proustove fatalne opčinjenosti Vermeerom, figurirane "malom frazom" *petit pan de mur jaune*, Didi-Huberman zapisuje sljedeće: „Proust je bio daleko od traganja za nekakvim pseudo-'fotografskim nepomičnim vremenom' u vidljivome; naprotiv, on je tražio drhtavo trajanje, ono što je Blanchot nazvao ekstazom - 'ekstazom vremena'. Shodno tome, Proust u vidljivome nije tražio argumente *deskripcije* nego prije bljeskove *odnosa*."[29] I Lovro Artuković daleko je od traganja za takvim pseudo-fotografskim nepomičnim vremenom, premda svakoj njegovoj slici prethodi opsežni *foto-session*, ili, ako hoćemo, pomno režirani performans za kameru. Potom slijedi ono: kako iz petrificiranog trenutka, mortificirajuće snimke, pokrenuti događaj slike? Anne Carson izbrojala je da se u romanesknom ciklusu *U traganju za izgubljenim vremenom* Albertinino ime javlja 2363 puta, te da je ona prisutna ili se spominje na 807 stranica romana.[30] Trebam li pokušati izbrojiti koliko se puta i u koliko Artukovićevih slika pojavljuju likovi Ari, Jeannine, Charly, Natasche ili Lene? One, doduše, u tim uprizorenjima ne voze bicikle, međutim, pod noćnim svjetlom ulične rasvjete u slici *Ukazanje u Neuköll-*


29  Didi-Huberman, op. cit., str. 245.

30  Anne Carson, Vježba zvana Albertina, (prev. Miroslav Kirin), Kulturtreger i Multimedijalni institut, Zagreb, 2019.

nu (2019.), iza leđa žene odjevene u nešto nalik vjenčanici, zapravo obavijene plastičnom folijom sa zračnim mjehurićima kakvom se omataju umjetnine i drugi krhki predmeti, vidim biciklista i nekoliko parkiranih bicikla. Umjesto u umjetnikovu ateljeru, što je bio slučaj u slikama *Ari u trash kostimu* (2012.) i *Ari pleše s plastičnim čašama* (2013. - 2014.), Ari sada, jednako odjevena, sjedi posred ceste u berlinskoj četvrti *Neukölln*, leđima okrenuta terasi bara koja je u ovoj slici uklopljeni citat Van Goghove *Terrasse de café sur la place du Forum,* naslikane 1888. u Arlesu. Isti se citat, ali u posve drukčijoj intonaciji, pojavio desetljećima prije u slici *Moj prijatelj Vincent* koju je Lovro Artuković naslikao 1986. godine. U toj se slici ukazanje Van Goghove terase zbiva u zagrebačkoj Medulićevoj ulici.

Gdje se zbivaju *Kasnonoćni razgovori* (2019.)? U berlinskom baru *Tier* u čijem su interijeru snimljeni mnogobrojni fotografski kadrovi koji će biti transfigurirani i potom generirati eruptirajuće čestice u događaju slike? Odakle stiže muklo crveno svjetlo pod kojim Natascha, leđima okrenuta promatračima kroz dim cigarete promatra čudnu, ogromnu fotografiju, nalijepljenu s druge strane šanka poput zidne tapete? Charly i Anian začuđeno je gledaju, ona možda nešto i govori. U jednoj drugoj sekvenci Artukovićeva "filma", njezino će lice obasjano mješavinom barskog i uličnog svjetla zauzeti puni kadar slike *Noćna svjetla* (2019.). Zeleni odsjaj na granitnoj uličnoj kocki, vidljiv kroz barski prozor, povezat će tu sliku sa slikom *Haljina na cvjetove* (2019.) u kojoj Charly pri svjetlu mirisne svijeće, usredotočenom sporošću Vermeerove *Mljekarice* otresa pepeo cigarete u pepeljaru. U jednome drugom platnu naslovljenom *U baru* (2020.) slikarev će pogled blago otklizati unatrag i ponuditi prizor viđen s neznatno veće distance pa će slika pokazati da je Charly, odjevena u crnu haljinu sa žutim cvjetnim uzorkom, još uvijek u istoj pozi, istog izraza lica, ali sada za stolom uz koji ona stoji sjede Natascha i Anian, pogleda uprtih u nešto što se u slici ne vidi. U trećem će je kadru njih dvoje pozorno motriti, a slikar će tu sliku nasloviti *Pripovjedačica* (2020.).

Berlinčanin Walter Benjamin 1936. u pariškom egzilu piše esej *Pripovjedač* u kojemu tvrdi da je umjetnost pripovijedanja postala rijetka, i štoviše, približila se svom kraju zato što nam je oduzeta sposobnost koja se činila neotuđivom - sposobnost razmjene iskustva. Cijena iskustva je pala i dalje pada u bezdan - piše on - a slika ne samo vanjskog nego i moralnog svijeta preko noći je pretrpjela promjene koje nikada nismo smatrali mogućima.[31] Je li bezdan koji povodom cijene iskustva spominje Benjamin predmet *Kasnonoćnih razgovora* koje u drugom desetljeću 21. stoljeća slika Lovro Artuković? Kako naslikati razgovor? Ili izgovoreno koje nikad neće dospjeti do čujnosti. *Tragedia civile*?
U prednjem planu jednog od barskih prizora smjestio se autoportret Lovre Artkovića. Naslikao se iz profila kako sjedi za šankom, odjeven u vjetrovku, duboko zamišljen, pogleda usmjerenog prema praznoj čaši koju drži u desnoj ruci. Lice mu je s prednje strane obasjano crvenim barskim svjetlom, a

s bočne plavim odsjajem vjetrovke. Na sceni su još Natascha, Anian i Charly. Nitko od njih nikoga ne gleda i nitko ni sa kim ne razgovara; Natascha puši, Anian pere čaše, Charly se odsutna pogleda dlanovima upire o rub sudopera. Naslov te slike iz 2019. je *Closing Time (Bad Thoughts)*. I ovdje u podlozi slike obitava uklopljeni citat, međutim, ovaj put nije citiran određeni vizualni nego verbalni motiv - naslov serije performativnih foto-slika, koju su 1975. izveli Gilbert & George, a u kojoj je boja koja potapa figure performera, njih dvojice s čašama u ruci i njihov dom-studio, krvavo crvena. Toj je seriji prethodio niz radova objedinjenih naslovom *Drinking Pieces*. Ovdje nije na odmet spomenuti i to da su se na samom početku karijere Gilbert & George, koji sebe od tada do danas deklariraju kao živu skulpturu, "portretirali" u tipičnom engleskom krajoliku. Izvedeni u velikom formatu, njihovi crteži ugljenom i kredom na papiru naslovljeni su *The Nature of Our Looking* (1970.), a ulja na platnu naslikana godinu dana poslije nazvali su jednostavno slikama: *The Paintings (with Us in the Nature)*. Naslovi su, dakako, ironijski jer je predmet njihovog interesa bila i ostala kulturalno proizvedena naturalizacija diskursa moći. Te su slike onda, kao i radovi Lovre Artukovića danas, artikulirale pitanja o mjestu događaja slike; o vidljivim refleksijama i o bljeskovima što prolaze ispod praga percepcije.

Seriju *Izlet* Lovro Artuković izvodi istodobno serijama *Posjet ateljeu*, *Noćna svjetla* i *Odrazi*. Parafrazirajući, mogla bih reći da je i u njoj posrijedi pitanje o "prirodi našeg gledanja". Što i zašto vidim u slici *Jesenji izlet* (2017. - 2019.)? Luksuzni kabriolet na čijem se uglancanom limu i vjetrobranskom staklu zrcali šuma - poluogoljele krošnje i zlaćano lišće s tla? Kroz to se zrcaljenje jedva naziru likovi žene i muškarca koji, u odjeći primjerenijoj večernjem izlasku negoli izletu u prirodu, sjede u automobilu. Ona za volanom gledajući preda se, on glave okrenute ulijevo, prema šumi. Filmski kadar? Kojem žanru pripada? "Priča" će nastavak dobiti u kadru sljedeće slike koji "zumira" automobilski kotač, blatobran, vrata i prazno vozačko sjedalo. Naslovljena je *Hidra (u jesenjem pejzažu)*(2019. - 2020.). U nju slikar nije, poput Goye, umetnuo natpis *El sueño de la razón produce monstruos*, nego je na limu vanjskog retrovizora naslikao mikroskopski prizor nazvavši ga (interno) *Brandenburški krajolik s figurom (odraz)*. *Hidrom (u jesenjem pejzažu)* Lovro Artuković sinkopirao je fenomen anamorfoze. Anamorfoza se, dakako, događa u refleksiji. Zato je posve irelevantno hoću li na sjajnom blatobranu među odsjajima jesenjeg lišća prepoznati mitsko čudovište smrtonosnog zadaha, odsutnu vozačicu odjevenu u kariranu suknju ili nešto pedeseto jer i u *Proljeću* (2016.) i *U Grunewaldu* (2016.) i u *Jednog ljetnog dana u Heidelberškoj šumi* (2017.), u "drhtavom trajanju" ili "ekstazi vremena" obitava događaj slike - prisutnost koja u gustoći naslikanog slikaru "uzima sate i sate koji nekako neprimjetno prolaze".

---

31   Walter Benjamin, "Pripovjedač", prev. Truda Stamać, u: Estetički ogledi (Zagreb: Školska knjiga, 1986.), str. 166-167.

Kada sam predao te slike na jednu od onih žiriranih izložaba koje pokazuju što se aktualno događa na lokalnoj umjetničkoj sceni, bilo mi je drago da su moji radovi prihvaćeni i izloženi iako su odudarali od svega što se oko njih na izložbi dešavalo. Ne znam da li je to bio razlog ali kada bi mi se netko obratio, mogao se osjetiti posprdni ton u pitanju „aaa, kaj sad slikate portrete?“. Slikanje portreta nije se smatralo cool u to vrijeme.
Osobno, nisam te slike uopće doživljavao kao portrete. Nastale su potpuno prirodno nadovezujući se na moj prethodni rad, onako kako se razvijao slikarski postupak kojim sam radio i kako sam osjećao atmosferu trenutka u kojoj sam se nalazio. Ono po čemu su se razlikovale bilo je to što su likovi na slici ostali bez uloge u nekoj mojoj priči, te su time prisiljavali promatrača da se koncentrira isključivo na njih i na postupak kojim su bili naslikani. Kako je rekao jedan moj prijatelj, „kod portreta nema blefiranja“, to je to što je naslikano.

Moram priznati da sam i ja, dok sam bio mlad, svoje školske kolege iz finih zagrebačkih kuća u kojima su sa zidova buljili članovi obitelji, također malo posprdnim tonom, nazivao „oni koji imaju doma slike“. Tu se vjerojatno više radilo o frustraciji nekoga tko je bio dijete „dojdeka“ nego o ideološkom stavu, ili je ovaj proizlazio iz onog prvoga. Ne znam da li sam se već tada, kada bi mi netko „predstavio“ neki lik u austrougarskoj uniformi kao svog pokojnog pradjeda, a ja pritom vidio samo prilično loše naslikanu sliku, počeo pitati da li vrijeme čini da se portret oslobađa onog koji je na njemu naslikan i počinje biti samo slika? Dobra ili loša. Ili ostaju zauvijek povezani, te kad prolazimo salama nekog muzeja, ne gledamo portrete samo kao slike, nego i osjećamo čistu ljudsku znatiželju, privlačnost ili odbojnost prema naslikanima.

Naravno, ne treba smetnuti s uma da smo dresirani da u portretima gledamo i autora koji ih je naslikao. No čini mi se da sam počeo komplicirati, nisam baš neki mislilac. Gledajući s čisto praktične strane, zahvaljujući tim slikama s izložbe, počeo sam povremeno dobivati narudžbe ljudi koji su željeli da ih naslikam, i tako zaradio pokoju paru, što mi je bilo cool.



Kamerman, osvjetljivač i tonac uperili su svoja oružja u mene. Osjećao sam se nelagodno, svjetlo reflektora bolo me u oči. Novinarka je stajala pokraj mene. Kada smo dobili znak da možemo započeti razgovor, pogledala me očima blistavim od entuzijazma i izgovorila: „Eto, vi slikate. Zar nije slikarstvo mrtvo?“

Oh, neeeee! Kaj sad hoće od mene? Da to potvrdim? Ili da održim pledoaje u obranu slikarstva? Nek' je mrtvo, boli me k..., pustite me da na miru slikam. Bio sam ljut na sebe, mogao sam očekivati takvo pitanje i pripremiti se, znao sam da se teza o smrti slikarstva već mjesecima povlačila po domaćim novinama (a u literaturi o umjetnosti prisutna je već desetljećima). Bio sam naravno ljut i na novinarku. Zakaj moraju svi uvijek ponavljati jedno te isto k'o papagaji, kaj nema oči, zakaj ne pogleda malo oko sebe i ne pita me neš' o slikama?
Počeo sam petljati nešto o tome kako sam ja, eto, još živ i slikam i kako taj potok koji sam naslikao na slici iza nas (pokazao sam je rukom ne bi li možda obratila pažnju na nju) još uvijek živo teče niz brijeg u šumi. Ne znam što sam još baljezgao, vjerojatno je bilo katastrofalno. Morao sam hitno nešto popiti.



Dragi prijatelju,
nismo nikad uspjeli raspraviti što bi trebala značiti Tvoja česta primjedba da svakodnevno moraš nekoliko sati voziti bicikl kako bi sve iznojio i „stao čist pred sliku“. Kako sam ja to razumio, nisi pritom mislio da je svrha tog rituala iznojavanje otrova nakupljenih u tijelu, nego više očišćenje od samoga sebe, od svakodnevice

kako bi mogao stvoriti „čisto slikarstvo" (peinture pure) lišeno tragova boli obična života.

Pretpostavljam da sam dobro protumačio Tvoje riječi (iako to nismo nikad uspjeli raspraviti), jer ta mi je ezoterična priča poznata iz tekstova o slikarstvu prošloga stoljeća koje još uvijek anakrono nazivamo slikarstvom moderne. Mene, moram priznati, nekako nije uspjela privući. Nadam se da mi nećeš zamjeriti što sam izabrao suprotan put i što dopuštam da ono što živim, mislim i osjećam bude vidljivo na mojim slikama. Čini mi se da je u naše doba slikarstvo jedan od rijetkih otoka gdje je još moguća individualnost. I zato: ako se u nekom trenutku osjetim sam, izoliran, obzidan horizontom kao zatvorom, kao na otoku na kojemu život pomalo zamire - to će se sigurno pojaviti na mojim slikama, htio ja to ili ne htio. Možda nije posrijedi veliko slikarstvo (grande peinture), ali nas dvojica nismo nažalost nikad uspjeli raspraviti što bi to zapravo trebalo biti.

## 82
## Septic
## Septično

Mimoišli smo se na ulazu u kafić i pozdravili. Poznavali smo se iz viđenja, s otvorenja različitih izložaba. Čestitao mi je na mojoj izložbi. Ne znam je li bio liječnik, ali na moje pitanje kako mu se svidjela odgovorio je da ga se dojmila „malo septično". Nisam baš shvatio taj odgovor, pa sam odvratio da je to zato što volim grupu Septica. Po njegovu pogledu bilo mi je jasno da ni on nije shvatio što sam ja htio reći. Rastali smo se srdačno se smiješeći.

Septica mi je pala na pamet zato što sam bio na njihovu koncertu nekoliko dana prije. U tom sam trenutku osjetio djetinje zadovoljstvo što sam mu tako spremno odvratio (to za mene nije tipično). Ali umjesto toga trebao sam ga pitati što je time zapravo mislio, jer njegova me primjedba ipak kopkala. No bilo je kasno za to, pa sam se latio rječnika stranih riječi ne bih li dokučio njezin smisao. Septično je nešto što je „onečišćeno uzročnicima bolesti", „zahvaćeno klicama", „zaraženo", „otrovano" i sl., pa stoga mogu samo pretpostaviti da je izložbu, moj rad u cjelini ili nešto u njemu doživio kao nešto „nečisto".
Lagao bih kad bih tvrdio da me to ostavilo mrtvim-hladnim, ali sigurno bih se mnogo više uzrujao da mi je rekao da ga se izložba dojmila „malo aseptično".

## 84
## BEECH CRUST
## BUKVINA KORA

## 84
## Scar
## Ožiljak

Vidio sam s prozora kako netko grli brezu, jedino stablo u našem betoniranom, sa svih strana zatvorenom dvorištu. Ta se osoba tako čulno pripijala uz deblo da je motrenje tog prizora u meni izazvalo sličnu nelagodu kao da sam slučajno zatekao dva bića kako razmjenjuju intimne nježnosti. Pročitao sam poslije na internetu da ritualno „grljenje drveća" potječe iz Japana, da se zove dendroterapija i da je vrlo ljekovito.

Svojedobno sam i ja bio u prilično intenzivnom kontaktu s drvećem. Nisam grlio stabla, ali sam ih crtao, a te tri-četiri godine čestih odlazaka u šumu nedvojbeno su bile vrlo dobre za moje tjelesno zdravlje. Zbog kretanja na čistom zraku bio sam u dobroj kondiciji, dok je crtanje u tišini šume, pažljivo promatranje izabranog motiva i njegovih gotovo neprimjetnih, ali neprestanih mijena bilo oblik kontemplacije koji je godio mojem duševnom zdravlju.

Crtao sam različita stabla, mlada i stara, jasen, hrast i kesten; ali pišem sve ovo zbog jedne bukve. Rasla je uz planinarsku stazu, a sudeći po opsegu debla, bila je prilično stara. Njezina inače glatka kora, koju su tek blago nabirale ispupčene vodoravne pruge, bila je bila prepuna široko razjapljenih ožiljaka, urezanih imena i inicijala, jednostavnih recki i znakova. Svježe ugrebotine iskakale su intenzivnom narančastom na sivoj boji kore. Imala je takozvane „oči drveta" na mjestima gdje su joj otpale ili odsječene grane. Bila je na njoj također naličena planinarska markacija i još neke oznake - pretpostavljam, šumarske. Naslikao sam je više puta i u tom se ponavljanju postupno mijenjao način na koji sam slikao. Zahvaljujući tom novom iskustvu počeo sam drugačije razmišljati o površini slike i o slici kao takvoj, i za to sam joj beskrajno zahvalan. Ako ikad budem opet planinario tim putem i ako ona još bude ondje stajala, čvrsto ću je zagrliti.

## 88
## Artists in Nature
## Umjetnici u prirodi

### (1)
Oslikao sam platno kao da mu je jedna strana na svjetlu, a druga u sjeni. Slikao sam dugo i pažljivo bojama koje sam umiješao tako da je slika zračila težinom i djelovala kao olovna ploča koju s jedne strane obasjava slabo svjetlo. Istim sam bojama paralelno nanosio crtež koji se reljefno izdizao nad površinom.

### (2)
Uz šumski put kojim sam prolazio gotovo svakoga dana ležao je mjesecima nevješto posječen mladi hrastić. Uznemiravala me očita bezrazložnost te smrti - nisam nikako mogao dokučiti zašto bi netko posjekao mlado stablo, a potom ga ostavio da leži. Danima sam u glavi konstruirao različite priče tražeći mogući razlog za taj besmisleni čin. Nekako u to vrijeme vidio sam autoportret slikara Igora Rončevića, koji je sebe prikazao sa sjekirom u rukama.

(3)

Reljefna crta na obojenoj površini platna ističe posebnost kako nacrtanoga tako i površine, a površina pak stvara raspoloženje i određuje emotivni doživljaj nacrtanoga. Crtež je prikazivao slikara Igora Rončevića sa sjekirom. A onda sam na tako pripremljenoj podlozi naslikao posječeni hrastić.

## 91
## Zeko i potočić [32]
## The Rabbit and the Rivulet

U jednoj zimskoj noći
tam' gdje je visok brijeg
smrznuo se potočić
i pokrio ga snijeg.

A jedan mali zeko
taj potok traži svud,
gdje je, kud je nestao
to njemu tišti grud.

I plače, plače zeko mlad,
za potočićem tim
žali, žali zeko sad
žali srcem svim.

I tužan misli zeko
ta gdje je potok taj,
možda laste slijedi on
u dalek južni kraj.

## 92
## Stillness
## Tišina

## 94
## Pictures Seen by Someone Else
## Slike koje gleda netko drugi

Ustao sam u praskozorje. Preostajalo je još samo nekoliko dana do otvorenja izložbe, a činilo mi se da na slikama treba još mnogo toga doraditi. Odjenuo sam majicu koju je nosio model za sliku na kojoj sam radio već mjesecima i koja je trebala nositi cijelu izložbu te pošao u atelje. Na majici je pisalo: „Bože kako volim Botticellia".

Bilo je prekrasno lipanjsko jutro, sunce je bilo tek izišlo. Krupno, žarko, obasjavalo je krovove pod kraljevskoplavim nebom bez oblačka. Osim ptičjeg cvrkuta nije se čuo gotovo nikakav drugi zvuk. Na kružnom toku oko Džamije pojavio se odjednom biciklist, koji je intenzivno gledao u mom smjeru dok sam se spuštao stubama od fontane prema kolniku. Bio je to raznosač novina koji je uranio kao i ja. Mislim da je pokušavao pročitati što piše na mojoj majici, ali mu je po svoj prilici sunce išlo u oči, ili je možda bio kratkovidan. Nije gledao kuda vozi, pa mu je prednji

kotač upao u tramvajsku tračnicu. I on i novine što ih je vozio na prtljažniku rasuli su se po kolniku točno preda mnom.

Na svu sreću nije bilo prometa, a činilo se također da se biciklist nije ozlijedio. Pohitao sam mu upomoć da ustane i pokupi razasute novine. Zbog svoje majice osjećao sam se pomalo kriv za tu nezgodu. Pokušao sam objasniti da je nosim kako bih skrenuo pozornost na svoju izložbu. I da na slici na kojoj je majica prikazana taj moj izraz ljubavi prema Botticelliu sugerira promatraču da ima ključ za njezino tumačenje, dok ga time zapravo navodi na krivi put. Biciklist je odlučno odbio moju pomoć. U njegovu pogledu i držanju bilo je ne samo nelagode i ljutnje zbog glupe situacije u kojoj se našao nego i svojevrsne odbojnosti prema meni. Pustio sam ga stoga na miru i pošao dalje svojim putem. Nekako mi se učinilo da je pomislio da sam peder.

## 102
## FALSE SCENES
## LAŽNI PRIZORI

## 102
## Storage-Room
## Spremište

Slikarstvo je pohranjeno u Spremištu koje se nalazi u našoj zajedničkoj, ukupnoj duši. Svi načini nanošenja boje, svi zanatski trikovi, sve "novo" i sve "staro" postoji u tom Spremištu oduvijek i zauvijek, bezvremeno, i postojat će sve dok je te zajedničke, ukupne duše, tj. čovječanstva. Prvi slikar sadržavao je već u sebi sve slikare koji će se pojaviti nakon njega, baš kao što onaj koji se ovaj čas rađa sadrži u sebi sve one koji su mu predhodili. Slikar uzima iz Spremišta ono što mu treba ili ono do čega svojom sposobnošću može doći i to iznosi na svjetlo jedinstvenog trenutka u kojemu živi. O tome jedinstvenom isječku vremena i o samom slikaru ovisi što će iz Spremišta izaći i kako će biti upotrijebljeno, kako će se materijalizirati u Slici.

## 104
## Scene
## Prizor

Duboko u sebi nosimo potrebu za vlastitim odrazom, koji uključuje i sve ono što nas okružuje. Žudimo za tim da gledajući taj odraz smjestimo svoje postojanje u Ukupnosti, koja se bez pogleda na sebe čini nesavladivom. Imamo također potrebu da svoj odraz zaodjenemo specifičnom atmosferom trenutka u kojemu se nalazimo kako bismo ga uskladili s onime što prema sebi osjećamo i o sebi mislimo. Takav odraz, zaodjeven specifičnom atmosferom trenutka u kojemu je nastao, nazivam Prizorom.

106
Illusion
Privid

Slika je jednostavan, najčešće četverokutan predmet koji zauzima određeni prostor u stvarnom svijetu. No ono što je naslikano na njegovoj površini ulaz je u prostor koji postoji paralelno sa stvarnim, u prostor koji je izgrađen našim htijenjem da stvorimo vlastiti svijet unatoč stvarnome. Sve materijalne vrijednosti i duhovna značenja što ih za nas ima taj jednostavni predmet postoje samo u našem paralelnom, umjetnom prostoru. Isticanje te umjetne naravi slike nazivam Iluzijom.


110
OBSERVATION
PROMATRANJE

Nacrtao sam Alexa, Christiana, Constanze, Consuelo, Giacoma, Giuliana, Ernestinu, Eru, Fabienne, Irmu, Jeremyja, Jörga, Karin, Karstena, Katju, Laru, Manuelu, Michelea, Miriam, Sabinu, Stefana, Thorstena i još ću neke. Prvi su mi pozirali, a i drugi će.

Prije njih nacrtao sam Marijanu i Mateu, Miu i Dolinu, Fijolića i Švabu, Ivanu i Marka, Mirandu i Stanka, Barbaru i Luciju, Dešu, Ivanu, Jelenu i Zdravku, Igora i onog drugog Igora, Sanju i Neru. Nera je doduše pas, ali crtao sam također Bukvu i Potok sa sunčevim bljeskom i Mlado stablo i Stari kesten i Crvene stijene, koji su mi također pozirali. Ali to je bilo nekako drukčije, crtao sam ih zato što su mi ti crteži služili kao predlošci za slike (poput ljudi i stvari koje sam slikao prema fotografijama). Što zapravo želim kad se trudim vjerno prikazati lice koje promatram pred sobom? Na to pitanje zapravo ne mogu dati nikakav suvisli odgovor. Možda mi je važno biti s ljudima, sjediti sučelice s njima satima, iz dana u dan, i osjetiti onu laganu nelagodu, lagano uzbuđenje kad nam se pogledi sretnu.


116
AS IF
KAO DA


Mislio sam da sam uspio dokučiti svojstva onoga čime se bavim. Činilo mi se da su Iluzija i Prizor dobri termini, koji uglavnom pokrivaju ono što činim dok slikam. Kao i ono što slikam. Moram priznati - ne tako nevoljko, jer čovjek je naravno sretan kada otkrije nešto novo - da sam došao do toga da su Koncept i Postupak ipak važnija svojstva slikanja. Stanovitu nelagodu izaziva, međutim, činjenica da vrijeme leti. Neki dan morao sam otići do optičara jer više ne vidim jasno ono što crtam i potpuno sam prestao čitati, zubi su mi već dosta dugo porculanski, a i pomalo sam sebi počinjem mirisati natrulo. No i bez naočala vidim da slike koje slikam postaju bolje. Ne znam je li to zato što

sam Konceptu i Postupku dao prednost pred Iluzijom i Prizorom ili možda čak zbog prožimanja svih tih svojstava. Uglavnom, ako budem imao sreće da još koju godinicu poživim u zdravlju i snazi, trebao bih naslikati neke stvarno dobre slike.
Možda sam to ipak trebao napisati ovako:

Bila jednom u Humani jedna bijela spavaćica. Humana je robna kuća rabljene odjeće na Frankfurter Toru. Poslao sam Ernestine tamo s 20 eura da nabavi nešto bijelo, što je trebala odjenuti kako bih na nju projicirao kartu zvjezdanog neba. Trebalo je to izgledati kao da je noć, ali i da bude jasno da je to ipak samo projekcija karte zvjezdanog neba na model. Volim se kretati u tom prostoru između naslikane slike i one u nama na koju nas ta slika asocira. Možda je Luc Tuymans mislio na to kada je rekao da "taj mali prostor izmedju slike i njezinog tumačenja vidi kao jedinu mogućnost". Premda nije to ništa novo. U Caravaggiovu *Polaganju u grob*, npr., jasno se vidi da je cijeli prizor samo poza, iluzija, koji u nama treba pobuditi pravu sliku toga tragičnog trenutka. Uglavnom, da skratim, Ernestine je kupila baš tu bijelu spavaćicu iz Humane za 5 eura.


122
Place
Mjesto


Rekla je da osjeća potencijal u meni i da točno vidi kako će jednom izgledati moje slike. Da bi to potvrdila, rekla je da bih na slici *Mjesto* trebao izbaciti »onaj glupi šteker« i smanjiti površinu poda na samo 7 cm. Poslušao sam i naslikao sliku *Bijeli kvadrat*. Hmm, nije loše, mislio sam, izgleda ozbiljno, onako u stilu patent-slikara iz prošlog stoljeća. Možda bih tako i ja mogao dobiti svoje mjesto u povijesti umjetnosti; na platnu velika površina zida, lijepo naslikana, a dolje 7 do 10 cm poda . Jebi ga, al' nekako mi je falio moj »glupi šteker« i cijelo ono zadovoljstvo u slikanju te male diverzije iz realnog svijeta.

Bila je to zapravo tipična ženska »navlakuša«: ili si sa mnom, i onda si super, ili nisi sa mnom, i onda si govno. Izabrao sam ovo drugo i pobjegao glavom bez obzira.


126
STAGINGS
UPRIZORENJA


126
Fake News
Lažne vijesti

## 158
## SLOWING DOWN
## USPORAVANJE

### 158
### Slowing Down
### Usporavanje

Posljednjih godina  živim u neprestanoj unutarnjoj borbi. Naime, moje slike, ili ono što njima pokušavam dosegnuti, zahtijevaju sve više vremena. Mislim da razlog ne treba tražiti u tome što starim i postajem općenito sporiji. Nego se u slikama množe detalji, a način na koji slikam, to bezbrojno premazivanje jednog te istog mjesta na slici lazurom da bih dobio željenu prisutnost i gustoću naslikanog uzima sate i sate, koji nekako neprimjetno prolaze. Sjedeći danima pred istom slikom, zarobljen jednim jedinim detaljem, često pomišljam kako bih trebao ubrzati svoj slikarski postupak, biti produktivniji, raditi primjerenije dobu u kojemu se sve odvija sumanutom brzinom i u kojemu - avaj - ionako nitko neće imati ni strpljenja ni koncentracije da se upusti u promatranje moje slike sa staromodnim, sporim užitkom.

Zapravo sam se sâm doveo u tu - klopku, kako mi se ponekad čini. Dopuštao sam da me pri odabiru motiva vode životne okolnosti, umjesto kakva plana ili sistema. Kad, međutim, pogledam to što sam naslikao, vidim da je baš tako i trebalo biti naslikano. Radi energije, radi atmosfere, radi svega što sam svjesno i nesvjesno htio postići svakom od tih slika. Budući da (dosada) nisam iznašao patent koji bi mi omogućio da slikam brzo i jednostavno, a da pritom budem i zadovoljan naslikanim, nakraju uvijek ponizno prihvatim da je taj spori i tegobni način koji me katkad frustrira upravo moj osobni, prepoznatljivi način. Zato sam odlučio da slike nastale posljednjih godina prikažem pod naslovom »Usporavanje«.

Ovdje su prikazane slike koje naslov *Zlatne folije* možda ne opisuje najpreciznije. Osnovni razlog da ih počnem slikati nije bila zlatna boja folije, nego njezino svojstvo da iskrivljeno zrcali okoliš. Zahvaljujući njemu dobio sam predložak koji ovisno o udaljenosti modela ili predmeta od folije odražava prostor i likove više ili manje fragmentarno, tako da se više naslućuju nego što se razabiru. Ta slutnja onoga što bi trebalo biti prikazano stvara dojam da je slika oslobođena snažne opisne predmetnosti te da je slikarski postupak slobodniji, autonomniji, čime stjeće prednost pred prikazanim predmetom. Ali u biti je pristup predmetu i način slikanja pritom posve jednak kao u slučaju mojih drugih, "klasičnih, izrazito figurativnih" slika, kako su ih nazvali. Kad se folije promotre iz tog kuta, postaje jasno da je naslikani predmet zapravo zlatna folija, koja je prikazana izrazito figurativno, a sve drugo samo su odrazi u njoj.

### 160
### Reflections
### Odrazi

Moja prijateljica Leonida izbrojila je 432 pravokutnika na slici *Odraz ateljea u zlatnoj foliji*. Nisam provjeravao - ako ona kaže, onda je sigurno tako. Pravokutnici na foliji nastali su presavijanjem radi pakiranja. Naslikao sam ih onako kako sam ih vidio. Geometrijska struktura tih "pločica" i iskrivljeni odrazi koje stvaraju daju slici dojam modernističkog slikarstva. Pogotovo ako se neke od tih pločica promatraju izdvojeno, moglo bi se pomisliti da je posrijedi slagalica koja se sastoji od slika iz razdoblja moderne. Budući da su nastale istim slikarskim postupkom kojim i inače slikam, tvrdim da mi to nije bila namjera, kao što nisam htio ni ironizirati modernu niti je uopće komentirati (barem ne svjesno). Unatoč tome, zabavno je otkrivati i promatrati te fragmente.

### 166
### Studio Visit
### Posjet ateljeu

Može se bez pretjerivanja reći da su gotovo svi posjeti mojem ateljeu uredno zabilježeni na slikama. Vrlo je malo ljudi iz kruga mojih prijatelja i znanaca za koje se još nije našla neka uloga, neki razlog da budu naslikani. Što ne znači da jednog dana neće biti naslikani i ti koji dosad nisu. Slikarstvo je po sebi samotnjačko zanimanje, a moje slike trebaju ljude. Stoga se druženje u ateljeu, pa makar to bila i obična pijanka, može smatrati dijelom stvaralačkog procesa. Da se poslužim analogijom sa svijetom prirode, čini mi se ponekad da sam poput muholovke koja je simbiotski povezana s ateljeom. Posjetitelji rado dolaze privučeni atmosferom prostora, ne sluteći da će mi kad-tad morati pozirati. Poekad to traje kratko, a ponekad se razvuče na mjesece. Naravno, iz ateljea svi odlaze živi, zdravi i veseli, tako da je usporedba s muholovkom možda ipak neosnovana.

172
The Bar
Bar

U polumraku svjetluca na tisuće sitnih odbljesaka poput zvjez-
dica u nekom crvenkastom svemiru. Na čašama, flašama, na
šejkerima i jiggerima, na lijevcima likerskih bočica uredno
postrojenih na šanku, na metalnom i staklenom posuđu kojim
se osoblje bara služi s uzvišenom upućenošću dok mjeri, mu-
ćka, miješa, istače i pretače raznobojne tekućine (iz nekih se
još i puši, iz drugih palucaju plavičasti plamičci). Boce opojna
sadržaja na polici onkraj šanka zrače zemljanim bojama. Sred
svih tih zvjezdastih bljeskova lijeno se uvija, izvija duhanski
dim kao svemirska maglica na fotografiji Hubbleova teleskopa.
Ispod svjetiljaka što lebde nisko iznad šanka pramenovi dima
zasjaju i kao kakvim velom zastru lijepo lice koje promatram.
Lica se mijenjaju od večeri do večeri, od čaše do čaše, što me
najčešće navede na melankolično meditiranje o prolaznosti.


176
Night Light Melancholy
Melankolija noćnih svjetala

Noćna svjetla fascinirala su me i prije nego što sam se kao klinac
počeo noću smucati po gradu. Grad je bio područje u kojemu
sam otkrivao život. I filmovi. Filmovi u kojima je noć i pada kiša
i neonska se svjetla razlijevaju mokrim asfaltom u bezbrojnim
nijansama. Boje tih svjetala intenzivne su u kontrastu s tminom
noćnog okoliša. I u kojima strašno cool filmski likovi, tek djelo-
mice osvijetljeni, izranjaju iz mraka. Da, to sam oduvijek želio
slikati, i ne znam zašto je tako dugo trebalo da ta želja ispliva na
površinu. Bilo je i drugih stvari koje sam htio naslikati, svakako.
A osjećao sam usto da još nisam slikarski dorastao toj zadaći.
Dugo sam okolišao. Ali mislim da sam sada kadar naslikati noćnu
scenu kakva raskrižja u kojoj pada kiša, a svjetla se automobila
i semafora odražavaju na mokrom asfaltu.


180
Excursion
Izlet

Sanjao sam da sam s pjevačem grupe Victims of Women Intolerance na road tripu po Brandenburgu. Ne znam odakle to ime,
internet nije mogao potvrditi postojanje takve grupe. Moglo
bi imati veze s nečim dubljim, čime se sada ne bih bavio. A taj
pjevač nije sličio nijednom od nekolicine koju poznajem. Zapravo
nije imao nikakav konkretan lik. Krenuli smo autom od njegove
vikendice vozeći se uskim regionalnim cestama koje obrubljuju
drvoredi tako tipični za Brandenburg. Za vrijeme vožnje - dijelom zbog efekta kretanja, a dijelom zato što se to u snovima
naprosto događa - počeli su se oblici koje sam opažao prožimati i
međusobno pretapati. Tako bi, naprimjer, dio pejzaža s drvećem
najedanput poprimio oblik kuće ili automobila, posve raspoznat-
ljivo, kao da su ti oblici umotani u nešto na čemu je otisnuta slika
pejzaža. Pričam sve to zato što me jako podsjetilo na odraz šume
na ulaštenoj karoseriji mercedesa s moje slike »Jesenski izlet«.


184
UNDERWORLD PARTY
TULUM U PODZEMNOM SVIJETU

Htio sam u svojem ateljeu prirediti tulum pod naslovom
„Podzemni svijet“. Zamislio sam da prostor bude osvijetljen
ultraljubičastim, takozvanim "crnim" svjetlom. Na zidovima
crteži ugljenom na papiru, čije bjeline pod UV-osvjetljenjem
zrače neprirodnim plavičastim sjajem. Crteži su trebali biti
kopije slika starih majstora koje prikazuju scene iz podzemnog
svijeta grčke mitologije. Zamišljao sam kako gosti, za tu prigodu odjeveni samo u propisano bijelo ili crno, poput svjetlucavih duhova tumaraju ateljeom u maglici duhanskog dima.
Po sebi je to zapravo banalan prizor, kao iz kakva kluba ili
diska, ali činilo mi se da bi ipak mogao imati nešto mistično.

Kad sam počeo raditi na prvom crtežu, uvidio sam, međutim,
da sam, premda umišljam da sam nakupio dovoljno iskustva
u svojem poslu, još uvijek djetinjasto naivan. Vrijeme koje je
trebalo uložiti u izradu vjerne kopije pomicalo je, naime, termin
planiranog tuluma sve dalje u neodređenu budućnost. A i želja da
ga priredim polako je jenjavala. Ipak sam nastavio raditi, unatoč
osjećaju da činim nešto posve apsurdno. Zašto, zaboga, trošim
vrijeme na nekakve kopije? Da bi mi netko nadjenuo nadimak
„Rembrandt“? I stoji li koncept ako tuluma ne bude? Pritom
znam da bi „pravi profi-umjetnik“ prepustio taj mukotrpni posao
nekome drugom, a sâm se posvetio pametnijem poslu.

No kako je rad na kopijama tekao, tako je u meni rasla stanovita radost zbog toga što moj pothvat nije imao nikakva smisla ni svrhe.
A osim toga se nisam htio odreći užitka: kao prvo u crtanju ugljenom, a kao drugo u postupnom „ulaženju“ u orginalno djelo koje
mi je služilo kao predložak. Na kraju krajeva, to je iskustvo ipak
bilo poput silaska u podzemni svijet - ako već ne razuzdan tulum,
onda ipak neka vrst druženja s onima koji više ne kroče Zemljom.

# catalogue

# katalog

| nr | caption | legenda | photography / fotograf | series / serija |
|---|---|---|---|---|
| 1 | Orpheus and Eurydice (alias Hansel and Gretel<br>Charcoal on paper, 115 x 80,5 cm, 2021 | Orfej i Euridika (iliti Ivica i Marica-svejedno)<br>Crtež ugljenom na papiru, 115 x 80,5 cm, 2021. | Gunter<br>Lepkowski | SLOWING DOWN<br>USPORAVANJE |
| 2 | Signing of the Declaration on the Unification of Western Herzegovina and Popovo polje with the Republic of Croatia (Wer hat das Bier bestellt?)<br>Oil on canvas, 280 × 480 cm, 2008-11 | Potpisivanje deklaracije o pripajanju Zapadne Hercegovine i Popova polja Republici Hrvatskoj (Wer hat ds Bier bestellt?).<br>Ulje na platnu, 480 × 280 cm, 2008-11. | Damir<br>Žižić | STAGINGS<br>UPRIZORENJA |
| 3 | The Rape of Proserpine (after Rembrandt)<br>Charcoal on paper, 110 x 102,5 cm, 2019 | Otmica Proserpine (po Rembrandtu)<br>Crtež ugljenom na papiru, 110 x 102,5 cm, 2019. | – | UNDERWORLD PARTY  TULUM U PODZEMLJU |
| 4 | Women's Bath (Diana and Actaeon?)<br>Oil on canvas, 190 × 220 cm, 2014 | Ženska kupelj (Dijana i Akteon?).<br>Ulje na platnu, 190 × 220 cm, 2014. | Gunter<br>Lepkowski | STAGINGS<br>UPRIZORENJA |
| 5 | Gemini<br>Oil on canvas, 2 × 180 × 110 cm, 2007 | Blizanci<br>Ulje na platnu, 2 × 180 × 110 cm, 2007. | Gunter<br>Lepkowski | AS IF<br>KAO DA |
| 6 | Gold (First-aid Blanket).<br>Oil on canvas, 145 × 125 cm, 2009 | Zlato (pokrivač prve pomoći)<br>Ulje na platnu, 145 × 125 cm, 2009. | Damir<br>Žižić | AS IF<br>KAO DA |
| 7 | White square<br>Oil on canvas, 170 × 160 cm, 2009-11 | Bijeli kvadrat<br>Ulje na platnu, 170 × 160 cm, 2009-11. | Damir<br>Žižić | AS IF<br>KAO DA |
| 8 | Let Me Show You My Dream<br>Oil on canvas, 105 × 145 cm, 2019 | Da vam pokažem svoj san<br>Ulje na platnu, 105 × 145 cm, 2019. | Gunter<br>Lepkowski | STAGINGS<br>UPRIZORENJA |
| 9 | Underworld Party<br>UV light, charcoal drawings on paper of different dimensions, table, tablecloth, various dishes, paper flower, 2020 | Tulum u podzemnom svijetu<br>UV-svjetlo, crteži ugljenom na papiru različitih dimenzija, stol, stolnjak, različito posuđe, papirnati cvijet, 2020. | Gunter<br>Lepkowski | UNDERWORLD PARTY TULUM U PODZEMLJU |
| 10 | Persephone<br>Charcoal on paper, 97,5 x 97,5 cm, 2022 | Perzefona<br>Ugljen na papiru, 97,5 x 97,5 cm, 2022. | Gunter<br>Lepkowski | SLOWING DOWN<br>USPORAVANJE |
| 11 | On the Water I (after Odilon Redon's drawing Head of Orpheus Floating in the Water)<br>Charcoal on paper, 75 × 65 cm, 2020 | U vodi I (prema crtežu Odilona Redona »Orfejeva glava pluta na vodi ili Mistik«).<br>Crtež ugljenom na papiru, 75 × 65 cm, 2020. | Gunter<br>Lepkowski | SLOWING DOWN<br>USPORAVANJE |
| 12 | On the Water II (after Odilon Redon's drawing Head of Orpheus Floating in the Water)<br>Charcoal on paper, 75 × 65 cm, 2020 | U vodi II (prema crtežu Odilona Redona »Orfejeva glava pluta na vodi ili Mistik«)<br>Crtež ugljenom na papiru, 75 × 65 cm, 2020. | Gunter<br>Lepkowski | SLOWING DOWN<br>USPORAVANJE |
| 13 | Y<br>Four-colour lithograph, 67 × 50 cm, 1990.<br>Prints portfolio «Alphabet of Narcissism» | Y<br>Litografija u 4 boje, 67 × 50 cm, 1990.<br>Grafička mapa »Abeceda narcisoidnosti« | Fedor<br>Vučemilović | CONSTRUCTED EVERYDAY LIFE<br>KONSTRUIRANA SVAKODNEVNICA |
| 14 | Night Lights<br>Oil on MDF board, 33.5 × 22.5 cm, 2019 | Noćna svjetla<br>Ulje na MDF-ploči, 33,5 × 22,5 cm, 2019. | Gunter<br>Lepkowski | SLOWING DOWN<br>USPORAVANJE |
| 15 | Dispute About the Meaning of Figurative Representation<br>Oil on canvas, 100 × 60 cm, 2015 | Disput o smislu figurativnog prikaza.<br>Ulje na platnu, 100 × 60 cm, 2015. | Andrija<br>Zelmanović | SLOWING DOWN<br>USPORAVANJE |

| No. | English | Croatian | Photographer | Series |
|---|---|---|---|---|
| 16 | Dispute in the Studio.<br>Oil on canvas, 160 × 170 cm, 2015-20 | Disput u ateljeu<br>Ulje na platnu, 160 × 170 cm, 2015-20. | Gunter Lepkowski | SLOWING DOWN<br>USPORAVANJE |
| 17 | Spring (after Botticelli)<br>Guache on cardboard, 70 x 100 cm, 1985 | Proljeće (po Botticelliu)<br>Gvaš na papiru (više karton), 70 x 100 cm, 1985. | Vedran Braun | EARLY WORKS<br>RANI RADOVI |
| 18 | God, I love Botticelli<br>Oil and glass splinters on canvas,<br>2 × 145 × 86.5 cm, 2001 | Bože kako volim Botticellia<br>Ulje i krhotine stakla na platnu,<br>2 × 145 × 86,5 cm, 2001. | Fedor Vučemilović | BEECH CRUST<br>BUKVINA KORA |
| 19 | Painting for Teeth (Shhhhh)<br>Oil on canvas, 2 × 176 × 110 cm, 2002-09 | Slika za zube (ŠŠŠŠŠ)<br>Ulje na platnu, 2 × 176 × 110 cm, 2002-09. | Damir Žižić | BEECH CRUST<br>BUKVINA KORA |
| 20 | Beech<br>Oil on canvas, 116 × 85 cm, 1996 | Bukva<br>Ulje na platnu, 116 × 85 cm, 1996. | – | SCENES<br>PRIZORI |
| 21 | Scarred Beech<br>Oil on canvas, 120 × 100 cm, 1997 | Bukva s ožiljcima<br>Ulje na platnu, 120 × 100 cm, 1997. | Damir Žižić | SCENES<br>PRIZORI |
| 22 | Scar<br>Oil on canvas, 98 × 70 cm, 1997 | Ožiljak<br>Ulje na platnu, 98 × 70 cm, 1997. | Vedran Braun | BEECH CRUST<br>BUKVINA KORA |
| 23 | Self-Portrait (as a Beech Tree)<br>Oil on canvas, 120 × 85 cm, 1996 | Autoportret (kao bukva)<br>Ulje na platnu, 120 × 85 cm, 1996. | Fedor Vučemilović | BEECH CRUST<br>BUKVINA KORA |
| 24 | Solarium<br>Oil on canvas, 160 × 190 cm, 2013-14 | Solarij<br>Ulje na platnu, 160 × 190 cm, 2013-14. | Andrija Zelmanović | STAGINGS<br>UPRIZORENJA |
| 25 | Untitled<br>Oil on canvas, 145 × 105 cm, 2006 | Bez naslova<br>Ulje na platnu, 145 × 105 cm, 2006. | Damir Žižić | THE FACE OF THE PAINTING<br>LICE SLIKE |
| 26 | False Twins in the Night<br>Oil on canvas, 2 × 180 × 110 cm, 2007-14 | Lažne blizanke u noći<br>Ulje na platnu, 2 × 180 × 110 cm, 2007-14. | Gunter Lepkowski | AS IF<br>KAO DA |
| 27 | False Twins<br>Oil on canvas, 2 × 180 × 110 cm, 2009-14 | Lažne blizanke<br>Ulje na platnu, 2 × 180 × 110 cm, 2009-14. | Gunter Lepkowski | AS IF<br>KAO DA |
| 28 | As if it Were a Starry Night<br>Oil on canvas, 145 × 175 cm, 2007 | Kao da je zvjezdana noć<br>Ulje na platnu, 145 × 175 cm, 2007. | Gunter Lepkowski | AS IF<br>KAO DA |
| 29 | As if Floating (Blue)<br>Oil on canvas, 195 × 145 cm, 2005 | Kao da lebde (Plava)<br>Ulje na platnu, 195 × 145 cm, 2005. | Fedor Vučemilović | AS IF<br>KAO DA |
| 30 | As if Floating (White)<br>Oil on canvas, 195 × 145 cm, 2005 | Kao da lebde (Bijela)<br>Ulje na platnu, 195 × 145 cm, 2005. | Gunter Lepkowski | AS IF<br>KAO DA |
| 31 | As if Floating (Red)<br>Oil on canvas, 195 × 145 cm, 2005 | Kao da lebde (Crvena)<br>Ulje na platnu, 195 × 145 cm, 2005. | Gunter Lepkowski | AS IF<br>KAO DA |
| 32 | Winged<br>Oil on canvas, 180 × 125 cm, 2010 | Na krilima<br>Ulje na platnu, 180 × 125 cm, 2010. | – | AS IF<br>KAO DA |
| 33 | Pietà Inverted<br>Oil on canvas, 220 × 190 cm, 2011 | Pietà obrnuto<br>Ulje na platnu, 220 × 190 cm, 2011. | Damir Žižić | STAGINGS<br>UPRIZORENJA |
| 34 | Models Posing for a Pietà<br>Oil on canvas, 190 × 220 cm, 2011 | Modeli poziraju za Pietu<br>Ulje na platnu, 220 × 190 cm, 2011. | – | STAGINGS<br>UPRIZORENJA |
| 35 | Hanging Self-Portrait<br>Oil on canvas, 250 × 110 cm, 2009-13 | Viseći autoportret.<br>Ulje na platnu, 250 × 110 cm, 2009-13. | Gunter Lepkowski | STAGINGS<br>UPRIZORENJA |
| 36 | Apollo and Marsyas<br>(Triumph of the New Media over Painting).<br>Oil on canvas, 270 × 360 cm, 2009-11 | Apolon i Marsija<br>(Trijumf novih medija nad slikarstvom).<br>Ulje na platnu, 360 × 270 cm, 2009-11. | Damir Žižić | STAGINGS<br>UPRIZORENJA |
| 37 | Kitschmonger in the Shade<br>Oil on canvas, 145 × 122,5 cm, 1999 (missing) | Kičer u sjeni<br>Ulje na platnu, 145 × 122,5 cm, 1999. (nestalo) | Luka Mjeda | BEECH CRUST<br>BUKVINA KORA |
| 38 | Ari in a Trashy Costume<br>Oil on canvas, 195 × 145 cm, 2012 | Ari u trash kostimu<br>Ulje na platnu, 195 × 145 cm, 2012. | Damir Žižić | STAGINGS<br>UPRIZORENJA |
| 39 | Shy Cowboy<br>Oil on canvas, 145 × 125 cm, 2005-2010 | Sramežljivi kauboj<br>Ulje na platnu, 145 × 125 cm, 2005-2010. | Damir Žižić | FALSE SCENES<br>LAŽNI PRIZORI |
| 40 | Self-Portrait - Remembering Marino Tartaglia<br>Oil on MDF board, 45 × 26 cm, 2022-23 | Autoportret - u mislima na Marina Tartagliu.<br>Ulje na MDF-ploči, 45 × 26 cm, 2022-23. | Gunter Lepkowski | |
| 41 | New Year's Eve Gown<br>Oil on canvas, 145 × 115 cm, 2009 | Novogodišnja haljina<br>Ulje na platnu, 145 × 115 cm, 2009. | – | AS IF<br>KAO DA |

| 42 | The Bunny and the Creek<br>Oil and gold foil on canvas, 145 × 122.5 cm, 1999 | Zeko i potočić<br>Ulje i zlatni listići na platnu, 145 × 122,5 cm, 1999. | Fedor<br>Vučemilović | BEECH CRUST<br>BUKVINA KORA |
|---|---|---|---|---|
| 43 | The Bunny and the Frozen Creek<br>Oil and gold foil on canvas,<br>145 × 122.5 cm, 2000 (missing) | Zeko i smrznuti potočić<br>Ulje i zlatni listići na platnu,<br>145 × 122,5 cm, 2000. (nestalo) | Luka Mjeda | BEECH CRUST<br>BUKVINA KORA |
| 44 | Fairy Tale Creature - Cubist<br>Oil on MDF board, 33.5 × 22.5 cm, 2018 | Biće iz bajke - kubističko<br>Ulje na MDF-ploči, 33,5 × 22,5 cm, 2018. | Gunter<br>Lepkowski | SLOWING DOWN<br>USPORAVANJE |
| 45 | Captured Spectre<br>Charcoal on paper, 100,5 × 110 cm, 2019 | Zarobljeni duh<br>Ugljen na papiru, 100,5 × 110 cm, 2019. | Gunter<br>Lepkowski | SLOWING DOWN<br>USPORAVANJE |
| 46 | Studio Reflection in Gold Foil<br>Oil on canvas, 220 × 190 cm, 2018 | Odraz ateljea na zlatnoj foliji<br>Ulje na platnu, 220 × 190 cm, 2018. | Gunter<br>Lepkowski | SLOWING DOWN<br>USPORAVANJE |
| 47 | Io and Jupiter<br>Oil on canvas, 100 × 82 cm, 2019-20 | Io i Jupiter<br>Ulje na platnu, 100 × 82 cm, 2019-20. | Gunter<br>Lepkowski | SLOWING DOWN<br>USPORAVANJE |
| 48 | Full Moon in My Kitchen<br>Oil on MDF board, 45 × 26 cm, 2019 | Pun mjesec u mojoj kuhinji<br>Ulje na MDF-ploči, 45 × 26 cm, 2019. | Gunter<br>Lepkowski | SLOWING DOWN<br>USPORAVANJE |
| 49 | Lene in a Deluge<br>Oil on MDF board, 40 × 29 cm, 2019-20 | Lene u potopu<br>Ulje na MDF-ploči, 40 × 29 cm, 2019-20. | Gunter<br>Lepkowski | SLOWING DOWN<br>USPORAVANJE |
| 50 | Runar<br>Oil on canvas, 100 × 62 cm, 2015 | Runar<br>Ulje na platnu, 100 × 62 cm, 2015. | Gunter<br>Lepkowski | SLOWING DOWN<br>USPORAVANJE |
| 51 | Shower in the Yard<br>Oil on MDF board, 40 × 29.5 cm, 2019-20 | Pljusak u dvorištu<br>Ulje na MDF-ploči, 40 × 29,5 cm, 2019-20. | Gunter<br>Lepkowski | SLOWING DOWN<br>USPORAVANJE |
| 52 | Apparition in Neukölln<br>Oil on canvas, 125 × 80 cm, 2019-20 | Ukazanje u Neuköllnu<br>Ulje na platnu, 125 × 80 cm, 2019-20. | Gunter<br>Lepkowski | SLOWING DOWN<br>USPORAVANJE |
| 53 | At the Tier<br>Oil on canvas, 145 × 115 cm, 2020 | U Tieru<br>Ulje na platnu, 145 × 115 cm, 2020. | Gunter<br>Lepkowski | SLOWING DOWN<br>USPORAVANJE |
| 54 | Late Night Tales<br>Oil on canvas, 125 × 145 cm, 2019 | Kasnonoćne pripovijesti<br>Ulje na platnu, 125 × 145 cm, 2019. | Gunter<br>Lepkowski | SLOWING DOWN<br>USPORAVANJE |
| 55 | Closing Time (Bad Thoughts)<br>Oil on canvas, 105 × 145 cm, 2019-20 | Closing time (Bad Thougths)<br>Ulje na platnu, 105 × 145 cm, 2019-20. | Gunter<br>Lepkowski | SLOWING DOWN<br>USPORAVANJE |
| 56 | Autumn Excursion<br>Oil on canvas, 145 × 125 cm, 2017-19 | Jesenski izlet<br>Ulje na platnu, 145 × 125 cm, 2017-19. | Gunter<br>Lepkowski | SLOWING DOWN<br>USPORAVANJE |
| 57 | Hydra (in an Autumn Landscape)<br>Oil on canvas, 145 × 125 cm, 2019-20 | Hidra (u jesenskom pejzažu)<br>Ulje na platnu, 145 × 125 cm, 2019-20. | Gunter<br>Lepkowski | SLOWING DOWN<br>USPORAVANJE |
| 58 | On a Summer Day in the Heidelberg Forest<br>Oil on MDF board, 45 × 26 cm, 2017 | Jednog ljetnog dana u Heidelberškoj šumi<br>Ulje na MDF-ploči, 45 × 26 cm, 2017. | Gunter<br>Lepkowski | SLOWING DOWN<br>USPORAVANJE |
| 59 | Self-Portrait<br>Charcoal, chalk and red chalk on primed<br>natron paper, 68 x 52 cm, 1982 | Autoportret<br>Ugljen, sangvina, akril (polikolor) na natron papiru,<br>68 x 52 cm, 1982. | Gunter<br>Lepkowski | EARLY WORKS<br>RANI RADOVI |
| 60 | Self-Portrait Study, detail<br>Charcoal and chalk on natron paper, 63 x 46 cm, 1982 | Studija autoportreta, detalj<br>Ugljen, kreda, kreda u boji na natron papiru, 63 x 46 cm, 1982. | Lovro<br>Artuković | EARLY WORKS<br>RANI RADOVI |
| 61 | Sitting Figure in Space<br>Charcoal and chalk on natron paper, 121 x 82 cm. 1982 | Sjedeća figurau prostoru<br>Ugljen i kreda na natron papiru,121 x 82 cm, 1982. | Lovro<br>Artuković | EARLY WORKS<br>RANI RADOVI |
| 62 | Figure in Space<br>Charcoal and chalk on natron paper, 121 x 80,5 cm, 1982 | Figura u prostoru<br>Ugljen i kreda na natron papiru, 121 x 80,5 cm, 1982. | Damir<br>Žižić | EARLY WORKS<br>RANI RADOVI |
| 63 | Brawly Night<br>China ink and tempera on grey packing paper,<br>105 x 82 cm, 1982. | Bučna noć<br>Tuš i tempera na sivom papiru za omatanje,<br>105 x 82 cm, 1982. | – | EARLY WORKS<br>RANI RADOVI |
| 64 | Resurrection (after Grünewald)<br>Guache on handmade paper, 63 x 46 cm, 1986 | Uskrsnuće (po Grünewaldu)<br>Gvaš na ručno rađenom papiru, 63 x 46 cm, 1985. | Damir<br>Žižić | EARLY WORKS<br>RANI RADOVI |
| 65 | Shhhh<br>Egg tempera on canvas, 135 × 165 cm, 1988 | Šššš<br>Jajčana tempera na platnu, 135 × 165 cm, 1988. | Vedran<br>Braun | EARLY WORKS<br>RANI RADOVI |
| 66 | The Magic Flute<br>Combined technique on jute, 110 × 177 cm, 1986 | Čarobna frula<br>Kombinirana tehnika na jutenom platnu, 110 × 177 cm, 1986. | Fedor<br>Vučemilović | EARLY WORKS<br>RANI RADOVI |
| 67 | Study for My Friend Vincent<br>Charcoal and chalk on natron paper, 107 x 80 cm, 1986 | Studija za Moj prijatelj Vincent<br>Ugljen i kreda na natron papiru, 107 x 80 cm, 1986. | Damir<br>Žižić | EARLY WORKS<br>RANI RADOVI |

| 68 | My friend Vincent<br>Oil on canvas, 195 × 135 cm, 1986 | Moj prijatelj Vincent<br>Ulje na platnu, 195 × 135 cm, 1986. | Fedor<br>Vučemilović | EARLY WORKS<br>RANI RADOVI |
|---|---|---|---|---|
| 69 | Walk<br>Egg tempera and oil on plywood and plexiglas,<br>195 x 145 cm, 1986 | Šetnja<br>Jajčana tempera i ulje na šperploči i pleksigasu,<br>195 x 145 cm, 1986. | Pavle<br>Orbović | EARLY WORKS<br>RANI RADOVI |
| 70 | Silba Trip<br>Oil on canvas, 195 × 135 cm, 1987 | Film sa Silbe<br>Ulje na platnu, 195 × 135 cm, 1987. | Fedor<br>Vučemilović | EARLY WORKS<br>RANI RADOVI |
| 71 | Spring<br>Egg tempera on canvas, 135 × 195 cm, 1988 | Proljeće<br>Jajčana tempera na platnu, 135 × 195 cm, 1988. | Fedor<br>Vučemilović | EARLY WORKS<br>RANI RADOVI |
| 72 | Domestic Spring<br>Egg tempera on canvas, 195 × 135 cm, 1988 | Proljeće (domaće)<br>Jajčana tempera na platnu, 195 × 135 cm, 1988. | Fedor<br>Vučemilović | EARLY WORKS<br>RANI RADOVI |
| 73 | Domestic Spring<br>Egg tempera on canvas, 195 × 135 cm, 1988 | Proljeće (domaće)<br>Jajčana tempera na platnu, 195 × 135 cm, 1988. | Fedor<br>Vučemilović | EARLY WORKS<br>RANI RADOVI |
| 74 | Drawings with Portraits of Gallery Visitors (Duje).<br>Charcoal, chalk and acrylics, 113 x 78 cm on natron<br>paper, 1988. | Crteži s portretima posjetitelja galerije (Duje)<br>Ugljen, kreda, kreda u boji, akril, 113 x 78 cm<br>na natron papiru, 1988. | Damir<br>Žižić | CONSTRUCTED EVERYDAY LIFE<br>KONSTRUIRANA SVAKODNEVNICA |
| 75 | Drawings with Portraits of Gallery Visitors<br>(Edita and Galeta)<br>Charcoal, chalk and acrylics, 113 x 78 cm<br>on natron paper, 1988 | Crteži s portretima posjetitelja galerije<br>(Edita i Galeta)<br>Ugljen, kreda, kreda u boji, akril, 113 x 78 cm<br>na natron papiru, 1988. | Damir<br>Žižić | CONSTRUCTED EVERYDAY LIFE<br>KONSTRUIRANA SVAKODNEVNICA |
| 76 | U<br>Four-colour lithograph, 67 × 50 cm, 1990<br>Prints portfolio «Alphabet of Narcissism» | U<br>Litografija u 4 boje, 67 × 50 cm, 1990<br>Grafička mapa »Abeceda narcisoidnosti« | Fedor<br>Vučemilović | CONSTRUCTED EVERYDAY LIFE<br>KONSTRUIRANA SVAKODNEVNICA |
| 77 | W<br>Four-colour lithograph, 67 × 50 cm, 1990<br>Prints portfolio «Alphabet of Narcissism» | W<br>Litografija u 4 boje, 67 × 50 cm, 1990.<br>Grafička mapa »Abeceda narcisoidnosti« | Fedor<br>Vučemilović | CONSTRUCTED EVERYDAY LIFE<br>KONSTRUIRANA SVAKODNEVNICA |
| 78 | Adam<br>Oil on canvas, 80 × 65 cm, 1994 | Adam<br>Ulje na platnu, 80 × 65 cm, 1994. | Andrija<br>Zelmanović | CONSTRUCTED EVERYDAY LIFE<br>KONSTRUIRANA SVAKODNEVNICA |
| 79 | Embellishment - Blooming Garden / Earring<br>Oil on canvas, 2 × 142 × 88 cm, 1994 | Ukrašavanje - Vrt u cvatu / Naušnica<br>Ulje na platnu, 2 × 142 × 88 cm, 1994. | Fedor<br>Vučemilović | CONSTRUCTED EVERYDAY LIFE<br>KONSTRUIRANA SVAKODNEVNICA |
| 80 | Apple Tree<br>Oil on canvas, 120 × 90 cm, 1994 | Jabuka<br>Ulje na platnu, 120 × 90 cm, 1994. | Fedor<br>Vučemilović | CONSTRUCTED EVERYDAY LIFE<br>KONSTRUIRANA SVAKODNEVNICA |
| 81 | Entrance<br>Oil on canvas, 165 × 135 cm, 1993 | Ulazak<br>Ulje na platnu, 165 × 135 cm, 1993. | – | CONSTRUCTED EVERYDAY LIFE<br>KONSTRUIRANA SVAKODNEVNICA |
| 82 | Sisters<br>Oil on canvas, 100 × 80, 1994 | Sestre<br>Ulje na platnu, 100 × 80, 1994. | Fedor<br>Vučemilović | SCENES<br>PRIZORI |
| 83 | Friends<br>Oil on canvas, 195 × 145, 1996 (missing) | Prijatelji<br>Ulje na platnu, 195 × 145, 1996. (nestalo) | – | SCENES<br>PRIZORI |
| 84 | Marijana<br>Oil on canvas, 100 × 80, 1996 | Marijana<br>Ulje na platnu, 100 × 80, 1996. | Fedor<br>Vučemilović | SCENES<br>PRIZORI |
| 85 | Sisters<br>Oil on canvas, 100 × 80, 1994 | Sestre<br>Ulje na platnu, 100 × 80, 1994. | – | SCENES<br>PRIZORI |
| 86 | Sisters<br>Oil on canvas, 195 × 145, 1996 | Sestre<br>Ulje na platnu, 195 × 145, 1996. | Fedor<br>Vučemilović | SCENES<br>PRIZORI |
| 87 | Miranda and Stanko<br>Oil on canvas, 195 × 145, 1996 (missing) | Miranda i Stanko<br>Ulje na platnu, 195 × 145, 1996. (nestalo) | – | SCENES<br>PRIZORI |
| 88 | Sanja and Nera<br>Oil on canvas, 195 × 145, 1996 (missing) | Sanja i Nera<br>Ulje na platnu, 195 × 145, 1996. (nestalo) | – | SCENES<br>PRIZORI |
| 89 | Tina, Jan, Davor, Carlos and My Little<br>Conversation with Julije Knifer<br>Oil on canvas, 100 x 80 cm, 2022-23 | Tina, Jan, Davor, Carlos i moj mali razgovor<br>s Julijem Kniferom<br>Ulje na platnu, 100 x 80 cm, 2022-23. | Damir<br>Žižić | SCENES<br>PRIZORI |
| 90 | Scene in the Woods with Cobwebs<br>Oil on canvas, 195 × 145 cm, 2001 (missing) | Šumski prizor s paukovim mrežama<br>Ulje na platnu, 195 × 145 cm, 2001. (nestalo) | – | SCENES<br>PRIZORI |
| 91 | Scene in the Woods, as if Made for a Story<br>Oil on canvas, 195 × 145 cm, 1996 | Šumski prizor k'o stvoren za priču<br>Ulje na platnu, 195 × 145 cm, 1996. | Luka<br>Mjeda | SCENES<br>PRIZORI |

| 92 | Black Forest<br>Oil on canvas, 116 × 85 cm, 1995 | Crna šuma<br>Ulje na platnu, 116 × 85 cm, 1995. | Fedor<br>Vučemilović | SCENES<br>PRIZORI |
|---|---|---|---|---|
| 93 | Storm is Coming<br>Oil on canvas, 135 × 86 cm, 1998 | Dolazi nevera<br>Ulje na platnu, 135 × 86, 1998. | Zoran<br>Alajbeg | SCENES<br>PRIZORI |
| 94 | Dusk<br>Oil on canvas, 135 × 86 cm, 1998 | Suton<br>Ulje na platnu, 135 × 86, 1998. | – | SCENES<br>PRIZORI |
| 95 | Alone<br>Oil on canvas, 135 × 86 cm, 1998 (missing) | Sama<br>Ulje na platnu, 135 × 86, 1998. (nestalo) | – | SCENES<br>PRIZORI |
| 96 | Alone<br>Oil on canvas, 195 × 145 cm, 1998 | Sam<br>Ulje na platnu, 195 × 145 cm, 1998. | – | SCENES<br>PRIZORI |
| 97 | Night Scene with Shining House<br>Pencil on paper, 100 × 70 cm, 2001 | Noćni prizor s kućom koja svijetli<br>Olovka na papiru, 100 × 70 cm, 2001. | – | SCENES<br>PRIZORI |
| 98 | Mark<br>Oil on canvas, 98 × 70 cm, 1997 | Oznaka<br>Ulje na platnu, 98 × 70 cm, 1997. | – | BEECH CRUST<br>BUKVINA KORA |
| 99 | Self-Portrait<br>Oil on canvas, 120 × 85 cm, 1996 | Autoportret<br>Ulje na platnu, 120 × 85 cm, 1996. | Fedor<br>Vučemilović | BEECH CRUST<br>BUKVINA KORA |
| 100 | Scratches<br>Oil on canvas, 98 × 70 cm, 1997 | Ogrebotine<br>Ulje na platnu, 98 × 70 cm, 1997. | Damir Žižić | BEECH CRUST<br>BUKVINA KORA |
| 101 | Wound<br>Oil on canvas, 97 × 70 cm, 1997 | Rana<br>Ulje na platnu, 97 × 70 cm, 1997. | Vedran<br>Braun | BEECH CRUST<br>BUKVINA KORA |
| 102 | Shit Happens<br>Oil on canvas, 145 × 177 cm, 1999 (missing) | Jebi ga, desi se<br>Ulje na platnu, 145 × 177 cm, 1999. (nestalo) | Luka<br>Mjeda | BEECH CRUST<br>BUKVINA KORA |
| 103 | Dead Hare<br>Oil on canvas, 145 × 122.5 cm, 1997 | Mrtvi zec<br>Ulje na platnu, 145 × 122,5 cm, 1997. | Fedor<br>Vučemilović | BEECH CRUST<br>BUKVINA KORA |
| 104 | Stillness (Vegetable Garden)<br>Oil on canvas, 144 × 88 cm, 1999 (missing) | Tišina (Vrtal)<br>Ulje na platnu, 144 × 88 cm, 1999. (nestalo) | – | BEECH CRUST<br>BUKVINA KORA |
| 105 | Stillness (Ivy-Covered Wall)<br>Oil on canvas, 144 × 88 cm, 1999 | Tišina (Zid s bršljanom)<br>Ulje na platnu, 144 × 88 cm, 1999. | – | BEECH CRUST<br>BUKVINA KORA |
| 106 | Inside Herself<br>Oil on canvas, 80 × 99 cm, 2001 | U sebi unutra.<br>Ulje na platnu, 80 × 99 cm, 2001. | Damir<br>Fabijanić | BEECH CRUST<br>BUKVINA KORA |
| 107 | Hold Me Tight (on a Summer Night)<br>Oil on canvas, 100 x 80 cm, 1999-2005 | Stisni me (jedne ljetne noći)<br>Ulje na platnu, 100 x 80 cm, 1999-2005. | Damir<br>Žižić | FALSE SCENES<br>LAŽNI PRIZORI |
| 108 | The Deer Hunter's Dream<br>Pencil on paper, 70 × 100 cm, 2001 | San lovca na jelene.<br>Olovka na papiru, 70 × 100 cm, 2001. | – | BEECH CRUST<br>BUKVINA KORA |
| 109 | The Deer Hunter's Dream<br>Oil on canvas, 80 × 99 cm, 2001 | San lovca na jelene.<br>Ulje na platnu, 80 × 99 cm, 2001. | Fedor<br>Vučemilović | BEECH CRUST<br>BUKVINA KORA |
| 110 | 64<br>Oil on canvas, 2 × 176 × 110 cm, 2006 | 64<br>Ulje na platnu, 2 × 176 × 110 cm, 2006. | Gunter<br>Lepkowski | BEECH CRUST<br>BUKVINA KORA |
| 111 | God, I Wish I Were a Tough Guy!<br>Pencil and crayon on paper, 2 × 100 × 70 cm, 2002-03 | Bože, kako bih volio biti faca!<br>Olovka i olovke u boji na papiru, 2 × 100 × 70 cm, 2002-03. | Gunter<br>Lepkowski | FALSE SCENES<br>LAŽZNI PRIZORI |
| 112 | Basketball (for Jeff)<br>Oil on canvas, 145 × 115 cm, 2004 | Košarkaška lopta (za Jeffa)<br>Ulje na platnu, 145 × 115 cm, 2004. | Gunter<br>Lepkowski | FALSE SCENES<br>LAŽNI PRIZORI |
| 113 | Echo<br>Oil on canvas, 145 × 120 cm, 2003 | Eho<br>Ulje na platnu, 145 × 120 cm, 2003. | Gunter<br>Lepkowski | FALSE SCENES<br>LAŽNI PRIZORI |
| 114 | The Pendulum<br>Oil on canvas, 145 × 100 cm, 2004 | Njihalo<br>Ulje na platnu, 145 × 100 cm, 2004. | Gunter<br>Lepkowski | FALSE SCENES<br>LAŽNI PRIZORI |
| 115 | Giacomo<br>Oil on canvas, 70 x 50 cm, 2003 | Giacomo<br>Ulje na platnu, 70 x 50 cm, 2003. | Gunter<br>Lepkowski | FALSE SCENES<br>LAŽNI PRIZORI |
| 116 | Manuela<br>Oil on canvas, 70 x 50 cm, 2003 | Manuela<br>Ulje na platnu, 70 x 50 cm, 2003. | Gunter<br>Lepkowski | FALSE SCENES<br>LAŽNI PRIZORI |
| 117 | Who Is Looking at Whom Here<br>Oil on canvas, 145 × 125 cm, 2004 | Tko tu koga gleda<br>Ulje na platnu, 145 × 125 cm, 2004. | Gunter<br>Lepkowski | FALSE SCENES<br>LAŽNI PRIZORI |
| 118 | Totem Painting<br>Oil on canvas, 145 × 125 cm, 2005-2011 | Totem-slika<br>Ulje na platnu, 145 × 125 cm, 2005-2011. | Damir<br>Žižić | FALSE SCENES<br>LAŽNI PRIZORI |

| # | Title | Naslov | Artist | Series |
|---|---|---|---|---|
| 119 | Little Red Riding Hood (Evil?)<br>Oil on canvas, 145 × 120 cm, 2004 | Crvenkapica (zla?)<br>Ulje na platnu, 145 × 120 cm, 2004. | Gunter Lepkowski | FALSE SCENES<br>LAŽNI PRIZORI |
| 120 | Three-Eyed Painting<br>Oil on canvas, 145 × 145 cm, 2005 | Trooka slika<br>Ulje na platnu, 145 × 145 cm, 2005. | Gunter Lepkowski | FALSE SCENES<br>LAŽNI PRIZORI |
| 121 | Katja<br>Pencil and crayon on paper, 40 × 30 cm, 2005-07 | Katja<br>Olovka i olovke u boji na papiru, 40 × 30 cm, 2005-07. | Gunter Lepkowski | OBSERVATION<br>PROMATRANJE |
| 122 | Irma<br>Pencil and crayon on paper, 40 × 30 cm, 2005-07 | Irma<br>Olovka i olovke u boji na papiru, 40 × 30 cm, 2005-07. | Gunter Lepkowski | OBSERVATION<br>PROMATRANJE |
| 123 | Stefano<br>Pencil and crayon on paper, 40 × 30 cm, 2005-07 | Stefano<br>Olovka i olovke u boji na papiru, 40 × 30 cm, 2005-07. | Gunter Lepkowski | OBSERVATION<br>PROMATRANJE |
| 124 | Manuela<br>Pencil and crayon on paper, 40 × 30 cm, 2005-07 | Manuela<br>Olovka i olovke u boji na papiru, 40 × 30 cm, 2005-07. | Gunter Lepkowski | OBSERVATION<br>PROMATRANJE |
| 125 | Karsten<br>Pencil and crayon on paper, 40 × 30 cm, 2005-07 | Karsten<br>Olovka i olovke u boji na papiru, 40 × 30 cm, 2005-07. | Gunter Lepkowski | OBSERVATION<br>PROMATRANJE |
| 126 | Fabienne<br>Pencil and crayon on paper, 40 × 30 cm, 2005-07 | Fabienne<br>Olovka i olovke u boji na papiru, 40 × 30 cm, 2005-07. | Gunter Lepkowski | OBSERVATION<br>PROMATRANJE |
| 127 | Giuliano<br>Pencil and crayon on paper, 40 × 30 cm, 2005-07 | Giuliano<br>Olovka i olovke u boji na papiru, 40 × 30 cm, 2005-07. | Gunter Lepkowski | OBSERVATION<br>PROMATRANJE |
| 128 | Consuelo<br>Pencil and crayon on paper, 40 × 30 cm, 2005-07 | Consuelo<br>Olovka i olovke u boji na papiru, 40 × 30 cm, 2005-07. | Gunter Lepkowski | OBSERVATION<br>PROMATRANJE |
| 129 | Jörg<br>Pencil and crayon on paper, 40 × 30 cm, 2005-07 | Jörg<br>Olovka i olovke u boji na papiru, 40 × 30 cm, 2005-07. | Gunter Lepkowski | OBSERVATION<br>PROMATRANJE |
| 130 | Untitled<br>Oil on canvas, 145 × 105 cm, 2011-12 | Bez naslova<br>Ulje na platnu, 145 × 105 cm, 2011-12. | Damir Žižić | THE FACE OF THE PAINTING<br>LICE SLIKE |
| 131 | Untitled<br>Oil on canvas, 145 × 105 cm, 2006 | Bez naslova<br>Ulje na platnu, 145 × 105 cm, 2006. | Damir Žižić | THE FACE OF THE PAINTING<br>LICE SLIKE |
| 132 | Untitled<br>Oil on canvas, 145 × 105 cm, 2009 | Bez naslova<br>Ulje na platnu, 145 × 105 cm, 2009. | Damir Žižić | THE FACE OF THE PAINTING<br>LICE SLIKE |
| 133 | Untitled<br>Oil on canvas, 145 × 105 cm, 2006 | Bez naslova<br>Ulje na platnu, 145 × 105 cm, 2006. | Damir Žižić | THE FACE OF THE PAINTING<br>LICE SLIKE |
| 134 | Untitled<br>Oil on canvas, 145 × 105 cm, 2006 | Bez naslova<br>Ulje na platnu, 145 × 105 cm, 2006. | Damir Žižić | THE FACE OF THE PAINTING<br>LICE SLIKE |
| 135 | Untitled<br>Oil on canvas, 145 × 105 cm, 2006 | Bez naslova<br>Ulje na platnu, 145 × 105 cm, 2006. | Damir Žižić | THE FACE OF THE PAINTING<br>LICE SLIKE |
| 136 | Untitled<br>Oil on canvas, 145 × 105 cm, 2006 | Bez naslova<br>Ulje na platnu, 145 × 105 cm, 2006. | Damir Žižić | THE FACE OF THE PAINTING<br>LICE SLIKE |
| 137 | Sabine<br>Pencil and crayon on paper, 40 × 30 cm, 2005-07 | Sabine<br>Olovka i olovke u boji na papiru, 40 × 30 cm, 2005-07. | Gunter Lepkowski | OBSERVATION<br>PROMATRANJE |
| 138 | Giacomo<br>Pencil and crayon on paper, 40 × 30 cm, 2005-07 | Giacomo<br>Olovka i olovke u boji na papiru, 40 × 30 cm, 2005-07. | Gunter Lepkowski | OBSERVATION<br>PROMATRANJE |
| 139 | Ina<br>Pencil and crayon on paper, 40 × 30 cm, 2005-07 | Ina<br>Olovka i olovke u boji na papiru, 40 × 30 cm, 2005-07. | Gunter Lepkowski | OBSERVATION<br>PROMATRANJE |
| 140 | Ero<br>Pencil and crayon on paper, 40 × 30 cm, 2005-07 | Ero<br>Olovka i olovke u boji na papiru, 40 × 30 cm, 2005-07. | Gunter Lepkowski | OBSERVATION<br>PROMATRANJE |
| 141 | Karin<br>Pencil and crayon on paper, 40 × 30 cm, 2005-07 | Karin<br>Olovka i olovke u boji na papiru, 40 × 30 cm, 2005-07. | Gunter Lepkowski | OBSERVATION<br>PROMATRANJE |
| 142 | Georg<br>Pencil and crayon on paper, 40 × 30 cm, 2005-07 | Georg<br>Olovka i olovke u boji na papiru, 40 × 30 cm, 2005-07. | Gunter Lepkowski | OBSERVATION<br>PROMATRANJE |
| 143 | Constanze<br>Pencil and crayon on paper, 40 × 30 cm, 2005-07 | Constanze<br>Olovka i olovke u boji na papiru, 40 × 30 cm, 2005-07. | Gunter Lepkowski | OBSERVATION<br>PROMATRANJE |
| 144 | Untitled<br>Oil on canvas, 145 × 105 cm, 2011-12 | Bez naslova<br>Ulje na platnu, 145 × 105 cm, 2011-12. | Damir Žižić | THE FACE OF THE PAINTING<br>LICE SLIKE |
| 145 | Untitled<br>Oil on canvas, 145 × 105 cm, 2011-12 | Bez naslova<br>Ulje na platnu, 145 × 105 cm, 2011-12. | Damir Žižić | THE FACE OF THE PAINTING<br>LICE SLIKE |

| 146 | Untitled<br>Oil on canvas, 145 × 105 cm, 2011-12 | Bez naslova<br>Ulje na platnu, 145 × 105 cm, 2011-12. | Damir<br>Žižić | THE FACE OF THE PAINTING<br>LICE SLIKE |
|---|---|---|---|---|
| 147 | As if on a Starry Night<br>Oil on canvas, 170 × 160 cm, 2007 | Kao u zvjezdanoj noći<br>Ulje na platnu, 170 × 160 cm, 2007. | Gunter<br>Lepkowski | AS IF<br>KAO DA |
| 148 | As if She Were a (Flying) Doll<br>Oil on canvas, 145 × 125 cm, 2009 | Kao da je lutka (koja leti)<br>Ulje na platnu, 145 × 125 cm, 2009. | Lovro<br>Artuković | AS IF<br>KAO DA |
| 149 | Nightgown<br>Oil on canvas, 145 × 115 cm, 2006 | Spavaćica<br>Ulje na platnu, 145 × 115 cm, 2006. | Gunter<br>Lepkowski | AS IF<br>KAO DA |
| 150 | As if it Were Night<br>Oil on canvas, 145 × 180 cm, 2006 | Kao da je noć<br>Ulje na platnu, 145 × 180 cm, 2006. | Gunter<br>Lepkowski | AS IF<br>KAO DA |
| 151 | Night<br>Oil on canvas, 145 × 175 cm, 2006-09 | Noć<br>Ulje na platnu, 145 × 175 cm, 2006-09. | Damir<br>Žižić | AS IF<br>KAO DA |
| 152 | Night<br>Oil on canvas, 170 × 160 cm, 2009 | Noć<br>Ulje na platnu, 170 × 160 cm, 2009. | – | AS IF<br>KAO DA |
| 153 | Projection (Under Water)<br>Oil on canvas, 160 × 170 cm, 2011 | Projekcija (podvodna)<br>Ulje na platnu, 160 × 170 cm, 2011. | Damir<br>Žižić | AS IF<br>KAO DA |
| 154 | Projection (Baroque)<br>Oil on canvas, 175 × 115 cm, 2009 | Projekcija (barokna)<br>Ulje na platnu, 175 × 115 cm, 2009. | Lovro<br>Artuković | AS IF<br>KAO DA |
| 155 | Ernestine<br>Charcoal on paper, 123,5 x 53,5 cm,  2007-2008 | Ernestine<br>Crtež ugljenom na papiru, 123,5 x 53,5 cm,  2007-2008. | Lovro<br>Artuković | STAGINGS<br>UPRIZORENJA |
| 156 | Idriz<br>Charcoal on paper, 191,5 x 62,5 cm,  2007-2008 | Idriz<br>Crtež ugljenom na papiru, 191,5 x 62,5 cm, 2007-2008. | Lovro<br>Artuković | STAGINGS<br>UPRIZORENJA |
| 157 | Carsten<br>Charcoal on paper, 168 x 36,5 cm,  2007-2008 | Carsten<br>Crtež ugljenom na papiru, 168 x 36,5 cm,  2007-2008. | Lovro<br>Artuković | STAGINGS<br>UPRIZORENJA |
| 158 | Mario<br>Charcoal on paper, 150 x 98,5 cm, 2007-2008 | Mario<br>Crtež ugljenom na papiru, 150 x 98,5 cm, 2007-2008. | Lovro<br>Artuković | STAGINGS<br>UPRIZORENJA |
| 159 | Ero<br>Charcoal on paper, 149,5 x 82,5 cm,  2007-2008 | Ero<br>Crtež ugljenom na papiru, 149,5 x 82,5 cm, 2007-2008. | Lovro<br>Artuković | STAGINGS<br>UPRIZORENJA |
| 160 | Elena<br>Charcoal on paper, 165,5 x 88 cm, 2007-2008 | Elena<br>Crtež ugljenom na papiru, 165,5 x 88 cm, 2007-2008. | Lovro<br>Artuković | STAGINGS<br>UPRIZORENJA |
| 161 | Pero<br>Charcoal on paper, 150 x 39,5 cm, 2007-2008 | Pero<br>Crtež ugljenom na papiru, 150 x 39,5 cm, 2007-2008. | Lovro<br>Artuković | STAGINGS<br>UPRIZORENJA |
| 162 | Lara<br>Charcoal on paper, 65 x 54,5 cm,  2007-2008 | Lara<br>Crtež ugljenom na papiru, 65 x 54,5 cm, 2007-2008. | Lovro<br>Artuković | STAGINGS<br>UPRIZORENJA |
| 163 | Jeff<br>Charcoal on paper, 67 x 46,5 cm, 2007-2008 | Jeff<br>Crtež ugljenom na papiru, 67 x 46,5 cm, 2007-2008. | Lovro<br>Artuković | STAGINGS<br>UPRIZORENJA |
| 164 | Ari Dancing with Plastic Cups<br>Oil on canvas, 160 × 170 cm, 2013-14 | Ari pleše s plastičnim čašama<br>Ulje na platnu, 160 × 170 cm, 2013-14. | Gunter<br>Lepkowski | STAGINGS<br>UPRIZORENJA |
| 165 | Eight studies for a painting (Diana and Actaeon?) A<br>Charcoal on paper, 100 x 70 cm, 2014 | Osam studija za jednu sliku (Dijana i Akteon?) A<br>Ugljen na papiru, 100 x 70 cm, 2014. | – | STAGINGS<br>UPRIZORENJA |
| 166 | Eight studies for a painting (Diana and Actaeon?) B<br>Charcoal on paper, 142 x 42 cm, 2014 | Osam studija za jednu sliku (Dijana i Akteon?) B<br>Ugljen na papiru, 142 x 42 cm, 2014. | – | STAGINGS<br>UPRIZORENJA |
| 167 | Eight studies for a painting (Diana and Actaeon?) C<br>Charcoal on paper, 90,5 x 58 cm, 2014 | Osam studija za jednu sliku (Dijana i Akteon?) C<br>Ugljen na papiru, 90,5 x 58 cm, 2014. | – | STAGINGS<br>UPRIZORENJA |
| 168 | Eight studies for a painting (Diana and Actaeon?) D<br>Charcoal on paper, 90,5 x 68 cm, 2014 | Osam studija za jednu sliku (Dijana i Akteon?) D<br>Ugljen na papiru, 90,5 x 68 cm, 2014. | – | STAGINGS<br>UPRIZORENJA |
| 169 | Eight studies for a painting (Diana and Actaeon?) E<br>Charcoal on paper, 75 x 36 cm, 2014 | Osam studija za jednu sliku (Dijana i Akteon?) E<br>Ugljen na papiru, 75 x 36 cm, 2014. | – | STAGINGS<br>UPRIZORENJA |
| 170 | Eight studies for a painting (Diana and Actaeon?) F<br>Charcoal on paper, 95 x 95 cm, 2014 | Osam studija za jednu sliku (Dijana i Akteon?) F<br>Ugljen na papiru, 95 x 95 cm, 2014. | – | STAGINGS<br>UPRIZORENJA |
| 171 | Eight studies for a painting (Diana and Actaeon?) G<br>Charcoal on paper, 75,5 x 36,5 cm, 2014 | Osam studija za jednu sliku (Dijana i Akteon?) G<br>Ugljen na papiru, 75,5 x 36,5 cm, 2014. | – | STAGINGS<br>UPRIZORENJA |
| 172 | Eight studies for a painting (Diana and Actaeon?) H<br>Charcoal on paper, 175,5 x 36 cm, 2014 | Osam studija za jednu sliku (Dijana i Akteon?) H<br>Ugljen na papiru, 175,5 x 36 cm, 2014. | – | STAGINGS<br>UPRIZORENJA |

| 173 | Women's Bath (Empty)<br>Oil on canvas, 145 × 125 cm, 2017 | Ženska kupelj (prazna)<br>Ulje na platnu, 145 × 125 cm, 2017. | Gunter<br>Lepkowski | STAGINGS<br>UPRIZORENJA |
|---|---|---|---|---|
| 174 | Women's Bath<br>Oil on canvas, 220 × 190 cm, 2017 | Ženska kupelj<br>Ulje na platnu, 220 × 190 cm, 2017. | Gunter<br>Lepkowski | STAGINGS<br>UPRIZORENJA |
| 175 | Girl's Head<br>Oil on MDF board laminated with canvas,<br>35 × 25 cm, 2016 | Glava djevojke<br>Ulje na platnu kaširanom na dasku,<br>35 × 25 cm, 2016. | Gunter<br>Lepkowski | STAGINGS<br>UPRIZORENJA |
| 176 | Anne (Royal)<br>Oil on canvas, 200 × 130 cm, 2015 | Anne (Royal)<br>Ulje na platnu, 200 × 130 cm, 2015. | Gunter<br>Lepkowski | SLOWING DOWN<br>USPORAVANJE |
| 177 | Female Figure in Space (Teschi)<br>Oil on MDF board, 55 × 40 cm, 2018 | Ženski lik u prostoru (Teschi)<br>Ulje na MDF-ploči, 55 × 40 cm, 2018. | Gunter<br>Lepkowski | SLOWING DOWN<br>USPORAVANJE |
| 178 | At the Window<br>Oil on canvas, 60 × 40 cm, 2015 | Na prozoru<br>Ulje na platnu, 60 × 40 cm, 2015. | Gunter<br>Lepkowski | SLOWING DOWN<br>USPORAVANJE |
| 179 | Smoke<br>Oil on MDF board, 40 × 29.5 cm, 2016 | Dim<br>Ulje na MDF-ploči, 40 × 29,5 cm, 2016. | Gunter<br>Lepkowski | SLOWING DOWN<br>USPORAVANJE |
| 180 | Ivica Buljan and Robert Waltl<br>Oil on canvas, 180 x 145 cm, 2012 | Ivica Buljan i Robert Waltl<br>Ulje na platnu, 180 x 145 cm, 2012. | Miha<br>Fras | SLOWING DOWN<br>USPORAVANJE |
| 181 | Closing Time<br>Oil on MDF board, 26 × 22.5 cm, 2018 | Closing Time<br>Ulje na MDF-ploči, 26 × 22,5 cm, 2018. | Gunter<br>Lepkowski | SLOWING DOWN<br>USPORAVANJE |
| 182 | Two Women in the Bar<br>Charcoal on paper, 80 x 80 cm, 2022 | Dvije žene u baru<br>Ugljen na papairu, 80 x 80 cm, 2022. | Gunter<br>Lepkowski | SLOWING DOWN<br>USPORAVANJE |
| 183 | Apparition in Neukölln (Red, Yellow, Green).<br>Oil on MDF board, 55 × 40 cm, 2020 | Ukazanje u Neuköllnu (crveno, žuto, zeleno)<br>Ulje na MDF-ploči, 55 × 40 cm, 2020. | Gunter<br>Lepkowski | SLOWING DOWN<br>USPORAVANJE |
| 184 | Dusk<br>Oil on canvas, 105 × 145 cm, 2020 | U sumrak<br>Ulje na platnu, 105 × 145 cm, 2020. | Gunter<br>Lepkowski | SLOWING DOWN<br>USPORAVANJE |
| 185 | Summer Storm<br>Charcoal on paper , 110 × 69 cm, 2020 | Ljetna oluja<br>Crtež ugljenom na papiru, 110 × 69 cm, 2020. | Gunter<br>Lepkowski | SLOWING DOWN<br>USPORAVANJE |
| 186 | In Grunewald<br>Oil on plywood, diameter 40 cm, 2016 | U Grunewaldu<br>Ulje na šperploči, promjer 40 cm, 2016. | Gunter<br>Lepkowski | SLOWING DOWN<br>USPORAVANJE |
| 187 | Party<br>Charcoal and egg tempera on paper,<br>180 × 260 cm, 1985 | Tulum<br>Ugljen i jajčana tempera na papiru, 180 × 260 cm, 1985. | Fedor<br>Vučemilović | EARLY WORKS<br>RANI RADOVI |
| 188 | Floating Sauna - a Party of Berliners in the Countryside<br>During the Lockdown (Also Called Corona's Ark)<br>Oil on canvas, 190 × 210 cm, 2020-21 | Sauna na vodi - berlinsko društvo na izletu za<br>vrijeme lockdowna (zvana još i Koronina arka)<br>Ulje na platnu, 190 × 210 cm, 2020-21. | Gunter<br>Lepkowski | SLOWING DOWN<br>USPORAVANJE |
| 189 | Rainy Scene with a Toy Duck<br>Oil on canvas, 200 × 200 cm, 1999-2000 (missing) | Kišni prizor s plastičnom patkicom<br>Ulje na platnu, 200 × 200 cm, 1999-2000. (nestalo) | Luka<br>Mjeda | SCENES<br>PRIZORI |
| 190 | Art<br>Oil on canvas, 145 × 122.5 cm, 1999 (missing) | Umjetnost<br>Ulje na platnu, 145 × 122,5 cm, 1999. (nestalo) | Luka<br>Mjeda | BEECH CRUST<br>BUKVINA KORA |
| 191 | Stillness (Window)<br>Oil on canvas, 144 × 88 cm, 2000 | Tišina (Prozor)<br>Ulje na platnu, 144 × 88 cm, 2000. | Damir<br>Žižić | BEECH CRUST<br>BUKVINA KORA |
| 192 | Masks<br>Oil on canvas, 82 x 102 cm, 2001 | Maske<br>Ulje na platnu, 82 x 102 cm, 2001. | Damir<br>Žižić | BEECH CRUST<br>BUKVINA KORA |
| 193 | Picture of Light in the Dark<br>Oil on canvas, 145 × 100 cm, 2003 | Slika svjetla u mraku<br>Ulje na platnu, 145 × 100 cm, 2003. | Gunter<br>Lepkowski | FALSE SCENES<br>LAŽNI PRIZORI |
| 194 | The Little Match Girl<br>Oil on canvas, 145 × 145 cm, 2006 | Djevojčica sa žigicama<br>Ulje na platnu, 145 × 145 cm, 2006. | Gunter<br>Lepkowski | FALSE SCENES<br>LAŽNI PRIZORI |
| 195 | Brandenburg Palm Tree<br>Oil on canvas, 180 × 110 cm, 2021-23 | Brandenburška palma<br>Ulje na platnu, 180 × 110 cm, 2021-23. | Gunter<br>Lepkowski | FALSE SCENES<br>LAŽNI PRIZORI |
| 196 | Entrance to the New World<br>Oil on MDF board, 26 × 23.5 cm, 2019 | Ulaz u Novi svijet<br>Ulje na MDF-ploči, 26 × 23,5 cm, 2019. | Gunter<br>Lepkowski | SLOWING DOWN<br>USPORAVANJE |
| 197 | First Aid Blanket with Reflections<br>Oil on MDF board, 40 × 29.5 cm, 2018 | Pokrivač prve pomoći s odrazima<br>Ulje na MDF-ploči, 40 × 29,5 cm, 2018. | Gunter<br>Lepkowski | SLOWING DOWN<br>USPORAVANJE |

# catalogue, appendix

# katalog, dodatak

| nr | Artist | Caption | Legenda | Photography | Copyright |
|---|---|---|---|---|---|
| A | | Flyer:<br>Some Things Just Stick in Your Mind<br>Exhibition | Letak za izložbu:<br>Some Things Just Stick<br>in Your Mind | Sarah Blaßkiewitz | Lovro Artuković, Berlin |
| B | Leonora Carrington | Self-Portrait | Autoportret | – | bpk \| The Metropolitan Museum of Art, The Pierre and Maria-Gaetana Matisse Collection, New York |
| C | Odilon Redon | Head of Orpheus Floating in the Water | Orfejeva glava koja pliva na vodi | Rik Klein Gotink | Collection Kröller-Müller Museum, Otterlo |
| D | Sandro Botticelli | A Young Man Being Introduced to the Seven Liberal Arts | Mladić kojeg se upoznaje sa sedam slobodnih umijeća | Daniel Arnaudet | RMN-Grand Palais \| musée du Louvre, Paris |
| E | Sandro Botticelli | Venus and the Three Graces Presenting Gifts to a Young Woman | Venera i tri gracije donose darove mladoj ženi | Michel Urtado | RMN-Grand Palais \| musée du Louvre, Paris |
| F | Marino Tartaglia | Self-Portrait | Autoportret | – | Museum of Contemporary Art, Zagreb |
| G | | A Brandenburg Landscape with a Figure (Reflection), Detail of Hydra in an Autumn Landscape | Brandenburški krajolik s figurom (odraz): detalj sa slike Hidra u jesenjem pejzažu | Lovro Artuković | Lovro Artuković, Berlin |
| H | | Tableaux vivant: Signing of the declaration on the unification of Western Herzegovina and Popovo polje with the Republic of Croatia (Wer hat das Bier bestellt?), Galerie Meinblau, Berlin | Tableaux vivant za sliku: Potpisivanje deklaracije o pripajanju Zapadne Hercegovine i Popova polja Republici Hrvatskoj (Wer hat das Bier bestellt?), Galerie Meinblau, Berlin | Thomas Kierok | Lovro Artuković, Berlin |
| I | | Preparations for:<br>Apollo and Marsyas<br>(Triumph of the New Media Over Painting) | Pripreme za sliku:<br>Apolon i Marsija<br>(trijumf novih medija nad slikarstvom) | Lovro Artuković | Lovro Artuković, Berlin |
| J | | Preparations for:<br>Apollo and Marsyas (Triumph of the New Media Over Painting), Ari and Birgit Dancing | Pripreme za sliku:<br>Apolon i Marsija (trijumf novih medija nad slikarstvom), Ari i Birgit plešu | Thomas Kierok | Lovro Artuković, Berlin |
| K | | Scene:<br>Ari Dancing with Plastic Cups | Scena za sliku:<br>Ari pleše s plastičnim čašama | Jeannine Simon | Lovro Artuković, Berlin |
| L | | Detail:<br>Studio Reflection in Gold Foil | Detalji sa slike:<br>Odraz ateljea u zlatnoj foliji | Lovro Artuković | Lovro Artuković, Berlin |
| M | Lovro Artuković | Underworld Party<br>Grand Park Hotel,<br>Rovinj | Tulum u podzemnom svijetu<br>Grand Park Hotel,<br>Rovinj | Damir Žižić | Lovro Artuković, Berlin |